THE HOME BOOK
OF
HUMOROUS
QUOTATIONS

THE HOME BOOK
OF
HUMOROUS
QUOTATIONS

SELECTED AND ARRANGED BY

A. K. ADAMS

DODD, MEAD & COMPANY
NEW YORK

THE HOME BOOK OF HUMOROUS QUOTATIONS

PRINTED IN THE UNITED STATES OF AMERICA
BY VAIL-BALLOU PRESS, INC., BINGHAMTON, N. Y.

PREFATORY NOTE

THE HOME BOOK OF HUMOROUS QUOTATIONS is appropriately light in tone and, also appropriately, serious in intent and scope. The many editors on the Dodd, Mead staff who have contributed to this volume have striven to present much of the most memorable and usable humor, both spoken and written, from all lands and from ancient times to the present, in a single book, and to make it even more readily usable by categorizing it by topics, or subject headings. In outline and style, this book follows Burton Stevenson's THE HOME BOOK OF QUOTATIONS and the more recent THE HOME BOOK OF AMERICAN QUOTATIONS. In the tradition of those volumes, THE HOME BOOK OF HUMOROUS QUOTATIONS was compiled and edited on the principle that what is worth preserving for future quotation is worthy of accurate and well-documented presentation. Humor and care are not incompatible; together they can make a highly readable book that is also a dependable reference work.

Discussing the "how" of such a book is undoubtedly more appropriate than undertaking to explain the "why" of its origin. Every experienced speaker or writer knows that few things are welcomed more by an audience than humor, where it is appropriate. And how often it *is* appropriate: the more somber the subject, the heavier the going, as a rule, the more welcome a light touch. That humor is indeed coexistent with a wide range of subject matter is clear from an inspection of the table of contents, which lists some four hundred subject headings, varying from "gambling" to "grief" and from "love" to "war," under which quotations can be found inside.

This very range suggests another principle underlying the book. It is the recognition that humor exists in many forms and guises, as well as in many places, likely and unlikely. Defining and analyzing humor is a pastime of humorless people, Robert Benchley observed, so no attempt will be made here. It is enough to point out that more than a thousand authors and speakers are represented by the nearly nine thousand selections in THE HOME BOOK OF HUMOROUS QUOTATIONS, and since they range from the ancient Greeks and Romans to the masters of television, diversity of thought and treatment is the rule on the pages ahead.

Many of the contributors are indispensable to any comprehensive record of humor from its beginnings, and they are generously represented here. To name a few, in addition to the ancients, there are Shakespeare, Ben Jonson, Molière, Balzac, Wycherley, Sheridan, Farquhar, Dr. Johnson, W. S. Gilbert, Shaw, Wilde, Lewis Carroll, Sholom Aleichem, Mark Twain, Will Rogers, Artemus Ward, Josh Billings, Robert Benchley, and James Thurber. The reader also will find the political wit of Winston Churchill, John F. Kennedy, and Adlai E. Stevenson. He may be more surprised to find the writings and sayings of persons no less famous but not usually associated with humor—men such as Napoleon Bonaparte, Bismarck, Thomas Jefferson, Swift, Pope, Dickens, Nietzsche, Emerson, Hawthorne, Longfellow, Melville, Poe, Whitman, and Thoreau.

To serve the reader further, the subject headings have been made as specific as possible. Since many are closely related, however, they are tied together by a system of cross references, which will guide the reader to material that may prove equally helpful. Thus, at "marriage" he will find a suggestion that he see also the quotations under the headings "divorce," "husband," "mother-in-law," "widow," and "wife." Within a given section, the individual entries are listed alphabetically by author or speaker. Where entries are very closely related, in the sense of being paraphrases or variants, that information is given at the end of each individual entry, in the form of cross references to similar quotations within the section.

Finally, a concordance, or index of key words, is provided in the back of the book as an aid to the reader who knows a single key word or words from a quotation he is seeking. By referring to this listing of key words, arranged alphabetically, he can be guided to the appropriate quotation; each entry in the concordance is keyed to a page number (listed first) and a quotation number, which indicates the order in which the selection in placed on the page indicated.

A. K. ADAMS

TABLE OF CONTENTS

K

L

M

N

O

P

Q

R

S

A

ABILITY

1
A great unrecognized incapacity. (Une grande incapacite inconnue.)
> Otto von Bismarck. *Letter,* 1862, while minister to France. Reference is to Napoleon III.

2
A good rooster crows in any hen house.
> Frank C. Brown. *Collection of North Carolina Folklore.*

3
I would rather that the people should wonder why I wasn't President than why I am.
> Salmon P. Chase.

4
If a traveller were informed that such a man was leader of the House of Commons, he may begin to comprehend how the Egyptians worshipped an insect.
> Benjamin Disraeli. On Lord John Russell.

5
Talents differ; all is well and wisely put;
If I cannot carry forests on my back,
Neither can you crack a nut.
> Ralph Waldo Emerson. *Fable: The Mountain and the Squirrel.*

6
He who has no hands
Perforce must use his tongue;
Foxes are so cunning
Because they are not strong.
> Ralph Waldo Emerson. *Orator.*

7
It is all one to me if a man comes from Sing Sing or Harvard. We hire a man, not his history.
> Henry Ford.

8
That Carpenter is not the Best
Who makes More Chips than all the Rest.
> Arthur Guiterman. *A Poet's Proverbs.*

9
His worst is better than any other person's best.
> William Hazlitt. *English Literature,* ch. 14: *Sir Walter Scott.*

10
A feller who knows his business is allus reticent.
> Frank McKinney (Kin) Hubbard. *Abe Martin's Primer.*

11
The succession of Dr. Franklin at the court of France was an excellent school of humility. On being presented to anyone as the minister of America, the commonplace question used in such cases was *"C'est vous, Monsieur, qui remplace le Docteur Franklin?"*—"It is you, sir, who replace Dr. Franklin?" I generally answered, "No one can replace him, sir; I am only his successor."
> Thomas Jefferson, 1791.

12
A man may be so much of everything that he is nothing of anything.
> Samuel Johnson. Boswell's *Life,* Mar. 30, 1783.

13
Some ladies now make pretty songs,
And some make pretty nurses;
Some men are good for righting wrongs,
And some for writing verses.
> F. Locker-Lampson. *The Jester's Plea.*

14
In the battle of existence, talent is the punch; tact is the clever footwork.
> Wilson Mizner. Quoted in *Reader's Digest,* Feb., 1967.

15
Men take only their needs into consideration—never their abilities.
> Napoleon Bonaparte. (*The Mind of Napoleon,* ed. by J. Christopher Herold.)

16
Sometimes we do things badly on purpose because those who do them well are classed as our inferiors.
> Bernard Shaw. *The Intelligent Woman's Guide* (1928).

17
Ability—The art of getting credit for all the home runs somebody else hits.
> Casey Stengel.

18
You cannot define talent. All you can do is build the greenhouse and see if it grows.
> William P. Steven. Quoted in *Time,* Aug. 23, 1963, p. 36.

19
As easy as rolling off a log.
> Mark Twain. *A Connecticut Yankee in King Arthur's Court.*

1

ABSENCE

See also Parting

1

Absence is to love what wind is to a fire;
it puts out the little, it kindles the great.
ROGER DE BUSSY-RABUTIN. *Epigram.*

2

Wives in their husbands' absences grow subtler,
And daughters sometimes run off with the butler.
LORD BYRON. *Don Juan.* Canto III, st. 22.

3

A woman must never let a man get accustomed to her absence.
LUCAS CLEEVE. *The Rose Geranium.*

4

And when he is out of sight, quickly also is he out of mind.
THOMAS À KEMPIS. *The Imitation of Christ,* tr. by Benham. Bk. I, ch. 23.

5

"Presents," I often say, "endear absents."
CHARLES LAMB. *Essays of Elia: A Dissertation Upon Roast Pig.*

6

Everyone agrees that the absent are warned by a ringing in the ears when they are being talked about. (Absentes tinnitu aurium praesentire sermones de se receptum est.)
PLINY THE ELDER. *Historia Naturalis.* Bk. xxviii, sec. 2.

7

What is better than presence of mind in a railway accident? Absence of body.
Punch. Vol. xvi, p. 231 (1849).

8

Absence makes the heart grow fonder—of somebody else.
UNKNOWN.

ABSTINENCE

See also Chastity

9

If you don't eat garlic, they'll never smell it on your breath.
SHOLOM ALEICHEM. *Eternal Life.*

10

A teetotaller is the very worst sort of drunkard.
E. F. BENSON. *The House of Defense.*

11

Self-denial is a weak indulgence of a propensity to forgo.
AMBROSE BIERCE. *The Cynic's Word Book.*

12

Do not put off till tomorrow what can be enjoyed today.
JOSH BILLINGS.

13

That which Pythagoras said to his scholars of old, may be for ever applied to melancholy men, *A fabis abstinete,* eat no beans.
ROBERT BURTON. *The Anatomy of Melancholy.*

14

There was once a man who learnt to mind his own business. He went to heaven. I hope the teetotallers will remember that.
T. W. H. CROSLAND. *The Beautiful Teetotaller.*

15

Refin'd himself to Soul, to curb the Sense;
And made almost a sin of Abstinence.
JOHN DRYDEN. *The Character of a Good Parson.*

16

If thou wouldst not be known to do anything, never do it.
RALPH WALDO EMERSON. *Essays, First Series: Spiritual Laws.*

17

When I was a lad I pondered some
On the horrible effects of the Demon Rum;
I scorned to dally with the dread highball
And I never saw a bottle of champagne at all.
I kept away from guzzling men
And now I am the ruler of the U.S.N.
Caption of cartoon. Quoted by J. C. FURNAS in *The Life and Times of the Late Demon Rum.* The reference is to Josephus Daniels, Secretary of the Navy.

18

Indeed, so well I've learned to fast
That, sooth my love, I know not whether
I might not bring myself at last
To—do without you altogether.
MARTIAL. *Epigrams.* From *Roman Culture,* ed. by Garry Wills.

19

I'm only a beer teetotaller, not a champagne teetotaller.
BERNARD SHAW. *Candida,* Act 3.

20

Self-denial is not a virtue: it is only the effect of prudence on rascality.
BERNARD SHAW. *Maxims for Revolutionists.*

21

A man is rich in proportion to the number of things he can afford to let alone.
HENRY D. THOREAU. *Walden,* ch. 11.

ACT, ACTION

See also Deeds

22

And of all glad words of prose or rhyme,
The gladdest are, "Act while there yet is time."
FRANKLIN P. ADAMS. *Maud Muller Mutatur.*

1

When you see a snake, never mind where he came from.

W. G. BENHAM. *Proverbs.*

2

It was William Booth who explained the authoritarian framework of his Salvation Army by remarking that if Moses had operated through committees, the Israelites never would have got across the Red Sea.

TED MORELLO. *New York World-Telegram and Sun,* July 28, 1965.

3

I'd do it as soon as say Jack Robinson.

FANNY BURNEY. *Evelina.*

4

We all like people who do things, even if we only see their faces on a cigar-box lid.

WILLA CATHER. *The Song of the Lark.*

5

Sloths are not active because millions of years ago their ancestors discovered that activity did them no good.

WILL CUPPY. *How to Tell Your Friends from the Apes: The Sloth.*

6

Unless to Thought is added Will,
Apollo is an imbecile.

RALPH WALDO EMERSON. *Fragments on the Poetic Gift.*

7

Activity is contagious.

RALPH WALDO EMERSON. *Representative Men: Uses of Great Men.*

8

Miss Stein was a past master in making nothing happen very slowly.

CLIFTON FADIMAN. *The Selected Writings of Clifton Fadiman: Puzzlements* (1955). Referring to Gertrude Stein.

9

Actions speak louder than words—but not so often.

Farmer's Almanac, 1966.

10

Acting without thinking is like shooting without aiming.

B. C. FORBES. *Epigrams.*

11

A man's acts are usually right, but his reasons seldom are.

ELBERT HUBBARD. *The Philistine.* Vol. xix, p. 143.

12

Lyndon acts like there was never going to be a tomorrow.

CLAUDIA TAYLOR (MRS. LYNDON B.) JOHNSON. Referring to her husband. Quoted as an oft-spoken remark. (*The New York Times Magazine,* Nov. 29, 1964, p. 28.)

13

To do nothing is in every man's power.

SAMUEL JOHNSON. *The Rambler,* No. 155.

14

There are always twenty excellent reasons for doing nothing for every one reason for starting anything—especially if it has never been done before.

PRINCE PHILIP. From *The Wit of Prince Philip,* ed. by Peter Butler.

15

I took the Canal Zone and let Congress debate, and while the debate goes on the canal does also.

THEODORE ROOSEVELT. Referring to his action in recognizing the Republic of Panama. (*The New York Times,* Mar. 24, 1911.)

16

. . . Hitler pretends to be a man of action, but he mistakes acting for action, in fact, he's the ham actor.

BERNARD SHAW. Quoted in *Days with Bernard Shaw* by Stephen Winsten.

17

Mistrust first impulses, they are always good.

CHARLES MAURICE DE TALLEYRAND. Quoted in *Biographie Universelle.*

18

When we have fully discovered the scientific laws that govern life, we shall realize that the one person who has more illusions than the dreamer is the man of action.

OSCAR WILDE. *The Critic as Artist.*

19

No, Ernest, don't talk about action. It is a blind thing dependent on external influences, and moved by an impulse of whose nature it is unconscious. It is a thing incomplete in its essence, because limited by accident, and ignorant of its direction, being always at variance with its aim. Its basis is the lack of imagination. It is the last resource of those who know not how to dream.

OSCAR WILDE. *The Critic as Artist.*

ACTING, ACTORS

See also Movies, Stage

20

Actors don't rate very high in the studio echelon until they become important; then they rate very high. Often the actor carries a deep grievance dating from the early stages of his career, a resentment that his talents were not appreciated, a hurt pride because of past humiliations. Now when he suddenly finds that he is the one who can draw the public, he slaps a hammerlock on his old tormentors and pins them to the mat.

GEORGE ABBOTT. *Mister Abbott.*

1

Q. Do actors need brains?

A. If they can act, no. If they can't, yes.

James Agate. *The Later Ego.*

2

A professional is a man who can do his job when he doesn't feel like it. An amateur is a man who can't do his job when he does feel like it.

James Agate. *The Later Ego.*

3

The only thing I like about being an actress is acting.

Elizabeth Ashley.

4

For an actress to be a success she must have the face of Venus, the brains of Minerva, the grace of Terpsichore, the memory of Macaulay, the figure of Juno, and the hide of a rhinoceros.

Ethel Barrymore. Quoted by George Jean Nathan, *The Theatre in the Fifties.*

5

An actor is a sculptor who carves in snow.

Edwin Booth.

6

Brutus seems no more than a resounding set of vocal cords wrapped up in a toga.

John Mason Brown. *Two on the Aisle.*

7

His life was what the marquees describe as a "continuous performance."

John Mason Brown. *Introduction* to *The Portable Woollcott.*

8

The actor who took the role of King Lear played the king as though he expected someone to play the ace.

Eugene Field.

9

Yes, films are a director's medium, not an actor's. . . . And on the stage, in contrast to films, if you're clicking, it's like rising in an emotional graph to the end. . . . it's like an airplane rising from sluggish water, balanced on the step under its belly. . . . That's the feeling you can get, with luck. You're sailing. You say to yourself, "Tonight you're gonna soar, baby."

Henry Fonda. *Interview, The New York Times,* Apr. 26, 1964.

10

One of the most famous remarks ever made about a stage performance was [W. S.] Gilbert's summary of Beerbohm Tree's Hamlet as "funny without being vulgar."

Hesketh Pearson. *Lives of the Wits.*

11

On the stage he was natural, simple, affecting;

'Twas only that when he was off, he was acting.

Oliver Goldsmith. *Retaliation.* On David Garrick.

12

An actress's life is so transitory—suddenly you're a building.

Helen Hayes. *Comment* in Nov., 1955, on the news that a New York theater was being renamed for her.

13

It worries me to beat the band

To hear folks say our life is grand;

Wish they'd try some one-night stand.

Ain't it awful, Mabel?

John Edward Hazzard. *Ain't It Awful, Mabel?*

14

The actor—A paradox who plays when he works and works when he plays.

Toasts for All Occasions, ed. by Lewis C. Henry.

15

I deny I ever said that actors are cattle. What I said was "actors should be treated like cattle."

Alfred Hitchcock.

16

At one time I thought he wanted to be an actor. He had certain qualifications, including no money and a total lack of responsibility.

Hedda Hopper. *From Under My Hat.*

17

Another style o' four flushin' is applaudin' an imitation of an actor you never saw.

Frank McKinney (Kin) Hubbard. *Abe Martin's Primer.*

18

Unfortunately, most of them [actors] are compulsive quoters of people who originated the ideas which they have finally come to believe are entirely their own.

Alexander King. *Rich Man, Poor Man, Freud and Fruit,* ch. 12.

19

Alfred Lunt was once asked for the secret of his great talent as an actor. "I speak," he replied, "in a loud, clear voice, and try not to bump into the furniture."

From *H. Allen Smith's Almanac* (1965).

20

Indeed, irresolution being the keynote of Hamlet's soliloquy, a clever player could to some extent indicate the whole thirty lines by a silent working of the jaw.

A. A. Milne. *The Sunny Side.*

21

The great art of the stage-craftsman, as I have already shown, is to seem natural rather than to be natural.

A. A. Milne. *The Sunny Side.*

1

She [Katharine Hepburn] runs the gamut of emotions from A to B.

> DOROTHY PARKER. Quoted in Miss Parker's obituary in *Publishers' Weekly*, June 19, 1967.

2

I think one of the deaths of Hollywood is that producers tried to make everybody normal. Nobody would be in this business if he were normal. When you think of the people you knew—all the Barrymores, Errol Flynn, Charles Laughton—they were eccentrics. I don't want to read about some of these actresses who are around today. They sound like my niece in Scarsdale. I love my niece in Scarsdale, but I won't buy tickets to see her act.

> VINCENT PRICE. *Interview* with Joseph Finnigan, United Press International, Feb. 28, 1964.

3

No self-respecting actor would dream of being punctual.

> FRANK RICHARDSON. *2835 Mayfair.*

4

When an actress writes her memoirs, she impresses on you in every chapter how cruelly it tried her feeling to exhibit her person to the public gaze; but she does not forget to decorate the book with a dozen portraits of herself.

> BERNARD SHAW. *Three Plays for Puritans:* Preface.

5

Garrick, had he called Dr. Johnson Punch, would have spoken profoundly and wittily; whereas Dr. Johnson, in hurling that epithet at him, was but picking up the cheapest sneer an actor is subject to.

> BERNARD SHAW. *Plays Unpleasant:* Preface.

6

The actor who drinks is in a bad way: but the actor who eats is lost.

> BERNARD SHAW. *Dramatic Opinions.*

7

All sorts of people come here at times—gentlemen as well as actors. I didn't know which you was, sir, for the moment.

> HORACE WYNDHAM. *The Flare of the Footlights.*

ADAM AND EVE

8

When Adam dolve and Eve span,
Who was then the gentleman?

> JOHN BALL. *Text*, used by him in his speech at Blackheath to the rebels in Wat Tyler's insurrection, June 12, 1381. Ball was afterwards hanged.

9

I wish Adam had died with all his ribs in his body.

> DION BOUCICAULT.

10

A man without a navel yet lives in me.

> SIR THOMAS BROWNE. *Religio Medici*, pt. 2.

11

Where the apple reddens
    Never pry—
Lest we lose our Edens,
    Eve and I.

> ROBERT BROWNING. *Bells and Pomegranates.*

12

Her daughters ever since prefer to urge
"Adam so starved me I was fain to accept
The apple any serpent pushed my way."

> ROBERT BROWNING. *The Ring and the Book.*

13

As a priest, I listen to a lot of wifely discontent. Women have their faults, and I don't suppose there is a pastor on earth who doesn't at times wish he had the power to convert them all back into ribs—nice, quiet, uncomplaining ribs.

> FATHER ROBERT CAPON. *Bed and Board.*

14

Can you imagine Adam alone in the Garden of Eden? Even he had to go when Eve left.

> LUCAS CLEEVE. *The Rose Geranium.*

15

Did Adam forsake Eve after they lost their Paradise? . . . You forget that there were no other women outside the gates. There *are* other women outside Paradise to-day.

> JAMES DOUGLAS. *The Unpardonable Sin.*

16

The fall of the first Adam was the end of the beginning; the rise of the second Adam was the beginning of the end.

> S. W. DUFFIELD. *Fragments.*

17

What you have told us is all very good. It is indeed bad to eat apples. It is better to make them all into cider.

> BENJAMIN FRANKLIN. *Remarks Concerning the Savages of North America.* Quoting an Indian's response to a missionary's account of the story of Adam and Eve.

18

It is not fair to visit all
The blame on Eve, for Adam's fall;
The most Eve did was to display
Contributory negligé.

> OLIVER HERFORD. *Eve: Apropos de Rien.*

19

Adam's Rib—The original bone of contention.

> OLIVER HERFORD.

1

When Eve upon the first of Men
   The apple press'd with specious cant,
Oh! what a thousand pities then
   That Adam was not Adamant!
   THOMAS HOOD. *A Reflection.*

2

When Adam day by day
   Woke up in paradise,
He always used to say,
   "Oh, this is very nice."
But Eve from scenes of bliss
   Transported him for life.
The more I think of this
   The more I beat my wife.
   A. E. HOUSMAN. *When Adam Day by Day.*

3

Newton *saw* an apple fall and discovered the
Law of Gravity.
Eve *made* an apple fall and discovered the
Gravity of Law.
   ALEXANDER KING. *I Should Have Kissed
      Her More.*

4

The fall, like the serpent, was mythical: the
apple was sound and Eve hysterical.
   EVA LATHBURY. *Mr. Meyer's Pupil.*

5

The first world war started because of a
difference between Adam and Eve.
   ART LINKLETTER. *A Child's Garden of
      Misinformation.*

6

Before Eve did bite into the apple, she had
first to be alone with Adam under the tree
where the apple grew.
   VIRGILIA PETERSON. *A Matter of Life and
      Death.*

7

History credits Adam and Eve with being
the first bookkeepers, because they invented
the loose-leaf system.
   More Playboy's Party Jokes (1965).

8

Probably when Adam tried to explain his
fall to the Lord he declared he had slipped
on a fig leaf.
   Reflections of a Bachelor (1903).

9

Guess the serpent in the Garden of Eden
was a garter snake.
   Reflections of a Bachelor (1903).

10

Had God thought that sin would enter Eden,
He would have created a parson also.
   LAURENCE STERNE.

11

Whoever has lived long enough to find out
what life is, knows how deep a debt of gratitude we owe to Adam, the first great benefactor of our race. He brought death into
the world.
   MARK TWAIN. *Pudd'nhead Wilson's Calen-
      dar.*

12

Adam and Eve had many advantages, but
the principal one was, that they escaped
teething.
   MARK TWAIN. *Pudd'nhead Wilson's Calen-
      dar.*

13

Adam was but human—this explains it all.
He did not want the apple for the apple's
sake, he wanted it only because it was forbidden.
   MARK TWAIN. *Pudd'nhead Wilson's Calen-
      dar.*

14

Adam ate the apple, and our teeth still ache.
   UNKNOWN. Hungarian proverb.

ADMIRATION

15

Admiration is like champagne to a woman.
The more she gets the more she wants.
   W. BURTON BALDRY. *Stray Thoughts.*

16

I do not like thee, Dr. Fell.
The reason why I cannot tell,
But this I know, I know full well,
I do not like thee, Dr. Fell.
   SIR THOMAS BROWNE.

17

The prophet and the quack are alike admired for a generation, and admired for the
wrong reasons.
   G. K. CHESTERTON. *A Handful of Au-
      thors.*

18

I love Henry, but I cannot like him; and
as for taking his arm, I should as soon think
of taking the arm of an elm-tree.
   RALPH WALDO EMERSON. *Lectures and
      Biographical Sketches: Thoreau.* Quot-
      ing a friend of Thoreau.

19

Assuredly nobody will care for him who
cares for nobody.
   THOMAS JEFFERSON. *Letter to Maria Cos-
      way* (1786).

20

Although you may, and in fact must, tell a
singer that you love him for his voice and a
painter that you admire him for his talent,
you must never admit to a man with money
that the basis for your affection is his large
capital.
   ALEXANDER KING. *Rich Man, Poor Man,
      Freud and Fruit,* ch. 15.

1
Men are more lovable for the bad qualities they don't possess than for the good ones they do.
E. PHILLIPS OPPENHEIM. *Simple Peter Cradd*, p. 60.

2
Bernard Shaw is an excellent man; he has not an enemy in the world, and none of his friends like him.
OSCAR WILDE. Quoted in Shaw: *Sixteen Self Sketches*, ch. 17.

3
Ernest Harrowden, one of those middle-aged mediocrities so common in London clubs, who have no enemies but are thoroughly disliked by their friends.
OSCAR WILDE. *The Picture of Dorian Gray.*

ADULTERY

4
What men call gallantry, and gods adultery, Is much more common where the climate's sultry.
LORD BYRON. *Don Juan.*

5
Merely innocent flirtation, Not quite adultery, but adulteration.
LORD BYRON. *Don Juan.*

6
To set your neighbor's bed a-shaking is now an ancient and long-established custom. It was the silver age that saw the first adulterers.
JUVENAL. *Satires*, VI, 1.

7
When a woman who admits that she is "unhappily yoked" holds long conversations about the "soul" with a man not her husband, it isn't the soul either of them is thinking about.
DON MARQUIS. *New York Herald.*

8
I submit to my fellow dramatists that the unfaithfulness of a wife is no longer a subject for drama, but only for comedy.
W. SOMERSET MAUGHAM. *Collected Plays:* preface.

9
"Here's luck," say, "to the lady," and "Luck to him who sleeps with her!'": but in your silent soul let the prayer be "Deuce take the husband."
OVID. *The Art of Love,* bk. i. tr. by J. H. Mozley.

10
Papa loved mamma
Mamma loved men
Mamma's in the graveyard

Papa's in the pen.
CARL SANDBURG. Quoted by Harry Golden in *Carl Sandburg.*

11
Next to the pleasure of making a new mistress is that of being rid of an old one.
WILLIAM WYCHERLEY. *The Country Wife,* Act 1.

12
A mistress should be like a little country retreat near the town; not to dwell in constantly, but only for a night and away.
WILLIAM WYCHERLEY. *The Country Wife,* Act 1.

13
Harcourt, what a good cuckold is lost there for want of a man to make him one?
WILLIAM WYCHERLEY. *The Country Wife,* Act 3.

14
A pox! keeping a cuckold company, after you have had his wife is as tiresome as the company of a country squire to a witty fellow of the town, when he has got all his money.
WILLIAM WYCHERLEY. *The Country Wife,* Act 5.

ADVENTURE

15
History has always treasured a catalogue of adventurers—she has not changed her ways, though she may not, for business reasons, be allowed to publish it.
WILLIAM BOLITHO. *Twelve Against the Gods:* introduction.

16
Geography, as Columbus has explained, is Adventure's rich game preserve, where any muff with a gun may hope for sport in the season.
WILLIAM BOLITHO. *Twelve Against the Gods: Mahomet.*

17
. . . the adventures of the spirit is a great deal more interestin' than the adventures of the flesh. No man can do more'n about six things with his flesh. But he can have a heap of fun with his immortal soul.
SIDNEY HOWARD. *They Knew What They Wanted.*

18
What an adroit old adventurer the subject of this memoir was! In order to get a chance to fly his kite on Sunday he used to hang a key on the string and let on to be fishing for lightning.
MARK TWAIN. *The Late Benjamin Franklin.*

ADVERTISING

1
The only thing you can tell an advertising man is that he is fortunate that he isn't in some other business.
FRED ALLEN. *Treadmill to Oblivion.*

2
When business is good it pays to advertise; when business is bad you've got to advertise.
ANONYMOUS.

3
Good times, bad times, there will always be advertising. In good times, people want to advertise; in bad times, they have to.
BRUCE BARTON. *Town & Country,* Feb., 1955.

4
Although
We've sold
Six million others
We still can't sell
Those coughdrop brothers
BURMA SHAVE SIGN. From *The Verse by the Side of the Road:* Frank Rowsome, Jr.

5
Commercials on television are similar to sex and taxes; the more talk there is about them, the less likely they are to be curbed.
JACK GOULD. *Column, The New York Times,* Oct. 20, 1963.

6
You know why Madison Avenue advertising has never done well in Harlem? We're the only ones who know what it means to *be* Brand X.
DICK GREGORY. *From the Back of the Bus.*

7
Back in the days when American billboard advertising was in flower, there were two slogans that I always rated above all others: the old Cremo Cigar ad that proclaimed "Spit Is A Horrid Word—But Worse On The End of Your Cigar," and "Drink Schlitz In Brown Bottles and Avoid That Skunk Taste."
ERNEST HEMINGWAY. Quoted by A. E. Hotchner in the *Saturday Evening Post,* Mar. 26, 1966.

8
Even merit has t' be advertised before it pays.
FRANK MCKINNEY (KIN) HUBBARD. *Abe Martin's Primer.*

9
The watch that made the dollar famous.
Attributed to R. H. INGERSOLL. According to I. E. Lambert, in *The Public Accepts,* Ingersoll once discovered, at a social gathering, that his hostess could not recall his name but readily identified

him with the inexpensive watch his company made. Thus the slogan was born.

10
The lack of candor among these officially hired racketeers is generally mitigated by a suavity of manner and an impeccable wardrobe.
ALEXANDER KING. *Rich Man, Poor Man, Freud and Fruit,* ch. 9.

11
Most fairly successful advertising men like to think that the composition of their copy involves enormous esthetic skills and they have a tendency to excuse the collecting of their exorbitant bribes on the ground that for the first time in history true genius is, at last, finding adequate compensation.
ALEXANDER KING. *Rich Man, Poor Man, Freud and Fruit,* ch. 9.

12
Embarrassing moments: when you have been making funny remarks about the party—and find it's your hostess you are talking to—be nonchalant—light a Murad.
LENNEN AND MITCHELL (New York Agency). *Slogan,* 1928, for P. Lorillard Co. This was one of a series of advertisements that offered a variety of "embarrassing moments."

13
Advertising is a valuable economic factor because it is the cheapest way of selling goods, particularly if the goods are worthless.
SINCLAIR LEWIS. (*The New York Times,* Apr. 18, 1943.)

14
A well-dressed man asked merely that the President allow the use of his name for advertising a project in view. "No!" flashed the President. "No! I'll have nothing to do with this. Do you take the President of the United States to be a commission broker? You have come to the wrong place. There is the door!"
CARL SANDBURG. *Abraham Lincoln: The Prairie Years and the War Years,* ch. 30.

15
Who's kidding whom? What's the difference between Giant and Jumbo? Quart and *full* quart? Two-ounce and *big* two-ounce? What does Extra Long mean? What's a *tall* 24-inch? And what busy shopper can tell?
MARYA MANNES. *Life,* June 12, 1964.

16
Obey That Impulse.
THOMAS L. MASSON. *Subscription slogan* (1895), for the old *Life,* of which he was editor for many years.

17
It is a mistake to use highfalutin language when you advertise to uneducated people. I

once used the word *obsolete* in a headline, only to discover that 43 per cent of the housewives had no idea of what it meant. In another headline, I used the word *ineffable*, only to discover that I didn't know what it meant myself.

> DAVID OGILVY. *Confessions of an Advertising Man*, ch. 6, ii.

1
The consumer is not a moron. She is your wife.

> DAVID OGILVY. *Advice* to advertising copywriters. (*New York Herald Tribune*, Aug. 29, 1956.)

2
That "producer's economy," then beginning to prevail in America, which first creates articles and then attempts to create a demand for them; an economy that has flooded the country with breakfast foods, shaving soaps, poets, and professors of philosophy.

> GEORGE SANTAYANA. *Persons and Places.*

3
Samson had the right idea about advertising. He took two columns and brought down the house.

> *Speaker's Cyclopedia of Humor.*

4
. . . there is this slightly misworded ad, which has been reprinted in many different forms: "Why go elsewhere to be cheated? You can trust us to do the job."

> From *A Treasury of Laughter* by LOUIS UNTERMEYER.

5
As far as I'm concerned, Pierre Salinger is a bar of soap, and we're going to sell him as effectively as we can.

> CHRISTY WALSH, JR. *Statement* to reporters, May 20, 1964, describing his technique in publicizing Salinger during the latter's campaign for the Democratic senatorial nomination in California in 1964. Walsh, a former advertising executive, was referring to a "saturation technique" employing a series of "spot" television appearances by the candidate.

6
Half the money I spend on advertising is wasted, and the trouble is I don't know which half.

> JOHN WANAMAKER. Credited originally to the first Lord Leverhulme. (DAVID OGILVY, *Confessions of an Advertising Man*, ch. 3.)

ADVICE

7
A woman seldom asks advice before she has bought all her wedding clothes.

> JOSEPH ADDISON. *The Spectator*, No. 475.

8
Who is to bell the cat? It is easy to propose impossible remedies.

> AESOP. *Belling the Cat.*

9
Never trust the advice of a man in difficulties.

> AESOP. *The Fox and the Goat.*

10
In June the air is full of advice. People are graduating and getting married and setting out on vacations, and it is the fate of these people to be battered with advice until they scream for mercy.

> RUSSELL BAKER. *"Observer" Column, The New York Times,* June 8, 1965.

11
The easiest way to escape being hated is to mind your own business and refrain from giving good advice.

> W. BURTON BALDRY. *Stray Thoughts.*

12
No man has ever yet discovered the way to give friendly advice to any woman, not even to his own wife.

> HONORÉ DE BALZAC. *Petty Troubles of Married Life.*

13
Advice is like castor oil, easy enough to give but dreadful uneasy to take.

> JOSH BILLINGS (H. W. SHAW).

14
If the lion was advised by the fox, he would be cunning.

> WILLIAM BLAKE. *Proverbs of Hell.*

15
Do as we say, and not as we do.

> GIOVANNI BOCCACCIO. *Decameron.*

16
These are high times when a British general is to take counsel of a Virginia buckskin.

> GENERAL EDWARD BRADDOCK. *Comment* in 1755, upon rejecting advice from George Washington.

17
Who cannot give good counsel? 'Tis cheap, it costs them nothing.

> ROBERT BURTON. *The Anatomy of Melancholy*, pt. 2.

18
Of all the horrid, hideous notes of woe,
Sadder than owl-songs or the midnight blast,
Is that portentous phrase, "I told you so."

> LORD BYRON. *Don Juan.*

19
She generally gave herself very good advice (though she very seldom followed it).

> LEWIS CARROLL. *Alice's Adventures in Wonderland.*

20
A woman's advice has little value, but he

who won't take it is a fool.
> MIGUEL DE CERVANTES. *Don Quixote*. Pt.
> II, ch. 7.

1
Advice is seldom welcome; and those who want it the most always like it the least.
> LORD CHESTERFIELD. *Letters,* Jan. 29,
> 1748.

2
To profit from good advice requires more wisdom than to give it.
> JOHN CHURTON COLLINS. *Aphorisms.*

3
We ask advice but we mean approbation.
> C. C. COLTON. *Lacon.*

4
Advice is offensive, . . . because it shows us that we are known to others as well as to ourselves.
> SAMUEL JOHNSON. *The Rambler.* No. 155.

5
A wise man puts aside 10 percent of the money he gets—and 90 percent of the free advice.
> HARRY KARNS. *Newsday.*

6
You will always find some Eskimos ready to instruct the Congolese on how to cope with heat waves.
> STANISLAW J. LEC. *Unkempt Thoughts,* tr.
> from the Polish by JACEK GALASKA.

7
She has the answer to everything and the solution to nothing.
> OSCAR LEVANT. *Memoirs of an Amnesiac.*

8
Many years ago a very wise man named Bernard Baruch took me aside and put his arm around my shoulder. "Harpo, my boy," he said, "I'm going to give you three pieces of advice, three things you should always remember." My heart jumped and I glowed with expectation. I was going to hear the magic password to a rich, full life from the master himself. "Yes, sir?" I said. And he told me three things.
I regret that I've forgotten what they were.
> HARPO MARX. *Harpo Speaks!*

9
A fool gives counsel to others but is not himself on his guard. (Sibi non cavere, et aliis consilium dare, Stultum esse.)
> PHAEDRUS. *Fables.* Bk. I, fab. 9.

10
I have made it so perfectly clear in my tracts, articles, and books what was to be done that all Parliament has had to do was read my works and do the opposite.
> BERNARD SHAW. In *Days with Bernard
> Shaw* by STEPHEN WINSTEN.

11
If you want people to notice your faults, start giving advice.
> KELLY STEPHENS. *Reader's Digest,* Feb.,
> 1967.

12
How is it possible to expect that mankind will take advice, when they will not so much as take warning?
> JONATHAN SWIFT. *Thoughts on Various
> Subjects.*

13
I have found that the best way to give advice to your children is to find out what they want and then advise them to do it.
> HARRY S TRUMAN. *Interview* with his
> daughter, *Person to Person,* CBS-TV,
> May 27, 1955. Margaret Truman sub-
> stituted for Edward R. Murrow.

14
He had only one vanity; he thought he could give advice better than any other person.
> MARK TWAIN. *The Man That Corrupted
> Hadleyburg,* ch. 1.

15
Free advice is the kind that costs you nothing unless you act upon it.
> UNKNOWN.

16
The advice of a wife is worthless, but woe to the man who does not take it.
> UNKNOWN. Welsh proverb.

17
It is always a silly thing to give advice, but to give good advice is absolutely fatal.
> OSCAR WILDE. *Portrait of Mr. W. H.*

AGE

See also Youth

18
When I read the obituary page of the *Times* I never see any women's names or pictures. They must have some secret formula men don't know about.
> GOODMAN ACE. *The Fine Art of Hypo-
> chondria.*

19
Young men have a passion for regarding their elders as senile.
> HENRY ADAMS. *The Education of Henry
> Adams.*

20
When an unsuccessful man passes that magic number [forty] he reacts to frustration and unhappiness by eating himself out of shape. The successful man reacts to good fortune by becoming a glutton. Either way the body is the same, even if the tailoring is different.
> JOEY ADAMS. *Cindy and I,* ch. 22.

21
Was she old? When they lit all of the candles

on her birthday cake, six people were over-
come with the heat.
  FRED ALLEN. *Much Ado About Me.*

1
Everyone knows that old men are twice
boys.
  ARISTOPHANES. *The Clouds.*

2
Middle age is a time of life
That a man first notices in his wife.
  RICHARD ARMOUR.

3
Antiquities are history defaced, or some
remnants of history which have casually escaped the shipwrecks of time.
  FRANCIS BACON. *Advancement of Learning,* bk. 2.

4
If you know what a cowcatcher is you're
over forty.
  JEROME BEATTY, JR. *The Saturday Review,*
  Mar. 16, 1968.

5
Someone asked Frankie how old Bald Charlie
was, and he said: "I don't know, but when
he dies I understand they are going to saw
the top of his head off and count the rings."
  JIM BISHOP. *Some of My Very Best: The
  Scoop.*

6
A lady of a "certain age", which means
Certainly aged.
  LORD BYRON. *Don Juan.* Canto vi, st. 69.

7
A Purdue graduate returned home from his
twenty-fifth class reunion in a very chastened
mood. "My classmates," he told his wife
sadly, "have all gotten so fat and bald they
didn't even recognize me."
  BENNETT CERF. *The Laugh's on Me.*

8
Old age isn't so bad when you consider the
alternative.
  MAURICE CHEVALIER. (*The New York
  Times,* Oct. 9, 1960.)

9
When you hit seventy, you eat better, you
sleep sounder, you feel more alive than when
you were thirty. Obviously, it's healthier to
have women on your mind than on your
knees.
  MAURICE CHEVALIER. (BENNETT CERF,
  The Laugh's on Me.)

10
We come now to the third ground for abus-
ing old age, and that is, that it is devoid
of sensual pleasures. O glorious boon of age,
if it does indeed free us from youth's most
vicious fault.
  MARCUS TULLIUS CICERO. *De Senectute.*
  Ch. XII, sec. 39.

11
A man is as old as he's feeling,
  A woman as old as she looks.
  MORTIMER COLLINS. *The Unknown Quan-
  tity.*

12
Wrinkles are the crannies and footholds on
the smooth visage of life to which man can
cling and gain some comfort and security.
  Daily Mail, London, Jan. 20, 1961. Editorial: *In Praise of Wrinkles.*

13
Age is like love, it cannot be hid.
  THOMAS DEKKER. *Fortunatus.* Act II,
  sc. 1.

14
Youth is a blunder; Manhood a struggle;
Old Age a regret.
  BENJAMIN DISRAELI. *Coningsby,* ch. 6.

15
  My birthday!—"How many years ago?
  Twenty or thirty?" Don't ask me!
"Forty or fifty?"—How can I tell?
I do not remember my birth, you see!
  JULIA C. DORR. *My Birthday.*

16
I am resolved to grow fat and look young
till forty, and then slip out of the world
with the first wrinkle and the reputation of
five-and-twenty.
  JOHN DRYDEN. *The Maiden Queen.* Act 3.

17
Many a man who couldn't direct you to the
drugstore on the corner when he was thirty
will get a respectful hearing when age has
further impaired his mind.
  FINLEY PETER DUNNE. *Mr. Dooley Remembers.*

18
Old age is a disease like other infirmaties
and people are afraid they'll catch it from
you.
  FINLEY PETER DUNNE. *Mr. Dooley Remembers.*

19
When a man has a birthday he takes a day
off, but when a woman has a birthday she
takes a year off.
  Toaster's Handbook, compiled by Peggy
  Edmund and Harold Workman Williams.

20
I'm saving that rocker for the day when I
feel as old as I really am.
  DWIGHT D. EISENHOWER. *Interview* with
  United Press International, Oct. 13,
  1965, the day before his 75th birthday.

21
The years between fifty and seventy are the
hardest. You are always being asked to do
things and yet you are not decrepit enough

to turn them down.
> T. S. ELIOT. Quoted in *Time*, Oct. 23, 1950.

1

Age, like woman, requires fit surroundings.
> RALPH WALDO EMERSON. *Society and Solitude: Old Age.*

2

The age of a woman doesn't mean a thing. The best tunes are played on the oldest fiddles.
> SIGMUND ENGEL, love pirate. *Retort*, when asked why he concentrated on older women. (*Newsweek*, July 4, 1949.)

3

The same old charitable lie
Repeated as the years scoot by
Perpetually makes a hit . . .
"You really haven't changed a bit!"
> MARGARET FISHBACK. *The Lie of the Land.*

4

All would live long, but none would be old.
> BENJAMIN FRANKLIN. *Poor Richard's Almanac*, 1749. See also SWIFT, *Thoughts on Various Subjects*, in this section.

5

Many foxes grow gray but few grow good.
> BENJAMIN FRANKLIN. *Poor Richard*, 1749.

6

Old boys have their playthings as well as young ones; the difference is only in the price.
> BENJAMIN FRANKLIN. *Poor Richard*, 1752.

7

Age and wedlock we all desire and repent of.
> THOMAS FULLER. *Gnomologia*, No. 780.

8

The Pyramids themselves, doting with age, have forgotten the names of their founders.
> THOMAS FULLER. *The Holy and Profane States: Of Tombs.*

9

Ours seems to be the only nation on earth that asks its teen-agers what to do about world affairs, and tells its golden-agers to go out and play.
> JULIAN GEROW. *Worcester* (Mass.) *Gazette.*

10

To everybody's prejudice I know a thing or two;
I can tell a woman's age in half a minute—and I do.
> W. S. GILBERT. *Princess Ida*, Act 1.

11

The imperceptible process of age has a point which, once passed, cannot be retraced. I knew I had passed that point and was getting old the day I noticed that all the cops looked so young.
> HARRY GOLDEN. *For 2¢ Plain.*

12

Most people say that as you get old, you have to give up things. I think you get old because you give up things.
> SENATOR THEODORE F. GREEN of Rhode Island, at 87. *News summaries*, June 28, 1954.

13

To be seventy years young is sometimes far more cheerful and hopeful than to be forty years old.
> OLIVER WENDELL HOLMES. *Letter to Julia Ward Howe*, on her 70th birthday, May 27, 1889.

14

Middle age is when your age starts to show around your middle.
> BOB HOPE.

15

You've got to be fifty-nine years ole t'believe a feller is at his best at sixty.
> FRANK MCKINNEY (KIN) HUBBARD. *Abe Martin's Primer.*

16

At seventy-seven it is time to be earnest.
> SAMUEL JOHNSON. Boswell's *Life.*

17

It was near a miracle to see an old man silent, since talking is the disease of age.
> BEN JONSON. *Timber.*

18

The growing infirmities of age manifest themselves in nothing more strongly than in an inveterate dislike of interruption.
> CHARLES LAMB. *Last Essays of Elia.*

19

Presently I shall be introduced as "this venerable old gentleman" and the axe will fall when they raise me to the degree of "grand old man." That means on our continent any one with snow-white hair who has kept out of jail till eighty.
> STEPHEN LEACOCK. *Three Score and Ten.*

20

For you the To-come,
But for me the Gone-by;
You are panting to live,
I am waiting to die.
> RICHARD LE GALLIENNE. *An Old Man's Song.*

21

I tell you at forty a man's a fool or his doctor—I mean, his own doctor.
> SINCLAIR LEWIS. *Babbitt.*

22

Whatever poet, orator or sage may say of it, old age is still old age.
> HENRY WADSWORTH LONGFELLOW. *Morituri Salutamus.*

23

Middle age: the time when a man is always

thinking that in a week or two he will feel just as good as ever.
Don Marquis. *New York Sun.*

1
Forty and forty-five are bad enough; fifty is simply hell to face; fifteen minutes after that you are sixty; and then in ten minutes more you are 85.
Don Marquis. Quoted by Edward Anthony in *O Rare Don Marquis.*

2
I suppose it's difficult for the young to realize that one may be old without being a fool.
W. Somerset Maugham. *The Circle.*

3
Growing old is no more than a bad habit which a busy man has no time to form.
André Maurois. Quoted by Milton Barron in *The Aging American.*

4
The older I grow the more I distrust the familiar doctrine that age brings wisdom.
H. L. Mencken. *Prejudices,* ser. 3.

5
Old age plants more wrinkles in the mind than in the face. (La vieillesse nous attache plus des rides en l'esprit qu'en visage.)
Michel de Montaigne. *Essays.* Bk. I, ch. 57.

6
King David and King Solomon
Led merry, merry lives,
With many, many lady friends
And many, many wives;
But when old age crept over them,
With many, many qualms,
King Solomon wrote the Proverbs
And King David wrote the Psalms.
James Ball Naylor. *David and Solomon.*

7
The maturity of man—that means, to have reacquired the seriousness that one had as a child at play.
Friedrich Wilhelm Nietzsche. *Beyond Good and Evil,* tr. by Helen Zimmern.

8
Generally money lies nearest them that are nearest their graves.
William Penn. *Fruits of Solitude.*

9
She's six-and-forty, and I wish nothing worse to happen to any woman.
Sir Arthur Wing Pinero. *The Second Mrs. Tanqueray,* Act. 2.

10
The years that a woman subtracts from her age are not lost. They are added to the ages of other women.
Diane de Poitiers.

11
Old men are twice children.
Thomas Randolph. *Jealous Lovers.* See also Aristophanes in this section.

12
An old man is a bed full of bones.
John Ray. *English Proverbs.*

13
First women subtract from their age, then they divide it, and then they extract its square root.
Reflections of a Bachelor.

14
The young man who has not wept is a savage, and the old man who will not laugh is a fool.
George Santayana. *Dialogues in Limbo.*

15
To be interested in the changing seasons is, in this middling zone, a happier state of mind than to be hopelessly in love with spring.
George Santayana. *Little Essays.*

16
Old age is an incurable disease.
Seneca. *Works: Epistles,* No. 108.

17
O Excellent! I love long life better than figs.
William Shakespeare. *Antony and Cleopatra.* Act I, sc. 2.

18
When the age is in, the wit is out.
William Shakespeare. *Much Ado About Nothing.* Act III, sc. 5.

19
She began to ask herself whether she had not overrated white beards and old age and nightshirts as divine credentials.
Bernard Shaw. *The Adventures of the Black Girl in Her Search for God.*

20
There are people who are beautiful in dilapidation, like houses that were hideous when new.
Logan Pearsall Smith. *All Trivia.*

21
You've heard of the three ages of man—youth, age and "you are looking wonderful."
Cardinal Francis Joseph Spellman. Quoted in *The New York Times,* Mar. 9, 1967.

22
Age may have one side, but assuredly Youth has the other. There is nothing more certain than that both are right, except perhaps that both are wrong.
Robert Louis Stevenson. *Virginibus Puerisque.*

23
I'm as old as my tongue and a little older than my teeth.
Jonathan Swift.

1
I swear she's no chicken; she's on the wrong side of thirty, if she be a day.
> JONATHAN SWIFT. *Polite Conversation,* Dialogue 1.

2
Every man desires to live long; but no man would be old.
> JONATHAN SWIFT. *Thoughts on Various Subjects.*

3
Old men and comets have been reverenced for the same reason: their long beards, and pretences to foretell events.
> JONATHAN SWIFT. *Works.* Vol. III, p. 409.

4
Old the proverb, old, but true;—
Age should think, and Youth should do.
> D'ARCY THOMPSON. *Sales Attici.*

5
Most of the visitors come here to see if the animal is still alive. But I fool 'em; I stay in my office most of the time.
> HARRY S TRUMAN. *Comment* on visitors to Truman Library, Sept. 13, 1959.

6
She had achieved a veritable triumph of art over middle age.
> G. F. TURNER. *The Conversion of Claude.*

7
Threescore years and ten!
It is the Scriptural statute of limitations.
> MARK TWAIN. *Essays: Seventieth Birthday.*

8
A youthful figure is what you get when you ask a woman her age.
> UNKNOWN.

9
A head that's white
To maids brings no delight.
> UNKNOWN. In *Berkeley Mss.,* III.

10
The old age of an eagle is better than the youth of a sparrow.
> UNKNOWN. Greek proverbial saying.

11
For a woman, the wrong side of forty is thirty-five.
> UNKNOWN. *Meditations in Wall Street.*

12
Soon ripe, soon rotten. (Cito maturum cito putridum.)
> UNKNOWN. Latin proverb.

13
Middle age is when a man figures he has enough financial security to wear the flashy sports coats he didn't have the courage to wear when he was young.
> BILL VAUGHAN. *Kansas City Star.*

14
Nothing is so ridiculous as an antique face in a juvenile drawing-room.
> HORACE WALPOLE. *Letter* to Sir Horace Mann, Dec. 31, 1780.

15
No woman should be quite accurate about her age. It looks so calculating.
> OSCAR WILDE. *The Importance of Being Earnest,* Act 3.

16
One should never trust a woman who tells one her real age. A woman who would tell one that, would tell one anything.
> OSCAR WILDE. *A Woman of No Importance,* Act I.

17
The gods bestowed on Max the gift of perpetual old age.
> OSCAR WILDE. Quoted by R. Aldington in his edition of Wilde. Referring to Max Beerbohm.

18
Middle Age—Later than you think and sooner than you expect.
> EARL WILSON.

AMBITION

See also Aspiration

19
A tomb now suffices him for whom the whole world was not sufficient.
> *Epitaph* on Alexander the Great.

20
I have found some of the best reasons I ever had for remaining at the bottom simply by looking at the men at the top.
> FRANK MOORE COLBY. *Essays,* vol. 2.

21
Most of the trouble in the world is caused by people wanting to be important.
> T. S. ELIOT. *The Cocktail Party.*

22
Every man who can be a first-rate something—as every man can be who is a man at all—has no right to be a fifth-rate something; for a fifth-rate something is no better than a first-rate nothing.
> JOSIAH G. HOLLAND. *Plain Talks: Self-Help.*

23
What's become o' th' ole fashioned feller who wuz willin' t' begin at th' bottom?
> FRANK MCKINNEY (KIN) HUBBARD. *Abe Martin's Primer.*

24
Here are mountains which I should once have climbed—[but] am now content with knowing that by scrambling up a rock, I shall see only other rocks.
> SAMUEL JOHNSON. *Letter* from Skye to Mrs. Thrale.

1
Ambition is but avarice on stilts and masked.
WALTER SAVAGE LANDOR. *Imaginary Conversations.*

2
Many go out for wool and come back shorn.
(Vendran por lana y volveran transquilados.)
Old Spanish Proverb.

3
The great quality of Dullness is to be unalterably contented with itself.
WILLIAM MAKEPEACE THACKERAY. *Miscellanies: Men's Wives: Dennis Haggarty's Wife.*

4
The dynamite of California was composed of one part vigor and one part unsatisfied passion.
FRANKLIN WALKER. *San Francisco's Literary Horizons.*

AMERICA AND THE AMERICANS

**See also Boston; New York;
Washington, D.C.**

5
No one should be required to see America for the first time.
ANONYMOUS. Quoted by Ashley Montagu on the Today show, Feb. 23, 1967.

6
The way to see America is from a lower berth about two in the morning. You've just left a station—it was the jerk of pulling out that woke you—and you raise the curtain a bit between thumb and forefinger to look out.
JACQUES BARZUN. *God's Country and Mine.*

7
Washington, Franklin, Hamilton, and Jefferson are wonderful legends—who will ever know or believe all that Jefferson did?—but match these names with Alexander, Borgia, Henry VIII, Luther, or Napoleon, and our heroes pale into unreality. For one thing, they have no wickedness to speak of. All we can muster as villains are Benedict Arnold and Aaron Burr—a pitiful showing of borderline cases.
JACQUES BARZUN. *God's Country and Mine.*

8
But then, Americans are always boasting about bribery and corruption, as if it was their own special invention, and as if nobody else had any.
BRENDAN BEHAN. *Where We All Came into Town; Evergreen Review.* Vol. V, No. 18.

9
Any well-established village in New England or the Northern Middle West could afford a town drunkard, a town atheist, and a few Democrats.
DENIS WILLIAM BROGAN. *The American Character.*

10
The American mind, unlike the English, is not formed by books, but, as Carl Sandburg once said to me . . . by newspapers and the Bible.
VAN WYCK BROOKS. *The Nation,* Aug. 14, 1954.

11
The swaggering underemphasis of New England.
HEYWOOD BROUN. *Collected Edition* (1941).

12
We send missionaries to China so the Chinese can get to heaven, but we won't let them into our country.
PEARL BUCK.

13
A people who are still, as it were, but in the gristle, and not yet hardened into the bone of manhood.
EDMUND BURKE. *Second Speech on Conciliation with America,* Apr. 19, 1774.

14
Don't get the idea that I'm one of these goddam radicals. Don't get the idea that I'm knocking the American system.
AL CAPONE, gangster. *Interview,* quoted by Claud Cockburn, *In Time of Trouble.*

15
Most Americans are born drunk . . . They have a sort of permanent intoxication from within, a sort of invisible champagne. . . . Americans do not need to drink to inspire them to do anything.
G. K. CHESTERTON. *The New York Times Magazine,* June 28, 1931.

16
There is nothing wrong with Americans except their ideals. The real American is all right; it is the ideal American who is all wrong.
G. K. CHESTERTON. Quoted in *The New York Times,* Feb. 1, 1931.

17
The American never imitates the Englishman in simply taking for granted both his own patriotism and his own superiority.
G. K. CHESTERTON. *Generally Speaking.*

18
The Pilgrim mothers, he said, not only had to bear with all the hardships—they also had to bear with the Pilgrim Fathers.
JOSEPH HODGES CHOATE. (Cleveland Amory, *The Last Resorts.*)

1
The semi-colon of the Eastern seaboard—
that's modern New Jersey.
    IRVIN S. COBB. *Some United States.*

2
We're a great people. We are that. And the
best of it is, we know we are.
    FINLEY PETER DUNNE. *Mr. Dooley Re-
    members.*

3
The enthusiasm of this country always makes
me think of a bonfire on an ice floe. It
burns bright as long as you feed it, and it
looks good, but it doesn't take hold, somehow, on the ice.
    FINLEY PETER DUNNE. *Mr. Dooley Re-
    members.*

4
The American nation in the sixth ward is a
fine people; they love the eagle—on the back
of the dollar.
    FINLEY PETER DUNNE.

5
Some people do not believe in California. I
do. There are now anonymous signboards in
Iowa announcing: "There is no California."
I don't go along with that.
    GEORGE P. ELLIOTT. *Why They Are Driv-
    ing Me Crazy.* From *First Person Sin-
    gular,* ed. by Herbert Gold.

6
A hundred years ago Cincinnati was often
called Porkopolis because so many hogs were
butchered and processed there.
    J. C. FURNAS. *The Late Demon Rum.*

7
Knavery seems to be so much the striking
feature of its [America's] inhabitants that
it may not in the end be an evil that they
will become aliens to this kingdom.
    GEORGE III, KING OF ENGLAND.

8
North Carolina has been referred to as "the
valley of humility between two mountains of
conceit" (Virginia and South Carolina).
    HARRY GOLDEN. *For 2¢ Plain.*

9
But the boys up in Boston were writing the
early histories of our country, and so they
made a big deal out of Bunker Hill, where
the Americans were on top of the hill, and
lost—and they forgot about Kings Mountain,
where the Americans were at the bottom of
the hill, and won.
    HARRY GOLDEN. *For 2¢ Plain.*

10
You may be Southern—but you're no Comfort.
    DICK GREGORY. *From the Back of the Bus.*

11
Everybody looks on this Civil War Centennial in a different light. Up in Harlem, all it

means is the 100th anniversary of separate
rest rooms. . . . That's why the South never
suffered from the Recession. Too busy building washrooms.
    DICK GREGORY. *From the Back of the Bus.*

12
I know a Southerner who owned an amusement park and almost went out of his mind
—over where to put us on a merry-go-
round.
    DICK GREGORY. *From the Back of the Bus.*

13
Isn't it fantastic that George Washington
Carver found over 300 uses for the lowly
peanut—but the South never had any use
for George Washington Carver?
    DICK GREGORY. *From the Back of the Bus.*

14
Are you aware that over 1½ million of my
people have left the South since 1950? 1½
million! It's like *Exodus* with pork chops instead of matzohs. . . . And why not? We
couldn't get treated any worse down there if
we came up with a substitute for cotton. . . .
That fine old Southern song says it: Way
down South in the land of cotton; where
civil rights are soon forgotten.
    DICK GREGORY. *From the Back of the Bus.*

15
Isn't this the most fascinating country in
the world? Where else would I have to ride
on the back of the bus, have a choice of going to the worst schools, eating in the worst
restaurants, living in the worst neighborhoods
—and average $5,000 a week just talking
about it?
    DICK GREGORY. *From the Back of the Bus.*

16
I was made by a Dago and presented to the
American people on behalf of the French
Government for the purpose of welcomin'
Irish immigrants into the Dutch city of New
York.
    O. HENRY. *Sixes and Sevens: The Lady
    Higher Up,* referring to the Statue of
    Liberty.

17
One thing I'll say fer the West is that in
this country there is more cows and less
butter, more rivers and less water, and you
can look farther and see less than in any
other place in the world.
    Complaint of a Southwestern rancher,
    quoted in *The Humor of the American
    Cowboy* by STAN HOIG.

18
The United States is the greatest law factory
the world has ever known.
    CHARLES EVANS HUGHES.

19
Kansas was once the butt of many a sena-

torial gibe but all that ended when John J. Ingalls in 1873 took his seat in the upper chamber. To a Delaware Senator who risked criticism of Kansas, Senator Ingalls flashed back: "Mr. President, the gentleman who has just spoken represents a state which has two counties when the tide is up—and only three when it is down."

> *The Wit and Wisdom of Congress*, ed. by EDWARD BOYKIN.

1

A Pennsylvania Senator made the mistake of drawing a disparaging comparison between "bleak Kansas" and the glorious Keystone State which he represented. Ingalls' reply was instant: "Mr. President, Pennsylvania has produced only two great men—Benjamin Franklin of Massachusetts and Albert Gallatin of Switzerland."

> *The Wit and Wisdom of Congress*, ed. by EDWARD BOYKIN. Referring to John J. Ingalls of Kansas.

2

America has not always been kind to its artists and scholars. Somehow the scientists always seem to get the penthouse while the arts and humanities get the basement.

> LYNDON B. JOHNSON. *Speech*, upon signing the Arts and Humanities Act of 1965, Sept. 29, 1965.

3

I am willing to love all mankind, *except an American.*

> SAMUEL JOHNSON. Boswell's *Life of Johnson.*

4

His great aim was to escape from civilization, and, as soon as he had money, he went to Southern California.

> ALVA JOHNSTON. *How To Become a Great Writer.* Reference to Edgar Rice Burroughs.

5

It is hard for a man who has enjoyed both the taste of our beer and the flavor of our politics to say which of these national glories has gone flatter in his lifetime.

> MURRAY KEMPTON. *America Comes of Middle Age.*

6

We cannot reform the world . . . Uncle Sugar is as dangerous a role for us to play as Uncle Shylock.

> JOHN F. KENNEDY. *Speech* to Boston Chamber of Commerce, Nov. 19, 1951.

7

You remember the very old story about a citizen of Boston who heard a Texan talking about the glories of Bowie, Davy Crockett, and all the rest, and finally said, "Haven't you heard of Paul Revere?" To which the Texan answered, "Well, he is the man who ran for help."

> JOHN F. KENNEDY. *Speech* in Houston, Sept. 12, 1960.

8

You can always tell the Irish,
  You can always tell the Dutch.
You can always tell a Yankee;
  But you cannot tell him much.

> ERIC KNIGHT. *All Yankees Are Liars.*

9

America was not discovered by Americans —shame on them.

> STANISLAW J. LEC. *Unkempt Thoughts,* tr. from the Polish by JACEK GALASKA.

10

Any man who wants to disrupt this Union needs all the religion in sight to save him.

> ABRAHAM LINCOLN. *Reply* to a Southern woman who asked for her husband's release from a Northern prison because he was a religious man. In *The Humorous Mr. Lincoln* by KEITH W. JENNISON.

11

America is the last abode of romance and other medieval phenomena.

> ERIC LINKLATER. *Juan in America.*

12

If Fascism came to America it would be on a program of Americanism.

> HUEY P. LONG. *Orientation Fact Sheet 64,* U.S. War Department, Mar. 24, 1945.

13

Our Pilgrim stock wuz pithed with hardihood.

> JAMES RUSSELL LOWELL. *The Biglow Papers.* Ser. ii, No. 6.

14

Americans don't think, they calculate: they are amazingly clever, but not very wise: they have no statesmen, only politicians.

> CHARLES MARRIOTT. *The House on the Sands.*

15

I don't blame our Indians for being discouraged. They are the only ones to be conquered by the United States and not come out ahead.

> HARRY OLIVER. *The Desert Rat Scrap Book.*

16

In writing a sketch of Washington a pupil ended her essay by saying: "Washington married a famous belle, Martha Custis, and in due time became the father of his country."

> WILLIAM PATTEN. *Among the Humorists.*

17

The situation is one something like living

with your wife. Sometimes it is difficult and even irritating to live with her but it is always impossible to live without her.

> LESTER PEARSON, as Canadian Secretary of State for External Affairs. Defining the Canadian attitude toward the United States. *News summaries*, March 15, 1955.

1
We are always watching Big Brother to see what trouble he might get us in—while at the same time protesting the fact that Big Brother is not watching us.

> LESTER PEARSON, as Prime Minister of Canada. *Commencement address* at Notre Dame University. (*The New York Times*, June 10, 1963.)

2
Asking one of the States to surrender part of her sovereignty is like asking a lady to surrender part of her chastity.

> JOHN RANDOLPH of Roanoke. From *The Wit and Wisdom of Congress*.

3
We have bought ten million Malays at two dollars a head unpicked, and nobody knows what it will cost to pick them.

> THOMAS B. REED. Referring to the purchase of the Philippines.

4
Nations talk about what they lack; America is talking about peace, Germany about unity, France about glory, Russia about freedom and India about food.

> JAMES RESTON. *The New York Times*, Dec. 15, 1965.

5
I attended a dinner the other morning given for the Old Settlers of California. No one was allowed to attend unless he had been in the State 2 and one half years.

> WILL ROGERS. *The Illiterate Digest*. (1924).

6
All Wrigley had was an idea. He was the first man to discover that American jaws must wag. So why not give them something to wag against?

> WILL ROGERS. *The Illiterate Digest*.

7
We don't know what we want, but we are ready to bite somebody to get it.

> WILL ROGERS. *Autobiography*.

8
Mr. [Henry L.] Stimson told me, "You go home, Will, and announce that one of America's muchly advertised talents has been overestimated. We are not the masters of bunk."

> WILL ROGERS. *Autobiography*. The remark was made in 1930, and referred to the London disarmament conference.

9
Americans are getting like a Ford car—they all have the same parts, the same upholstering and make exactly the same noises.

> WILL ROGERS. *Autobiography*.

10
The United States never lost a war or won a conference.

> WILL ROGERS. Quoted in *Life*, July 18, 1949.

11
There is a small articulate minority in this country which advocates changing our national symbol which is the eagle to that of the ostrich and withdrawing from the UN.

> ELEANOR ROOSEVELT. *Speech* before the Democratic national convention in Chicago, July 23, 1952. See also H. G. WELLS in this section.

12
Nations are known for the things they are not. Russia for its soul; Germany for its *Gemütlichkeit;* France for its logic; Spain for its religious compassion—and the United States for its efficiency.

> HARRY ROSKOLENKO. *When I Was Last on Cherry Street*.

13
In the years following the publication of the *Chicago Poems* [Carl] Sandburg used to say publicly, "Here is the difference between Dante, Milton, and me. They wrote about hell and never saw the place. I wrote about Chicago after looking the town over for years and years."

> HARRY GOLDEN. *Carl Sandburg*.

14
All his life he [the American] jumps into the train after it has started and jumps out before it has stopped; and he never once gets left behind or breaks a leg.

> GEORGE SANTAYANA. *Character and Opinion in the United States*.

15
To hell with Europe and the rest of those nations.

> SENATOR THOMAS D. SCHALL of Minnesota. From *The Wit and Wisdom of Congress*, ed. by EDWARD BOYKIN.

16
America is a "happy-ending" nation.

> DORE SCHARY. *Address* to the Harvard Club of Los Angeles. Quoted as foreword in Louis Kronenberger, *Company Manners*.

17
When you find some country gentleman keeping up the old English customs at Christmas and so forth, who is he? An American who has bought the place.

> BERNARD SHAW. *The Apple Cart*, Act 2.

1

You are right in your impression that a number of persons are urging me to come to the United States. But why on earth do you call them my friends?

BERNARD SHAW. *Letter* to Oswald Garrison Villard, Aug. 4, 1921.

2

If I owned Texas and Hell, I would rent out Texas and live in Hell.

GENERAL PHILIP H. SHERIDAN. Spoken at officers' mess at Fort Clark, Tex., in 1855.

3

Not many Americans have been around the world but their money sure has.

WALTER SLEZAK. From *Complete Toastmaster,* by HERBERT PROCHNOW.

4

In the United States there is more space where nobody is than where anybody is. This is what makes America what it is.

GERTRUDE STEIN. *The Geographical History of America.*

5

Yellowstone National Park is no more representative of America than is Disneyland.

JOHN STEINBECK. *Travels with Charley,* pt. 3.

6

Texas is a state of mind.

JOHN STEINBECK. *Travels with Charley,* pt. 4.

7

Like most passionate nations Texas has its own private history based on, but not limited by, facts.

JOHN STEINBECK. *Travels with Charley,* pt. 4.

8

The reason American cities are prosperous is that there is no place to sit down.

ALFRED J. TALLEY. *Interview,* on returning from Europe.

9

I do not object if the Easterner believes that the aurora borealis is only the glow in the sky from the factories of the East. I do not object if the Westerners believe as they do, that the glow of the setting sun is but a reflection of the grain fields of the West. Then why should they object if I believe, as I do, that the great Milky Way is but a reflection in the sky of the rice and cotton fields of Dixie?

SENATOR ROBERT TAYLOR of Tennessee.

10

October 12, the Discovery. It was wonderful to find America, but it would have been more wonderful to miss it.

MARK TWAIN. *Pudd'nhead Wilson's Calendar.*

11

[An Englishman is] a person who does things because they have been done before. [An American is] a person who does things because they haven't been done before.

MARK TWAIN.

12

A foreigner can photograph the exteriors of a nation, but I think that it is as far as he can get. No foreigner can report its interior—its soul, its life, its speech, its thought.

MARK TWAIN. *What Paul Bourget Thinks of Us.*

13

Nevada was discovered many years ago by the Mormons, and was called Carson county. It only became Nevada in 1861, by act of Congress. There is a popular tradition that the Almighty created it; but when you come to see it . . . you will think differently.

MARK TWAIN. *Information for the Million.*

14

Every time Europe looks across the Atlantic to see the American eagle, it observes only the rear end of an ostrich.

H. G. WELLS. *America.*

15

America is one long expectoration.

OSCAR WILDE. *Newspaper Interview,* during his visit to America in 1882.

16

When I went to America I had two secretaries, one for autographs, the other for locks of hair. Within six months the one had died of writer's cramp, the other was completely bald.

OSCAR WILDE. Quoted by HESKETH PEARSON in *Lives of the Wits.*

17

After all, this is a nation that, except for a hard core of winos at the bottom and a hard crust of aristocrats at the top, has been going gloriously middle class for two decades.

TOM WOLFE. *The Kandy-Colored Tangerine-Flake Streamline Baby* (1965).

18

The South has preaching and shouting, the South has grits, the South has country songs, old mimosa traditions, clay dust, Old Bigots, New Liberals—and all of it, all of that old mental cholesterol, is confined to the Sunday radio.

TOM WOLFE. *The Kandy-Colored Tangerine-Flake Streamline Baby.*

ANCESTRY

See also Aristocracy

19

Always select the right sort of parents before you start to be rough.

GEORGE ADE. *Fables.*

1
I don't have to look up my family tree, because I know that I'm the sap.
FRED ALLEN. *Much Ado About Me.*

2
It is hereditary in my family to have no children.
ANONYMOUS.

3
There was a young man in Rome, that was very like Augustus Caesar; Augustus took knowledge of it, and sent for the man, and asked him, "Was your mother never at Rome?" He answered, "No, sir, but my father was."
FRANCIS BACON. *Apothegms*, No. 87.

4
There were human beings aboard the
Mayflower,
Not merely ancestors.
STEPHEN VINCENT BENÉT. *Western Star.*

5
Nothing is so soothing to our self-esteem as to find our bad traits in our forbears. It seems to absolve us.
VAN WYCK BROOKS. *From a Writer's Notebook* (1958).

6
He was not merely a chip of the old block, but the old block itself.
EDMUND BURKE. Referring to Pitt, 1781. See also MILTON AND ROWLEY in this section.

7
I'd rather have an inch of dog than miles of pedigree.
DANA BURNET. *The Road to Vagabondia*, st. 3.

8
A degenerate nobleman, or one that is proud of his birth, is like a turnip. There is nothing good of him but that which is underground.
SAMUEL BUTLER. *"Characters": A Degenerate Nobleman* (c. 1660).

9
A hen is only an egg's way of making another egg.
SAMUEL BUTLER. *Life and Habit* (1877).

10
I cannot help reflecting that if my father had been American and my mother British, instead of the other way around, I might have got here on my own.
WINSTON CHURCHILL. *Address to Congress of United States*, Dec. 26, 1941.

11
Gentility is what is left over from rich ancestors after the money is gone.
JOHN CIARDI. *The Saturday Review*, Sept. 24, 1966.

12
. . . the thing a child gets from the other side of the family.
MARCELINE COX. Referring to heredity. (CLEVELAND AMORY, *Who Killed Society?*)

13
The pride of ancestry increases in the ratio of distance.
GEORGE WILLIAM CURTIS. *Prue and I*, ch. 6.

14
The pedigree of honey
Does not concern the bee;
A clover, any time, to him
Is aristocracy.
EMILY DICKINSON. *Poems*, pt. 2.

15
Very likely my ancestry begins where yours ends.
Attributed to ALEXANDER DUMAS, *père.* When asked if he was not descended from an ape, a covert sneer at his Negro grandmother.

16
Ancestors are initiators. Descendants too often are imitators.
B. C. FORBES. *Epigrams.*

17
. . . Years ago I heard somebody say that being a Roumanian was not a nationality, but a profession.
LILLIAN HELLMAN. *Watch on the Rhine*, Act 3.

18
It will not out of the flesh that is bred in the bone.
JOHN HEYWOOD. *Proverbs.*

19
Many a family tree needs trimmin'.
FRANK MCKINNEY (KIN) HUBBARD. *Abe Martin's Primer.*

20
There is no king who has not had a slave among his ancestors, and no slave who has not had a king among his.
HELEN KELLER. *Story of My Life.*

21
The stairway of time ever echoes with the wooden shoe going up and the polished boot coming down.
JACK LONDON. *What Life Means to Me; Cosmopolitan Magazine*, Mar. 1906.

22
Somehow I've always had a sort of sneakin'
Idee that peddygrees is purty much
Like monkeys' tails—so long they're apt to
weaken
The yap that drags 'em round.
ROBERTUS LOVE. *The Boy From Hodgensville.*

1

They talk about their Pilgrim blood,
  Their birthright high and holy!
A mountain-stream that ends in mud
  Methinks is melancholy.
  JAMES RUSSELL LOWELL. *Interview with
  Miles Standish.*

2

We pay for the mistakes of our ancestors,
and it seems only fair that they should leave
us the money to pay with.
  DON MARQUIS. *New York Sun.*

3

i have often noticed that
ancestors never boast
of the descendants who boast
of ancestors i would
rather start a family than
finish one blood will tell but often
it tells too much
  DON MARQUIS. *a roach of the taverns.*

4

How well dost thou now appear to be a
chip of the old block?
  JOHN MILTON. *Apology for Smectymnuus,*
  sec. 7 (1642). See also ROWLEY in this
  section.

5

Sire, I am my own Rudolph of Hapsburg.
  NAPOLEON BONAPARTE. To his prospective
  father-in-law, the Emperor of Austria,
  when the latter wished to trace his ancestry to a prince. Rudolph was the
  founder of the Hapsburg family.

6

The best blood will sometimes get into a fool
or a mosquito.
  AUSTIN O'MALLEY.

7

The man who has not anything to boast of
but his illustrious ancestors is like a potato,
—the only good belonging to him is underground.
  SIR THOMAS OVERBURY. *Characters.*

8

Blood is thicker than water.
  JOHN RAY. *English Proverbs* (1670).

9

Generally when a man brags about his pedigree he has nothing else to brag about.
  Reflections of a Bachelor.

10

You have read of the San Blas Indians. You
can land and visit them but you must get
away before night. The old chief won't let
you stop after dark. Due to his foresight,
they are the only 100 percent pure Indians.
  WILL ROGERS. *Autobiography.*

11

It's kinder funny, but no matter how common our blood is, we hate to lose any of it.
  WILL ROGERS. *The Illiterate Digest.*

12

"Ancestors don't mean a thing in the human
tribe," Will Rogers once commented.
"They're as unreliable as a political promise.
A western range mare is liable to produce a
Man o' War. You won't know what will
happen. You just raise 'em and then start
guessing. They no more take after Father
and Mother than a Congressman will take
after a good example."
  DONALD DAY. *Will Rogers: A Biography.*

13

My folks didn't come over on the *Mayflower,* but they were there to meet the boat.
  WILL ROGERS.

14

He's a chip o' th' old block.
  WILLIAM ROWLEY. *A Match at Midnight*
  (1633).

15

He who boasts of his descent, praises the
deeds of another. (Qui genus jactat suum,
Aliena laudat.)
  SENECA. *Hercules Furens,* l. 340.

16

Let who will preen himself on his Mother
Hubbard's bare cupboard, and play for sympathy as an upstart: I was a downstart and
the son of a downstart.
  BERNARD SHAW. *Immaturity:* preface.

17

Our ancestors are very good kind of folks;
but they are the last people I should choose
to have a visiting acquaintance with.
  RICHARD BRINSLEY SHERIDAN. *The Rivals,*
  Act 4.

18

The Smiths never had any arms, and have
invariably sealed their letters with their
thumbs.
  SYDNEY SMITH. Quoted in Lady Holland,
  Memoir, vol. 1.

19

Not long ago it was proved that Dwight D.
Eisenhower was descended from the royal
line of Britain, a proof if one were needed
that everyone is descended from everyone.
  JOHN STEINBECK. *Travels with Charley,*
  pt. 2.

20

Nothing like blood, sir, in hosses, dawgs,
and men.
  WILLIAM MAKEPEACE THACKERAY. *Vanity
  Fair,* ch. 35.

21

Paul Bourget: "When an American has
nothing to do, he can always spend a few

years trying to find out who his grand-father was."
Mark Twain: "Quite right, Mr. Bourget. And when all other interests fail a French-man, he can always try to find out who his father was."
  Speaker's Cyclopedia of Humor, ed. by
    JACOB BRAUDE.

1
A great many family trees were started by grafting.
  UNKNOWN.

2
A man who boasts of his ancestors con-fesses that he belongs to a family that is better off dead than alive.
  UNKNOWN.

3
John Carnegie lies here,
  Descended from Adam and Eve.
If any can boast of a pedigree higher,
  He will willingly give them leave.
  UNKNOWN. Ancient Scotch epitaph.

4
The first king was a successful soldier;
He who serves his country well has no need
  of ancestors.
(Le premier qui fut roi, fut un soldat
  heureux;
Qui sert bien son pays, n'a pas besoin
  d'aieux.)
  VOLTAIRE. *Mérope.* Act I, sc. 3.

ANGER

5
Anger makes dull men witty, but it keeps them poor.
  FRANCIS BACON. *Apothegms,* No. 4.
    Quoted as by Queen Elizabeth I.

6
The tigers of wrath are wiser than the horses of instruction.
  WILLIAM BLAKE. *Proverbs of Hell.*

7
The anger of fools is my favorite crown.
  MAXWELL BODENHEIM. Quoted by Ben
    Hecht in *Letters From Bohemia.*

8
Nursing her wrath to keep it warm.
  ROBERT BURNS. *Tam o' Shanter.*

9
Betsy, like all good women, had a temper of her own.
  WILL CARLETON. *Betsy and I Are Out.*

10
Anger helps complexion, saves paint.
  WILLIAM CONGREVE. *The Way of the
    World,* Act 1.

11
Anger is an expensive luxury in which only men of a certain income can indulge.
  GEORGE WILLIAM CURTIS. *Prue and I.*

12
There is something about a roused woman, especially if she add to all her other strong passions, the fierce impulses of recklessness and despair, which few men like to provoke.
  CHARLES DICKENS. *Oliver Twist,* ch. 16.

13
Like women's anger, impotent and proud.
  JOHN DRYDEN. *To Sir Godfrey Kneller.*

14
A man in a passion rides a mad horse.
  BENJAMIN FRANKLIN. *Poor Richard,* 1749.

15
When angry, count ten before you speak; if very angry, an hundred.
  THOMAS JEFFERSON. *Writings,* vol. 16.

16
He looked at me as if I was a side dish he hadn't ordered.
  RING LARDNER.

17
Powerless rage can work miracles.
  STANISLAW J. LEC. *Unkempt Thoughts,*
    tr. from the Polish by JACEK GALASKA.

18
Peace of mind is better than giving them "a piece of your mind."
  J. P. McEVOY. *Charlie Would Have
    Loved This.*

19
Every normal man must be tempted, at times, to spit on his hands, hoist the black flag, and begin slitting throats.
  H. L. MENCKEN. *Prejudices,* ser. 1.

20
Bridle your tongue and you saddle your temper.
  Reflections of a Bachelor.

21
Anger wishes all mankind had only one neck; love, that it had only one heart.
  J. P. F. RICHTER. *Flower, Fruit and Thorn,*
    IV.

22
When angry, count four; when very angry, swear.
  MARK TWAIN. *Pudd'nhead Wilson's Calen-
    dar.*

23
The elephant is never won with anger,
  Nor must that man who would reclaim a
    lion
  Take him by the teeth.
  JOHN WILMOT. *Valentinian,* Act 1.

ANIMALS

See also Ape, Ass, Cat, Cow, Dog, Horse

24
I could descant in all candor on the glories of the worm, when I look at its glancing

color, its perfect corporal rotundity, its in-
termeshing of end with middle, middle with
end, each contributing something to a thrust
toward one-ness in this lowest of things, so
that there is no part that does not answer to
another part harmoniously.
> St. Augustine. *The True Religion,* 77.
> From *Roman Culture,* ed. by Garry
> Wills.

1
Animals are such agreeable friends—they
ask no questions, they pass no criticisms.
> George Eliot. *Scenes of Clerical Life:
> Mr. Gilfil's Love Story.*

2
The fox has many tricks and the hedgehog
only one, but that is the best of all.
> Desiderius Erasmus. *Adagia.*

3
Some reptiles are helpful to man by eating
harmful bugs and little animals. Some other
reptiles are harmful to man by eating him.
> Art Linkletter. *A Child's Garden of
> Misinformation.*

4
All Aesop's Fables are libels on the animal
kingdom and would not have a chance of
being understood by the animals if they
could read them.
> Lin Yutang. *With Love and Irony.*

5
If you lift a guinea-pig up by the tail
His eyes drop out!
> F. Locker-Lampson. *A Garden Lyric.*

6
                    Th' unwieldy elephant,
To make them mirth, us'd all his might, and
        wreath'd
His lithe proboscis.
> John Milton. *Paradise Lost.*

7
Man isn't so smart. Thousands of years
before he began to have afternoon headaches
from trying to think, the desert tortoise had
a streamlined body, turret top, retractable
landing gear, and a portable house.
> Harry Oliver. *The Desert Scrap Book.*

8
Pity the Unicorn
Pity the Hippogriff.
Souls that were never born
Out of the land of If!
> Martha Ostenso.

9
We have no intention of campaigning against
mousetraps or flypapers.
> Prince Philip. When speaking as presi-
> dent of the World Wildlife Fund's
> British National Appeal, Nov., 1962,
> he emphasized that their purpose was
> not to protect all animals against every-
> thing.

10
The mouse that trusts to one poor hole,
Can never be a mouse of any soul.
> Alexander Pope. *The Wife of Bath.*

11
. . . when one loves animals and children
too much, one loves them against human
beings.
> Jean-Paul Sartre. *The Words.*

12
Nature teaches beasts to know their friends.
> William Shakespeare. *Coriolanus.* Act
> II, sc. 1.

13
The behavior of men to the lower animals,
and their relationship to each other, bear
a constant relationship.
> Herbert Spencer. *Social Statics.* Pt. iv,
> ch. 30, sec. 2.

14
It often happens that a man is more hu-
manely related to a cat or dog than to any
human being.
> Henry D. Thoreau. *Journal,* Apr. 29,
> 1851.

15

A Hop Toad
He practiced, with a calm the saints might
        prize,
Faith—that he would receive his daily flies;
Hope—for a share in common garden joys,
And charity—even toward small tormenting
        boys.
But for a little slip in Nature's plan,
Here would be lying a Christian gentleman.
> Nancy Byrd Turner. *Poems Selected and
> New.*

16

Rabbit
God wrought him well, of silk and tempered
        steel,
Amber and ivory, and shod his heel
With wind, and gave him wit to understand
Lore of the wood and wisdom of the land.
"Ashes to ashes" for mortals, "Dust to dust."
These bones lie light beneath a pastry crust.
> Nancy Byrd Turner. *Poems Selected and
> New.*

17
Mules and donkeys and camels have appetites that anything will relieve temporarily,
but nothing satisfy.
> Mark Twain.

18
I have been studying the traits and dispositions of the "lower animals" (so called)
and contrasting them with the traits and
dispositions of man. I find the result humili-
ating to me.
> Mark Twain. *Letters from the Earth.*

1

The refreshing definition of a camel: a horse planned by a committee.

Vogue, July, 1958.

2

Animals have these advantages over man: they have no theologians to instruct them, their funerals cost them nothing, and no one starts lawsuits over their wills.

VOLTAIRE.

APE

See also Evolution

3

The Chimpanzee is found in equatorial Africa and vaudeville.

WILL CUPPY. *How to Tell Your Friends from the Apes.*

4

Young Gorillas are friendly but they soon learn.

WILL CUPPY. *How to Tell Your Friends from the Apes.*

5

Orang-utans teach us that looks are not everything but darned near it.

WILL CUPPY. *How to Tell Your Friends from the Apes.*

6

An ape's an ape, a varlet's a varlet, Tho' they be clad in silk or scarlet.

THOMAS FULLER. *Gnomologia,* No. 6391.

7

I believe that our Heavenly Father invented man because he was disappointed in the monkey.

MARK TWAIN.

APOLOGY

8

Apologize—to lay the foundation for a future offense.

AMBROSE BIERCE.

9

Apology is only egotism wrong side out.

OLIVER WENDELL HOLMES. *The Professor at the Breakfast Table.*

10

I guess he [former President Truman] will apologize for calling me an S.O.B. and I will apologize for being one.

JOHN F. KENNEDY. Quoted by VICTOR LASKY in *J.F.K.: The Man and the Myth.*

11

. . . I asked Tom if countries always apologized when they had done wrong, and he says: "Yes, the little ones does."

MARK TWAIN. *Tom Sawyer Abroad,* ch. 12.

APPEARANCE

See also Bearing, Face, Mirror

12

There's less in this than meets the eye.

TALLULAH BANKHEAD.

13

Merely as an observer of natural phenomena, I am fascinated by my own personal appearance. This does not mean that I am pleased with it, mind you, or that I can even tolerate it. I simply have a morbid interest in it.

ROBERT BENCHLEY. *My Face. (The Benchley Roundup,* ed. by NATHANIEL BENCHLEY.)

14

It is sometimes the man who opens the door who is the last one to enter the room.

ELIZABETH BIBESCO. *The Fur and the Palm,* ch. 13.

15

Passport Picture—A photo of a man that he can laugh at without realizing that it looks exactly the way his friends see him.

Boston Herald.

16

Keep up appearances; there lies the test;
The world will give thee credit for the rest.
Outward be fair, however foul within;
Sin, if thou wilt, but then in secret sin.

CHARLES CHURCHILL (1731–1764). *Night.*

17

He is a sheep in sheep's clothing.

SIR WINSTON CHURCHILL. *Remark* attributed in 1945, with reference to CLEMENT ATTLEE.

18

The hippopotamus looks monogamous. He looks as if he would have to be.

WILL CUPPY. *How to Tell Your Friends from the Apes: The Hippopotamus.*

19

When I see a bird that walks like a duck and swims like a duck and quacks like a duck, I call that bird a duck.

RICHARD CARDINAL CUSHING. Comment on the propriety of calling Fidel Castro a Communist. In *The New York Times,* Mar. 1, 1964.

20

To be plain with you, friend, you don't carry in your countenance a letter of recommendation.

CHARLES DICKENS. *Barnaby Rudge,* ch. 2.

21

To say I always look my best can only mean the worst.

T. S. ELIOT. *The Cocktail Party,* Act 2.

1
The trouble is, the more it resembles me, the worse it looks.
> RALPH WALDO EMERSON. To Daniel Chester French, who was making a bust of him. (CABOT, *A Memoir of Ralph Waldo Emerson.*)

2
Things are seldom what they seem.
Skim milk masquerades as cream.
> W. S. GILBERT. *H.M.S. Pinafore,* Act 2.

3
Hit look lak sparrer-grass, hit feel like sparrer-grass, hit tas'e lak sparrer-grass, en I bless ef 'taint sparrer-grass.
> JOEL CHANDLER HARRIS. *Nights with Uncle Remus.*

4
Those awful goddesses, Appearances, are to us what the Fates were to the Greeks.
> SIR ARTHUR HELPS. *Friends in Council.* Bk. I, ch. 5.

5
The outward forms the inward man reveal,—
We guess the pulp before we cut the peel.
> OLIVER WENDELL HOLMES. *A Rhymed Lesson.*

6
Some folks, like most resturints, seem t' think a clean front is all that's necessary.
> FRANK McKINNEY (KIN) HUBBARD. *Abe Martin's Primer.*

7
It must be great t' be rich and let th' other feller keep up appearances.
> FRANK McKINNEY (KIN) HUBBARD. *Abe Martin's Primer.*

8
Ther's gittin' t' be too many thirty-cent people that look like a million dollars.
> FRANK McKINNEY (KIN) HUBBARD. *Abe Martin's Primer.*

9
You look wise. Pray correct that error.
> CHARLES LAMB. *Essays of Elia: All Fools' Day.*

10
The Lord prefers common-looking people. That is the reason He makes so many of them.
> ABRAHAM LINCOLN. Quoted by JAMES MORGAN, *Our Presidents.* C. T. WETTSTEIN, *Was Lincoln an Infidel?*

11
In a certain way, like the men in the breakfast-food ads, he is quite handsome.
> RUTH McKENNEY. *The Sock Hunt.* Reference to RANDOLPH CHURCHILL.

12
He bears an unmistakable resemblance to a cornered rat.
> NORMAN MAILER. *Advertisements for My-*

self. Description of photograph of himself.

13
Famous last words of Ned Rorem, crushed by a truck, gnawed by the pox, stung by wasps, in dire pain: "How do I look?" It's harder to maintain a reputation for being pretty than for being a great artist.
> NED ROREM. *Paris Diary.*

14
Mellow nuts have the hardest rind.
> SIR WALTER SCOTT. *Lord of the Isles,* canto 3.

15
Looked as if she had walked straight out of the ark.
> SYDNEY SMITH. Quoted in LADY HOLLAND's *Memoir.*

16
Don't rely too much on labels,
For too often they are fables.
> CHARLES HADDON SPURGEON. *Salt-Cellars.*

17
Twenty-four years ago, Madam, I was incredibly handsome. The remains of it are still visible through the rift of time. I was so handsome that women became spellbound when I came in view. In San Francisco, in rainy seasons, I was frequently mistaken for a cloudless day.
> MARK TWAIN. *Letter* written toward the end of his life.

18
It is only shallow people who do not judge by appearances.
> OSCAR WILDE. *Picture of Dorian Gray,* ch. 2.

ARCHITECTURE

See also Furnishings

19
He that builds a fair house upon an ill seat, committeth himself to prison.
> FRANCIS BACON. *Essays: Of Building.*

20
Sir Christopher Wren
Said, "I am going to dine with some men.
If anybody calls
Say I am designing St. Paul's."
> EDMUND CLERIHEW BENTLEY.

21
We shape our buildings; thereafter they shape us.
> SIR WINSTON CHURCHILL. In *Time,* Sept. 12, 1960.

22
Under this stone, reader, survey
Dead Sir John Vanbrugh's house of clay.
Lie heavy on him, earth! for he

Laid many heavy loads on thee.
ABEL EVANS. *On Sir John Vanbrugh.* Vanbrugh was the architect of Blenheim Palace.

1
That miracle of a youth, Mr. Christopher Wren.
JOHN EVELYN. *Diary,* July 11, 1654.

2
Too many stairs and back-doors makes thieves and whores.
BALTHAZAR GERBIER. *Discourse of Building,* ch. 14.

3
There are possibilities in a door always, for how can you know what is on the other side?
ANTHONY HOPE. *Tales of Two People.*

4
Architecture is the art of how to waste space.
PHILIP JOHNSON. From *The New York Times,* "Ideas and Men," Dec. 27, 1964.

5
Modern buildings tend to look like call girls who came out of it intact except that their faces are a touch blank and the expression in their eyes is as lively as the tip of a filter cigarette.
NORMAN MAILER. *The Presidential Papers.*

6
He couldn't design a cathedral without it looking like the First Supernatural Bank.
EUGENE O'NEILL. *The Great God Brown.*

7
To talk of architecture is a joke
Till you build a chimney that won't smoke.
JAMES ROBINSON PLANCHÉ. Paraphrasing ARISTOPHANES, *The Birds.*

8
Political anecdotes are rife, like the one about the monstrous Palace of Culture, Stalin's gift in the middle of Warsaw: the best view of Warsaw, they say, is the one from the Palace, because it is the only place in Warsaw from which you can't see the Palace.
ADLAI STEVENSON. *Friends and Enemies.*

9
Everything betrays us as a bunch of catchpenny materialists devoted to a blatant, screeching insistence on commercialism. If you look around you, and you give a damn, it makes you want to commit suicide.
EDWARD DURELL STONE. *Interview, The New York Times,* Aug. 27, 1964.

10
The dome of St. Paul's is supported by eight peers, all of which are unfortunately cracked.
LOUIS UNTERMEYER. *A Treasury of Laughter.* Quoted as a student boner.

11
It is no accident that Las Vegas and Versailles are the only two architecturally uniform cites in Western history.
TOM WOLFE. *The Kandy-Kolored Tangerine-Flake Streamline Baby.*

12
Builds himself a name; and, to be great,
Sinks in a quarry an immense estate.
EDWARD YOUNG. *Love of Fame,* satire 1.

ARGUMENT

13
Let the long contention cease!
Geese are swans and swans are geese!
MATTHEW ARNOLD. *The Last Word.*

14
Sentiment is not argument, reason is not pleasure, and pleasure is certainly not a reason.
HONORÉ DE BALZAC. *Petty Troubles of Married Life.*

15
An heretic, my dear sir, is a fellow who disagrees with you regarding something neither of you knows anything about.
WILLIAM C. BRANN. Quoted by CHARLES CARVER, *Brann and the Iconoclast.*

16
A woman who is confuted is never convinced.
JOHN CHURTON COLLINS. *Aphorisms.*

17
Don't try to argue with a million dollars.
HARRISON COWAN.

18
The tree of knowledge blasted by dispute,
Produces sapless leaves instead of fruit.
SIR JOHN DENHAM. *Progress of Learning.*

19
Argeyment is a gift of Natur.
CHARLES DICKENS. *Barnaby Rudge,* ch. 1.

20
I am bound to furnish my antagonists with arguments, but not with comprehension.
BENJAMIN DISRAELI. *Speech,* House of of Commons. See also JOHNSON in this section.

21
If you wish to win a man's heart, allow him to confute you.
BENJAMIN DISRAELI. *Vivian Grey.*

22
He argued high, he argued low,
He argued round about him.
W. S. GILBERT. *Sir Macklin.*

23
There's no arguing with Johnson; for when his pistol misses fire, he knocks you down with the butt end of it.
OLIVER GOLDSMITH. *Remark.* From BOSWELL's *Life of Johnson,* Oct. 26, 1769.

24
In arguing, too, the parson own'd his skill,

For e'en though vanquished, he could argue
  still;
While words of learned length, and thund'ring
  sound,
Amazed the gazing rustics rang'd around;
And still they gaz'd, and still the wonder
  grew,
That one small head could carry all he knew.
  OLIVER GOLDSMITH. *The Deserted Village,*
  l. 211.

1
And, Sir, there is a gratification of pride.
Though we cannot out-vote them we will
out-argue them.
  SAMUEL JOHNSON. BOSWELL'S *Life,* Apr.
  3, 1778.

2
Sir, I have found you an argument; but I
am not obliged to find you an understanding.
  SAMUEL JOHNSON. BOSWELL'S *Life,* June
  19, 1784.

3
Abel was the first to discover that dead
victims do not protest.
  STANISLAW J. LEC. *Unkempt Thoughts,*
  tr. from the Polish by JACEK GALASKA.

4
According to Governor Andrew, Lincoln was
asked what he would reply to McClellan's
earlier advice on how to carry on the affairs
of the nation. And Lincoln answered: "Nothing—but it made me think of the man whose
horse kicked up and stuck his foot through
the stirrup. He said to the horse, 'If you are
going to get on I will get off.' "
  CARL SANDBURG. *Abraham Lincoln: The
  Prairie Years and the War Years,* ch. 27.

5
There is no good in arguing with the in-
evitable. The only argument available with
an east wind is to put on your overcoat.
  JAMES RUSSELL LOWELL. *Democracy and
  Addresses.*

6
He [Don Marquis] once said that no one
had ever won an argument—that when a ver-
bal battle is over the adversaries think as
they did when they started trading insults.
The one that backs down is merely trying to
protect his eardrums.
  EDWARD ANTHONY. *O Rare Don Marquis.*

7
Con was a thorn to brother Pro—
  On Pro we often sicked him:
Whatever Pro would claim to know
  Old Con would contradict him!
  CHRISTOPHER MORLEY. *The Twins.*

8
Only a fool argues with a skunk, a mule or
the cook.

HARRY OLIVER. *The Desert Rat Scrap
  Book.*

9
Discussion is an exchange of knowledge;
argument an exchange of ignorance.
  ROBERT QUILLEN.

10
One of the best ways to persuade others is
with your ears—by listening to them.
  DEAN RUSK. In *Reader's Digest,* July,
  1961.

11
To strive with an equal is a doubtful thing
to do; with a superior, a mad thing; with
an inferior, a vulgar thing. (Cum pare con-
tendre, anceps est; cum superiore, furiosum;
cum inferiore, sordidum.)
  SENECA. *De Ira.* Quoted by CHAUCER,
  Melibeus.

12
They are yet but ear-kissing arguments.
  WILLIAM SHAKESPEARE. *King Lear.* Act
  ii, sc. 1.

13
A man never tells you anything until you
contradict him.
  BERNARD SHAW. *Letter* to Ellen Terry.

14
You may say, I am hot; I say I am not,
Only warm, as the subject on which I am
  got.
  JONATHAN SWIFT. *The Famous Speech-
  maker.*

15
The itch of disputation will break out
Into a scab of error.
  ROWLAND WATKYNS. *Flamma Sine Fumo:
  The New Illiterate Late Teachers.* A
  paraphrase of SIR HENRY WOTTON:
  "The itch of disputation will prove the
  scab of the Church."

16
Never argue at the dinner table, for the one
who is not hungry always gets the best of
the argument.
  ARCHBISHOP RICHARD WHATELY.

17
I am not arguing with you—I am telling you.
  JAMES MCNEILL WHISTLER. *The Gentle
  Art of Making Enemies.*

18
The man who sees both sides of a question
is a man who sees absolutely nothing at all.
  OSCAR WILDE. *The Critic as Artist,* pt. 2.

19
Ah, don't say that you agree with me. When
people agree with me I always feel that I
must be wrong.
  OSCAR WILDE. *The Critic as Artist,* pt. 2.
  Lady Windermere's Fan, Act 2.

ARISTOCRACY

See also Ancestry, Kings

1
An earl by right, by courtesy a man.
ALFRED AUSTIN. *The Season.*

2
Sorry pre-eminence of high descent,
Above the vulgar born, to rot in state!
ROBERT BLAIR. *The Grave,* l. 154.

3
Strip majesty of its exteriors (the first and last letters) and it becomes a jest.
EDMUND BURKE.

4
Great families of yesterday we show,
And lords whose parents were the Lord knows who.
DANIEL DEFOE. *The True-Born English-man,* pt. 1.

5
Any king or queen may make a lord, but only the devil himself—and the graces—can make a Chesterfield.
CHARLES DICKENS. *Barnaby Rudge,* ch. 23.

6
How those rooks bore! I hate staying with ancient families; you are always cawed to death.
BENJAMIN DISRAELI. *Vivian Grey.*

7
My nobility begins in me, but yours ends in you.
IPHICRATES, a shoemaker's son. When reviled by Harmodius for his mean birth. (PLUTARCH, *Apothegms.*)

8
The castle-bred brat is a senator born,
Or a saint, if religion's in vogue.
CHARLES KINGSLEY. *Saint's Tragedy,* Act 2.

9
To the Caliph I may be dirt, but to dirt I am the Caliph.
EDWARD KNOBLOCK. *Kismet.*

10
In an old civilization things come and go. Knighthood came and went; it was in the flower, then in the pod and then all went to seed. Now it seems to be gentlemen that are going. It appears that the upper classes are being so depressed and the lower classes so pushed up, and both shifting sideways so fast, that you simply can't distinguish an upper birth from a lower. It fact it is hard to make up their births at all.
STEPHEN LEACOCK. *The Struggle to Make Us Gentlemen.*

11
Friend, my patent of nobility comes from Montenotte.

NAPOLEON BONAPARTE. To a genealogist, referring to his first victory.

12
Earls as goes mad in their castles,
And females what settles their hash.
GEORGE ROBERT SIMS. *Dagonet Ballads: Polly.*

13
Learning in a Prince is like a dangerous knife in the hands of a madman.
DANIEL TUVILL. *Vade Mecum.*

14
. . . Titles of honor and dignity once acquired in a democracy . . . are as permanent here as eternity is in heaven . . . We adore titles and heredities in our hearts, and ridicule them with our mouths. This is our democratic privilege.
MARK TWAIN. *Autobiography.*

15
The peerage—is the best thing in fiction the English have ever done.
OSCAR WILDE. *A Woman of No Importance,* Act I.

ART AND ARTISTS

See also Painting

16
You let art alone. She's got enough guys sleeping with her.
SHERWOOD ANDERSON. *Letter to Ben Hecht.*

17
Believe it or not, there is even an artistic way to pick up a garbage can.
FRED ASTAIRE. *Steps in Time.*

18
Those who dwell in ivory towers
Have heads of the same material.
LEONARD BACON. *Tower of Ivory.*

19
To be an artist is a great thing, but to be an artist and not know it is the most glorious plight in the world.
JAMES M. BARRIE. *Tommy and Grizel.*

20
Early in life, Duveen—who became Lord Duveen of Millbank before he died in 1939, at the age of sixty-nine—noticed that Europe had plenty of art and America had plenty of money, and his entire astonishing career was the product of that simple observation.
S. N. BEHRMAN. *Duveen.*

21
PATRON—The last resort of a scoundrel.
SAMUEL JOHNSON.

22
PATRON—The first resort of a scoundrel.
AMBROSE BIERCE.

23
If art moralizes, how is it that the lives of

so precious few great artists will bear looking into?

HUBERT BLAND. *The Happy Moralist.*

1

Art, like morality, consists in drawing the line somewhere.

GILBERT KEITH CHESTERTON.

2

Art is science in the flesh.

JEAN COCTEAU. *Le Rappel à l'Ordre.*

3

There is no way to success in art but to take off your coat, grind paint, and work like a digger on the railroad, all day and every day.

RALPH WALDO EMERSON. *Conduct of Life: Power.*

4

To me nature is everything that man is born to, and art is the difference he makes in it.

JOHN ERSKINE. *Gentle Reader,* Dec. 1931.

5

Art is either a plagiarist or a revolutionist.

PAUL GAUGUIN. Quoted by JAMES HUNE-KER in *The Pathos of Distance.*

6

Art is the collaboration between God and the artist, and the less the artist does the better.

ANDRÉ GIDE.

7

New artists must break a hole in the sub-conscious and go fishing there.

ROBERT BEVERLY HALE. In *Time,* Apr. 11, 1960.

8

The word "artists" offered a picture of fellows with odd haircuts who were partial to floors rather than chairs as sitting places.

BEN HECHT. *Letters from Bohemia.*

9

One of those queer artistic dives,
Where funny people had their fling.
Artists, and writers, and their wives—
Poets, all that sort of thing.

OLIVER HERFORD. *The Women of the Better Class.*

10

Build your art horse-high, pig-tight and bull-strong.

ELBERT HUBBARD. *Epigrams.*

11

Bohème is not down on the map because it is not a money-order office.

ELBERT HUBBARD. *The Philistine.*

12

Scratch an artist and you surprise a child.

JAMES G. HUNEKER. *Chopin.*

13

Patron: Commonly, a wretch who supports with insolence, and is paid with flattery.

SAMUEL JOHNSON. *Dictionary.*

14

Is not a patron, my Lord, one who looks with unconcern on a man struggling for life in the water, and when he has reached ground, encumbers him with help?

SAMUEL JOHNSON. *Letter* to the Earl of Chesterfield, Feb. 7, 1755.

15

Gauguin is an excellent standby in any event. He has for years been the consolation of procrastinators, jobholders, and hopeful weaklings below forty.

ALEXANDER KING. *Rich Man, Poor Man, Freud and Fruit,* ch. 3.

16

To complete the design of the Gods we have to put a stitch here and there.

GEORGE MOORE. *Aphrodite in Aulis.*

17

All loved art in a seemly way
With an earnest soul and a capital A.

JAMES JEFFREY ROCHE. *The V-A-S-E.*

18

Engraving is, in brief terms, the art of scratch.

JOHN RUSKIN. *Ariadne.*

19

An artist is a dreamer consenting to dream of the actual world.

GEORGE SANTAYANA. *The Life of Reason.*

20

An artist may visit a museum but only a pedant can live there.

GEORGE SANTAYANA. *The Life of Reason.*

21

The true artist will let his wife starve, his children go barefoot, his mother drudge for his living at seventy, sooner than work at anything but his art.

BERNARD SHAW. *Man and Superman,* Act 1.

22

The Muses are vindictive virgins and avenge themselves without mercy on those who weary of their charms.

LOGAN PEARSALL SMITH. *All Trivia.*

23

The misfortune of the "artistic temperament" is that so many people have the temperament, and so few the art.

J. A. SPENDER. *The Comments of Bagshot.*

24

Statues and pictures and verse may be grand,
But they are not the life for which they stand.

JAMES THOMSON. *Sunday up the River.*

1
Whenever I enjoy anything in art it means that it is mighty poor.
> MARK TWAIN. *Essays: At the Shrine of St. Wagner.*

2
Donatello's interest in the female nude made him the father of the Renaissance.
> LOUIS UNTERMEYER. *A Treasury of Laughter.* Quoted as a student boner.

3
In my youth people talked about Ruskin; now they talk about drains.
> MRS. HUMPHRY WARD. *Robert Elsmere.* Bk. ii, ch. 12.

4
Art is like religion. As long as you do your best to stamp it out of existence, it flourishes in spite of you, like weeds in a garden. But if you try and cultivate it, and it becomes a popular success, it goes to the dogs at once.
> JANE WARDLE. *The Artistic Temperament.*

5
Art happens—no hovel is safe from it, no Prince may depend upon it, the vastest intelligence cannot bring it about.
> JAMES MCNEILL WHISTLER. *Ten O'Clock.*

6
Bad artists always admire each other's work. They call it being large-minded and free from prejudice.
> OSCAR WILDE. *The Critic as Artist.*

7
The best that one can say of most modern creative art is that it is just a little less vulgar than reality.
> OSCAR WILDE. *The Critic as Artist.*

8
Most women are so artificial that they have no sense of art. Most men are so natural that they have no sense of beauty.
> OSCAR WILDE. *Saturday Review,* Nov. 17, 1894.

9
A subject that is beautiful in itself gives no suggestion to the artist. It lacks imperfection.
> OSCAR WILDE. *Saturday Review,* Nov. 17, 1894.

10
The only thing that the artist cannot see is the obvious. The only thing that the public can see is the obvious. The result is the Criticism of the Journalist.
> OSCAR WILDE. *Saturday Review,* Nov. 17, 1894.

11
Art is the only serious thing in the world. And the artist is the only person who is never serious.
> OSCAR WILDE. *Saturday Review,* Nov. 17, 1894.

ASPIRATION

12
The tyranny of the commonplace, which seems to accompany civilization.
> WALTER BAGEHOT. *The English Constitution.*

13
All women marry gods, but sadly consent afterwards to live with men.
> HENRY WARD BEECHER. *Norwood.* Quoted by PAXTON HIBBEN in *Henry Ward Beecher: An American Portrait.*

14
Castles in the air cost a vast deal to keep up.
> SIR EDWARD BULWER-LYTTON. *Lady of Lyons.* Act i, sc. 3.

15
My life was spent in one long effort to escape from the commonplaces of existence.
> SIR ARTHUR CONAN DOYLE. *The Red Headed League.* The line is spoken by Sherlock Holmes.

16
It is better to be a "has been" than one of the "never wases."
> H. GORDON-BROWNE. *Conclusions of an Everyday Woman.*

17
There never lived a mortal man who bent
His appetite beyond his natural sphere,
But starved and died.
> JOHN KEATS. *Endymion.* Bk. iv, 1. 646.

18
If you cannot catch a bird of paradise, better take a wet hen.
> NIKITA KHRUSHCHEV. In *Time,* Jan. 6, 1958.

19
Because it's there.
> GEORGE MALLORY, mountain climber. When asked, "Why do you climb this mountain?" (*Time,* July 6, 1953.)

20
Better a brutal starving nation,
Than men with thoughts above their station.
> JOHN MASEFIELD. *The Everlasting Mercy.*

21
He hated all pretension save his own pretension.
> H. L. MENCKEN. *Prejudices:* ser. 2. Comment on Theodore Roosevelt.

22
If a man wants his dreams to come true he must wake up.
> *The Public Speaker's Treasure Chest,* ed. by HERBERT PROCHNOW.

23
We must not look for a golden life in an iron age.
> JOHN RAY. *English Proverbs.*

1

We are all in the gutter, but some of us are looking at the stars.

OSCAR WILDE. *Lady Windermere's Fan,* Act 3.

ASS

2

The Mule is haf hoss and haf Jackass, and then comes to a full stop, natur diskovering her mistake . . . Tha are the strongest creeturs on earth, and heaviest ackording to their sise: I herd tell ov one who fell oph from the tow path, on the Eri kanawl, and sunk as soon as he touched bottom, but he kept rite on towing the boat to the nex stashun, breathing thru his ears, which stuck out of the water about 2 feet 6 inches; i didn't see this did, but an auctioneer told me ov it, and I never knew an auctioneer to lie unless it was absolutely convenient.

JOSH BILLINGS (Henry Wheeler Shaw). *The Mule.*

3

The Boston *Post* says: "The person who sent us a copy of the Boston *Post,* with 'Jackass' written upon the margin, is requested to inform us at what stable he can be found."

The Library of Wit and Humor, ed. by A. R. SPOFFORD.

4

When the prophet beats the ass,
The angel intercedes.

E. B. BROWNING. *Aurora Leigh,* bk. 8.

5

Play with an ass, and he will whisk his tail in your face.

JACOB CATS. *Moral Emblems.*

6

Yuh gotta treat people jes' like yuh do mules. Don't try to drive 'em. Jes' leave the gate open a mite an' let 'em bust in.

EDWARD EVERETT DALE. *Cow Country,* an adaptation.

7

The ass thinks one thing, and he that rides him another.

THOMAS D'URFEY. *Quixote.* Pt. iii, Act 3, Sc. 2.

8

An ass may bray a good while before he shakes the stars down.

GEORGE ELIOT. *Romola.* Bk. iii, ch. 50.

9

Who washes an ass's head loseth both labor and soap.

JOHN FLORIO. *First Fruites.* Fo. 34.

10

Mules kick. Who wants to become known as a mule?

B. C. FORBES. *Epigrams.*

11

Only asses bray.

B. C. FORBES. *Epigrams.*

12

Better strive with an ill ass than carry the wood one's self.

THOMAS FULLER. *Gnomologia,* No. 930.

13

Every ass loves to hear himself bray.

THOMAS FULLER. *Gnomologia,* No. 1404.

14

He that makes himself an ass must not take it ill if men ride him.

THOMAS FULLER. *Gnomologia,* No. 2232.

15

Because a Donkey takes a whim
To Bray at You, why Bray at Him?

ARTHUR GUITERMAN. *A Poet's Proverbs.*

16

If a donkey bray at you, don't bray at him.

GEORGE HERBERT. *Jacula Prudentum.*

17

I had rather ride on an ass that carries me than on a horse that throws me.

GEORGE HERBERT. *Jacula Prudentum.*

18

Give an ass oats and he runs after thistles.

GEORGE HERBERT. *Jacula Prudentum.*

19

Better an ass that carries us, than a horse that throws us.

J. G. HOLLAND. *Gold-Foil.* See also GEORGE HERBERT above.

20

A mule has neither pride of ancestry nor hope of posterity.

ROBERT G. INGERSOLL.

21

When a jackass brays, no one pays any attention to him, not even other jackasses. But when a lion brays like a jackass, even the lions in the neighborhood may be pardoned for exhibiting a little surprise.

GEORGE JEAN NATHAN. *Testament of a Critic.*

22

A man who cannot beat his ass beats the saddle. (Sedqui asinum no potest stratum caedit.)

PETRONIUS. *Satyricon,* sec. 45.

23

It is recorded of Mahomet, that, upon a visit he was going to pay in Paradise, he had an offer of several vehicles to conduct him upwards; as fiery chariots, winged horses, and celestial sedans; but he refused them all, and would be borne to heaven upon nothing but his ass.

JONATHAN SWIFT. *The Operation of the Spirit.*

1
One ass names another "Long-ears." (Ein Esel schimpft den andern Lang-Ohr.)
UNKNOWN. German proverb.

ATHEISM

2
Atheism is rather in the lip than in the heart of man.
FRANCIS BACON. *Essays: of Atheism.*

3
The materialist is a Calvinist without a God.
EDUARD BERNSTEIN. *Evolutionary Socialism.*

4
An atheist is a man who has no invisible means of support.
JOHN BUCHAN.

5
Two goldfish, relates Walter Cronkite, were swimming around and around in a glass bowl. One announced crankily that he had become an atheist. "Fine, fine," scoffed the other. "Now just explain to me who changes the water in this bowl!"
BENNETT CERF. *The Laugh's on Me.*

6
I don't believe in God because I don't believe in Mother Goose.
CLARENCE DARROW.

7
An atheist is a guy who watches a Notre Dame-SMU football game and doesn't care who wins.
DWIGHT D. EISENHOWER. *News summaries,* Nov. 6, 1954.

8
Atheism is the last word of theism.
HEINRICH HEINE. *MS. Papers.*

9
A priest came up to Ingersoll's table and asked: "Mr. Ingersoll, how can you disagree with Sir Isaac Newton? He believed in God." Ingersoll asked: "How can you dare disagree with Newton? He was a Protestant."
The World of Haldeman-Julius, compiled by ALBERT MORDELL. Referring to ROBERT G. INGERSOLL.

10
I do not know, Sir, that the fellow is an infidel; but if he be an infidel, he is an infidel as a dog is an infidel; that is to say, he has never thought upon the subject.
SAMUEL JOHNSON. Boswell's *Life,* Oct. 19, 1769.

11
An atheist is a man who has no invisible means of support.
BISHOP FULTON SHEEN. (*Look,* Dec. 14, 1955.) See also BUCHAN in this section.

AUTOMOBILE

12
It's nice to keep in touch—besides, it's the only place in London where you can park a car.
LORD ATTLEE, former Prime Minister, on reasons for attending the House of Lords. (*The Times,* London, Feb. 4, 1962.)

13
True, it raises haunting visions to discover from a sign outside a gas station at Murphy, North Carolina, that here De Soto and his men encamped in 1540. One can imagine the swampy ground sloping toward the river—under the present concrete and asphalt that stretches to the bridge. But for the ordinary traveler the reminiscence is barren. De Soto is a car and so is La Salle.
JACQUES BARZUN. *God's Country and Mine.*

14
One of the measures suggested to aid in the reduction of the number of automobile accidents is the prohibition of gasoline sales to intoxicated drivers. Another good way would be the prohibition of liquor sales to intoxicated drivers.
ROBERT BENCHLEY. *Easy Tests.* (*The Benchley Roundup,* ed. by NATHANIEL BENCHLEY.)

15
. . . in American towns, it was thought more important to have a car which is a public asset than a bathroom which is private.
DENIS WILLIAM BROGAN. *The American Character.*

16
"There were just as many foolhardy drivers fifty years ago," the San Francisco *Chronicle* reminds us, "but in those days they drove something that had more sense than they did."
BENNETT CERF. *The Laugh's on Me.*

17
Washington, D.C. safety slogan urging slower driving: "Nice guys may finish last. But they finish."
Reader's Digest. Feb., 1967.

18
Here lies G. Whilken's friends, all five,
He took them along when he learned to drive.
LEONARD H. ROBBINS. *Epitaphs for the Speed Age.*

19
Stranger, pause and shed a tear
For one who leaves no mourners.

D. F. Sapp reposes here:
  He would cut corners.
  LEONARD H. ROBBINS. *Epitaphs for the Speed Age.*

1
It is with real regret that we learn of Mr. Wayne's recovery from an automobile accident.

From *A Treasury of Laughter* by LOUIS UNTERMEYER. A minor classic among newspaper reports.

2
The driver of a hearse has the advantage of never having to put up with backseat driving.
  DOUGLAS YATES. *Works.*

B

BABY

3
I just noticed that more twins are being born these days. Maybe it's because kids lack the courage to come into this world alone.
  STAN BURNS. *Parade Magazine*, Apr. 9, 1967.

4
Nothing is more absurd than begetting. Having fits is more reasonable than having children.
  FATHER ROBERT CAPON. *Bed and Board.*

5
It is useless to go to bed to save the light, if the result is twins.
  Chinese Proverb.

6
A newborn baby is merely a small, noisy object, slightly fuzzy on one end, with no distinguishing marks to speak of except a mouth, and in color either a salmon pink or a deep sorrel, depending on whether it is going to grow up a blonde or a brunette. But to its immediate family it is without question the most phenomenal, the most astonishing, the most absolutely unparalleled thing that has yet occurred in the entire history of this planet.
  IRVIN S. COBB. *Shakespeare's Seven Ages and Mine.*

7
Every baby born into the world is a finer one than the last.
  CHARLES DICKENS. *Nicholas Nickleby*, ch. 36.

8
About the only thing we have left that actually discriminates in favor o' the plain people is the stork.
  FRANK MCKINNEY (KIN) HUBBARD. *Sayings.*

9
This afternoon at 4:15 at the Imperial Household Hospital, Her Highness the Crown Princess honorably effecting delivery, the honorable birth of a son occurred. The exalted mother and child are honorably healthy.
  Japanese Radio announcement of the birth of a Prince. (*Newsweek*, Mar. 7, 1960.)

10
My wife is home and we are having a baby, a boy, in November.
  JOHN F. KENNEDY. (*The Quotable Mr. Kennedy*, ed. by GERALD GARDNER.)

11
A tight little bundle of wailing and flannel, Perplex'd with the newly-found fardel of life.
  F. LOCKER-LAMPSON. *The Old Cradle.*

12
If you please, ma'am, it was a very little one. [The nurse excusing her illegitimate baby.]
  FREDERICK MARRYAT. *Midshipman Easy*, ch. 3.

13
For what she does not know, she eats,
  A worm, a twig, a block, a fly,
And every novel thing she meets
  Is bitten into by and by.
  ROBERT NATHAN. *The Daughter of Evening.*

14
If men bore the children, there would be only one born in each family.
  Reflections of a Bachelor (1903).

15
When a woman has had nine children she begins to have suspicions about some of the beautiful passages in love stories.
  Reflections of a Bachelor (1903).

16
The birth of a baby brings joy into the house: it might have been twins.
  FRANK RICHARDSON. *Love, and All About It.*

17
Man, a dunce uncouth,
Errs in age and youth:
Babies know the truth.
  ALGERNON CHARLES SWINBURNE. *Cradle Songs*, No. 4.

1
"Young mother."—And so you think a baby is a thing of beauty and a joy forever? Well, the idea is pleasing, but not original; every cow thinks the same of its own calf.
MARK TWAIN. *Answers to Correspondents.*

2
Today a premature baby is one that's born before its parents are married.
EARL WILSON. *Syndicated Column.*

BACHELOR

3
The ideal woman . . . the dream of a man who will be a bachelor all his life.
W. BURTON BALDRY. *Stray Thoughts.*

4
If a mistaken marriage can be purgatory, mistaken celibacy is hell.
R. H. BENSON. *The Conventionalists.*

5
Any man may be a celibate who has never had the opportunity to be anything else.
COSMO HAMILTON. *Adam's Clay.*

6
To the bachelors: may they never impale their freedom on the point of a steel pen.
Toasts for All Occasions, ed. by LEWIS C. HENRY.

7
The only comfort of my life
Is that I never yet had wife.
ROBERT HERRICK. *His Comfort.*

8
Praise a wife but remain a bachelor. (Lauda la moglie e tienti donzello.)
Old Italian Proverb.

9
Marriage has many pains, but celibacy has no pleasures.
SAMUEL JOHNSON. *Works,* xi, 74.

10
Bachelors know more about women than married men. If they didn't they'd be married, too.
H. L. MENCKEN. *Chrestomathy.*

11
Our Unabashed Dictionary defines:
Bachelor as one who's foot-loose and fiancée free.
More Playboy's Party Jokes (1965).

12
You can be a married man many times, but a bachelor only once.
Reflections of a Bachelor (1903).

13
Bachelors could have a fine time if there weren't any maidens or husbands to get in their way.
Reflections of a Bachelor (1905).

14
A bachelor has to have inspiration for making love to a woman—a married man needs only an excuse.
HELEN ROWLAND. Quoted in *The Book of Diversion,* ed. by FRANKLIN P. ADAMS.

15
Never trust a husband too far, nor a bachelor too near.
HELEN ROWLAND.

16
. . . if you wish the pick of men and women, take a good bachelor and a good wife.
ROBERT LOUIS STEVENSON. *Virginibus Puerisque.*

17
Bachelor's fare: bread and cheese and kisses.
JONATHAN SWIFT. *Polite Conversation.*

18
A bachelor is one who enjoys the chase but does not eat the game.
UNKNOWN.

19
The happy marrid man dies in good stile at home, surrounded by his weeping wife and children. The old bachelor don't die at all— he sort of rots away, like a pollywog's tail.
ARTEMUS WARD. *The Draft in Baldinsville.*

20
Bachelor—A man who never makes the same mistake once.
ED WYNN.

BEARD

21
A beard creates lice, not brains.
AMMIANUS. From *Greek Anthology.* Bk. xi, epig. 156.

22
Dear Lover Boy
Your photo came
But your doggone beard
Won't fit
The frame
BURMA SHAVE SIGN. From *The Verse by the Side of the Road:* FRANK ROWSOME, JR.

23
Grandpa's beard
Was stiff and coarse
And that's what
Caused his
Fifth Divorce
BURMA SHAVE SIGN. From *The Verse by the Side of the Road:* FRANK ROWSOME, JR.

24
Whiskers long
Made Sampson strong
But Sampson's gal

She done
Him wrong
> Burma Shave Sign. From *The Verse by the Side of the Road:* Frank Rowsome, Jr.

1
Since I have dealt in suds, I could never discover more than two reasons for shaving; the one is to get a beard, the other is to get rid of one.
> Henry Fielding. *Tom Jones.* Bk. viii, ch. 4.

2
'Tis not the beard that makes the philosopher.
> Thomas Fuller. *Gnomologia,* No. 5102.

3
My grandfather had the longest beard in the Bronx. It had buttons down the front and a belt in the back.
> George Jessel. Quoted in *Treadmill to Oblivion* by Fred Allen.

4
You know, in most towns of any size, when a man is dead and needs a shave, why the barber that shaves him soaks him five dollars for the job; that is, he don't soak *him,* but whoever ordered the shave. I just charge three dollars because personally I don't mind much shavin' a dead person. They lay a whole lot stiller than live customers. The only thing is that you don't feel like talkin' to them and you get kind of lonesome.
> Ring Lardner. *Haircut.*

5
Where did I read one the other day that said: Every time Sir Thomas More was executed he used to have a clean shave.
> Stephen Leacock. *The Saving Grace of Humor.*

6
Even the prophet's beard can be shaved.
> Stanislaw J. Lec. *Unkempt Thoughts,* tr. from the Polish by Jacek Galaska.

7
If by growing a goatee you hope to come upon wisdom,
then, O wise friend, any smelly goat in a handsome beard
is at once Plato.
> Lucian (Loukianos). *On Magical Whiskers,* tr. by William Barnstone.

8
How wonderful it is to have a perfectly safe place to throw worn-out safety razor blades.
> Ross W. Lynn. *Letter to F.P.A.,* from Hotel El Tovar, Grand Canyon of the Colorado, Oct. 5, 1916.

9
If the beard were all, a goat might preach.
> Unknown. A Danish proverb.

10
When your razor is dull
And you need to shave
Think of the man
That lays in this grave,
For there was a time
It might have been whet,
You was afeard of a dime
And now it's too late.
> Unknown. *Epitaph* on tombstone of August Hefner, in a cemetery in Waverly, Ohio.

BEARING

11
He [General Grant] does not march, nor quite walk, but pitches along as if the next step would bring him on his nose.
> Richard Henry Dana.

12
Horatio looked handsomely miserable, like Hamlet slipping on a piece of orange-peel.
> Charles Dickens. *Sketches by Boz: Horatio Sparkins.*

13
He was close on to six feet tall, of military bearing, and of such extraordinary vitality that young ladies asserted they could feel him ten feet away.
> C. Hartley Grattan. *Bitter Bierce,* p. 39. The reference is to Ambrose Bierce.

14
. . . an improbable creature, like a human giraffe, sniffing down his nostrils at mortals beneath his gaze.
> Lord Moran. *Diaries,* Jan. 22, 1943. The description is of Charles de Gaulle.

15
Daniel Webster struck me much like a steam engine in trousers.
> Sydney Smith.

16
He walked among men a bronze statue, for thirty years determinedly looking for his pedestal.
> William Allen White. On President McKinley. Quoted by Ralph G. Martin in *Ballots and Bandwagons: Republican Convention of 1900.*

17
I turned to Aunt Agatha, whose demeanor was now rather like that of one who, picking daisies on the railway, has just caught the down express in the small of the back.
> P. G. Wodehouse.

BEAUTY

18
Beauty may be said to be God's trademark in creation.
> Henry Ward Beecher. *Proverbs from Plymouth Pulpit.*

1
Observing a number of pretty working girls on holiday at Broadstairs he [Max Beerbohm] remarked: "I don't think the lower orders ought to be attractive—it brings Beauty into disrepute."
HESKETH PEARSON. *Lives of the Wits.*

2
If things were seen as they truly are, the beauty of bodies would be much abridged.
SIR THOMAS BROWNE. *Christian Morals.* Pt. ii, sec. 9.

3
Beauty, in a modest woman, is like fire, or a sharp sword at a distance: neither doth the one burn, nor the other wound those that come not too near them.
MIGUEL DE CERVANTES. *Don Quixote.* Pt. i, bk. 2, ch. 14.

4
Women have, in general, but one object, which is their beauty; upon which, scarce any flattery is too gross for them to swallow.
LORD CHESTERFIELD. *Letters,* Oct. 16, 1747.

5
Every woman who is not absolutely ugly thinks herself handsome.
LORD CHESTERFIELD. *Letters,* Sept. 5, 1748.

6
Women's beauty, like men's wit, is generally fatal to the owners.
LORD CHESTERFIELD. *Miscellaneous Works,* vol. 2.

7
Beauty hath created been
T' undo or be undone.
SAMUEL DANIEL. *Ulysses and the Syren.*

8
Beauty, what is that? There are phalanxes of beauty in every comic show. Beauty neither buys food nor keeps up a home.
MAXINE ELLIOT. *Newspaper interview,* 1908.

9
Beauty's the thing that counts
In women; red lips
And black eyes are better than brains.
MARY J. ELMENDORF. *Beauty's the Thing.*

10
Beauty without grace is the hook without the bait.
RALPH WALDO EMERSON. *Conduct of Life: Beauty.*

11
No woman can be a beauty without a fortune.
GEORGE FARQUHAR, *The Beaux' Stratagem.* Act ii, sc. 2.

12
If Jack's in love, he's no judge of Jill's beauty.
BENJAMIN FRANKLIN, *Poor Richard,* 1748.

13
Beauty will buy no beef.
THOMAS FULLER, *Gnomologia,* No. 956.

14
A poor beauty finds more lovers than husbands.
GEORGE HERBERT, *Jacula Prudentum.*

15
The homely pure hate the beautiful bad in self-defense, so we are told . . .
HUBERT HOWE, *Popular Tribunals.* (CURT GENTRY, *Madams of San Francisco.*)

16
I'm tired of all this nonsense about beauty being only skin-deep. That's deep enough. What do you want—an adorable pancreas?
JEAN KERR, *The Snake Has All the Lines: Mirror, Mirror, on the Wall, I Don't Want to Hear One Word Out of You.*

17
Not every woman in old slippers can manage to look like Cinderella.
DON MARQUIS, *New York Herald.*

18
Beauty makes idiots sad and wise men merry.
GEORGE JEAN NATHAN, *House of Satan.*

19
When the candles are out all women are fair.
PLUTARCH, *Conjugal Precepts.*

20
Even now, mad girl, dost ape the painted Briton and wanton with foreign dyes upon thy cheek? The face is ever best as nature made it; foul shows the Belgian rouge on Roman cheeks!
SEXTUS PROPERTIUS, *Elegies,* bk. 2.

21
No girl is ever so pretty as her mirror pictures her to herself.
Reflections of a Bachelor.

22
There are more pretty photographs of women than there are photographs of pretty women.
Reflections of a Bachelor (1903).

23
Remember that the most beautiful things in the world are the most useless; peacocks and lilies for instance.
JOHN RUSKIN, *The Stones of Venice.* Vol. I, ch. 2.

24
The noble grotesque involves the true appreciation of beauty.
JOHN RUSKIN, *The Stones of Venice,* ch. 3.

1

Those proud, modest bourgeois were of the opinion that beauty was beyond their means or below their station; it was all right for a marquise or a whore.

JEAN-PAUL SARTRE, *The Words.*

2

For honesty coupled to beauty, is to have honey a sauce to sugar.

WILLIAM SHAKESPEARE, *As You Like It.* Act iii, sc. 3.

3

Beauty is all very well at first sight; but who ever looks at it when it has been in the house three days?

BERNARD SHAW, *Man and Superman,* Act 4.

4

Beauty vanishes like a vapor,
Preach the men of musty morals.

HARRIET PRESCOTT SPOFFORD, *Evanescence.*

5

Every woman would rather be beautiful than good. (Jedes Weib will lieber schön als fromm sein.)

UNKNOWN, German proverb.

6

If a man hears much that a woman says, she is not beautiful.

UNKNOWN, *Meditations in Wall Street.*

7

Beauty is altogether in the eye of the beholder.

LEW WALLACE, *The Prince of India.* Bk. iii, ch. 6.

8

It is better to be beautiful than to be good, but it is better to be good than to be ugly.

OSCAR WILDE, *The Picture of Dorian Gray,* ch. 17.

9

The only beautiful things are the things that do not concern us.

OSCAR WILDE, *The Decay of Lying.*

10

Dandyism is the assertion of the absolute modernity of Beauty.

OSCAR WILDE, *Saturday Review,* Nov. 17, 1894.

11

A beautiful woman who is pleasing to men is good only for frightening fish when she falls into the water.

Zen Proverb. Quoted by HELEN S. CHASIN, *The Atlantic,* May, 1966.

BED

See also Sleep

12

In bed we laugh, in bed we cry,
  And born in bed, in bed we die;

The near approach a bed may show
Of human bliss to human woe.

ISAAC DE BENSERADE, tr. by SAMUEL JOHNSON.

13

Wedlock—The deep, deep peace of the double bed after the hurly-burly of the chaise-longue.

MRS. PATRICK CAMPBELL.

14

The bed comprehends our whole life, for we were born in it, we live in it, and we shall die in it.

GUY DE MAUPASSANT, *The Bed.*

15

The only interesting thing that can happen in a Swiss bedroom is suffocation by a feather mattress.

DALTON TRUMBO, advising a teen-age daughter about to tour Europe. (*Time,* Jan. 2, 1961.)

16

I always think a bed that hasn't been slept in looks sort of forlorn in the morning.

JOHN VAN DRUTEN, *The Voice of the Turtle.*

17

Turn out more ale, turn up the light;
I will not go to bed tonight.
Of all the foes that man should dread
The first and worst one is a bed.

CHARLES HENRY WEBB, *Dum Vivimus Vigilamus.*

BEE

18

Nature's confectioner, the bee.

JOHN CLEVELAND, *Fuscara.*

19

Honey is sweet but the bee stings.

GEORGE HERBERT, *Jacula Prudentum.*

20

No good sensible working bee listens to the advice of a bedbug on the subject of business.

ELBERT HUBBARD, *Epigrams.*

21

Even bees, the little almsmen of spring bowers,
Know there is richest juice in poison-flowers.

JOHN KEATS, *Isabella,* st. 13.

22

God's little epigrams, the Bees,
Are pointed and impartial.
Could Martial rival one of these?
No, not even Martial.

RICHARD R. KIRK, *The Bees.*

23

The bee that hath honey in her mouth, hath a sting in her tail.

JOHN LYLY, *Euphues,* 79.

1

The bee and the serpent often sip from the selfsame flower. (*L'ape e la serpe spesso Suggon L'istesso unmore.*)
 METASTASIO, *Morte d'Abele*, pt. 1.

2

He has a bee in his bonnet.
 JOHN RAY, *English Proverbs.*

3

Bee scientists always speak of the bee as she. It is because all the important bees are of that sex.
 MARK TWAIN, *Essays: The Bee.*

BEHAVIOR

See also Abstinence, Gentleman, Manners, Morality

4

"Do you mean to say," he joshed, "that the Union Club has come to a day when a man can bring his mistress to the club?" Along with the great club revolution, the doorman remembered the great club tradition. "You may, Sir," he replied stiffly, "if the lady is the wife of one of the members."
 CLEVELAND AMORY, *Who Killed Society?*

5

God's men are better than the devil's men, and they ought to act as though they were.
 HENRY WARD BEECHER, *Proverbs from Plymouth Pulpit.*

6

Neither crow nor croak.
 W. G. BENHAM, *Proverbs.*

7

The age of chivalry is gone: that of sophisters, economists, and calculators has succeeded.
 EDMUND BURKE, *Reflections on the Revolution in France.*

8

Let them cant about decorum
Who have characters to lose.
 ROBERT BURNS, *The Jolly Beggars.*

9

We're not primarily put on this earth to see through one another, but to see one another through.
 PETER DE VRIES, *Let Me Count the Ways.*

10

"It is always best on these occasions to do what the mob do."—"But suppose there are two mobs?" suggested Mr. Snodgras.—"Shout with the largest," replied Mr. Pickwick.
 CHARLES DICKENS, *Pickwick Papers*, ch. 13.

11

Don't jump on a man unless he's down.
 FINLEY PETER DUNNE, *Mr. Dooley Remembers.*

12

When, at a recent convention, the American Legion, instead of acting like teen-agers, comported itself as grown men normally do, the fact was thought worthy of front-page notice, as if somehow the Legion had reverted to an extinct form of behavior.
 CLIFTON FADIMAN, *Enter, Conversing.*

13

All that hot stuff that happened in the Bible is happening today on every street.
 ROBERT FONTAINE, *That's a Good Question.*

14

The rounder usually ends in a square hole.
 B. C. FORBES, *Epigrams.*

15

As innocent as a new-laid egg.
 W. S. GILBERT, *Engaged.*

16

Self-Sacrifice is Noble, it is true,
 But Sacrifice Yourself, not Others too.
 ARTHUR GUITERMAN, *A Poet's Proverbs.*

17

How is it that innocent people remain innocent? . . . They wilfully neglect their opportunities.
 COSMO HAMILTON, *Brummell.*

18

Walk groundly, talk profoundly, drink roundly, sleep soundly.
 WILLIAM HAZLITT, *English Proverbs*, No. 446.

19

Life, not the parson, teaches conduct.
 OLIVER WENDELL HOLMES, JR., *Letter to Sir Frederick Pollock*, Apr. 2, 1926.

20

They called it a family hotel, but as far as I could see, Ella and I was the only ones there that had ever forced two dollars on the clergy.
 RING LARDNER, *The Big Town.*

21

My behavior has been impeccable; I've been unconscious for the past six months.
 OSCAR LEVANT, *The Memoirs of an Amnesiac.*

22

Nothing is more adroit than irreproachable conduct.
 MADAME DE MAINTENON, *Maxims.*

23

You is sharks, sartin, but if you gobern de shark in you, why den you be angel; for all angel is not'ing more dan de shark well goberned.
 HERMAN MELVILLE, *Moby Dick*, ch. 64.

24

Home is heaven and orgies are vile,

But I like an orgy, once in a while.
OGDEN NASH, *Home, 99 44/100% Sweet Home.*

1
Our Unabashed Dictionary defines:
Orgy as group therapy.
More Playboy's Party Jokes (1965).

2
Our unabashed dictionary defines *wolf* as a man with a little black book of cancelled chicks.
Playboy, Feb., 1966.

3
Though one admires disinterested chivalry . . . it never won a woman yet.
E. R. PUNSHON, *Rhoda in Between.*

4
So live that you wouldn't be ashamed to sell the family parrot to the town gossip.
WILL ROGERS.

5
It is said of me that when I was young I divided my time impartially among wine, women and song. I deny this categorically. Ninety per cent of my interests were women.
ARTUR RUBINSTEIN. (*Rubinstein Speaking; The New York Times Magazine*, Jan. 26, 1964.)

6
Be self-indulgent, and those who are also self-indulgent will like you. Tear your neighbor to pieces, and the other neighbors will laugh. But if you beat your soul, all souls will cry out.
JEAN-PAUL SARTRE, *The Words.*

7
Third Fisherman: Master, I marvel how the fishes live in the sea.
First Fisherman: Why, as men do a-land: the great ones eat up the little ones.
WILLIAM SHAKESPEARE, *Pericles.* Act ii, sc. 1.

8
Keep thy foot out of brothels, thy hand out of plackets, thy pen from lenders' books, and defy the foul fiend.
WILLIAM SHAKESPEARE, *King Lear.* Act iii, sc. 4.

9
Decency is Indecency's Conspiracy of Silence.
BERNARD SHAW, *Maxims for Revolutionists.*

10
Self-sacrifice enables us to sacrifice other people without blushing.
BERNARD SHAW, *Maxims for Revolutionists.*

11
. . . cruelty must be whitewashed by a moral excuse, and a pretense of reluctance.
BERNARD SHAW, *Parents and Children.*

12
Do not unto others as you would that they should do unto you. Their tastes may not be the same.
BERNARD SHAW, *Revolutionist's Handbook.*

13
My only policy is to profess evil and do good.
BERNARD SHAW, quoted in *Days with Bernard Shaw* by STEPHEN WINSTEN.

14
As of 1965, all is fair in love and war . . . and politics, and retail business, and wholesale, and agriculture, and advertising and the fine arts, and the humanities.
H. ALLEN SMITH, *H. Allen Smith's Almanac* (1965).

15
Never practice what you preach. If you're going to practice it, why preach it?
LINCOLN STEFFENS, *Autobiography.*

16
Be good (if you can't be good, be careful).
HARRINGTON TATE, *Refrain* of popular song (1907).

17
The greater part of what my neighbors call good I believe in my soul to be bad, and if I repent of anything it is very likely to be my good behavior.
HENRY D. THOREAU, *Walden*, ch. 1.

18
Let us endeavor so to live that when we come to die even the undertaker will be sorry.
MARK TWAIN, *Pudd'nhead Wilson's Calendar.*

19
The fatality of good resolutions is that they are always too late.
OSCAR WILDE, *The Picture of Dorian Gray.*

BELIEF

See also Faith

20
A belief is not true because it is useful.
AMIEL, *Journal*, Nov. 15, 1876.

21
People only think a thing's worth believing in if it's hard to believe.
ARMIGER BARCLAY, *The Kingmakers.*

22
More persons, on the whole, are humbugged by believing nothing, than by believing too much.
PHINEAS T. BARNUM, quoted in *Ladies' Home Journal*, Sept., 1957.

1
Absurdity, n. A statement or belief manifestly inconsistent with one's own.
AMBROSE BIERCE, *The Devil's Dictionary.*

2
Sometimes I've believed as many as six impossible things before breakfast
LEWIS CARROLL (CHARLES LUTWIDGE DODGSON), *Through the Looking-Glass,* ch. 5.

3
All you've got to do is believe what you hear, and if you do that enough, after a while you'll hear what you believe.
FINLEY PETER DUNNE, *Mr. Dooley Remembers.*

4
We believe that mustard bites the tongue, that pepper is hot, friction-matches incendiary, revolvers are to be avoided, and suspenders hold up the pantaloons.
RALPH WALDO EMERSON, *Representative Men: Montaigne.*

5
As with guns we kill the crow,
For spoiling our relief,
The devil so must we o'erthrow,
With gunshot of belief.
GEORGE GASCOIGNE, *Good-Morrow.*

6
Believe what you have Proved. They most deceive
Themselves who try to Prove what they Believe.
ARTHUR GUITERMAN, *A Poet's Proverbs.*

7
We are inclined to believe those whom we do not know, because they have never deceived us.
SAMUEL JOHNSON, *The Idler,* No. 8.

8
Some like to understand what they believe in. Others like to believe in what they understand.
STANISLAW J. LEC, *Unkempt Thoughts,* tr. from the Polish by JACEK GALASKA.

9
He is an incorrigible believer. He believes in everything that works.
JAMES RESTON, *What's He Like? And How Will He Do?; The New York Times Magazine,* Jan. 17, 1965, p. 8. The reference is to Lyndon B. Johnson.

10
A thing that nobody believes cannot be proved too often.
BERNARD SHAW, *The Devil's Disciple,* Act 3.

11
Seeing is deceiving. It's eating that's believing.

JAMES THURBER, *Further Fables for Our Time.*

12
If you believe that you will believe anything.
THE DUKE OF WELLINGTON, to a man who stopped him on the street saying, "Mr. Jones, I believe."

13
I can believe anything, provided it is incredible.
OSCAR WILDE, *The Picture of Dorian Gray.*

BIRDS

14
A bird in the hand may be worth two in the bush, but remember also that a bird in the hand is a positive embarrassment to one not in the poultry business.
GEORGE ADE, *Fables.*

15
I do not consider pigeons birds . . . They are more in the nature of people; people who mooch.
ROBERT BENCHLEY, *Down with Pigeons.* (*The Benchley Roundup,* ed. by NATHANIEL BENCHLEY.)

16
. . . if you can't hold onto a bird in a cage, you're not likely to catch one in the air.
GIORDANO BRUNO, *The Candle Bearer.* Act ii, sc. 3. English version by J. R. HALE.

17
All our geese are swans.
ROBERT BURTON, *The Anatomy of Melancholy.*

18
The average sparrow is something of a bore and the trouble is that all sparrows are average.
WILL CUPPY, *How to Tell Your Friends from the Apes: The Sparrow.*

19
The Robin is called the harbinger of spring because he makes so much noise.
WILL CUPPY, *How to Tell Your Friends from the Apes: The Robin.*

20
The Nightingale is a familiar figure in poems beginning "Oh, Nightingale!" . . . He is much loved by persons who are slightly deaf.
WILL CUPPY, *How to Tell Your Friends from the Apes: The Nightingale.*

21
The Crow is tough. He uses no baby talk even in mating season. During courtship the male feeds the female but he soon gets wise to himself.
WILL CUPPY, *How to Tell Your Friends from the Apes: The Crow.*

1

The love bird or Connubial Parakeet is one hundred percent faithful to his mate who is locked into the same cage.

> WILL CUPPY, *How to Tell Your Friends from the Apes: The Love Bird.*

2

The Pewee is famous for catching flies and going *pee-a-wee pee-a-wee* all day long. His melancholy call is greatly enjoyed by those who enjoy that sort of thing.

> WILL CUPPY, *How to Tell Your Friends from the Apes: The Pewee.*

3

The loon bobs up in the surf on dark nights, ruins your summer with a burst of wild maniacal laughter, then dives and waits for the next victim. And he wonders why people shoot at him.

> WILL CUPPY, *How to Tell Your Friends from the Apes: The Loon.*

4

"Is it weakness of intellect, birdie?" I cried,
"Or a rather tough worm in your little inside?"
With a shake of his poor little head he replied,
"Oh, willow, titwillow, titwillow!"

> SIR WILLIAM SCHWENCK GILBERT, *The Mikado*, Act 2.

5

Jay-bird don't rob his own nes'.

> JOEL CHANDLER HARRIS, *Plantation Proverbs.*

6

Crows are pardoned, but the pigeons are found guilty.

> JUVENAL, *Satires: Hypocrisy and Vice.*

7

What's so special about capon? It's just a rooster that's had an operation.

> FREDERICK LAING, *The Giant's House.*

8

As the birds do, so do we,
Bill our mate, and choose our tree.

> GEORGE MEREDITH, *The Three Singers to Young Blood.*

9

If there is anything in being first, man must acknowledge the supremacy of the goose, for according to Genesis the fowl was first created.

> PETROLEUM V. NASBY (DAVID ROSS LOCKE).

BLESSING

10

Matthew, Mark, Luke and John,
The bed be blest that I lie on.

> THOMAS ADY, *A Candle in the Dark.*

11

God Bless the King,—I mean the Faith's defender!
God bless—no harm in blessing—the Pretender!
But who pretender is, or who is king,—
God bless us all!—that's quite another thing.

> JOHN BYROM, *Miscellaneous Poems* (1773).

12

May the good Lord receive ye—but not too soon.

> FATHER FRANCIS PATRICK DUFFY, quoted by GENE FOWLER in *Skyline.*

13

Sun that givest all things birth
Shine on every thing on earth!
If that's too much to demand
shine at least on this our land.
If even that's too much for thee,
shine at any rate on me.

> PIET HEIN, *Grooks.*

14

God bless the Duke of Argyle.

> UNKNOWN. A phrase supposed to be addressed to Scots when they scratch themselves. The story is that the Duke erected posts on his land for cattle to rub against, and his herdsmen uttered this as they used the posts.

BLUSHING

15

Mr. Phunky, blushing into the very whites of his eyes, tried to look as if he didn't know that everybody was gazing at him: yet a thing which no man ever succeeded in doing yet, or, in all reasonable probability, ever will.

> CHARLES DICKENS, *Pickwick Papers*, ch. 34.

16

The blush is beautiful but it is sometimes inconvenient.

> CARLO GOLDONI, *Pamela*. Act i, sc. 3.

17

. . . she blushed like a well-trained sunrise.

> MARGARET HALSEY, *With Malice Toward Some.*

18

The blush that flies at seventeen
Is fixed at forty-nine.

> RUDYARD KIPLING, *My Rival.*

19

A lobster blushes after it dies; what rare subtlety in a victim!

> STANISLAW J. LEC, *Unkempt Thoughts*, tr. from the Polish by JACEK GALASKA.

1
Man is the only animal that blushes. Or needs to.
MARK TWAIN, *Pudd'nhead Wilson's New Calendar*.

2
Blushes are badges of imperfection.
WILLIAM WYCHERLEY, *Love in a Wood*. Act i, sc. 1.

BOASTING

3
The empty cask makes the most sound.
JACOB CATS (b. 1577), *Moral Emblems*. See also LYLY and WRIGHT in this section.

4
Cunning egotism. If I cannot brag of knowing something, then I brag of not knowing it. At any rate, brag.
RALPH WALDO EMERSON, *Journals*, 1866.

5
The rooster makes more racket than the hen that lays the egg.
JOEL CHANDLER HARRIS.

6
Before you tell someone how good you are, you must tell him how bad you used to be.
SEMON E. KNUDSEN. (*Time*, May 25, 1959.)

7
The empty vessel giveth a greater sound than the full barrel.
JOHN LYLY, *Euphues*, p. 15 (1579).

8
Who knows himself a braggart,
Let him fear this, for it will come to pass
That every braggart shall be found an ass.
WILLIAM SHAKESPEARE, *All's Well That Ends Well*. Act iv, sc. 3.

9
She understood how much louder a cock can crow in its own farmyard than elsewhere.
ANTHONY TROLLOPE, *The Last Chronicle of Barset*. Vol. i, ch. 17.

10
Empty barrels make the most noise.
E. M. WRIGHT, *Rustic Speech*. See also CATS and LYLY in this section.

BODY

See also Face, Fatness, Size

11
His arm looks like a buggy whip with fingers.
FRED ALLEN, *Treadmill to Oblivion*. Reference to JACK BENNY.

12
Have you ever noticed, Harry, that many jewels make women either incredibly fat or incredibly thin?
JAMES M. BARRIE, *The Twelve-Pound Look*.

13
We sit at breakfast, we sit on the train on the way to work, we sit at work, we sit at lunch, we sit all afternoon . . . a hodgepodge of sagging livers, sinking gall bladders, drooping stomachs, compressed intestines, and squashed pelvic organs.
DR. JOHN BUTTON, JR., *Address* to American Osteopathic Association. (*Newsweek*, Aug. 6, 1956.)

14
Would that the Roman populace had but one neck. (Utinam populus Romanus unum cervicem haberet.)
CALIGULA, when incensed at the people of Rome. (SUETONIUS, *Life*.)

15
A leg and foot, to speak more plain,
Rests here of one commanding;
Who though his wits he might retain,
Lost half his understanding.
GEORGE CANNING, *Epitaph for the Tombstone Erected Over the Marquis of Anglesea's Leg, Lost at Waterloo*.

16
How funny it'll seem to come out among the people who walk with their heads downwards. The antipathies, I think.
LEWIS CARROLL, *Alice's Adventures in Wonderland*.

17
Neck or nothing.
COLLEY CIBBER, *The Lady's Last Stake*, Act 3.

18
He [Irvin S. Cobb] frankly admitted he was "an outstanding writer—when viewed edgeways." Once he said in profile he "looked like a rolltop desk."
FRED G. NEUMAN, *Irvin S. Cobb*.

19
Let him value his hands and feet, he has but one pair.
RALPH WALDO EMERSON, *Conduct of Life: Fate*.

20
It is tragic when a man outlives his body.
SIGMUND FREUD, quoted in *The New York Times* obituary of Freud, Sept. 24, 1939.

21
The female knee is a joint and not an entertainment.
PERCY HAMMOND, *Review*, in the *Chicago Tribune*, of a Shubert musical show with a "preponderance of leg."

22
The average human body looks either like a monkey or an overfed horse, and only clothes

help some to look like colonels and others like bank presidents. Strip them and farewell to the colonels and the bank presidents!
LIN YUTANG, *With Love and Irony*.

1
Ballygullion girls have dispension from the Pope to wear the thick end of their legs downward.
SEUMAS MACMANUS, *Heavy Hangs the Golden Grain*.

2
Now, I consider that the phrenologists have omitted an important thing in not pushing their investigations from the cerebellum through the spinal canal. For I believe that much of a man's character will be found betokened in his backbone. I would rather feel your spine than your skull, whoever you are. A thin joist of a spine never yet upheld a full and noble soul. I rejoice in my spine, as in the firm audacious staff of that flag which I fling half out to the world.
HERMAN MELVILLE, *Moby Dick*, ch. 80.

3
She whose body's young and cool
Has no need of dancing-school.
DOROTHY PARKER, *Salome's Dancing Lesson*.

4
Generally when women are careless about the way their legs can be seen there is a good reason for it.
Reflections of a Bachelor.

5
It takes an awful lot of faith to believe that a woman is built like her clothes make her seem to be.
Reflections of a Bachelor.

6
Nice joint you have, said the doctor as he examined the pretty girl's knee.
DOUGLAS YATES, *Works*.

BOLDNESS

7
Bold knaves thrive, without one grain of sense,
But good men starve for want of impudence.
JOHN DRYDEN, *Constantine the Great: epilogue*.

8
I dip my pen in the blackest ink, because I am not afraid of falling into my inkpot.
RALPH WALDO EMERSON, *Conduct of Life: Worship*.

9
He flies through the air with the greatest of ease,
This daring young man on the flying trapeze;
His figure is handsome, all girls he can please,

And my love he purloined her away.
GEORGE LEYBOURNE, *The Man on the Flying Trapeze* (1860).

10
I don't believe in circumstances. The people who get on in this world are the people who get up and look for the circumstances they want and, if they can't find them, make them.
BERNARD SHAW, *Mrs. Warren's Profession*, Act 2.

11
This bosom friend of senators and congressmen was about as daring as an early Shirley Temple movie.
JAMES THURBER, on WILL ROGERS. From *Fred Allen's Letters*, ed. by JOE MCCARTHY.

BOOKS

See also Library, Reading

12
What is even a wise book but a blast from the lungs made visible to the eyes?
HERVEY ALLEN, *Anthony Adverse*.

13
Great store of all sorts of good books (through the great mercy of God) are common among us. He that cannot buy, may borrow.
RICHARD BAXTER, *Compassionate Counsel to Young Men*.

14
Where is human nature so weak as in the book-store!
HENRY WARD BEECHER, *Star Papers*.

15
When I am dead, I hope it may be said:
"His sins were scarlet but his books were read."
HILAIRE BELLOC, *On His Books*.

16
Child! do not throw this book about;
Refrain from the unholy pleasure
Of cutting all the pictures out!
Preserve it as your chiefest treasure.
HILAIRE BELLOC, *A Bad Child's Book of Beasts*.

17
Memories are like books; a few live in our hearts through life, and the rest, like the bills we pay, are read, and then forgotten.
GERALD BENDALL, *Mrs. Jones' Bonnet*.

18
Of all odd crazes, the craze to be forever reading new books is one of the oddest.
AUGUSTINE BIRRELL, *Essays: Books Old and New*.

19
'Tis pleasant, sure, to see one's name in print;

A book's a book, although there's nothing in't.
LORD BYRON, *English Bards and Scotch Reviewers.*

1
So essential did I consider an index to be to every book, that I proposed to bring a bill into parliament to deprive an author who publishes a book without an index of the privilege of copyright, and, moreover, to subject him for his offense to a pecuniary penalty.
JOHN CAMPBELL, *Lives of the Chief Justices of England*, vol. 3: preface.

2
No good Book, or good thing of any sort, shows its best face at first.
THOMAS CARLYLE, *Essays: Novalis.*

3
Books are the blessed chloroform of the mind.
ROBERT W. CHAMBERS, *What English Literature Gives Us.*

4
The success of many books is due to the affinity between the mediocrity of the author's ideas and those of the public.
NICHOLAS CHAMFORT.

5
Due attention to the inside of books, and due contempt for the outside, is the proper relation between a man of sense and his books.
LORD CHESTERFIELD, *Letters*, Mar. 19, 1750.

6
He never completed his History of Ephesus,
But his name got mentioned in numerous prefaces.
W. CRADDLE.

7
His books are selling like wildfire. Everybody's burning them.
GEORGE DEWITT. (JOEY ADAMS, *Cindy and I*, ch. 27.)

8
There are books of which the backs and covers are by far the best parts.
CHARLES DICKENS, *Oliver Twist*, ch. 14.

9
Books are fatal; they are the curse of the human race. Nine-tenths of existing books are nonsense, and the clever books are the refutation of that nonsense.
BENJAMIN DISRAELI, *Lothair.*

10
Beware of the man of one book. (Cave ab homine unius Libri.)
ISAAC D'ISRAELI, *Curiosities of Literature.*

11
Who, without books, essays to learn,
Draws water in a leaky urn.
AUSTIN DOBSON, *A Bookman's Budget.*

12
Every burned book enlightens the world.
RALPH WALDO EMERSON, *Compensation.*

13
Never lend books, for no one ever returns them; the only books I have in my library are books that other folk have lent me.
ANATOLE FRANCE.

14
Woe be to him that reads but one book.
GEORGE HERBERT, *Jacula Prudentum.*

15
Ever'thing comes t' him who waits but a loaned book.
FRANK MCKINNEY (KIN) HUBBARD, *Abe Martin's Primer.*

16
It is just those books which a man possesses, but does not read, which constitute the most suspicious evidence against him.
VICTOR HUGO, *The Toilers of the Sea*. Pt. I, bk. i, ch. 4.

17
When I emptied the top drawer of my mind I had a book.
GEORGE JESSEL, quoted in *Treadmill to Oblivion* by FRED ALLEN.

18
Any simpleton may write a book, but it requires high skill to make an index.
ROSSITER JOHNSON. Quoted, by ANNA L. WARD, in *A Dictionary of Quotations in Prose.*

19
I mean your borrowers of books—those mutilators of collections, spoilers of the symmetry of shelves, and creators of odd volumes.
CHARLES LAMB, *Essays of Elia: The Two Races of Man.*

20
The prices paid for first editions are no real evidence of the value of a book or the eminence of the author. Indeed the "first edition" hobby is one of the minor forms of mental derangement, seldom ending in homicide, and outside the scope of the law.
STEPHEN LEACOCK, *Charles Dickens.*

21
Of course one has to have an Index. Authors themselves would prefer not to have any. Having none would save trouble and compel reviewers to read the whole book instead of just the Index.
STEPHEN LEACOCK, *Index: There Is No Index.*

22
Reading all these long-gone-with-the-winded novels, some people are going gaga;
What this country needs is a good five-cent saga.
DAVID MCCORD, *Of Time and the Reader.*

1
If books did good, the world would have been converted long ago.
GEORGE MOORE, *Impressions and Opinions.*

2
Please return this book; I find that though many of my friends are poor arithmeticians, they are nearly all good bookkeepers.
SIR WALTER SCOTT.

3
There is no quite good book without a good morality; but the world is wide, and so are morals.
ROBERT LOUIS STEVENSON, *A Gossip on a Novel of Dumas.*

4
Digressions in a book are like foreign troops in a state, which argue the nation to want a heart and hands of its own, and often either subdue the natives, or drive them into the most unfruitful corners.
JONATHAN SWIFT, *A Tale of a Tub.*

5
The most accomplished way of using books at present is two-fold: either, first, to serve them as some men do lords, learn their titles exactly, and then brag of their acquaintance. Or, secondly, which is indeed the choicer, the profounder, and politer method, to get a thorough insight into the index, by which the whole book is governed and turned, like fishes by the tail.
JONATHAN SWIFT, *A Tale of a Tub.*

6
The multitude of books is making us ignorant.
VOLTAIRE.

7
Wisdom is wealth, and every good book is equivalent to a wise head—the head may die, but the book may live forever.
REPRESENTATIVE JOSEPH WHEELER of Alabama. From *The Wit and Wisdom of Congress*, ed. by EDWARD BOYKIN.

8
In old days books were written by men of letters and read by the public. Nowadays books are written by the public and read by nobody.
OSCAR WILDE, *Saturday Review*, Nov. 17, 1894.

BORES, BOREDOM

9
There is nothing that people get tired of so quickly as the things they like the most.
W. BURTON BALDRY, *Stray Thoughts.*

10
Practice makes—monotony.
W. BURTON BALDRY, *Stray Thoughts.*

11
He's the kind of bore who's here today and here tomorrow.
BINNIE BARNES.

12
I have not had my hearing aid open to that man for years.
BERNARD M. BARUCH, on how to handle a bore. (*The New York Times*, June 21, 1965.)

13
If only those old walls could talk, how boring they would be!
ROBERT BENCHLEY, *If These Old Walls Could Talk!* Inspired by the wrecking of the old Waldorf-Astoria Hotel in New York City, where, as a young reporter, Benchley had covered many an uninspiring banquet and meeting.

14
Bore: a person who talks when you want him to listen.
AMBROSE BIERCE, *The Devil's Dictionary.*

15
Are You a Bromide?
GELETT BURGESS, Title of essay in *Smart Set*, Apr., 1906. "Bromide" is now applied both to commonplace people and to their ideas and statements.

16
Society is now one polished horde
Form'd of two mighty tribes, the *Bores* and *Bored*.
LORD BYRON, *Don Juan.*

17
He'd be sharper than a serpent's tooth, if he wasn't as dull as ditch water.
CHARLES DICKENS, *Our Mutual Friend.* Bk. iii. ch. 10.

18
Bores have succeeded to dragons.
BENJAMIN DISRAELI, *The Young Duke.* Bk. ii, ch. 5.

19
The bore is usually considered a harmless creature, or of that class of irrational bipeds who hurt only themselves.
MARIA EDGEWORTH, *Thoughts on Bores.*

20
Never to be bored is an active form of imbecility.
CLIFTON FADIMAN, *The Selected Writings of Clifton Fadiman: The Reading Lamp* (1955).

21
A bore is a fellow who opens his mouth and puts his feats in it.
HENRY FORD.

22
I fell asleep reading a dull book, and I

dreamt that I was reading on, so I awoke
from sheer boredom.
HEINRICH HEINE.

1
It is a peculiarity of the bore that he is the
last person to find himself out.
OLIVER WENDELL HOLMES, from *Wit and
Wisdom of Oliver Wendell Holmes*, ed.
by LESTER E. DENONN.

2
It is only people of importance who can
afford to be dull.
CONSTANCE JONES, *The Ten Years' Agreement*.

3
We often forgive those who bore us; we
cannot forgive those whom we bore.
FRANÇOIS, DUC DE LA ROCHEFOUCAULD,
Maximes, No. 304.

4
Bores bore each other too; but it never
seems to teach them anything.
DON MARQUIS, *New York Sun*.

5
I am never bored anywhere: being bored is
an insult to oneself.
JULES RENARD, *Journal*.

6
I do not tremble when I meet
The stoutest of my foes,
But heaven defend me from the friend
Who comes—but never goes!
JOHN GODFREY SAXE, *My Familiar*.

7
A bore is a man who, when you ask him how
he is, tells you.
BERT LESTON TAYLOR, *The So-Called Human Race*.

8
He is an old bore; even the grave yawns
for him.
SIR HERBERT BEERBOHM TREE, quoted by
HESKETH PEARSON in *Lives of the Wits*.

9
The secret of being a bore is to tell every-
thing.
VOLTAIRE, *The Enfant Prodigy:* preface.

BORROWING AND LENDING

See also Debt

10
A moneylender serves you in the present
tense, lends you in the conditional mood,
keeps you in the subjunctive, and ruins you
in the future.
JOSEPH ADDISON.

11
Give, and you may keep your friend if you
lose your money; lend, and the chances are
that you lose your friend if ever you get
back your money.
SIR EDWARD BULWER-LYTTON, *Caxtoniana*,
essay 21.

12
Public credit means the contracting of debts
which a nation can never pay.
WILLIAM COBBETT, *Advice to Young Men*.

13
Great collections of books are subject to
certain accidents besides the damp, the
worms, and the rats; one not less common
is that of the *borrowers*, not to say a word
of the *purloiners*.
ISAAC D'ISRAELI, *Curiosities of Literature:
The Bibliomania*.

14
If you would know the value of money, go
and try to borrow some.
BENJAMIN FRANKLIN, *Poor Richard*, 1758.

15
Lend only what you can afford to lose.
GEORGE HERBERT, *Jacula Prudentum*.

16
Boswell, lend me sixpence—not to be repaid.
SAMUEL JOHNSON, Boswell's *Life*, Mar.
30, 1783.

17
The human species, according to the best
theory I can form of it, is composed of two
distinct races, the men who borrow, and
the men who lend.
CHARLES LAMB, *Essays of Elia*.

18
I am well acquainted with Mr. ___, and
know his circumstances. First of all, he has
a wife and baby; together they ought to be
worth $50,000 to any man. Secondly, he has
an office in which there is a table worth
$1.50 and three chairs worth, say, $1.00.
Last of all there is in one corner a large rat
hole, which will bear looking into. Respectfully, A. Lincoln.
ABRAHAM LINCOLN, *Reply* to a request
about the financial rating of a Springfield neighbor. From *The Humorous Mr.
Lincoln* by KEITH W. JENNISON.

19
My dear, I'll be economically independent
if I have to borrow every cent!
The Masses. Caption of cartoon, quoted
by MAX EASTMAN in *Enjoyment of
Laughter*.

20
The three degrees of comparison—begging,
borrowing and stealing.
JOHN RANDOLPH of Roanoke. From *The
Wit and Wisdom of Congress*, ed. by
EDWARD BOYKIN.

1
The more men you lend money to, the less there are from whom you can borrow.
Reflections of a Bachelor.

2
He was an incorrigible borrower of money; he borrowed from all his friends; if he ever repaid a loan the incident failed to pass into history.
MARK TWAIN, *Autobiography*, ch. 61. Referring to Bret Harte.

3
No man's credit is as good as his money.
HENRY VAN DYKE.

4
He that shows his wife or money will be in danger of having them borrowed sometimes.
WILLIAM WYCHERLEY, *The Country Wife,* Act 3.

BOSTON

5
Then here's to the City of Boston,
  The town of the cries and the groans,
Where the Cabots can't see the Kabotschniks
  And the Lowells won't speak to the Cohns.
FRANKLIN P. ADAMS, *Revised.* (For the original on which this is based, see BOSSIDY quotation in this section.)

6
Portland: Does every boy born in Boston *have* to go to Harvard?
Fred: It isn't compulsory. If you know the right people you can get out of it.
FRED ALLEN, *Treadmill to Oblivion.*

7
And this is good old Boston
  The home of the bean and the cod,
Where the Lowells talk to the Cabots
  And the Cabots talk only to God.
JOHN C. BOSSIDY, *Toast,* midwinter dinner, Holy Cross Alumni (1910).

8
Boston runs to brains as well as to beans and brown bread. But she is cursed with an army of cranks whom nothing short of a strait-jacket or a swamp-elm club will ever control.
WILLIAM COWPER BRANN, from *The Iconoclast,* a paper published in Austin, Tex., and later in Waco.

9
On another occasion a guest at a White House reception eased up to the President and remarked: "Mr. President, I'm from Boston."
His blue eyes rested only briefly on her as he said: "You'll never get over it."
ISHBEL ROSS, *Grace Coolidge and Her Era,* ch. 11.

10
We say the cows laid out Boston. Well, there are worse surveyors.
RALPH WALDO EMERSON, *Conduct of Life: Wealth.*

11
Boston State-house is the hub of the solar system. You couldn't pry that out of a Boston man if you had the tire of all creation straightened out for a crow-bar.
OLIVER WENDELL HOLMES, *The Autocrat of the Breakfast Table.*

12
The Bostonian who leaves Boston ought to be condemned to perpetual exile.
WILLIAM DEAN HOWELLS, *The Rise of Silas Lapham.*

13
A solid man of Boston;
With comfortable dividends,
And the first salmon and the first green peas.
HENRY WADSWORTH LONGFELLOW, *John Endicott,* Act 4.

14
Boston is a moral and intellectual nursery always busy applying first principles to trifles.
GEORGE SANTAYANA, from *Santayana: The Later Years,* ed. by DANIEL CORY.

15
Wendell Phillips. He was about the only Bostonian of his time who wore no middle name and he was therefore considered half naked.
FRANK SULLIVAN, *A Garland of Ibids.*

16
In Boston they ask, How much does he know? In New York, How much is he worth? In Philadelphia, Who were his parents?
MARK TWAIN, *What Paul Bourget Thinks of Us.*

17
Solid men of Boston, make no long orations;
Solid men of Boston, drink no long potations;
Solid men of Boston, go to bed at sundown;
Never lose your way like the logger heads of London.
UNKNOWN, *Billy Pitt and the Farmer.* (DEBRETT, *Asylum for Fugitive Pieces,* 1786.)

18
Well-bred Bostonians today deprecate the dourness, grimness, and bigotry of their forefathers—but they are intensely proud of them.
DIXON WECTER, *Saga of American Society.*

BOY

19
A good man dies when a boy goes wrong.
Boys' Ranch Roundup. Quoted in *Reader's Digest,* Sept. 1966.

1
I know only two sorts of boys. Mealy boys, and beef-faced boys.
CHARLES DICKENS, *Oliver Twist*, ch. 14.

2
"Boys will be boys." "And even that," I interposed, "wouldn't matter if we could only prevent girls from being girls."
ANTHONY HOPE, *The Dolly Dialogues*, No. 16.

3
The parent who could see his boy as he really is would shake his head and say: "Willie is no good: I'll sell him."
STEPHEN LEACOCK, *The Lot of the Schoolmaster*.

4
As a boy gets old he likes to have a man around to do the work.
STEPHEN LEACOCK, *Laugh with Leacock*.

5
Of course all boys are not full of tricks, but the best of them are. That is, those who are readiest to play innocent jokes, and who are continually looking for chances to make Rome howl, are the most apt to be first-class business men.
GEORGE W. PECK, quoted in *A Treasury of American Folklore* by B. A. BOTKIN.

6
A boy with head enough to amount to anything in the world can't help wondering how he is going to do it when everybody tells him how much like his father he is.
Reflections of a Bachelor.

7
A good way to get a boy to cut the grass is to forbid him to touch the lawn mower.
Reflections of a Bachelor.

8
Up to fifteen a boy has only two ambitions —to smoke and to shave.
Reflections of a Bachelor.

9
One of the best things in the world to be is a boy; it requires no experience, but needs some practice to be a good one.
CHARLES DUDLEY WARNER. *Being a Boy*, ch. 1.

BRAVERY

See also Boldness

10
It is easy to be brave from a safe distance.
AESOP, *The Wolf and the Kid*.

11
He has all the courage of a lame mouse in a lion's cage.
JIM BISHOP, *Some of My Very Best: The Male Animal*.

12
Here comes courage! that seized the lion absent, and ran away from the present mouse.
BENJAMIN FRANKLIN, *Poor Richard's Almanac*, 1775.

13
How valiantly the buzzing Gnat defies
The Eagle—who disdains to swoop on Flies!
ARTHUR GUITERMAN, *A Poet's Proverbs*.

14
Even cowards can endure hardship; only the brave can endure suspense.
MIGNON MCLAUGHLIN, *The Neurotic's Notebook*.

15
Two o'clock in the morning courage.
NAPOLEON BONAPARTE, quoted in LAS CASES, *Napoleon at St. Helena*.

16
Courage is doing what you're afraid to do. There can be no courage unless you're scared.
EDWARD V. (EDDIE) RICKENBACKER. (PEGGY STREIT, *What Is Courage?*; *The New York Times Magazine*, Nov. 24, 1963.)

17
The notable ferocity of non-combatants.
ARTHUR RIMBAUD, *Letter* to Izambard.

18
That's a valiant flea that dare eat his breakfast on the lip of a lion.
WILLIAM SHAKESPEARE, *Henry V*. Act iii, sc. 7.

19
The three-o'-clock in the morning courage, which Bonaparte thought was the rarest.
HENRY DAVID THOREAU, *Walden*. See Napoleon Bonaparte in this section.

20
FLEA. The bravest of all the creatures of God, if ignorance of fear were courage.
MARK TWAIN.

BREVITY

21
Bilin' down his repoort, wuz Finnigin!
An' he writed this here: "Musther Flannigan:
Off agin, on agin,
Gone agin.—Finnigin."
STRICKLAND GILLILAN, *Finnigin to Flannigan*.

22
Hubert, to be eternal you don't have to be endless.
MURIEL HUMPHREY (MRS. HUBERT HUMPHREY).

1
If there be any man cursed with the itch to compress a whole book into a page, a whole page into a phrase, and that phrase into a word, it is I.
JOSEPH JOUBERT, *Pensées.*

2
Brevity is the soul of drinking, as of wit.
CHARLES LAMB, *John Woodvil,* ch. 3. See also Shakespeare in this section.

3
A report having much useless language lay on his desk, the work of a Congressional committee regarding a newly devised gun. "I should want a new lease of life to read this through," groaned the President. "Why can't an investigating committee show a grain of common sense? If I send a man to buy a horse for me, I expect him to tell me that horse's points—not how many hairs he has in his tail."
CARL SANDBURG, *Abraham Lincoln: The Prairie Years and the War Years,* ch. 34.

4
Brevity is the soul of lingerie.
DOROTHY PARKER, quoted by ALEXANDER WOOLLCOTT in *While Rome Burns.*

5
Brevity is the soul of wit.
WILLIAM SHAKESPEARE, *Hamlet.* Act ii, sc. 2.

BRIBERY

6
It is patent to the mob,
That my being made a nob,
Was effected by a job.
W. S. GILBERT, *Trial by Jury.*

7
I needed the good will of the legislature of four states. I "formed" the legislative bodies with my own money. I found that it was cheaper that way.
JAY GOULD, *Testimony* to Congressional committee. (ANDRÉ SIEGFRIED, *America at Mid-Century.*)

8
Instead of paying lawyers to battle for them, they bought their freedom from city and state officials, and thus had to waste no time in courtrooms.
BEN HECHT, *Gaily, Gaily.*

9
I think I can say, and say with pride, that we have some legislatures that bring higher prices than any in the world.
MARK TWAIN, *After-Dinner Speech* in London, July 4, 1875.

BUSINESS

10
A conference is a gathering of important people who singly can do nothing, but together can decide that nothing can be done.
FRED ALLEN.

11
On ships they call them barnacles; in radio they attach themselves to desks, and are called vice-presidents.
FRED ALLEN.

12
Echo men are very important in the field of advertising. They are men who follow in the wake of the big executive and echo his sentiments as they are expressed.
FRED ALLEN, *Treadmill to Oblivion.*

13
The new brooms in the organization would just make a sweeping decision and there we were standing in the dust.
FRED ALLEN, *Treadmill to Oblivion.*

14
The idea of strictly minding our own business is moldy rubbish. Who could be so selfish?
MYRTIE BARKER, *I Am Only One.*

15
To mind my own business.
BERNARD M. BARUCH, *Reply,* when asked the most important lesson he had learned during his life. (*St. Louis Post-Dispatch,* June 21, 1965.)

16
A committee is a group that keeps minutes and loses hours.
MILTON BERLE, *News summaries,* July 1, 1954.

17
Mr. Morgan buys his partners; I grow my own.
ANDREW CARNEGIE. (HENDRYCK, *Life.*)

18
"Do other men for they would do you." That's the true business precept.
CHARLES DICKENS, *Martin Chuzzlewit.*

19
It is well known what a middleman is: he is a man who bamboozles one party and plunders the other.
BENJAMIN DISRAELI, *Speech,* Apr. 11, 1845.

20
A pretty good firm is "Watch & Waite,"
And another is "Attit, Early & Layte;"
And still another is "Doo & Dairet;"
But the best is probably "Grinn & Barrett."
WALTER G. DOTY, *The Best Firm.*

1
Business? That's very simple—it's other people's money. (Les affaires? C'est bien simple, c'est l'argent des autres.)
ALEXANDRE DUMAS, *fils, La Question d'Argent*. Act ii, sc. 7.

2
Don't forget until too late that the business of life is not business, but living.
B. C. FORBES, *Epigrams*.

3
A tip for girls in business: Pay more attention to making up your minds than to making up your faces.
B. C. FORBES, *Epigrams*.

4
A man who makes a one-dollar profit on his expense account is dishonest. A man who loses five cents on one is a damned fool.
GENE FOWLER, *Skyline*.

5
Drive thy business or it will drive thee.
BENJAMIN FRANKLIN, *Poor Richard*, 1758.

6
A man loseth his time that comes early to a bad bargain.
THOMAS FULLER, *Gnomologia*, No. 286.

7
He who thinks his business below him will always be above his business.
THOMAS FULLER, *Gnomologia*, No. 2333.

8
There's a firm that specializes in packaging materials—it's called Wrapture, Inc.
BILL GOLD, *Washington Post*.

9
A secretary came to Goldwyn saying, "Our files are so crowded that I suggest destroying all correspondence more than six years old."
"By all means," said Goldwyn. "But be sure to make copies."
SAM GOLDWYN, attributed.

10
A man is likely to mind his own business when it is worth minding. When it is not, he takes his mind off his own meaningless affairs by minding other people's business.
ERIC HOFFER, *The True Believer*.

11
Once in a long while some feller retires from th' poultry business instead o' quittin'.
FRANK MCKINNEY (KIN) HUBBARD, *Abe Martin's Primer*.

12
It seems like one o' the hardest lessons t' be learned in this life is where your business ends an' somebuddy else's begins.
FRANK MCKINNEY (KIN) HUBBARD, *Abe Martin's Primer*.

13
Th' trouble with mixin' business with plea-sure is that th' pleasure allus comes t' th' top.
FRANK MCKINNEY (KIN) HUBBARD, *Abe Martin's Primer*.

14
Th' feller who refuses t' neglect his business an' foller th' crowd is called a grouch.
FRANK MCKINNEY (KIN) HUBBARD, *Abe Martin's Primer*.

15
You don't have t' peddle a good thing.
FRANK MCKINNEY (KIN) HUBBARD, *Abe Martin's Primer*.

16
A trust is known by the companies it keeps.
ELLIS O. JONES. (*Toastmaster's Handbook*, compiled by PEGGY EDMUND and HAROLD WORKMAN WILLIAMS.)

17
No one ever won an interview.
GARSON KANIN. (RICHARD MANEY, *Fanfare*, p. 195.)

18
"Big businessmen are the most over-rated people in the country," Joe [Joseph P. Kennedy] would tell his sons. "Here I am, a boy from East Boston and I took 'em. So don't be impressed."
VICTOR LASKY, *J.F.K.: The Man and the Myth*.

19
Many of the bold buccaneers of trade become timid as mice in the presence of any female who is not working for them.
ALEXANDER KING, *Rich Man, Poor Man, Freud and Fruit*, ch. 2.

20
A salesman is got to dream, boy. It comes with the territory.
ARTHUR MILLER, *Death of a Salesman: requiem*.

21
When I see a merchant over-polite to his customers, begging them to taste a little brandy and throwing half his goods on the counter—thinks I, that man has an axe to grind.
CHARLES MINER, *Who'll Turn the Grindstones?*

22
The trouble with senior management to an outsider is that there are too many one-ulcer men holding down two-ulcer jobs.
PRINCE PHILIP, from *The Wit of Prince Philip*, compiled by PETER BUTLER.

23
She was "honeychile" in New Orleans,
The hottest of the bunch;
But on the old expense account,
She was gas, cigars, and lunch.
More Playboy's Party Jokes (1965).

1

I've noticed that men are awfully funny and fussy over what they call business, and take hours and hours to do a thing any woman could settle in five minutes.

    E. R. PUNSHON, *Rhoda in Between.*

2

Will you please tell me what you do with all the Vice Presidents a bank has? I guess that's to get you more discouraged before you can see the President. Why, the United States is the biggest business institution in the world and they only have one Vice President and nobody has ever found anything for him to do.

    WILL ROGERS, *Autobiography.* Speech to International Bankers Association, New York, 1922.

3

He talked shop like a tenth muse.

    G. W. E. RUSSELL, *Collections and Recollections.* Referring to the speeches of Prime Minister Gladstone.

4

Mind your till and till your mind.

    CHARLES HADDON SPURGEON, *Salt-Cellars.*

5

We were to do more business after dinner; but after dinner is after dinner—an old saying and a true, 'much drinking, little thinking.'

    JONATHAN SWIFT, *Journal to Stella,* Feb. 26, 1712.

6

Have you so much leisure from your own business, that you can take care of other people's that does not at all belong to you?

    P. T. A. TERENCE, quoted in *Classic Quotations,* ed. by JAMES ELMES.

7

In doing of aught let your wit bear a stroke
For buying or selling of pig in a poke.

    THOMAS TUSSER, *Five Hundred Points of Good Husbandry:* September (1557).

8

Statistics indicate that as a result of overwork, modern executives are dropping like flies on the nation's golf-courses.

    IRA WALLACH, *How to Be Deliriously Happy.*

9

I remember that a wise friend of mine did usually say, "That which is everybody's business is nobody's business."

    IZAAK WALTON, *The Compleat Angler.* Pt. i, ch. 2. (Third Edition.)

C

CANDOR

10

Always be ready to speak your mind, and a base man will avoid you.

    WILLIAM BLAKE, *Proverbs of Hell.*

11

I can call nothing by a name if that is not his name. I call a cat a cat, and Rolet a rogue. (Je ne puis rien nommer si ce n'est pas son nom; j'appelle un chat un chat, et Rolet un fripon.)

    BOILEAU, *Satires,* Satire 1.

12

A loose, plain, rude writer, I call a spade a spade.

    ROBERT BURTON, *The Anatomy of Melancholy: Democritus to the Reader.*

13

Pigs Is Pigs.

    ELLIS PARKER BUTLER, *Title* of story dealing with guinea pigs.

14

I don't complain of Betsy or any of her acts
Exceptin' when we've quarreled and told each other facts.

    WILL CARLETON, *Betsy and I Are Out.*

15

Frankness is the backbone of friendship—when it is covered by the flesh of tact.

    G. G. COLMORE, *The Angel and the Outcast.*

16

"Frank and explicit"—that is the right line to take when you wish to conceal your own mind and to confuse the minds of others.

    BENJAMIN DISRAELI, *Sybil,* bk. 6.

17

A man that should call everything by its right name, would hardly pass the streets without being knocked down as a common enemy.

    LORD HALIFAX, *Works,* p. 246.

18

The man who says what he thinks is finished and the man who thinks what he says is an idiot.

    ROLF HOCHHUTH, *The Deputy.* Act i, sc. 3.

19

To say what you think will certainly damage you in society; but a free tongue is worth more than a thousand invitations.

    LOGAN PEARSALL SMITH, *Afterthoughts.*

20

On an occasion of this kind it becomes more than a moral duty to speak one's mind. It becomes a pleasure.

> Oscar Wilde, *The Importance of Being Earnest*, Act 2.

1

Penny was always frank, outspoken and never tried to conceal his feelings. He had no friends whatsoever.

> Douglas Yates, *The Courage of His Convictions.*

CAT

2

My mistress turned into a ghost,
I reign supreme and rule the roast;
Yet I cannot claim to be.
Half so great a cat as she.

> Martin Armstrong, *54 Conceits: A Cat on Her Late Mistress.*

3

It is a very inconvenient habit of kittens (Alice had once made the remark) that, whatever you say to them, they *always* purr.

> Lewis Carroll, *Through the Looking-Glass*, ch. 9.

4

"Not like cats!" cried the Mouse in a shrill, passionate voice. "Would *you* like cats if you were me?"

> Lewis Carroll, *Alice in Wonderland*, ch. 2.

5

In the dark all cats are grey.

> Miguel de Cervantes, *Don Quixote*. Pt. ii, ch. 33. (See also Heywood in this section.)

6

The cat may look at a King, they say,
But rather would look at a Mouse at Play.

> Arthur Guiterman, *A Poet's Proverbs.*

7

The Cat that always wears Silk Mittens
Will catch no Mice to feed her Kittens.

> Arthur Guiterman, *A Poet's Proverbs.*

8

When all candles be out, all cats be gray.

> John Heywood, *Proverbs.*

9

Then, my boy, beware of Daphne. Learn a lesson from a rat:
What is cunning in the kitten may be cruel in the cat.

> R. U. Johnson, *Daphne.*

10

There are more ways to kill a cat than choking her with cream.

> Charles Kingsley, *Westward Ho*, ch. 20.

11

When I play with my cat, who knows whether I do not make her more sport than she makes me?

> Michel de Montaigne, *Essays.* Bk. ii, ch. 12.

12

I cannot agree that it should be the declared public policy of Illinois that a cat visiting a neighbor's yard or crossing the highway is a public nuisance. It is in the nature of cats to do a certain amount of unescorted roaming . . . to escort a cat abroad on a leash is against the nature of the owner. Moreover, cats perform useful service, particularly in the rural areas. The problem of the cat vs. the bird is as old as time. If we attempt to resolve it by legislation, who knows but what we may be called upon to take sides as well in the age-old problems of dog vs. cat, bird vs. bird, or even bird vs. worm. In my opinion, the State of Illinois and its local governing bodies already have enough to do without trying to control feline delinquency.

> Adlai E. Stevenson, *Message* to Illinois Senate, Apr. 23, 1949, accompanying his veto of a bill that would have punished owners of cats who permitted the animals to roam at large without leashes. Stevenson was governor of the state when he wrote this, one of his most widely quoted passages.

13

Cruel Clever Cat

Sally, having swallowed cheese,
Directs down holes the scented breeze,
Enticing thus with baited breath
Nice mice to an untimely death.

> Geoffrey Taylor.

CAUSE

14

Obstinacy in a bad cause is but constancy in a good.

> Sir Thomas Browne, *Religio Medici*, sec. 25.

15

My advice to a young man seeking deathless fame would be to espouse an unpopular cause and devote his life to it.

> George William Curtis, *Wendell Phillips.*

16

Faith in a holy cause is to a considerable extent a substitute for the lost faith in ourselves.

> Eric Hoffer, *The True Believer.*

17

The less justified a man is in claiming excellence for his own self, the more ready is he to claim all excellence for his nation, his religion, his race or his holy cause.

> Eric Hoffer, *The True Believer.*

1
It is more important to know that we are on God's side.
> ABRAHAM LINCOLN, *Retort,* to a deputation of Southerners during the Civil War, whose spokesman had remarked, "We trust, sir, that God is on our side."

2
I realize that one man's cliché can be another man's conviction.
> ADLAI STEVENSON, *Speech,* Harvard Business School, June 6, 1959.

CENSORSHIP

3
Censor—A self-appointed snoophound who sticks his noes into other people's business.
> BENNETT CERF, *The Laugh's on Me.*

4
Television executives issue a "forbidden sheet" to editors. You must not buy a script in which a man loses limbs. Never show a murdered body. Adultery is a permissible subject, provided it is not committed with the husband's best friend. (Whom do television executives think women commit adultery with?)
> HARRY GOLDEN, *For 2¢ Plain.*

5
The smile of the Goat has a meaning that few
Will mistake, and explains in a measure
The Censor attending a risqué Revue
And combining Stern Duty with pleasure.
> OLIVER HERFORD, *The Smile of the Goat.*

6
A writer owned an asterisk,
And kept it in his den,
Where he wrote tales (which had large sales)
Of frail and erring men;
And always, when he reached the point
Where carping censors lurk,
He called upon the asterisk
To do his dirty work.
> STODDARD KING, *The Writer and the Asterisk.*

7
A sodomite got very excited looking at a zoology text. Does this make it pornography?
> STANISLAW J. LEC, *Unkempt Thoughts,* tr. from the Polish by JACEK GALASKA.

8
I'm going to introduce a resolution to have the Postmaster General stop reading dirty books and deliver the mail.
> SENATOR GALE McGEE, on censorship. (*Quote,* Sept. 13, 1959.)

9
The artist and the censor differ in this wise: that the first is a decent mind in an indecent body and that the second is an indecent mind in a decent body.
> GEORGE JEAN NATHAN, *The Autobiography of an Attitude.*

10
It is remarkable how many impure things a prude can discover that nobody else can discover.
> *Reflections of a Bachelor* (1903).

11
Assassination is the extreme form of censorship.
> BERNARD SHAW. *The Shewing-Up of Blanco Posnet:* preface.

12
I never knew a girl who was ruined by a book.
> JAMES J. WALKER, *Debate* on censorship, in New York Senate.

CHANGE

See also Consistency

13
Nought endures but change.
> LUDWIG BOURNE, *Address,* Dec. 2, 1825.

14
Some things, of course, you can't change. Pretending that you have is like painting stripes on a horse and hollering "Zebra!"
> EDDIE CANTOR, *The Way I See It.*

15
The only difference between a rut and a grave is their dimensions.
> ELLEN GLASGOW.

16
Better far to die in the old harness than to try to put on another.
> J. G. HOLLAND, *Gold-Foil.*

17
I do not allow myself to suppose that either the convention or the League have concluded to decide that I am either the greatest or best man in America, but rather they have concluded it is not best to swap horses while crossing the river, and have further concluded that I am not so poor a horse that they might not make a botch of it in trying to swap.
> ABRAHAM LINCOLN, *Address* to a delegation of the National Union League, which had called to congratulate him on his renomination as Republican presidential candidate, June 9, 1864.

18
Truly there is a tide in the affairs of men; but there is no gulf-stream setting forever in one direction.
> JAMES RUSSELL LOWELL, *Among My Books.*

1
Let a man proclaim a new principle. Public sentiment will surely be on the other side.
  THOMAS B. REED, quoted in W. A. ROBINSON, *Life*.

2
They are the weakest-minded and the hardest-hearted men, that love most variety and change.
  JOHN RUSKIN, *Modern Painters*. Pt. ii, ch. 6, sec. 7.

3
It is the nature of a man as he grows older, a small bridge in time, to protest against change, particularly change for the better.
  JOHN STEINBECK, *Travels with Charley*, pt. 2.

4
There is nothing in the world constant, but inconstancy.
  JONATHAN SWIFT, *On the Faculties of the Mind*.

5
Change everything except your loves.
  VOLTAIRE, *Sur l'Usage de la Vie*.

CHARACTER

6
Underneath this flabby exterior is an enormous lack of character.
  OSCAR LEVANT, *Memoirs of an Amnesiac*.

7
A man far oftener appears to have a decided character from persistently following his temperament than from persistently following his principles.
  FRIEDRICH WILHELM NIETZSCHE, *Human, All Too Human*, vol. 1, tr. by HELEN ZIMMERN.

8
Character is made by what you stand for; reputation, by what you fall for.
  ROBERT QUILLEN.

9
Lax in their gaiters, laxer in their gait.
  HORACE and JAMES SMITH, *Rejected Addresses: The Theatre*.

10
The fate of the country . . . does not depend on what kind of paper you drop into the ballot-box once a year, but on what kind of man you drop from your chamber into the street every morning.
  HENRY D. THOREAU, *Slavery in Massachusetts* (1854).

11
There is no character, howsoever good and fine, but it can be destroyed by ridicule, howsoever poor and witless. Observe the ass, for instance: his character is about perfect, he is the choicest spirit among all the humbler animals, yet see what ridicule has brought him to. Instead of feeling complimented when we are called an ass, we are left in doubt.
  MARK TWAIN, *Pudd'nhead Wilson's Calendar*.

CHARITY

12
Do not give alms promiscuously. Select the unworthy poor and make them happy. To give to the deserving is a duty, but to help the improvident, drinking class is clear generosity, so that the donor has a right to be warmed by a selfish pride and count on a most flattering obituary.
  GEORGE ADE, *Fables*.

13
Beggars must be no choosers.
  BEAUMONT AND FLETCHER, *Scornful Lady*, Act 3.

14
Charity begins at home, and justice begins next door.
  CHARLES DICKENS, *Martin Chuzzlewit*, ch. 27.

15
Sue a beggar and get a louse.
  EDMUND GAYTON, *Festivous Notes on Don Quixote*, 83.

16
Brother, can you spare a dime?
  E. Y. HARBURG, *Title and refrain* of song (1932).

17
He is one of those wise philanthropists who, in a time of famine, would vote for nothing but a supply of toothpicks.
  DOUGLAS JERROLD, *Wit and Opinions of Douglas Jerrold* (1859).

18
I do not give alms; I am not poor enough for that.
  FRIEDRICH WILHELM NIETZSCHE, *Thus Spake Zarathustra:* introductory.

19
The organized charity, scrimped and iced,
In the name of a cautious, statistical Christ.
  JOHN BOYLE O'REILLY, *In Bohemia*.

20
With one hand he put
A penny in the urn of poverty,
And with the other took a shilling out.
  ROBERT POLLOCK, *The Course of Time*.

21
God's servants making a snug living
By guiding Mammon in smug giving.
  KEITH PRESTON, *Professional Welfare Workers*.

22
Charity eggs don't seem to hatch.
  Reflections of a Bachelor (1903).

1

Benevolence is a natural instinct of the human mind; when A sees B in distress, his conscience always urges him to entreat C to help him.
SYDNEY SMITH.

2

Feel for others—in your pocket.
CHARLES HADDON SPURGEON, *Salt-Cellars*.

3

The milk of human kindness ran
In rich abundance in his breast,
It left thin grease stains on the tan
Of his asbestos vest.
PAUL TANAQUIL, *Philanthropist*.

CHARM

4

He had no more charm than an old knothole.
CLIFTON FADIMAN, *The Selected Writings of Clifton Fadiman: The Book-Reviewing Business* (1955).

5

She was a woman who, between courses, could be graceful with her elbows on the table.
HENRY JAMES, *The Ambassadors*.

6

Do you know the difference between a beautiful woman and a charming one? A beauty is a woman you notice; a charmer is one who notices you.
ADLAI STEVENSON, *Speech* at Radcliffe College in 1963.

7

A woman must beware of speaking the truth to a man: he loves her the less for it. Men are wilfully blind to our faults. It is only in being enigmatical that we charm.
J. M. STUART-YOUNG, *Passion's Peril*.

8

It is absurd to divide people into good and bad. People are either charming or tedious.
OSCAR WILDE, *Lady Windermere's Fan*, Act. 1.

CHASTITY

9

Chaste women are often proud and forward, as presuming upon the merits of their chastity.
FRANCIS BACON, *Essays: Of Marriage and Single Life*.

10

. . . the simple feat of keeping her legs crossed was a structural impossibility.
MAXWELL BODENHEIM, *Replenishing Jessica*.

11

A woman's honor is concerned with one thing only, and it is a thing with which the honor of a man is not concerned at all.
JAMES BRANCH CABELL, *Jurgen*, p. 63.

12

From hence let those be warned, who mean to wed;
Lest mutual falsehood stain the bridal-bed:
For each deceiver to his cost may find,
That marriage frauds too oft are paid in kind.
WILLIAM CONGREVE, *The Way of the World*, Act 5.

13

Elyot: It doesn't suit women to be promiscuous.
Amanda: It doesn't suit men for women to be promiscuous.
NOEL COWARD, *Private Lives*.

14

Are there still virgins? One is tempted to answer no. There are only girls who have not yet crossed the line, because they want to preserve their market value, having been told that desirable customers buy only unused merchandise; and girls who are afraid of men, of *Man*, the enemy who must be avoided because he wounds or must be captured in order to make him a husband. Call them virgins if you wish, these travelers in transit.
FRANÇOISE GIROUD, *Coronet*, Nov., 1960.

15

A woman's chastity consists, like an onion, of a series of coats.
NATHANIEL HAWTHORNE, *Journals*, Mar. 16, 1854.

16

I may not be exactly what some people consider a virgin, but I've been chaste. Chased by every man.
Line from movie version of CHRISTOPHER ISHERWOOD's *I Am a Camera*.

17

Virgin me no virgins.
PHILIP MASSINGER, *A New Way to Pay Old Debts*.

18

Chaste is she whom no one has asked. (Casta est, quam nemo rogavit.)
OVID, *Amores*, bk. 1.

19

If she seem not chaste to me,
What care I how chaste she be?
SIR WALTER RALEIGH, *Shall I, Like a Hermit, Dwell?*

20

The very ice of chastity is in them.
WILLIAM SHAKESPEARE, *As You Like It*. Act iii, sc. 4.

21

I will find you twenty lascivious turtles ere one chaste man.
WILLIAM SHAKESPEARE, *The Merry Wives of Windsor*. Act ii, sc. 1.

1
It is not politic in the commonwealth of nature to preserve virginity.
  WILLIAM SHAKESPEARE, *All's Well That Ends Well.* Act i, sc. 1.

2
Women enjoy'd (whate'er before they've been)
Are like romances read, or sights once seen.
  SIR JOHN SUCKLING, *Against Fruition.*

CHEATING

3
Thou shalt not steal: an empty feat,
When it's so lucrative to cheat.
  ARTHUR HUGH CLOUGH, *The Latest Decalogue.*

4
The hand that rocks the scales in the grocery store is the hand that rules the world.
  FINLEY PETER DUNNE, *Mr. Dooley Remembers.*

5
Three things are men most likely to be cheated in, a horse, a wig, and a wife.
  BENJAMIN FRANKLIN, *Poor Richard,* 1736.

6
Men may *swallow* the being cheated, but no man can ever endure to chew it.
  LORD HALIFAX, *Works.*

7
In trade you are either afraid that the other fellow will cheat you or that you won't cheat him.
  Reflections of a Bachelor.

CHILDREN

See also Baby, Boy, Girl

8
You can do anything with children if you only play with them.
  OTTO VON BISMARCK, *Sayings of Bismarck.*

9
Children rule, old men go to school, women wear the breeches.
  ROBERT BURTON, *The Anatomy of Melancholy.*

10
Children can stand vast amounts of sternness. They rather expect to be wrong and are quite used to being punished. It is injustice, inequity and inconsistency that kill them.
  FATHER ROBERT CAPON, *Bed and Board.*

11
Speak roughly to your little boy,
  And beat him when he sneezes:
He only does it to annoy,
  Because he knows it teases.
  LEWIS CARROLL, *Alice's Adventures in Wonderland,* ch. 6.

12
So she set the little creature down, and felt quite relieved to see it trot away quietly into the wood. "If it had grown up," she said to herself, "it would have been a dreadfully ugly child: but it makes rather a handsome pig, I think." And she began thinking over other children she knew, who might do very well as pigs.
  LEWIS CARROLL, *Alice's Adventures in Wonderland,* ch. 6.

13
When children stand still,
They have done some ill.
  A. B. CHEALES, *Proverbial Folk-lore.*

14
I have monsters of my own who pose as children of mine, and I have learned as a first principle to encourage them in nothing.
  JOHN CIARDI, *The Saturday Review,* Aug. 14, 1965.

15
I know a lot about children. Not being an author, I'm a great critic.
  FINLEY PETER DUNNE, *Mr. Dooley Remembers.*

16
Some have children—some have none—
Here lies the mother of twenty-one.
  Epitaph of ANN JENNINGS, Wolstanton, England. (*Curious Epitaphs,* collected by WILLIAM ANDREWS.)

17
Being a child is in itself a profession.
  CLIFTON FADIMAN. *The Selected Writings of Clifton Fadiman: Children's Reading* (1955).

18
When children are doing nothing, they are doing mischief.
  HENRY FIELDING, *Tom Jones.* Bk. xv, ch. 2.

19
Teach your child to hold his tongue; he'll learn fast enough to speak.
  BENJAMIN FRANKLIN, *Poor Richard,* 1734.

20
Kids lead a tough life. Nobody takes them seriously. Nobody listens to them. They're always getting pushed aside. Kids and my people have a lot in common. . . . Only our problems aren't solved by getting older. . . . If man could only get a little older a little later, and a little wiser a little younger.
  DICK GREGORY, *From the Back of the Bus.*

21
Marry your son when you will, your daughter when you can.
  GEORGE HERBERT, *Jacula Prudentum.*

1
Many kiss the child for the nurse's sake.
JOHN HEYWOOD, *Proverbs.*

2
A child enters your home and makes so much noise for twenty years you can hardly stand it—then departs, leaving the house so silent you think you will go mad.
DR. J. A. HOLMES, quoted in *Dynamic Maturity.*

3
The daughter begins to bloom before the mother can be content to fade, and neither can forbear to wish for the absence of the other.
SAMUEL JOHNSON, *Rasselas,* ch. 29.

4
Parents do not know what they do when they leave tender babes alone to go to sleep in the dark.
CHARLES LAMB, *Essays of Elia.*

5
I never knows the children. It's just six of one and a half-dozen of the other.
FREDERICK MARRYAT, *The Pirate,* ch. 4.

6
A mother loves her child more than the father does, because she knows it's her own, while the father only thinks it's his.
MENANDER, *Fragments,* No. 657.

7
Children are in the number of things that need not greatly bee desired; especially in these corrupted daies, wherein it would be so hard a matter to make them good.
MICHEL DE MONTAIGNE, *Essays,* tr. by JOHN FLORIO.

8
Parents were invented to make children happy by giving them something to ignore.
OGDEN NASH, quoted in *Horse Sense in American Humor,* by WALTER BLAIR.

9
Heredity is what a man believes in until his son begins to behave like a delinquent.
Presbyterian Life.

10
An easy way not to get rich is to have plenty of children.
Reflections of a Bachelor.

11
Two of anything but children make a pair; two of them make a mob.
Reflections of a Bachelor.

12
It prevents a great deal of suspicion to have a child look like its father.
Reflections of a Bachelor.

13
Before I got married I had six theories about bringing up children; now I have six children and no theories.
LORD ROCHESTER (1647–1680).

14
I was not a child prodigy, because a child prodigy is a child who knows as much when it is a child as it does when it grows up.
WILL ROGERS, *Autobiography.*

15
All children know they are progressing. Moreover, they're not allowed to forget it.
JEAN-PAUL SARTRE, *The Words.*

16
The Chinese (they say) make physical monsters. We revile them for it and proceed to make moral monsters of our own children.
BERNARD SHAW, *Parents and Children.*

17
If you strike a child, take care that you strike it in anger, even at the risk of maiming it for life. A blow in cold blood neither can nor should be forgiven.
BERNARD SHAW, *Maxims for Revolutionists.*

18
No child should be unaware that if it provokes its elders beyond endurance, it will get its head clouted without regard to the possible consequences.
BERNARD SHAW, quoted in *Days with Bernard Shaw* by STEPHEN WINSTEN.

19
I must have been an insufferable child; all children are.
BERNARD SHAW, quoted in *Days with Bernard Shaw* by STEPHEN WINSTEN.

20
Every child should have an occasional pat on the back as long as it is applied low enough and hard enough.
BISHOP FULTON J. SHEEN. (*Farmer's Almanac,* 1966.)

21
Men dress their children's minds as they do their bodies in the prevailing fashion.
HERBERT SPENCER, *The Education of a Gentleman.*

22
Give a child his will and a whelp his fill,
Both will surely turn out ill.
CHARLES HADDON SPURGEON, *Ploughman's Pictures.*

23
A child should always say what's true
And speak when he is spoken to,
And behave mannerly at table;
At least as far as he is able.
ROBERT LOUIS STEVENSON, *Whole Duty of Children.*

1
I 'spect I growed. Don't think nobody never made me.
> HARRIET BEECHER STOWE, *Uncle Tom's Cabin*, ch. 21.

2
Childhood used to end with the discovery that there is no Santa Claus. Nowadays, it too often ends when the child gets his first adult, the way Hemingway got his first rhino, with the difference that the rhino was charging Hemingway, whereas the adult is usually running from the child.
> JAMES THURBER, *The Darlings at the Top of the Stairs*.

3
If your mother tells you to do a thing, it is wrong to reply that you won't. It is better and more becoming to intimate that you will do as she bids you, and then afterward act quietly in the matter according to the dictates of your best judgment.
> MARK TWAIN, *Advice to Little Girls*.

4
Children begin by loving their parents. After a time they judge them. Rarely, if ever, do they forgive them.
> OSCAR WILDE, *A Woman of No Importance*, Act 2.

5
The thing that impresses me most about America is the way parents obey their children.
> DUKE OF WINDSOR, quoted in *Look*, Mar. 5, 1957.

6
Few things so speedily modify an uncle's love as a nephew's air-gun bullet in the fleshy part of the leg.
> P. G. WODEHOUSE.

CHRISTMAS

7
Christmas itself may be called into question
If carried so far it creates indigestion.
> RALPH BERGENGREN, *The Unwise Christmas*.

8
'Most all the time, the whole year round,
   there ain't no flies on me,
But jest 'fore Christmas I'm as good as I
   kin be!
> EUGENE FIELD, *Jest 'Fore Christmas*.

9
I once asked a Christmas Eve group of children if they believed in Santa Claus. The very smallest ones answered without hesitation, "Why, of course!" The older ones shook their heads. The little girls smiled sadly but said nothing. One future scientist asserted boldly, "I know who it is"; and

a little make-strong with his eye on gain said: "I believe in it all; I can believe anything." That boy, I realized, would one day be a bishop.
> STEPHEN LEACOCK, *War-Time Santa Claus*.

10
Our Unabashed Dictionary defines beatnik as Santa Claus the day after Christmas.
> *More Playboy's Party Jokes* (1965).

11
Christmas is coming, the geese are getting fat,
Please to put a penny in the old man's hat;
If you haven't got a penny, a ha'penny will do,
If you haven't got a ha'penny, God Bless You!
> UNKNOWN, *Beggar's Rhyme*.

CHURCH

See also Clergy, Religion

12
Don't stay away from church because there are so many hypocrites. There's always room for one more.
> A. R. ADAMS.

13
Churches, like women, don't improve with age . . . and like women both need tight lacing to hold them together.
> MAX BARING, *The Shattered Idol*.

14
While Beecher's church holds out to burn
The vilest sinner may return!
> Reported to have been sung by firemen at the burning of Lyman Beecher's church in Boston. (*Henry Ward Beecher: An American Portrait* by PAXTON HIBBEN.)

15
Wherever God erects a house of prayer,
The Devil always builds a chapel there;
And 'twill be found, upon examination,
The latter has the largest congregation.
> DANIEL DEFOE, *The True-born Englishman*.

16
A lady, if undrest at church, looks silly,
One cannot be devout in dishabilly.
> GEORGE FARQUHAR, *The Stage Coach:* prologue.

17
The Bell calls others to Church, but itself never minds the sermon.
> BENJAMIN FRANKLIN, *Poor Richard*, 1754.

18
Bells call others, but themselves enter not into the Church.
> GEORGE HERBERT, *Jacula Prudentum*.

1
A church is God between four walls.
  VICTOR HUGO, *Ninety-Three*. Pt. ii, bk. 3, ch. 2.

2
While I can not be regarded as a pillar, I must be regarded as a buttress of the church, because I support from the outside.
  WILLIAM LAMB, attributed.

3
There can be no church in which the demon does not have his chapel.
  THOMAS NASHE, *Have With You to Saffron-Walden*.

4
Even a warm church can't compete successfully with a cold barroom.
  Reflections of a Bachelor (1903).

5
A great many more men would want to go to church if there was a law against it.
  Reflections of a Bachelor (1903).

6
Opium is not so stupefying to many persons as an afternoon sermon.
  JONATHAN SWIFT, *A Sermon on Sleeping in Church*.

7
The church and clergy, here no doubt,
  Are very much akin;
Both weather-beaten are without,
  Both empty are within.
  JONATHAN SWIFT, *Extempore Verses*.

8
There warn't anybody at the church, except maybe a hog or two, . . . If you notice, most folks don't go to church only when they've got to; but a hog is different.
  MARK TWAIN, *Adventures of Huckleberry Finn*, ch. 18.

CITIES
9
Cambridge people rarely smile,
Being urban, squat, and packed with guile.
  RUPERT BROOKE, *The Old Vicarage, Grantchester*.

10
I love capitals. Everything is best at capitals.
  LORD CHESTERFIELD, *Letters*, Oct. 2, 1749.

11
The chicken is the country's, but the city eats it.
  GEORGE HERBERT, *Jacula Prudentum*, No. 113.

12
The mobs of great cities add just so much to the support of pure government as sores do to the strength of the human body.
  THOMAS JEFFERSON, *Writings*, vol. 2.

13
All cities are mad: but the madness is gallant. All cities are beautiful: but the beauty is grim.
  CHRISTOPHER MORLEY, *Where the Blue Begins*.

14
In a real estate man's eye, the most exclusive part of the city is wherever he has a house to sell.
  WILL ROGERS, *The Illiterate Digest*.

15
As for these communities, I think I had rather keep bachelor's hall in hell than go to board in heaven.
  HENRY DAVID THOREAU, *Journal*, March 3, 1841.

16
City life: Millions of people being lonesome together.
  HENRY DAVID THOREAU.

17
This poor little one-horse town.
  MARK TWAIN, *The Undertaker's Story*.

18
Las Vegas is the only town in the world whose skyline is made up neither of buildings, like New York, nor of trees, like Wilbraham, Massachusetts, but signs.
  TOM WOLFE, *The Kandy-Kolored Tangerine-Flake Streamline Baby*.

19
A hick town is one where there is no place to go where you shouldn't be.
  ALEXANDER WOOLLCOTT.

20
I doubt if there is anything in the world uglier than a midwestern city.
  FRANK LLOYD WRIGHT, *Address*, Evanston, Ill., Aug., 1954.

CIVILIZATION
21
The deformation of the human foot by the shoe is the test of ripeness in civilization— not heat but feet.
  JACQUES BARZUN, *God's Country and Mine*.

22
The Neanderthal Man had fires, caves, marrow bones, mosquitoes, love and arthritis. What more can you ask?
  WILL CUPPY, *How to Tell Your Friends from the Apes*.

23
Every prison is the exclamation point and every asylum is the question mark in the sentences of civilization.
  SAMUEL DUFFIELD, *Essay*.

1
The end of the human race will be that it will eventually die of civilization.
RALPH WALDO EMERSON.

2
You gotta say this for the white race—its self-confidence knows no bounds. Who else could go to a small island in the South Pacific where there's no poverty, no crime, no unemployment, no war and no worry— and call it a "primitive society"?
DICK GREGORY, *From the Back of the Bus.*

3
The path of civilization is paved with tin cans.
ELBERT HUBBARD.

4
You can't say civilization don't advance, however, for in every war they kill you a new way.
WILL ROGERS, *Autobiography.*

5
It is strange that the last men of intellectual eminence before the dark ages were concerned, not with saving civilization or expelling the barbarians or reforming the abuses of the administration, but with preaching the merit of virginity and the damnation of unbaptized infants.
BERTRAND RUSSELL, *A History of Western Philosophy,* ch. 4.

CLEANLINESS

6
Cleanliness is almost as bad as godliness.
SAMUEL BUTLER.

7
When Ministers of the Crown speak like this on behalf of His Majesty's Government, the Prime Minister and his friends have no need to wonder why they are getting universally into bad odour.
SIR WINSTON CHURCHILL, *Speech* in House of Commons, Oct. 28, 1947. Hugh Gaitskell, then Minister of Fuel, advocated fewer baths to save fuel. He said he did not take many baths himself.

8
Cleaning your house while your kids are still growing
Is like shoveling the walk before it stops snowing.
PHYLLIS DILLER, *Phyllis Diller's Housekeeping Hints.*

9
O the moon shines bright on Mrs. Porter
And on her daughter
They wash their feet in soda water.
T. S. ELIOT, *The Waste Land: The Fire Sermon.*

10
They who bathe in May will soon be laid in clay;
They who bathe in June will sing a merry tune;
They who bathe in July will dance like a fly.
WILLIAM HONE, *Table-Book.*

11
If you wish, Faustinus, that a bath, so hot that even Julianus could scarcely get into it, should be called, ask the rhetorician Sabineius to bathe in it. He makes icy the warm baths of Nero.
MARTIAL, *Epigrams,* bk. 3.

12
The Romans started this bath gag . . . now look what became of them.
WILL ROGERS, *The Illiterate Digest.*

13
If anyone desires a glass of bottled ale; first shake the bottle, to see whether anything be in it; then taste it, to know what liquor it is, that you may not be mistaken; and lastly, wipe the mouth of the bottle with the palm of your hand, to shew your cleanliness.
JONATHAN SWIFT, *Directions to Servants.*

14
When you are in lodgings, and no shoe-boy to be got, clean your master's shoes with the bottom of the curtains, a clean napkin, or your landlady's apron.
JONATHAN SWIFT, *Directions to Servants.*

15
Soap and education are not as sudden as a massacre, but they are more deadly in the long run.
MARK TWAIN, *The Facts Concerning the Recent Resignation. Sketches New & Old* (1900), p. 350.

CLERGY

16
Clergyman: a man who undertakes the management of our spiritual affairs as a method of bettering his temporal ones.
AMBROSE BIERCE, *The Devil's Dictionary.*

17
Most parsons like to be persecuted; it gives 'em a better chance in the next world, something to howl about in this.
G. B. BURGIN, *Fanuela.*

18
One great reason why clergymen's households are generally unhappy is because the clergyman is so much at home and close about the house.
SAMUEL BUTLER, *The Way of All Flesh,* ch. 24.

1

Sally Salter, she was a young teacher who taught,
And her friend, Charley Church, was a preacher who praught,
Though his enemies called him a screecher who scraught.

PHOEBE CARY, *The Lovers.*

2

A clergyman goes a-fishing and comes home well browned and ten pounds fatter. So he sits down and writes a book full of trite compliments to nature interspersed with a good deal of self-congratulation.

FRANK MOORE COLBY, *The Colby Essays.*

3

A country preacher was once asked to explain his success in preaching. "First," he said, "I tell them what I'm going to tell them. Then I tell it to them. Then I tell them what I've just told them."

IRWIN EDMAN, *Philosopher's Quest.* See also HILAIRE BELLOC in section headed "Writing."

4

Among provocatives, the next best thing to good preaching is bad preaching. I have even more thoughts during or enduring it than at other times.

RALPH WALDO EMERSON, *Journal,* May 22, 1837.

5

Oh, Lord! thou art the clay and we are the Potters.

WILLIAM M. EVARTS, *Speech,* referring to the celebrated Potter family of which Bishop Potter was a member.

6

None preaches better than the ant, and she says nothing.

BENJAMIN FRANKLIN, *Poor Richard,* 1736.

7

To the philosophic eye the vices of the clergy are far less dangerous than their virtues.

EDWARD GIBBON, *Decline and Fall of the Roman Empire,* ch. 49.

8

I would not do for a Methodist preacher, for I am a poor horseman. I would not suit the Baptists, for I dislike water. I would fail as an Episcopalian, for I am no ladies' man.

JOHN HAY, *Letter.* (THAYER, *Life and Letters of John Hay.*)

9

A country clergyman with a one story intellect and a one-horse vocabulary.

OLIVER WENDELL HOLMES, *The Autocrat of the Breakfast Table,* ch. 2.

10

If you become a nun, dear,

A friar I will be;
In any cell you run, dear,
Pray look behind for me.

LEIGH HUNT, *The Nun.*

11

There would never have been an infidel, if there had never been a priest.

THOMAS JEFFERSON, *Letter to Mrs. Harrison Smith.*

12

Anybody can be pope; the proof of this is that I have become one.

POPE JOHN XXIII, *Letter* to a boy who wanted to know if he should be a pope or a policeman. (*Wit and Wisdom of Good Pope John.*)

13

A man who is good enough to go to heaven is good enough to be a clergyman.

SAMUEL JOHNSON, Boswell's *Life of Johnson,* Apr. 5, 1777.

14

When the clergyman's daughter drinks nothing but water, she's certain to finish on gin.

RUDYARD KIPLING.

15

We have to treat him as they are sometimes obliged to treat a Methodist minister I know of out West. He gets wrought up to so high a pitch of excitement in his prayers and exhortations, that they are obliged to put bricks in his pockets to keep him down. We may be obliged to serve Stanton in the same way, but I guess we'll let him jump awhile first.

ABRAHAM LINCOLN, quoted by CARL SANDBURG in *Abraham Lincoln: The Prairie Years and the War Years,* ch. 23.

16

There was no one there but the priest and the parson but I lost my purse.

SEUMAS MACMANUS, *Heavy Hangs the Golden Grain.*

17

We dislike the man who tries
To give us title clear
To any mansion in the skies
An' grab our title here.

DOUGLAS MALLOCH, *Behind a Spire.*

18

Talks much, and says just nothing for an hour.
Truth and the text he labors to display,
Till both are quite interpreted away.

CHRISTOPHER PITT, *On the Art of Preaching.*

19

Take heed of an ox before, an ass behind, and a monk on all sides.

JOHN RAY, *English Proverbs.* Cited as from the Spanish.

1
As a preacher he [Henry Ward Beecher] is a landscape painter of Christianity.
SENATOR OLIVER H. SMITH of Indiana. Quoted in *Henry Ward Beecher: An American Portrait* by PAXTON HIBBEN.

2
When I am in the pulpit, I have the pleasure of seeing my audience nod approbation while they sleep.
SYDNEY SMITH.

3
I must believe in the Apostolic Succession, there being no other way of accounting for the descent of the Bishop of Exeter from Judas Iscariot.
SYDNEY SMITH.

4
There is not the least use in preaching to anyone, unless you chance to catch them ill.
SYDNEY SMITH, from *Bon-Mots of Sydney Smith*, ed. by JERROLD.

5
Let the Dean and Canons lay their heads together and the thing will be done.
SYDNEY SMITH, when it was proposed that St. Paul's Cathedral be surrounded by a wooden pavement.

6
As the French say, there are three sexes, —men, women, and clergymen.
SYDNEY SMITH, in LADY HOLLAND, *Memoir*, vol. 1.

7
Some ministers would make good martyrs: they are so dry they would burn well.
CHARLES HADDON SPURGEON.

8
There is a certain class of clergyman whose mendicity is only equalled by their mendacity.
ARCHBISHOP FREDERICK TEMPLE, *Remark* at a meeting of the Ecclesiastical Commissioners, quoted by SIR GEORGE LEVESON GOWER, *Years of Endeavour*.

9
A little, round, fat oily man of God.
JAMES THOMSON, *The Castle of Indolence*.

10
. . . it is not a new thing for a thoroughly good and well-meaning preacher's soft heart to run away with his soft head.
MARK TWAIN, *Essays: The Temperance Crusade and Woman's Rights*.

11
He charged nothing for his preaching, and it was worth it too.
MARK TWAIN.

12
It takes a long tall brown-skin gal to make a preacher lay his Bible down.
MARSHALL WALKER, *Title and refrain of Song* (1917).

13
Preach not because you have to say something, but because you have something to say.
ARCHBISHOP RICHARD WHATELY, *Apothegms*.

14
. . . a middlin' doctor is a pore thing, and a middlin' lawyer is a pore thing; but keep me from a middlin' man of God.
OWEN WISTER, *The Virginian*.

CLEVERNESS

15
I always did think that cleverness was the art of hiding ignorance.
SHELLAND BRADLEY, *An American Girl in India*.

16
It is very clever to know how to hide one's cleverness.
FRANÇOIS, DUC DE LA ROCHEFOUCAULD.

17
He's as clever as a bagful of monkeys.
W. SOMERSET MAUGHAM, *The Circle*.

18
Too clever is dumb.
OGDEN NASH, *When the Mood Shines*.

19
One begins to distrust very clever persons when they become embarrassed.
FRIEDRICH WILHELM NIETZSCHE, *Beyond Good and Evil*, tr. by HELEN ZIMMERN.

20
The Athenians do not mind a man being clever, so long as he does not impart his cleverness to others.
PLATO, *Euthyphro*, sc. 3.

21
Mr. Hannaford's utterances have no meaning; he's satisfied if they sound clever.
ALFRED SUTRO, *The Walls of Jericho*, Act 1.

COAL

22
Salt to Dysart, or coals to Newcastle.
SIR JAMES MELVILLE, *Autobiography* (1583).

23
It is easy to find fault, if one has that disposition. There was once a man who, not being able to find any other fault with his coal, complained that there were too many prehistoric toads in it.
MARK TWAIN, *Pudd'nhead Wilson's Calendar*.

COFFEE

24
After insisting on coffee, I realized why the

English are big tea drinkers. Just taste their coffee and you'll see the reason.
> JOEY ADAMS, *Cindy and I*, ch. 9.

1
Even the Turkish coffee turned out to be deadly. If you don't believe me, make it at home some time. Dig up some dirt from your backyard, add a teaspoon of mud, a drop of fertilizer, add hot water, presto!—instant Turkish coffee.
> JOEY ADAMS, *Cindy and I*, ch. 31.

2
English coffee tastes like water that has been squeezed out of a wet sleeve.
> FRED ALLEN, *Treadmill to Oblivion*.

3
We prefer our coffee as strong as love, as black as sin, and as hot as hades.
> REPRESENTATIVE HALE BOGGS of Louisiana, during debate of the free tariff list of 1960.

4
Coffee in England is just toasted milk.
> CHRISTOPHER FRY, quoted in *New York Post*, Nov. 29, 1962.

5
Actually this seems to be the basic need of the human heart in nearly every great crisis —a good hot cup of coffee.
> ALEXANDER KING, *I Should Have Kissed Her More*.

6
Look here, Steward, if this is coffee, I want tea; but if this is tea, then I wish for coffee.
> *Punch*, Vol. cxxiii, p. 44 (1902).

COMFORT

7
His first struggle with a sleeping car made him doubt the value—to him—of a Pullman civilization.
> HENRY ADAMS, *The Education of Henry Adams*.

8
Lodgings—free from bugs and fleas, if possible,
If you know any such.
> ARISTOPHANES, *The Frogs*.

9
Truly, one gets easier accustomed to a silken bed, than to a sack of leaves.
> BERTHOLD AUERBACH, *On the Heights*.

10
It is grand, and you canna expect to be baith grand and comfortable.
> JAMES M. BARRIE, *The Little Minister*, ch. 10.

11
The neon glow of the age of comfort and violence.
> HENRY BRESTON, *Review* of *John Bur-*

roughs's America; The Freeman, Feb. 11, 1952.

12
You will recall what Senator Dirksen said about the rocking chair—it gives you a sense of motion without any sense of danger.
> JOHN F. KENNEDY, *Note* to Arthur Hays Sulzberger, May 1, 1961.

13
It is better to dwell in a corner of the housetop than with a brawling woman in a wide house.
> OLD TESTAMENT, *Proverbs: XXI*, 9.

14
In this country [England] everything has to be done with the maximum of discomfort.
> BERNARD SHAW, quoted in *Days with Bernard Shaw* by STEPHEN WINSTEN.

COMMUNISM

15
What is a communist? One who has yearnings for equal division of unequal earnings.
> EBENEZER ELLIOT, *Epigram*.

16
They were black sheep in a good herd—we took the black sheep by the tail and threw them out.
> NIKITA KHRUSHCHEV, *Comment* on Russian leaders ousted from Soviet Presidium, July 10, 1957.

17
After the liquidation of classes we have a monolithic society. Therefore, why found another party? That would be like voluntarily letting someone put a flea in your shirt.
> NIKITA KHRUSHCHEV, quoted in *Der Monat*, June, 1957.

18
If we could have the revolution over again, we would carry it out more sensibly and with smaller losses. But history does not repeat itself. The situation is favorable for us. If God existed, we would thank Him for it.
> NIKITA KHRUSHCHEV, to Western Ambassadors, Moscow, November 18, 1956.

19
Zsa Zsa . . . is the only lady who ever left the Iron Curtain wearing it.
> OSCAR LEVANT, *Memoirs of an Amnesiac*.

20
This guy Marx, why, he was one of these efficiency experts. He could explain to you how you could save a million dollars, yet he couldn't save enough himself to eat on.
> WILL ROGERS, *Autobiography*.

21
Communism to me is one-third practice and two-thirds explanation.
> WILL ROGERS, *Autobiography*.

1
If the Communists worked just as hard as they talked, they'd have the most prosperous style of government in the world.
WILL ROGERS, *Saturday Evening Post*, 1926.

2
It is hard to make Communists of Poles: they are too Catholic and they have a sense of humor.
ADLAI STEVENSON, *Friends and Enemies*.

3
Communist: one who has nothing, and is eager to share it with others.
UNKNOWN.

COMPANIONS

See also Friend, Friendship

4
A man is known by the company he keeps out of.
A. CRAIG, *Work of the Wits*.

5
Hail! Hail! the gang's all here,—
What the hell do we care,
What the hell do we care?
Hail! Hail! we're full of cheer,—
What the hell do we care, Bill!
D. A. ESTROM, *Hail! Hail! the Gang's All Here* (1897). Song first popular during the war with Spain.

6
Who friendship with a knave has made
Is judged a partner in the trade.
JOHN GAY, *Fables*. Pt. i, No. 24.

7
Ez soshubble ez a baskit er kittens.
JOEL CHANDLER HARRIS, *Legends of the Old Plantation*, ch. 3.

8
The most delightful of companions is he who combines the mind of a gentleman with the emotions of a bum. . . . Toward men, ever an aristocrat; toward women, ever a commoner—that way lies success.
GEORGE JEAN NATHAN, *The Autobiography of an Attitude*.

9
Three is company—two is merely compromising.
FRANK RICHARDSON, *2835 Mayfair*.

10
Man is the only animal that esteems itself rich in proportion to the number and voracity of its parasites.
BERNARD SHAW, *Maxims for Revolutionists*.

11
Hearts that are delicate and kind and tongues that are neither—these make the finest company in the world.
LOGAN PEARSALL SMITH, *All Trivia*.

12
What men call social virtue, good fellowship, is commonly but the virtue of pigs in a litter, which lie close together to keep each other warm.
HENRY D. THOREAU, *Journal*, Oct. 23, 1852.

13
Associate with well-mannered persons, and your own manners will improve. Run with decent folk and your own decent instincts will be strengthened. Keep the company of bums and you will become a bum. *But* hang around with rich people and you will end by picking up the tab and dying broke.
STANLEY WALKER, quoted by GENE FOWLER in *Skyline*.

COMPARISONS

14
Comparisons are odious.
JOHN FORTESCUE, *De Laudibus Legum Angliae*, ch. 19.

15
Joan is as good as my lady in the dark.
DUCHESS OF NEWCASTLE, *Sociable Companions*. II.

16
Compare her face with some that I shall show,
And I will make thee think thy swan a crow.
WILLIAM SHAKESPEARE, *Romeo and Juliet*. Act i, sc. 2.

17
No caparisons, miss, if you please. Caparisons don't become a young woman.
RICHARD BRINSLEY SHERIDAN, *The Rivals*. Act iv, sc. 2. Mrs. Malaprop speaking.

CONCEIT

See also Egotism, Vanity

18
Conceit is God's gift to little men.
BRUCE BARTON, *Conceit*.

19
The world tolerates conceit from those who are successful, but not from anybody else.
JOHN BLAKE, *Uncommon Sense*.

20
Every man has a right to be conceited until he is successful.
BENJAMIN DISRAELI, *The Young Duke*.

21
The fellow who gets too big for his shoes is apt to finish up barefooted.
B. C. FORBES, *Epigrams*.

1
What a dust have I rais'd! quoth the fly upon the coach.
THOMAS FULLER, *Gnomologia*, No. 5476.

2
We can bear to be deprived of everything but our self-conceit.
WILLIAM HAZLITT, *Characteristics*, No. 421.

3
Many a zero thinks it is the ellipse on which the earth travels.
STANISLAW J. LEC. (*The Mathematical Magpie*, ed. by CLIFTON FADIMAN.)

4
A swelling head always contains a shrinking brain.
Reflections of a Bachelor.

5
Conceit may puff a man up, but never prop him up.
JOHN RUSKIN, *True and Beautiful: Morals and Religion.*

6
Woman's dearest delight is to wound Man's self-conceit, though Man's dearest delight is to gratify hers.
BERNARD SHAW, *An Unsocial Socialist*, ch. 5.

7
Remark of Dr. Baldwin's, concerning upstarts: We don't care to eat toadstools that think they are truffles.
MARK TWAIN, *Pudd'nhead Wilson's Calendar.*

CONFIDENCE

8
With all the confidence of a man dialing his own telephone number.
JOHN BELL, of Associated Press. Description of Robert A. Taft's manner in handling political crises, in *The Splendid Misery* (1960).

9
The men who really believe in themselves are all in lunatic asylums.
GILBERT KEITH CHESTERTON.

10
He rarely Hits the Mark or Wins the Game, Who says, "I Know I'll Miss!" while taking Aim.
ARTHUR GUITERMAN, *A Poet's Proverbs.*

11
All you need is to tell a man that he is no good ten times a day, and very soon he begins to believe it himself.
LIN YUTANG, *With Love and Irony.*

12
You cannot learn to skate without being ridiculous. . . . The ice of life is slippery.
BERNARD SHAW, *Fanny's First Play*: induction.

CONSCIENCE

13
Lost in the spiral of his conscience, he Detachedly takes rest.
LAURA BENÉT, *The Snail.*

14
Much industry and little conscience make a man rich.
W. G. BENHAM, *Proverbs.*

15
The world has achieved brilliance without conscience. Ours is a world of nuclear giants and ethical infants.
GENERAL OMAR BRADLEY, *Address*, Armistice Day, 1948.

16
There is another man within me that's angry with me.
SIR THOMAS BROWNE, *Religio Medici*, pt. 2.

17
Conscience was born when man had shed his fur, his tail, his pointed ears.
SIR RICHARD BURTON, *The Kasîdah*. Pt. v, st. 19.

18
They have cheveril consciences that will stretch.
ROBERT BURTON, *The Anatomy of Melancholy.*

19
Conscience is thoroughly well-bred and soon leaves off talking to those who do not wish to hear it.
SAMUEL BUTLER, *Notebooks.*

20
The trouble is, his chest is a cage in which two squirrels are at war, his conscience and his career.
WINSTON CHURCHILL, quoted by LORD MORAN, *Diaries*. The reference to Sir Stafford Cripps was made by Churchill in a talk with Joseph Stalin.

21
The unknown is an ocean. What is conscience? The compass of the unknown.
JOSEPH COOK, *Boston Monday Lectures.*

22
Conscience is the inner voice that warns us that someone may be looking.
H. L. MENCKEN, *A Mencken Chrestomathy.*

23
Conscience has no more to do with gallantry than it has with politics.
RICHARD BRINSLEY SHERIDAN, *The Duenna*. Act ii, sc. 4.

1
We grow with years more fragile in body, but morally stouter, and we can throw off the chill of a bad conscience almost at once.
LOGAN PEARSALL SMITH, *Afterthoughts.*

2
I have noticed my conscience for many years, and I know it is more trouble and bother to me than anything else I started with.
MARK TWAIN.

3
Conscience makes egotists of us all.
OSCAR WILDE, *The Picture of Dorian Gray,* ch. 8.

CONSERVATISM

4
It seems to me a barren thing, this Conservatism—an unhappy cross-breed, the mule of politics that engenders nothing.
BENJAMIN DISRAELI, *Coningsby,* ch. 5.

5
Men are conservative when they are least vigorous, or when they are most luxurious. They are conservatives after dinner.
RALPH WALDO EMERSON, *Essays, Second Series: New England Reformers.*

6
I never dared be radical when young
For fear it would make me conservative when old.
ROBERT FROST, *Precaution.*

7
A conservative is a man who is too cowardly to fight and too fat to run.
ELBERT HUBBARD, *One Thousand and One Epigrams.*

8
A reactionary is a somnambulist walking backward.
FRANKLIN DELANO ROOSEVELT.

9
A conservative is a man who does not think that anything should be done for the first time.
FRANK VANDERLIP.

10
    That staid, conservative,
Came-over-with-the-Conqueror type of mind.
WILLIAM WATSON, *A Study in Contrasts,* pt. 1.

CONSISTENCY

11
Life is not a static thing. The only people who do not change their minds are incompetents in asylums, who can't, and those in cemeteries.
EVERETT M. DIRKSEN, *News Conference,* Washington, D.C., Jan. 1, 1965.

12
A foolish consistency is the hobgoblin of little minds.
RALPH WALDO EMERSON, *Essays, First Series: Self-Reliance.*

13
A woman's mind is cleaner than a man's— she changes it oftener.
OLIVER HERFORD, *Epigram.*

14
The foolish and the dead alone never change their opinion.
JAMES RUSSELL LOWELL, *My Study Windows: Abraham Lincoln.*

15
I always reserve to myself the privilege of changing my mind. It's the only one elderly gentlemen share with pretty women.
W. SOMERSET MAUGHAM, *The Circle.*

16
There is nothing I so hardly believe to be in man as consistancie, and nothing so easie to be found in him, as inconstancy.
MICHEL DE MONTAIGNE, *Essays,* tr. by JOHN FLORIO.

CONVERSATION

See also Speech

17
Debate is angular, conversation circular and radiant of the underlying unity.
A. BRONSON ALCOTT, *Concord Days.*

18
Debate is masculine; conversation is feminine.
A. BRONSON ALCOTT, *Concord Days.*

19
Many can argue; not many converse.
A. BRONSON ALCOTT, *Tablets.*

20
In dinner talk it is perhaps allowable to fling any faggot rather than let the fire go out.
JAMES M. BARRIE, *Tommy and Grizel.*

21
He never spares himself in conversation. He gives himself so generously that hardly anybody else is permitted to give anything in his presence.
ANEURIN BEVAN, *News summaries,* Apr. 26, 1954. Referring to SIR WINSTON CHURCHILL.

22
A good conversationalist is not one who remembers what was said, but says what someone wants to remember.
JOHN MASON BROWN, *Esquire,* Apr., 1960.

23
Conversation is a game of circles.
RALPH WALDO EMERSON, *Essays: Circles.*

1
One of the marks of mediocrity of understanding, is to be always telling stories. (L'une des marques de la mediocrite de l'esprit de toujours conter.)
Old French Proverb.

2
Though I'm anything but clever,
I could talk like that forever.
    W. S. GILBERT, *H.M.S. Pinafore*, Act 2.

3
These people [the English] do not talk, as so many Americans do, to make a good impression on themselves by making a good impression on somebody else. They have already made a good impression on themselves and talk simply because they think sound is more manageable than silence.
    MARGARET HALSEY, *With Malice Toward Some*.

4
The boneless quality of English conversation, which, so far as I have heard it, is all form and no content. Listening to Britons dining out is like watching people play first-class tennis with imaginary balls.
    MARGARET HALSEY, *With Malice Toward Some*.

5
He [Coleridge] talked on for ever; and you wished him to talk on for ever.
    WILLIAM HAZLITT, *Lectures on the English Poets:* lecture 8, *On the Living Poets.*

6
Silence: A conversation with an Englishman.
    HEINRICH HEINE, *Works.*

7
It takes a great man to make a good listener.
    SIR ARTHUR HELPS, *Brevia.*

8
Inject a few raisins of conversation into the tasteless dough of existence.
    O. HENRY, *Complete Life of John Hopkins.*

9
Look out fer th' feller who lets you do all th' talkin'.
    FRANK MCKINNEY (KIN) HUBBARD, *Abe Martin's Primer.*

10
Th' feller that tells a good story allus has t' listen t' a couple o' poor ones.
    FRANK MCKINNEY (KIN) HUBBARD, *Abe Martin's Primer.*

11
Sir, you have but two topics, yourself and me. I am sick of both.
    SAMUEL JOHNSON, BOSWELL'S *Life of Johnson.*

12
He speaketh not; and yet lies
A conversation in his eyes.
    HENRY WADSWORTH LONGFELLOW, *The Hanging of the Crane,* sec. 3.

13
How many men think of improving their talk as well as their golf handicap?
    F. L. LUCAS, *What Is Style?; Holiday,* Mar., 1960.

14
The art of conversation is not knowing what you ought to say, but what one ought not to say.
    Reflections of a Bachelor (1903).

15
The trouble with her is that she lacks the power of conversation but not the power of speech . . .
    BERNARD SHAW, quoted in *Days with Bernard Shaw* by STEPHEN WINSTEN.

16
Macaulay has occasional flashes of silence that make his conversation perfectly delightful.
    SYDNEY SMITH.

17
All natural talk is a festival of ostentation; and by the laws of the game each accepts and fans the vanity of the other.
    ROBERT LOUIS STEVENSON, *Memories and Portraits: Talk and Talkers.*

18
It is as foolish to say something brilliant with intention as it is to be silent by compulsion.
    J. M. STUART-YOUNG, *Passion's Peril.*

19
There are two faults in conversation, which appear very different, yet arise from the same root, and are equally blameable; I mean an impatience to interrupt others; and the uneasiness of being interrupted ourselves.
    JONATHAN SWIFT, *Hints Toward an Essay on Conversation.*

20
There are some people whose good manners will not suffer them to interrupt you, but, what is almost as bad, will discover an abundance of impatience, and lie upon the watch until you have done, because they have started something in their own thoughts, which they long to be delivered of.
    JONATHAN SWIFT, *Hints Toward an Essay on Conversation.*

21
Another general fault in conversation is that of those who affect to talk of themselves: some, without any ceremony, will run over the history of their lives; will relate the annals of their diseases, with the several

symptoms and circumstances of them; will enumerate the hardships and injustice they have suffered in court, in parliament, in love, or in law.

> JONATHAN SWIFT, *Hints Toward an Essay on Conversation.*

1
The time to stop talking is when the other person nods his head affirmatively but says nothing.

> UNKNOWN, *Meditations in Wall Street.*

2
Talking to her is about as hard as talking in church.

> PETER USTINOV, *Romanoff and Juliet,* Act 2.

3
Conversation should touch everything, but should concentrate itself on nothing.

> OSCAR WILDE, *The Critic as Artist.*

4
When people talk to us about others they are usually dull. When they talk to us about themselves they are nearly always interesting . . .

> OSCAR WILDE, *The Critic as Artist.*

5
Learned conversation is either the affectation of the ignorant or the profession of the mentally unemployed.

> OSCAR WILDE, *The Critic as Artist.*

COOKING

6
No mean woman can cook well. It calls for a generous spirit, a light hand and a large heart.

> A. M., *The Irish Digest.*

7
Cooking has become an art, a noble science; cooks are gentlemen.

> ROBERT BURTON, *The Anatomy of Melancholy.*

8
Bigamist—A man who marries a beautiful girl and a good cook.

> *Chicago Herald-American.*

9
There is one thing more exasperating than a wife who can cook and won't, and that's a wife who can't cook and will.

> ROBERT FROST.

10
The more cooks the worse broth.

> THOMAS FULLER, *Gnomologia,* No. 4657 (1732). See also GERBIER in this section.

11
Many excellent cooks are spoiled by going into the arts.

> PAUL GAUGUIN, quoted by COURNOS, *Modern Plutarch.*

12
Too many cooks spoil the broth.

> SIR BALTHAZAR GERBIER, *Discourse of Building* (1662).

13
We may live without poetry, music and art;
We may live without conscience, and live without heart;
We may live without friends; we may live without books;
But civilized man cannot live without cooks.

> OWEN MEREDITH (EDWARD ROBERT BULWER, Earl of Lytton), *Lucile.* Pt. i, canto 2, st. 19.

14
The cook was a good cook, as cooks go; and as cooks go she went.

> HECTOR HUGH MUNRO (SAKI), *Reginald: Reginald on Besetting Sins.*

15
If a lump of soot falls into the soup, and you cannot conveniently get it out, stir it well in, and it will give the soup a high *French* taste.

> JONATHAN SWIFT, *Advice to Servants.*

16
God sends meat, and the Devil sends cooks.

> JOHN TAYLOR, *Works,* vol. 2.

17
Cooking is like love. It should be entered into with abandon or not at all.

> HARRIET VAN HORNE, *Vogue,* Oct. 15, 1956.

18
When I first told my cooks we would make frozen foods, they protested—explaining that they were cooks, not mechanics.

> LOUIS VAUDABLE, quoted in *Life,* Jan. 7, 1966. Referring to Maxim's in Paris.

19
The wonderful world of home appliances now makes it possible to cook indoors with charcoal and outdoors with gas.

> BILL VAUGHAN, *Kansas City Star.*

20
There is no spectacle on earth more appealing than that of a beautiful woman in the act of cooking dinner for someone she loves.

> THOMAS WOLFE, *The Web and the Rock.*

COUNTRY, THE

See also Farming

21
You can take a boy out of the country but you can't take the country out of a boy.

> ARTHUR (BUGS) BAER.

22
There is nothing good to be had in the

country, or, if there be, they will not let you have it.

WILLIAM HAZLITT, *Lectures: Mr. Words-worth's "Excursion."*

1
A pretty country retreat is like a pretty wife —one is always throwing away money decorating it.

WASHINGTON IRVING, *Letter* to a friend, quoted by R. DEARDORFF in *North of Broadway; Redbook*, Oct., 1963.

2
He looks like some hayseed from Kansas.

JOSEPH P. KENNEDY, referring to his son JOHN F. KENNEDY. Quoted by VICTOR LASKY in *J.F.K.: The Man and the Myth.*

3
Like so many country people who lead a natural outdoor life, his features had hardly any definition. He gave me the impression of an underdone veal cutlet.

ALEXANDER KING, *Mine Enemy Grows Older.*

4
One boob may die, but deathless is
The royal race of hicks—
When Ahab went to Ascalon
They sold him gilded bricks.

DON MARQUIS, *Boob Ballad.*

5
Country life is very good; in fact, the best —for cattle.

SYDNEY SMITH, from *Bon-Mots of Sydney Smith*, ed. by JERROLD.

6
Anybody can be good in the country. There are no temptations there.

OSCAR WILDE, *The Picture of Dorian Gray*, ch. 19.

7
I see a little time in the country makes a man turn wild and unsociable, and only fit to converse with his horses, dogs, and his herds.

WILLIAM WYCHERLEY, *The Country Wife*, Act 3.

COURAGE, see Bravery

COW
8
Condensed milk is wonderful. I don't see how they can get a cow to sit down on those little cans.

FRED ALLEN, *Much Ado About Me.*

9
I never saw a purple cow,
I never hope to see one;
But I can tell you anyhow,
I'd rather see than be one.

GELETT BURGESS, *The Purple Cow; The Lark*, San Francisco, May, 1895.

10
Ah, yes! I wrote the PURPLE COW—
I'm sorry, now, I wrote it!
But I can tell you anyhow
I'll kill you if you quote it!

GELETT BURGESS.

11
The piper he piped on the hill-top high
(*Butter and eggs and a pound of cheese*)
Till the cow said, "I die," and the goose said, "Why?"
And the dog said nothing, but searched for fleas.

CHARLES STUART CALVERLEY, *Ballad of the Period.*

12
My cow milks me.

RALPH WALDO EMERSON, *Journals*, vol. 5.

13
And when the jug is empty quite,
I shall not mew in vain,
The friendly cow, all red and white,
Will fill her up again.

OLIVER HERFORD, *The Milk Jug.*

14
Any of us would kill a cow rather than not have beef.

SAMUEL JOHNSON, BOSWELL'S *Life of Johnson.*

15
Cows do not "give" milk. If you are wily and strong and ruthless, you can have it for the taking.

J. P. MCEVOY, *Charlie Would Have Loved This.*

16
God's jolly cafeteria
With four legs and a tail.

E. M. ROOT, *The Cow.*

COWARDICE

See also Fear
17
If Almighty God gives a man a cowardly pair of legs how can he help their running away with him?

ABRAHAM LINCOLN, *Explanation* of why he could not approve the death sentence of a soldier charged with cowardice on the battlefield. In *The Humorous Mr. Lincoln* by KEITH W. JENNISON.

18
I would rather be a philosopher and a coward than a hero and a fool.

AMBROSE PRATT, *The Leather Mask.*

19
We have heard of men celebrating their

country's battles who in war were celebrated for keeping out of them.
> GEORGE D. PRENTICE.

1
McKinley has a chocolate éclair backbone.
> THEODORE ROOSEVELT, quoted in *Ballots & Bandwagons* by RALPH G. MARTIN.

2
It is not seemly for any man who has weapons in his hands to resort to the help of his unarmed feet. (Nec quemquam decere, qui manus armaverit, ab inermis pedibus auxilium petere.)
> SULLA. (SALLUST, *Jugurtha*, ch. 107.)

3
There are several good protections against temptation: but the surest is cowardice.
> MARK TWAIN.

4
I have seen their backs before.
> WELLINGTON, when French marshals turned their backs on him at a reception.

CRIME

5
Lizzie Borden took an axe
And gave her mother forty whacks;
When she saw what she had done,
She gave her father forty-one.
> ANONYMOUS, *Lizzie Borden*. Lizzie Borden was accused of murdering her father and stepmother in Fall River, Mass., on Aug. 4, 1892.

6
There's no evidence of guilt,
    Lizzie Borden,
That should make your spirit wilt,
    Lizzie Borden;
Many do not think that you,
Chopped your father's head in two,
It's so hard a thing to do,
    Lizzie Borden.
> A. L. BIXBY, *To Lizzie*.

7
Prisons are built with stones of law, brothels with bricks of religion.
> WILLIAM BLAKE, *Proverbs of Hell*.

8
If his home is happy—if a kid is cared *about*, not merely cared for—he can cope. When I see the "Ten Most Wanted" lists—the Wanted posters—I always have this thought. If we'd made them feel wanted earlier, they wouldn't be wanted now.
> EDDIE CANTOR, *The Way I See It*.

9
My rackets are run on strictly American lines and they're going to stay that way.
> AL CAPONE, gangster. *Interview*, quoted by CLAUD COCKBURN, *In Time of Trouble*.

10
A racket's a line you adopt to make money you don't deserve.
> JOHN COATES, *Time for Tea*.

11
No matter how you seem to fatten on a crime, that can never be good for the bee which is bad for the hive.
> RALPH WALDO EMERSON, *Lectures and Biographical Studies: The Sovereignty of Ethics*.

12
The long and distressing controversy over capital punishment is very unfair to anyone meditating murder.
> GEOFFREY FISHER. (*Sunday Times*, London, Feb. 24, 1957.)

13
It's not the people in prison who worry me. It's the people who aren't.
> CARL OF ARRAN (ARTHUR GORE), London columnist. (*The New York Times*, Jan. 7, 1962.)

14
The eagerness of a knave maketh him often as catchable as ignorance maketh a fool.
> LORD HALIFAX, *Works*, p. 232.

15
If their "offence be rank", should mine be *rancour?*
> THOMAS HOOD, *Ode to Rae Wilson*.

16
They cut his throat from ear to ear,
    His brains they battered in;
His name was Mr. William Weare,
    He dwelt in Lyon's Inn.
> THEODORE HOOK, *William Weare*. On the authority of John Lockhart. The lines, which refer to the murder of William Weare by John Thurtell in 1823, have also been ascribed to LORD WILLIAM LENNOX.

17
The reason the way of the transgressor is hard is because it's so crowded.
> FRANK McKINNEY (KIN) HUBBARD.

18
Juvenile delinquents do not have an assured future. They may become decent people.
> STANISLAW J. LEC, *Unkempt Thoughts*, tr. from the Polish by JACEK GALASKA.

19
Murder, like talent, seems to run in families.
> GEORGE HENRY LEWES, *Philosophy of Common Life*, ch. 12.

20
Typewriter Heiress XXX's out Husband.
> *Los Angeles Times. Headline*, quoted in *Reader's Digest*, Feb., 1967.

21
Juvenile delinquency starts in the high chair

and ends in the death chair.
> JAMES D. C. MURRAY, lawyer. (*New York World-Telegram and Sun,* Sept. 8, 1956.)

1
A switch in time saves crime.
> ROY B. NEWELL. (*Speaker's Sourcebook,* ed. by ELEANOR DOAN.)

2
One murder makes a villain, millions a hero.
> BISHOP BEILBY PORTEUS, *Death.*

3
The first prison I ever saw had inscribed on it "Cease to do evil: learn to do well"; but the inscription was on the outside, the prisoners could not read it.
> BERNARD SHAW, *Imprisonment.*

4
When we want to read of the deeds done for love, whither do we turn? To the murder column; and there we are rarely disappointed.
> BERNARD SHAW, *Three Plays for Puritans:* preface.

5
When a man wants to murder a tiger he calls it sport: when the tiger wants to murder him he calls it ferocity. The distinction between Crime and Justice is no greater.
> BERNARD SHAW, *Maxims for Revolutionists.*

6
His crimes are the only great thing about him, and these are contrasted by the littleness of his motives.
> RICHARD BRINSLEY SHERIDAN, *Speech,* at the trial of Warren Hastings, June, 1788. The reference is to Hastings.

7
People who deserve it always believe in capital punishment.
> LINCOLN STEFFENS, *Autobiography.*

8
Jesse James had a wife,
She's a mourner all her life;
  His children they were brave;
Oh, the dirty little coward
That shot Mr. Howard,
  Has laid poor Jesse in his grave.
> UNKNOWN, *Jesse James.* The song commemorates the murder of Jesse James by Bob Ford in St. Joseph, Mo., Apr. 3, 1882. James had been living under the name of Thomas Howard.

9
Two brothers in our town did dwell:
Hiram sought Heaven, but Isaac Sawtell.
> UNKNOWN, *The Sawtell Murder.* A New Hampshire crime of the 1890s, in which Isaac Sawtell murdered his brother, Hiram.

10
It is well for our vanity that we slay the criminal, for if we suffered him to live he might show us what we had gained by his crime.
> OSCAR WILDE, *The Critic as Artist.*

11
The criminal classes are so close to us that even the policeman can see them. They are so far away from us that only the poet can understand them.
> OSCAR WILDE, *Saturday Review,* Nov. 17, 1894.

CRITICISM

I: General

12
Ridicule is the deadliest of weapons against a lofty cause.
> SAMUEL HOPKINS ADAMS, *Tenderloin.*

13
Sir Henry Wotton used to say that critics are like the brushers of noblemen's clothes.
> FRANCIS BACON, *Apothegms,* No. 64.

14
When God protested, they rocked the boat,
  And dumped him into the sea,
"For you have no critical facultee,"
Said Mencken and Nathan to God.
> BERTON BRALEY, quoted in *O Rare Don Marquis* by EDWARD ANTHONY.

15
A man must serve his time to every trade
Save censure—critics are all ready made.
> LORD BYRON, *English Bards and Scotch Reviewers.*

16
If enough people told enough people to put their heads under trucks, I'm sure they would do so. I wonder why no one has thought of doing that.
> NOEL COWARD, on lukewarm reception given by critics to his *Look after Lulu.* (*New York Journal-American,* Apr. 29, 1959.)

17
This shows how much easier it is to be critical than to be correct.
> BENJAMIN DISRAELI, *Speech,* House of Commons, Jan. 15, 1860.

18
Those who do not read criticism will rarely merit to be criticized.
> ISAAC D'ISRAELI, *Literary Character of Men of Genius.*

19
I could travel from Boston to Chicago by the light of my own effigies.
> STEPHEN A. DOUGLAS, in 1854, after passage of the Kansas-Nebraska bill, which he supported. (RHODES, *History of the United States.*)

1

The British critics—be it to their glory,
When they abuse us, do it *con amore.*
A. J. H. DUGANNE, *Parnassus in Pillory.*

2

Criticizing, like charity, should begin at home.
B. C. FORBES, *Epigrams.*

3

The first man who objected to the general nakedness, and advised his fellows to put on clothes, was the first critic.
E. L. GODKIN, *Problems of Modern Democracy.*

4

If I've said anything to upset you, maybe it's what I'm here for. Lenny Bruce shakes up the puritans, Mort Sahl the Conservatives, and me—almost everybody!
DICK GREGORY, *From the Back of the Bus.*

5

The Stones that Critics hurl with Harsh Intent
A Man may use to build his Monument.
ARTHUR GUITERMAN, *A Poet's Proverbs.*

6

He edited a magazine called "The Smart Set", which is like calling Cape Kennedy "Lovers' Lane."
BEN HECHT, *Letters from Bohemia.* Reference to H. L. MENCKEN.

7

The absence of humility in critics is something wonderful.
SIR ARTHUR HELPS, *Friends in Council,* bk. 2.

8

To escape criticism—do nothing, say nothing, be nothing.
ELBERT HUBBARD.

9

The false elephant's hide that he always wore was quickly stripped away and his own tender skin was revealed.
DALE KRAMER, *Ross and the New Yorker.* Comment on Harold Ross, the editor.

10

Criticism of our contemporaries is not criticism; it is conversation.
FRANÇOIS LEMAÎTRE.

11

I have never found in a long career of politics that criticism is ever inhibited by ignorance.
HAROLD MACMILLAN. (*Wall Street Journal,* Aug. 13, 1963.)

12

If the critics were always right we should be in deep trouble.
ROBERT MORLEY.

13

Any jackass can kick down a barn, but it takes a good carpenter to build one.
Attributed to SAM RAYBURN, and quoted by Lyndon B. Johnson in 1952, in response to Texas' swing to Dwight D. Eisenhower in the presidential election of that year. (HENRY A. ZEIGER, *Lyndon B. Johnson: Man and President,* p. 47.)

14

One mustn't criticize other people on grounds where he can't stand perpendicular himself.
MARK TWAIN, *A Connecticut Yankee in King Arthur's Court.*

15

It is the will of God that we must have critics, and missionaries, and congressmen, and humorists, and we must bear the burden.
MARK TWAIN, *Autobiography.*

16

When I did well, I heard it never;
When I did ill, I heard it ever.
UNKNOWN.

17

Things have come to a helluva pass
When a man can't cudgel his own jackass.
HENRY WATTERSON, *Retort,* when accused of unduly criticizing the governor of Kentucky.

II: Criticism, the Arts

18

The Jukes family of journalism.
MAXWELL ANDERSON, on drama critics. (*The Passionate Playgoer,* ed. by GEORGE OPPENHEIMER, p. 602.)

19

Critics sipping cups of tea
Praise, between their crumpets,
Drunken poets—men who cried
Ha, ha among the strumpets:
It's sad kind words are seldom said
Until a rake is safely dead.
ANTHONY BRODE, *Obituary.*

20

To many people dramatic criticism must seem like an attempt to tattoo soap bubbles.
JOHN MASON BROWN, *Broadway in Review.*

21

You know who the critics are? The men who have failed in literature and art.
BENJAMIN DISRAELI, *Lothair.*

22

They who write ill, and they who ne'er durst write,
Turn critics out of mere revenge and spite.
JOHN DRYDEN, *Conquest of Granada:* prologue.

1
A reviewer is not a whole man. He is that partial man, an expert. All experts are monsters.
> CLIFTON FADIMAN, *The Selected Writings of Clifton Fadiman* (1955).

2
Literary criticism is an art, like the writing of tragedies or the making of love, and, similarly, does not pay.
> CLIFTON FADIMAN, *The Selected Writings of Clifton Fadiman: The Book-Reviewing Business* (1955).

3
What a blessed thing it is that nature, when she invented, manufactured and patented her authors, contrived to make critics out of the chips that were left.
> OLIVER WENDELL HOLMES, *The Professor at the Breakfast Table*, ch. 1.

4
Critics are sentinels in the grand army of letters, stationed at the corners of newspapers and reviews, to challenge every new author.
> HENRY WADSWORTH LONGFELLOW, *Kavanagh*, ch. 13.

5
Nature fits all her children with something to do,
He who would write and can't write, can surely review.
> JAMES RUSSELL LOWELL, *A Fable for Critics*.

6
The dramatic critic who is without prejudice is on the plane with the general who does not believe in taking human life.
> GEORGE JEAN NATHAN, *Comedians All*.

7
There are two kinds of dramatic critics: destructive and constructive. I am a destructive. There are two kinds of guns: Krupp and pop.
> GEORGE JEAN NATHAN, *The World in Falseface*.

8
Impersonal criticism is like an impersonal fist fight or an impersonal marriage, and as successful.
> GEORGE JEAN NATHAN, in *The World of George Jean Nathan*, ed. by CHARLES ANGOFF.

9
Tonstant Weader fwowed up.
> DOROTHY PARKER, in her "Constant Reader" column in *The New Yorker*, after reading one of the "Pooh" stories by A. A. MILNE. (*Newsweek*, June 19, 1967, p. 43.)

10
I never read a book before reviewing it; it prejudices me so.
> HESKETH PEARSON, *The Smith of Smith*, ch. 3.

11
A critic is a legless man who teaches running.
> CHANNING POLLOCK, *The Green Book*.

12
Can't a critic give his opinion of an omelette without being asked to lay an egg?
> CLAYTON RAWSON, *No Coffin for the Corpse*.

13
A drama critic is a man who leaves no turn unstoned.
> BERNARD SHAW, quoted in *The New York Times*, Nov. 5, 1950.

14
As a bankrupt thief turns thief-taker, so an unsuccessful author turns critic.
> PERCY BYSSHE SHELLEY, *Adonais*: preface.

15
I have just read your lousy review buried in the back pages. You sound like a frustrated old man who never made a success, an eight-ulcer man on a four-ulcer job, and all four ulcers working. I have never met you, but if I do you'll need a new nose and plenty of beefsteak and perhaps a supporter below. Westbrook Pegler, a guttersnipe, is a gentleman compared to you. You can take that as more of an insult than as a reflection on your ancestry.
> HARRY S TRUMAN, *Note* to Paul Hume, music critic of the *Washington Post*, Dec. 6, 1950, in reply to Hume's unfavorable review of Margaret Truman's concert in the capital on Dec. 5, 1950. This famous example of criticism of a critic was signed "HST," but the White House acknowledged its authorship. Hume had granted Miss Truman's attractiveness on stage, but added: "Yet Miss Truman cannot sing very well. She is flat a good deal of the time. . . . She communicates almost nothing of the music she presents. . . ." See also HUME in section headed "Music."

16
You should not say it is not good. You should say you do not like it; and then, you know, you're perfectly safe.
> JAMES MCNEILL WHISTLER, quoted by DON SEITZ, *Whistler Stories*.

17
The critic leaves at curtain fall
To find, in starting to review it,
He scarcely saw the play at all
For watching his reaction to it.
> E. B. WHITE, *Critic*.

1
The first duty of an art critic is to hold his tongue at all times and upon all occasions.
   OSCAR WILDE, *The English Renaissance of Art: Lecture,* New York, Jan. 9, 1882.

2
A certain columnist has been barred from all Shubert openings. Now he can wait three days and go to their closings.
   WALTER WINCHELL, writing of himself. Quoted in SAMUEL HOPKINS ADAMS, *A. Woollcott, His Life and World,* ch. 6.

3
Has anybody ever seen a drama critic in the daytime? Of course not. They come out after dark, up to no good.
   P. G. WODEHOUSE, quoted in the *New York Mirror,* May 27, 1955.

CULTURE

4
Great cultural changes begin in affectation and end in routine.
   JACQUES BARZUN, *The House of Intellect.*

5
Culture is the product of versatility and leisure, aided and abetted by some cash.
   Crossett (Ark.) *News-Observer.*

6
Culture is what your butcher would have if he were a surgeon.
   MARY PETTIBONE POOLE, *A Glass Eye at the Keyhole.*

7
"If Lyndon says we're going to have culture," a Texas friend said to us the other day, "then by God we're going to have culture."
   ROGER H. SMITH, *Publishers' Weekly,* Oct. 4, 1965. Referring to Lyndon B. Johnson.

8
An Aristotle was but the rubbish of an Adam, and Athens but the rudiments of Paradise.
   REV. ROBERT SOUTH, *Sermons,* vol. 1.

9
We have on radio every Sunday a stroke of culture, a symphony concert from New York or somewhere with a tooth-wash. That's the culture part, the tooth-wash.
   LINCOLN STEFFENS, *Autobiography.*

CURIOSITY

See also Question

10
Ask me no questions, and I'll tell you no fibs.
   OLIVER GOLDSMITH, *She Stoops to Conquer,* Act 3.

11
Talk to him of Jacob's ladder, and he would ask the number of the steps.
   DOUGLAS JERROLD, *A Matter-of-Fact Man.*

12
Talkativeness has another plague attached to it, even curiosity; for praters wish to hear much that they may have much to say.
   PLUTARCH, *Morals: Of Talkativeness.*

13
The things most people want to know are usually none of their business.
   BERNARD SHAW.

14
You know what a woman's curiosity is. Almost as great as a man's!
   OSCAR WILDE, *An Ideal Husband,* Act 1.

CYNICISM

15
The cynic is one who never sees a good quality in a man, and never fails to see a bad one. He is the human owl, vigilant in darkness, and blind to light, mousing for vermin, and never seeing noble game.
   HENRY WARD BEECHER, *Proverbs from Plymouth Pulpit.*

16
Cynic: a blackguard whose faulty vision sees things as they are, not as they ought to be.
   AMBROSE BIERCE.

17
Cynicism is an unpleasant way of saying the truth.
   LILLIAN HELLMAN, *The Little Foxes,* Act 1.

18
"I like him," I replied. "He restores my cynicism about the human race."
   CHARLES MERCER, *The Trespassers.*

19
What is a cynic? A man who knows the price of everything and the value of nothing.
   OSCAR WILDE, *Lady Windermere's Fan,* Act 1. See also WILDE in section headed "Price."

D

DANCE

1
Look at that gal
  Shake that thing.
We cannot all be
  Martin Luther King . . .
> JULIAN BOND, quoted by LANGSTON
> HUGHES in *The Book of Negro Humor*,
> 1966.

2
Many will not allow men and women to dance together, because it is a provocation to lust; they may as well forbid the drinking of wine, for that it makes some men drunk.
> ROBERT BURTON, *The Anatomy of Melancholy.*

3
They are waiting on the shingle—will you come and join the dance?
Will you, won't you, will you, won't you, will you join the dance?
Will you, won't you, will you, won't you, won't you join the dance?
> LEWIS CARROLL, *Alice in Wonderland: The Whiting and the Snail.*

4
Oh, how we danced on the night we were wed,
We danced and we danced 'cause the room had no bed.
> EDDIE DAVIS, of the famous night club
> Leon and Eddie's. The words are sung
> to the tune of *Anniversary Waltz.*
> Quoted by JOEY ADAMS in *Cindy and I*,
> ch. 4.

5
A good education is usually harmful to a dancer. A good calf is better than a good head.
> AGNES DE MILLE, *News summaries*, Feb.
> 1, 1954.

6
Dancing is such a despised and dishonored trade that if you tell a doctor or a lawyer you do choreography he'll look at you as if you were a hummingbird. Dancers don't get invited to visit people. It is assumed a boy dancer will run off with the spoons and a girl with the head of the house.
> AGNES DE MILLE. (JANE HOWARD, *The
> Grande Dame of Dance; Life*, Nov. 15,
> 1963.)

7
And we love to dance—especially that new one called the Civil War Twist. The Northern part of you stands still while the Southern part tries to secede.
> DICK GREGORY, *From the Back of the Bus.*

8
The greater the fool the better the dancer.
> THEODORE EDWARD HOOK, *Epigram.* (BARHAM, *Life and Reminiscences.*)

9
Fred Astaire, when his miraculous feet are quiet, gives a curious impression of unemployment.
> HAROLD LOCKRIDGE, *Review* of *The Gay
> Divorce* in the New York *Sun.*

10
o i should worry and fret
death and i will coquette
there's a dance in the old dame yet
toujours gai toujours gai
> DON MARQUIS, *archy and mehitabel.*

11
Dancing is wonderful training for girls, it's the first way you learn to guess what a man is going to do before he does it.
> CHRISTOPHER MORLEY, *Kitty Foyle*, ch.
> 11.

12
Once a jolly swagman camped by a billy-bong,
Under the shade of a kulibar tree,
And he sang as he sat and waited for his billy-boil,
"You'll come a-waltzing, Matilda, with me."
> ANDREW PATERSON, *Waltzing Matilda.*

13
Our Unabashed Dictionary defines:
Hula dance as a shake in the grass.
> *More Playboy's Party Jokes* (1965).

DANGER

14
The lamb that belonged to the sheep, whose skin the wolf was wearing, began to follow the wolf in the sheep's clothing.
> AESOP, *The Wolf in Sheep's Clothing.*

15
There was a young lady of Niger
Who smiled as she rode on a tiger.
They returned from the ride
With the lady inside
And the smile on the face of the tiger.
> ANONYMOUS.

16
The executioner is, I believe, very expert and my neck is very slender.
> ANNE BOLEYN.

1
If a man proves too clearly and convincingly to himself that the tiger is an optical illusion—well, he will find out that he is wrong. The tiger will himself intervene in the discussion.
G. K. Chesterton, *Illusions.*

2
Young normal tigers do not eat people. If eaten by a tiger you may rest assured that he was abnormal.
Will Cuppy, *How to Tell Your Friends from the Apes: The Tiger.*

3
Some people lose all respect for the lion unless he devours them instantly. There is no pleasing some people.
Will Cuppy, *How to Tell Your Friends from the Apes: The Lion.*

4
Young man, you are standing on the brink of an abscess.
Andrew Freedman, *Retort* to a sports writer, Charley Dryden, who had offended him. Freedman was owner of the New York Giants baseball team.

5
"De place wharbouts you spill de grease,
   Right dar youer boun' ter slide,
An' whar you fine a bunch er ha'r,
   You'll sholy fine de hide."
Joel Chandler Harris, *The Wonderful Tar Baby Story.*

6
Holland . . . lies so low, they're only saved by being damned.
Thomas Hood, *Up the Rhine.*

7
It's always the feller that's lookin' on that gits hit.
Joseph Lincoln, *Mr. Pratt.*

8
Sometimes a man has to stick out his neck, but there's no point to stretching it.
New York World-Telegram and Sun. The reference is to Lyndon Johnson during the campaign for the Democratic nomination for the presidency in 1960.

9
I will try my best to look like a fool—it is the safest way when one lives in the tiger's mouth.
John Oxenham, *A Long Road.*

10
When a woman in New York finds out about a panther having escaped in California, she goes and brings the baby in out of the yard, just to be sure.
Reflections of a Bachelor.

11
A lion among ladies is a most dreadful thing.
William Shakespeare, *A Midsummer Night's Dream.* Act iii, sc. 1.

12
Anybody who ever says he was et by a wolf is a damn liar.
H. Allen Smith, *We Went Thataway.*

13
Glass and a maid are ever in danger.
Torriano, *Piazza Universale.*

14
Get a bicycle. You will not regret it, if you live.
Mark Twain, *Essays: Taming the Bicycle.*

15
Beware how you give any edged tool
Unto a young child and unto a fool.
William Wagner, *Longer Thou Livest* (1568).

DEATH

See also Epitaphs, Grave, Suicide

16
My uncle is a Southern planter. He's an undertaker in Alabama.
Fred Allen, *Much Ado About Me.*

17
Here I lie at the chancel door,
Here I lie because I'm poor;
The farther in the more you pay,
Here I lie as warm as they.
William Andrews, *Curious Epitaphs.*

18
Gaily I lived, as ease and nature taught,
And spent my little life without a thought;
And am amazed that Death, that tyrant grim,
Should think of me, who never thought of him.
Anonymous, *Epitaph.*

19
Applaud friends, the comedy is over.
Ludwig van Beethoven, on his death bed.

20
When Sir Joshua Reynolds died
   All nature was degraded;
The king dropped a tear into the Queen's ear,
   And all his pictures faded.
William Blake, *Sir Joshua Reynolds.*

21
An undertaker does not have much use for a living man but he has great respect for a dead one.
Representative Charles A. Boutelle of Maine (1900).

1
Someone at this banquet [a banquet of undertakers] got up and sang the Indian plague song, with a glass in his hand, and the others with glasses in theirs:
So stand to your glasses steady;
'Tis here the revival lies;
A cup to the dead already—
Hurrah for the next that dies!
REPRESENTATIVE CHARLES A. BOUTELLE of Maine (1900).

2
He cannot read his tombstone when he's dead.
BERTON BRALEY, *Do It Now*.

3
The fence around a cemetery is foolish, for those inside can't come out and those outside don't want to get in.
ARTHUR BRISBANE.

4
It costs a lot of money to die comfortably.
SAMUEL BUTLER, *Notebooks*.

5
I am ready to meet my Maker. Whether my Maker is prepared for the ordeal of meeting me is another matter.
SIR WINSTON CHURCHILL, *Comment* on 75th anniversary, upon being asked if he feared death.

6
          then
laugh, leaning back in my arms
for life's not a paragraph

and death i think is no parenthesis
E. E. CUMMINGS, *Since Feeling Is First*, st. 4.

7
The Dodo never had a chance. He seems to have been invented for the sole purpose of becoming extinct and that was all he was good for.
WILL CUPPY, *How to Become Extinct*.

8
We cannot put the face of a person on a stamp unless said person is deceased. My suggestion, therefore, is that you drop dead.
JAMES EDWARD DAY, *Letter* dictated but not mailed to a petitioner who wanted his likeness on a postage stamp. (*The New York Times*, Mar. 7, 1962.)

9
Old Marley was as dead as a doornail . . .
The wisdom of our ancestors is in the simile.
CHARLES DICKENS, *A Christmas Carol*.

10
He'd make a lovely corpse.
CHARLES DICKENS, *Martin Chuzzlewit*, ch. 19.

11
Dead men tell no tales.
JOHN DRYDEN, *Spanish Friar*. Act iv, sc. 1. See also WILSON in this section.

12
Fear of death has gone farther with me in two minutes, than my conscience would have gone in two months.
JOHN DRYDEN, *Don Sebastian*. Act iii, sc. 2.

13
It's a good thing that funeral sermons are not composed in the confessional.
FINLEY PETER DUNNE, *Mr. Dooley Remembers*.

14
To be enjoyable, a will must be at one and the same time a practical joke on the heirs and an advertisement of the man that made it.
FINLEY PETER DUNNE, *Mr. Dooley Remembers*.

15
The only place a man can't hide . . . is at his own funeral. Every scoundrel and bore he's spent his life in avoiding is privileged to step up, view the carcass and tell the world what a dear friend he has lost in good old What's-his-name.
FINLEY PETER DUNNE, *Mr. Dooley Remembers*.

16
Having read the inscriptions
Upon the tombstones
Of the great and the little cemeteries,
Wang Peng advised the Emperor
To kill all the living
And resurrect the dead.
PAUL ELDRIDGE, *Wang Peng, Famous Sociologist, Suggests to the Emperor the Only Positive Means of Improving the People of the Empire*.

17
The reason so many people showed up at his funeral was because they wanted to make sure he was dead.
SAMUEL GOLDWYN, reference to Louis B. Mayer. (BOSLEY CROWTHER, *Hollywood Rajah*.)

18
Death possesses a good deal of real estate, namely the graveyard in every town.
NATHANIEL HAWTHORNE, *Twice-Told Tales*.

19
More than one mourner has laughed at a funeral.
THAYER HOBSON, *Morrow's Almanac* (1929).

1
When a man dies and his kin are glad of it, they say, "He's better off."
E. W. HOWE.

2
It is better to die on your feet than to live on your knees.
DOLORES IBARRURI (La Passionara). *Speech*, Paris, Sept. 3, 1936. The phrase has been claimed for Emiliano Zapata, but Pinchon claims Zapata said, "Better a fighting death than a slave's life."

3
My bed-fellows are cramp and cough—we three all in one bed.
CHARLES LAMB, his last words.

4
You can die on St. Helena without being Napoleon.
STANISLAW J. LEC, *Unkempt Thoughts*, tr. from Polish by JACEK GALASKA.

5
If we could only sleep off death on the installment plan.
STANISLAW J. LEC, *Unkempt Thoughts*, tr. by JACEK GALASKA.

6
If the General had known how big a funeral he was going to have, he would have died years ago.
ABRAHAM LINCOLN, from *The Humorous Mr. Lincoln* by KEITH W. JENNISON.

7
The young may die, but the old must!
HENRY WADSWORTH LONGFELLOW.

8
I think that maybe threescore years and ten is subject to change without notice.
JOHN MCNULTY, quoted by JAMES THURBER in *Credos and Curios*.

9
It's nature's way of telling you to slow down. Madison avenue definition of death. (*Newsweek*, April 25, 1960.)

10
Promotion cometh neither from east nor west, but from the cemetery.
EDWARD SANFORD MARTIN. (*Toaster's Handbook*, compiled by PEGGY EDMUND and HENRY WORKMAN WILLIAMS.)

11
If you are small, death may quite likely overlook you.
W. SOMERSET MAUGHAM. (*Time*, Feb. 3, 1958.)

12
Now, had Tashtego perished in that head [of a whale], it had been a very precious perishing; smothered in the very whitest and daintiest of fragment spermaceti; coffined, hearsed, and tombed in the secret inner chamber and sanctum sanctorum of the whale. Only one sweeter end can readily be recalled—the delicious death of an Ohio honey-hunter, who seeking honey in the crotch of a hollow tree, found such exceeding store of it, that leaning too far over, it sucked him in, so that he died embalmed. How many, think ye, have like-wise fallen into Plato's honey head, and sweetly perished there?
HERMAN MELVILLE, *Moby Dick*, ch. 78.

14
One of the crying needs of the time is for a suitable Burial Service for the admittedly damned.
H. L. MENCKEN, *Prejudices*, ser. 6.

15
Today if death did not exist, it would be necessary to invent it. (Aujourd'hui si la mort n'existait pas, il faudrait l'inventer.)
JEAN BAPTISTE MILHAUD, when voting for the death of Louis XVI, Jan. 19, 1793. (*Le Moniteur*, Jan. 20, 1793.)

16
O death where is thy sting? O grave where is thy victory? Where, indeed? Many a badly stung survivor, faced with the aftermath of some relative's funeral, has ruefully conceded that the victory has been won hands down by a funeral establishment—in disastrously unequal battle.
JESSICA MITFORD, *The American Way of Death*.

17
Over the legend "Beautiful Bodies by Chambers" appears an unusually well endowed, and completely naked, young lady.
JESSICA MITFORD, *The American Way of Death*. Referring to a calendar issued by the W. W. Chambers Mortuary.

18
Chambers' caskets are just fine,
Made of sandalwood and pine.
If your loved ones have to go
Call Columbus 690.
If your loved ones pass away,
Have them pass the Chambers way.
Chambers' customers all sing:
"Death, oh death, where is thy sting?"
JESSICA MITFORD, *The American Way of Death*. Quoting a radio commercial for an undertaker.

19
"In keeping with our high standard of living, there should be an equally high standard of dying," says the past president of the Funeral Directors of San Francisco.
JESSICA MITFORD, *The American Way of Death*.

1

Told that his death was only a few hours away, [Wilson] Mizner rallied strength to send a postcard notifying a friend. "They're going to bury me at 9 A.M.," wrote Mizner. "Don't be a sucker and get up."

ALVA JOHNSTON, *Legend of a Sport; The New Yorker* (1942).

2

Coming out of a coma shortly before his death, [Wilson Mizner] waved a priest away disdainfully. "Why should I talk to you?" he said. "I've just been talking to your boss."

ALVA JOHNSTON, *Legend of a Sport; The New Yorker.*

3

I want a priest, a rabbi, and a Protestant clergyman. I want to hedge my bets.

WILSON MIZNER, quoted by ALVA JOHNSTON in *Legend of a Sport; The New Yorker.*

4

I pray you give me your aid in my going up; as for my coming down I can make shift for myself.

SIR THOMAS MORE, as he was about to ascend the scaffold.

5

Waldo is one of those people who would be enormously improved by death.

HECTOR HUGH MUNRO (SAKI), *Beasts and Super-Beasts: The Feast of Nemesis.*

6

What an artist the world is losing! (Qualis artifex pereo!)

EMPEROR NERO, as he drove a dagger into his throat, rather than be taken alive. (SUETONIUS, *Lives of the Caesars.*)

7

All victory ends in the defeat of death. That's sure. But does defeat end in the victory of death? That's what I wonder.

EUGENE O'NEILL, *Mourning Becomes Electra*, Act 3.

8

Remember, men of guns and rhymes,
 And kings who kill so fast,
That men you kill too many times
 May be too dead at last.

ROSE O'NEILL, *When the Dead Men Die.*

9

I went out to Charing Cross, to see Major-general Harrison hanged, drawn, and quartered; which was done there, he looking as cheerful as any man could do in that condition.

SAMUEL PEPYS, *Diary*, Oct. 13, 1660.

10

He [the author's father] said he was dying of fast women, slow horses, crooked cards and straight whiskey.

KENNETH REXROTH, *An Autobiographical Novel* (1966).

11

Men have died from time to time and worms have eaten them, but not for love.

WILLIAM SHAKESPEARE, *As You Like It.* Act iv, sc. 1.

12

A man may fish with the worm that hath eat of a king, and eat of the fish that hath fed of the worm.

WILLIAM SHAKESPEARE, *Hamlet.* Act iv, sc. 3.

13

To what base uses we may return, Horatio! Why may not imagination trace the noble dust of Alexander, till we find it stopping a bung-hole?

WILLIAM SHAKESPEARE, *Hamlet.* Act v, sc. 1.

14

Death is for many of us the gate of hell; but we are inside on the way out, not outside on the way in.

BERNARD SHAW, *Parents and Children.*

15

Life does not cease to be funny when people die any more than it ceases to be serious when people laugh.

BERNARD SHAW, *The Doctor's Dilemma*, Act 5.

16

Since we have to speak well of the dead, let's knock them while they're alive.

JOHN SLOAN, quoted by ALLEN CHURCHILL in *The Improper Bohemians.*

17

To have to die is a distinction of which no man is proud.

ALEXANDER SMITH, *Dreamthorp: On the Writing of Essays.*

18

At the door of life by the gate of breath, There are worse things waiting for men than death.

ALGERNON CHARLES SWINBURNE, *The Triumph of Time.*

19

Die, my dear Doctor, that's the last thing I shall do!

HENRY JOHN TEMPLE, Viscount Palmerston.

20

When a pious visitor inquired sweetly, "Henry, have you made your peace with

God?" he replied, "We have never quarrelled."

BROOKS ATKINSON, *Henry Thoreau, the Cosmic Yankee.*

1
Why is it that we rejoice at a birth and grieve at a funeral? It is because we are not the person involved.

MARK TWAIN, *Pudd'nhead Wilson's Calendar.*

2
He is useless on top of the ground; he ought to be under it, inspiring the cabbages.

MARK TWAIN, *Pudd'nhead Wilson's Calendar.*

3
The reports of my death are greatly exaggerated.

MARK TWAIN.

4
Death, the only immortal who treats us all alike, whose pity and whose peace and whose refuge are for all—the soiled and the pure, the rich and the poor, the loved and the unloved.

MARK TWAIN, *Memorandum*, written on his deathbed.

5
The last one [funeral] I went to had people in the front pew that I wouldn't have to my funeral over my dead body.

UNKNOWN, quoted in *Who Killed Society* by CLEVELAND AMORY.

6
Many of the Indian heroes were killed, which proved very fatal to them.

LOUIS UNTERMEYER, *A Treasury of Laughter.* Quoted as a student boner.

7
They gave William IV a lovely funeral. It took six men to carry the beer.

LOUIS UNTERMEYER, *A Treasury of Laughter.* Quoted as a student boner.

8
I suppose that I shall have to die beyond my means.

OSCAR WILDE, when a fee for an operation was discussed. Quoted in SHERARD'S *Life.*

9
'Twere best to knock them in the head. . . .
The dead do tell no tales.

JOHN WILSON, *Andronicus Commenius,* Act 1 (1664).

DEBT

See also Borrowing and Lending

10
Nothing (except having a baby) makes a woman feel more important than paying bills.

HAL BOYLE, *Column,* Associated Press, datelined New York, Oct. 21, 1964.

11
Running into debt isn't so bad. It's running into creditors that hurts.

JACOB M. BRAUDE, *Treasury of Wit and Humor.*

12
You can't get blood out of a turnip, but you can get the turnip.

FRANK C. BROWN, *Collection of North Carolina Folklore.*

13
The proverb says, "If you want Lent to go quickly, contract a debt you'll have to pay at Easter."

GIORDANO BRUNO, *The Candle Bearer.* Act iv, sc. 13. English version by J. R. HALE.

14
Debt is to a man what the serpent is to the bird; its eye fascinates, its breath poisons, its coil crushes both sinew and bone, its jaw is the pitiless grave.

SIR EDWARD BULWER-LYTTON, *Caxtoniana,* essay 21.

15
He'd run in debt by disputation,
And pay with ratiocination.

SAMUEL BUTLER, *Hudibras,* pt. 1.

16
Dreading that climax of all human ills,
The inflammation of his weekly bills.

LORD BYRON, *Don Juan.* Canto III, st. 35.

17
A person who can't pay, get another person who can't pay, to guarantee that he can pay.

CHARLES DICKENS, *Little Dorrit.* Bk. i, ch. 23.

18
Wilt thou seal up the avenues of ill?
Pay every debt as if God wrote the bill!

RALPH WALDO EMERSON, *Suum Cuique.*

19
Creditors have better memories than debtors.

BENJAMIN FRANKLIN, *Poor Richard's Almanac,* 1758.

20
Creditors are a superstitious set, great observers of set days and times.

BENJAMIN FRANKLIN, *Poor Richard.*

21
Let the world slide, let the world go;
A fig for care, and a fig for woe!
If I can't pay, why I can owe,
And death makes equal the high and low.

JOHN HEYWOOD, *Be Merry, Friends.*

1
In the midst of life we are in debt.
ETHEL WATTS MUMFORD.

2
I owe much; I have nothing; the rest I leave
to the poor.
FRANÇOIS RABELAIS.

3
I've often known people more shocked be-
cause you are not bankrupt than because
you are.
MRS. BAILLIE SAUNDERS, *A Shepherd of
Kensington.*

4
He that dies pays all debts.
WILLIAM SHAKESPEARE, *The Tempest.* Act
iii, sc. 2.

5
You know it is not in my *interest* to pay the
principal; nor is it my *principle* to pay the
interest.
RICHARD BRINSLEY SHERIDAN, *Reply* to
a creditor.

6
[Bret] Harte owed me fifteen hundred dollars at that time; later he owed me three
thousand. He offered me his note but I was
not keeping a museum and didn't take it.
MARK TWAIN, *Autobiography,* ch. 61.

7
Today any man who owes $25,000 has ar-
rived. His material worries will disappear.
He will find that he can command the best
of everything, and head waiters will have a
special bow for him. He has put himself in
a situation in which his creditors have a
vested interest in him. They cannot afford
to let him down.
IRA WALLACH, *How to Be Deliriously
Happy* (1950).

8
It is only by not paying one's bills than one
can hope to live in the memory of the com-
mercial classes.
OSCAR WILDE, quoted by HESKETH PEAR-
SON in *Lives of the Wits.*

DECEIT

See also Hypocrisy, Lies and Lying

9
Like the strawberry wives that laid two or
three great strawberries at the mouth of
their pot, and all the rest were little ones.
FRANCIS BACON, *Apothegms,* No. 54.

10
There is a cunning which we in England
call "the turning of the cat in the pan";
which is, when that which a man says to
another, he lays it as if another had said
it to him.
FRANCIS BACON, *Of Cunning.*

11
Some people cultivate a simple manner. It
is a useful thing to cultivate, when one
wishes to throw dust into other people's
eyes.
RICHARD BAGOT, *Temptation.*

12
Even a fool can deceive a man—if he be a
bigger fool than himself.
MARJORIE BOWEN, *The Glen O'Weeping.*

13
The world is full of women, and the women
full of wile.
GELETT BURGESS, *Willy and the Lady.*

14
How cheerfully he seems to grin,
  How neatly spreads his claws,
And welcomes little fishes in
  With greatly smiling jaws!
LEWIS CARROLL, *Alice in Wonderland,* ch.
2.

15
Fraud is the homage that force pays to
reason.
CHARLES P. CURTIS, *A Commonplace
Book.*

16
In trickery, evasion, procrastination, spolia-
tion, botheration, under false pretenses, of
all sorts, there are influences that can never
come to good.
CHARLES DICKENS, *Bleak House,* ch. 1.

17
Experience teaches us that the man who
looks you straight in the eye, particularly if
he adds a firm handshake, is hiding something.
CLIFTON FADIMAN, *Enter, Conversing.*

18
Which I wish to remark,
And my language is plain,
That for ways that are dark
And for tricks that are vain,
The heathen Chinee is peculiar,
Which the same I would rise to explain.
BRET HARTE, *Plain Language from Truth-
ful James.*

19
You can fool some of the people all of the
time, and all of the people some of the time,
but you cannot fool all of the people all the
time.
ABRAHAM LINCOLN, *Speech* in Bloomington, Ill., May 29, 1856. William P. Kel-
logg is the authority for this. Other
students of Lincoln are in fundamental
agreement about the substance of the
quotation, but differ on the date and
place of delivery. The quotation has also
been attributed, much less frequently, to
P. T. Barnum.

1

As real drunkenness does harm, so will feigned bring profit: make your crafty tongue stumble in stammering talk, so that, whatever you do or say more freely than you should, may be put down to too much wine.
> OVID, *The Art of Love*, bk. 1, tr. by J. H. MOZLEY.

2

Innocence quits being it just as soon as it knows what innocence is.
> *Reflections of a Bachelor.*

3

I want that glib and oily art,
To speak and purpose not.
> WILLIAM SHAKESPEARE, *King Lear*. Act i, sc. 1.

4

Nothing doing. That's just baloney. Everybody knows I can't lay bricks.
> ALFRED E. SMITH, when governor of New York. He was laying the cornerstone of the New York State Office Building, when asked to permit the taking of a motion picture showing him actually laying the brick.

5

One dupe is as impossible as one twin.
> JOHN STERLING, *Essays and Tales.*

6

You can fool too many of the people too much of the time.
> JAMES THURBER, *Fables for Our Time.*

7

When a person cannot deceive himself the chances are against his being able to deceive other people.
> MARK TWAIN.

DECISION

8

I'm giving you a definite maybe.
> SAM GOLDWYN. (E. ESAR, *The Humor of Humor.*)

9

The trouble with Howard is that he won't take yes for an answer.
> OSCAR HAMMERSTEIN II, referring to HOWARD REINHEIMER. (GEORGE ABBOTT, *Mister Abbott.*)

10

It often happens that I wake at night and begin to think about a serious problem and decide I must tell the Pope about it. Then I wake up completely and remember that I am the Pope.
> POPE JOHN XXIII.

11

Give your decisions, never your reasons; your decisions may be right, but your reasons are sure to be wrong.
> WILLIAM MURRAY, Earl of Mansfield. *Advice* to judges.

12

When you guess wrong it is crazy irresponsibility; when you guess right it is sound judgment.
> *Reflections of a Bachelor* (1903).

13

I am Sir Oracle,
And, when I ope my lips, let no god bark!
> WILLIAM SHAKESPEARE, *The Merchant of Venice*. Act i, sc. 1.

14

The buck stops here.
> UNKNOWN, *Motto* mounted on the desk of Harry S Truman while he was President, as a reminder of the ultimate responsibility inherent in that post. (*American Heritage*, Aug., 1964, p. 49.)

DEEDS

See also Act, Action

15

And when I lie in the green kirkyard,
With the mould upon my breast,
Say not that she did well or ill,
Only, "She did her best."
> DINAH MARIA MULOCK CRAIK, *Epitaph.*

16

He did nothing in particular,
And did it very well.
> W. S. GILBERT, *Iolanthe*, Act 2.

17

He that leaveth nothing to chance will do few things ill, but he will do very few things.
> LORD HALIFAX, *Works*, p. 247.

18

The Italians are wise before the deed; the Germans in the deed; the French after the deed.
> GEORGE HERBERT, *Jacula Prudentum.*

19

It is as folk do, and not as folk say.
> JOHN HEYWOOD, *Proverbs*. Pt. ii, ch. 5.

20

A man of words and not of deeds
Is like a garden full of weeds.
> JAMES HOWELL, *Proverbs*, 20. HALLIWELL, *Nursery Rhymes*, No. 166.

21

The greatest pleasure I know is to do a good action by stealth, and to have it found out by accident.
> CHARLES LAMB, *Table Talk: In the Athenaeum.*

22

Talkers are no good doers.
> WILLIAM SHAKESPEARE, *Richard III*. Act i, sc. 3.

23

Your dad will never be reckoned among the great. But you can be sure he did his level

best and gave all he had to his country.
There is an epitaph in Boothill Cemetery in
Tombstone, Arizona, which reads, "Here lies
Jack Williams; he done his damndest." What
more can a person do?

> HARRY S TRUMAN, *Note* to his daughter
> Margaret, written shortly before his sec-
> ond term as President expired early in
> 1953. (ALFRED STEINBERG, *The Man
> from Missouri*, p. 418.)

DELAY

1
When a man's life is at stake no delay is too
long. (Nulla umquam de morte hominis
cunctatio longa est.)

> JUVENAL, *Satires.* Sat. vi, l. 221.

2
Delay is a great procuress. (Maxima lena
mora est.)

> OVID, *Ars Amatoria.* Bk. iii, l. 752.

DEMOCRACY

3
Democracy means government by the uneducated, while aristocracy means government by the badly educated.

> G. K. CHESTERTON, *The New York Times,*
> Feb. 1, 1931.

4
Democracy is the will of the governed after
it has been subjected to federal probate.

> JOHN CIARDI, *The Saturday Review*, Sept.
> 24, 1966.

5
A monarchy is like a man-of-war,—bad shots
between wind and water hurt it exceedingly;
there is danger of capsizing. But democracy
is a raft. You cannot easily overturn it. It
is a wet place, but a pretty safe one.

> JOSEPH COOK, *Boston Monday Lectures:
> Labor.* See also FISHER AMES, quoted in
> section headed "Government."

6
Democracy becomes a government of bullies
tempered by editors.

> RALPH WALDO EMERSON, *Journals.* Vol.
> vii, p. 193.

7
There are some things so elastic that even
the heavy roller of democracy cannot flatten
them altogether down.

> JAMES RUSSELL LOWELL, *On a Certain
> Condescension in Foreigners.*

8
Democracy means not "I am as good as you
are," but "You are as good as I am."

> THEODORE PARKER.

9
The whole thing is gloriously unpredictable,
occasionally tragic, often frustrating and

sometimes uproariously funny. How democracy works nobody quite knows. It is the
worst system of government in the world,
says Winston Churchill, "except all those
other systems."

> JAMES RESTON, *Washington Column, The
> New York Times,* Jan. 20, 1964.

10
Democracy substitutes election by the in-
competent many for appointment by the
corrupt few.

> BERNARD SHAW, *Maxims for Revolution-
> ists.*

11
The Republican form of government is the
highest form of government: but because of
this it requires the highest type of human
nature—a type nowhere at present existing.

> HERBERT SPENCER, *The Americans.*

DETERMINATION

12
Determination is all right if you are not the
victim of it.

> ANONYMOUS.

13
Hold-fast is a good dog.

> JACOB CATS, *Moral Emblems.*

14
When I am determined, I always listen to
reason, because it can then do no harm.

> OLIVER GOLDSMITH.

15
One morning [Oliver] Herford arrived at the
Club wearing an exaggerated, not to say impossible, hat. Derided for it, he explained
that the choice had not been his. "It was a
whim of my wife's," he said. "Disregard all
that, and throw the hat away," his friends
said. "You don't know her," he said, "she
has a whim of iron."

> FRANK CROWNINSHIELD, *A Wit with a
> Whim of Iron.*

16
Hold on with a bulldog grip, and chew and
choke as much as possible.

> ABRAHAM LINCOLN, *Telegram* to General
> Grant during the siege of Petersburg,
> Aug. 17, 1864.

DEVIL

See also Hell

17
The devil take the hindmost.

> BEAUMONT AND FLETCHER, *Philaster,* Act
> 5.

18
The meanest thing in the world is—the
Devil.

> HENRY WARD BEECHER, *Proverbs from
> Plymouth Pulpit.*

1

If two New Hampshire men aren't a match for the devil, we might as well give the country back to the Indians.

STEPHEN VINCENT BENÉT, *The Devil and Daniel Webster.*

2

The Christians were the first to make the existence of Satan a dogma of the church. What is the use in a Pope if there is no Devil?

MADAME BLAVATSKY, founder of theosophy.

3

The devil himself, which is the author of confusion and lies.

ROBERT BURTON, *The Anatomy of Melancholy.*

4

Nick Machiavel had ne'er a trick,
Though he gave his name to our
Old Nick.

SAMUEL BUTLER, *Hudibras*, pt. 3.

5

An apology for the devil: it must be remembered that we have heard only one side of the case; God has written all the books.

SAMUEL BUTLER, *Notebooks.*

6

Neutral men and the devil's allies.

EDWIN HUBBEL CHAPIN, *American Clergyman.*

7

Talk of the devil, and his horns appear.

SAMUEL TAYLOR COLERIDGE, *Biographia Literaria*, ch. 23.

8

Give the devil his due.

JOHN DRYDEN, *Short Studies on Great Subjects.*

9

If you keep painting the Devil on the wall he will presently appear in person.

Old French Proverb.

10

The duchess thinking to have gotten God by the foot, when she had the devil by the tail.

EDWARD HALL, *Chronicles* (1548).

11

Why should the devil have all the good tunes?

ROWLAND HILL, *Sermons.* (BROOME, *Life.*)

12

        At Nineteen, Plagued by the Devil
This very day [Christmas, 1762, at Fairfield plantation], to others the day of greatest mirth and jollity, sees me overwhelmed with more and greater misfortunes than have fallen a descendant of Adam for these thousand years past, I am sure; and perhaps, after excepting Job, since the creation of the world. . . . You must know, dear Page [John Page of Rosewell, a college friend], that I am now in a house surrounded with enemies who take counsel together against my soul; and when I lay me down to rest they say among themselves, come let us destroy him. I am sure if there is such a thing as a Devil in this world, he must have been here last night and have had some hand in contriving what happened to me.

Do you think the cursed rats (at his instigation, I suppose) did not eat up my pocket-book, which was in my pocket within a foot of my head? And not contented with plenty for the present, they carried away my jemmy-worked silk garters and half a dozen new minuets I had just got, to serve, I suppose, as provision for the winter. But of this I should not have accused the Devil (because you know rats will be rats, and hunger, without the addition of his instigations, might have urged them to do this), if something worse, and from a different quarter, had not happened.

You know it rained last night, or if you do not know it, I am sure I do. When I went to bed I laid my watch in the usual place, and going to take her up after I arose this morning, I found her in the same place, it's true, but *Quantum mutatus ab illo!* all afloat in water, let in at a leak in the roof of the house, and as silent and still as the rats that had eat my pocket-book. Now you know if chance had had anything to do in this matter, there were a thousand other spots where it might have chanced to leak as well as this one, which was perpendicularly over my watch. But I'll tell you, it's my opinion that the Devil came and bored a hole over it on purpose.

THOMAS JEFFERSON.

13

It is by the Vicar's skirts that the Devil climbs into the belfry.

HENRY WADSWORTH LONGFELLOW, *The Spanish Student.* Act i, sc. 2.

14

In all systems of theology the devil figures as a male person . . . Yes, it is women who keep the churches going.

DON MARQUIS, *New York Sun.*

15

The devil was sick, the devil a monk would be;
The devil was well, the devil a monk was he.

FRANÇOIS RABELAIS, *How Pantagruel Met with a Great Storm at Sea.*

1
He had needed a long spoon that eats with the devil.
JOHN RAY, *English Proverbs.*

2
The devil pulls the string that winks the eye.
Reflections of a Bachelor (1903).

3
The devil can cite scripture for his purpose.
WILLIAM SHAKESPEARE, *The Merchant of Venice.* Act i, sc. 3.

4
The devil hath power to assume a pleasing shape.
WILLIAM SHAKESPEARE, *Hamlet.* Act ii, sc. 2.

5
I have always felt friendly toward Satan. Of course that is ancestral; it must be in the blood, for I could not have originated it.
MARK TWAIN.

6
It may be that I lean a little his way, on account of his not having a fair show. All religions issue bibles against him, and say the most injurious things about him, but we never hear *his* side.
MARK TWAIN, *Essays: Concerning the Jews.* Referring to the devil.

DIAMOND

7
When Mrs Claude K. Boettcher, who had been voted one of the ten best-dressed ladies of Denver, arrived in Palm Beach, she was challenged by an elderly Eastern *grande dame* who spotted her one morning wearing diamonds. "Oh, no, my dear," said the Eastern lady patronizingly, "you mustn't. One simply doesn't wear diamonds in the daytime." Mrs Boettcher smiled. "I thought not, too," she said pleasantly, "until I had them."
CLEVELAND AMORY, *The Last Resorts.*

8
Diamonds are chunks of coal that stuck to their job.
B. C. FORBES, *Epigrams.*

9
Diamonds are a girl's best friend.
ANITA LOOS, *Gentlemen Prefer Blondes.*

10
Let us not be too particular. It is better to have old second-hand diamonds than none at all.
MARK TWAIN.

11
I never knew but one woman who would not take gold—and she took diamonds.
HORACE WALPOLE.

DIETING

See also Fatness

12
If you want to feel important, go on a diet.
JOEY ADAMS, *Cindy and I,* ch. 22.

13
It was . . . dangerous to have people over to the house. I would greet visitors with such uplifting statements as, "You're getting a little flabby there, boy." Or my big hilarious joke to a woman was, "If you don't watch your figure the men won't."
JOEY ADAMS, *Cindy and I,* ch. 22.

14
More often, however, unnecessary dieting is because everything from television to fashion ads have made it seem wicked to cast a shadow. This wild, emaciated look appeals to some women, though not to many men, who are seldom seen pinning up a *Vogue* illustration in a machine shop.
PEG BRACKEN, *Appendix* to the *I Hate to Cook Book; Ladies' Home Journal,* Feb., 1967.

15
I wish my ulcers and I could get together on a mutually satisfactory diet. What suits me seems to disagree with them. I claim a stomach ulcer should be like a tapeworm or a boarding house guest—take what's put before it and raise no rumpuses.
IRVIN S. COBB, *Exit Laughing,* ch. 42.

16
Eat, drink and be merry, for tomorrow ye diet.
Toasts for All Occasions, ed. by LEWIS C. HENRY.

17
I feel about airplanes the way I feel about diets. It seems to me that they are wonderful things for other people to go on.
JEAN KERR, *The Snake Has All the Lines.*

18
Fred Allen used to talk about a man who was so thin he could be dropped through a piccolo without striking a single note. Well, I'm glad I never met *him;* I'd hate to have to hear about *his* diet.
JEAN KERR, *Please Don't Eat the Daisies.*

19
Another good reducing exercise consists in placing both hands against the table edge and pushing back.
ROBERT QUILLEN.

20
Mother Goose
Jack Sprat could eat no fat,
His wife could eat no lean.
A real sweet pair of neurotics.
JACK SHARKEY, *Playboy,* May, 1965.

1
Dietitians are the worst enemy of the great cuisine; it is impossible to have low calories in excellent food.
> LOUIS VAUDABLE, quoted in *Life*, Jan. 7, 1966.

DIGNITY

2
It is only people of small moral stature who have to stand on their dignity.
> ARNOLD BENNETT.

3
We have exchanged the Washingtonian dignity for the Jeffersonian simplicity, which was in truth only another name for the Jacksonian vulgarity.
> BISHOP HENRY C. POTTER, *Address*, Washington Centennial Service, New York City, Apr. 30, 1889.

4
Place confers no dignity upon such a man as the new Missouri senator. Like a balloon, the higher he rises the smaller he looks.
> GEORGE D. PRENTICE, *Louisville Journal*, c. 1860.

5
The butler entered the room, a solemn procession of one.
> P. G. WODEHOUSE.

DIPLOMACY

6
Diplomacy. The patriotic art of lying for one's country.
> AMBROSE BIERCE, *The Devil's Dictionary*.

7
No one, not even the most malevolent democrat, has any idea how much nullity and charlatanism there is in diplomacy.
> OTTO VON BISMARCK.

8
Diplomacy—The art of saying "Nice doggie" till you can find a rock.
> WYNN CATLIN. (BENNETT CERF, *The Laugh's on Me*.)

9
I have discovered the art of fooling diplomats; I speak the truth and they never believe me.
> BENSO DI CAVOUR.

10
It is fortunate that diplomats generally have long noses, since usually they cannot see beyond them.
> Attributed to PAUL CLAUDEL, while Ambassador to Washington, but denied by him in letter to Burton Stevenson.

11
He was a clever diplomat—principally because he was a good liar—paid to lie in a foreign country.
> LUCAS CLEEVE, *The Rose Geranium*.

12
American diplomacy is easy on the brain but hell on the feet.
> CHARLES G. DAWES, attributed.

13
'Tis startin' a polis foorce to prevint war. . . . How'll they be ar-med? What a foolish question. They'll be ar-med with love, if coorse.
> FINLEY PETER DUNNE, *On Making a Will*. The reference is to William Jennings Bryan's speech on the League of Nations in 1920.

14
As a general thing, T.R. didn't like the diplomats. He thought few of them knew their own business. They were almost as stupid as our own ambassadors.
> FINLEY PETER DUNNE, *Mr. Dooley Remembers*.

15
A diplomat is a man who always remembers a woman's birthday but never remembers her age.
> ROBERT FROST.

16
Diplomats are useful only in fair weather. As soon as it rains they drown in every drop.
> GENERAL CHARLES DE GAULLE, quoted by a former cabinet aide, CONSTANTIN MELNICK, in *Newsweek*, Oct. 1, 1962.

17
Modern diplomats approach every problem with an open mouth.
> ARTHUR GOLDBERG, U.S. Ambassador to the United Nations. (*The New York Times*, Apr. 19, 1967.)

18
Diplomacy is to do and say
The nastiest thing in the nicest way.
> ISAAC GOLDBERG, *The Reflex*.

19
The only summit meeting that can succeed is one that does not take place.
> BARRY M. GOLDWATER, *Why Not Victory?* Winston Churchill first used "summit," with reference to present-day diplomacy, in 1954, a year before the first such meeting.

20
Conferences at the top level are always courteous. Name-calling is left to the foreign ministers.
> W. AVERELL HARRIMAN, *News summaries*, Aug. 1, 1955.

1

When they seem going they come:
Diplomats, women and crabs.
JOHN HAY, *Distichs*.

2

Diplomacy—Lying in state.
OLIVER HERFORD.

3

I wish there were some giant economy-size aspirin tablet that would work on international headaches. But there isn't. The only cure is patience with reason mixed in.
LYNDON B. JOHNSON, *Speech* in Belleville, Ill., during the presidential campaign, Oct. 21, 1964.

4

My God, in this job, he's got the nerve of a burglar.
JOHN F. KENNEDY, on Adlai Stevenson as United Nations ambassador. (*Time*, Feb. 24, 1961.)

5

This organization is created to prevent you from going to hell. It isn't created to take you to heaven.
HENRY CABOT LODGE, JR., U.S. Ambassador to the United Nations. On the purpose of the UN. *News summaries* of Jan. 28, 1954.

6

We are being rushed pell-mell into this thing so that Senor Ab Jab or some other something from Japan can pass upon our controversies.
SENATOR HUEY LONG of Louisiana, commenting on Franklin D. Roosevelt's message urging U.S. entry into the World Court, 1935. (*The Wit and Wisdom of Congress*, ed. by EDWARD BOYKIN.)

7

Ambassadors are, in the full meaning of the term, titled spies.
NAPOLEON BONAPARTE. (*The Mind of Napoleon*, ed. by J. CHRISTOPHER HEROLD.)

8

Joe Robinson [U.S. Senator Joseph Robinson of Arkansas] said to me, "Will, the whole thing is no different from old Arkansaw politics, only the food is a little fancier."
WILL ROGERS, *Autobiography*. The remark was made in 1930 and referred to the London disarmament conference.

9

Diplomats are just as essential to starting a war as soldiers are for finishing it.
WILL ROGERS, *Autobiography*.

10

You take diplomacy out of war and the thing would fall flat in a week.
WILL ROGERS, *Autobiography*.

11

A diplomat and a stage magician are the two professions that have to have a high silk hat. All the tricks that either one of them have are in that hat, and are all known to other diplomats and magicians.
WILL ROGERS, *Autobiography*.

12

There's the one thing no nation can ever accuse us of and that is secret diplomacy. Our foreign dealings are an open book, generally a check book.
WILL ROGERS, *Autobiography*.

13

I think the only real diplomacy ever performed by a diplomat is in deceiving their own people after their dumbness has got them into a war.
WILL ROGERS, *Autobiography*.

14

I can tell by observation that it does not come under civil service or competitive examination.
WILL ROGERS, *The Illiterate Digest*. Reference to the ambassadorship to the court of St. James.

15

All ambassadors make love and are very nice and useful to people who travel.
BERNARD SHAW, *Misalliance*.

16

A diplomat's life is made up of three ingredients: protocol, Geritol and alcohol.
ADLAI E. STEVENSON. (*The New York Times Magazine*, Feb. 7, 1965, p. 22.)

17

The League of Nations is a declaration of love without the promise of marriage.
ADMIRAL ALFRED VON TIRPITZ.

18

I am not a gentleman. I am representative of the Soviet Union here.
SEMYON TSARAPKIN, Soviet delegate to the United Nations. Reply to Ambassador Lodge's inquiry on why "the gentleman" was asking for the floor. Lodge then replied, "The two are not necessarily mutually exclusive." Quoted in news reports of June 26, 1954.

19

Look at John Hay and me . . . He is Secretary of State and I am a gentleman.
MARK TWAIN, *Speech*, Nov. 28, 1902.

20

A diplomat these days is nothing but a headwaiter who's allowed to sit down occasionally.
PETER USTINOV, *Romanoff and Juliet*, Act 1.

21

It's not without reason that diplomats dress like this. Gloves, walking stick, portfolio, three articles to leave behind, if necessary. Sometimes, in the world of diplomacy, it is very important to have a pretext to return after having said goodbye.

> PETER USTINOV, *Romanoff and Juliet,* Act 2.

1

An ambassador is an honest man, sent to lie abroad for the good of his country. (Legatus est vir bonus peregre missus ad mentiendum Reipublicae causa.)

> SIR HENRY WOTTON, *Inscription* in the album of a friend, Christopher Flecka-more, 1604.

DISAPPOINTMENT

2

The best laid schemes o' mice and men
  Gang aft a-gley;
And leave us nought but grief and pain
  For promised joy.

> ROBERT BURNS, *To a Mouse.*

3

Many things happen between the cup and the lip.

> ROBERT BURTON, *The Anatomy of Melancholy.*

4

Nothing is so good as it seems beforehand.

> GEORGE ELIOT, *Silas Marner,* ch. 18.

5

The fathers have eaten sour grapes, and the children's teeth are set on edge.

> *Ezekiel,* XVIII, 2.

6

Leslie's Weekly itemized: When Colonel Forney inquired of him [Lincoln] how he felt about New York, he replied: "Somewhat like that boy in Kentucky, who stubbed his toe while running to see his sweetheart. The boy said he was too big to cry, and far too badly hurt to laugh."

> CARL SANDBURG, *Abraham Lincoln: The Prairie Years and the War Years,* ch. 27. The reference is to the outcome of the elections in 1862.

7

Blessed is he who expects nothing, for he shall never be disappointed.

> ALEXANDER POPE, *Letter* to John Gay, Oct. 16, 1727.

DISEASE

See also Doctors, Medicine

8

There is no curing a sick man who believes himself in health.

> AMIEL, *Journal,* Feb. 6, 1877.

9

Cure the disease and kill the patient.

> FRANCIS BACON, *Essays: Of Friendship.*

10

One foot in the grave.

> BEAUMONT AND FLETCHER, *The Little French Lawyer.* Act i, sc. 1.

11

"Ye can call it influenza if ye like," said Mrs Machin. "There's no influenza in my young days. We called a cold a cold."

> ARNOLD BENNETT, *The Card,* ch. 8.

12

How holy people look when they are seasick!

> SAMUEL BUTLER, *Truth and Convenience.*

13

I reckon being ill is one of the great pleasures of life, provided one is not too ill and is not obliged to work till one is better.

> SAMUEL BUTLER, *The Way of All Flesh,* ch. 80.

14

Self-contemplation is infallibly the symptom of disease.

> THOMAS CARLYLE, *Characteristics.*

15

You see, in those primitive times germs had not been invented yet and so he did not have to take any steps to avoid them.

> IRVIN S. COBB, *Speaking of Operations.*

16

I've just learned about his illness; let's hope it's nothing trivial.

> IRVIN S. COBB.

17

Though I have patches on me pantaloons, I've ne'er a wan on me intestines.

> FINLEY PETER DUNNE, *Thanksgiving.*

18

Illness offers him a double advantage:
To escape from himself—and get the better of his wife.

> T. S. ELIOT, *The Cocktail Party,* Act ii, sc. 1.

19

Adam
Had 'em.

> STRICKLAND GILLILAN, *Lines on the Antiquity of Microbes.*

20

I have been laid up with intentional flu.

> SAM GOLDWYN. (E. ESAR, *The Humor of Humor.*)

21

Don't tell your Friends about your Indigestion:
"How are you!" is a Greeting, not a Question.

> ARTHUR GUITERMAN, *A Poet's Proverbs.*

22

The patient raised a frightened head from

the bed. "Who is you?" his voice quavered. "Friend or enema?"

LANGSTON HUGHES, *The Book of Negro Humor.*

1
A person's age is not dependent upon the number of years that have passed over his head, but upon the number of colds that have passed through it.

DR. WOODS HUTCHINSON, quoted by DR. SHIRLEY WYNNE.

2
What can a sick man say, but that he is sick?

SAMUEL JOHNSON, Boswell's *Life.*

3
If there be a regal solitude, it is a sick bed.

CHARLES LAMB, *Last Essays of Elia.*

4
He is . . . the only man I know who has had two appendectomies with thirty years intervening.

OSCAR LEVANT, *Memoirs of an Amnesiac.* The reference is to Ira Gershwin.

5
A slight case of apoplexy may be called a retaining fee on the part of death.

GILLES DE MÉNAGE, *Epigram.*

6
A cold is both positive and negative; sometimes the Eyes have it and sometimes the Nose.

WILLIAM LYON PHELPS.

7
Some people have such a habit of being in hard lines that they can get rid of one disease only by catching another.

Reflections of a Bachelor.

8
I have a horror of the hospital, that blend of penitentiary and third-class hotel.

DR. HENRY E. SIGERIST, quoted by ERIC HODGINS in *Episode.*

9
We are so fond of each other, because our ailments are the same.

JONATHAN SWIFT, *Letters to Stella*, Feb. 1, 1710.

10
Did you ever have the measles, and if so, how many?

ARTEMUS WARD, *The Census.*

DISGRACE

11
The disgrace of the strong man is sacred . . . Would anyone care to see a great general having his tooth pulled out?

R. N. DICKINSON, *Keddie.*

12
Love and scandal are the best sweeteners of tea.

HENRY FIELDING, *Love in Several Masques.* Act iv, sc. 2.

13
The vain man makes a merit of misfortune, and triumphs in his disgrace.

WILLIAM HAZLITT, *Characteristics*, No. 113.

14
There is so much good in the worst of us,
And so much bad in the best of us,
That it hardly becomes any of us
To talk about the rest of us.

UNKNOWN.

15
The king [Frederick the Great] has sent me some of his dirty linen to wash. I will wash yours another time.

VOLTAIRE, to General Manstein, 1732.

16
For your bigots in honour are just like those in religion; they fear the eye of the world more than the eye of heaven; and think there is no virtue but railing at vice, and no sin, but giving scandal.

WILLIAM WYCHERLEY, *The Country Wife,* Act 4.

DISPOSITION

See also Feeling

17
Sourness spoils men as well as milk.

B. C. FORBES, *Epigrams.*

18
Gravity is the ballast of the soul, which keeps the mind steady.

THOMAS FULLER, *Holy and Profane States: Gravity.*

19
Nowadays, if men are more serious than women, it's because their clothes are darker.

ANDRÉ GIDE, *The Counterfeiters.* Pt. i, ch. 7.

20
Make two grins grow where there was only a grouch before.

ELBERT HUBBARD, *Pig-Pen Pete.*

21
Th' first thing some folks put on after they git up in th' mornin' is a fresh grouch.

FRANK MCKINNEY (KIN) HUBBARD, *Abe Martin's Primer.*

22
A good many women are good tempered simply because it saves the wrinkles coming too soon.

BARONESS VON HUTTEN, *The Halo.*

1
I shall be sending on to Philadelphia a grandson [Thomas Jefferson Randolph, sent for his education] of about fifteen years of age. . . . Without that bright fancy which captivates, I am in hopes he possesses sound judgment and much observation, and, what I value more than all things, good humor. For thus I estimate the qualities of the mind: 1, good humor; 2, integrity; 3, industry; 4, science. The preference of the first to the second quality may not at first be acquiesced in; but certainly we had all rather associate with a good-humored, light-principled man than with an ill-tempered rigorist in morality.
THOMAS JEFFERSON, to Dr. Benjamin Rush, Jan. 3, 1808.

2
He was as serious as an overdue mortgage . . .
ALEXANDER KING, Mine Enemy Grows Older.

3
The most gregarious handshaker likes to think that his noisy and effusive gestures are but a cover for deep philosophical misgivings which he bravely hides from everyone.
ALEXANDER KING, Rich Man, Poor Man, Freud and Fruit, ch. 23.

4
He slapped the backs of all men, he tickled the ribs of almost all the current ideas, and he kissed a surprising proportion of the women.
SINCLAIR LEWIS, Introduction to Henry Ward Beecher: An American Portrait, by PAXTON HIBBEN.

5
Well I reckon he ought to be. He's about the meanest man in town.
ABRAHAM LINCOLN, Reply to an inquiry as to whether a neighbor was a man of means. The Humorous Mr. Lincoln by KEITH W. JENNISON.

6
As savage as a bear with a sore head.
FREDERICK MARRYAT, The King's Own.

7
His bow-wow way.
LORD PEMBROKE, referring to Dr. Johnson. (BOSWELL's Life, 1775.)

8
A very little vinegar makes a poor salad of love.
Reflections of a Bachelor.

9
Some men are so mean they wouldn't give a drowning man a drink of water.
Reflections of a Bachelor.

10
As merry as the day is long.
WILLIAM SHAKESPEARE, Much Ado About Nothing. Act ii, sc. 1. Also King John. Act iv, sc. 1.

11
As headstrong as an allegory on the banks of the Nile.
RICHARD BRINSLEY SHERIDAN, The Rivals. Act iii, sc. 3.

12
You and I are exceptions to the laws of nature; you have risen by your gravity, and I have sunk by my levity.
SYDNEY SMITH.

DIVORCE

13
Alimony is like buying oats for a dead horse.
ARTHUR (BUGS) BAER, New York American.

14
You never realize how short a month is until you pay alimony.
JOHN BARRYMORE.

15
Both happy in their several states we find,
Those parted by consent, and those conjoined.
Consent, if mutual, saves the lawyer's fee.
Consent is law enough to set you free.
GEORGE FARQUHAR, The Beaux' Stratagem, Act 5.

16
I sincerely regret all my divorces because I don't like anything to be unsuccessful.
JOHN PAUL GETTY. (Time, Feb. 24, 1958.)

17
Divorce is the sacrament of adultery. (Le divorce est le sacrement de l'adultère.)
JEAN FRANÇOIS GUICHARD, Maximes.

18
Bigamy is one way of avoiding the painful publicity of divorce and the expense of alimony.
OLIVER HERFORD.

19
The divorcee is like a side dish that nobody remembers having ordered.
ALEXANDER KING, I Should Have Kissed Her More.

20
In Reno, there is always a bull market, never a bear market, for the stocks and bonds of happiness.
VIRGILIA PETERSON, A Matter of Life and Death.

21
The wife of a pal of ours is suing for divorce. She claims he was spending his nights sitting up with a chic friend.
More Playboy's Party Jokes (1965).

1

Christ saw a wedding once, the Scripture
    says,
And saw but one, 'twas thought, in all his
    days;
Whence some infer, whose conscience is too
    nice,
No pious Christian ought to marry twice.
    ALEXANDER POPE, *The Wife of Bath*, I, 9.

2

Grass widows are not so green as their
    names.
    Reflections of a Bachelor.

3

What a holler would ensue if people had to
pay the minister as much to marry them as
they have to pay a lawyer to get them a
divorce.
    CLAIRE TREVOR, actress. Quoted in *New
    York Journal-American*, Oct. 12, 1960.

DOCTORS

See also Medicine

4

I am dying with the help of too many physicians.
    ALEXANDER THE GREAT.

5

A minor operation is one that was performed
on the other fellow.
    RUSSELL PETTIS ASKUE.

6

All doctors know what great influence women
have on their reputation; thus we meet with
few doctors who do not study to please the
ladies.
    HONORÉ DE BALZAC, *The Physiology of
    Marriage.*

7

Before undergoing a surgical operation arrange your temporal affairs. You may live.
    AMBROSE BIERCE, *The Cynic's Word Book.*

8

The first physicians by debauch were made:
Excess began, and sloth sustains the trade.
    JOHN DRYDEN, *To John Driden*, Epis.
    xiv, 1. 73.

9

Most of my patients begin, Miss Coplestone,
By telling me exactly what is the matter
    with them,
And what I am to do about it.
    T. S. ELIOT, *The Cocktail Party*, Act 2.

10

One wrong step. On Wachusett, I sprained
my foot. It was slow to heal, and I went to
the doctors. Dr. Henry Bigelow said, "Splint
and absolute rest." Dr. Russell said, "Rest,
yes but a splint, no." Dr. Bartlett said,

"Neither splint nor rest, but go and walk."
Dr. Russell said, "Pour water on the foot,
but it must be warm." Dr. Jackson said,
"Stand in a trout brook all day."
    RALPH WALDO EMERSON, *Journal*, Aug.,
    1859.

11

The body is well but the purse is sick.
(Corpus valet sed aegrotat crumena.)
    GERARD DIDIER ERASMUS, *Adagia.*

12

Every physician, almost, hath his favorite
disease.
    HENRY FIELDING, *Tom Jones.* Bk. ii, ch. 9.

13

Physicians are the cobblers, rather the
botchers, of men's bodies; as one patches
our tattered clothes, so the other solders
our diseased flesh.
    JOHN FORD, *The Lover's Melancholy.* Act
    i, sc. 2.

14

Beware of the young doctor and the old
barber.
    BENJAMIN FRANKLIN, *Poor Richard*, 1733.

15

He's a fool that makes his doctor his heir.
    BENJAMIN FRANKLIN, *Poor Richard*, 1733.

16

God heals and the doctor takes the fee.
    BENJAMIN FRANKLIN, *Poor Richard*, 1774.

17

Commonly physicians, like beer, are best
when they are old; and lawyers, like bread,
when they are young and new.
    THOMAS FULLER, *The Holy State.* Bk. ii,
    ch. 1.

18

"Is there no hope," the sick man said,
The silent doctor shook his head,
And took his leave with signs of sorrow,
Despairing of his fee tomorrow.
    JOHN GAY, *The Sick Man and the Angel.*

19

Oh, it's easy to fool a woman. But you can't
fool a doctor.
    SIDNEY HOWARD, *They Knew What They
    Wanted.*

20

If a doctor cures, the sun sees it; if he kills,
the earth hides it.
    JAMES KELLY, *Scottish Proverbs*, p. 184.
    See also QUARLES in this section.

21

With a doctor, you can afford to appear
slightly hoydenish, just enough to make him
think he's saving you from something worse
than death.
    ALEXANDER KING, *Rich Man, Poor Man,
    Freud and Fruit*, ch. 4.

1
When I was young and full of life
I loved the local doctor's wife,
And ate an apple every day
To keep the doctor far away.
> THOMAS W. LAMONT, *My Boyhood in a Parsonage.*

2
When people's ill, they comes to I,
I physics, bleeds, and sweats 'em;
Sometimes they live, sometimes they die.
What's that to I? I lets 'em.
> DR. J. C. LETTSOM, *On Himself.*

3
Dialus, lately a doctor, is now an undertaker; what he does as an undertaker, he used to do as a doctor.
> MARTIAL, *Epigrams.* Bk. i, epig. 47.

4
Specialist—A man who knows more and more about less and less.
> DR. WILLIAM J. MAYO.

5
In my opinion physicians kill as many people as we generals.
> NAPOLEON BONAPARTE. (*The Mind of Napoleon,* ed. by J. CHRISTOPHER HEROLD.)

6
They were gabbing, at the Pen & Pencil, about a medical specialist in Greenwich who is so suspicious of late he gets the feeling someone's listening in on his stethoscope.
> HARRY NEIGHER, *Connecticut Sunday Herald,* Feb. 19, 1967.

7
God and the doctor we alike adore
But only when in danger, not before;
The danger o'er, both are alike requited,
God is forgotten, and the Doctor slighted.
> JOHN OWEN, *Epigrams.*

8
Cur'd yesterday of my disease,
I died last night of my physician.
> MATTHEW PRIOR, *The Remedy Worse Than the Disease.*

9
Physicians are of all men most happy; what good success they have the world proclaimeth and what faults they commit the earth covereth.
> FRANCIS QUARLES.

10
Personally, I have always felt that the best doctor in the world is the veterinarian. He can't ask his patients what is the matter—he's got to just know.
> WILL ROGERS, *Autobiography.*

11
Bernard Shaw recorded that he [William Wilde, father of Oscar Wilde and a noted eye specialist of his time] "operated on my father to correct a squint and overdid the correction so much that my father squinted the other way all the rest of his life."
> HESKETH PEARSON, *Lives of the Wits.*

12
The best doctors in the world are Doctor Diet, Doctor Quiet, and Doctor Merriman.
> JONATHAN SWIFT, *Polite Conversation,* II.

13
Apollo was held the God of physic, and sender of diseases. Both were originally the same trade, and still continue.
> JONATHAN SWIFT, *Thoughts on Various Subjects.*

14
Every man at thirty is either a fool or a physician.
> EMPEROR TIBERIUS, quoted in Plutarch, *De Canitae,* ii; Suetonius, *Tiberius,* sec. 68.

15
He has been a doctor a year now and has had two patients—no, three, I think—yes, it was three; I attended their funerals.
> MARK TWAIN.

16
Doctors pour drugs of which they know little, to cure diseases of which they know less, into human beings of whom they know nothing.
> VOLTAIRE.

DOG

17
The dogs bark but the caravan passes.
> Arab proverb. Quoted by GEORGE TABORI in *The Caravan Passes.*

18
There is no doubt that every healthy, normal boy (if there is such a thing in these days of Child Study) should own a dog at some time in his life, preferably between the ages of 45 and 50.
> ROBERT BENCHLEY. (*The New York Times Magazine,* May 14, 1967.)

19
Newfoundland dogs are good to save children from drowning, but you must have a pond of water handy and a child, or else there will be no profit in boarding a Newfoundland.
> JOSH BILLINGS. (*The New York Times Magazine,* May 14, 1967.)

20
A dog starved at his master's gate
Predicts the ruin of the state.
> WILLIAM BLAKE, *Auguries of Innocence.*

21
If dogs could talk, perhaps we'd find it just as hard to get along with them as we do with people.
> KAREL ČAPEK.

1

Dogs bark as they are bred, and fawn as they are fed.

A. B. CHEALES, *Proverbial Folk-Lore*, 140.

2

"Is there any point to which you would wish to draw my attention?" [asked Inspector Gregory.]

"To the curious instance of the dog in the night-time." [said Holmes.]

"The dog did nothing in the night-time." [retorted Gregory.]

"That was the curious incident," remarked Sherlock Holmes.

SIR ARTHUR CONAN DOYLE, the famous riposte of Sherlock Holmes in *Silver Blaze*.

3

Dogs laugh, but they laugh with their tails.

MAX EASTMAN, *Enjoyment of Laughter*.

4

A living dog is better than a dead lion.

Ecclesiastes, IX, 4.

5

A dog is loved by Old and Young
He wags his tail, and not his tongue.

Farmer's Almanac, 1966.

6

Who sleepeth with dogs shall rise with fleas.

JOHN FLORIO, *First Fruites*. Fo. 29 (1578). See also HERBERT and RAY in this section.

7

The Span of Life

The old dog barks backward without getting up,
I can remember when he was a pup.

ROBERT FROST.

8

The man recovered of the bite,
The dog it was that died.

OLIVER GOLDSMITH, *Elegy on the Death of a Mad Dog*.

9

Cut off his tail behind his ears.

HORACE GREELEY, when asked how to cure a dog of killing sheep.

10

He who lies with the dogs, riseth with fleas.

GEORGE HERBERT, *Jacula Prudentum*, No. 343.

11

To his dog, every man is Napoleon; hence the constant popularity of dogs.

ALDOUS HUXLEY.

12

When a dog barks at the moon, then it is religion; but when he barks at strangers, it is patriotism.

DAVID STARR JORDAN, quoted in CARDIFF, *What Great Men Think of Religion*.

13

The more I see of the representatives of people, the more I admire my dogs.

ALPHONSE DE LAMARTINE. See also MADAME DE STAËL in section headed "Man."

14

A good many people has police dogs, and brags about them and how nice they are for children etc. but personally I would just as leaf have my kids spend their week-end swimming in the State Shark Hatchery.

RING LARDNER, *Red Riding Hood*.

15

Killing the dog does not cure the bite.

ABRAHAM LINCOLN.

16

Ev'ry time I come to town,
The boys keep kickin' my dawg aroun'
Makes no difference if he is a houn'
They gotta quit kickin' my dawg aroun'.

WEBB M. OUNGST, *They Gotta Quit Kickin' My Dawg Aroun'*. Published in 1912, and the slogan of the campaign for Champ Clark that year.

17

I am his Highness' dog at Kew;
Pray tell me, Sir, whose dog are you?

On the collar of a dog presented by Alexander Pope to the Prince of Wales.

18

He that lies down with dogs must rise up with fleas.

JOHN RAY, *English Proverbs*.

19

The probable view of the fox terrier or dachshund which lies upon our hearthrug is that he is one of a pack, the other members of which are the human inhabitants of the house. From the dog's point of view his master is an elongated and abnormally cunning dog.

LOUISE ROBINSON, *The New York Times Magazine*, May 14, 1967.

20

No man who hates dogs or babies can be all bad.

LEO ROSTEN, *Remark* at a Friars Club testimonial banquet for W. C. Fields, Hollywood, 1938. This is often incorrectly attributed to Fields himself. In a letter to the compiler, Rosten said, "I *think* the remark was entirely spontaneous, and one of those happy *ad libs* God sends you. I didn't have the faintest inkling that I would be called upon to make any remarks, and those I made were uttered in an almost total daze."

21

In the streets of New York between 7 and 9 in the morning you will see the slow procession of dog and owner proceeding from street to tree to hydrant to trash basket. They are apartment dogs. They are taken out twice a day and, while it is a cliché, it is truly amazing how owner and dog resemble each other. They grow to walk alike, have the same set of head.

JOHN STEINBECK, *The New York Times Magazine,* May 14, 1967.

1
Pray steal me not, I'm Mrs. Dingley's,
Whose heart in this four-footed thing lies.
JONATHAN SWIFT, *Inscription* on the collar of Mrs. Dingley's lap-dog.

2
A dog, I will maintain, is a very tolerable judge of beauty, as appears from the fact that any liberally educated dog does, in a general way, prefer a woman to a man.
FRANCIS THOMPSON, quoted in *The New York Times Magazine,* May 14, 1967.

3
Let sleeping dogs lie, but why let lying dogs sleep?
SIR HERBERT BEERBOHM TREE, quoted by HESKETH PEARSON in *Lives of the Wits.*

4
A reasonable amount o' fleas is good fer a dog—keeps him from broodin' over *bein'* a dog.
EDWARD NOYES WESCOTT, *David Harum.*

5
Lots of people have a rug.
Very few have a pug.
E. B. WHITE, *Fashions in Dogs.*

6
An airdale, erect beside the chauffeur of a Rolls-Royce,
Often gives you the impression he's there from choice.
E. B. WHITE, *Fashions in Dogs.*

DOUBT

7
He is a dull man who is always sure, and a sure man who is always dull.
H. L. MENCKEN, *Prejudices.* Ser. ii, ch. 1.

8
Corvisart [Napoleon's personal physician] had many doubts and did not always answer my questions. Horeau was sure of everything and explained everything. The one was a learned physician, the other an ignoramus.
NAPOLEON BONAPARTE. (*The Mind of Napoleon,* ed. by J. CHRISTOPHER HEROLD.)

9
Four be the things I'd been better without:
Love, curiosity, freckles, and doubt.
DOROTHY PARKER, *Inventory.*

DREAMS

10
Don't tell me what you dream'd last night, for I've been reading Freud.
FRANKLIN P. ADAMS, *Don't Tell Me What You Dreamed Last Night.*

11
Once a gushing admirer approached Mr. Pullman and asked him if in his early days he ever dreamed of his vast company "with its palaces on wheels scurrying over the face of the earth." Replied Pullman gruffly, "No, I did not. If I had dreamed them, I'd be dreaming still."
CLEVELAND AMORY, *Who Killed Society?*

12
Once upon a time, I, Chuang Chou, dreamt I was a butterfly, fluttering hither and thither, to all intents and purposes a butterfly. I was conscious only of my happiness as a butterfly, unaware that I was Chou. Soon I awaked, and there I was, veritably myself again. Now I do not know whether I was then a man dreaming I was a butterfly, or whether I am now a butterfly, dreaming I am a man.
CHUANG-TZE, disciple of Lao-tze. Columbia University Forum, summer, 1966.

13
Dreaming permits each and every one of us to be quietly and safely insane every night of our lives.
DR. WILLIAM DEMENT. (*Newsweek,* Nov. 30, 1959.)

14
Castles in the air—they are so easy to take refuge in. And so easy to build, too.
HENRIK IBSEN, *The Master Builder,* Act 3.

15
He felt like a nightmare that had yet to be dreamt.
STANISLAW J. LEC, *Unkempt Thoughts,* tr. from the Polish by JACEK GALASKA.

16
I had a dream about reality. It was such a relief to wake up.
STANISLAW J. LEC, *Unkempt Thoughts,* tr. from the Polish by JACEK GALASKA.

DRESS

See also Fashion, Hat, Shoes

17
It is not only fine feathers that make fine birds.
AESOP, *The Jay and the Peacock.*

18
I have never seen a pair of slacks that had very much slack in them.
FRED ALLEN.

1
A pair of female slacks represents the triumph of moral courage over vanity.
  Cream of Wit, compiled by ROD ASKELL.

2
        The Big Baboon
The Big Baboon is found upon
The plains of Cariboo;
He goes about with nothing on
(A shocking thing to do.)
But if he dressed respectably
And let his whiskers grow
How like this Big Baboon would be
To Mister So and So!
  HILAIRE BELLOC.

3
It has the subtle flavor of an old pair of sox.
  WILLIAM COWPER BRANN, *The Iconoclast.*

4
God makes and the tailor shapes.
  JOHN BULWER, *Anthropomet.*

5
This same Miss McFlimsey of Madison Square,
The last time we met was in utter despair,
Because she had nothing whatever to wear!
  WILLIAM ALLEN BUTLER, *Nothing to Wear.*

6
He was old-fashioned enough to be a trifle shocked on beholding a grandmother with one leg in the grave and the other in knee-pants.
  IRWIN S. COBB, *If I Were a Woman.*

7
One of our unfavorite sights is a mini skirt on a maxi mum.
  HAROLD COFFIN, *San Francisco Examiner.*

8
Trousers, trousers, why do women—with the lovely shape which God has given them —want to wear trousers?
  LORD CURZON, quoted by LEONARD MOSLEY in *The Glorious Fault.*

9
Some women grow old gracefully—others wear stretch pants.
  ROGER DEVLIN, *Tulsa Tribune.*

10
Your age and my discretion.
  MARY GARDEN, to Chauncey Depew when he asked her what was holding up her daringly low-cut gown. (*Time,* Jan. 13, 1967.)

11
The more a feller really amounts to th' worse his clothes fit.
  FRANK McKINNEY (KIN) HUBBARD, *Abe Martin's Primer.*

12
Z stands fer Zanibar, in th' tropical zone

Where th' belles dress as scantily as our girls here at home.
  FRANK McKINNEY (KIN) HUBBARD, *Abe Martin's Primer.*

13
A man made by God and not by a tailor.
  ANDREW JACKSON, referring to Sam Houston. (McELROY, *Grover Cleveland.*)

14
Once at a banquet the Apostolic Nuncio to France [later Pope John XXIII] found himself seated next to an elegant lady in a dress cut overgenerously low in the neck. When the dessert was served, he invited her to take the apple which he held out to her. Since the lady showed surprise at this gesture, Msgr. Roncalli added:
"Do take it, Madame, please do. It was only after Eve ate the apple that she became aware of how little she had on!"
  From *Wit and Wisdom of Good Pope John,* compiled by HENRI FESQUET.

15
Tell him to go ahead with the blue suit. We can use that no matter what happens.
  LYNDON B. JOHNSON, *Reply* to a query from a tailor from whom Johnson had ordered two suits shortly before the latter was stricken with a severe heart attack in July, 1955. While Johnson was in a Washington hospital, the tailor called to inquire whether he should proceed with the order. (HENRY A. ZEIGER, *Lyndon B. Johnson: Man and President,* p. 59.)

16
The uniform 'e wore
Was nothin' much before,
An' rather less than 'arf o' that be'ind.
  RUDYARD KIPLING, *Gunga Din.*

17
A sensational event was changing from the brown suit to the gray the contents of his pockets. He was earnest about these objects. They were of eternal importance, like baseball or the Republican Party.
  SINCLAIR LEWIS, *Babbitt.*

18
I can not contribute to the end in view.
  ABRAHAM LINCOLN, *Reply* to a request to contribute to buying a Bloomington man a new pair of pants. From *The Humorous Mr. Lincoln* by KEITH W. JENNISON.

19
The miniskirt is a functional thing. It enables young ladies to run faster—and because of it they may have to.
  JOHN V. LINDSAY, quoting *Time.*

20
I have a hankering to go back to the Orient

and discard my necktie. Neckties strangle clear thinking.
> LIN YUTANG, *News summaries*, Feb. 22, 1954.

1
I got a coat lined with hamster. You couldn't do that kind of thing in America. All the Boy Scouts would go on strike.
> SUZY PARKER, actress. (*Newsweek*, Feb. 18, 1963.)

2
She wore a silk jersey dress that held fast going around curves.
> CHANNING POLLOCK.

3
To fifty chosen sylphs of special note,
We trust th' important charge, the petticoat.
Oft have we known that sev'n-fold fence to fail,
Tho' stiff with hoops, and arm'd with ribs of whale.
> ALEXANDER POPE, *The Rape of the Lock.*

4
No man is esteemed for gay garments, but by fools and women.
> SIR WALTER RALEIGH, in *Classic Quotations*, ed. by JAMES ELMES.

5
Whether a woman is too fat or too thin, she can dress to fool everybody about it except her husband.
> *Reflections of a Bachelor.*

6
A woman in rubber boots is as harmonious as a statue in petticoats.
> *Reflections of a Bachelor.*

7
The amount of money that some women think they can afford to put into stockings would enable them to wear underclothes that wouldn't fall to pieces.
> *Reflections of a Bachelor.*

8
The birds that fly the strongest don't have the finest plumage.
> *Reflections of a Bachelor.*

9
It's funny that women's clothes that are never seen are mostly made for show.
> *Reflections of a Bachelor.*

10
Every time a woman leaves off something she looks better, but every time a man leaves off something he looks worse.
> WILL ROGERS, *Autobiography.*

11
"You got to be awful rich to dress as bad as you do," he said.
> JOHN STEINBECK, *Travels with Charley*, pt. 4.

12
I say, beware of all enterprises that require new clothes, and not rather a new wearer of clothes.
> HENRY DAVID THOREAU, *Walden*, ch. 1.

13
She looked as if she had been poured into her clothes and had forgotten to say "when."
> P. G. WODEHOUSE.

DRINKING

See also Abstinence, Prohibition, Wine

14
Were I to prescribe a rule for drinking, it should be formed upon a saying quoted by Sir William Temple: the first glass for myself, the second for my friends, the third for good humor, and the fourth for mine enemies.
> JOSEPH ADDISON, *The Spectator*, No. 195.

15
If all be true that I do think,
There are five reasons we should drink:
Good wine—a friend—or being dry—
Or lest we should be by and by—
Or any other reason why.
> HENRY ALDRICH, *Five Reasons for Drinking.*

16
Philosophers tell you that many things can happen as a result of shock. A woman can have a miscarriage because of a sudden fright. If the shock is great enough a person can go out of his mind, and in some cases—Heaven forbid!—it has even been suggested that it was possible for a drunkard to become suddenly sober.
> SHOLOM ALEICHEM, *Two Dead Men.*

17
Drunkard.

The black earth drinks
and trees suck rain.
The seas drink brooks
and sun the sea
and moon the sun.
Why do you rage, friends,
when I want to drink?
> ANONYMOUS. See ANACREON, *Odes*, No. 21.

18
Although man is already ninety per cent water, the Prohibitionists are not yet satisfied.
> JOHN KENDRICK BANGS.

19
I don't know about being steeped in spiritual apathy, but I reckon they are steeped in beer and skittles.
> MAX BARING, *The Shattered Idol.*

1
It is said that Gen. Grant is a drunkard. I do not believe a word of it. But if it were so, I had rather have Gen. Grant a drunkard than Horatio Seymour sober.
HENRY WARD BEECHER, quoted by PAXTON HIBBEN, *Henry Ward Beecher: An American Portrait*. See also Lincoln on Grant in section headed WAR.

2
. . . much is said about the prudent use of spirits, but we might as well speak of the prudent use of the plague—of fire handed prudently round among powder—of poison taken prudently every day . . .
LYMAN BEECHER, *Six Sermons*.

3
Oh. Georgia booze is mighty fine booze,
The best yuh ever poured yuh,
But it eats the soles right offen yore shoes,
For Hell's broke loose in Georgia.
STEPHEN VINCENT BENÉT, *The Mountain Whippoorwill*.

4
He drinks beer, a habit no more bacchanalian than taking enemas.
MAXWELL BODENHEIM, quoted by BEN HECHT in *Letters from Bohemia*.

5
When the liquor's out, why clink the cannikin?
ROBERT BROWNING, *Bells and Pomegranates*.

6
The Admiral has won his victories on water, and so I shall drink to him with water; when the Admiral wins his victories on champagne, I shall drink to him with champagne.
WILLIAM JENNINGS BRYAN, quoted in *They Also Ran*, by IRVING STONE. The occasion for the remark was a reception for a Japanese admiral.

7
My! but these long times between the drinks! . . . If it wasn't for the long drinks between the times!
G. B. BURGIN, *Fanuela*.

8
For he by geometric scale
Could take the size of pots of ale.
SAMUEL BUTLER, *Hudibras*, pt. 1.

9
What's drinking?
A mere pause from thinking!
LORD BYRON, *The Deformed Transformed*, Act 3.

10
I am willing to taste any drink once.
JAMES BRANCH CABELL, *Jurgen*.

11
Always remember, that I have taken more out of alcohol than alcohol has taken out of me.
SIR WINSTON CHURCHILL, quoted in *By Quentin Reynolds*, 1963.

12
There is nothing wrong with sobriety in moderation.
JOHN CIARDI, *The Saturday Review*, Sept. 24, 1966.

13
Some men are like musical glasses: to produce their finest tones you must keep them wet.
SAMUEL TAYLOR COLERIDGE.

14
Leave a bottle on the chimley-piece, and don't ask me to take none, but let me put my lips to it when I am so disposed.
CHARLES DICKENS, *Martin Chuzzlewit*, ch. 19.

15
People can't tell us apart, we stagger so much alike.
FINLEY PETER DUNNE, *Cross-Examinations*.

16
Many a miss would not be a missus
If liquor did not add a spark to her kisses.
E.L.C., *Listen; Life*, Mar., 1933.

17
As I was drinkin' gin and water,
And me bein' the One Eyed Riley,
Who came in but the landlord's daughter
And she took my heart entirely.
T. S. ELIOT, *The Cocktail Party*. Act i, sc. 1.

18
There is this much to be said in favor of drinking, that it takes the drunkard first out of society, then out of the world.
RALPH WALDO EMERSON, *Journal*, 1866.

19
I never drink anything stronger than gin before breakfast.
W. C. FIELDS, quoted by ROBERT LEWIS TAYLOR in *W. C. Fields*.

20
I always keep a supply of stimulant handy in case I see a snake—which I also keep handy.
W. C. FIELDS, from *The Time of Laughter* by CAREY FORD.

21
Drink today, and drown all
        sorrow:
You shall perhaps not do it
        tomorrow.
JOHN FLETCHER, *The Bloody Brother*.

22
There are more old drunkards than old doctors.
BENJAMIN FRANKLIN.

1
. . . 'Twas honest old Noah first planted the Vine
And mended his Morals by drinking its Wine . . .
    BENJAMIN FRANKLIN, *A Drinking Song.*

2
The [Anti-Saloon] League succeeded where others had failed because it learned to jettison scruples. "Why," it asked in effect, "should the Devil throw all the sneaky curves?"
    J. C. FURNAS, *The Life and Times of the Late Demon Rum.*

3
No matter what anyone says, no matter what anyone thinks,
If you want to be happy the rest of your life,
    Don't marry a man if he drinks!
    Temperance song, quoted by J. C. FURNAS in *The Life and Times of the Late Demon Rum.*

4
In at least one Massachusetts township in the 1820's the list of "posted drunkards" was so long that a stranger mistook it for the local roster of eligible voters.
    J. C. FURNAS, *The Life and Times of the Late Demon Rum.*

5
What key will unlock the door to hell?
Whis-*key.*
    National Temperance Almanac, quoted by J. C. FURNAS in *The Life and Times of the Late Demon Rum.*

6
One of life's puzzling oddities is that every centenarian has either used alcohol most of his life or has let it strictly alone.
    ARNOLD H. GLASOW, quoted in *Reader's Digest,* July, 1966.

7
Let schoolmasters puzzle their brain,
With grammar, and nonsense, and learning;
Good liquor, I stoutly maintain,
Gives *genus* a better discerning.
    OLIVER GOLDSMITH, *She Stoops to Conquer,* Act i, sc. 2.

8
Call things by their right names. . . . Glass of brandy and water! That is the current, but not the appropriate, name: ask for a glass of liquid fire and distilled damnation.
    ROBERT HALL. (GREGORY, *Life of Hall.*)

9
Here's to good old Whiskey
So amber and clear,
'Tis not so sweet as woman's lips

But a damned sight more sincere.
    Toasts for All Occasions, ed. by LEWIS C. HENRY.

10
I saved shoe-leather by keeping one foot on the foot-rest.
    O. HENRY, *The Four Million: Memoirs of a Yellow Dog.*

11
Drink always rubbed him the right way.
    O. HENRY, *The Rubaiyat of a Scotch Highball.*

12
There are two times when you can never tell what is going to happen. One is when a man takes his first drink; and the other is when a woman takes her latest.
    O. HENRY, *The Gentle Grafter.*

13
In shallow waters heav'n doth show;
But who drinks on, to hell may go.
    GEORGE HERBERT, *Charms and Knots.*

14
The warm, champagny, old-particular, brandy-punchy feeling.
    OLIVER WENDELL HOLMES, *The Banker's Secret.*

15
If wine tells truth,—and so have said the wise,—
It makes me laugh to think how brandy lies!
    OLIVER WENDELL HOLMES, *The Banker's Secret.*

16
Alcoholic psychosis is nothin' more or less'n ole D.T.s in a dinner suit.
    FRANK MCKINNEY (KIN) HUBBARD, *Abe Martin's Broadcast.*

17
They who drink beer will think beer.
    WASHINGTON IRVING, *Sketch Book: Stratford.* Quoted.

18
No nation is drunken where wine is cheap; and none sober where the dearness of wine substitutes ardent spirits as the common beverage.
    THOMAS JEFFERSON, *Writings,* vol. xv, p. 179.

19
The man who called it "near beer" was a bad judge of distance.
    PHILANDER JOHNSON, *Shooting Stars.* Also attributed to Luke McLuke, columnist of the Cincinnati *Enquirer.*

20
There are some sluggish men who are improved by drinking, as there are fruits that are not good until they are rotten.
    SAMUEL JOHNSON, Boswell's *Life.*

1
Claret is the liquor for boys; port for men; but he who aspires to be a hero [smiling] must drink brandy.
SAMUEL JOHNSON, Boswell's *Life*, Apr. 7, 1779.

2
Half as sober as a judge.
CHARLES LAMB, *Popular Fallacies*.

3
The rapturous, wild and ineffable pleasure of drinking at somebody else's expense.
HENRY SAMBROOKE LEIGH, *Stanzas to an Intoxicated Fly*.

4
I don't drink. I don't like it. It makes me feel good.
OSCAR LEVANT. (*Time*, May 5, 1950.)

5
A man takes a drink, the drink takes another, and the drink takes the man.
SINCLAIR LEWIS, to Dorothy Thompson. (VINCENT SHEEAN, *Dorothy and Red*.) See also E. R. SILL in this section.

6
I reminded him of that old saying: "There are more old drunkards than old doctors."
J. P. McEVOY, *Charlie Would Have Loved This*. See also FRANKLIN in this section.

7
It was the first drop that kilt me; the last was harmless.
SEUMAS MACMANUS, *Heavy Hangs the Golden Grain*.

8
I drink only to make my friends seem interesting.
DON MARQUIS, quoted in *O Rare Don Marquis* by EDWARD ANTHONY. See also NATHAN in this section.

9
By the time a bartender knows what drink a man will have before he orders, there is little else about him worth knowing.
DON MARQUIS, quoted by EDWARD ANTHONY, *O Rare Don Marquis*.

10
One day, after fulfilling the first month of his pledge to stay on the water wagon forever and a day, [Don] Marquis was seen entering the taproom of the Players Club. Advancing to the bar he announced, "I've conquered my goddam will power. A double scotch, please."
EDWARD ANTHONY, *O Rare Don Marquis*.

11
Oh some are fond of Spanish wine and some are fond of French,
And some 'ill swallow tay and stuff fit only for a wench.
JOHN MASEFIELD, *Captain Stratton's Fancy*.

12
I've made it a rule never to drink by daylight and never to refuse a drink after dark.
H. L. MENCKEN.

13
I drank at every vine.
The last was like the first.
I came upon no wine
So wonderful as thirst.
EDNA ST. VINCENT MILLAY, *Feast*.

14
Candy is dandy
But liquor is quicker.
OGDEN NASH, *Reflection on Ice-Breaking*.

15
I drink to make other people interesting.
GEORGE JEAN NATHAN, *News summaries*, Apr. 8, 1958.

16
Kentucky tailor: What size shall I make your hip pockets, Colonel, pint or quart?
WILLIAM PATTEN, *Among the Humorists*.

17
Not drunk is he, who from the floor
Can rise alone, and still drink more;
But drunk is he, who prostrate lies,
Without the power to drink or rise.
THOMAS LOVE PEACOCK, *The Misfortunes of Elphin*.

18
There are two reasons for drinking: one is, when you are thirsty, to cure it; the other, when you are not thirsty, to prevent it.
THOMAS LOVE PEACOCK.

19
Let us wet our whistles. (Tengomenas faciamus.)
PETRONIUS, *Satyricon*, sec. 34.

20
A hot drink is as good as an overcoat. (Tamen calda potio vestiarius est.)
PETRONIUS, *Satyricon*, sec. 41.

21
Our Unabashed Dictionary defines *hangover* as the wrath of grapes.
More Playboy's Party Jokes (1965).

22
The passers-by whom Cato met when drunk, blushed when they discovered who it was, and (says Cicero) "You would have thought they had been found out by Cato, not Cato by them." What better tribute to Cato's prestige than to show him still awe-inspiring when drunk . . .
PLINY THE YOUNGER, *Letters*. III, 12. From *Roman Culture*, ed. by GARRY WILLS.

23
One swallow doesn't make a summer but too many swallows make a fall.
GEORGE D. PRENTICE.

1
Many a man keeps on drinking till he hasn't
a coat to either his back or his stomach.
GEORGE D. PRENTICE.

2
I do not drink more than a sponge. (Je ne
boy en plus qu'une esponge.)
FRANÇOIS RABELAIS, *Works*. Bk. i, ch. 5.

3
When I drink, I think; and when I think,
I drink.
FRANÇOIS RABELAIS.

4
To drink like a funnel.
JOHN RAY, *English Proverbs*.

5
Cider is the devil's kindling-wood.
HENRY A. REYNOLDS, M.D., quoted by
J. C. FURNAS in *The Life and Times of
the Late Demon Rum*.

6
There is a story from Trieste of a drunk
who mistook his wife's canary for a lemon
and put it in the squeezer.
NED ROREM, *Paris Diary*.

7
Men fished for women, and women for men,
in muddy water, and drink was the bait they
used.
WILLIAM ROTHSTEIN, *Men and Memories,
1872–1900*.

8
A torchlight procession marching down your
throat.
G. W. E. RUSSELL, *Collections and Recollections*, ch. 19. Description of whisky.

9
Drunkenness is nothing else than a voluntary
madness.
SENECA, *Epistles*, No. 83.

10
Lechery, sir, it [drink] provokes, and un-
provokes. It provokes the desire, but it takes
away from the performance.
WILLIAM SHAKESPEARE, *Macbeth*. Act ii,
sc. 3.

11
A man may surely be allowed to take a glass
at his own fireside.
RICHARD BRINSLEY SHERIDAN, when found
at the Piazza Coffee House, following
the fire at the nearby Drury Lane
Theater in which Sheridan had invested
heavily.

12
Anybody that can't get drunk by midnight
ain't trying.
TOOTS SHOR, quoted by JOEY ADAMS in
Cindy and I, ch. 11.

13
First the man takes a drink
Then the drink takes a drink
Then the drink takes a man!
EDWARD ROWLAND SILL, *An Adage from
the Orient*.

14
At the first cup man drinks wine; at the
second cup wine drinks wine; at the third
cup wine drinks man.
UNKNOWN, Old Japanese proverb.

15
Whiskey is a bad thing—especially bad
whiskey.
CHARLES HADDON SPURGEON, quoted as a
Highland saying.

16
When at length they rose to go to bed, it
struck each man as he followed his neighbour upstairs that the one before him walked
very crookedly.
ROBERT SMITH SURTEES, *Mr. Sponge's
Sporting Tour*, ch. 35.

17
Better belly be burst than good liquor be
lost.
JONATHAN SWIFT, *Polite Conversation*.

18
There are two things that will be believed of
any man whatsoever, and one of them is that
he has taken to drink.
BOOTH TARKINGTON, *Penrod*, ch. 10.

19
The seller of liquor is the only man who is
ashamed of his best customers.
HERBERT W. THOMPSON, quoted in *Speaker's Sourcebook*, ed. by ELEANOR DOAN.

20
After supper pap took the jug, and said he
had enough whiskey there for two drunks
and one delirium tremens.
MARK TWAIN, *Huckleberry Finn*.

21
Scotch whisky to a Scotchman is as innocent
as milk is to the rest of the human race.
MARK TWAIN.

22
Every man that had any respect for himself
would have got drunk, as was the custom of
the country on all occasions of public moment.
MARK TWAIN, *Innocents at Home*, ch. 10.

23
When I was two years of age she asked me
not to drink, and then I made a resolution
of total abstinence. That I have adhered to
it and enjoyed the beneficent effects of it
through all time, I owe to my grandmother.
I have never drunk a drop from that day
to this of any kind of water.
MARK TWAIN, *History Repeats Itself*.

1
An alcoholic is someone who drinks too much—and you don't like anyway.
UNKNOWN.

2
They drink with impunity, or anybody who invites them.
ARTEMUS WARD, *Moses the Sassy: Programme.*

3
Why don't you get out of that wet coat and into a dry Martini?
BILLY WILDER, *The Major and the Day.* The line was actually written by Wilder but spoken by Robert Benchley in the play and so attributed to him.

4
Drink makes men hungry, or it makes them lie.
GEORGE WILKINS, *The Miseries of Enforced Marriage,* Act 2.

5
While beer brings gladness, don't forget
That water only makes you wet.
HARRY LEON WILSON, *The Spenders.*

6
He that drinks well, sleeps well.
THOMAS WILSON, *Rule of Reason.*

7
Said Aristotle unto Plato,
"Have another sweet potato?"
Said Plato unto Aristotle,
"Thank you, I prefer the bottle."
OWEN WISTER, *Philosophy 4.* Quoted.

8
He was white and shaken, like a dry martini.
P. G. WODEHOUSE, *Cocktail Time.*

9
If for beauties you'd pass,
Take a lick of the glass,
'Twill mend your complexions, and when they are gone,
The best red we have is the red of the grape:
Then sisters, lay't on,

And damn a good shape.
WILLIAM WYCHERLEY, *The Country Wife,* Act 5.

10
My final warning to you is always pay for your own drinks . . . All the scandals in the world of politics have their cause in the despicable habit of swallowing free drinks.
Y. YAKIGAWA, President, Kyoto (Japan) University. To a graduating class. Quoted in news summaries, June 13, 1954.

DUTY

11
Duty is all very well when it doesn't upset other folks: when it does, it's better to forget it.
G. H. BURGIN, *Fanuela.*

12
The burning conviction that we have a holy duty toward others is often a way of attaching our drowning selves to a passing raft. What looks like giving a hand is often a holding on for dear life.
ERIC HOFFER, *The True Believer.*

13
As President, I have no eyes but constitutional eyes; I cannot see you.
ABRAHAM LINCOLN, *Reply* to South Carolina Commissioners.

14
Where it is a duty to worship the sun it is pretty sure to be a crime to examine the laws of heat.
JOHN MORLEY, *Miscellanies: Voltaire.*

15
I will do human nature the justice to say that we are all prone to make *other* people do their duty.
SYDNEY SMITH, from *Bon-Mots of Sydney Smith,* ed. by JERROLD.

16
It is just as hard to do your duty when men are sneering at you as when they are shooting at you.
WOODROW WILSON, *Speech,* 1914.

E

EARS

17
One eare it heard, at the other out it went.
GEOFFREY CHAUCER, *Troilus and Cryseyde.* Bk. iv, l. 1625.

18
Went in one ear and out at the other.
JOHN HEYWOOD, *Proverbs.* Pt. ii, ch. 9.

19
In one ear and out the other. (Nec quae dicentur superfluent aures.)
QUINTILIAN, *De Institutione Oratoria,* bk. 2.

20
This cuff was but to knock at your ear, and beseech listening.
WILLIAM SHAKESPEARE, *The Taming of the Shrew.* Act iv, sc. 1.

1
One should never listen. To listen is a sign of indifference to one's hearers.
OSCAR WILDE, *Saturday Review*, Nov. 17, 1894.

2
We have two ears and one mouth that we may listen the more and talk the less.
ZENO, quoted in DIOGENES LAERTIUS, *Zeno*, bk. 7.

EATING

See also Dieting

3
. . . I hadn't eaten anything that morning so I walked over to a restaurant and made short Schrafft of breakfast.
GOODMAN ACE, *The Fine Art of Hypochondria*.

4
You can't expect a person to dance before he's eaten.
SHOLOM ALEICHEM, *Tevye Wins a Fortune*.

5
Automat—The first restaurant to make it possible for the poor man to enjoy food served under glass.
FRED ALLEN.

6
Acorns were good until bread was found.
FRANCIS BACON, *Colours of Good and Evil*, sec. 6.

7
'Tis not *her* coldness, father
    That chills my labouring breast;
It's that confounded cucumber
    I've ate and can't digest.
R. H. BARHAM, *The Confession*.

8
Root, hog, or die. This is the refrain of each of the nine verses of the Bull-Whacker's epic.
J. H. BEADLE, *Life in Utah*.

9
The extra calories needed for one hour of mental effort would be completely met by the eating of one oyster cracker or one half of a salted peanut.
FRANCIS G. BENEDICT, *The Energy Requirement of Intense Mental Effort*.

10
Cannibal—A guy who goes into a restaurant and orders the waiter.
JACK BENNY.

11
Cabbage—A familiar kitchen-garden vegetable about as large and wise as a man's head.
AMBROSE BIERCE.

12
Thank you for inviting me to dine at your house, he wrote a well-to-do lady who fancied she was running a salon, but I prefer to dine in the Greek restaurant at Wabash Avenue and 12th Street where I will be limited to finding dead flies in my soup.
MAXWELL BODENHEIM, quoted by BEN HECHT in *Letters From Bohemia*.

13
Tell me what you eat and I'll tell you what you are.
ANTHELME BRILLAT-SAVARIN, *Physiologie du Goût*.

14
The discovery of a new dish does more for the happiness of man than the discovery of a star.
ANTHELME BRILLAT-SAVARIN, *Physiologie du Goût*.

15
Good dinners are so much rarer than good women: and far more piquant.
G. B. BURGIN, *Which Woman?*

16
That all-softening, over-powering knell,
The tocsin of the soul—the dinner bell.
LORD BYRON, *Don Juan*. Canto V, st. 49.

17
All human history attests
That happiness for man—the hungry sinner—
    Since Eve ate apples, much depends on dinner!
LORD BYRON, *Don Juan*. Canto XIII, st. 99.

18
Which may be a bone for you to pick on.
JAMES CALFHILL, *Answer to Martial*, 277 (1565).

19
Soup of the evening, beautiful soup!
LEWIS CARROLL (Charles Lutwidge Dodgson). *Alice's Adventures in Wonderland*, ch. 10, "Turtle Song," st. 1.

20
The Queen of Hearts, she made some tarts,
    All on a summer day;
The Knave of Hearts, he stole those tarts,
    And took them quite away!
LEWIS CARROLL, *Alice's Adventures in Wonderland*, ch. 11.

21
A loaf of bread, the Walrus said,
    Is what we chiefly need:
Pepper and vinegar besides
    Are very good indeed.
LEWIS CARROLL, *The Walrus and the Carpenter*. (*Through the Looking-Glass*, ch. 4.)

1
"O Looking-Glass creatures," quoth Alice,
"draw near!
Tis an honor to see me, a favor to hear;
'Tis a privilege high to have dinner and tea
Along with the Red Queen, the White Queen
and me!"
LEWIS CARROLL, *Through the Looking-Glass*, ch. 9.

2
All people are made alike.
They are made of bones, flesh and dinners.
Only the dinners are different.
GERTRUDE LOUISE CHENEY, *People*.

3
Jack Sprat will eat no fat,
And Jill doth love no lean,
Yet betwixt them both,
They lick the dishes clean.
JOHN CLARKE, *Paraemiologia*.

4
A man may as well expect to grow stronger
by always eating, as wiser by always reading.
JEREMY COLLIER. (*Classic Quotations*, ed.
by JAMES ELMES.)

5
Strange how one's thoughts turn to food
when there is nothing else to think of.
JOHN COLTON and CLEMENCE RANDOLPH,
Rain.

6
She is a wise woman—she knows that ten
minutes after consummation it won't matter
whether one has dined on truffled grouse or
hamburg steak—so why bother?
JOHN COLTON and CLEMENCE RANDOLPH,
Rain.

7
Some people have food but no appetite;
others have an appetite, but no food. I have
both. The Lord be praised.
Attributed to OLIVER CROMWELL, *Grace*.

8
For my part, now, I consider supper as a
turnpike through which one must pass, in
order to get to bed.
(Boswell's *Note:* I am not absolutely sure
but this was my own suggestion, though it
is truly in the character of Edwards.)
OLIVER EDWARDS, from Boswell's *Johnson*, Apr. 17, 1778.

9
Cheese—milk's leap toward immortality.
CLIFTON FADIMAN, *Any Number Can Play*.

10
The way to a man's heart is through his
stomach.
FANNY FERN, *Willis Parton*.

11
When I demanded of my friend what viands
he preferred

He quoth: "A large cold bottle, and a small
hot bird!"
EUGENE FIELD, *The Bottle and the Bird*,
st. 1.

12
We must eat to live, not live to eat.
HENRY FIELDING, *The Miser*, Act 3. See
also SOCRATES in this section.

13
Many dishes, many diseases. Many medicines, few cures.
BENJAMIN FRANKLIN, *Poor Richard*, 1734.

14
I saw few die of hunger; of eating, a hundred thousand.
BENJAMIN FRANKLIN, *Poor Richard*, 1735.

15
The bagel, an unsweetened doughnut with
rigor mortis.
BEATRICE and IRA FREEMAN. (*The New
York Times*, May 22, 1960.)

16
He that banquets every day never makes a
good meal.
THOMAS FULLER, *Gnomologia*, No. 2043.

17
It was a saying of his that no man was sure
of his supper until he had eaten it.
OLIVER GOLDSMITH, *She Stoops to Conquer*.

18
So much of this segregation bit is in the
mind. People aren't just segregating us.
They're segregating themselves too. Like,
how many of you have ever tested hominy
grits? Black-eyed peas? Chitlins? No law
against it. . . . You try it tomorrow, and I
guarantee you won't turn one shade darker.
. . . It doesn't make sense—prejudice
against foods. I mean, I've been eating
gefilte fish for years—even before I knew
Sammy Davis, Jr.
DICK GREGORY, *From the Back of the Bus*.

19
A gourmet is just a glutton with brains.
PHILLIP W. HABERMAN, JR., *Vogue*, Jan.
15, 1961.

20
Lazy foks' stummucks don't git tired.
JOEL CHANDLER HARRIS, *Plantation Proverbs*.

21
He who does not mind his belly will hardly
mind anything else.
SAMUEL JOHNSON, Boswell's *Life*, 1763.

22
". . . What do you think a citizen of Hamburg, Germany, for instance, would say if
you served him one of our hamburgers? You
know what he would say?"

"Yes," I said, "he'd say it lost a lot in translation."

ALEXANDER KING, *Mine Enemy Grows Older.*

1
A fair sepulchre in the grateful stomach of the judicious epicure.

CHARLES LAMB, *Essays of Elia: A Dissertation Upon Roast Pig.*

2
The waiter roars it through the hall, "We don't give bread with one fishball!"

GEORGE MARTIN LANE, *The Lay of the One Fishball.* The ballad was used as the basis of a mock Italian opera, *Il Pesceballo,* by PROFESSOR FRANCIS JAMES CHILD and JAMES RUSSELL LOWELL.

3
A man should have dinner with his friends, and the commanding general has no friends.

GENERAL CURTIS LEMAY, refusing a dinner invitation from fellow officers. (*Look,* Nov. 2, 1965.)

4
Your supper is like the Hidalgo's dinner, very little meat, and a great deal of table-cloth.

HENRY WADSWORTH LONGFELLOW, *The Spanish Student.* Act i, sc. 4.

5
Go to the meat-market of a Saturday night and see the crowds of live bipeds staring up at the long rows of dead quadrupeds. Does not that sight take a tooth out of the cannibal's jaw? Cannibals? who is not a cannibal?

HERMAN MELVILLE, *Moby Dick,* ch. 65.

6
Dr. Middleton misdoubted the future as well as the past of the man who did not, in becoming gravity, exult to dine. That man he deemed unfit for this world and the next.

GEORGE MEREDITH, *The Egoist,* ch. 20.

7
He may live without books,—what is knowledge but grieving?
He may live without hope,—what is hope but deceiving?
He may live without love,—what is passion but pining?
But where is the man that can live without dining?

OWEN MEREDITH, *Lucile.* Pt. i, canto 2.

8
I have never been able to sacrifice my appetite on the altar of appearance.

ROBERT MORLEY.

9
I never had a piece of toast
Particularly long and wide,
But fell upon the sanded floor,
And always on the buttered side.

JAMES PAYN, *Chambers's Journal,* Feb. 2, 1884.

10
The Receipts of cookery are swelled to a Volume, but a good Stomach excels them all.

WILLIAM PENN, *Fruits of Solitude.*

11
No man in the world has more courage than the man who can stop after eating one peanut.

CHANNING POLLOCK.

12
Middle-aged rabbits don't have a paunch, do have their own teeth and haven't lost their romantic appeal.

DR. AURELIA POTER, endocrinologist. On why "rabbit food" may be good for executives. (*The New York Times,* Sept. 22, 1956.)

13
A bellyful is a bellyful.

FRANÇOIS RABELAIS, *Works,* bk. 5.

14
Diner at Café Français to waiter: "Do you have a menu with English subtitles?"

Register and Tribune Syndicate. Caption for cartoon.

15
It takes much art
To choose à la carte
For less than they quote
For the table d'hôte.

JUSTIN RICHARDSON, *La Carte.*

16
I often wished that all my causes were apple-pie causes.

JOHN SCOTT, LORD ELDON, referring to a complaint made to him when he was resident fellow of University College. Some of the undergraduates complained that the cooks had sent to table an apple-pie which could not be eaten. Lord Eldon ordered the cook to bring the pie before him, but the cook informed him that the pie was eaten, whereupon Lord Eldon gave judgment for the defendant, saying to the complainants: "You complain that the pie could not be eaten, but the pie *has* been eaten, and therefore *could* be eaten."

17
Everything I eat has been proved by some doctor or other to be a deadly poison, and everything I don't eat has been proved to be indispensable for life. . . . But I go marching on.

BERNARD SHAW, quoted by STEPHEN WINSTEN in *Days with Bernard Shaw.*

1
They consumed the whole animal kingdom at each meal.
> BERNARD SHAW, quoted in *Days with Bernard Shaw* by STEPHEN WINSTEN. The reference is to Pepys and the enormous eating described in his diary.

2
Madam, I have been looking for a person who disliked gravy all my life; let us swear eternal friendship.
> SYDNEY SMITH. (LADY HOLLAND, *Memoir*.)

3
Other men live to eat, while I eat to live.
> SOCRATES, quoted by DIOGENES LAERTIUS.

4
Sweets to the sweet have made much business for dentists.
> UNKNOWN.

5
I can never resist a delicatessen. I hate eating alone, except things you can sort of cuddle up on the couch with . . . like potato salad.
> JOHN VAN DRUTEN, *The Voice of the Turtle*.

6
People who appreciate gastronomic miracles never worry about their insides while they eat—any more than a man worries about his heart while making love.
> LOUIS VAUDABLE, quoted in *Life*, Jan. 7, 1966.

7
The fate of a nation has often depended upon the good or bad digestion of a prime minister.
> VOLTAIRE.

8
The breast of veal had a sweater on it.
> BERT WHEELER, quoted in *Treadmill to Oblivion* by FRED ALLEN.

9
I have heard that people eat most heartily of another man's meat, that is, what they do not pay for.
> WILLIAM WYCHERLEY, *The Country Wife*, Act 5.

ECONOMICS

See also Money, Price, Prosperity, Taxes

10
Economist—A guy with a Phi Beta Kappa key on one end of his watch chain and no watch on the other end.
> ALBEN W. BARKLEY.

11
Inflation might be called prosperity with high blood pressure.
> ARNOLD H. GLASOW, quoted in *Reader's Digest*, Sept., 1966.

12
Guns will make us powerful; butter will only make us fat.
> HERMANN GOERING, *Radio broadcast*, summer of 1936.

13
If ignorance paid dividends most Americans could make a fortune out of what they don't know about economics.
> LUTHER HODGES, Secretary of Commerce. (*Wall Street Journal*, Mar. 14, 1962.)

14
I learned more about economics from one South Dakota dust storm than I did in all my years in college.
> HUBERT HUMPHREY, quoted in *This Is Humphrey* by MICHAEL AMRINE.

15
Under the new math, 2 and 2 sometimes make 22. Obviously the new math is well suited for interpreting the new economics.
> HARRY KARNS, *Newsday*.

16
Economist—A man who states the obvious in terms of the incomprehensible.
> ALFRED A. KNOPF.

17
It's called political economy because it has nothing to do with either politics or economy.
> STEPHEN LEACOCK.

18
If the cost of living continues to rise, dollars to doughnuts will soon be an even bet.
> The Man Next Door, *Better Homes and Gardens*, Sept., 1965.

19
Socialism is simply the degenerate capitalism of bankrupt capitalists. Its one genuine object is to get more money for its professors.
> H. L. MENCKEN, *Prejudices*, ser. 3.

20
Some idea of inflation comes from seeing a youngster get his first job at a salary you dreamed of as the culmination of your career.
> BILL VAUGHAN, *Kansas City Star*.

ECONOMY

21
If you must economize, dispense with some of the necessities. You can bear up under the realization that the gas company knows of your keeping the jets turned low, but if you go out of a café followed by the reproachful gaze of a waiter who regards you as stingy, you will feel small and unhappy for hours afterward and your work will suffer.
> GEORGE ADE, *Fables*.

1
He would skin a flint.
JOHN BERTHELSON (1754).

2
Wise men say
Keep somewhat till a rainy day.
NICHOLAS BRETON, *Works,* vol. i (1581).

3
The boys are in such a mood that if someone introduced the Ten Commandments,
they'd cut them down to eight.
SENATOR NORRIS COTTON, reference to
economy-minded Senate. (*Newsweek,*
Feb. 3, 1958.)

4
Thrifty! Man, she'd skin a flea for his hide.
JAMES DUFFY, *The Coiner,* sc. 7.

5
We're too poor to economize. Economy is a
luxury . . . Our only salvation is in ex-
travagance
F. SCOTT FITZGERALD, quoted by PAUL
SANN in *The Lawless Decade.*

6
He would have flayed a louse to save the
skin of it.
JOHN FLORIO, *Second Frutes,* 117.

7
We now have a President who tries to save
money by turning off lights in the White
House, even as he heads toward a staggering
addition to the national debt. "L.B.J." should
stand for Light Bulb Johnson.
BARRY M. GOLDWATER, *Speech* in Chicago,
Apr. 10, 1964.

8
Economy is going without something you do
want in case you should, some day, want
something you probably won't want.
ANTHONY HOPE, *The Dolly Dialogues,*
No. 12.

9
I have said that I believe in the tight fist and
the open mind—a tight fist with money and
an open mind to the needs of America.
LYNDON B. JOHNSON, *Speech,* Washington,
D.C., Dec. 4, 1964.

10
Thrift cannot be too highly commended.
Teach all those with whom you come in
contact to be saving. You never know when
you may need their savings to finance one
of your ventures.
DON MARQUIS, Parody of Dale Carnegie.
From *O Rare Don Marquis* by EDWARD
ANTHONY.

11
"I had" is a heartache, "I have" is a foun-
tain,
You're worth what you saved, not the mil-
lion you made.
JOHN BOYLE O'REILLY, *Rules of the Road.*

12
Take care of the pennies and the dollars will
be blown in by your heirs.
Puck.

13
The only time most people can save money
by not spending it is when they haven't got
any.
Reflections of a Bachelor.

14
Economy is the art of making the most of
life. The love of economy is the root of all
virtue.
BERNARD SHAW, *Maxims for Revolutionists.*

15
Let us all be happy and live within our
means, even if we have to borrow the money
to do it.
ARTEMUS WARD, *Natural History.*

EDUCATION

See also Knowledge, Teaching

16
The chief wonder of education is that it does
not ruin everybody concerned in it, teachers
and taught.
HENRY ADAMS, *The Education of Henry
Adams.*

17
Nothing in education is so astonishing as
the amount of ignorance it accumulates in
the form of inert facts.
HENRY ADAMS, *The Education of Henry
Adams.*

18
"Whom are you?" said he, for he had been
to night school.
GEORGE ADE, *Bang! Bang: The Steel Box.*

19
Education is a fine thing and doubtless de-
serves the high reputation it enjoys, particu-
larly with the uneducated.
GEORGE E. ALLEN, *Presidents Who Have
Known Me.*

20
One of the problems of child education
which is not generally included in books on
the subject is the Visiting Schoolmate. By
this is meant the little friend whom your
child brings home for the holidays. What is
to be done with him, the Law reading as
it does?
ROBERT BENCHLEY, *The Stranger Within
Our Gates.* (*The Benchley Roundup,* ed.
by NATHANIEL BENCHLEY.)

21
Part of the American myth is that people
who are handed the skin of a dead sheep at

graduating time think that it will keep their minds alive forever.
JOHN MASON BROWN.

1
There's a new tribunal now,
Higher than God's—the educated man's!
ROBERT BROWNING, *The Ring and the Book*, bk. 10.

2
What's a' your jargon o' your schools,
  Your Latin names for horns and stools;
If honest nature made you fools.
ROBERT BURNS, *First Epistle to J. Lapraik.*

3
A mere scholar, a mere ass.
ROBERT BURTON, *The Anatomy of Melancholy.*

4
He learned the arts of riding, fencing, gunnery,
And how to scale a fortress—or a nunnery.
LORD BYRON, *Don Juan.* Canto i, st. 38.

5
"Tut, tut, child!" said the Duchess. "Everything's got a moral, if you only can find it."
LEWIS CARROLL, *Alice's Adventures in Wonderland*, ch. 9.

6
"That's the reason they're called lessons," the Gryphon remarked; "because they lessen from day to day."
LEWIS CARROLL, *Alice's Adventures in Wonderland*, ch. 9.

7
"Reeling and Writhing, of course, to begin with," the Mock Turtle replied, "and the different branches of Arithmetic—Ambition, Distraction, Uglification, and Derision."
LEWIS CARROLL, *Alice's Adventures in Wonderland*, ch. 10.

8
Swallow all your learning in the morning, but digest it in company in the evenings.
LORD CHESTERFIELD, *Letters*, Feb. 22, 1748.

9
Perhaps it is inevitable that the colleges which had so long taught the dead languages as if they were buried should now teach the living ones as if they were dead.
FRANK MOORE COLBY, *Confessions of a Gallomaniac.*

10
Examinations are formidable even to the best prepared, for the greatest fool may ask more than the wisest man can answer.
C. C. COLTON, *Lacon: Reflections*, No. 322.

11
The ancient seat of pedantry [Oxford] where they manufacture prigs as fast as butchers in Chicago handle hogs.
R. B. CUNNINGHAME-GRAHAM, *With the North-West Wind.*

12
When eras die, their legacies
  Are left to strange police;
Professors in New England guard
  The glory that was Greece.
CLARENCE DAY, *Thoughts Without Words.*

13
The self-educated are marked by stubborn peculiarities.
ISAAC D'ISRAELI, *Literary Character*, ch. 6.

14
The average Ph. D. Thesis is nothing but a transference of bones from one graveyard to another.
J. FRANK DOBIE, *A Texan in England*, ch. 1.

15
Ye can lade a man up to th' university, but ye can't make him think.
FINLEY PETER DUNNE, *Mr. Carnegie's Gift.*

16
Would I send a boy to college? Well, at the age when a boy is fit to be in college I wouldn't have him around the house.
FINLEY PETER DUNNE, *Mr. Dooley Remembers.*

17
He was so learned that he could name a horse in nine languages; so ignorant that he bought a cow to ride on.
BENJAMIN FRANKLIN.

18
A learned blockhead is a greater blockhead than an ignorant one.
BENJAMIN FRANKLIN, *Poor Richard*, 1734.

19
Learning makes a good man better and an ill man worse.
THOMAS FULLER, *Gnomologia*, No. 3162.

20
. . . One of the greatest educational swindles ever perpetrated on American youth.
WHITNEY GRISWOLD, president, Yale University. On athletic scholarships. (*The New York Times*, Apr. 20, 1963.)

21
He might be a very clever man by nature, for all I know, but he laid so many books upon his head that his brains could not move.
ROBERT HALL. (GREGORY, *Life of Hall.*)

22
It is better to be able neither to read nor write than to be able to do nothing else.
WILLIAM HAZLITT, *On the Ignorance of the Learned.*

1

Anyway, a certain kind of good mind does resist education.

WILLIAM RANDOLPH HEARST, alluding to the fact that the Hearst sons were in and out of various schools. (CLEVELAND AMORY, *Who Killed Society?*)

2

A college degree does not lessen the length of your ears: it only conceals it.

ELBERT HUBBARD, *Epigrams.*

3

The college graduate is presented with a sheepskin to cover his intellectual nakedness.

ROBERT MAYNARD HUTCHINS.

4

I understand that Harvard University is making its diplomas larger or smaller. I have forgotten which. This is a step in the right direction.

ROBERT MAYNARD HUTCHINS, quoted by MAX EASTMAN, *Enjoyment of Laughter.*

5

Colleges are places where pebbles are polished and diamonds are dimmed.

ROBERT G. INGERSOLL, *Abraham Lincoln.*

6

There is less flogging in our great schools than formerly,—but then less is learned there; so that what the boys get at one end they lose at the other.

SAMUEL JOHNSON, Boswell's *Life,* Nov. 5, 1775.

7

Here's to the town of New Haven,
   The home of the Truth and the Light,
Where God talks to Jones in the very same
      tones
   That He uses with Hadley and Dwight.

F. S. JONES, *On the Democracy of Yale.*

8

It is the essence of our educational system that whatever part of the institution is not run by the inmates is reserved for the parents of the inmates.

MURRAY KEMPTON, *New York Post,* Mar. 31, 1960.

9

It might be said now that I have the best of both worlds: a Harvard education and a Yale degree.

JOHN F. KENNEDY, upon getting an honorary degree from Yale University, June, 1962.

10

I find that the three major administrative problems on a campus are sex for the students, athletics for the alumni, and parking for the faculty.

CLARK KERR, President of University of California. (*Time,* Nov. 17, 1958.)

11

The red-letter days, now become, to all intents and purposes, dead-letter days.

CHARLES LAMB, *Essays of Elia.* The reference is to Oxford during vacation.

12

I'm still waiting for some college to come up with a march protesting student ignorance.

PAUL LARMER, *Chicago Tribune.*

13

"We sit round with him," said another, "and he simply smokes and goes over our exercises with us." From this and other evidence I gather that what an Oxford tutor does is to get a little group of students together and smoke at them. Men who have been systematically smoked at for four years turn into ripe scholars. If anybody doubts this, let him go to Oxford and he can see the thing actually in operation. A well-smoked man speaks and writes English with a grace that can be acquired in no other way.

STEPHEN LEACOCK, *Laugh with Leacock: Oxford As I See It.*

14

If the lectures are called for they give them; if not, the professor's feelings are not hurt. He merely waits and rests his brain until in some later year the students call for his lectures. There are men at Oxford who have rested their brains this way for over thirty years: the accumulated brain power thus dammed up is said to be colossal.

STEPHEN LEACOCK, *Laugh with Leacock: Oxford As I See It.*

15

If I were founding a university—and I say it with all the seriousness of which I am capable—I would found first a smoking room; then when I had a little more money in hand I would found a dormitory; then, after that, or more probably with it, a decent reading room and a library. After that, if I still had money over that I couldn't use, I would hire a professor and get some textbooks.

STEPHEN LEACOCK, *My Discovery of England: Oxford As I See It.*

16

Very few people can stand the strain of being educated without getting superior over it.

STEPHEN LEACOCK, *Who Canonizes the Classics?*

17

When you educate a man you educate an individual; when you educate a woman you educate a whole family.

DR. CHARLES D. McIVER, *Address* at North Carolina College for Women.

1
A highbrow is a person educated beyond his intelligence.
BRANDER MATTHEWS, *Epigram.*

2
He is piping hot from the university. He smells of buttered loaves yet.
THOMAS MIDDLETON, *Your Five Gallants.*

3
Show me the man who has enjoyed his school days, and I will show you a bully and a bore.
ROBERT MORLEY.

4
You can't expect a boy to be depraved until he has been to a good school.
HECTOR HUGH MUNRO (SAKI). *A Baker's Dozen.*

5
So I wonder a woman, the mistress of hearts,
Should descend to aspire to be Master of arts;
A ministering angel in woman we see,
And an angel need covet no other degree.
CHARLES NEAVES, *O Why Should a Woman Not Get a Degree?*

6
The students would be much better off if they could take a stand against taking a stand.
DAVID RIESMAN, *Individualism Reconsidered.*

7
If you send somebody to teach somebody, be sure that the system you are teaching is better than the system they are practicing.
WILL ROGERS, *Autobiography.*

8
A man who has never gone to school may steal from a freight car; but if he has a university education, he may steal the whole railroad.
THEODORE ROOSEVELT.

9
Pency Prep is this school that's in Agerstown, Pennsylvania. You probably heard of it. You've probably seen the ads anyway. They advertise in about a thousand magazines, always showing some hot-shot guy on a horse jumping over a fence. Like as if all you ever did at Pency was play polo all the time. I never even once saw a horse anywhere *near* the place. And underneath the guy on the horse's picture, it always says: "Since 1888 we have been molding boys into splendid, clear-thinking young men." Strictly for the birds. They don't do any damn more *molding* at Pency than they do at any other school. And I didn't know anybody there that was splendid and clear-thinking and all.

Maybe two guys. If that many. And they probably *came* to Pency that way.
J. D. SALINGER, *The Catcher in the Rye.*

10
You ought not to educate a woman as if she were a man, or to educate her as if she were not.
GEORGE SHUSTER, president emeritus, Hunter College. *The Ground I Walked On.*

11
. . . there is, on the whole, nothing on earth intended for innocent people so horrible as a school. To begin with, it is a prison. But it is in some respects more cruel than a prison. In a prison, for instance, you are not forced to read books written by the warders and the governor. . . . In prison they may torture your body; but they do not torture your brains.
BERNARD SHAW, *Parents and Children.*

12
I'm not a teacher: only a fellow-traveller of whom you asked the way. I pointed ahead—ahead of myself as well as of you.
BERNARD SHAW, *Getting Married.*

13
A fool's brain digests philosophy into folly, science into superstition, and art into pedantry. Hence University education.
BERNARD SHAW, *Maxims for Revolutionists.*

14
A learned man is an idler who kills time with study.
BERNARD SHAW, *Maxims for Revolutionists.*

15
Self-education is fine when the pupil is a born educator.
JOHN A. SHEDD, *Salt from My Attic*, p. 28.

16
Some men are graduated from college *cum laude*, some are graduated *summa cum laude*, and some are graduated *mirabile dictu*.
WILLIAM HOWARD TAFT.

17
What does education often do? It makes a straight-cut ditch of a free, meandering brook.
HENRY D. THOREAU, *Journal*, Oct., 1850.

18
Waggish non-Yale men never seem to weary of calling "For God, for Country and for Yale," the outstanding single anti-climax in the English language.
Time. June 11, 1951.

19
An overeducated s.o.b.
HARRY S TRUMAN, referring to Senator J.

W. Fulbright. This description followed the release, Feb. 5, 1951, of a report by a Senate committee, headed by Fulbright, that charged irregularities in the functioning of the Reconstruction Finance Corporation, and connected them to "an influence ring with White House contacts."

1
Training is everything. The peach was once a bitter almond; cauliflower is nothing but cabbage with a college education.
MARK TWAIN, *Pudd'nhead Wilson's Calendar*.

2
In the first place God made idiots. This was for practice. Then He made school boards.
MARK TWAIN.

3
Education is something you get when your father sends you to college. But it isn't complete until you send your son there.
Washington Journal, quoted in *Chicago Tribune*.

4
Celibacy does not suit a university. It must mate itself with action.
ALFRED NORTH WHITEHEAD.

5
Learning preserves the errors of the past, as well as its wisdom. For this reason, dictionaries are public dangers, although they are necessities.
ALFRED NORTH WHITEHEAD.

6
Intelligence appears to be the thing that enables a man to get along without education. Education enables a man to get along without the use of his intelligence.
ALBERT EDWARD WIGGAM, *The New Decalogue of Science*.

7
Education is an admirable thing, but it is well to remember from time to time that nothing that is worth knowing can be taught.
OSCAR WILDE, *The Critic as Artist*.

8
They say that we are better educated than our parents' generation. What they mean is that we go to school longer. They are not the same thing.
DOUGLAS YATES, *Works*.

EGGS

9
Going as if he trod upon eggs.
ROBERT BURTON, *The Anatomy of Melancholy*.

10
All the goodness of a good egg cannot make up for the badness of a bad one.
CHARLES A. DANA, *The Making of a Newspaper Man*, maxim 5.

11
You can't unscramble eggs.
J. P. MORGAN, when rejecting a proposal to dissolve the trusts.

12
Hardboiled as a picnic egg.
EDWARD E. PARAMORE, *The Ballad of Yukon Jake*, st. 5.

13
Put all your eggs in one basket, and—watch the basket.
MARK TWAIN, *Pudd'nhead Wilson's Calendar*.

EGOTISM

See also Conceit, Vanity

14
Had I been present at the creation, I would have given some useful hints for the better ordering of the universe.
ALFONSO THE WISE.

15
One of my chief regrets during my years in the theater is that I couldn't sit in the audience and watch me.
JOHN BARRYMORE.

16
The myth of Narcissus haunts me. Did he fall in love with his own image in the pool? If he had never seen it before, how did he know it was himself?
BERNARD BERENSON, *Diaries*.

17
The most humane of the group was Alfred Adler, a stout cherub with a pursed mouth and a gay sparkle in his eyes. When he heard that an egocentric had fallen in love, he said: "Against whom?"
JIM BISHOP, *Some of My Very Best: Exponent of the Soul*.

18
That favorite subject, Myself.
JAMES BOSWELL, *Letter* to Temple, July 26, 1763.

19
He is a self-made man, and worships his creator.
JOHN BRIGHT, reference to Disraeli. See also COWPER in this section.

20
I had to deal in the peace conference with two men, one of whom thought he was Napoleon and the other Jesus Christ.
GEORGES CLEMENCEAU, referring to Lloyd George and Woodrow Wilson.

1
A self-made man? Yes—and worships his creator.
WILLIAM COWPER.

2
Talk to a man about himself and he will listen for hours.
BENJAMIN DISRAELI.

3
He was a cock who thought the sun had risen to hear him crow.
GEORGE ELIOT, *Adam Bede*, ch. 23. See also ROSTAND in this section.

4
Gertrude [Stein] has always done justice to Gertrude, but this book sets a high-water mark in the delicate art of self-appreciation.
CLIFTON FADIMAN, *Review* of *The Autobiography of Alice B. Toklas.*

5
He that falls in love with himself will have no rivals.
BENJAMIN FRANKLIN.

6
I: The most popular letter in the alphabet.
OLIVER HERFORD, *Cupid's Cyclopedia.*

7
When a man tries himself, the verdict is usually in his favor.
E. W. HOWE.

8
You haf too much Ego in your Cosmos.
RUDYARD KIPLING, *Life's Handicap: Bertran and Bimi.*

9
One prefers to speak evil of himself rather than not speak of himself at all. (On aime mieux dire du mal de soi-meme de n'en point parler.)
FRANÇOIS, DUC DE LA ROCHEFOUCAULD, *Maximes*, No. 138.

10
We know well enough that we should not talk of our wives, but we seem not to know that we should talk still less of ourselves. (On sait assez qu'il ne faut guere parler de sa femme, mais on ne sait pas assez qu'on devrait encore moins parler de soi.)
FRANÇOIS, DUC DE LA ROCHEFOUCAULD, *Maximes*. No. 364.

11
Egotism is the anesthetic that dulls the pain of stupidity.
FRANK LEAHY, former Notre Dame football coach. (*Look*, Jan. 10, 1955.)

12
Of all speculations the market holds forth,
   The best that I know, for the lover of pelf,
Is to buy Marcus up at the price he is worth,

And sell him at that which he sets on himself.
THOMAS MOORE, *A Speculation.*

13
Edith was a little country bounded on the north, south, east and west by Edith.
MARTHA OSTENSO.

14
I recoil dazzled at beholding myself all rosy red, at having, I myself, caused the sun to rise. (Je recule Ebloui de me voir moi meme tout vermeil Et d'avoir, moi le coq, fait elever le soleil.)
EDMOND ROSTAND, *Chanticler*. Act ii, sc. 3.

15
The egoist does not tolerate egoism.
JOSEPH ROUX, *Meditations of a Parish Priest.*

16
When a man is wrapped up in himself he makes a pretty small package.
JOHN RUSKIN.

17
He that is giddy thinks the world turns round.
WILLIAM SHAKESPEARE, *The Taming of Shrew*. Act v, sc. 2.

18
Oscar Wilde: When you and I are together, we never talk about anything except ourselves.
Whistler: No, no, Oscar, you forget—when you and I are together, we never talk about anything except me.
JAMES MCNEILL WHISTLER, *The Gentle Art of Making Enemies.*

19
To love oneself is the beginning of a lifelong romance.
OSCAR WILDE, *An Ideal Husband*, Act 3.

END

20
That's all there is: There ain't any more.
ETHEL BARRYMORE, *Curtain line* to *Sunday.*

21
This is the short and the long of it.
WILLIAM SHAKESPEARE, *The Merry Wives of Windsor*. Act ii, sc. 2.

22
Anybody can start something.
JOHN A. SHEDD, *Salt from My Attic.*

23
It's a long stretch between that first birthday speech and this one. That was my cradle song, and this is my swan song, I suppose. I am used to swan songs; I have sung them several times.
MARK TWAIN, *Essays, Seventieth Birthday.*

ENEMY

1
Never soar aloft on an enemy's pinions.
AESOP, *The Tortoise and the Birds.*

2
Better make a weak man your enemy than your friend.
JOSH BILLINGS (HENRY WHEELER SHAW). *Affurisms.*

3
I wish my deadly foe no worse
Than want of friends, and empty purse.
NICHOLAS BRETON, *A Farewell to Town.*

4
Love your enemy—it will drive him nuts.
Speaker's Sourcebook. Ed. by ELEANOR DOAN.

5
H. L. Mencken's war aims, according to the handful of observers who deigned to notice his conflict, were the overthrow of American Democracy, the Christian religion, and the YMCA. He was also credited with trying to wipe out poets and luncheon orators.
BEN HECHT, *Letters from Bohemia.*

6
You know, if I were on a desert island with Madame Nhu, I would quickly make friends with the natives.
OSCAR LEVANT, *Memoirs of an Amnesiac.*

7
I never hold a grudge, especially when I'm wrong.
OSCAR LEVANT, *Memoirs of an Amnesiac.*

8
Do not speak ill of an enemy, but think it.
(De inimico non loquaris male, sed cogites.)
PUBLILIUS SYRUS, *Sententiae,* No. 147.

9
Take heed of enemies reconciled, and of meat twice boiled.
JOHN RAY, *Spanish Proverbs.*

10
'Twas one of my most intimate enemies.
DANTE GABRIEL ROSSETTI, *Fragment.*

11
I do desire we may be better strangers.
WILLIAM SHAKESPEARE, *As You Like It.* Act III, sc. 2.

12
It's a sure sign somebody has been thinking about you when you find a tack in your chair.
UNKNOWN, quoted by Max Eastman in *Enjoyment of Laughter.*

13
I'm lonesome. They are all dying. I have hardly a warm personal enemy left.
J. A. McNEILL WHISTLER, quoted by D. C. SEITZ in *Whistler Stories.*

ENGLAND AND THE ENGLISH

14
I think the British have the distinction above all other nations of being able to put new wine into old bottles without bursting them.
CLEMENT ATTLEE, Prime Minister, on rebuilt House of Commons. (*Time,* Nov. 6, 1950.)

15
Britons, who will never be slaves, must have that cup of tea; they will turn vicious for lack of it; and the whole world is now tobacco-stained.
JACQUES BARZUN, *God's Country and Mine.*

16
We will never have Fascism in England. No Englishman will dress up, not even for a revolution.
WILLIAM BOLITHO, *Conversation* with Walter Duranty, George Seldes, and others, Paris, 1930.

17
"London!" It has the sound of distant thunder.
JAMES BONE, *The London Perambulator.*

18
I always think it such a pity that the gods didn't bestow just that one more favour on Englishwomen . . . the knack of putting on their clothes.
SHELLAND BRADLEY, *An American Girl in India.*

19
England is a paradise for women and hell for horses; Italy a paradise for horses, hell for women, as the proverb goes.
ROBERT BURTON, *The Anatomy of Melancholy.* See also FLORIO in this section.

20
The world is a bundle of hay,
Mankind are the asses who pull;
Each tugs it a different way,—
And the greatest of all is John Bull!
LORD BYRON, *Epigram.*

21
There are in England sixty different religions and only one gravy, melted butter.
MARQUIS CARACCIOLI, Neapolitan Ambassador.

22
Of all the nations in the world, at present, the English are the stupidest in speech, the wisest in action.
THOMAS CARLYLE, *Past and Present.* Bk. iii, ch. 5.

1
England has been divided into three classes: knaves, fools, and revolutionists.
G. K. CHESTERTON, *Victorian Age in English Literature.*

2
When I warned them [the French] that Britain would fight on alone whatever they did, their generals told their Prime Minister and his divided cabinet, "In three weeks England will have her neck wrung like a chicken." Some chicken! Some neck!
SIR WINSTON S. CHURCHILL, *Speech* to Canadian Parliament, Dec. 30, 1941.

3
But English gratitude is always such,
To hate the hand which doth oblige too much.
DANIEL DEFOE, *The True-Born Englishman*, pt. 2.

4
O! What a snug little island!
A right little, tight little island.
THOMAS JOHN DIBDIN, *The Snug Little Island.*

5
London is a roost for every bird.
BENJAMIN DISRAELI, *Lothair.*

6
When the British nation is at once grateful and enthusiastic, they always call you "my lord."
BENJAMIN DISRAELI, *Lothair.*

7
The well-bred Englishman is about as agreeable a fellow as you can find anywhere— especially, as I have noted, if he is an Irishman or a Scotchman.
FINLEY PETER DUNNE, *Mr. Dooley Remembers.*

8
The English are not an inventive people; they don't eat enough pie.
THOMAS A. EDISON, from *Golden Book,* Apr., 1931.

9
England is the paradise of women, the purgatory of men, and the hell of horses.
JOHN FLORIO, *Second Fruites.* See also ROBERT BURTON in this section.

10
No one can be as calculatedly rude as the British, which amazes Americans, who do not understand studied insult and can only offer abuse as a substitute.
PAUL GALLICO. (*The New York Times,* Jan. 14, 1962.)

11
Not Angles, but Angels! (Non Angli, sed Angeli!)
Attributed to GREGORY THE GREAT, on seeing some handsome British captives offered for sale at Rome.

12
An Englishman is a man who lives on an island in the North Sea governed by Scotsmen.
PHILIP GUEDALLA, *Supers and Superman.*

13
Living in England is curing me with almost alarming rapidity of being shy. Even with the Olympians, there is no need to worry about appearing stupid, because it takes a great deal to produce ennui in an Englishman and if you do, he only takes it as convincing proof that you are well-bred.
MARGARET HALSEY, *With Malice Toward Some.*

14
Toward people with whom they disagree, the English gentry, or at any rate that small cross section of them I have seen, are tranquilly good-natured. It is not *comme il faut* to establish the supremacy of an idea by smashing in the faces of all the people who try to contradict it. The English never smash in a face. They merely refrain from asking it to dinner.
MARGARET HALSEY, *With Malice Toward Some.*

15
The attitude of the English . . . toward English history, reminds one a good deal of the attitude of a Hollywood director toward love.
MARGARET HALSEY, *With Malice Toward Some.*

16
We are much invited out and we take our meals everywhere—in other hostels, in restaurants and in private houses. I was well warned about English food, so it did not surprise me, but I do wonder, sometimes, how they ever manage to prise it up long enough to get a plate under it.
MARGARET HALSEY, *With Malice Toward Some.*

17
Back from dinner, where I sat next to a young Canadian architect who lives and works in the next county. We got along well. I asked him, in comparing notes on English and American civilization, whether there is much graft in this country [England]. He smiled. "They don't call it graft," he said. "It's all done with so much Old World charm that it's quite painless. The Rape of the Sabine Women set to a minuet."
MARGARET HALSEY, *With Malice Toward Some.*

18
Englishwomen's shoes look as if they had

been made by someone who had often heard shoes described, but had never seen any . . .
> MARGARET HALSEY, *With Malice Toward Some.*

1
Living in England, provincial England, must be like being married to a stupid but exquisitely beautiful wife.
> MARGARET HALSEY, *With Malice Toward Some.*

2
England is my wife—America, my mistress. It is very good sometimes to get away from one's wife.
> SIR CEDRIC HARDWICKE. (Associated Press obituary of Sir Cedric, datelined New York City, Aug. 6, 1964.)

3
The English (it must be owned) are rather a foul-mouthed nation.
> WILLIAM HAZLITT, *Table Talk: XXII, On Criticism.*

4
An Englishman is never so natural as when he's holding his tongue.
> HENRY JAMES, *The Portrait of a Lady,* ch. 10.

5
The best thing I know between France and England is the sea.
> DOUGLAS JERROLD, *The Anglo-French Alliance.*

6
As thorough an Englishman as ever coveted his neighbor's goods.
> CHARLES KINGSLEY, *The Water Babies,* ch. 1.

7
Our England is a garden, and such gardens are not made
By singing: "Oh how beautiful!" and sitting in the shade.
> RUDYARD KIPLING, *The Glory of the Garden.*

8
We had a kettle: we let it leak:
Our not repairing it made it worse.
We haven't had any tea for a week . . .
The bottom is out of the universe!
> RUDYARD KIPLING, *Natural Theology.*

9
. . . nearly all people in England are of the superior sort, superiority being an English ailment.
> D. H. LAWRENCE, *The Last Laugh.*

10
In the United States they need a whole constitution of thousands and thousands of words, and they get tangled up in the clauses. The British constitution is just "the thing." Of course, there are no rules to guide private morals. I mean to say one learnt one's catechism when one was young, but as a matter of fact it is rather the thing to forget it.
> STEPHEN LEACOCK, *L'Envoi: A Salutation Across the Sea.*

11
You ask, what was that song they sang at the opening—that's *God Save the King.* You thought it was *Sweet Land of Liberty?* So it is. You Yankees took it from us and put new words to it. As a matter of fact we took it from the Ancient Britons—they had it, *England-may-go-to-Hell*—and the English liked it so much they took it over and made it *God Save the King.*
> STEPHEN LEACOCK, *A Welcome to a Visiting American.*

12
In order to appreciate England one has to have a certain contempt for logic.
> LIN YUTANG, *With Love and Irony.*

13
The British Commonwealth is actually a league of nations, with the difference that it is a league of nations which really works. The English people are probably unaware that it is a league of nations, for they have the knack of doing a thing without knowing what it is.
> LIN YUTANG, *With Love and Irony.*

14
England—An island entirely surrounded by hot water.
> London *Opinion.*

15
Three things to beware of: The hoof of a horse, the horn of a bull, and the smile of an Englishman.
> SEUMAS MACMANUS, *Heavy Hangs the Golden Grain.*

16
In England, the Garden of Beauty is kept By a dragon of prudery placed within call.
> THOMAS MOORE, *We May Roam Through This World.*

17
The people of England are never so happy as when you tell them they are ruined.
> ARTHUR MURPHY, *The Upholsterer.* Act ii, sc. 1.

18
Wherever wood can swim there I am sure to find this flag of England.
> NAPOLEON BONAPARTE, at Rochefort, July, 1815.

19
The English are mentioned in the Bible: Blessed are the meek, for they shall inherit the earth.
> MARK TWAIN, *Pudd'nhead Wilson's New Calendar.*

1
There is no good shutting your eyes and saying "Britain is Best" three times a day after meals, and expect it to be so.
    PRINCE PHILIP, *Remark* at the opening of the Design Center for British Industries, Apr. 1956.

2
An English noble has one son. All the rest are bastards.
    JOHN RANDOLPH of Roanoke. From *The Wit and Wisdom of Congress,* ed. by EDWARD BOYKIN.

3
Englishmen live slow and move fast; we live fast and move slow. Englishmen are the only race of people that never travel for just fun.
    WILL ROGERS, *Autobiography.*

4
Have you ever been to a country where I have the largest following? England.
    BERNARD SHAW, *Don Juan in Hell.* The Devil speaking.

5
Englishman—A creature who thinks he is being virtuous when he is only being uncomfortable.
    BERNARD SHAW.

6
. . . Englishmen will never be slaves: they are free to do whatever the Government and public opinion allow them to do.
    BERNARD SHAW, *Man and Superman,* Act 3.

7
. . . it seems impossible to root out of an Englishman's mind the notion that vice is delightful, and that abstention from it is a privation.
    BERNARD SHAW, *Mrs. Warren's Profession:* preface.

8
Ten years of cheap reading have changed the English from the most stolid nation in Europe to the most theatrical and hysterical.
    BERNARD SHAW, *Three Plays for Puritans:* preface.

9
How can what an Englishman believes be heresy? It is a contradiction in terms.
    BERNARD SHAW, *St. Joan,* sc. 4.

10
No Englishman is ever fairly beaten.
    BERNARD SHAW, *Saint Joan,* sc. 4.

11
We don't bother much about dress and manners in England, because, as a nation, we don't dress well and we've no manners.
    BERNARD SHAW, *You Never Can Tell,* Act 1.

12
I am a snob. Why not? The whole strength of England lies in the fact that the enormous majority of the English people are snobs.
    BERNARD SHAW, *Getting Married.*

13
The world is as full of fools as a tree is full of leaves. Well, the Englishman does what the caterpillar does. He instinctively makes himself look like a fool, and eats up all the real fools at his ease while his enemies let him alone and laugh at him for being a fool like the rest.
    BERNARD SHAW, *John Bull's Other Island,* Act 1.

14
An Englishman has some sense about working: he never does more than he can help— and hard enough to get him to do that without scamping it; but an Irishman will work as if he'd die the moment he stopped.
    BERNARD SHAW, *John Bull's Other Island,* Act 3.

15
There is nothing in this world so exquisitely comic as an Englishman's seriousness.
    BERNARD SHAW, *Dramatic Opinions.*

16
The English do not know what to think until they are coached, laboriously and insistently for years, in the proper and becoming opinion.
    BERNARD SHAW, *Dramatic Opinions.*

17
. . . If the British can survive their meals, they can survive anything.
    BERNARD SHAW, quoted in *Days with Bernard Shaw* by STEPHEN WINSTEN.

18
When a man is a fool, in England we only trust him with immortal concerns of human beings.
    SYDNEY SMITH.

19
What a pity it is that in England we have no amusements but vice and religion.
    SYDNEY SMITH, from *Bon-Mots of Sydney Smith,* ed. by JERROLD.

20
England is not governed by logic, but by acts of Parliament.
    UNKNOWN.

21
In this country they put an admiral to death from time to time to encourage the others. (Dans ce pays-ci il est bon de tuer de temps en temps un amiral pour encourager les autres.)
    VOLTAIRE, *Henriade:* preface. *Candide,* ch. 23. Referring to the execution of Admiral Byng by the English for failing to relieve Minorca, besieged by the French, in 1756.

1
Froth at the top, dregs at bottom, but the middle excellent.
VOLTAIRE.

2
The English never abolish anything. They put it in cold storage.
ALBERT NORTH WHITEHEAD, *Dialogues of Alfred North Whitehead.*

3
Those things which the English public never forgives—youth, power, and enthusiasm.
OSCAR WILDE, *The English Renaissance.*

4
The English public always feels perfectly at its ease when a mediocrity is talking to it.
OSCAR WILDE, *The Critic as Artist.*

5
Those comfortably padded lunatic asylums, which are known, euphemistically, as the stately homes of England.
VIRGINIA WOOLF, *The Common Reader.*

6
The English have an extraordinary ability for flying into a great calm.
ALEXANDER WOOLLCOTT.

ENTHUSIASM

See also Zeal

7
In things pertaining to enthusiasm, no man is sane who does not know how to be insane on proper occasions.
HENRY WARD BEECHER, *Proverbs from Plymouth Pulpit.*

8
Latins are tenderly enthusiastic. In Brazil they throw flowers at you. In Argentina they throw themselves.
MARLENE DIETRICH, quoted in *Newsweek,* Aug. 24, 1959.

9
One of my old formulas is to be an enthusiast in the front part of your heart and ironical in the back.
OLIVER WENDELL HOLMES, JR. (*The Holmes-Einstein Letters,* ed. by JAMES BISHOP PEABODY.)

10
We act as though comfort and luxury were the chief requirements of life, when all that we need to make us really happy is something to be enthusiastic about.
CHARLES KINGSLEY, quoted in *Reader's Digest,* July, 1966.

11
Opposition may inflame the enthusiast, but it never converts him.
JOHANN VON SCHILLER, *Love and Intrigue.* Act iii, sc. 1.

ENVY

See also Jealousy

12
The dullard's envy of brilliant men is always assuaged by the suspicion that they will come to a bad end.
MAX BEERBOHM, *Zuleika Dobson,* ch. 4.

13
The apples on the other side of the wall are the sweetest.
W. G. BENHAM, *Proverbs.*

14
Better to be envied than pitied.
HERODOTUS, *Thalia.* Bk. iii, sec. 52.

15
The fathers have eaten sour grapes, and the children's teeth are set on edge.
Jeremiah, XXXI, 29.

16
Diophon was being crucified,
but when he saw another near him on a higher cross,
he died of envy.
LUCILIUS (Loukillios). *On the Hard Luck of Diophon,* tr. by WILLIAM BARNSTONE.

17
He's no-way covetous, but he'd fain have what is yours.
SEUMAS MACMANUS, *Heavy Hangs the Golden Grain.*

18
It is the practice of the multitude to bark at eminent men, as little dogs do at strangers.
SENECA, *Of a Happy Life.*

19
Anyone can sympathize with the sufferings of a friend, but it requires a very fine nature to sympathize with a friend's success.
OSCAR WILDE.

EPIGRAM

20
The diamond's virtues well might grace
    The epigram, and both excel
In brilliancy in smallest space,
    And power to cut as well.
GEORGE BIRDSEYE, *The Epigram.*

21
Many men can make an epic who cannot make an epigram.
G. K. CHESTERTON, *A Handful of Authors.*

22
What is an epigram? A dwarfish whole,
Its body brevity, and wit its soul.
    Attributed to SAMUEL TAYLOR COLERIDGE, but not in his works.

23
An epigram is only a wisecrack that's played Carnegie Hall.
OSCAR LEVANT.

1

But, with the imprecise arrow
　　The intended acorn fairly struck—
Such is epigram, requiring
　　Wit, occasion, and good luck!
CHRISTOPHER MORLEY, *The Epigram.*

EPITAPHS

2

Here lie I, Master Elginbrod.
Have mercy on my soul, O God,
As I would have if I were God
And thou wert Master Elginbrod.
ANONYMOUS.

3

Here lies a poor woman, who always was
　　tired;
She lived in a house where help was not
　　hired.
Her last words on earth were: "Dear friends,
　　I am going
Where washing ain't done, nor sweeping, nor
　　sewing;
But everything there is exact to my wishes;
For where they don't eat there's no washing
　　of dishes.
I'll be where loud anthems will always be
　　ringing,
But, having no voice, I'll be clear of the
　　singing.
Don't mourn for me now; don't mourn for
　　me never—
I'm going to do nothing forever and ever."
ANONYMOUS.

4

Here Huntington's ashes long have lain
Whose loss is our external gain,
For while he exercised all his powers,
Whatever he gained, the loss was ours.
AMBROSE BIERCE, *Epitaph on Collis P.
Huntington.* From *The Devil's Dictionary.*

5

Epitaph: a belated advertisement for a line
of goods that has been permanently discontinued.
IRVIN SHREWSBURY COBB.

6

Alas, poor Tom! How oft with merry heart,
Have we beheld thee play the Sexton's part;
Each comic heart must now be grieved to see
The Sexton's dreary part performed on thee.
ROBERT FERGUSSON, *Epigram on the Death
of Mr. Thomas Lancashire, Comedian.*

7

On the whole, I'd rather be in Philadelphia.
W. C. FIELDS, proposed as his epitaph.

8

The body of Benjamin Franklin, Printer,
(like the cover of an old book, its contents
torn out and stripped of its lettering and
gilding), lies here, food for worms; but the
work shall not be lost, for it will (as he
believed) appear once more in a new and
more elegant edition, revised and corrected
by the Author.
BENJAMIN FRANKLIN, *Epitaph on Himself.* Written by him in 1728, at the age
of twenty-two. It was not placed on his
monument.

9

Here Reynolds is laid, and, to tell you my
　　mind,
He has not left a wiser or better behind:
His pencil was striking, resistless, and grand;
His manners were gentle, complying, and
　　bland.
OLIVER GOLDSMITH, *On Sir Joshua Reynolds.*

10

His name was Calvin.
What could you expect
From one whose namesake
Was of God's elect.
KENSAL GREEN, *Premature Epitaphs.* On
Calvin Coolidge.

11

Here Einstein lies;
　　At least, they laid his bier
Just hereabouts—
　　Or relatively near.
KENSAL GREEN, *Premature Epitaphs.*

12

He thwarted time and space . . .
　　. . . But what a bore
It is to hear
The Gramophone next door.
KENSAL GREEN, *Premature Epitaphs.* On
Thomas Edison.

13

Let his detractors dare deny the fact
That Mussolini well knew how to act.
He slept from ten till six, and in between, he
Acted the play entitled Mussolini.
KENSAL GREEN, *Premature Epitaphs.*

14

His fame endures; we shall not forget
The name of Baldwin until we're out of debt.
KENSAL GREEN, *Premature Epitaphs.*

15

Here England buries her grudge against
Columbus.
KENSAL GREEN, *Premature Epitaphs.* On
Lady Astor.

16

But here's the sunset of a tedious day.
These two asleep are; I'll but be undrest,
And so to bed. Pray wish us all good rest.
ROBERT HERRICK, *Epitaph on Sir Edward
Giles.*

17

When fades at length our lingering day

Who cares what pompous tombstones say?
Read on the hearts that love us still,
Hic jacet Joe. *Hic jacet* Bill.
 OLIVER WENDELL HOLMES, *Bill and Joe.*

1
The writer of an epitaph should not be considered as saying nothing but what is strictly true. Allowance must be made for some degree of exaggerated praise. In lapidary inscriptions a man is not upon oath.
 SAMUEL JOHNSON, Boswell's *Life,* Nov. 5, 1775.

2
Here lie the bones of Robert Lowe:
Where he's gone to I don't know.
If the realms of peace and love,
Farewell to happiness above.
If he's gone to a lower level,
I can't congratulate the Devil.
 E. KNATCHBULL-HUGESSEN, *Epitaph on Robert Lowe.*

3
Here lies a nuisance dedicated to sanity.
 DAVID LOW, *Epitaph* on himself. Quoted in obituary, *The New York Times,* Sept. 29, 1963.

4
He died pied.
Reset and stet,
HE NAPS IN CAPS.
 DAVID MCCORD, *Remainders.*

5
By and by
God caught his eye.
 DAVID MCCORD, *Epitaph to a Waiter.*

6
If, after I depart this vale, you remember me and have thought to please my ghost, forgive some sinner and wink your eye at a homely girl.
 H. L. MENCKEN, *The Smart Set,* Dec., 1921.

7
Rest in peace—until we meet again.
 A widow's epitaph for her husband. From *The American Way of Death* by JESSICA MITFORD.

8
Excuse my dust.
 DOROTHY PARKER, *Her Own Epitaph.*

9
Here lies Lord Coningsby—be civil!
The rest God knows—perhaps the devil.
 ALEXANDER POPE, *Epitaph on Lord Coningsby.*

10
Nobles and heralds, by your leave,
 Here lies what once was Matthew Prior;
The son of Adam and of Eve,
 Can Bourbon or Nassau go higher?
 MATTHEW PRIOR, *Epitaph.*

11
As a general thing, the writer of epitaphs is a monumental liar.
 JOHN E. ROSSER.

12
Hotten
Rotten
Forgotten
 GEORGE AUGUSTUS HENRY SALA, *Epitaph for John Camden Hotten.*

13
Traveller, let your step be light,
 So that sleep these eyes may close,
For poor Scarron, till to-night,
 Ne'er was able e'en to doze.
 PAUL SCARRON, *Epitaph Written by Himself.*

14
Here lies that peerless paper peer Lord Peter,
Who broke the laws of God and man and metre.
 SIR WALTER SCOTT, *Epitaph for Patrick ("Peter"), Lord Robertson.*

15
In heart a Lydia, and in tongue a Hannah,
In zeal a Ruth, in wedlock a Susanna,
Prudently simple, providently wary,
To the world a Martha, and to heaven a Mary.
 Epitaph on Dame Dorothy Selby (d. 1641), Ightham Church near Sevenoaks, England.

16
Like a worn out type, he is returned to the Founder in the hope of being recast in a better and more perfect mold.
 UNKNOWN, *Epitaph on Peter Gedge.* Parish Church, Bury St. Edmund's, England.

17
Here lies the mother of children seven,
Four on earth and three in heaven;
The three in heaven preferring rather
To die with mother than live with father.
 UNKNOWN, *Epitaph,* graveyard in Birmingham, England.

18
Here lies DuVall; reader if male thou art,
Look to thy purse; if female to thy heart.
 UNKNOWN, Epitaph of the famous highwayman Claude DuVall, in Covent Garden Church.

19
Friend, in your epitaph I'm grieved
 So very much is said:
One-half will never be believed.
 The other never read.
 UNKNOWN. Sometimes ascribed to Pope.

20
Reader, John Newter, who erst played

The Jack of both sides, here is laid.
UNKNOWN, *Wits' Recreations* (1654).

1

Long of interest was an inadvertent error in the inscription in a Presbyterian churchyard. The stonecutter, apparently crowded for space, omitted a final letter in a pious sentiment with this unusual result:

Lord, she is Thin.

An "e" has recently been added to the line.
CHARLES L. WALLIS, *Stories in Stone: A Book of American Epitaphs.*

2

To the Memory
of
Abraham Beaulieu
Born 15 September
1822
Accidentally shot
4th April 1844
As a mark of affection
from his brother
CHARLES L. WALLIS, *Stories in Stone: A Book of American Epitaphs.*

3

Here lies Jane Smith, wife of Thomas Smith, marble cutter. This monument was erected by her husband as a tribute to her memory and a specimen of his work. Monuments of the same style 350 dollars.
CHARLES L. WALLIS, *Stories in Stone: A Book of American Epitaphs.*

EQUALITY

4

All men are equal on the turf and under it.
LORD GEORGE BENTINCK.

5

What is sauce for the goose is sauce for the gander.
TOM BROWN, *New Maxims.*

6

Death and the dice level all distinctions.
SAMUEL FOOTE, *The Minor.* Act i, sc. 1.

7

Inequality is as dear to the American heart as liberty itself.
W. D. HOWELLS, *Impressions and Experiences: New York Streets.*

8

For the colonel's lady an' Judy O'Grady,
Are sisters under the skin.
RUDYARD KIPLING, *Barrack-Room Ballads.*

9

All animals are equal, but some animals are more equal than others.
GEORGE ORWELL (ERIC HUGH BLAIR), *Animal Farm.*

10

One man is as good as another—and a great

dale betther, as the Irish philosopher said.
WILLIAM MAKEPEACE THACKERAY, *Roundabout Papers: On Ribbons.*

ERROR

11

If frequently I fret and fume,
And absolutely will not smile,
I err in company with Hume,
Old Socrates and T. Carlyle.
FRANKLIN P. ADAMS, *Erring in Company.*

12

A blunderer is a man who starts a meat market during Lent.
JAMES MONTGOMERY BAILEY.

13

I have made mistakes but I have never made the mistake of claiming that I never made one.
JAMES GORDON BENNETT.

14

Wise men learn by other men's mistakes, fools by their own.
H. G. BOHN, *Handbook of Proverbs.*

15

My opinion is that the Northern States will manage somehow to muddle through.
JOHN BRIGHT, spoken during the American Civil War. (JUSTIN McCARTHY, *Reminiscences.*)

16

They defend their errors as if they were defending their inheritance.
EDMUND BURKE, *Speech,* House of Commons, Feb. 11, 1780.

17

There are few virtues which the Poles do not possess and there are few errors they have ever avoided.
SIR WINSTON CHURCHILL, *Speech,* House of Commons, after Potsdam Conference.

18

Truth is a good dog; but beware of barking too close to the heels of an error, lest you get your brains kicked out.
SAMUEL TAYLOR COLERIDGE, *Table Talk,* June 7, 1830.

19

No one rises so high as he who knows not whither he is going.
OLIVER CROMWELL, quoted by WILLIAM OSLER in lectures to students.

20

Whatever was required to be done, the Circumlocution Office was beforehand with all the public departments in the art of perceiving—How Not To Do It.
CHARLES DICKENS, *Little Dorrit.* Bk. i, ch. 10.

1
Every absurdity has a champion to defend it, for error is always talkative.
OLIVER GOLDSMITH.

2
Admitting Error clears the Score
And proves you Wiser than before.
ARTHUR GUITERMAN, *A Poet's Proverbs.*

3
The man who makes no mistakes does not usually make anything.
BISHOP W. C. MAGEE, *Sermon,* 1868.

4
A man whose errors take ten years to correct is quite a man.
J. ROBERT OPPENHEIMER, *Comment* on errors in the early scientific work of Albert Einstein, which delayed for ten years the publication of Einstein's collected works. Dr. Oppenheimer's remark was made during a symposium on Einstein in Paris, Dec. 13, 1965.

5
The best may slip, and the most cautious fall;
He's more than mortal that ne'er err'd at all.
JOHN POMFRET, *Love Triumphant Over Reason.*

6
Nothing is more boring than an account of errors one has not committed.
EZRA POUND, *ABC of Reading.*

7
He wanted Li Wing
But we winged Willie Wong.
A sad but excusable
Slip of the Tong.
KEITH PRESTON, *Lapsus Linguae.*

8
A life spent in making mistakes is not only more honorable but more useful than a life spent in doing nothing.
BERNARD SHAW, *The Doctor's Dilemma:* Preface.

9
If you find a mistake in this paper, please consider that it was there for a purpose. We publish something for everyone, including those who are always looking for mistakes.
UNKNOWN, *Weekly Bulletin* of the First Congregational Church, San Diego. Reported by Associated Press in dispatch datelined San Diego, Oct. 16, 1963.

10
Whoever undertakes to rectify error must have done much erring to be good at it.
UNKNOWN, *Meditations in Wall Street.*

EVIL

11
The most pathetic object is . . . the man

who wants to be a degenerate and can't quite make it.
GEORGE ADE, *Fables.*

12
There's something about a closet that makes a skeleton terribly restless.
JOHN BARRYMORE.

13
For ways that are dark
And tricks that are vain,
I name Speaker Blaine,
And that I dare maintain.
REPRESENTATIVE BENJAMIN F. BUTLER of Massachusetts, in a controversy with Speaker James G. Blaine of Maine. A paraphrase of Bret Harte.

14
What is bad cannot endure: it must grow worse.
NED ROREM, *Paris Diary.*

15
Only one-third of the people of the world are asleep at any given moment. The other two-thirds are awake and probably stirring up mischief somewhere.
DEAN RUSK, SECRETARY OF STATE, explaining to the House Foreign Affairs Committee that he starts his day by reading a summary of overnight reports. (*The New York Times,* Feb. 6, 1966.)

16
No man means evil but the Devil, and we shall know him by his horns.
WILLIAM SHAKESPEARE, *The Merry Wives of Windsor.* Act v, sc. 2.

17
I think the devil will not have me damned, lest the oil that is in me should set hell on fire.
WILLIAM SHAKESPEARE, *The Merry Wives of Windsor.* Act v, sc. 5.

18
A bad man is not so bad as a worse.
BERNARD SHAW, *Dramatic Opinions.*

19
Of two evils, choose neither.
CHARLES HADDON SPURGEON, *John Ploughman.*

20
'Cause I's wicked, I is. I's mighty wicked, anyhow, I can't help it.
HARRIET BEECHER STOWE, *Uncle Tom's Cabin.*

21
All the evil in the world was brought in by means of an apple. (Mala mali malo mala contulit omnia mundo.)
UNKNOWN, Medieval proverb.

22
A dunghill covered with flowers.
HENRY WATTERSON, referring to Henry

Ward Beecher. (*Beecher-Tilton Scandal*, p. 143.)

EVOLUTION

See also Ape

1
The evolutionists seem to know everything about the missing link except the fact that it is missing.
G. K. CHESTERTON, *Evolution.*

2
"The unfit die—the fit both live and thrive."
Alas, who says so? They who do survive.
SARAH N. CLEGHORN, *The Survival of the Fittest.*

3
I confess freely to you, I could never look long upon a monkey, without very mortifying reflections.
WILLIAM CONGREVE, *Letter*, to Dennis, 1695.

4
All modern men are descended from wormlike creatures, but it shows more on some people.
WILL CUPPY.

5
I grant you that there are plenty of old-fashioned and pretty effective ways to tell one's friends from the apes. What could be simpler, for instance, when you are at the zoo? The apes are in cages.
WILL CUPPY, *How to Tell Your Friends from the Apes:* preface.

6
The Peking Man shows that people were living in Asia long long ago as most of us knew already. He was discovered near Peking or Peiping and was named *Sinanthropus pekinensis* to keep certain persons from calling him Peiping Tom.
WILL CUPPY, *How to Tell Your Friends from the Apes.*

7
For my part I would as soon be descended from [a] baboon . . . as from a savage who delights to torture his enemies . . . treats his wives like slaves . . . and is haunted by the grossest superstitions.
CHARLES DARWIN, *The Descent of Man.*

8
The question is this: Is man an ape or an angel? I, my lord, am on the side of the angels.
BENJAMIN DISRAELI, *Speech*, Oxford Diocesan Conference, 1864.

9
I am very proud of those bright-eyed, furry, four-footed or feathered progenitors, and not at all ashamed of my cousins, the tigers and apes and peacocks.
LOGAN PEARSALL SMITH, *Trivia: Desires.*

10
Each has his own tree of ancestors, but at the top of all sits Probably Arboreal.
ROBERT LOUIS STEVENSON, *Memories and Portraits: Pastoral.*

EXAMPLE

11
To follow foolish precedents, and wink
With both our eyes, is easier than to think.
WILLIAM COWPER, *Tirocinium*, l. 255.

12
I wish that practicing was not
So different from preaching.
JOHN GODFREY SAXE, *Wishing.*

13
Few things are harder to put up with than the annoyance of a good example.
MARK TWAIN, *Pudd'nhead Wilson's Calendar.*

14
As a rule, there is no surer way to the dislike of men than to behave well where they have behaved badly.
LEW WALLACE, *Ben Hur.* Bk. iv, ch. 9.

EXCUSE

15
A woman's excuses are like her apron, easily lifted.
FRANK C. BROWN, *Collection of North Carolina Folklore.*

16
The usual excuse a man makes for doing one an injury is that he wishes one well.
ROBERT W. CHAMBERS, *The Fighting Chance.*

17
The most profitless thing to manufacture is excuses.
B. C. FORBES, *Epigrams.*

18
"Impossible"—Oh, Heart confess!—
Is Man's Excuse for Laziness.
ARTHUR GUITERMAN, *A Poet's Proverbs.*

19
A person who is going to commit an inhuman act invariably excuses himself by saying, "I'm only human, after all."
SYDNEY J. HARRIS, *Strictly Personal.*

20
You needn't try to reason,
Your excuse is out of season,
Just kiss yourself goodbye.
WILLIAM JEROME, *His Sweet Face She Never Saw More.*

1
I can't help it . . . that's what we all say when we don't want to exert ourselves.
    EVA LATHBURY, *Mr. Meyer's Pupil.*

2
He reminds me of the man who murdered both his parents, and then, when sentence was about to be pronounced, pleaded for mercy on the grounds that he was an orphan.
    ABRAHAM LINCOLN. (GROSS, *Lincoln's Own Stories*, p. 179.)

3
It is a great consolation for a man who has made a muddle of his life, to throw the blame on his wife, especially if he can get his wife to believe it.
    FRANK RICHARDSON, *2835 Mayfair.*

4
There are many scapegoats for our sins, but the most popular is providence.
    MARK TWAIN, *More Tramps Abroad.*

5
That's like blaming the Johnstown flood on a leaky toilet in Altoona, Pennsylvania.
    STANLEY WOODWARD, commenting acidly on the reason given by the Army football coach, Earl (Red) Blaik, for the Cadets' loss to the University of Michigan. Blaik had seemed to put the blame for the rout on a single Army player's inadequacy.

EXPERIENCE

6
It takes longer to hard-boil a man or a woman than an egg.
    FREDERICK LEWIS ALLEN, *Only Yesterday.*

7
An expert is one who knows more and more about less and less.
    NICHOLAS MURRAY BUTLER, *Commencement Address*, Columbia University.

8
Experience is the best of schoolmasters, only the school fees are heavy.
    THOMAS CARLYLE, *Miscellaneous Essays.*

9
A proverb is a short sentence based on long experience.
    MIGUEL DE CERVANTES, *Don Quixote.*

10
Experience keeps a dear school but a fool will learn in no other.
    BENJAMIN FRANKLIN, *Poor Richard's Almanac.*

11
You owe the World for all you learn;
    In Payment you should Teach in turn.
    ARTHUR GUITERMAN, *A Poet's Proverbs.*

12
I know a banker who served thirty years as president of a bank. He had more experience, until his bank went broke, than any other banker in Massachusetts. But if I ever go into the banking business, I do not plan to hire him, and he knows the operation from top to bottom.
    JOHN F. KENNEDY, *Remark* made at Muskegon, Mich., Sept. 5, 1960, in answer to questions about the relative experience of Kennedy and his opponent, Richard M. Nixon. (*The Kennedy Wit*, ed. by BILL ADLER.)

13
The man in the audience said that I should tell Mr. Nixon that experience is what he will have left after this campaign is over. I don't know why we never think of these things.
    JOHN F. KENNEDY, *Speech* in New York City, Oct. 27, 1960.

14
He who neglects to drink of the spring of experience is apt to die of thirst in the desert of ignorance.
    LING PO, Chinese philosopher. *Epigram.*

15
One thorn of experience is worth a whole wilderness of warning.
    JAMES RUSSELL LOWELL, *Among My Books.*

16
Our unabashed Dictionary defines *experience* as the wonderful knowledge that enables you to recognize a mistake when you make it again.
    More Playboy's Party Jokes (1965).

17
Experience may not be worth what it costs but I can't seem to get it for any less.
    Presbyterian Life.

18
The first fall hurts, the others harden.
    Reflections of a Bachelor (1903).

19
I had rather have a fool to make me merry than experience to make me sad.
    WILLIAM SHAKESPEARE, *As You Like It.* Act iv, sc. 1.

20
We learn from experience that men never learn anything from experience.
    BERNARD SHAW, quoted in *The Quintessence of G.B.S.*, ed. by STEPHEN WINSTEN.

21
Experience—A comb life gives you after you lose your hair.
    JUDITH STERN, from *The Laugh's on Me* by BENNETT CERF.

1
War talk by men who have been in a war is always interesting, whereas moon talk by a poet who has not been in the moon is likely to be dull.
MARK TWAIN.

2
I will now teach, offering my way of life to whosoever desires to commit suicide by the scheme which has enabled me to beat the doctor and the hangman for seventy years.
MARK TWAIN, *Essays: Seventieth Birthday.*

3
We should be careful to get out of an experience only the wisdom that is in it—and stop there; lest we be like the cat that sits down on a hot stove-lid. She will never sit down on a hot stove-lid again—and that is well; but also she will never sit down on a cold one anymore.
MARK TWAIN, *Pudd'nhead Wilson's New Calendar.*

4
Experience is of no ethical value. It is merely the name men give to their mistakes.
OSCAR WILDE, *The Picture of Dorian Gray*, ch. 4.

5
Experience is the name everyone gives to his mistakes.
OSCAR WILDE, *Lady Windermere's Fan*, Act 1.

EXTREMES

6
Extremes meet, as the Whiting said with its tail in its mouth.
THOMAS HOOD, *The Doves and the Crows.*

7
Every white shall have its blacke,
And every sweet its soure.
THOMAS PERCY, *Reliques of Ancient Poetry.*

8
We are apt to make the usual blunder of emptying the baby out with the bath.
BERNARD SHAW, *Parents and Children.*

EYES

9
In the country of the blind, the one-eyed man is king. (Caecorum in patria luscus rex imperat omnis.)
MICHAEL APOSTOLIUS, *Proverbs.* An old proverb taken from the Greek, its earliest English use probably in the translation by JOHN PALSGRAVE, in 1540, of the *Comedye of Acolastus*, by FULLENIUS.

10
Nor brighter was his eye, nor moister
Than a too-long opened oyster.
ROBERT BROWNING, *The Pied Piper*, sec. 4.

11
The dragonfly:
  his face is very nearly
    only eye!
CHISOKU, *An Introduction to Haiku*, tr. by HAROLD G. HENDERSON.

12
He had but one eye, and the popular prejudice runs in favour of two.
CHARLES DICKENS, *Nicholas Nickleby*, ch. 4.

13
If you give up wearing glasses you look better but you don't see as well.
EVAN ESAR.

14
Keep your eyes wide open before marriage, and half-shut afterwards.
BENJAMIN FRANKLIN.

15
Clara's blue eyes were as innocent as if they had entered their sockets a half-hour ago.
BEN HECHT, *Gaily, Gaily.*

16
Inanimate objects sometimes appear endowed with a strange power of sight. A statue notices, a tower watches, the face of an edifice contemplates.
VICTOR HUGO, *Ninety-Three.* Pt. iii, bk. 5, ch. 6.

17
We looked into each other's eyes. I saw myself, she saw herself.
STANISLAW J. LEC, *Unkempt Thoughts*, tr. from the Polish by JACEK GALASKA.

18
Why has not man a microscopic eye?
For this plain reason, man is not a fly.
ALEXANDER POPE, *Essay on Man.*

F

FACE

See also Ears, Eyes, Mouth, Nose

19
He had a profile like a set of keys and a nose like a bicycle seat.
JOEY ADAMS, *Cindy and I*, ch. 3.

20
The faces in New York remind me of people who played a game and lost.
Daughter of LANE ADAMS, quoted by MURRAY KEMPTON, *New York Post*, May 16, 1957.

1
He has features that you women would call handsome . . . that is, with nothing more distinctive about them than a row of telegraph poles along a railway line.
MAX BARING, *The Shattered Idol.*

2
He wore a sterilized, disinfected expression, yet he could suddenly confront a person or a camera with a momentary expression of almost lover-like understanding and affection.
WILLIAM C. BULLITT, *Introduction to Thomas Woodrow Wilson: Twenty-eighth President of the United States— A Psychological Study by William C. Bullitt and Sigmund Freud.*

3
Yet even her tyranny had such a grace,
The women pardoned all, except her face.
LORD BYRON, *Don Juan.* Canto v, st. 113.

4
Nature gives you the face you have at twenty; it is up to you to merit the face you have at fifty.
GABRIELLE CHANEL, *Ladies' Home Journal,* Sept., 1956.

5
A man with a face that looks like someone had thrown it at him in anger nearly always marries before he is old enough to vote.
FINLEY PETER DUNNE, *Mr. Dooley Remembers.*

6
For Beauty I am not a star
There are others more handsome by far.
But my face I don't mind it,
For I am behind it,
It's the people in front that I jar.
Attributed to ANTHONY EUWER, quoted by WILLIAM C. BULLITT AND SIGMUND FREUD in *Thomas Woodrow Wilson: Twenty-eighth President of the United States—A Psychological Study.* Wilson was fond of quoting this limerick.

7
That woman is one of the Lee sisters—and her first name is Ug.
LANGSTON HUGHES, *The Book of Negro Humor.*

8
Her face was her chaperone.
RUPERT HUGHES.

9
A woman, the more curious she is about her face, is commonly the more careless about her house.
BEN JONSON, *Explorata: Munda et Sordida.*

10
The apple-pie hat which she wore, surmounted with black willow plumes, concealed from view a face so face-like in its appearance as to be positively facial.
STEPHEN LEACOCK, *Laugh with Leacock.*

11
Nobody ever expected me to be President. In my poor, lean, lank face nobody has ever seen that any cabbages were sprouting.
ABRAHAM LINCOLN, *Speech* against Douglas, in the campaign of 1860.

12
Lady, you went to the market
and picked up hair, rouge, honey, wax and teeth.
For a like amount
you might have bought a face.
LUCILIUS (LOUKILLIOS), *Shopping Tip,* tr. by WILLIAM BARNSTONE.

13
I never forget a face—
But I am willing to make an exception in your case.
GROUCHO MARX, from *The Silver Treasury of Light Verse,* ed. by OSCAR WILLIAMS.

14
His face was of that doubtful kind
That wins the eye, but not the mind.
SIR WALTER SCOTT, *Rokeby.* Canto v, st. 16.

15
You have such a February face,
So full of frost, of storm, and cloudiness.
WILLIAM SHAKESPEARE, *Much Ado About Nothing.* Act v, sc. 4.

16
He had the sort of face that, once seen, is never remembered.
OSCAR WILDE.

FAILURE

17
A fool often fails because he thinks what is difficult is easy, and a wise man because he thinks what is easy is difficult.
JOHN CHURTON COLLINS, *Aphorisms.*

18
According to everyone a man is either a fool or a knave if he fails; a Solon if he succeeds. Nobody goes by anything except results.
G. G. COLMORE, *The Angel and the Outcast.*

19
Half the failures in life arise from pulling in one's horse as he is leaping.
J. C. AND A. W. HARE, *Guesses at Truth.*

20
A failure must have a hard time tracin' his downfall in a dry town.
FRANK MCKINNEY (KIN) HUBBARD, *Abe Martin's Primer.*

1
Face-saving, the President [Lyndon B. Johnson] observed, was not his major purpose in life. "While you're trying to save your face," he declared, "you're losing your ass."
PHILIP GEYELIN, *Lyndon B. Johnson and the World.*

2
You never know where bottom is until you plumb for it.
FREDERICK LAING, *The Giant's House.*

3
Failure has gone to his head.
WILSON MIZNER, quoted by ALVA JOHNSTON, *Legend of a Sport; The New Yorker.*

4
From the sublime to the ridiculous is but a step. (Du sublime au ridicule il n'y a qu'un pas.)
NAPOLEON BONAPARTE, to the ABBÉ DU PRADT, on his return from Russia, with reference to the retreat from Moscow. (DU PRADT, *Histoire de l'Ambassade dans la Grande Duché de Varsovie,* p. 215.)

5
I can not give you the formula for success, but I can give you the formula for failure— which is: Try to please everybody.
HERBERT BAYARD SWOPE.

6
He had read of the keen critical rejection of failures such as Wagner's operas, Lincoln's Gettysburg Address, Walt Whitman's poems, and Christ's Sermon on the Mount, and he was sensibly impressed.
ROBERT LEWIS TAYLOR, *W. C. Fields.*

7
In the game of life it's a good idea to have a few early losses, which relieves you of the pressure of trying to maintain an undefeated season.
BILL VAUGHAN, *Kansas City Star.*

FAITH

See also Belief

8
Faith is nothing but spiritualized imagination.
HENRY WARD BEECHER, *Proverbs from Plymouth Pulpit.*

9
'Tis well averred,
Scientific faith's absurd.
ROBERT BROWNING, *Easter Day,* pt. 6.

10
You can do very little with faith, but you can do nothing without it.
SAMUEL BUTLER, *Notebooks.*

11
Faith is believing the dentist when he says it isn't going to hurt.
Toaster's Handbook, compiled by PEGGY EDMUND AND HAROLD WORKMAN WILLIAMS.

12
The way to see by Faith is to shut the Eye of Reason.
BENJAMIN FRANKLIN, *Poor Richard,* 1758.

13
After all, to the disbeliever, no refutation of a faith is necessary; to the believer, none is possible.
JOHN GREENWAY, *The Inevitable Americans,* ch. 5.

14
A man must be faithless to something— either a woman, or his god, or his firmest belief.
JOHN OLIVER HOBBES, *Life and Tomorrow.*

15
You can change your faith without changing your gods. And vice versa.
STANISLAW J. LEC, *Unkempt Thoughts,* tr. from the Polish by JACEK GALASKA.

16
Faith may be defined briefly as an illogical belief in the occurrence of the improbable.
H. L. MENCKEN, *Prejudices,* ser. 3.

17
Mysticism suits displaced persons and superfluous children.
JEAN-PAUL SARTRE, *The Words.*

FAME

See also Reputation

18
A celebrity is a person who works hard all his life to become well known, and then wears dark glasses to avoid being recognized.
FRED ALLEN, *Treadmill To Oblivion.* See also MURPHY in this section.

19
There's a wonderful family called Stein—
There's Gert, and there's Epp, and there's Ein;
Gert's poems are bunk,
Epp's statues are junk,
And no one can understand Ein.
ANONYMOUS, *The Steins.*

20
I think immortality is an overrated commodity.
S. N. BEHRMAN, *Biography.*

21
In the march up to the heights of fame there comes a spot close to the summit in which man reads "nothing but detective stories."
HEYWOOD BROUN, *G.K.C.* (1922).

1
Herostratus lives that burnt the temple of Diana; he is almost lost that built it.
> Sir Thomas Browne, *Hydriotaphia: Urn Burial,* ch. 5.

2
Fame creates its own standards. A guy who twitches his lips is just another guy with a lip twitch—unless he's Humphrey Bogart.
> Sammy Davis, Jr., *Yes I Can.*

3
Fame is a food that dead men eat,—
I have no stomach for such meat.
> Austin Dobson, *Fame Is a Food.*

4
Fame without aim is a soap-bubble.
> B. C. Forbes, *Epigrams.*

5
In short, whoever you may be,
To this conclusion you'll agree,
When everyone is somebodee,
  Then no one's anybody!
> W. S. Gilbert, *The Gondoliers,* Act 2.

6
Fame is delightful, but as collateral it does not rank high.
> Elbert Hubbard, *Epigrams.*

7
Celebrity—One who works all his life to be recognized—then hides behind dark glasses so no one will know who he is.
> Dudley Murphy, from *The Laugh's on Me* by Bennett Cerf.

8
As he rose like a rocket, he fell like a stick.
> Thomas Paine, *Letter to His Addressers.* The reference is to Edmund Burke.

9
Fame—The aggregate of all the misunderstandings that collect around a new name.
> Rainer Maria Rilke.

10
We toil for fame,
  We live on crusts,
We make a name,
  Then we are busts.
> Leonard H. Robbins, *Lines,* intended for delivery at the unveiling of the memorials to Monroe, Maury, Whitman and Whistler in the Hall of Fame.

11
I would give all my fame for a pot of ale and safety.
> William Shakespeare, *King Henry V.* Act iii, sc. 2.

12
There's hope a great man's memory may outlive his life half a year.
> William Shakespeare, *Hamlet.* Act iii, sc. 2.

13
Imperious Caesar, dead and turn'd to clay,
Might stop a hole to keep the wind away:
O, that that earth, which kept the world in awe,
Should patch a wall to expel the winter's flaw!
> William Shakespeare, *Hamlet.* Act v, sc. 1.

14
Fame is the perfume of heroic deeds.
> Socrates.

15
Of some for glory such the boundless rage,
That they're the blackest scandal of their age.
> Edward Young, *Love of Fame.* Satire iv, l. 65.

FAMILY

16
Where does the family start? It starts with a young man falling in love with a girl—no superior alternative has yet been found.
> Sir Winston Churchill, *Speech,* House of Commons, Nov. 6, 1950.

17
It is a melancholy truth that even great men have their poor relations.
> Charles Dickens, *Bleak House,* ch. 28.

18
Every day when he looked into the glass, and gave the last touch to his consummate toilette, he offered thanks to Providence that his family was not unworthy of him.
> Benjamin Disraeli, *Lothair,* ch. 1.

19
I let my relatives support me. I never flinched. I knew they could do it.
> Robert Fontaine, *That's a Good Question.*

20
In the drinking well
  Which the plumber built her,
Aunt Eliza fell.
  We must buy a filter.
> Harry Graham, *Aunt Eliza.*

21
Good families are generally worse than any others.
> Anthony Hope, *The Prisoner of Zenda,* ch. 1.

22
The hardest thing is to disguise your feelings when you put a lot of relatives on the train for home.
> Frank McKinney (Kin) Hubbard.

23
Next t' a city th' loneliest place in th' world when you're broke is among relatives.
> Frank McKinney (Kin) Hubbard, *Abe Martin's Primer.*

1
Th' richer a relative is th' less he bothers you.
> FRANK MCKINNEY (KIN) HUBBARD, *Abe Martin's Primer.*

2
Prithee, my dear, have done with canting; how would the world be worse for it, I may ask, if all your relations were at once spitted like larks, and roasted for Presta's [the dog's] supper?
> SAMUEL JOHNSON, to MRS. THRALE, who lamented a first cousin lost in America. BOSWELL'S *Life,* June 30, 1784.

3
A poor relation—is the most irrelevant thing in nature.
> CHARLES LAMB, *Poor Relations.*

4
None but a mule denies his family.
> MOROCCAN PROVERB.

5
It costs more money to keep up your own family than it does to break up another man's.
> *Reflections of a Bachelor.*

6
If a family didn't have at least eight children in those days the Father was either in jail or deceased.
> WILL ROGERS, *Autobiography.*

7
Be a tramp or be a millionaire—it matters little which: what does matter is being a poor relation of the rich; and that is the very devil.
> BERNARD SHAW, *Who I Am, and What I Think,* pt. 1; *The Candid Friend,* May 11, 1901.

8
Nobody with that awful wife and those ugly children could be anything but normal.
> GORE VIDAL, *The Best Man.*

9
Relations are simply a tedious pack of people who haven't got the remotest knowledge of how to live, nor the smallest instinct about when to die.
> OSCAR WILDE, *The Importance of Being Earnest.*

FANATICISM

10
A fanatic is one who can't change his mind and won't change the subject.
> SIR WINSTON CHURCHILL, from *Reader's Digest,* Dec. 1954.

11
A fanatic is a man that does what th' Lord wud do if he knew the facts iv the case.
> FINLEY PETER DUNNE, *Mr. Dooley Remembers.*

12
Fanaticism consists in redoubling your effort when you have forgotten your aim.
> GEORGE SANTAYANA, *The Life of Reason.* Vol. i, p. 13.

13
I don't want to send them to jail. I want to send them to school.
> ADLAI STEVENSON, on pickets who attacked him in Dallas. (*Time,* Nov. 1, 1963.)

FARMING

14
And out in Iowa, where the black loam is twenty feet deep, the corn grows so high they have to climb ladders to get down the ears.
> MAX ADELER (CHARLES HEBER CLARK), *Ten Tall Tales.*

15
He that sows his grain upon marble will have many a hungry belly before his harvest.
> JOHN ARBUTHNOT. (*Classic Quotations,* ed. by JAMES ELMES.)

16
To dig and delve in nice clean dirt
Can do a mortal little hurt.
> JOHN KENDRICK BANGS, *Gardening.*

17
Tools were made and born were hands,
Every farmer understands.
> WILLIAM BLAKE, *Proverbs.*

18
A farmer, according to this definition, is a man who makes his money on the farm and spends it in town. An agriculturist is a man who makes his money in town and spends it on the farm.
> *Toaster's Handbook,* compiled by PEGGY EDMUND AND HAROLD WORKMAN WILLIAMS.

19
Farming looks mighty easy when your plow is a pencil, and you're a thousand miles from the corn field.
> DWIGHT D. EISENHOWER, *Address* in Peoria, Ill., Sept. 25, 1956. Referring to "synthetic farmer" experts.

20
The Boldest Farmer heeds the Cautious Rule
To stand Behind the Bull, Before the Mule.
> ARTHUR GUITERMAN, *A Poet's Proverbs,* p. 106.

21
A Farmer on his Feet, the World agrees,
Is taller than a Prince upon his Knees.
> ARTHUR GUITERMAN, *A Poet's Proverbs: Old Irish Proverbs.*

22
Some folks tell us there ain't no hell,

But they never farmed, so how can they tell?
> *Toasts for All Occasions,* ed. by LEWIS C. HENRY.

1
The best compost for the lands
Is the wise master's feet and hands.
> ROBERT HERRICK, *The Country Life.*

2
Earth here is so kind, that just tickle her with a hoe and she laughs with a harvest.
> DOUGLAS JERROLD, *A Land of Plenty.* The reference is to Australia.

3
Italians come to ruin generally in three ways —women, gambling, and farming. My family chose the slowest one.
> POPE JOHN XXIII, quoted in *Newsweek,* Dec. 17, 1962.

4
The best fertilizer for a piece of land is the footprints of its owner.
> LYNDON B. JOHNSON, *Remark* during an inspection of his Texas ranch. (JAMES RESTON, Washington Column, *The New York Times,* Jan. 8, 1964.) See also HERRICK in this section.

5
As Abraham Lincoln used to say, when you want to do gardening, you've got to take your coat off, a sentiment shared by his fellow enthusiast, the exiled Napoleon, who, after conquering all Europe, retaining only the sovereignty of the spade in his garden plot at St. Helena, longed only for more fertilizer.
> STEPHEN LEACOCK, *Index: There Is No Index.*

6
What you Kansas farmers ought to do is to raise less corn and raise more hell.
> MRS. MARY ELIZABETH CLYENS LEASE, *Speech,* during campaign against J. J. Ingalls, 1890.

7
The master's eye is the best fertilizer. (Majores fertilieium in agro orculum domini.)
> PLINY THE ELDER, *Historia Naturalis.* Bk. xviii, sec. 18. See also HERRICK AND JOHNSON in this section.

8
I believe the first receipt to farm well is to be rich.
> SYDNEY SMITH, *Letter* to John Wishaw, Apr. 13, 1818.

9
He was a very inferior farmer when he first began, and he is now fast rising from affluence to poverty.
> MARK TWAIN, *Rev. Henry Ward Beecher's Farm.*

10
The farmer works the soil,
The agriculturist works the farmer.
> EUGENE FITCH WARE (IRONQUILL), *The Kansas Bandit.*

11
Blessed be agriculture! If one does not have too much of it.
> CHARLES DUDLEY WARNER, *My Summer in a Garden.*

FASHION

See also Dress

12
Many are clothed, but few are dressed.
> W. BURTON BALDRY, *Stray Thoughts.*

13
He is only fantastical that is not in fashion.
> ROBERT BURTON, *The Anatomy of Melancholy.*

14
Fashionability is a kind of elevated vulgarity.
> GEORGE DARLEY, *Introduction to Works of Beaumont and Fletcher.*

15
Fashions in sin change.
> LILLIAN HELLMAN, *Watch on the Rhine.*

16
When we read about th' spring styles we almost dread t' see th' first robin.
> FRANK MCKINNEY (KIN) HUBBARD, *Abe Martin's Primer.*

17
The Venus of Milo represents an ideal, but modistes with their bread to earn do not cut their material to suit the Venus of Milo.
> FRANKFORT MOORE, *The Marriage Lease.*

18
High Heels—Invented by a woman who had been kissed on the forehead.
> CHRISTOPHER MORLEY.

19
The fashion wears out more apparel than the man.
> WILLIAM SHAKESPEARE, *Much Ado About Nothing.* Act iii, sc. 3.

20
You cannot be both fashionable and first-rate.
> LOGAN PEARSALL SMITH, *Afterthoughts.*

21
In the East, women religiously conceal that they have faces; in the West, that they have legs. In both cases they make it evident that they have but little brains.
> HENRY D. THOREAU, *Journal,* Jan. 31, 1852.

22
The first thing the first couple did after committing the first sin was to get dressed.

Thus Adam and Eve started the world of fashion, and styles have been changing ever since.
Time, Nov. 8, 1963.

1
Give feminine fashions time enough and they will starve all the moths to death.
UNKNOWN, *Detroit Free Press,* June, 1925.

2
Women's styles may change but their designs remain the same.
OSCAR WILDE.

3
After all, what is a fashion? From the artistic point of view, it is usually a form of ugliness so intolerable that we have to alter it every six months.
OSCAR WILDE, *Suitable Dress for Women Workers.*

FATE

4
Resolved to take fate by the throat and shake a living out of her.
LOUISA MAY ALCOTT, quoted in EDNAH D. CHENEY, *Louisa May Alcott, Her Life, Letters, and Journals.*

5
If you are destined to draw the winning ticket in the lottery, Mr. Sholom Aleichem, it will come right to your house without your asking for it. As King David says, "It never rains but it pours." You don't need wisdom or skill.
SHOLOM ALEICHEM, *Tevye Wins a Fortune.*

6
Whenever you're in the bathtub and the telephone rings, it invariably is the wrong number.
ANONYMOUS.

7
Destiny, n. A tyrant's authority for crime and a fool's excuse for failure.
AMBROSE BIERCE, *The Devil's Dictionary.*

8
I do not believe in a fate that falls on men however they act; but I do believe in a fate that falls on them unless they act.
G. K. CHESTERTON, quoted in *Reader's Digest,* Feb. 1967.

9
He that's born to be hanged shall never be drowned.
THOMAS FULLER, *Gnomologia,* No. 2279.

10
At length the fox is brought to the furrier.
GEORGE HERBERT, *Jacula Prudentum.*

11
Were it not for Czolgosz [the assassin of President McKinley], we'd all be back in our brownstone-front houses. That's where we'd be. And I would have married for money and been divorced for good cause.
ALICE ROOSEVELT LONGWORTH, *Interview* with JEAN VANDEN HEUVEL; *Saturday Evening Post,* Dec. 4, 1965.

12
As the old hermit of Prague, that never saw pen and ink, very wittily said to a niece of King Gorboduc, "That that is, is."
WILLIAM SHAKESPEARE, *Twelfth Night.* Act iv, sc. 2.

13
Apparently there is nothing that cannot happen.
MARK TWAIN, *Autobiography,* vol. 1.

FATHER

14
Most fathers would rather see their sons dead than either cultivated or devout.
LOUIS AUCHINCLOSS, *The Rector of Justin.*

15
Diogenes struck the father when the son swore.
ROBERT BURTON, *The Anatomy of Melancholy.*

16
As fathers commonly go, it is seldom a misfortune to be fatherless; and considering the general run of sons, as seldom a misfortune to be childless.
LORD CHESTERFIELD, *Letters,* May 27, 1752.

17
Some time before his death, he had stamped his likeness upon a little boy.
CHARLES DICKENS, *Pickwick Papers,* ch. 34.

18
Father is also, in our country, The Boy We Left Behind Us.
MARGARET HALSEY, *The Folks at Home.*

19
I was the same kind of father as I was a harpist—I played by ear.
HARPO MARX, *Harpo Speaks!*

20
We think our fathers fools, so wise we grow;
Our wiser sons, no doubt, will think us so.
ALEXANDER POPE, *Essay on Criticism.*

21
Men who are ashamed of the way their fathers made their money are never ashamed to spend it.
Reflections of a Bachelor.

22
A wise son knows enough to pretend it is his father who is wise.
Reflections of a Bachelor.

1

There is no good father, that's the rule.
Don't lay the blame on men but on the bond
of paternity, which is rotten.

    JEAN-PAUL SARTRE, *The Words.*

2

It is a wise father that knows his own child.

    WILLIAM SHAKESPEARE, *The Merchant of
    Venice.* Act ii, sc. 2.

3

I was not a staff to my father's old age: I
hung on to his coat tails.

    BERNARD SHAW, *The Irrational Knot:*
    preface.

4

A lady who had gallantries and several children told her husband he was like the aus-
tere man, who reaped where he did not sow.

    JONATHAN SWIFT, *Thoughts on Various
    Subjects.*

5

He pleased the ladies round him,—with
    manners soft and bland;
With reason good, they named him,—the
    father of his land.

    WILLIAM MAKEPEACE THACKERAY, *The
    King of Brentford.* (After Beranger.)

6

No man is responsible for his father. That is
entirely his mother's affair.

    MARGARET TURNBULL, *Alabaster Lamps.*

7

Perhaps host and guest is the happiest relation for father and son.

    EVELYN WAUGH, *Father and Son; The
    Atlantic,* Mar., 1963.

8

The child had every toy his father wanted.

    ROBERT C. WHITTEN, from *Complete
    Toastmaster,* by HERBERT V. PROCHNOW.

9

The booby father craves a booby son,
And by Heaven's blessing thinks himself
    undone.

    EDWARD YOUNG, *Love of Fame,* satire 2.

FATNESS

See also Dieting

10

Fat bodies, lean brains!

    BEAUMONT AND FLETCHER, *Love's Cure.*
    Act ii, sc. 1.

11

He had a paunch so big that he had to lean
backwards just to stand up.

    JIM BISHOP, *Some of My Very Best: The
    Voters—Just Like the People.*

12

When a 220-pound man laughs, there is
twice as much of him having a good time

as when a 110-pound man laughs. This is
one of the advantages of being fat.

    HAL BOYLE, *Column,* Associated Press,
    datelined Oct. 1, 1964.

13

The reason everybody loves a fat man is
that everyone feels superior to him; if you
give a fellow a reason to feel superior to
you he can't help liking you.

    HAL BOYLE, *Column,* Associated Press,
    datelined Oct. 14, 1965. See also ED-
    MUND DAY in this section.

14

Who's your fat friend?

    GEORGE BRYAN BRUMMELL, referring to
    the Prince of Wales. (Gronow's *Remi-
    niscences.*)

15

Nobody loves a fat man.

    EDMUND DAY, *The Round-Up.* Made fa-
    mous by MACKLYN ARBUCKLE, as Sher-
    iff "Slim" Hoover.

16

Jeshurun waxed fat, and kicked.

    Deuteronomy. xxxii, 15.

17

Yes, my fat goes under my belt, but yours
goes under your hat.

    FINLEY PETER DUNNE, *Mr. Dooley Re-
    members.* Comment to NICHOLAS MUR-
    RAY BUTLER.

18

I see no objection to stoutness—in moderation.

    W. S. GILBERT, *Iolanthe,* Act 1.

19

The cooler a fat man dresses th' hotter he
looks.

    FRANK MCKINNEY (KIN) HUBBARD, *Abe
    Martin's Primer.*

20

A corpulent Adonis of fifty.

    LEIGH HUNT, who was imprisoned for
    this remark about George IV of En-
    gland, when Regent. (*Examiner,* 1813.)

21

A Courtier Elegantly Presents Two Pairs
of Corsets

Mr. Jefferson has the honor to present his
compliments to Mrs. Smith [John Adams's
daughter] and to send her the two pair of
corsets she desired. He wishes they may be
suitable, as Mrs. Smith omitted to send her
measure. Times are altered since Mademoiselle de Sanson had the honor of knowing
her; should they be too small, however, she
will be so good as to lay them by a while.
There are ebbs as well as flows in this
world.

    THOMAS JEFFERSON, to MRS. WILLIAM S.
    SMITH, Jan. 15, 1787.

1
Years ago when a man began to notice that if he stood up on the subway he was immediately replaced by *two* people, he figured he was getting too fat.
JEAN KERR, *Please Don't Eat the Daisies.*

2
An optimist is a girl who mistakes a bulge for a curve.
RING LARDNER.

3
No gentleman ever weighs more than two hundred pounds.
THOMAS B. REED, when his statement of his own weight as 199 pounds was questioned.

4
Two leans never make a fat.
Reflections of a Bachelor.

5
Fair, fat, and forty.
SIR WALTER SCOTT, *St. Ronan's Well,* ch. 7. The Prince Regent's description of what a wife should be.

FAULTS

6
Every man should keep a fair-sized cemetery in which to bury the faults of his friends.
HENRY WARD BEECHER.

7
Faultless to a fault.
ROBERT BROWNING, *The Ring and the Book.*

8
The greatest of faults, I should say, is to be conscious of none.
THOMAS CARLYLE, *Heroes and Hero-Worship: The Hero as Prophet.*

9
A knowing wife if she is worth her salt
Can always prove her husband is at fault.
GEOFFREY CHAUCER, *The Wife of Bath's Prologue.*

10
People in general will much better bear being told of their vices and crimes than of their failings and weaknesses.
LORD CHESTERFIELD, *Letters,* Nov. 26, 1749.

11
Intoxication is revolting in everyone except a gentleman. Cheating at cards is revolting in everyone except a woman.
R. N. DICKINSON, *Keddie.*

12
He has not a single redeeming defect.
BENJAMIN DISRAELI. The reference is to Gladstone.

13
The first faults are theirs that commit them; The second theirs that permit them.
THOMAS FULLER, *Gnomologia,* No. 4228.

14
In other men we faults can spy,
And blame the mote that dims their eye;
Each little speck and blemish find;
To our own stronger errors blind.
JOHN GAY, *The Turkey and the Ant,* pt. 1.

15
Who brags about his Faults, no doubt
Has little else to brag about.
ARTHUR GUITERMAN, *A Poet's Proverbs.*

16
All the faults of the age come from Christianity and journalism.
FRANK HARRIS, quoted by MARGOT ASQUITH in her autobiography.

17
It is well that there is no one without a fault, for he would not have a friend in the world. He would seem to belong to a different species.
WILLIAM HAZLITT, *Characteristics,* No. 46.

18
Most of his faults brought their excuse with them.
SAMUEL JOHNSON, *Lives of the Poets.* Reference to MATTHEW PRIOR.

19
In friendship we see only those faults which may be prejudicial to our friends. In love we see no faults but those by which we suffer ourselves.
JEAN DE LA BRUYÈRE, *Les Caracteres,* ch. 5.

20
Great men too often have greater faults than little men can find room for.
WALTER SAVAGE LANDOR, *Imaginary Conversations: Diogenes and Plato.*

21
If we had no faults, we should not take so much pleasure in remarking them in others. (Si nous n'avions point de defauts, nous ne prendrions pas tant de plaisir a en remarquer dans les autres.)
FRANÇOIS, DUC DE LA ROCHEFOUCAULD, *Maximes,* No. 31.

22
We can easily forget our faults when no one but ourselves knows them.
FRANÇOIS, DUC DE LA ROCHEFOUCAULD, *Maximes,* No. 196.

23
We never confess our faults except through vanity. (Nous n'avouons jamais nos defauts que par vanite.)
FRANÇOIS, DUC DE LA ROCHEFOUCAULD, *Maximes,* No. 202.

1
Mistakes remember'd are not faults forgot.
R. H. NEWELL, *The Orpheus C. Kerr Papers: Columbia's Agony.*

2
With names you can soften shortcomings; let her be called swarthy, whose blood is blacker than Illyrian pitch; if cross-eyed, she is like Venus: yellow-haired, like Minerva; call her slender whose thinness impairs her health; if short, call her trim; if stout, of full body; let its nearness to a virtue conceal a fault.
OVID, *The Art of Love,* bk. 2, tr. by J. H. MOZLEY.

3
Jupiter has loaded us with two wallets: the one, filled with our own faults, he has placed at our backs; the other, heavy with the faults of others, he has hung before.
PHAEDRUS, *Fables,* X.

4
Be to her virtues very kind,
Be to her faults a little blind.
MATTHEW PRIOR, *An English Padlock.*

5
Let's develop our faults: they're our true nature.
NED ROREM, *Paris Diary.*

6
Don't tell your friends their social faults; they will cure the fault and never forgive you.
LOGAN PEARSALL SMITH, *Trivia.*

7
When you have done a fault, be always pert and insolent, and behave yourself as if you were the injured person; this will immediately put your master or lady off their mettle.
JONATHAN SWIFT, *Directions to Servants.*

8
Men have many faults;
    Women have but two:
There's nothing good they say,
    And nothing right they do.
UNKNOWN, *Women's Faults.*

FEAR

See also Cowardice, Meekness, Timidity

9
A good scare is worth more to a man than good advice.
E. W. HOWE, *Howe's Monthly.*

10
Fears is about all some people ever entertain.
FRANK McKINNEY (KIN) HUBBARD, *Abe Martin's Primer.*

11
Dodgers often dodge into the danger they would avert. Don't dodge anything except sin, sir, and you will be all right.
STONEWALL JACKSON, quoted in *Southern Punch.*

12
Stage fright of a martyr: the simple Christian fears the lions less than his first public appearance.
NED ROREM, *Paris Diary.*

FEELING

See also Disposition, Manners

13
Sensitive beings are not sensible beings.
HONORÉ DE BALZAC, *Petty Troubles of Married Life.*

14
As cold as cucumbers.
BEAUMONT AND FLETCHER, *Cupid's Revenge,* Act 1.

15
Length must be measured by sensations, not by yards. The channel, for instance, if you are seasick, is longer than the Atlantic if you are not.
HUBERT BLAND, *The Happy Moralist.*

16
It is universally understood that, as if it were nothing more substantial than vapour floating in the sky, every emotion of a woman is bound to end in a shower.
JOSEPH CONRAD, *The Secret Agent.*

17
Passion, though a bad regulator, is a powerful spring.
RALPH WALDO EMERSON, *Conduct of Life: Considerations by the Way.*

18
Laughter and tears are meant to turn the wheels of the same sensibility; one is wind-power and the other water-power, that is all.
OLIVER WENDELL HOLMES, *The Autocrat of the Breakfast-Table,* ch. 4.

19
Melancholy is the pleasure of being sad.
VICTOR HUGO, *The Toilers of the Sea.* Pt. iii, bk. 1, ch. 1.

20
It is curious that we should be more anxious to conceal our best passions than our worst.
WALTER SAVAGE LANDOR, *Letter to Southey,* 1811.

21
Watch out that someone else's emotion does not grip your throat.
STANISLAW J. LEC, *Unkempt Thoughts,* tr. from the Polish by JACEK GALASKA.

1
Passions are likened to floods and streams:
The shallow murmur, but the deep are dumb.
SIR WALTER RALEIGH, *The Silent Lover.*

2
It is just as well to be a little giddy-pated,
if you are to feel at home on this turning
earth.
LOGAN PEARSALL SMITH.

3
When I walk with you I feel as if I had a
flower in my buttonhole.
WILLIAM MAKEPEACE THACKERAY.

4
For sometimes she would laugh, and some-
    times cry,
Then sudden waxed wroth, and all she knew
    not why.
JAMES THOMSON, *The Castle of Indolence.*

5
The prevailin' weakness of most public men
is to Slop Over! . . . G. Washington never
slopt over.
ARTEMUS WARD, *Fourth of July Oration.*

6
The advantage of the emotions is that they
lead us astray.
OSCAR WILDE, *The Picture of Dorian
Gray,* ch. 3.

7
The secret of life is never to have an emotion that is unbecoming.
OSCAR WILDE, *A Woman of No Importance,* Act 3.

FIGHTING

See also Quarreling, War

8
Mr. President, I never quarrel, sir. But
sometimes I fight, sir, and whenever I fight,
sir, a funeral follows.
SENATOR THOMAS HART BENTON of Missouri, 1850. (*The Wit and Wisdom of
Congress,* ed. by EDWARD BOYKIN.)

9
Men should stop fighting among themselves
and start fighting insects.
LUTHER BURBANK.

10
You can refuse to love a man or to lend
him money, but if he wants to fight you
have got to oblige him.
FINLEY PETER DUNNE.

11
After having worked like horses, don't set
about to fight like dogs.
MARIA EDGEWORTH, *Parent's Assistant.*

12
Many a man has fought because he feared to
run away.
RICHARD HOVEY, *The Marriage of Guen-
evere.* Act iv, sc. 3.

13
As the poet Dante once said: "The hottest
places in hell are reserved for those who, in
a time of great moral crisis, maintain their
neutrality."
JOHN F. KENNEDY, from *The Quotable
Mr. Kennedy,* ed. by GERALD C. GARD-
NER.

14
I don't want to hear of any of you men
getting into any fights with the British. But
if you do, you'd better not get whipped.
CURTIS E. LEMAY, to his Air Force officers during World War II, while he was
stationed in England. (*The New York
Times,* Dec. 8, 1964.)

15
These bears, being so hard to die, rather
intimidate us all. I must confess that I do
not like the gentleman and had rather fight
two Indians than one grizzly bear.
MERIWETHER LEWIS, quoted in *The Legend of Grizzly Adams* by RICHARD DIL-
LON.

16
We're eyeball to eyeball, and the other
fellow just blinked.
DEAN RUSK, *Comment,* Oct., 1962, during the Cuban missile crisis.

17
Received a blushing crow.
WILLIAM A. SPOONER, warden of New
College, Oxford, who transposed the
sound of words. (Received a crushing
blow.)

18
"Now we are even," quoth Steven, when he
gave his wife six blows to one.
JONATHAN SWIFT, *Letters to Stella,* Jan.
20, 1711.

19
At the end of a French duel the pair hug
and kiss and cry, and praise each other's
valor; then the surgeons make an examination and pick out the scratched one, and the
other one helps him on to the litter and pays
his fare; and in return the scratched one
treats to champagne and oysters in the evening, and then "the incident is closed," as
the French say. It is all polite, and gracious,
and pretty, and impressive.
MARK TWAIN, *Essays: Dueling.*

20
Much as the modern French duel is ridi-
culed by certain smart people, it is in reality
one of the most dangerous institutions of

our day. Since it is always fought in the open air, the combatants are nearly sure to catch cold.

MARK TWAIN, *A Tramp Abroad.*

1
By a sudden and adroit movement I placed my left eye agin the Secesher's fist . . . The ground flew up and hit me in the hed.

ARTEMUS WARD, *Thrilling Scenes in Dixie.*

FINANCE

See also Money

2
Great is Bankruptcy: the great bottomless gulf into which all Falsehoods, public and private, do sink, disappearing.

THOMAS CARLYLE, *The French Revolution,* vol. 1.

3
They throw cats and dogs together and call them elephants.

ANDREW CARNEGIE, *Interview,* referring to industrial promoters.

4
What's this draft whistling through your house?—
no East wind dank;
an overdraft is blowing coldly
from the bank.

CATULLUS, *Songs,* 26. From *Roman Culture,* ed. by GARRY WILLS.

5
Buy an annuity cheap, and make your life interesting to yourself and everybody else that watches the speculation.

CHARLES DICKENS, *Martin Chuzzlewit.*

6
A titan of finance, said Mr. Dooley, is a man that's got more money than he can carry without being disorderly.

FINLEY PETER DUNNE, *Mr. Dooley Remembers.*

7
A big head and a big bank account don't keep company very long.

B. C. FORBES, *Epigrams.*

8
A bank is a place where they lend you an umbrella in fair weather and ask for it back again when it begins to rain.

ROBERT FROST. See also TWAIN in this section.

9
I was even thinking of dabbling in the stock market, only the broker everybody recommended had a very disturbing word in the name—Lynch!

DICK GREGORY, *From the Back of the Bus.*

10
Put not your trust in money, but put your money in trust.

OLIVER WENDELL HOLMES, *The Autocrat of the Breakfast-Table,* ch. 2.

11
The safest way to double your money is to fold it over once and put it in your pocket.

FRANK MCKINNEY (KIN) HUBBARD, quoted in *Horse Sense in American Humor.*

12
Wall street, observed the Detroit *Free Press,* is paralyzed at the thought that a President of the United States would sink so low as to try to enforce the law.

WALTER LORD, *The Good Years: Big Stick, Big Business.* Reference is to President Theodore Roosevelt's filing of an antitrust suit.

13
Bankers Are Just Like Anybody Else, Except Richer.

OGDEN NASH, *Title* of poem from the collection *I'm a Stranger Here Myself.*

14
I'm sure it's easy enough to make a fortune if you have a decent share of brains and a bigger one of capital.

MAX PEMBERTON, *The Lodestar.*

15
A bad man's credit is as shifty as himself.

PLINY THE YOUNGER, *Letters.* Bk. i, letter 5.

16
Men put money into stocks and women into stockings.

Reflections of a Bachelor.

17
It is speculation when you lose; investment when you win.

Reflections of a Bachelor.

18
One-third of the people in the United States promote, while the other two-thirds provide.

WILL ROGERS, *The Illiterate Digest.*

19
A holding company is the people you give your money to while you're being searched.

WILL ROGERS, quoted by ALISTAIR COOKE in *One Man's America.*

20
Never invest your money in anything that eats or needs repainting.

BILLY ROSE, *New York Post,* Oct. 26, 1957.

21
. . . it is more dangerous to be a great prophet or poet than to promote twenty companies for swindling simple folk out of their savings.

BERNARD SHAW, *Misalliance:* preface.

1
Next to reading somebody else's love letters, there's nothing quite so delightful as being privy to the facts of his financial life, especially if they tend toward the disastrous.
A. C. SPECTORSKY, *The Exurbanites.*

2
In the whole art of painting is there anything uglier than the shape of a banker's mouth who is afraid of losing his money?
STENDHAL (MARIE HENRI BEYLE), *Memoirs of a Tourist,* tr. by ALLAN SEAGER.

3
Banker—A fellow who lends you his umbrella when the sun is shining and wants it back the minute it begins to rain.
MARK TWAIN.

4
A banker is a fellow who will lend you money if you can prove that you don't need it.
UNKNOWN.

5
Wall Street Lays An Egg.
Variety. Headline referring to the stock-market crash of 1929.

6
The way to stop financial joy-riding is to arrest the chauffeur, not the automobile.
WOODROW WILSON, from LINTHICUM, *Wit and Wisdom of Woodrow Wilson.*

FIRE

7
Billy, in one of his nice new sashes,
Fell in the fire and was burned to ashes;
Now, although the room grows chilly,
I haven't the heart to poke poor Billy.
HARRY GRAHAM.

8
There is no fire without some smoke.
JOHN HEYWOOD, *Proverbs.*

9
Out of the frying pan into the fire.
JOHN HEYWOOD, *Proverbs.* Pt. ii, ch. 5.

10
When the house is on fire the good girls have to get out as well as the bad ones.
J. P. MORGAN, quoted by Cleveland Amory in *The Last Resorts.*

11
Better a little fire that warms than a big one that burns.
JOHN RAY, *English Proverbs.*

FISH

12
How can you stop a dead fish from smelling? Cut off its nose.
FRED ALLEN, *Much Ado About Me.*

13
A sardine is a herring's pup.
FRED ALLEN, *Much Ado About Me.*

14
But four young Oysters hurried up,
All eager for the treat:
Their coats were brushed, their faces washed,
Their shoes were clean and neat—
And this was odd, because, you know,
They hadn't any feet.
LEWIS CARROLL, *Through the Looking-Glass,* ch. 4.

15
"O Oysters," said the Carpenter,
"You've had a pleasant run!
Shall we be trotting home again?"
But answer came there none—
And this was scarcely odd, because
They'd eaten every one.
LEWIS CARROLL, *Through the Looking-Glass,* ch. 4.

16
"Will you walk a little faster?" said a whiting to a snail,
"There's a porpoise close behind us, and he's treading on my tail!"
LEWIS CARROLL, *Alice's Adventures in Wonderland,* ch. 10.

17
Damned neuters, in their
Middle way of steering,
Are neither Fish, nor Flesh,
Nor good Red Herring.
JOHN DRYDEN, *Duke of Guise.*

18
Here we have an Oyster. It is Going to a Church Fair. When it gets to the Fair, it will Swim around in a big Kettle of Warm Water. A Lady will Stir it with a Spoon and sell the Warm Water for Forty Cents a pint. Then the Oyster will move on to the next Fair. In this Way, the Oyster will visit all the Church Fairs in Town and Bring a great many Dollars into the Church Treasury. The Oyster goes a great Way in a Good Cause.
EUGENE FIELD, *The Tribune Primer.*

19
If you would make little fishes talk, they would talk like whales.
OLIVER GOLDSMITH, to Dr. Johnson. (BOSWELL, *Life,* 1773.)

20
"The Folks on Land are Dumb," the Fish declare;
"How can they speak?—their Mouths are full of Air!"
ARTHUR GUITERMAN, *A Poet's Proverbs.*

21
Oh, man! admire and model thyself after the whale! Do thou, too, remain warm among

ice. Do thou, too, live in this world without being of it. Be cool at the equator; keep thy blood fluid at the Pole. Like the great dome of St. Peter's, and like the great whale, retain, O man! in all seasons a temperature of thine own.
> HERMAN MELVILLE, *Moby Dick*, ch. 68.

1
Only the game fish swims upstream,
But the sensible fish swims down.
> OGDEN NASH, *When You Say That, Smile.*

2
I can tell you why a snail has a house . . .
To put his head in.
> WILLIAM SHAKESPEARE, *King Lear.* Act i, sc. 5.

3
It is the sick oyster which possesses the pearl.
> JOHN A. SHEDD, *Salt from My Attic.*

4
"The snail," says the Hindoo, "sees nothing but his own shell, and thinks it the grandest palace in the universe."
> SYDNEY SMITH, *Peter Plymley Letters*, No. 10.

5
He was a bold man that first eat an oyster.
> JONATHAN SWIFT, *Polite Conversation*, Dial. 2.

FLATTERY

6
Flattery is like Kolone water, tew be smelt of, not swallowed.
> JOSH BILLINGS, *Philosophy.*

7
Flatterers look like friends, as wolves like dogs.
> GEORGE CHAPMAN.

8
One catches more flies with a spoonful of honey than with twenty casks of vinegar.
> HENRY IV of France, *Maxim.*

9
Madam, before you flatter a man so grossly to his face, you should consider whether or not your flattery is worth his having.
> SAMUEL JOHNSON, *Remark* to Hannah More. (FANNY BURNEY, *Diary*, 1778.)

10
Of all wild beasts preserve me from a tyrant;
And of all tame, a flatterer.
> BEN JONSON, *Fall of Sejanus*, Act 1.

11
Flattery very seldom changes a woman's character, though it may sway her judgment. She accepts it as her right, but seldom believes it.
> ORPHEUS C. KERR. (*Civil War Humor*, ed. by DORIS BENARDETE.)

12
When my friend, Judge Douglas, came to Chicago, . . . he complimented me as being a "kind, amiable and intelligent gentleman." . . . I was not very much accustomed to flattery, and it came the sweeter to me. I was rather like the Hoosier with the gingerbread, when he said he reckoned he loved it better than any other man, and got less of it.
> ABRAHAM LINCOLN, *Speech* in Ottawa, Ill., in reply to Stephen Douglas, July 31, 1858.

13
It is possible to be below flattery, as well as above it.
> THOMAS BABINGTON MACAULAY, *History of England*, ch. 2.

14
Well said: that was laid on with a trowel.
> WILLIAM SHAKESPEARE, *As You Like It.* Act i, sc. 2.

15
But when I tell him he hates flatterers,
He says he does; being then most flattered.
> WILLIAM SHAKESPEARE, *Julius Caesar.* Act ii, sc. 1.

16
They do abuse the King that flatter him,
For flattery is the bellows blows up sin.
> WILLIAM SHAKESPEARE, *Pericles.* Act i, sc. 2.

17
What really flatters a man is that you think him worth flattering.
> BERNARD SHAW, *John Bull's Other Island*, Act 4.

18
Oh, flattery—it's like a cigaret; it is all right if you don't inhale.
> ADLAI STEVENSON, quoted by ARCHIBALD MACLEISH.

19
'Tis an old maxim in the schools,
That flattery's the food of fools;
Yet now and then your men of wit
Will condescend to take a bit.
> JONATHAN SWIFT, *Cadenus and Vanessa.*

20
Nothing is so great an instance of ill manners as flattery. If you flatter all the company, you please none: if you flatter only one or two, you affront the rest.
> JONATHAN SWIFT, *Hints on Good Manners.*

21
Flattery is the worst and falsest way of showing our esteem.
> JONATHAN SWIFT, *Hints on Good Manners.*

1
Even the disciple has his uses. He stands behind one's throne, and at the moment of one's triumph whispers in one's ear that, after all, one is immortal.

OSCAR WILDE, *Saturday Review*, Nov. 17, 1894.

FLOWERS

2
Any nose
May ravage with impunity a rose.

ROBERT BROWNING, *Sordello*.

3
What is a weed? A plant whose virtues have not yet been discovered.

RALPH WALDO EMERSON, *Fortune of the Republic*.

4
For each pure Rose
  That now the Bust adorns,
The patient Gardener knows
  A Hundred Thorns.

ARTHUR GUITERMAN, *A Poet's Proverbs*.

5
Rose is a rose is a rose is a rose.

GERTRUDE STEIN, *Geography and Plays: Sacred Emily*.

6
What a man needs in gardening is a cast-iron back with a hinge on it.

CHARLES DUDLEY WARNER, *My Summer in a Garden*.

FOOL AND FOLLY

7
A good folly is worth whatever you pay for it.

GEORGE ADE, *Fables in Slang: The Fable of the Visitor Who Got a Lot for Three Dollars*.

8
A prosperous fool is a grievous burden.

AESCHYLUS, *Fragment 383*.

9
He that makes himself an ass must expect to be rode.

G. L. APPERSON, *English Proverbs and Proverbial Phrases*.

10
She would rather fool with a bee than be with a fool.

JOHN KENDRICK BANGS.

11
There's a sucker born every minute.

PHINEAS T. BARNUM.

12
A Jerk is someone who is overly sensitive to Parental influences.

ERIC BERNE, *Games People Play*, ch. 14.

13
A fool sees not the same tree as a wise man sees.

WILLIAM BLAKE, *Proverbs of Hell*.

14
If the fool would persist in his folly he would become wise.

WILLIAM BLAKE, *Proverbs of Hell*.

15
There's no fool like an old fool—you can't beat experience.

JACOB M. BRAUDE, *Treasury of Wit and Humor*.

16
The picture placed the busts between
  Adds to the thought much strength;
Wisdom and Wit are little seen,
  But Folly's at full length.

JANE BRERETON, *On Beau Nash's Picture at Full Length between the Busts of Sir Isaac Newton and Mr. Pope*.

17
To swallow gudgeons ere
  they're catch'd.
And count their chickens ere
  they're hatch'd.

SAMUEL BUTLER, *Hudibras*.

18
There are more fools than knaves in the world, or else the knaves would not have enough to live upon.

SAMUEL BUTLER, *Remains*.

19
A fool is like other men as long as he is silent.

JACOB CATS, *Moral Emblems*.

20
After their [knaves' and fools'] friendship, there is nothing so dangerous as to have them for enemies.

LORD CHESTERFIELD, *Letters*, Feb. 17, 1754.

21
Those who did not think her a fool thought her a saint. There is a certain similarity between the two.

LUCAS CLEEVE, *Selma*.

22
Nobody can describe a fool to the life, without much patient self inspection.

FRANK MOORE COLBY, *The Colby Essays*, vol. 1.

23
A fool's paradise is better than a wiseacre's purgatory.

GEORGE COLEMAN, THE ELDER, *The Deuce Is in Him*.

24
A rogue is a roundabout fool.

SAMUEL TAYLOR COLERIDGE, *Table Talk*, Jan. 4, 1823.

1
He who at fifty is a fool,
Is far too stubborn grown for school.
CHARLES COTTON, *Visions*, No. 1.

2
A fool must now and then be right by chance.
WILLIAM COWPER, *Conversation*.

3
Someone once told me that the world is composed of 1) Fools; 2) Damned fools, and 3) Bloody fools. The least one can do is try to stick to the first class.
LORD CURZON. (LEONARD MOSLEY, *The Glorious Fault*.)

4
I'm not denyin' the women are foolish: God Almighty made 'em to match the men.
GEORGE ELIOT, *Adam Bede*.

5
If you can successfully guard against it the other 364 days of the year, you can afford to be made a fool of on April 1st.
B. C. FORBES, *Epigrams*.

6
If fifty million people say a foolish thing, it is still a foolish thing.
ANATOLE FRANCE.

7
Who knows a fool must know his brother;
One fop will recommend another.
JOHN GAY, *Fables*. Pt. i, fab. 9.

8
It might be argued, that to be a knave is the gift of fortune, but to play the fool to advantage it is necessary to be a learned man.
WILLIAM HAZLITT, *Table Talk:* Intellectual Superiority.

9
The wisest fool in Christiandom.
HENRY IV of France, of James I of England, when the latter abandoned him for an alliance with Spain.

10
Mix with your sage counsels some brief folly. In due place to forget one's wisdom is sweet.
HORACE, *Odes*, xii.

11
He dares be a fool, and that is the first step in the direction of wisdom.
JAMES HUNEKER, *Pathos of Distance*.

12
The silliest woman can manage a clever man; but it takes a very clever woman to manage a fool.
RUDYARD KIPLING, *Plain Tales*.

13
But because a man is fooling some of the time, it does not follow that he is fooling all of the time.
STEPHEN LEACOCK, *Charles Dickens*.

14
Fine B— observes no other rules
    Than those the coterie prize;
She thinks, whilst lords continue fools,
    'Tis vulgar to be wise.
EDWARD LOVIBOND, *On a Very Fine Lady*.

15
A blockhead, bit by fleas, put out the light,
And chucking cried, "Now you can't see to bite!"
LUCIAN, *Epigram*.

16
It needs brains to be a real fool.
GEORGE MACDONALD, *Weighed and Wanting*, ch. 26.

17
Even a fool may be efficient, if his foolishness fits the office.
CHARLES MARRIOTT, *The House on the Sands*.

18
Into a Limbo large and broad, since call'd
The Paradise of Fools, to few unknown.
JOHN MILTON, *Paradise Lost*, III.

19
A fellow who is always declaring he's no fool usually has his suspicions.
WILSON MIZNER.

20
An erudite fool is a greater fool than an ignorant fool. (Un sot savant est sot plus qu'un sot ignorant.)
MOLIÈRE (JEAN BAPTISTE POQUELIN), *Les Femmes Savantes*.

21
A whip for the horse, a bridle for the ass, and a rod for the fool's back.
Old Testament, *Proverbs: xxvi*, 3.

22
I have great faith in fools; self-confidence my friends call it.
EDGAR ALLAN POE.

23
No creature smarts so little as a fool.
ALEXANDER POPE, *Satires:* Prologue.

24
The traditional fool and his money are lucky ever to have got together in the first place.
Puck, quoted in *Toaster's Handbook*, compiled by PEGGY EDMUND AND HAROLD WORKMAN WILLIAMS.

25
Fools are fond o' flittin', and wise men o' sittin'.
JOHN RAY, *Proverbs: Scottish*.

26
Even the wisest men make fools of themselves about women, and even the most foolish women are wise about men.
DR. THEODORE REIK, *The Need to Be Loved*.

1

A fool, Sir, at a woman's service, and a knave at a man's.

> WILLIAM SHAKESPEARE, *All's Well That Ends Well.* Act iv, sc. 5.

2

Folly is the direct pursuit of Happiness and Beauty.

> BERNARD SHAW, *Maxims for Revolutionists.*

3

The ultimate result of shielding men from the effects of folly is to fill the world with fools.

> HERBERT SPENCER, *State Tamperings with Money Banks.*

4

April 1. This is the day upon which we are reminded of what we are on the other three hundred and sixty-four.

> MARK TWAIN, *Pudd'nhead Wilson's Calendar.*

5

Let us be thankful for the fools. But for them the rest of us could not succeed.

> MARK TWAIN, *Pudd'nhead Wilson's New Calendar.*

6

Hain't we got all the fools in town on our side? And ain't that a big enough majority in any town?

> MARK TWAIN, *The Adventures of Huckleberry Finn,* ch. 26.

7

Fools' names, like fools' faces,
Are often seen in public places.

> UNKNOWN.

8

I only desire to have follies that are amusing, and am sorry Cervantes laughed chivalry out of fashion.

> HORACE WALPOLE, *Letter* to Horace Mann, July 10, 1774.

9

Follies cease to attract the elect when cultivated by the many.

> PERCY WHITE, *The Eight Guests.*

10

The best way to silence any friend of yours whom you know to be a fool is to induce him to hire a hall.

> WOODROW WILSON, *Speech* in New York, Jan. 27, 1916.

11

Our police system can protect us from our criminals, but only public opinion can protect us from our fools.

> WALTER WINCHELL, in *Let's Go to Press* by ED WEINER.

12

A fool at forty is a fool indeed.

> EDWARD YOUNG, *Love of Fame, the Universal Passion.* Satire ii, 1. 282.

13

Nothing exceeds in ridicule, no doubt,
A fool in fashion, but a fool that's out;
His passion for absurdity's so strong,
He cannot bear a rival in the wrong.

> EDWARD YOUNG, *Love of Fame.* Satire iv, l. 105.

FORGIVENESS

14

The offender never pardons.

> GEORGE HERBERT, *Jacula Prudentum.*

15

Nobuddy ever fergits where he buried a hatchet.

> FRANK McKINNEY (KIN) HUBBARD, *Abe Martin's Broadcast.*

16

I think all men are born with the knowledge that when they have wounded a woman's soul—and our souls are easily wounded—the only cure is a trifling, but expensive, jewel.

> W. SOMERSET MAUGHAM, *The Constant Wife.*

17

A woman will never forgive a man if she is wrong.

> *Pana* (Ill.) *News-Palladium.*

18

Nothing is ever forgiven you in the place you were born in.

> SIR ARTHUR WING PINERO, *The Thunderbolt,* Act 1.

19

We can forgive most anything except the person who has to forgive us.

> *Reflections of a Bachelor* (1903).

20

No woman will deny herself the romantic luxury of self-sacrifice and forgiveness when they take the form of doing something agreeable.

> BERNARD SHAW, *Fanny's First Play,* Act 3.

21

For my part I believe in the forgiveness of sin and the redemption of ignorance.

> ADLAI E. STEVENSON, *Reply* to a heckler during a United Nations Day speech delivered by Stevenson in Dallas, Oct. 24, 1963.

FORTUNE

See also Luck

22

He that waits upon fortune, is never sure of a dinner.

> BENJAMIN FRANKLIN, *Poor Richard,* 1734.

23

He seldom lives frugally who lives by

chance. Hope is always liberal; and they that trust her promises make little scruple of revelling to-day on the profits of the morrow.

> SAMUEL JOHNSON, *Works*, vol. 7 (Oxford Edition, 1825).

1
Watch out you don't get crushed under somebody else's wheel of fortune.

> STANISLAW J. LEC, *Unkempt Thoughts*, tr. from the Polish by JACEK GALASKA.

2
The blanks as well as the prizes must be drawn in the cheating lottery of life.

> ALAIN RENÉ LE SAGE, *Gil Blas*. Bk. iv, ch. 2.

3
There are many in this old world of ours who hold that things break about even for all of us. I have observed for example that we all get the same amount of ice. The rich get it in the summertime and the poor get it in the winter.

> BAT MASTERSON, quoted by GENE FOWLER in *Skyline*.

4
Nowadays everybody forgets there are other kinds of fortune than the money kind.

> *Reflections of a Bachelor.*

5
A woman goes and gets her fortune told so as not to be discouraged when it doesn't come true.

> *Reflections of a Bachelor.*

6
If chance will have me king, why, chance may crown me.

> WILLIAM SHAKESPEARE, *Macbeth*. Act i, sc. 3.

7
It was very prettily said that we may learn the little value of fortune by the persons on whom Heaven is pleased to bestow it.

> SIR RICHARD STEELE, *The Tatler*, No. 203.

8
I must complain the cards are ill shuffled till I have a good hand.

> JONATHAN SWIFT, *Thoughts on Various Subjects.*

FRANCE AND THE FRENCH

9
Forty million Frenchmen can't be wrong.

> ANONYMOUS. In the version attributed to TEXAS GUINAN, the figure is fifty million.

10
France, fam'd in all great arts, in none supreme.

> MATTHEW ARNOLD, *To a Republican Friend.*

11
The French are wiser than they seem, and the Spaniards seem wiser than they are.

> FRANCIS BACON, *Essays: Of Seeming Wise.*

12
In reading French newspapers there is always one consolation: no matter how little of the meaning you are able to get, you aren't missing a thing.

> ROBERT BENCHLEY, *La Presse Perverse.*

13
Maybe the French will get a manned craft into space if they can get a rocket strong enough to lift a bottle of wine.

> DAVID BRINKLEY, *Newscast on NBC-TV*, Dec. 15, 1965.

14
A bad liver is to a Frenchman what a nervous breakdown is to an American. Everyone has had one and everyone wants to talk about it.

> ART BUCHWALD, *New York Herald Tribune*, Jan. 16, 1958.

15
A Frenchwoman has so much imagination that she can even warm her heart at the cold ashes of a dead love.

> G. B. BURGIN, *Which Woman?*

16
France without an army is a cock without a comb.

> WINSTON CHURCHILL, quoted in the *Diaries* of Lord Moran, July 9, 1945.

17
The French woman says, "I am a woman and a Parisienne, and nothing foreign to me appears altogether human."

> RALPH WALDO EMERSON, *Lectures: Table-Talk.*

18
Paris is terribly derisive of all absurd pretensions but its own.

> RALPH WALDO EMERSON, *Lectures: Table-Talk.*

19
I hate the French because they are all slaves and wear wooden shoes.

> OLIVER GOLDSMITH, *Essays: The History of a Disabled Soldier.*

20
Everything is on such a clear financial basis in France. It is the simplest country to live in. No one makes things complicated by becoming your friend for any obscure reason. If you want people to like you, you have only to spend a little money.

> ERNEST HEMINGWAY, *The Sun Also Rises.*

21
Paris is well worth a Mass. (Paris vaut bien une Messe.)

> HENRY IV, referring to his conversion to

Catholicism in order to gain Paris and the crown of France. Fournier doubts if Henry was so undiplomatic as to have said this.

1

We have given you Lafayette and French fried potatoes.
O. HENRY, *Tictocq*.

2

Good! I need no sand!
MARSHALL ANDOCHE JUNOT, when a bursting shell threw some dirt on a dispatch he was writing from Bonaparte's dictation, Toulon, Dec., 1793.

3

Parasites are residents of Paris.
ART LINKLETTER, *A Child's Garden of Misinformation*.

4

Half artist and half anchorite,
Part siren and part Socrates.
PERCY MACKAYE, *France*.

5

A Frenchman loves his mother—in the abstract.
HENRY SETON MERRIMAN, *The Sowers*, ch. 3.

6

. . . men of his race do not find it easy to accept any foreigner as a superior being, and Winston does not like that kind of agnosticism.
LORD MORAN, *Diaries*, Jan. 22, 1943. Referring to Charles de Gaulle and Winston Churchill, respectively.

7

It is easy to govern the French through vanity.
NAPOLEON BONAPARTE. (*The Mind of Napoleon*, ed. by J. CHRISTOPHER HEROLD.)

8

Have the French for friends, but not for neighbors.
EMPEROR NICEPHORUS, when treating with the Ambassadors of Charlemagne in 803.

9

Paris is the middle-aged woman's paradise.
SIR ARTHUR WING PINERO, *The Princess and the Butterfly*, Act 1.

10

Paris today is a city asleep. And snoring loudly.
NED ROREM, *Paris Diary*.

11

John Ashberry says: "Once you've been happy in Paris you can never be happy anywhere else—not even in Paris."
NED ROREM, *Paris Diary*.

12

A mademoiselle from Armentières,

13

She hasn't been kissed in forty years,
Hinky, dinky, par-lee-voo.
EDWARD ROWLAND, *Mademoiselle from Armentières*.

13

You who have ever been to Paris, know;
And you who have not been to Paris—go!
JOHN RUSKIN, *A Tour Through France*, st. 12.

14

A nation of monkeys with the throat of parrots.
JOSEPH SIEYÈS, *Letter* to Mirabeau.

15

There is always one thing which a Frenchman respects more than his mistress, that is, his vanity.
STENDHAL (MARIE HENRI BEYLE), *De l'Amour*, ch. 41.

16

Paris seems to be full of American girls who are hiding out from their mothers.
JAMES THURBER, *Credos and Curios*.

17

French morality is not of that strait-laced description which is shocked at trifles.
MARK TWAIN.

18

The cross of the Legion of Honor has been conferred upon me. However, few escape that distinction.
MARK TWAIN, *A Tramp Abroad*, ch. 8.

19

The Parisian travels but little, he knows no language but his own, reads no literature but his own, and consequently he is pretty narrow and pretty self-sufficient. However, let us not be too sweeping; there are Frenchmen who know languages not their own: these are the waiters.
MARK TWAIN, *Paris Notes* (1882).

20

The king of France with twenty thousand men
Went up the hill, and then came down again;
The king of Spain with twenty thousand more,
Climbed the same hill the French had climbed before.
UNKNOWN, *The King of France*. Reference to Henry IV of France. (Sloane Ms. No. 1489.) An earlier version of *Old Tarleton's Song*. For other versions see HALLIWELL, *Nursery Rhymes*.

21

Most of the houses in France are made of Plaster of Paris.
LOUIS UNTERMEYER, *A Treasury of Laughter*. Quoting a student boner.

22

Your nation is divided into two species: the

one of idle monkeys who mock at everything; and the other of tigers who tear.
> VOLTAIRE, *Letter* to Madame du Deffand, Nov. 21, 1776.

FREEDOM

See also Liberty

1
We are not free; it was not intended we should be. A book of rules is placed in our cradle, and we never get rid of it until we reach our graves. Then we are free, and only then.
> E. W. HOWE, *Howe's Monthly.*

2
A man should never put on his best trousers when he goes out to battle for freedom and truth.
> HENRIK IBSEN, *An Enemy of the People,* Act 4.

3
Many a boomerang does not return but chooses freedom instead.
> STANISLAW J. LEC, *Unkempt Thoughts,* tr. from the Polish by JACEK GALASKA.

4
Most men have a tendency to imprison themselves—without the help of the authorities.
> HENRY MILLER, *Introduction* to *Really the Blues* by MEZZ MEZZROW AND BERNARD WOLFE.

5
Nathan Leopold walked out of Stateville Prison Thursday into the wonderful world of free men. He promptly got sick.
> JOHN JUSTIN SMITH, *Story* on release of Leopold after 33 years in prison; *Chicago Daily News,* Mar. 13, 1958.

6
We have confused the free with the free and easy.
> ADLAI STEVENSON, *Putting First Things First: A Democratic View.*

7
There be four things that keep us from having our own way,—
Money, Fortune, Mrs Grundy, and Policeman A.
> D'ARCY THOMPSON, *Sales Attici.*

8
It is by the goodness of God that in our country we have those three unspeakably precious things: freedom of speech, freedom of conscience, and the prudence never to practise either of them.
> MARK TWAIN, *Pudd'nhead Wilson's New Calendar,* ch. 20.

FRIEND, FRIENDSHIP

See also Companions

9
We're insufferable friends.
> JANE ACE, quoted in *The Fine Art of Hypochondria* by GOODMAN ACE.

10
A friend in power is a friend lost.
> HENRY ADAMS, *The Education of Henry Adams.*

11
You, sir, are a foul-weather friend.
> BERNARD BARUCH. (HARPO MARX, *Harpo Speaks!*)

12
While your friend holds you affectionately by both your hands you are safe, for you can watch both his.
> AMBROSE BIERCE, *The Cynic's Word Book.*

13
Until harsh experience taught him the folly of it, he was always willing to endorse a friend's note, and surely greater love hath no man than this: laying down one's life is nothing in comparison.
> GAMALIEL BRADFORD, *As God Made Them: Henry Clay,* p. 63.

14
Love is only chatter,
Friends are all that matter.
> GELETT BURGESS, *Willy and the Lady.*

15
Friendship is like money, easier made than kept.
> SAMUEL BUTLER, *Notebooks* (c. 1890).

16
Many a friend who will tell us our faults without reserve will not so much as hint at our follies.
> LORD CHESTERFIELD, *Letters,* July 1, 1748.

17
Friendship often ends in love; but love, in friendship—never.
> C. C. COLTON, *Lacon.*

18
'Tis a lamentable thing, I swear, that one has not the liberty of choosing one's acquaintance as one does one's clothes.
> WILLIAM CONGREVE, *The Way of the World,* Act 3.

19
Fate makes our relatives, choice makes our friends.
> JACQUES DELILLE, *Misfortune and Pity,* canto 1.

20
Explanations are the essence of friendship —yet, if you've got to have a dose of castor oil, you needn't lick the spoon.
> R. N. DICKINSON, *Keddie.*

1
There is a magic in the memory of school-boy friendships; it softens the heart, and even affects the nervous system of those who have no heart.
> BENJAMIN DISRAELI, *Endymion,* ch. 52.

2
There are no friends at cards or world politics.
> FINLEY PETER DUNNE, *Mr. Dooley Remembers.*

3
There are three faithful friends—an old wife, an old dog, and ready money.
> BENJAMIN FRANKLIN, *Poor Richard,* 1738.

4
Friendship is a disinterested commerce between equals; love, an abject intercourse between tyrants and slaves.
> OLIVER GOLDSMITH, *The Good-Natured Man.*

5
He cast off his friends as a huntsman his pack,
For he knew when he pleas'd he could whistle them back.
> OLIVER GOLDSMITH, *Retaliation.*

6
I have no trouble with my enemies. But my goddam friends, White, they are the ones that keep me walking the floor nights.
> WARREN G. HARDING, to WILLIAM ALLEN WHITE, 1923. (COHN, *The Fabulous Democrats.*)

7
Friendship is cemented by interest, vanity, or the want of amusement; it seldom implies esteem, or even mutual regard.
> WILLIAM HAZLITT, *Characteristics,* No. 412.

8
There's one thing that keeps surprising you about stormy old friends after they die—their silence.
> BEN HECHT, *Letters from Bohemia.*

9
Here's champagne to our real friends,
And real pain to our sham friends.
> *Toasts for All Occasions,* ed. by LEWIS C. HENRY.

10
A platonic friendship is an unhealthy lie.
> JOHN OLIVER HOBBES, *Life and Tomorrow.*

11
Those who have never tried, think it pleasant to court a friend in power; one who has tried dreads it.
> HORACE, *Epistles.* I, 18.

12
A friend married is a friend lost.
> HENRIK IBSEN, *Love's Comedy,* Act 2. Quoted as a proverb.

13
The feeling of friendship is like that of being comfortably filled with roast beef; love, like being enlivened with champagne.
> SAMUEL JOHNSON, BOSWELL'S *Life,* Apr. 16, 1775.

14
No friendship is so cordial or so delicious as that of girl for girl; no hatred so intense and immovable as that of woman for woman.
> WALTER SAVAGE LANDOR, *Imaginary Conversations.*

15
If you want to make a dangerous man your friend, let him do you a favor.
> LEWIS E. LAWES, former warden of Sing Sing.

16
God gives us relatives; thank God, we can choose our friends.
> ADDISON MIZNER, *The Cynics' Calendar,* p. 1. Also attributed to ETHEL WATTS MUMFORD. See also DELILLE in this section.

17
There is no stronger bond of friendship than a mutual enemy.
> FRANKFORT MOORE, *The Marriage Lease.*

18
Fellowship in joy, and not sympathy in sorrow, makes people friends.
> FRIEDRICH WILHELM NIETZSCHE, *Human, All Too Human,* vol. 2, tr. by PAUL V. COHN.

19
The familiarity of superiors embitters one, because it may not be returned.
> FRIEDRICH WILHELM NIETZSCHE, *Beyond Good and Evil,* tr. by HELEN ZIMMERN.

20
Let us embrace, and from this very moment vow an eternal misery together.
> THOMAS OTWAY, *The Orphan.* Act iv, sc. 2.

21
Reporter: Now that you are wealthy are you ever bothered by the friends you had when you were poor?
Man of Wealth: I never had any friends when I was poor.
> HERBERT PROCHNOW, *Complete Toastmaster.*

22
Stick to a friend a little in the wrong.
> JOHN RANDOLPH of Roanoke, from *The Wit and Wisdom of Congress,* ed. by EDWARD BOYKIN.

1
Friends: people who borrow books and set wet glasses on them.
EDWIN ARLINGTON ROBINSON.

2
One's old acquaintances sometimes come upon one like ghosts—and most people hate ghosts.
MRS. BAILLIE SAUNDERS, *A Shepherd of Kensington.*

3
Old friends are best. King James us'd to call for his old shoes, they were easiest for his feet.
JOHN SELDEN, *Table Talk.*

4
No friendship can survive the gift of gold. The generous can indeed forget that they have given, but the grateful can never forget that they have received.
WILLIAM SMITH, *Thorndale.* Bk. ii, ch. 6.

5
Choose a good disagreeable friend, if you are wise—a surly, steady, economical, rigid fellow.
WILLIAM MAKEPEACE THACKERAY, *Sketches and Travels in London.*

6
The holy passion of Friendship is of so sweet and steady and loyal and enduring a nature that it will last through a whole lifetime, if not asked to lend money.
MARK TWAIN, *Pudd'nhead Wilson's Calendar.*

7
Familiarity breeds contempt—and children.
MARK TWAIN, *Unpublished Diaries.*

8
Do not use a hatchet to remove a fly from your friend's forehead.
UNKNOWN. Chinese proverb, quoted in *H. Allen Smith's Almanac* (1965).

9
Friendship is far more tragic than love. It lasts longer.
OSCAR WILDE, *Saturday Review*, Nov. 17, 1894.

10
All men's friend, no man's friend.
JOHN WODROEPHE, *Spared Hours.*

FURNISHINGS

11
The chandelier is the great abomination of furniture; it makes a noble apartment look dull.
BENJAMIN DISRAELI, *Lothair.*

12
Anyone can buy new things, but only a strong man can throw out old things.
WILLIAM FEATHER.

13
American interiors tend to have no happy medium between execrable taste and what is called "good taste" and is worn like a wart.
MARGARET HALSEY, *With Malice Toward Some.*

14
The titanic vulgarity of the interior design is so tremendous, so assured, and so absolutely unconscious of its own absurdity, that it comes off triumphantly.
BERNARD LEVIN, *London Daily Mail* columnist. His impression of the new Metropolitan Opera. Quoted in *The New York Times,* Jan. 22, 1967.

15
My copper lamps, at any rate,
For being true antique I bought;
Yet wisely melted down my plate,
On modern models to be wrought;
And trifles I alike pursue,
Because they're old, because they're new.
MATTHEW PRIOR, *Alma*, Canto 3.

16
No furniture so charming as books.
SYDNEY SMITH, quoted by LADY HOLLAND, *Memoir,* vol. 1.

17
Carpets are bought by the yard and worn by the foot.
A. R. SPOFFORD, *The Library of Wit and Humor.*

FUTURE

18
By and by never comes. (Modo et modo non habebant modum.)
ST. AUGUSTINE, *Confessions.* VIII, 5.

19
It often occurs to me to envy the future for what it will know about the past.
BERNARD BERENSON, *Notes* (1950).

20
The future is an opaque mirror. Anyone who tries to look into it sees nothing but the dim outlines of an old and worried face.
JIM BISHOP, *New York Journal-American,* Oct. 15, 1959.

21
And Hobbs, Nobbs, Stokes, and Nokes combine
To paint the future from the past,
Put blue into their line.
ROBERT BROWNING, *Popularity.*

22
The future is but dressing and undressing.
JAMES BRANCH CABELL, *Jurgen.*

23
I never think of the future. It comes soon enough.
ALBERT EINSTEIN, *Interview*, Dec., 1930

1
Neither a wise man nor a brave man lies down on the tracks of history to wait for the train of the future to run over him.
DWIGHT D. EISENHOWER, *Speech*, Oct. 6, 1957.

2
We should all be concerned about the future because we will have to spend the rest of our lives there.
CHARLES F. KETTERING, *Seed for Thought*.

3
I believe the future is only the past again, entered through another gate.
SIR ARTHUR WING PINERO, *The Second Mrs. Tanqueray*.

G

GAMBLING

4
There are two people who bet, Mutke explained. One is an idiot. The other is a bastard. An idiot bets because he's not sure and a bastard bets because he is sure.
JOEY ADAMS, *Cindy and I*, ch. 11.

5
The blue ribbon goes to the boy who never changes his underwear or his shirt while he's on a winning streak. In one week he can become the wealthiest, dirtiest gambler in Las Vegas. That's where they get the expression, "filthy rich." The moment he goes on a losing streak he can be clean in short order—inside and out.
JOEY ADAMS, *Cindy and I*, ch. 24.

6
The urge to gamble is so universal and its practice is so pleasurable that I assume it must be evil.
HEYWOOD BROUN.

7
Quoth she, I've heard old cunning stagers
Say fools for arguments use wagers.
SAMUEL BUTLER, *Hudibras*, pt. 2.

8
And remember, dearie, never give a sucker an even break.
Attributed to W. C. FIELDS.

9
Gaming is the son of avarice, and the father of despair. (Le jeu le fils d'avarice, et le pere du desespoir.)
Old French Proverb.

10
When in doubt, win the trick.
EDMOND HOYLE, *Twenty-four Rules for Learners*.

11
Why they call a feller that keeps losin' all the time a good sport gits me.
FRANK McKINNEY (KIN) HUBBARD, *Abe Martin's Broadcast*.

12
Gambling is a disease of barbarians superficially civilized.
DEAN W. R. INGE. (Merchant, *Wit and Wisdom of Dean Inge*, No. 116.)

13
If dirt was trumps, what hands you would hold!
CHARLES LAMB, *Lamb's Suppers*, vol. 2, last ch.

14
Gambling—The sure way of getting nothing for something.
WILSON MIZNER.

15
Bookie—A pickpocket who lets you use your own hands.
HENRY MORGAN.

16
I know nothing about racing and any money I put on a horse is a sort of insurance policy to prevent it winning.
FRANK RICHARDSON, *Bunkum*.

17
The race is not always to the swift, nor the battle to the strong—but that's the way to bet.
DAMON RUNYON, attributed.

18
If you bet on a horse, that's gambling. If you bet you can make three spades, that's entertainment. If you bet cotton will go up three points, that's business. See the difference?
BLACKIE SHERROD, *Dallas Times Herald*.

19
The story is not founded on fact . . . My education in that field did not come until I went to France (as an artillery officer in World War I). P.S.—I found it rather costly.
HARRY S TRUMAN, refuting accusation that he cleaned up at poker in Oklahoma during the early 1900's. (*Newsweek*, Sept. 30, 1957.)

20
There are two times in a man's life when he should not speculate: when he can't afford it, and when he can.
MARK TWAIN, *Pudd'nhead Wilson's New Calendar*.

GENIUS

21
Fifty percent of Winston [Churchill] is

genius, fifty percent bloody fool. He will behave like a child.
> CLEMENT ATTLEE, quoted in the *Diaries of Lord Moran*, ch. 72.

1
What is genius? It is the power to be a boy again at will.
> JAMES M. BARRIE, *Tommy and Grizel*.

2
Men ov genius are like eagles, tha live on what tha kill, while men ov talents is like crows, tha live on what has been killed for them.
> JOSH BILLINGS, *Talent and Genius*.

3
Genius . . . has been defined as a supreme capacity for taking trouble. . . . It might be more fitly described as a supreme capacity for getting its possessors into trouble of all kinds and keeping them therein so long as the genius remains.
> SAMUEL BUTLER, *The Way of All Flesh*.

4
Genius, in one respect, is like gold,—numbers of persons are constantly writing about both, who have neither.
> C. C. COLTON, *Lacon*. Vol. ii, No. 133.

5
Genius is one percent inspiration and ninety-nine percent perspiration.
> THOMAS A. EDISON, *Newspaper Interview*. Quoted in *Golden Book*, Apr., 1931.

6
Great geniuses have the shortest biographies.
> RALPH WALDO EMERSON, *Representative Men: Plato*.

7
Genius without education is like silver in the mine.
> BENJAMIN FRANKLIN, *Poor Richard*.

8
Genius is the capacity of evading hard work.
> ELBERT HUBBARD, *The Philistine*. Vol. xi, p. 14.

9
In the republic of mediocrity genius is dangerous.
> ROBERT G. INGERSOLL, *Liberty in Literature*.

10
There is the same difference between talent and genius that there is between a stone mason and a sculptor.
> ROBERT G. INGERSOLL, *Shakespeare*.

11
There is a thin line between genius and insanity; I have erased that line.
> OSCAR LEVANT, *The Memoirs of an Amnesiac*.

12
At least once a year everyone is a genius.
> GEORGE C. LICHTENBERG, *Reflections*.

13
Men of genius are often dull and inert in society, as the blazing meteor when it descends to the earth is only a stone.
> HENRY WADSWORTH LONGFELLOW, *Kavanagh*, ch. 13.

14
Geniuses should always be given dinners when they are struggling; it gives them encouragement. If you wait till they are recognized it only gives them indigestion.
> CHARLOTTE MANSFIELD, *Girl and the Gods*.

15
Do not pity the unsuccessful lover of a woman of genius. Save your sympathy for the man who marries her.
> DON MARQUIS, *New York Herald*.

16
Genius in the Sperm Whale? Has the Sperm Whale ever written a book, spoken a speech? No, his great genius is declared in his doing nothing particular to prove it.
> HERMAN MELVILLE, *Moby Dick*, ch. 79.

17
Genius, cried the commuter,
As he ran for the 8:13,
Consists of an infinite capacity
For catching trains.
> CHRISTOPHER MORLEY, *An Ejaculation*.

18
The function of genius is not to give new answers, but to pose new questions which time and mediocrity can resolve.
> H. R. TREVOR-ROPER, *Men and Events*.

19
Thousands of geniuses live and die undiscovered—either by themselves or by others.
> MARK TWAIN.

20
Antony was not a genius; he was a gigantic commonplace.
> ARTHUR WEIGALL, *Life and Times of Cleopatra*.

21
To the question: "Do you think genius is hereditary?" he replied: "I can't tell you; heaven has granted me no offspring."
> HESKETH PEARSON, *Lives of the Wits*. Quoting J. A. MCNEILL WHISTLER.

22
I have nothing to declare except my genius.
> OSCAR WILDE, *Remark* to customs officers on his arrival in the United States. Quoted by HESKETH PEARSON in *Lives of the Wits*.

GENTLEMAN

23
I am a gentleman, though spoiled i' the breeding. The Buzzards are all gentlemen.

We came in with the Conqueror.
RICHARD BROME, *English Moor.* Act ii,
sc. 4.

1
Manners and money make a gentleman.
THOMAS FULLER, *Gnomologia.*

2
Whatever the rest of the world thinks of
the English gentleman, the English lady regards him apprehensively as something between God and a goat, and equally formidable on both scores.
MARGARET HALSEY, *With Malice Toward
Some.*

3
A gentleman is one who understands and
shows every mark of deference to the claims
of self-love in others, and exacts it in return
from them.
WILLIAM HAZLITT, *Table-Talk: On the
Look of a Gentleman.*

4
A gentleman is one who never hurts any-
one's feelings unintentionally.
OLIVER HERFORD.

5
He was the product of an English public
school and university. . . . He had little
education and highly developed muscles—
that is to say, he was no scholar, but essentially a gentleman.
H. S. MERRIMAN, *The Sowers,* ch. 1.

6
You can do business with anyone, but you
can only sail a boat with a gentleman.
J. P. MORGAN, THE ELDER, quoted by
CLEVELAND AMORY in *The Last Resorts.*

7
When Adam delved and Eve span
Who was then the gentleman?
JOHN RAY, *English Proverbs.*

8
Since every Jack became a gentleman,
There's many a gentle person made a Jack.
WILLIAM SHAKESPEARE, *Richard III.* Act
i, sc. 3.

9
A gentleman of our days is one who has
money enough to do what every fool would
do if he could afford it: consume without
producing.
BERNARD SHAW, *Maxims for Revolutionists.*

10
It don't cost nothin' to be a gentleman.
JOHN L. SULLIVAN, reproving a rowdy.

11
The only infallible rule we know is, that the
man who is always talking about being a
gentleman never is one.
ROBERT SMITH SURTEES, *Ask Mamma,* ch.
1.

12
He was a gentleman who was generally
spoken of as having nothing a-year, paid
quarterly.
ROBERT SMITH SURTEES, *Mr. Sponge's
Sporting Tour,* ch. 24.

13
He is every other inch a gentleman.
REBECCA WEST.

14
If a man is a gentleman, he knows quite
enough, and if he is not a gentleman, whatever he knows is bad for him.
OSCAR WILDE, *A Woman of No Importance,* Act 3.

GERMANY AND THE GERMANS

15
With friends like them we don't need any
enemies.
JOEY ADAMS, *Cindy and I,* ch. 30.

16
It is untrue that Germans are bad drivers.
They hit everything they aim at.
JOEY ADAMS, *Cindy and I,* ch. 30.

17
By its sudden collapse, the proud German
army has once again proved the truth of
the saying, "The Hun is always either at
your throat or at your feet."
SIR WINSTON CHURCHILL, *Speech,* to the
U.S. Congress, May 19, 1943.

18
The German mind has a talent for making
no mistakes but the very greatest.
CLIFTON FADIMAN.

19
Germans have a way of protecting themselves from an awareness of their own in-
coherence by telling themselves lies.
ROBERT GRAVES, *The Crowning Privilege.*

20
Luther convulsed Germany—but Francis
Drake calmed it down again. He gave us the
potato.
HEINRICH HEINE, quoted in *The Nation,*
Feb. 11, 1956.

21
Think of the man who first tried German
sausage.
JEROME K. JEROME, *Three Men in a Boat.*

22
Did the skies the Lord dressed in Prussian
blue
Make the Kaiser dream that He was Prus-
sian too?
ALFRED KREYMBORG, *God Complex.*

1
"Voila un homme!"—that was as much to say: "But this is a *man!* And I only expected to see a German!"

FRIEDRICH WILHELM NIETZSCHE, *Beyond Good and Evil*, tr. by HELEN ZIMMERN. The quotation in French is attributed to Napoleon at his meeting with Goethe.

2
It was a dictum of Porson, that "Life is too short to learn German," meaning, I apprehend, not that it is too difficult to be acquired within the ordinary space of life, but that there is nothing in it to compensate for the portion of life bestowed on its acquirement.

THOMAS LOVE PEACOCK, *Gryll Grange*, ch. 3.

3
The great majority of Germans, realizing the practical impossibility of talking their language with any degree of success, abandon it altogether, and communicate with one another on brass bands. German sounds better on a band, but not much.

FRANK RICHARDSON, *Love, and All About It.*

4
One thing I will say for the Germans, they are always perfectly willing to give somebody else's land to somebody else.

WILL ROGERS, *Autobiography.*

5
German: a good fellow, maybe; but it is better to hang him.

Russian Proverb.

6
Germany, the diseased world's bathhouse.

MARK TWAIN, *Autobiography*, vol. 1.

7
The only way to treat a Prussian is to step on his toes until he apologizes.

UNKNOWN, an Austrian proverb.

8
The people of Germany are just as responsible for Hitler as the people of Chicago are for the *Chicago Tribune.*

ALEXANDER WOOLLCOTT, *Remark* on radio program "People's Platform," Jan. 23, 1943. These were Woollcott's last words; he died a few hours after speaking them and after collapsing at the microphone. The subject of the forum was "Is Germany Incurable?"

GHOST

9
What would you charge to haunt a house?

FRED ALLEN, *Much Ado About Me.* This line has been used many times by many comedians, but Allen says he used it first, in Toledo, Ohio, in 1926.

10
From ghoulies and ghosties and long-leggety beasties
And things that go bump in the night,
   Good Lord, deliver us!

ANONYMOUS, Scottish.

11
I don't believe in ghosts, but I've been afraid of them all my life.

CHARLES A. DANA.

12
I hope not. If I did I should frighten the ghost.

SAMUEL JOHNSON, when asked if he would start as Mr. Garrick did if he saw a ghost.

GIFTS, GIVING

13
Wives like to open packages more than they care what's inside them. So bring her home many inexpensive presents each year, but only one that really strains your pocketbook. The big one is for her to show to her friends, the others just for her to know that you thought of her often.

HAL BOYLE, *Column*, Associated Press, datelined New York, Oct. 21, 1964.

14
A man there was, though some did count him mad,
The more he cast away the more he had.

JOHN BUNYAN, *Pilgrim's Progress*, pt. 2.

15
It is always pleasant to be generous, though very vexatious to pay debts.

RALPH WALDO EMERSON, *Essays, Second Series: Gifts.*

16
Be generous, yet not too free;
   Don't give the Fox the Henhouse Key.

ARTHUR GUITERMAN, *A Poet's Proverbs.*

17
A Gift that's given hesitating
Is not a Gift, but bought with Waiting.

ARTHUR GUITERMAN, *A Poet's Proverbs.*

18
Benefits please like flowers while they are fresh.

GEORGE HERBERT, *Jacula Prudentum.*

19
No man ought to looke a given horse in the mouth.

JOHN HEYWOOD, *Proverbs.*

20
He is very fond of making things which he doesn't want, and then giving them to people who have no use for them.

ANTHONY HOPE (SIR ANTHONY HOPE HAWKINS), *The Dolly Dialogues*, No. 17.

1

It's sweet to be remembered, but it's often cheaper t' be fergotten.

FRANK MCKINNEY (KIN) HUBBARD, *Abe Martin's Primer.*

2

Treating her handsomely buttered no parsnips.

HENRY JAMES, *The Ambassadors.*

3

Yet Foote [the actor] used to say of him [David Garrick] that he walked out with an intention to do a generous action; but turning the corner of a street, he met with the ghost of a half penny, which frightened him.

BOSWELL'S *Life of Johnson,* Apr. 10, 1778.

4

Kissing your hand may make you feel very good but a diamond bracelet lasts forever.

ANITA LOOS, *Gentlemen Prefer Blondes.*

5

Never let your inferiors do you a favor. It will be extremely costly.

H. L. MENCKEN, *A Mencken Chrestomathy.*

6

Princely gifts don't come from princes any more. They come from tycoons.

PRINCE PHILIP, *Remark,* Nov., 1963.

7

I depended on him for everything: what he worshipped in me was his generosity.

JEAN-PAUL SARTRE, *The Words.*

8

Full o' beans and benevolence!

ROBERT SMITH SURTEES, *Handley Cross,* ch. 27.

9

Few men, drinking at a rivulet, stop to consider its source.

M. F. TUPPER, *Proverbial Philosophy: Of Gifts.*

10

It's cheaper to buy than to receive a gift.

UNKNOWN, Japanese proverb, from *Oriental Humor,* ed. by R. H. BLYTH.

11

I fear the Greeks even when they bring gifts. (Timeo Danaos et dona ferentes.)

VIRGIL, *Aeneid,* bk. 2.

GIRL

12

I'd rather have two girls at 17 than one at 34.

FRED ALLEN, *Much Ado About Me.*

13

Those sweetly smiling angels with pensive looks, innocent faces, and cash-boxes for hearts.

HONORÉ DE BALZAC, *Cousin Bette,* ch. 15.

14

Whether men will make passes at girls who wear glasses, depends quite a bit on the shape of the chassis.

S. OMAR BARKER, *U.S. Lady.* See DOROTHY PARKER in this section.

15

Cécile: Do you think it wrong for a girl to know Latin?

Pierre: Not if she can cook a hare or a partridge as well as Mademoiselle Auclaire! She may read all the Latin she pleases.

WILLA CATHER, *Shadows on the Rock.*

16

A girl is certainly the best idea any boy has had to date.

JOHN CIARDI, *The Saturday Review,* Sept. 24, 1966.

17

After a girl gits too big fer Santy Claus she begins t' cast around fer an easy mark.

FRANK MCKINNEY (KIN) HUBBARD, *Abe Martin's Primer.*

18

Well, one or two times they was a little gal that lived in the suburbs who they called her little Red Riding Hood because she always wore a red riding hood in the hopes that sometime a fresh guy in a high power roadster would pick her up and take her riding.

RING LARDNER, *Red Riding Hood.*

19

So this gentleman said a girl with brains ought to do something else with them besides think.

ANITA LOOS, *Gentlemen Prefer Blondes.*

20

. . . I always say that a girl never really looks as well as she does on board a steamship, or even a yacht.

ANITA LOOS, *Gentlemen Prefer Blondes.*

21

Few girls are as well shaped as a good horse.

CHRISTOPHER MORLEY.

22

Men seldom make passes
At girls who wear glasses.

DOROTHY PARKER, *News Item.*

23

A girl should use what Mother Nature gave her before Father Time takes it away.

More Playboy's Party Jokes (1965).

24

A pretty young maiden of France
Decided she'd "just take a chance."
  She let herself go
  For an hour or so,
And now all her sisters are aunts.

More Playboy's Party Jokes (1965).

1
It's usually a girl's geography that determines her history.
More Playboy's Party Jokes (1965).

2
Our Unabashed Dictionary defines:
Well-proportioned girl as one with a narrow waist and a broad mind.
More Playboy's Party Jokes (1965).

3
All it really takes to separate the men from the boys is girls.
More Playboy's Party Jokes (1965).

4
Many a young tomato has been cultivated by an old rake.
More Playboy's Party Jokes (1965).

5
Whether or not a girl can be had for a song depends on a man's pitch.
More Playboy's Party Jokes (1965).

6
When a young girl begins to confide to her mother how silly it is for other young girls to pay any attention to boys, that is the time for her mother to look out for her own little girl.
Reflections of a Bachelor.

7
Most any girl with a good figure learns to swim young.
Reflections of a Bachelor.

8
After a girl has got a good figure and wavy hair and a smooth complexion and attractive teeth it will be time enough to worry about brains.
Reflections of a Bachelor.

9
Young ladies: You shouldn't go strolling
    about
When your anxious mamas don't know you
    are out;
And remember that accidents often befall
From kissing young fellows through holes in
    the wall.
JOHN GODFREY SAXE, *Pyramus and Thisbe: Moral.*

10
She was an extremely beautiful girl and as innocent as a rose. When Watts kissed her, she took for granted she was going to have a baby.
BERNARD SHAW, quoted in *Days with Bernard Shaw* by STEPHEN WINSTEN. The reference is to the actress Ellen Terry.

11
From birth to age eighteen, a girl needs good parents. From eighteen to thirty-five, she needs good looks. From thirty-five to fifty-

five, she needs a good personality. From fifty-five on, she needs good cash.
SOPHIE TUCKER.

12
My son, I've traveled round the world
    And many maids I've met:
There are two kinds you should avoid—
    The blonde and the brunette.
UNKNOWN, *A Warning.*

13
Every good American girl wants to marry a doctor.
TOM WOLFE, *The Kandy-Kolored Tangerine-Flake Streamline Baby.*

GLAMOUR

14
My grandfather, Frank Lloyd Wright, wore a red sash on his wedding night. That is glamour!
ANNE BAXTER, quoted in *Time*, May 5, 1952.

15
Glamour is what makes a man ask for your telephone number. But it also is what makes a woman ask for the name of your dressmaker.
LILLY DACHÉ, quoted in *Woman's Home Companion*, July, 1955.

GOD

16
But there is a God in heaven who looks after everything, "a Lord merciful and compassionate" who has His way with me summer and winter, in season and out. And He says to me, "Tevye, don't talk like a fool. Leave the management of the world to Me."
SHOLOM ALEICHEM, *Modern Children.*

17
Man proposes, and God disposes.
ARIOSTO, *Orlando Furioso.* See also THOMAS À KEMPIS in this section.

18
The God to whom little boys say their prayers has a face very like their mothers.
JAMES M. BARRIE.

19
All those who came here this morning to worship Henry Ward Beecher may now withdraw from the church; all who came to worship God may remain.
THOMAS BEECHER, in Plymouth Church, Brooklyn, when some of the congregation, who had expected to hear his brother, Henry Ward, preach, started to walk out.

20
If there is no God for thee
Then there is no God for me.
ANNA H. BRANCH, *To a Dog.*

1

I fear God, yet am not afraid of him.
SIR THOMAS BROWNE, *Religio Medici*, Bk.
1.

2

All things are artificial, for nature is the art
of God.
SIR THOMAS BROWNE, *Religio Medici*, sec.
16.

3

If the Lord would only send something interesting, I wouldn't mind if it was only a
plaid pig.
GELETT BURGESS.

4

An honest God's the noblest work of man.
SAMUEL BUTLER, *Further Extracts from
the Notebooks* (1934). See also INGER-
SOLL in this section. Both paraphrase
POPE: "An honest man's the noblest
work of God," *Essay on Man*.

5

God was satisfied with his own work, and
that was fatal.
SAMUEL BUTLER, *Notebooks*.

6

Doubtless God could have made a better
berry (strawberry), but doubtless God never
did.
WILLIAM BUTLER, from IZAAK WALTON,
The Compleat Angler. Pt. i, ch. 5.

7

We are all as God made us, and oftentimes
a great deal worse.
MIGUEL DE CERVANTES, *Don Quixote*. Pt.
ii, ch. 4.

8

God is for men and religion for women.
JOSEPH CONRAD, *Nostromo*.

9

We are glad to have God on our side to
maul our enemies, when we cannot do the
work ourselves.
JOHN DRYDEN. (INGE, *Wit and Wisdom:*
preface.)

10

God is clever but not dishonest.
ALBERT EINSTEIN, engraved over a fire-
place in Fine Hall, Princeton, N.J.

11

God is not a cosmic bell-boy for whom we
can press a button to get things.
HARRY EMERSON FOSDICK, *Prayer*.

12

They that worship God merely from fear,
Would worship the devil too, if he appear.
THOMAS FULLER, *Gnomologia*, No. 6419.

13

God will pardon me; it is his trade. (Dieu
me pardonnera; c'est son métier.)
HEINRICH HEINE, *Remark*, Feb. 17, 1856,
the day before his death.

14

An Act of God was defined as something
which no reasonable man could have expected.
A. P. HERBERT, *Uncommon Law*.

15

I have never understood why it should be
considered derogatory to the Creator to suppose that He has a sense of humor.
DEAN W. R. INGE. (MARCHANT, *Wit and
Wisdom of Dean Inge*, No. 235.)

16

An honest God is the noblest work of man.
ROBERT G. INGERSOLL, *The Gods*.

17

Man proposes, but God disposes. (Homo
proponit, sed Deus desponit.)
THOMAS À KEMPIS, *The Imitation of
Christ*. I, 19.

18

The vengeful God is a stallion; in [Billy]
Graham's hands he is a gelding.
MURRAY KEMPTON, *New York Post*, May
16, 1957.

19

I don't object to Gladstone always having
the ace of trumps up his sleeve, but merely
to his belief that the Almighty put it there.
HENRY LABOUCHERE. (HESKETH PEARSON,
Lives of the Wits.)

20

Do not make gods in your own images.
STANISLAW J. LEC, *Unkempt Thoughts*, tr.
from the Polish by JACEK GALASKA.

21

All gods *were* immortal.
STANISLAW J. LEC, *Unkempt Thoughts*, tr.
from the Polish by JACEK GALASKA.

22

Whoever falls from God's right hand
Is caught into his left.
EDWIN MARKHAM, *The Divine Strategy*.

23

If we assume that man actually does resemble God, then we are forced into the
impossible theory that God is a coward, an
idiot and a bounder.
H. L. MENCKEN, quoted by BENJAMIN
DE CASSERES in *Mencken and Shaw*.

24

We are most dishonorable towards our God:
he is not *permitted to sin*.
FRIEDRICH WILHELM NIETZSCHE, *Beyond
Good and Evil*, tr. by HELEN ZIMMERN.

25

God often visits us, but most of the time we
are not at home.
JOSEPH ROUX, *Meditations of a Parish
Priest: God*, No. 65.

26

For several years more I maintained public
relations with the Almighty. But privately,

I ceased to associate with him.
JEAN-PAUL SARTRE, *The Words.*

1
Beware of the man whose god is in the skies.
BERNARD SHAW, *Man and Superman: Maxims for Revolutionists.*

2
God's only excuse is that he does not exist.
STENDHAL (MARIE HENRI BEYLE), quoted by NIETZSCHE in *Ecce Homo.*

3
God is only the president of the day, and Webster is his orator.
HENRY D. THOREAU, *Walden:* conclusion.

4
It is said that God is always for the big battalions.
VOLTAIRE, *Letter* to M. de Riche, Feb. 6, 1770.

5
If God did not exist, it would be necessary to invent him.
VOLTAIRE, *Epître à l'Auteur du Livre des Trois Imposteurs*, Nov. 10, 1770.

6
God and other artists are always a little obscure.
OSCAR WILDE, to Ada Leverson, Dec., 1894.

GOODNESS

See also Morality, Saints, Virtue

7
Those who wish to lead a good life ought to have genuine friends or red-hot enemies; for the former deterred you from what was wrong by reproof, the latter, by abuse.
ANTISTHENES, *Plutarch's Morals*, sec. 5.

8
The good die young—because they see it's no use living if you've got to be good.
JOHN BARRYMORE.

9
Life has taught me that it is not for our faults that we are disliked and even hated, but for our qualities.
BERNARD BERENSON, *Diaries* (1957).

10
There should be some schools called deformatories to which people are sent if they are too good to be practical.
SAMUEL BUTLER (1835–1902).

11
When people get it into their heads that they are being specially favored by the Almighty, they had better as a general rule mind their p's and q's.
SAMUEL BUTLER, *The Way of All Flesh*, ch. 71.

12
Good to animals . . . the bad man's invariable characteristic.
ROBERT W. CHAMBERS, *The Fighting Chance.*

13
The word "good" has many meanings. For example, if a man were to shoot his grandmother at a range of five hundred yards, I should call him a good shot, but not *necessarily* a good man.
G. K. CHESTERTON. (HESKETH PEARSON, *Lives of the Wits.*)

14
We are ne'er like angels till our passion dies.
THOMAS DEKKER, *The Honest Whore*, pt. 2.

15
If you wish to be good, first believe that you are bad.
EPICTETUS, *Fragments*, 3.

16
A halo has to fall only a few inches to become a noose.
Farmer's Almanac, 1966.

17
A real Christian is a person who can give his pet parrot to the town gossip.
BILLY GRAHAM.

18
Few persons have courage enough to appear as good as they really are.
J. C. AND A. W. HARE, *Guesses at Truth.*

19
A man is as good as he has to be, and a woman as bad as she dares.
ELBERT HUBBARD, *Epigrams.*

20

> Abraham Lincoln
> his hand and pen
> he will be good but
> god knows When.

ABRAHAM LINCOLN, in one of his schoolbooks. From *The Humorous Mr. Lincoln* by KEITH W. JENNISON.

21
If there were many more like her, the stock of halos would give out.
SIR ARTHUR WING PINERO.

22
Being good is an awful lonesome job.
Reflections of a Bachelor.

23
The golden rule is that there are no golden rules.
BERNARD SHAW, *Maxims for Revolutionists.*

24
He has more goodness in his little finger

than you have in your whole body.
JONATHAN SWIFT, *Mary the Cookmaid's Letter to Dr. Sheridan.*

1
A bad woman always has something she regards as a curse—a real bit of goodness hidden away somewhere.
LADY TROUBRIDGE, *The Millionaire.*

2
To be good is noble, but to teach others how to be good is nobler—and less trouble.
MARK TWAIN.

3
Oft the statesman and the saint
Think they're doing good, but ain't.
EUGENE FITCH WARE, *Aesop's Fables.*

4
I am as bad as the worst, but thank God I am as good as the best.
WALT WHITMAN.

GOSSIP

See also Slander

5
Rumor, that most efficient of press agents . . .
BRUCE BARTON, JR., art editor of *Time.*

6
Everybody says it, and what everybody says must be true.
JAMES FENIMORE COOPER, *Miles Wallingford,* ch. 30.

7
A gossip is a person with a keen sense of rumor.
Speaker's Sourcebook. Ed. by ELEANOR DOAN.

8
Gossip is a sort of smoke that comes from the dirty tobacco-pipes of those who diffuse it; it proves nothing but the bad taste of the smoker.
GEORGE ELIOT, *Daniel Deronda.*

9
Sir, if they should cease to talk of me I must starve.
SAMUEL JOHNSON, BOSWELL'S *Life of Johnson.*

10
When gossip grows old it becomes myth.
STANISLAW J. LEC, *Unkempt Thoughts,* tr. from the Polish by JACEK GALASKA.

11
Gossips are people who have only one relative in common, but that relative the highest possible; namely God.
CHRISTOPHER MORLEY, *Religio Journalistici.*

12
There are two kinds of people who blow through life like a breeze,

And one kind is gossipers, and the other kind is gossipees.
OGDEN NASH, *I'm a Stranger Here Myself: I Have It on Good Authority.*

13
I lay it down as a fact that, if all men knew what others say of them, there would not be four friends in the world.
BLAISE PASCAL, *Pensees,* sec. 2.

14
Tale-bearers, as I said before, are just as bad as the tale-makers.
RICHARD BRINSLEY SHERIDAN, *The School for Scandal.* Act i, sc. 1.

15
How awful to reflect that what people say of us is true.
LOGAN PEARSALL SMITH, *Afterthoughts.*

16
A preacher cannot look round from the pulpit without observing that some are in a perpetual whisper, and by their air and gesture give occasion to suspect that they are in those very minutes defaming their neighbour.
JONATHAN SWIFT, *A Sermon on Sleeping in Church.*

17
In order to learn the secrets of other families, tell your brethren those of your master's; thus you will grow a favourite both at home and abroad, and regarded as a person of importance.
JONATHAN SWIFT, *Directions to Servants.*

18
But her friends stand by her: when she prematurely published the claim that a certain actress was pregnant, the actress' husband hastened to prove her correct.
Time. Nov. 24, 1961. On columnist Louella Parsons.

19
Tattlers also and busybodies, speaking things which they ought not.
I Timothy. V, 13.

20
There is only one thing in the world worse than being talked about, and that is not being talked about.
OSCAR WILDE, *The Picture of Dorian Gray,* ch. 1.

21
If only when my epitaph is readied, they will say: "Here is Walter Winchell—with his ear to the ground—as usual."
WALTER WINCHELL, from *Let's Go to Press* by ED WEINER.

22
A word to the wives is sufficient.
DOUGLAS YATES, *How to Start Gossip.*

GOVERNMENT

See also Democracy, Politics

1
A monarchy is a merchantman which sails well, but will sometimes strike on a rock, and go to the bottom; a republic is a raft which will never sink, but then your feet are always in the water.

> FISHER AMES, *Speech*, House of Representatives, 1795. (A paraphrase of this quotation, by JOSEPH COOK, appears in section headed "Democracy.")

2
Whenever you read about the unearthing of a big international spy ring in some European country, you may be pretty sure that the government of that country has been naughty and is trying to give the people something else to think about for a minute or two.

> ROBERT BENCHLEY, *Spy Scares*. (*The Benchley Roundup*, ed. by NATHANIEL BENCHLEY.)

3
I think that when God created this country He certainly intended to see, or at least had an idea, that the people should have some rights of self-government. But about the only thing they have left in the country in the way of self-government is how many children the women shall have, and I suppose after a while they will want to regulate even that.

> SENATOR COLEMAN L. BLEASE of South Carolina, 1926. (*The Wit and Wisdom of Congress*, ed. by EDWARD BOYKIN.)

4
Congress has largely abrogated the creative role—[it's] a sort of Grand Exalted Potentate of the Cash Box and nothing more.

> DAVID BRINKLEY, *Foreword to Congress Needs Help* by PHILIP DONHAM AND R. J. FAHEY.

5
France is an absolute monarchy, tempered by songs.

> NICHOLAS CHAMFORT, *Characters and Anecdotes*.

6
If it were not for the government, we should have nothing left to laugh at in France.

> NICHOLAS CHAMFORT.

7
Government has been a fossil: it should be a plant.

> RALPH WALDO EMERSON, *Miscellanies: Lecture*, Boston, Feb. 7, 1844.

8
In 1910, except in backward countries such as Russia, the world was virtually passport-less. Today the papers are more important than the man; what is public is essential.

> CLIFTON FADIMAN, *The Selected Writings of Clifton Fadiman* (1955).

9
It's getting harder and harder to support the government in the style to which it has become accustomed.

> *Farmer's Almanac*, 1966.

10
For a statesman—any school child knows that hot air rises to the top.

> F. SCOTT FITZGERALD, *The Crack-up*.

11
A government that is big enough to give you all you want is big enough to take it all away.

> BARRY M. GOLDWATER, *Speech* in West Chester, Pa., during the presidential campaign, 21 Oct., 1964.

12
It's political Daddyism, and it's as old as demagogues and despotism.

> BARRY M. GOLDWATER, *Speech* in New York City during the presidential campaign, 26 Oct., 1964. He was referring to the paternalism of the "everlastingly growing Federal government."

13
The whole flavor and quality of the American representative government turn to ashes on the tongue, if one regards the government as simply an inferior and rather second-rate sort of corporation.

> MARGARET HALSEY, *The Folks at Home*.

14
In other countries when a citizen becomes dissatisfied with his government he emigrates; in France he requests the government to emigrate.

> HEINRICH HEINE. (*The Humor of Germany*, ed. and trans. by HANS MULLER CASENOV.)

15
No public man can be just a little crooked.

> HERBERT HOOVER, 1951. (*Herbert Hoover in His Own Words*, compiled by LOUIS P. LOCHNER; *The New York Times Magazine*, Aug. 9, 1964, p. 15.)

16
I am against government by crony.

> HAROLD ICKES, *Remark*, on resigning as Secretary of the Interior, Feb., 1946, referring to President Truman's propensity toward rewarding old friends with jobs.

17
It is really more questionable than may at first be thought, whether Bonaparte's dumb legislature, which said nothing and did much,

may not be preferable to one which talks much and does nothing.

THOMAS JEFFERSON, *Writings*, vol. i, p. 86.

1

I believe a woman's place not only is in the home, but in the House and Senate and throughout the government. One thing we are insisting on is that we not have this stag government.

LYNDON B. JOHNSON, *Speech* in Washington, D.C., 3 Mar., 1964, commending career women in government service.

2

Government is an Irish boy from Boston who grew up to be President. Government is the son of a German immigrant from Pekin, Ill., who became a leader of the American Senate. Government is a rancher from Montana, a banker from New York, an automobile maker from Detroit; government is the son of a tenant farmer from Texas who is speaking to you tonight.

LYNDON B. JOHNSON, *Address* before annual Boy Scout jamboree, Valley Forge, Pa., July 24, 1964. He was referring, respectively, to John F. Kennedy, Everett M. Dirksen, Mike Mansfield, C. Douglas Dillon (then Secretary of the Treasury), Robert S. McNamara (then Secretary of Defense), and himself.

3

It is much safer to obey, than to govern. (Multo tutius est stare in subcectione quam in prolatura.)

THOMAS À KEMPIS, *The Imitation of Christ*, ch. 9, tr. by ANTHONY HOSKINS.

4

My experience in government is that when things are non-controversial, beautifully coordinated and all the rest, it must be that there is not much going on.

JOHN F. KENNEDY. (*The Kennedy Wit*, ed. by BILL ADLER.)

5

It is easy to hang puppets. The strings are already there.

STANISLAW J. LEC, *Unkempt Thoughts*, tr. from the Polish by JACEK GALASKA.

6

A lesson that our country learned early and well, and which some countries unfortunately never learned or learned too late, is that each citizen had better take an active interest in running his country or he may suddenly find the country running him.

ART LINKLETTER, *A Child's Garden of Misinformation.*

7

We trust a man with making constitutions on less proof of competence than we should

demand before we gave him our shoe to patch.

JAMES RUSSELL LOWELL, *On a Certain Condescension in Foreigners.*

8

Despotism is often the effort of nature to cure herself from a worse disease.

ROBERT LORD LYTTON, *Speeches of Edward Lord Lytton:* prefatory memoir.

9

The Commons, faithful to their system, remained in a wise and masterly inactivity.

SIR JAMES MACKINTOSH, *Vindiciae Gallicae.*

10

Socialist—A man suffering from an overwhelming compulsion to believe what is not true.

H. L. MENCKEN.

11

Metternich comes close to being a statesman: he lies very well.

NAPOLEON BONAPARTE. (*The Mind of Napoleon*, ed. by J. CHRISTOPHER HEROLD.)

12

The American government is a rule of the people, by the people, for the boss.

AUSTIN O'MALLEY.

13

As long as you keep the present turtle at the head of the government you make a pit with one hand and fill it with the other.

WENDELL PHILLIPS, quoted by CARL SANDBURG in *Abraham Lincoln: The Prairie Years and The War Years*, ch. 26. The reference, to Abraham Lincoln, was made in 1862.

14

It is an axiom of statecraft that you can always give the public anything but you can never take away what you have once given, without enormous trouble.

WALTER B. PITKIN, *Twilight of the American Mind.*

15

Government is like a baby—an alimentary canal with a big appetite at one end and no sense of responsibility at the other.

RONALD REAGAN, quoted by STEWART ALSOP in *The Saturday Evening Post*, Nov. 20, 1965.

16

The Federal Power Commission sent a questionnaire to the gas producers which weighed ten pounds and required seventeen thousand accountant man-hours to complete.

RONALD REAGAN, quoted by STEWART ALSOP in *The Saturday Evening Post*, Nov. 20, 1965.

1
I don't make jokes; I just watch the government and report the facts.
    WILL ROGERS.

2
Thou little thinkest what a little foolery governs the world.
    JOHN SELDEN, *Table-Talk.*

3
A government which robs Peter to pay Paul can always depend on the support of Paul.
    BERNARD SHAW, *Everybody's Political What's What* (1944).

4
Surely if a president kills anyone it's an execution; but if anyone kills a president it's an assassination.
    BERNARD SHAW, *Geneva,* Act 1.

5
When you come to examine the American constitution, you found it was not really a constitution, but a Charter of Anarchism.
    BERNARD SHAW, *Address,* New York, Apr. 11, 1933.

6
The Constitution provides for every accidental contingency in the Executive—except a vacancy in the mind of the President.
    SENATOR SHERMAN of Ohio, referring to President JAMES BUCHANAN.

7
What a man that would be had he . . . the least knowledge of the value of red tape.
    SYDNEY SMITH, referring to SIR JAMES MACKINTOSH. (LADY HOLLAND, *Memoir.*)

8
A motto for Cabinets: Twenty wise men may easily add up into one fool.
    J. A. SPENDER, *The Comments of Bagshot.*

9
Customarily absolute sovereigns know that they can maintain themselves by sharing with their nobility the enjoyment of vice.
    STENDHAL (MARIE HENRI BEYLE), *Memoirs of a Tourist,* tr. by ALLAN SEAGER.

10
The notorious "do-nothing" Republican 80th Congress.
    HARRY S TRUMAN, *Speech* in Dexter, Ia., Sept. 18, 1948.

11
In these latter days it seems hard to realize that there was ever a time when the robbing of our government was a novelty.
    MARK TWAIN.

12
But no, that would be common sense—and out of place in a government.
    MARK TWAIN, *Following the Equator.*

13
Congress is the most interesting body I have found yet. It does more crazy things, and does them with a graver earnestness, than any State Legislature that exists, perhaps.
    MARK TWAIN, *Chicago Republican,* Jan. 31, 1868.

14
Noble system, truly . . . where it is impossible to reward the most illustrious and fittest citizen with the presidency.
    MARK TWAIN, *Notebook,* ch. 13.

15
. . . all Congresses and Parliaments have a kindly feeling for idiots and a compassion for them, on account of personal experience and heredity.
    MARK TWAIN, *Autobiography,* ch. 57.

16
I guess the government that robs its own people earns the future it is preparing for itself.
    MARK TWAIN, *Letter* to John Bigelow.

17
In statesmanship get the formalities right, never mind about the moralities.
    MARK TWAIN, *Pudd'nhead Wilson's New Calendar.*

18
The government of England is a limited mockery.
    LOUIS UNTERMEYER, *A Treasury of Laughter.* Quoted as a student boner.

19
When a government project is described as "imaginative" you know it is going to be almost as expensive as those that are called "bold."
    BILL VAUGHAN, *Kansas City Star.*

20
. . . in its idiot way our system, though it usually keeps us from having the very best man as President, does protect us from the worst.
    GORE VIDAL, *Rocking the Boat.*

21
In general the art of government consists in taking as much money as possible from one class of citizens to give to the other.
    VOLTAIRE, *Dictionnaire Philosophique: Money.*

22
My movements to the chair of Government will be accompanied by feelings not unlike those of a culprit who is going to the place of his execution.
    GEORGE WASHINGTON, *Letter* to Henry Knox, Apr. 1, 1789.

23
Influence is not government.
    GEORGE WASHINGTON, *Political Maxims.*

GRAMMAR

1
So hath man sought to come forth of the second general curse, which was the confusion of tongues, by the art of grammar.
FRANCIS BACON, *Advancement of Learning,* bk. 2.

2
The grammar has a rule absurd
Which I would call an outworn myth:
"A preposition is a word
You mustn't end a sentence with!"
BRETON BRALEY, *No Rule to Be Afraid Of.*

3
More fault of those who had the hammering
Of prosody into me, and syntax,
And did it, not with hobnails but tintacks!
ROBERT BROWNING, *The Flight of the Duchess.*

4
This is the sort of English up with which I will not put.
Attributed to SIR WINSTON S. CHURCHILL, on avoiding ending a sentence with a preposition. Marginal comment on a document, quoted by SIR ERNEST GOWERS in *Plain Words.*

5
Do not feel bad when you hear the broadcaster say he feels badly. Just remember that all men are created equally.
CLIFTON FADIMAN, *Enter, Conversing.*

6
For there be women, fair as she,
Whose verbs and nouns do more agree.
BRET HARTE, *Mrs. Judge Jenkins.*

7
Grammar, which knows how to lord it over kings, and with high hands makes them obey its laws. (La grammaire, qui sait régenter jusqu'aux rois. Et les fait, la main haute, obéir à ses lois.)
MOLIÈRE, *Les Femmes Savantes.* Act ii, sc. 6.

8
The greater part of the world's troubles are due to questions of grammar. (La plus part des occasions des troubles du monde sont grammairiennes.)
MICHEL DE MONTAIGNE, *Essays.* Bk. ii, ch. 12.

9
A grammarian's daughter made love with a man, and the poor creature gave birth to a child who was, in orderly sequence:
masculine, feminine, & neuter.
PALLADAS, tr. by WILLIS BARNSTONE.

10
Mr. Speaker, I smell a rat; I see him forming in the air and darkening the sky; but I'll nip him in the bud.
SIR BOYLE ROCHE, attributed. A classic example of mixing metaphors.

11
I am the King of Rome, and above grammar.
THE EMPEROR SIGISMUND, at the Council of Constance (1414–1418).

12
When I read some of the rules for speaking and writing the English language correctly, . . . I think—
Any fool can make a rule
And every fool will mind it.
HENRY D. THOREAU, *Journal,* Feb. 3, 1860.

13
I don't give a damn for a man that can spell a word only one way.
MARK TWAIN.

14
The heart of our trouble is with our foolish alphabet. It doesn't know how to spell, and can't be taught. In this it is like all other alphabets except one—the phonographic. That is the only competent alphabet in the world.
MARK TWAIN, *Essays: A Simplified Alphabet.*

15
A metaphor is a thing you shout through.
LOUIS UNTERMEYER, *A Treasury of Laughter.* Quoted as a student boner.

16
I was never allowed to read the popular American children's books of my day because, as my mother said, the children spoke bad English *without the author's knowing it.*
EDITH WHARTON.

17
George Moore: he wrote excellent English until he discovered grammar.
OSCAR WILDE.

GRATITUDE

18
Be thankful f'r what ye have not, Hinnissy —'tis the on'y safe rule.
FINLEY PETER DUNNE, *Thanksgiving.*

19
Revenge is profitable, gratitude is expensive.
EDWARD GIBBON, *The Decline and Fall of the Roman Empire.*

20
To John I ow'd great obligation;
But John, unhappily, thought fit
To publish it to all the nation;
Sure John and I are more than quit.
MATTHEW PRIOR, *Epigram.*

1
Our God and soldiers we alike adore
Ev'n at the brink of danger; not before:
After deliverance, both alike requited,
Our God's forgotten, and our soldiers
  slighted.
FRANCIS QUARLES, *Epigram.*

2
It is safer to affront some people than to
oblige them; for the better a man deserves,
the worse they will speak of him.
SENECA.

3
Now in art, as in politics, there is no such
thing as gratitude.
BERNARD SHAW, *Our Theatres in the
  Nineties.*

4
If you pick up a starving dog and make him
prosperous, he will not bite you; that is the
principal difference between a dog and a
man.
MARK TWAIN.

GRAVE

5
Only on the edge of the grave can a man
conclude anything.
HENRY ADAMS, *The Education of Henry
  Adams.*

6
I say that if Lincoln were living today, he
would turn over in his grave.
HOUSE MINORITY LEADER GERALD FORD.
  Spoken at a Lincoln Day Republican
  rally. (*Time*, Feb. 17, 1967.)

7
Tombs are the clothes of the dead; a grave
is but a plain suit, and a rich monument is
one embroidered.
THOMAS FULLER, *The Holy and Profane
  States.*

8
And now he has no single plot of ground,
Excepting that in which he sleeps so sound!
HENRY HARRISON, *Epitaph for a Real-
  Estate Dealer.*

9
The grave's a fine and private place,
But none, I think, do there embrace.
ANDREW MARVELL, *To His Coy Mistress.*

GREATNESS

10
Calvin Coolidge—The greatest man who ever
came out of Plymouth Corner, Vermont.
CLARENCE DARROW.

11
If greatness and goodness went hand in hand,
it's small chance any of us would have of

seeing our picture in the papers.
FINLEY PETER DUNNE, *Mr. Dooley Remembers.*

12
Great Caesar's bust is on the shelf,
And I don't feel so well myself.
ARTHUR GUITERMAN, *On the Vanity of
  Earthly Greatness.*

13
Great eaters and great sleepers are incapable
of anything else that is great. (Les grands
manageurs et les grands dormeurs sont in-
capables de rien faire de grand.)
HENRY IV of France, *Epigram.*

14
He [Thomas Gray] was dull in a new way,
and that made many people think him great.
SAMUEL JOHNSON, Boswell's *Life of Johnson*, Mar. 28, 1775.

15
The majority of great men are the offspring
of unhappy marriages.
HERMANN VON KEYSERLING, *Works.*

16
And the talk slid north and the talk slid
  south,
With the sliding puffs from the hookah-
  mouth.
Four things greater than all things are,—
Women, and Horses and Power and War.
RUDYARD KIPLING, *Ballad of the King's
  Jest.*

17
What? A great man? I always see merely
the play-actor of his own ideal.
FRIEDRICH WILHELM NIETZSCHE, *Beyond
  Good and Evil*, tr. by HELEN ZIMMERN.

18
Greatness is its own torment.
THEODORE PARKER, *Ten Sermons of Reli-
  gion: Of Justice and the Conscience.*

19
That man is great who can use the brains
of others to carry on his work.
DONN PIATT, *Memories of the Men Who
  Saved the Union.*

20
It's great to be great but it's greater to be
human.
WILL ROGERS, *Autobiography.*

GREED

21
Vile avarice and pride from Heaven accurst,
In all are ill, but in a church-man worst.
WILLIAM ALEXANDER, *Doomsday: The
  Sixth Hour*, st. 86.

22
A miser is a guy who lives within his in-
come. He's also called a magician.
Alliston (Ontario) *Herald.*

1
"I ain't greedy for land," the old farmer said, "I only want what jines mine."
ANONYMOUS.

2
The bird of paradise alights only upon the hand that does not grasp.
JOHN BERRY, *Flight of White Crows.*

3
Spare all I have, and take my life!
GEORGE FARQUHAR, *The Beaux' Stratagem.* Act iv, sc. 2.

4
If I knew a miser, who gave up every kind of comfortable living, all the pleasure of doing good to others, all the esteem of his fellow-citizens, and the joys of benevolent friendship, for the sake of accumulating wealth, Poor man, said I, you pay too much for your whistle.
BENJAMIN FRANKLIN, *The Whistle.*

5
Avarice and happiness never saw each other, how then should they become acquainted?
BENJAMIN FRANKLIN, *Poor Richard,* 1734.

6
A covetous man does nothing well till he dies.
THOMAS FULLER, *Gnomologia,* No. 51.

7
Scheme not to make what's Another's your own;
Be not a Dog for the sake of a Bone.
ARTHUR GUITERMAN, *A Poet's Proverbs.*

8
Punishment of a miser,—to pay the drafts of his heir in his tomb.
NATHANIEL HAWTHORNE, *American Notebooks,* July 10, 1838.

9
You cannot flay a stone.
GEORGE HERBERT, *Jacula Prudentum.*

10
Just what's the matter with the whole world.
I've got three walnuts and each wants two.
ABRAHAM LINCOLN, *Reply* to a friend who asked him what his two sons were fighting about. From *The Humorous Mr. Lincoln* by KEITH W. JENNISON.

11
After spending some money in his sleep, Hermon the miser was so hopping mad, he hanged himself.
LUCILIUS (LOUKILLIOS), *On Hermon the Miser,* tr. by WILLIAM BARNSTONE.

12
The beautiful eyes of my money-box!
He speaks of it as a lover of his mistress.
(Les beaux yeux de ma cassette!
Il parle d'elle comme un amant d'une maitresse.)
MOLIÈRE, *L'Avare,* Act 5.

13
The miser is as much in want of what he has as of what he has not. (Tam deest avaro quod habet, quam quod non habet.)
PUBLILIUS SYRUS, *Sententiae,* No. 440.

14
Some people are so mean they wouldn't even spend a counterfeit bill.
Reflections of a Bachelor.

15
One of the weaknesses of our age is our apparent inability to distinguish our needs from our greeds.
DON ROBINSON, *Phi Delta Kappan,* May, 1963. Reprinted in *The Reader's Digest,* Dec., 1963.

16
'T would make one scratch where 't does not itch,
To see fools live poor to die rich.
THOMAS SHADWELL, *Woman Captain,* Act 1.

GRIEF

See also Sorrow

17
Woman's grief is like a summer storm,
Short as it is violent.
JOANNA BAILLE, *Basil.*

18
Grief is a species of idleness.
SAMUEL JOHNSON, *Letters,* vol. 1.

19
A plague of sighing and grief! it blows a man up like a bladder.
WILLIAM SHAKESPEARE, *King Henry IV, Pt. i.* Act ii, sc. 4.

20
Every one can master a grief but he that has it.
WILLIAM SHAKESPEARE, *Much Ado About Nothing.* Act iii, sc. 2.

GUILT

21
Vouchsafe, O Lord, to keep us this day without being found out.
SAMUEL BUTLER, *Notebooks.*

22
Guilt and sin are only a fear of the past.
CHARLES P. CURTIS, *A Commonplace Book.*

23
Stubborn audacity is the last refuge of guilt.
SAMUEL JOHNSON, *Works,* ix.

24
Let he who is without guilt cast the first stone. A trap. Because he will be no longer without guilt.
STANISLAW J. LEC, *Unkempt Thoughts,* tr. from the Polish by JACEK GALASKA.

1
It is indecent to suspect a man when you are sure of his guilt.
STANISLAW J. LEC, *Unkempt Thoughts,*
tr. from the Polish by JACEK GALASKA.

2
No burglar goes about with a face that in itself amounts to a previous conviction.
FRANK RICHARDSON, *Bunkum.*

3
Give me six lines written by the most honorable of men, and I will find an excuse in them to hang him.
CARDINAL RICHELIEU, *Mirame.*

4
When you are chidden for a fault, as you go out of the room, and down stairs, mutter loud enough to be plainly heard; this will make him believe you are innocent.
JONATHAN SWIFT, *Directions to Servants.*

5
If your master or lady happen once in their lives to accuse you wrongfully, you are a happy servant, for you have nothing more to do, than for every fault you commit, while you are in their service, to put them in mind of that false accusation, and protest yourself equally innocent in the present case.
JONATHAN SWIFT, *Directions to Servants.*

6
The Eleventh Commandment: thou shalt not be found out.
G. J. WHYTE-MELVILLE, *Holmby House.*

H

HABIT

7
Our second mother, habit, is also a good mother.
BERTHOLD AUERBACH, *On the Heights.*

8
It's repetitious to eat or to make love, isn't it? You keep on doing it.
S. N. BEHRMAN, *Biography.*

9
Free yourself from the slavery of tea and coffee and other slopkettle.
WILLIAM COBBETT, *Advice to Young Men,*
ch. 1.

10
You see what will happen to you if you keep on biting your nails.
NOEL COWARD, written on a postcard which contained a photograph of the Venus de Milo.

11
Cultivate only the habits that you are willing should master you.
ELBERT HUBBARD, *The Philistine,* vol. xxv, p. 62.

12
If you will walk with lame men you'll soon limp yourself.
SEUMAS MACMANUS, *Heavy Hangs the Golden Grain.*

13
There is nothing so habit-forming as money.
DON MARQUIS, quoted in *O Rare Don Marquis* by EDWARD ANTHONY.

14
It makes a wife shudder to think what bad habits her husband might acquire if he did not smoke, drink, and swear.
Reflections of a Bachelor.

15
I bite away my fingernails and cuticle, realizing I'm practicing a sort of auto-cannibalism. We shed our skin completely every seven years; and I'm sure that without knowing it, we eat our own weight of ourselves during our lifetime.
NED ROREM, *Paris Diary.*

16
Habit is habit, and not to be flung out of the window by any man, but coaxed downstairs a step at a time.
MARK TWAIN, *Pudd'nhead Wilson's Calendar.*

17
Nothing so needs reforming as other people's habits.
MARK TWAIN, *Pudd'nhead Wilson's Calendar.*

18
Have a place for everything and keep the thing somewhere else; this is not advice, it is merely custom.
MARK TWAIN.

HAIR

See also Beard, Mustache

19
I'd rather have Fingers than Toes,
I'd rather have Eyes than a Nose;
  And as for my Hair
  I'm glad it's all there,
I'll be awfully sad when it goes.
GELETT BURGESS, *Nonsense Verses.*

20
He used to cut his hair, but now his hair has cut him.
THEODORE HOOK, of Planché. (THOMAS, *Nineteenth Century,* Dec., 1881.)

1
Bob's hirsute adornment having been disturbed by one of his spouse's digits during one of the orgies, he went upstairs ten minutes before dinner-time to effect repairs.
RING LARDNER, *The Facts.*

2
Not ten yoke of oxen
Have the power to draw us
Like a woman's hair!
HENRY WADSWORTH LONGFELLOW, *The Saga of King Olaf.*

3
Better a bald head than no head at all.
SEUMAS MACMANUS, *Heavy Hangs the Golden Grain.*

4
As I was letting down my hair
I met a guy who didn't care;
He didn't care again today—
I *love* 'em when they get that way!
HUGHES MEARNS, *The Lady with Technique.*

5
She knows her man, and when you rant and swear,
Can draw you to her with a single hair.
(Ne trepidare velis atque artos rodere casses.)
PERSIUS, *Satires.* Sat. v., l. 170.

6
You can mix any color with some other color and get a different one except when you mix red hair.
Reflections of a Bachelor.

7
All is not blonde that bleaches.
Reflections of a Bachelor.

8
It got to a point where I had to get a haircut or a violin.
FRANKLIN DELANO ROOSEVELT.

9
There's no time for a man to recover his hair that grows bald by nature.
WILLIAM SHAKESPEARE, *The Comedy of Errors.* Act ii, sc. 2.

10
When red-haired people are above a certain social grade their hair is auburn.
MARK TWAIN.

11
Gray hair is a sign of age, not of wisdom.
UNKNOWN, Greek proverb.

12
Why don't you get a haircut; you look like a chrysanthemum.
P. G. WODEHOUSE.

HAPPINESS

13
No misery is more genuine than false joy.
ST. BERNARD, *Concerning Grace and Freewill.*

14
Happiness is the natural flower of duty.
PHILLIPS BROOKS, *Sermons.*

15
The pursuit of happiness belongs to us, but we must climb around or over the church to get it.
HEYWOOD BROUN, *The Nation.*

16
We do not believe in having happiness imposed upon us.
SIR ANDREW COHEN, *Comment* as British representative, UN Trustee Council. (*Quote,* Feb. 23, 1958.)

17
Happiness makes up in height for what it lacks in length.
ROBERT FROST, *Title* of poem (1942).

18
All happiness depends on a leisurely breakfast.
JOHN GUNTHER. (*Newsweek,* Apr. 14, 1958.)

19
Most of the disappointments of later life could be lightened immeasurably if we could learn—and truly believe—early in life that what we confusedly call "happiness" is a direction and not a place.
SYDNEY J. HARRIS, Publishers Newspaper Syndicate. (*The Reader's Digest,* Dec., 1963, p. 205.)

20
Happiness is a habit—cultivate it.
ELBERT HUBBARD, *Epigrams.*

21
It's pretty hard to tell what does bring happiness. Poverty an' wealth have both failed.
FRANK MCKINNEY (KIN) HUBBARD, *Abe Martin's Broadcast.*

22
Happiness is the legal tender of the soul.
ROBERT G. INGERSOLL, *The Liberty of Man, Woman and Child.*

23
There is no private house in which people can enjoy themselves so well, as at a capital tavern. Let there be ever so great plenty of good things, ever so much grandeur, ever so much eloquence, ever so much desire that everybody should be easy; in the nature of things it cannot be: there must always be some degree of care and anxiety. . . . Whereas, at a tavern, there is a general freedom from anxiety . . . No, Sir, there

is nothing which has yet been contrived by man by which so much happiness is produced as by a good tavern or inn.
> SAMUEL JOHNSON, Boswell's *Life,* Mar. 21, 1776.

1
Happiness is the interval between periods of unhappiness.
> DON MARQUIS, *Notes and Comment.*

2
He's simply got the instinct for being unhappy highly developed.
> HECTOR HUGH MUNRO (SAKI), *Chronicles of Clovis: The Match-Maker.*

3
What trifles constitute happiness! The sound of a bagpipe. Without music life would be a mistake.
> FRIEDRICH WILHELM NIETZSCHE, *The Twilight of the Idols,* tr. by A. M. LUDOVICI.

4
Happiness is a good bank account, a good cook, and a good digestion.
> JEAN-JACQUES ROUSSEAU.

5
Happiness is not having what you want, but wanting what you have.
> HYMAN JUDAH SCHACHTEL, *The Real Enjoyment of Living.*

6
But a lifetime of happiness! No man alive could bear it: it would be hell on earth.
> BERNARD SHAW, *Man and Superman,* Act 1.

7
Happiness is never my aim. Like Einstein I am not happy and do not want to be happy: I have neither time nor taste for such comas, attainable at the price of a pipeful of opium or a glass of whiskey, though I have experienced a very superior quality of it two or three times in dreams.
> BERNARD SHAW, *Sixteen Self Sketches.*

8
We are never happy: we can only remember that we were so once.
> ALEXANDER SMITH, *Dreamthorp.*

9
A happy man or woman is a better thing to find than a five-pound note.
> ROBERT LOUIS STEVENSON, *An Apology for Idlers.*

10
One of the oldest and quietest roads to contentment lies through the conventional trinity of wine, woman and song.
> REXFORD GUY TUGWELL, *Address* to the Woman's National Democratic Club, Washington, D.C., May, 1934.

11
Grief can take care of itself; but to get the full value of a joy you must have somebody to divide it with.
> MARK TWAIN.

12
Felicity is happiness with its hair combed straight.
> UNKNOWN, *Meditations in Wall Street.*

13
No talent, no self-denial, no brains, no character is required to set up in the grumbling business.
> ROBERT WEST.

14
A man can be happy with any woman as long as he does not love her.
> OSCAR WILDE, *The Picture of Dorian Gray,* ch. 15.

HASTE

15
What's the use of running when you are on the wrong road?
> W. G. BENHAM, *Proverbs.*

16
There was a young lady named Bright,
Whose speed was faster than light;
    She set out one day
    In a relative way,
And returned home the previous night.
> ARTHUR H. BULLER, *Punch,* Dec. 19, 1923.

17
Who will try to catch the Hare
    When the Deer is standing there?
> ARTHUR GUITERMAN, *A Poet's Proverbs.*

18
Here lies, extinguished in his prime,
a victim of modernity;
but yesterday he hadn't time—
and now he has eternity.
> PIET HEIN, *Grooks.* On speeding.

19
You can't set a hen in one morning and have chicken salad for lunch.
> GEORGE HUMPHREY, Secretary of the Treasury. On the impossibility of quick economic change. (*Time,* Jan. 26, 1953.)

20
Lord Ronald said nothing: he flung himself from the room, flung himself upon his horse and rode madly off in all directions.
> STEPHEN LEACOCK, *Nonsense Novels: Gertrude the Governess.*

21
Stay your haste: the Man who made time made plenty of it.
> SEUMAS MACMANUS, *Heavy Hangs the Golden Grain.*

1
The haste of a fool is the slowest thing in the world.
> THOMAS SHADWELL, *A True Widow*, Act 3.

2
Some people who jump at conclusions lose sight of the hurdles.
> *The Pun Book* by T.B. and T.C. (c. 1906).

3
Put your hand quickly to your hat and slowly to your purse.
> UNKNOWN, *Danish Proverb*.

HAT

4
There is not so variable a thing in nature as a lady's head-dress.
> JOSEPH ADDISON, *The Spectator*, No. 98.

5
Life is futile and the man who wears a toupee should take his hat off to no one.
> FRED ALLEN, in *Fred Allen's Letters*, ed. by JOE MCCARTHY.

6
Here's your hat, what's your hurry?
> BARTLEY C. COSTELLO, *Title and refrain* of popular song (1904).

7
When I was six I made my mother a little hat—out of her new blouse.
> LILLY DACHÉ, designer. *News summaries,* Dec. 3, 1954.

8
I have a theory about their [Englishwomen's] hats. I think they keep them suspended on pulleys from the bedroom ceiling and when they want to put one on, they go and stand directly under it, pull on a rope, and it drops down, smack, squarely on top of the head. Then, without touching a finger to it, they march out of the house.
> MARGARET HALSEY, *With Malice Toward Some.*

9
Virtue may flourish in an old cravat,
But man and nature scorn the shocking hat.
> OLIVER WENDELL HOLMES, *A Rhymed Lesson.*

10
Where did you get that hat?
Where did you get that tile?
Isn't it a nobby one,
  And just in proper style?
> JOSEPH J. SULLIVAN, *Where Did You Get That Hat?* A popular song, written in 1888.

HATE

11
Of all the objects of hatred, a woman once loved is the most hateful.
> MAX BEERBOHM, *Zuleika Dobson*, ch. 13.

12
Ay, do despise me, I'm the prouder for it;
I likes to be despised.
> ISAAC BICKERSTAFFE, *The Hypocrite*, Act 5.

13
The mayor was a man you had to know to dislike.
> JIM BISHOP, *Some of My Very Best: The Voters—Just Like the People.*

14
Now hatred is by far the longest pleasure;
Men love in haste, but they detest at leisure.
> LORD BYRON, *Don Juan.* Canto xiii, st. 6.

15
Hating people is like burning down your own house to get rid of a rat.
> HARRY EMERSON FOSDICK, *The Wages of Hate.*

16
It is because people do not know each other that they hate each other so little.
> REMY DE GOURMONT, *Decadence.*

17
I decided that [Arthur] Brisbane was a member of the 7-H club—Holy howling hell, how he hates himself.
> HEDDA HOPPER, *From Under My Hat.*

18
To love you was pleasant enough,
And, oh! 'tis delicious to hate you!
> THOMAS MOORE, *To* ——.

19
Any kiddie in school can love like a fool,
But hating, my boy, is an art.
> OGDEN NASH, *Plea for Less Malice Toward None.*

20
. . . the two women exchanged the kind of glance women use when there is no knife handy.
> ELLERY QUEEN, *Man Bites Dog.*

21
The greatest hatred, like the greatest virtue, and the worst dogs, is quiet.
> J. P. F. RICHTER, *Hesperus*, 12.

22
What ages most women of thirty are the hateful passions that war in their faces. If women in love with love age less, it is because this dominant emotion preserves them from hatred.
> STENDHAL (MARIE HENRI BEYLE), *Memoirs of a Tourist*, tr. by ALLAN SEAGER.

1
All men kill the thing they hate, too, unless, of course, it kills them first.

> JAMES THURBER, quoted in *Fred Allen's Letters.*

HEALTH

See also Disease, Doctors, Medicine

2
There iz lots ov people in this world who spend so mutch time watching their healths that they hain't got no time to enjoy it.

> JOSH BILLINGS (HENRY WHEELER SHAW), in *Civil War Humor,* ed. by DORIS BENARDETE.

3
The humorous thief who drank a pot of beer at the gallows blew off the foam because he had heard it was unhealthy.

> RALPH WALDO EMERSON, *Society and Solitude: Old Age.*

4
All wealth is founded on health. To squander money is foolish; to squander health is murder in the second degree.

> B. C. FORBES, *Epigrams.*

5
The good old days! I won't say I'm out of condition now—but I even puff going downstairs.

> DICK GREGORY, *From the Back of the Bus.*

6
We er sorter po'ly, Sis Tempy, I'm oblige ter you. You know w'at de jay-bird say ter der squinch-owl! "I'm sickly but sassy."

> JOEL CHANDLER HARRIS, *Uncle Remus: Legends of the Old Plantation,* ch. 2, *Tar-Baby Story.*

7
Those obsessed with health are not healthy: the first requisite of good health is a certain calculated carelessness about oneself.

> SYDNEY J. HARRIS, *Last Things First.*

8
The only exercise I get is when I take the studs out of one shirt and put them in another.

> RING LARDNER.

9
Joy and Temperance and Repose
Slam the door on the doctor's nose.

> HENRY WADSWORTH LONGFELLOW, *The Best Medicines.*

10
The doctor is sure that my health is poor, he says that I waste away; so bring me a can of the shredded bran, and a bale of the toasted hay.

> WALT MASON, *Health Food.*

11
The water tasted like a solution of a dozen disagreeable things, and was sufficiently nauseous to have made the fortune of the proprietor, had the spa been situated in the midst of any civilized community.

> HERMAN MELVILLE, *Typee,* ch. 21.

12
Health of body and mind is a great blessing, if we can bear it.

> CARDINAL JOHN HENRY NEWMAN, *Parochial and Plain Sermons.*

13
Avoid fried meats which angry up the blood. If your stomach disputes you, lie down and pacify it with cool thoughts. Keep the juices flowing by jangling around gently as you move. Go very light on the vices, such as carrying on in society. The social ramble ain't restful. Avoid running at all times. Don't look back. Someone might be gaining on you.

> LEROY (SATCHEL) PAIGE, the ageless baseball pitcher's prescription for staying young. (*Collier's,* June 13, 1953.)

14
I have gout, asthma, and seven other maladies, but am otherwise very well.

> SYDNEY SMITH.

15
He had had much experience of physicians, and said, "The only way to keep your health is to eat what you don't want, drink what you don't like, and do what you'd druther not."

> MARK TWAIN, *Pudd'nhead Wilson's New Calendar.*

16
Eat an apple on going to bed,
And you'll keep the doctor from earning his bread.

> UNKNOWN.

17
If you would the doctor pay,
Leave your flannels off in May.

> UNKNOWN, from *West Somersetshire Word-Book.*

HEART

18
An advantage of having a hard heart is that it will take a lot to break it.

> W. BURTON BALDRY, *Stray Thoughts.*

19
In each human heart are a tiger, a pig, an ass and a nightingale. Diversity of character is due to their unequal activity.

> AMBROSE BIERCE, *The Devil's Dictionary.*

20
If a good face is a letter of recommendation, a good heart is a letter of credit.

> SIR EDWARD BULWER-LYTTON, *What Will He Do with It?* Bk. ii, ch. 11.

1
More people are killed by bad dinners than by broken hearts. A heart mends quicker than a digestion.
> G. B. Burgin, *Which Woman?*

2
The tramp and the millionaire, these two alone know what it is to live according to the dictates of the heart.
> Lucas Cleeve, *Selma.*

3
Nothing agreeth worse
Than a lady's heart and a beggar's purse.
> John Heywood, *Proverbs.* Pt. i, ch. 10.

4
The heart of man is made to reconcile contradictions.
> David Hume, *Essays, IX: Of the Parties of Great Britain.*

5
The surest way to hit a woman's heart is to take aim kneeling.
> Douglas Jerrold.

6
Give God thy broken heart, He whole will make it:
Give woman thy whole heart, and she will break it.
> Edmund Prestwich, *The Broken Heart.*

7
A man who desires to soften another man's heart, should always abuse himself. In softening a woman's heart, he should abuse her.
> Anthony Trollope, *The Last Chronicle of Barset.*

HEAVEN

8
If we were treated in this world as we deserve, I am afraid we should have to alter our ideas of a heaven hereafter.
> W. Burton Baldry, *Stray Thoughts.*

9
The New Jerusalem, when it comes, will probably be found so far to resemble the old as to stone its prophets freely.
> Samuel Butler, *Notebooks.*

10
At any rate there will be no wedding presents in heaven.
> Samuel Butler.

11
To appreciate Heaven well
'Tis good for a man to have some fifteen minutes of Hell.
> Will Carleton, *Gone with a Handsomer Man.*

12
Heaven—The Coney Island of the Christian imagination.
> Elbert Hubbard.

13
Heaven protects children, sailors, and drunken men.
> Thomas Hughes, *Tom Brown at Oxford.*

14
Pity that the only way to paradise is in a hearse.
> Stanislaw J. Lec, *Unkempt Thoughts,* tr. from the Polish by Jacek Galaska.

15
The prophet ill sustains his holy call,
Who finds not heav'n to suit the tastes of all.
> Thomas Moore, *Lalla Rookh: The Veiled Prophet of Khorassan.*

16
Men have fiendishly conceived a heaven only to find it insipid, and a hell to find it ridiculous.
> George Santayana, *Little Essays.*

17
In heaven an angel is nobody in particular.
> Bernard Shaw, *Maxims for Revolutionists.*

18
When he [Robert Benchley] died, one of them said, "They're going to have to stay up late in heaven now."
> James Thurber, *Credos and Curios.*

19
When I reflect upon the number of disagreeable people who I know have gone to a better world, I am moved to lead a different life.
> Mark Twain, *Pudd'nhead Wilson's Calendar.*

HELL

See also Devil

20
So this is Utopia, is it? Well
I beg your pardon, I thought
It was hell.
> Max Beerbohm, *Max in Verse.*

21
They're very strict on etiquette in hell.
> Hilaire Belloc, *To Dives.*

22
They order things so damnably in hell.
> Hilaire Belloc, *To Dives.*

23
. . . No saint, however, in the course of his religious warfare, was more sensible of the unhappy failure of pious resolves, than Johnson. He said one day, talking to an acquaintance on this subject, "Sir, Hell is paved with good intentions."
> James Boswell, *The Life of Samuel Johnson, LL.D.* See also Shaw in this section.

1

Hell is paved with great granite blocks hewn from the hearts of those who said, "I can do no other."

HEYWOOD BROUN, *Syndicated Column,* Jan. 20, 1934.

2

In digging up your bones, Tom Paine,
  Will Cobbett has done well:
You visit him on earth again,
  He'll visit you in hell.

LORD BYRON, *Epigram.*

3

Hell may have a worse climate [than heaven] but undoubtedly the company is sprightlier.

IRVIN S. COBB, *Letter* written late in 1943 to the editor of the *Paducah* (Ky.) *Sun-Democrat.*

4

From Hell, Hull, and Halifax, good Lord deliver us.

ANTHONY COPLEY, *Wits, Fits, etc.*

5

Hell and Chancery are always open.

THOMAS FULLER, *Gnomologia.*

6

Said Conan when set with the Devils to dwell,
" 'Tis hard upon me, but 'tis harder on Hell!"

ARTHUR GUITERMAN, *A Poet's Proverbs.*

7

Hell is full of good desires.

EDWARD HELLOWES, *Guevara's Epistles.*

8

Satan the envious said with a sigh:
Christians know more of their hell than I.

ALFRED KREYMBORG, *Envious Satan.*

9

Dirce

Stand close around, ye Stygian set,
  With Dirce in one boat conveyed!
Or Charon, seeing, may forget,
  That he is old and she a shade.

WALTER SAVAGE LANDOR.

10

Hell is empty
And all the devils are here.

WILLIAM SHAKESPEARE, *The Tempest.* Act i, sc. 2.

11

Hell is paved with good intentions, not with bad ones.

BERNARD SHAW, *Maxims for Revolutionists.*

12

The first time the Deity came down to earth, he brought life and death; when he came the second time, he brought hell.

MARK TWAIN, *Letters from the Earth.*

13

Hell is paved with good intentions and roofed with lost opportunities.

UNKNOWN. Portuguese proverb.

14

Hell is given up so reluctantly by those who don't expect to go there.

HARRY LEON WILSON, *The Spenders.*

HERO, HEROISM

15

No man is a hero to his own wife; no woman is a wife to her own hero.

ANONYMOUS.

16

No man is a hero to his undertaker.

FINLEY PETER DUNNE, *Mr. Dooley Remembers.*

17

Every hero becomes a bore at last.

RALPH WALDO EMERSON, *Representative Men.*

18

To a valet no man is a hero. (Es gibt für den Kammerdiener keinen Helden.)

JOHANN WOLFGANG VON GOETHE, *Wahlverwandtschaften: Aus Ottilien's Tagebuche.*

19

Jesse James shot children, but only in fact, not in folklore.

JOHN GREENWAY, *The Inevitable Americans,* ch. 5.

20

Ultimately a hero is a man who would argue with the Gods, and so awakens devils to contest his vision.

NORMAN MAILER, *The Presidential Papers:* special preface.

21

Great Chieftain, who takest such pains
  To prove—what is granted, *nem. con.*—
With how mod'rate a portion of brains
  Some heroes contrive to get on.

THOMAS MOORE, *Dog-Day Reflections.* Referring to the Duke of Wellington.

22

Hail, the conquering hero comes,
Surrounded by a bunch of bums.

GEORGE E. PHAIR, quoted by GENE FOWLER in *Skyline.*

23

This thing of being a hero, about the main thing to do is to know when to die. Prolonged life has ruined more men than it ever made.

WILL ROGERS, *Autobiography.* See also ROUSSEAU below.

24

How many illustrious and noble heroes have lived too long by one day! (Combien de

héros, glorieux, magnanimes, out vécu trop d'un jour!)
JEAN-JACQUES ROUSSEAU.

1
Formerly we used to canonize our heroes. The modern method is to vulgarize them. Cheap editions of great books may be delightful, but cheap editions of great men are absolutely detestable.
OSCAR WILDE, *The Critic as Artist.*

HISTORY

See also Past

2
History is a pageant and not a philosopher.
AUGUSTINE BIRRELL, *Obiter Dicta.*

3
History is simply a piece of paper covered with print; the main thing is still to make history, not to write it.
OTTO VON BISMARCK, *Prussian Chamber.*

4
History, a distillation of rumor.
THOMAS CARLYLE, *French Revolution.*

5
History is only a confused heap of facts.
LORD CHESTERFIELD, *Letters to His Son,* Feb. 5, 1750.

6
History shows you prospects by starlight, or at best, by the waning moon.
RUFUS CHOATE, *New England History.*

7
History is but little more than a graveyard in which one reads the epitaphs of buried states.
SENATOR EDGAR COWAN of Pennsylvania.

8
The further you get away from any period the better you can write about it. You aren't subject to interruptions by people that were there.
FINLEY PETER DUNNE, *Mr. Dooley Remembers.*

9
History is a post-mortem examination. It tells you what a country died of. But I'd like to know what it lived of.
FINLEY PETER DUNNE, *Mr. Dooley Remembers.*

10
The happiest women, like the happiest nations, have no history.
GEORGE ELIOT, *The Mill on the Floss.* Bk. vi, ch. 3.

11
History is bunk.
HENRY FORD, spoken on witness stand at Mt. Clemens, Mich., in his libel suit against the *Chicago Tribune,* July, 1919.

12
All the historical books which contain no lies are extremely tedious.
ANATOLE FRANCE, *The Crime of Sylvestre Bonnard.*

13
Historians relate, not so much what is done, as what they would have believed.
BENJAMIN FRANKLIN, *Poor Richard,* 1739.

14
History is the unrolled scroll of prophecy.
JAMES A. GARFIELD, *The Province of History; Williams Quarterly,* June, 1856.

15
We used to root for the Indians against the cavalry, because we didn't think it was fair in the history books that when the cavalry won it was a great victory, when the Indians won it was a massacre.
DICK GREGORY, *Nigger: An Autobiography.*

16
There is no Gibbon but Gibbon and Gibbon is his prophet. The solemn march of his cadences, the majestic impropriety of his innuendo are without rivals in the respective annals of British eloquence and British indelicacy.
PHILIP GUEDALLA, *Supers and Supermen.*

17
History repeats itself; historians repeat each other.
PHILIP GUEDALLA.

18
The horse, the mass of human intelligence, draws along the cart of history in which stands the professor, looking backward and explaining the scenery.
STEPHEN LEACOCK, *Who Canonizes the Classics?*

19
A foreign diplomat demurred at Lincoln's condemning a certain Greek history as tedious. "The author of that history, Mr. President, is one of the profoundest scholars of the age. Indeed, it may be doubted whether any man of our generation has plunged more deeply in the sacred fount of learning." "Yes," said Lincoln, "or come up dryer."
CARL SANDBURG, *Abraham Lincoln: The Prairie Years and the War Years,* ch. 34.

20
Historian: An unsuccessful novelist.
H. L. MENCKEN, *A Mencken Chrestomathy.*

21
What is history but a fable agreed upon?
NAPOLEON BONAPARTE. (*Sayings.*)

1

Legend—a lie that has attained the dignity of age.

HARRY OLIVER, *The Desert Rat Scrap Book*.

2

I doubt if there is a thing in the world as wrong or unreliable as history. History ain't what it is; it's what some writer wanted it to be, and I just happened to think I remember ours is as cock-eyed as the rest. I bet we have started just as much devilment as was ever started against us—maybe more. So far as facts are concerned, the better educated you are the less you know.

WILL ROGERS, *Autobiography*.

3

Statesmen think they make history; but history makes itself and drags the statesmen along.

WILL ROGERS, quoted by ALISTAIR COOKE in *One Man's America*.

4

Alas! Hegel was right when he said that we learn from history that men never learn anything from history.

BERNARD SHAW, *Heartbreak House:* preface.

5

Dates are hard to remember because they consist of figures; figures are monotonously unstriking in appearance, and they don't take hold, they form no pictures, and so they give the eye no chance to help. Pictures are the thing. Pictures can make dates stick. They can make nearly anything stick—particularly *if you make the pictures yourself*.

MARK TWAIN, *Essays: How to Make History Dates Stick*.

6

History is something that never happened, written by someone who wasn't there.

UNKNOWN.

7

This agglomeration which was called and which still calls itself the Holy Roman Empire is neither holy, nor Roman, nor an Empire.

VOLTAIRE, *Essai sur les Moeurs*, 1756.

8

More difficult to do a thing than to talk about it? Not at all. That is a gross popular error. It is very much more difficult to talk about a thing than to do it. In the sphere of actual life that is of course obvious. Anyone can make history. Only a great man can write it.

OSCAR WILDE, *The Critic as Artist*.

HOME

9

A House Is Not a Home.

POLLY ADLER, *Title* of memoir.

10

"Home, sweet home," must surely have been written by a bachelor.

SAMUEL BUTLER, *Note Books*.

11

The snail, which everywhere doth roam,
Carrying his own house still, still is at home.

JOHN DONNE, *To Sir Henry Wotton*.

12

Many a man who thinks to found a home discovers that he had merely opened a tavern for his friends.

NORMAN DOUGLAS, *South Wind*.

13

You can't appreciate home till you've left it, money till it's spent, your wife till she's joined a woman's club, nor Old Glory till you see it hanging on a broomstick on the shanty of a consul in a foreign town.

O. HENRY, *Roads of Destiny*.

14

The truth is that Mr. James's cosmopolitanism is, after all, limited; to be really cosmopolitan, a man must be at home even in his own country.

THOMAS W. HIGGINSON, *Short Studies of American Authors: Henry James, Jr.*

15

It must make some folks mad t' feel at home.

FRANK MCKINNEY (KIN) HUBBARD, *Abe Martin's Primer*.

16

The fellow that owns his own home is always just coming out of a hardware store.

FRANK MCKINNEY (KIN) HUBBARD.

17

. . . If I read one more piece about a $100,-000-a-year man who is unhappy because he came from a broken home, I'm going to feel that I owe it to the kids to break up my home.

MURRAY KEMPTON, *New York Post*, Aug. 10, 1956.

18

There's no place like home, and many a man is glad of it.

F. M. KNOWLES, *A Cheerful Year Book*.

19

Not many sounds in life, and I include all urban and all rural sounds, exceed in interest a knock at the door.

CHARLES LAMB, *Essays of Elia*.

20

The longest way home is the shortest road to a family row.

Reflections of a Bachelor.

1
Every cock is at his best on his own dunghill. (Gallum in suo sterquilinio plurimum
posse.)
SENECA, *Apocolocyntosis.*

2
Home is the girl's prison and the woman's
workhouse.
BERNARD SHAW, *Maxims for Revolutionists.*

3
Bret Harte's poetic dictum that nobody
shoulder a rifle in defense of a boarding
house.
ADLAI STEVENSON, *Address,* Newark, N.J.,
May 5, 1959.

4
Of the home economists we have met in
our lifetime, all had one trait in common:
not one of them was at home.
E. B. WHITE, *The Second Tree from the
Corner.*

5
The modern idea of home has been well
expressed as the place one goes from the
garage.
GEORGE WICKERSHAM.

HONESTY

6
No man, the late Charles May Oelrichs used
to say, ever made more than a million
dollars honestly.
CLEVELAND AMORY, *The Last Resorts.*

7
He was honest except when he went out to
rob (there was no paradox in that to him).
HOMER CROY, *Jesse James Was My Neighbor.* Reference to JESSE JAMES.

8
The louder he talked of his honor, the faster
we counted our spoons.
RALPH WALDO EMERSON, *Conduct of Life:
Worship.*

9
To rise, be on the level.
B. C. FORBES, *Epigrams.*

10
Be on the level and you're not likely to
go downhill.
B. C. FORBES, *Epigrams.*

11
He that resolves to deal with none but
honest men must leave off dealing.
THOMAS FULLER, *Gnomologia,* No. 2530.

12
And whether you're an honest man or
whether you're a thief
Depends on whose solicitor has given me my
brief.
SIR WILLIAM SCHWENCK GILBERT, *Utopia,
Limited,* Act 1.

13
In this age, when it is said of a man, He
knows *how to live,* it may be implied he is
not very honest.
LORD HALIFAX, *Works,* p. 232.

14
Be honest as the day is long
And pay for every piece of cheese.
But after dark there's nothing wrong
In grabbing anything you please.
ROLF HOCHHUTH, *The Deputy.* Act i, sc.
2, tr. by RICHARD AND CLARA WINSTON.

15
An Oxford scholar, meeting a porter who
was carrying a hare through the streets, ac-
costs him with this extraordinary question:
"Prithee, friend, is that thy own hare, or a
wig?"
CHARLES LAMB, *Popular Fallacies.*

16
It is prudent to look on every man as a
rogue until you know him to be honest.
FRANK MARRYAT, *Mountains and Mole-
hills.*

17
There's one way to find out if a man is
honest—ask him. If he says "yes," you know
he is crooked.
GROUCHO MARX, *News summaries,* July
28, 1954.

18
When you find a man too honest to steal
an umbrella it is sure betting that he has
his eye on something worth a sight more.
Reflections of a Bachelor.

19
Shrewdness in public life all over the world
is always honored, while honesty in public
men is generally attributed to dumbness and
is seldom rewarded.
WILL ROGERS, *Autobiography.*

20
A man can build a staunch reputation for
honesty by admitting he was in error, especially when he gets caught at it.
ROBERT RUARK, quoted by VICTOR LASKY
in *J.F.K.: The Man and the Myth.* The
reference is to SENATOR TED KENNEDY
and the fact that he was caught cheating while at Harvard.

21
Hamlet: What's the news?
Rosencranz: None, my lord; but that the
world's grown honest.
Hamlet: Then is dooms-day near.
WILLIAM SHAKESPEARE, *Hamlet.* Act ii,
sc. 2.

22
Ay, sir; to be honest, as this world goes,
is to be one man picked out of ten thousand.
WILLIAM SHAKESPEARE, *Hamlet.* Act ii,
sc. 2.

1
Rich honesty dwells like a miser, sir, in a poor house.
> WILLIAM SHAKESPEARE, *As You Like It.* Act v, sc. 4.

2
I thank God I am as honest as any man living that is an old man and no honester than I am.
> WILLIAM SHAKESPEARE, *Much Ado About Nothing.* Act iii, sc. 5.

3
Barring that natural expression of villainy which we all have, the man looked honest enough.
> MARK TWAIN, *A Mysterious Visit.*

4
For those who believe the old saw that an honest man must have a direct gaze, I refer them to a contemporary's report that the shiftiest-eyed man he had ever met was Thomas Jefferson.
> GORE VIDAL.

5
"Honesty is the best policy," but he who acts on that principle is not an honest man.
> ARCHBISHOP RICHARD WHATELY, *Thoughts and Apothegms.* Pt. ii, ch. 18.

HONOR

6
Gods for themselves are monuments enough.
> ALFRED AUSTIN, *On the Proposal to Erect a Statue to Shakespeare in London.*

7
Shakespeare was not accounted great
When good Queen Bess ruled England's state,
So why should I today repine
Because the laurel is not mine?
> JOHN KENDRICK BANGS, *Consolation.*

8
The strongest poison ever known
Came from Caesar's laurel crown.
> WILLIAM BLAKE, *Auguries of Innocence.*

9
Let not a monument give you or me hopes,
Since not a pinch of dust remains of Cheops.
> LORD BYRON, *Don Juan.* Canto i, st. 219.

10
I had rather men should ask why no statue has been erected in my honor, than why one has.
> CATO MARCUS PORCIUS ("the Censor").

11
I do honor the very flea of his dog.
> BEN JONSON, *Every Man in His Humour.*

12
Glory's no compensation for a belly-ache.
> RUDYARD KIPLING, *Life's Handicap: The Courting of Dinah Shadd.*

13
We no longer know how to distinguish monuments from tombstones.
> STANISLAW J. LEC, *Unkempt Thoughts,* tr. from the Polish by JACEK GALASKA.

14
If glory comes after death, I am in no hurry. (Si post fata venit gloria non propero.)
> MARTIAL, *Epigrams.* Bk. v, ep. 10.

15
The top of honor is a slippery place.
> JONATHAN MITCHELL, *Sermon,* 1677.

16
Honour will buy no beef.
> THOMAS SHADWELL, *Sullen Lovers.* Act v, sc. 3.

17
I find honorary degrees always tempting, and often bad for me: tempting because we all —even ex-politicians—hope to be mistaken for scholars, and bad because if you then make a speech the mistake is quickly exposed.
> ADLAI STEVENSON, *Speech,* on acceptance of honorary degree from McGill University, May 29, 1959.

18
If somebody throws a brick at me I can catch it and throw it back. But when somebody awards a decoration to me, I am out of words.
> HARRY S TRUMAN, on receiving the Gold Grand Cross of Merit, Austria's highest decoration, in Washington, D.C., May 7, 1964, the day before his 80th birthday.

HOPE

19
Hope is merely disappointment deferred.
> W. BURTON BALDRY, *Stray Thoughts.*

20
Hope is the most treacherous of human fancies.
> JAMES FENIMORE COOPER, *Homeward Bound,* ch. 22.

21
He that lives upon hope will die fasting.
> BENJAMIN FRANKLIN, *Poor Richard,* 1758.

22
Hope is the poor man's bread.
> GEORGE HERBERT, *Jacula Prudentum.*

23
In all the wedding cake hope is the sweetest of plums.
> DOUGLAS JERROLD, *Specimens of Jerrold's Wit.*

24
All our lives we are putting pennies—our

most golden pennies—into penny-in-the-slot machines that are almost always empty.

LOGAN PEARSALL SMITH, *All Trivia.*

HORSE

1
What has four legs and flies?
A dead horse.

FRED ALLEN, *Much Ado About Me.*

2
Italy is a paradise for horses, hell for women, as the proverb goes.

ROBERT BURTON, *The Anatomy of Melancholy.* Pt. iii, sec. 3.

3
The seat on a horse makes gentlemen of some and grooms of others.

MIGUEL DE CERVANTES, *Don Quixote.* Pt. ii, ch. 43.

4
God forbid that I should go to any heaven in which there are no horses.

R. B. CUNNINGHAME-GRAHAM, *Letter* to Theodore Roosevelt.

5
They say Princes learn no art truly, but the art of horsemanship. The reason is, the brave beast is no flatterer. He will throw a Prince as soon as his groom.

BEN JONSON, *Explorata: Illiteratus Princeps.*

6
Never give up. For 50 years they said the horse was through. Now look at him—a status symbol.

FLETCHER KNEBEL, *Register and Tribune Syndicate.*

7
Well, Uncle, now tell us how many short breaths he drew.

ABRAHAM LINCOLN, *Reply* to a friend's boast that his horse had galloped nine miles without drawing a long breath. (KEITH W. JENNISON, *The Humorous Mr. Lincoln.*)

8
Never go to the fair to swap horses with the Hungarians or you will walk home carrying your saddle.

Proverb quoted by J. P. McEVOY in *Charlie Would Have Loved This.*

9
The only time a horse gets scared on the road nowadays is when he meets another horse.

HARRY OLIVER, *The Desert Rat Scrap Book.*

10
The best thing for the inside of a man is the outside of a horse.

LORD PALMERSTON.

11
It's a poor horse that falls on the ice and doesn't want to get up.

STENDHAL (MARIE HENRI BEYLE), *Memoirs of a Tourist,* tr. by ALLAN SEAGER.

HOSPITALITY

12
Sweet courtesy has done its most
If you have made each guest forget
That he himself is not the host.

THOMAS BAILEY ALDRICH, *Hospitality.*

13
Then fill up the glasses as quick as you can,
And sprinkle the table with buttons and bran;
Put cats in the coffee, and mice in the tea—
And welcome Queen Alice with thirty-times-three!

LEWIS CARROLL, *Through the Looking-Glass,* ch. 9.

14
Then fill up the glasses with treacle and ink,
Or anything else that is pleasant to drink;
Mix sand with the cider, and wool with the wine—
And welcome Queen Alice with ninety-times-nine!

LEWIS CARROLL, *Through the Looking-Glass,* ch. 9.

15
Hospitality reaches its greatest heights in Virginia, Mr. [Irvin S.] Cobb avers. Distant relatives who visit there "are like the inflammatory rheumatism—arrive in the fall and stay right on through the spring—stay on forever, sometimes."

FRED G. NEUMAN, *Irvin S. Cobb.*

16
Come in the evening, or come in the morning;
Come when you're looked for, or come without warning.

THOMAS OSBORNE DAVIS, *The Welcome.*

17
Some fellers' idea o' being funny is breakin' a few bones when they shake your hand.

FRANK McKINNEY (KIN) HUBBARD, *Abe Martin's Primer.*

18
In contradistinction to those, who, having a wife and children, prefer domestick enjoyments to those which a tavern affords, I have heard him [Samuel Johnson] assert that a tavern chair was the throne of human felicity. "As soon as I enter the door of a tavern, I experience an oblivion of care, and a freedom from solicitude: when I am seated, I find the master courteous and the servants obsequious to my call; anxious to know and ready to supply my wants; wine

there exhilarates my spirits and prompts me
to free conversation and an interchange of
discourse with those whom I most love: I
dogmatise and am contradicted and in this
conflict of opinion and sentiments I find
delight."
> SIR JOHN HAWKINS, *Memorabilia.*

1
It will never do, Sir. There is nothing served
about there, neither tea, nor coffee, nor
lemonade, nor anything whatever, and depend upon it, Sir, a man does not love to
go to a place from whence he comes out
exactly as he went in.
> SAMUEL JOHNSON, to James Boswell about
> a certain house which was proposed for
> a series of conversations.

2
I appreciate your welcome. As the cow said
to the Maine farmer, "Thank you for a
warm hand on a cold morning."
> JOHN F. KENNEDY, *Speech* in Los Angeles,
> Nov. 2, 1960.

3
Fish and guests in three days are stale.
> JOHN LYLY, *Euphues.*

4
The art of being a good guest is to know
when to leave.
> PRINCE PHILIP, *Comment* in Argentina,
> Mar. 1962.

5
Unbidden guests are often welcomest when
they are gone.
> WILLIAM SHAKESPEARE, *Henry VI,* pt. i.
> Act ii, sc. 2.

HUMILITY

See also Modesty

6
Ocean, wherein the whale
Swims minnow-small.
> WILLIAM ROSE BENÉT, *Whale,* st. 1.

7
You're not the only pebble on the beach.
> HARRY BRAISTED, *Title* and refrain of song
> (1896).

8
She takes me for a mountain, that am but a
molehill.
> RICHARD BROME, *City Wit,* Act iv, sc. 1.

9
When I am dead and buried, on my tombstone I would like to have it written, "I
have arrived." Because when you feel that
you have arrived, you are dead.
> YUL BRYNNER, in *New York Post,* Sept.
> 30, 1956.

10
There's no sense in having both cheeks

smitten, although some people have such a
love of uniformity.
> G. B. BURGIN, *Fanuela.*

11
They are proud in humility, proud in that
they are not proud.
> ROBERT BURTON, *The Anatomy of Melan-
> choly.*

12
I ate umble pie with an appetite.
> CHARLES DICKENS, *David Copperfield,* ch.
> 39.

13
Humility is not my forte, and whenever I
dwell for any length of time on my own
shortcomings, they gradually begin to seem
mild, harmless, rather engaging little things,
not at all like the staring defects in other
people's characters.
> MARGARET HALSEY, *With Malice Toward
> Some.*

14
If humble pie has to be eaten, that's the
best way to eat it—bolt it whole.
> MAURICE HEWLETT, *The Stooping Lady.*

15
The biggest dog has been a pup.
> JOAQUIN MILLER (CINCINNATUS HINER
> MILLER), *William Brown of Oregon.*

16
Some editors ate crow and left the feathers
on.
> HARRY S TRUMAN, *Comment* on the
> friendly tone of newspaper editorials
> just after he returned to private life
> early in 1953—in marked contrast to
> the widespread criticism of his adminis-
> tration. (ALFRED STEINBERG, *The Man
> from Missouri,* p. 420.)

17
What small potatoes we all are.
> CHARLES DUDLEY WARNER, *My Summer
> in a Garden.*

HUMOR

See also Wit

18
One of the places we enjoyed most was the
Stork Club [London], run by an English
Milton Berle named Al Burnett. Burnett is
the British version of the Thief of Bad Gags.
> JOEY ADAMS, *Cindy and I,* ch. 9.

19
A fellow-writer called Shakespeare once said,
"The play's the thing." But Willy didn't
know the modern comics. If the Bard of
Avon were bred on Broadway instead of
Stratford Avenue, he might have said, "The
gag's the thing."
> JOEY ADAMS, *Cindy and I,* ch. 27.

1

There are only three basic jokes, but since the mother-in-law joke is not a joke but a very serious question, there are only two.

GEORGE ADE.

2

The Australian audiences felt about jokes the way they did about friends: the old ones were the best.

FRED ALLEN, *Much Ado About Me.*

3

And Milton Berle for years has been bragging to audiences that he has stolen jokes from other comedians. There has been no reason to doubt his word.

FRED ALLEN, *Much Ado About Me.*

4

The average radio gag writer is an emaciated nonentity with a good memory and a pencil.

FRED ALLEN, *Footnote* to *Fred Allen: Strictly From Misery,* by MAURICE ZOLOTOW.

5

There seems to be no lengths to which humorless people will not go to analyze humor. It seems to worry them. They can't believe that anything could be funny just on its own hook.

ROBERT BENCHLEY, *What Does It Mean? (The Benchley Roundup,* ed. by NATHANIEL BENCHLEY.)

6

I think funny.

ABE BURROWS, quoted by LEWIS FUNKE, drama-news column, *The New York Times,* Mar. 29, 1964.

7

A little levity will save many a good heavy thing from sinking.

SAMUEL BUTLER, quoted by BERNARD SHAW in *Days with Bernard Shaw,* by STEPHEN WINSTEN.

8

They that are serious in ridiculous things will be ridiculous in serious affairs.

CATO THE ELDER. (PLUTARCH, *Roman Apothegms.*)

9

A pompous gentleman once asked the sharp-tongued British actress, Mrs. Patrick Campbell, "Why do you suppose it is that women are so utterly lacking in a sense of humor?"

"God did it on purpose," Mrs. Campbell answered without batting an eyelash, "so that we may love you men instead of laughing at you."

BENNETT CERF, *The Laugh's on Me.*

10

Men will confess to treason, murder, arson, false teeth, or a wig. How many of them will own up to a lack of humor?

FRANK MOORE COLBY, *Essays,* vol. 1.

11

But still a pun I do detest,

'Tis such a paltry humbug jest;

They who've least wit can make them best.

WILLIAM COMBE, *Dr. Syntax in Search of the Picturesque,* canto 26.

12

Gnus—he said—are used chiefly by a certain class of authors for making atrocious puns, such as, "No Gnus is good Gnus," and "Happy Gnu Year!" This will go on forever, too, because you can't teach an old Gnu tricks.

WILL CUPPY, quoted by MAX EASTMAN in *The Enjoyment of Laughter.*

13

A man who would make so vile a pun would not scruple to pick a pocket.

JOHN DENNIS, *The Gentleman's Magazine.*

14

If Adam came on earth again the only thing he would recognize would be the old jokes.

THOMAS ROBERT DEWAR.

15

A woman's sense of humor is usually in her husband's name.

FINLEY PETER DUNNE, *Mr. Dooley Remembers.*

16

Strange that a Frenchman should be the one to invent the legend that "the comic appeals to the intelligence pure and simple." I wonder if Bergson would think the *poilu's* interpretation of the letters Y.M.C.A. on the uniforms of American war nurses—*y a moyen de choucher avec*—made no appeal to the emotions!

MAX EASTMAN, *Enjoyment of Laughter.* Referring to Henri Bergson, French philosopher.

17

We love a joke that hands us a pat on the back while it kicks the other fellow downstairs.

C. L. EDSON.

18

Humor is an affirmation of dignity, a declaration of man's superiority to all that befalls him.

ROMAIN GARY, *Promise at Dawn.*

19

The jests of the rich are ever successful.

OLIVER GOLDSMITH, *The Vicar of Wakefield,* ch. 7.

20

Mr. Hearst warned Smith, "Young man, the next time you do a story about *any* of my friends, please take your tongue out of your cheek."

GENE FOWLER, *Skyline.* Referring to the publisher William Randolph Hearst.

1
I never dare to write as funny as I can.
OLIVER WENDELL HOLMES, *Divided Hours.*

2
Ever'buddy seems t' think it's funny t' be
a bad speller.
FRANK McKINNEY (KIN) HUBBARD, *Abe
Martin's Primer.*

3
Humor is your own smile surprising you in
your mirror.
LANGSTON HUGHES, *The Book of Negro
Humor.*

4
Humor is laughing at what you haven't got
when you ought to have it.
LANGSTON HUGHES, *The Book of Negro
Humor.*

5
Humor is when the joke is on you but hits
the other fellow first—before it boomerangs.
LANGSTON HUGHES, *The Book of Negro
Humor.*

6
A pun is a pistol let off at the ear; not a
feather to tickle the intellect.
CHARLES LAMB, *Last Essays of Elia.*

7
I never knew an enemy to puns who was not
an ill-natured man.
CHARLES LAMB.

8
May my last breath be drawn through a pipe
and exhaled in a pun.
CHARLES LAMB.

9
Any man will admit, if need be, that his
sight is not good, or that he cannot swim, or
shoots badly with a rifle, but to touch upon
his sense of humor is to give him a mortal
affront.
STEPHEN LEACOCK, *Laugh with Leacock.*

10
Yet I admit we have to make a pretense at
humor in moments of trial. It is a sort of
survival quality that came down with us
through the ages that we must take adversity with a smile or a joke. Tell any man
that he has lost his job, and his "reaction,"
as they say in college, will be to make some
kind of a joke about having lots of time
now for golf.
STEPHEN LEACOCK, *The Saving Grace of
Humor.*

11
A pun is the lowest form of humor—when
you don't think of it first.
OSCAR LEVANT.

12
Many married couples have learned that a

joke can be the shortest distance between
two points of view.
J. P. McEVOY, *Charlie Would Have Loved
This.*

13
Think of what would happen to us in America if there were no humorists; life would be
one long Congressional Record.
THOMAS L. MASSON.

14
It [a sense of humor] always withers in
the presence of the messianic delusion, like
justice and truth in front of patriotic passion.
H. L. MENCKEN, *Prejudices*, ser. 1.

15
"If a Pole calls something funny," said
Stanley, "it means that he finds it bizarre.
He's too somber, too tragic, to appreciate
horseplay."
HENRY MILLER, *Plexus.*

16
Good taste and humor are a contradiction in
terms, like a chaste whore.
MALCOLM MUGGERIDGE, speaking of his
editorship of *Punch.* (*Time*, Sept. 14,
1953.)

17
Of puns it has been said that they who most
dislike them are least able to utter them.
EDGAR ALLAN POE.

18
The reason that there are so few women
comics is that so few women can bear being
laughed at.
ANNA RUSSELL, quoted in *Sunday Times*,
London, Aug. 25, 1957.

19
A jest loses its point when he who makes
it is the first to laugh.
JOHANN VON SCHILLER, *Fiesco.* Act i,
sc. 7.

20
For every ten jokes, thou hast got an hundred enemies.
LAURENCE STERNE, *Tristram Shandy*, ch.
2.

21
Humor is emotional chaos remembered in
tranquility.
JAMES THURBER, quoted by MAX EAST-
MAN.

22
Any man who has had the job I've had and
didn't have a sense of humor wouldn't still
be here.
PRESIDENT HARRY S TRUMAN, *News reports*, Apr. 19, 1955.

23
Everything human is pathetic. The secret

source of humor itself is not joy but sorrow.
There is no humor in heaven.
> MARK TWAIN.

1
Irony is jesting hidden behind gravity.
> JOHN WEISS, *Wit, Humor, and Shake-speare.*

2
Nothing spoils a romance so much as a sense
of humor in the woman.
> OSCAR WILDE, *A Woman of No Importance,* Act 1.

HUNGER

3
A gorged tiger, indeed, is much pleasanter
to meet than a hungry one.
> WILLIAM BOLITHO, *Twelve Against the Gods: Lucius Sergius Catiline.*

4
Poor men want meat for their stomachs,
rich men stomachs for their meat.
> ANTHONY COPLEY, *Wits, Fits, etc.*

5
The starving natives of the Bahamas frequently kill and eat Flamingoes although it
is against the law. We must educate these
persons to starve and like it.
> WILL CUPPY, *How to Tell Your Friends from the Apes: The Flamingo.*

6
At the workingman's house, hunger looks in
but dares not enter.
> BENJAMIN FRANKLIN, *Poor Richard's Almanac.*

7
Hunger is the best sauce.
(Il n'est sauce que d'appétit.)
> Old French Proverb.

8
To a man with an empty stomach food is
God.
> MOHANDAS GANDHI.

9
Hungry rooster don't cackle w'en he fine a
wum.
> JOEL CHANDLER HARRIS, *Plantation Proverbs.*

10
Ticker tape ain't spaghetti.
> FIORELLO H. LA GUARDIA, *Speech* to the United Nations Relief and Rehabilitation Commission, Mar. 29, 1946.

11
But somehow, when the dogs hed gut asleep,
Their love o' mutton beat their love o' sheep.
> JAMES RUSSELL LOWELL, *The Biglow Papers,* Ser. ii, No. 11.

12
One soldier letter to Lincoln pleaded, "I am
near starved if I get much thinner it will
take two of us to make one shadder."
> CARL SANDBURG, *Abraham Lincoln: The Prairie Years and the War Years,* ch. 30.

HUSBAND

See also Marriage, Wife

13
The most popular labor-saving device today
is still a husband with money.
> JOEY ADAMS, *Cindy and I,* ch. 3.

14
The fraternity of the henpecked.
> JOSEPH ADDISON, *The Spectator,* 1712.

15
Since you have given us the character of a
wife who wears the breeches, pray say something of a husband that wears the petticoat.
> JOSEPH ADDISON, *The Spectator,* 1712.

16
A husband is simply a lover with a two-
days' growth of beard, his collar off, and a
bad cold in the head.
> ANONYMOUS.

17
A husband should never let his wife visit
her mother unattended.
> HONORÉ DE BALZAC, *The Physiology of Marriage.*

18
A lover has all the good points and all the
bad points which are lacking in a husband.
> HONORÉ DE BALZAC, *The Physiology of Marriage.*

19
A husband should sleep as lightly as a
watch-dog, so as never to be caught with his
eyes shut.
> HONORÉ DE BALZAC, *The Physiology of Marriage.*

20
A husband should always know what is the
matter with his wife, for she always knows
what is not.
> HONORÉ DE BALZAC, *Petty Troubles of Married Life.*

21
I have nothing to say against Monsieur de
Fischtaminel: he does not gamble, he is
indifferent to women, he doesn't like wine,
and he has no expensive fancies: he possesses, as you said, all the negative qualities
which make husbands passable.
> HONORÉ DE BALZAC, *Petty Troubles of Married Life.*

22
Being a husband is a whole-time job.
> ARNOLD BENNETT, *The Title.*

1
She wears him like a charm bracelet.
>JIM BISHOP, *Some of My Very Best: A Very Proper Lady.*

2
A moderate income and a good temper—given these two, if any girl can't get on with any man, any girl must be a born fool.
>HUBERT BLAND, *The Happy Moralist.*

3
It is comforting to feel that one's husband never so much as smiles at another woman, of course: but it is rather cold comfort if he never smiles at you either.
>HUBERT BLAND, *The Happy Moralist.*

4
Vociferous Lady: Mr. Prime Minister, if I were your wife, I would put poison in your coffee.
Winston Churchill: Madame, if I were your husband, I'd drink it.
>*Roll Call,* July 19, 1961.

5
A husband should tell his wife everything that he is sure she will find out, and before anyone else does.
>THOMAS ROBERT DEWAR.

6
It's impossible for a woman to be married to the same man for 50 years. After the first 25, he's not the same man.
>*Farmer's Almanac,* 1966.

7
The Supreme Court of the United States gives a man a right to open his wife's letters, but it doesn't give him the courage.
>*Farmer's Almanac,* 1966.

8
O sister sister! if ever you marry, beware of a sullen, silent sot, one that's always musing, but never thinks. There's some diversion in talking to a blockhead; and since a woman must wear chains, I would have the pleasure of hearing 'em rattle a little.
>GEORGE FARQUHAR, *The Beaux' Stratagem,* Act 2.

9
One good husband is worth two good wives; for the scarcer things are, the more they are valued.
>BENJAMIN FRANKLIN.

10
He loves little who will tell his wife all he knows.
>THOMAS FULLER, *Holy and Profane State: The Good Husband.*

11
Husbands are like fires. They go out when unattended.
>ZSA ZSA GABOR, quoted in *Newsweek,* Mar. 28, 1960.

12
A reserved lover, it is said, always makes a suspicious husband.
>OLIVER GOLDSMITH, *She Stoops to Conquer.*

13
To the model husband—any other woman's.
>*Toasts for All Occasions,* ed. by LEWIS C. HENRY.

14
I should like to see any kind of a man, distinguishable from a gorilla, that some good and even pretty woman could not shape a husband out of.
>OLIVER WENDELL HOLMES, *The Professor at the Breakfast-Table,* ch. 7.

15
A man should be taller, older, heavier, uglier, and hoarser than his wife.
>E. W. HOWE, *Country Sayings.*

16
No woman cares how much her husband stays away from home in th' daytime.
>FRANK McKINNEY (KIN) HUBBARD, *Abe Martin's Primer.*

17
Weddings make a lot of people sad,
But if you're not the groom, they're not so bad, . . .
>GUS KAHN, *Makin' Whoopee* (1928).

18
Marrying a man is like buying something you've been admiring for a long time in a shop window. You may love it when you get it home, but it doesn't always go with everything else in the house.
>JEAN KERR, *The Snake Has All the Lines: The Ten Worst Things About a Man.*

19
A husband who shaves in front of his wife is either an idiot or a scoundrel.
>H. L. MENCKEN, *Prejudices:* ser. 2.

20
The man she had was kind and clean
And well enough for every day,
But, oh, dear friends, you should have seen
The one that got away.
>DOROTHY PARKER, *The Fisherwoman.*

21
When a woman's husband quits doing something he knows she doesn't like it is time for her to discover what he has been doing in its place.
>*Reflections of a Bachelor.*

22
When a woman says her husband is perfect, she means he suits her better than any perfect man could.
>*Reflections of a Bachelor.*

1
A husband is what is left of the lover after the nerve has been extracted.
HELEN ROWLAND.

2
A married man can do anything he likes if his wife don't mind. A widower can't be too careful.
BERNARD SHAW, *Misalliance.*

3
A little in drink, but at all times your faithful husband.
SIR RICHARD STEELE, *Letters to His Wife.*

4
A married lady was debating the subject with another lady. "You know, dear," said the first, "after ten years of marriage, if he is nothing else, your husband is always an old friend."
ROBERT LOUIS STEVENSON, *Virginibus Puerisque.*

5
The air of the fireside withers out all the fine wildings of the husband's heart. He is so comfortable and happy that he begins to prefer comfort and happiness to everything else on earth, his wife included.
ROBERT LOUIS STEVENSON, *Virginibus Puerisque.*

6
There is a well-known aphorism that men are different, but husbands are all alike.
WILLIAM HOWARD TAFT, *The President and His Powers.*

7
All husbands are alike, but they have different faces so you can tell them apart.
UNKNOWN.

HYPOCRISY

See also Deceit

8
I will have nought to do with a man who can blow hot and cold with the same breath.
AESOP, *The Man and the Satyr.*

9
It is the wisdom of crocodiles, that shed tears when they would devour.
FRANCIS BACON, *Essays.*

10
A bad man is worse when he pretends to be a saint.
FRANCIS BACON, *Moral and Historical Works.*

11
It will not do to be saints at meeting and sinners everywhere else.
HENRY WARD BEECHER, *Proverbs from Plymouth Pulpit.*

12
. . . Rich enough so you don't have to be a hypocrite.
SAUL BELLOW, *Orange Soufflé; Esquire,* Oct., 1965.

13
May the man be damned and never grow fat Who wears two faces under one hat.
H. G. BOHN, *Handbook of Proverbs.*

14
Saint abroad, and a devil at home.
JOHN BUNYAN, *Pilgrim's Progress.*

15
It was said of Pope Alexander VI and of his son the Duc de Valentinois, that the father never did what he said, and the son never said what he did.
JACOB CATS, *Moral Emblems.*

16
With affection beaming in one eye and calculation shining out of the other.
CHARLES DICKENS, *Martin Chuzzlewit,* ch. 8.

17
A hypocrite is in himself both the archer and the mark, in all actions shooting at his own praise or profit.
THOMAS FULLER, *The Holy and Profane States.*

18
We are not hypocrites in our sleep.
WILLIAM HAZLITT, *On Dreams.*

19
A hypocrite despises those whom he deceives, but has no respect for himself. He would make a dupe of himself, too, if he could.
WILLIAM HAZLITT, *Characteristics,* No. 398.

20
A wicked fellow is the most pious when he takes to it. He'll beat you all in piety.
SAMUEL JOHNSON, Boswell's *Life.*

21
They set the sign of the cross over their outer doors, and sacrifice to their gut and their groin in their inner closets.
BEN JONSON, *Explorata.*

22
To call him a hypocrite would be to attribute vices to his virtues; he is not so positive a character as that.
RUSSELL LYNES, *Snobs.*

23
A Pharisee is a man who prays publicly and preys privately.
DON MARQUIS, *New York Sun.*

24
A hypocrite is a person who—but who isn't?
DON MARQUIS, *New York Sun.*

1
I have heard of your paintings, too, well enough; God has given you one face, and you make yourselves another.
WILLIAM SHAKESPEARE, *Hamlet*. Act iii, sc. 1.

2
Making the world safe for hypocrisy.
THOMAS WOLFE, *Look Homeward, Angel!*, pt. 3.

I

IDEALS

3
Cling to your ideals, such as they are.
GEORGE ADE, *Fables in Slang*.

4
Ideals are the last refuge of the absolutely commonplace.
G. B. BURGIN, *Which Woman*.

5
There is nothing like an idealist for making hay.
JOHN GALSWORTHY, *The Country House*.

6
There are three Johns: 1, the real John, known only to his Maker; 2, John's ideal John, never the real one, and often very unlike him; 3, Thomas's ideal John, never the real John, nor John's John, but often very unlike either.
OLIVER WENDELL HOLMES, *The Autocrat of the Breakfast-Table*, ch. 3.

7
Architects, engineers and scientists are apt to consider themselves practical idealists, which means that they are really neither practical nor idealists.
ALEXANDER KING, *Rich Man, Poor Man, Freud and Fruit*, ch. 6.

8
When myth becomes reality, who wins? The idealists or the materialists?
STANISLAW J. LEC, *Unkempt Thoughts*, tr. from the Polish by JACEK GALASKA.

9
The Don Quixote of one generation may live to hear himself called the savior of society by the next.
JAMES RUSSELL LOWELL, *Essays: Don Quixote*.

10
The only way to save yourself from the pain of lost illusions is to have none.
CHARLES MARRIOTT, *The House on the Sands*.

11
An idealist is one who, on noticing that a rose smells better than a cabbage, concludes that it will also make better soup.
H. L. MENCKEN, *A Mencken Chrestomathy*.

12
I am an idealist. I don't know where I'm going but I'm on my way.
CARL SANDBURG, quoted by HARRY GOLDEN in *Carl Sandburg*.

13
Wiser not to come too near the glow, lest you see the worm.
HUGH DE SELINCOURT, *A Boy's Marriage*.

14
When they come downstairs from their Ivory Towers, Idealists are apt to walk straight into the gutter.
LOGAN PEARSALL SMITH, *All Trivia*.

IDEAS

15
If the ancients left us ideas, to our credit be it spoken that we moderns are building houses for them.
A. BRONSON ALCOTT, *Table Talk*.

16
One of the greatest pains to human nature is the pain of a new idea.
WALTER BAGEHOT, *Physics and Politics*.

17
Women, and especially married women, stick ideas into their brain-pan precisely as they stick pins into a pincushion, and the devil himself,—do you mind?—could not get them out: they reserve to themselves the exclusive right of sticking them in, pulling them out, and sticking them in again.
HONORÉ DE BALZAC, *Petty Troubles of Married Life*.

18
No grand idea was ever born in a conference, but a lot of foolish ideas have died there.
F. SCOTT FITZGERALD, *The Crack-up*.

19
An idea is planted with words, watered with words and plucked with words.
NORMAN FORD, *Headmasters Courageous*.

20
A word has been known to destroy a man's life. An idea has built a nation.
NORMAN FORD, *Headmasters Courageous*.

1
To die for an idea is to place a pretty high price upon conjecture.
ANATOLE FRANCE, *The Revolt of the Angels.*

2
A new and valid idea is worth more than a regiment and fewer men can furnish the former than can command the latter.
OLIVER WENDELL HOLMES, JR., *Letter* to John C. Wu, July 21, 1925.

3
We do not sell ideas if they are not good. Ideas are not salami.
NIKITA KHRUSHCHEV, quoted in *New York Herald Tribune,* Feb. 11, 1960.

4
An idea isn't responsible for the people who believe in it.
DON MARQUIS, *The Sun Dial.*

5
Give it only the fulcrum of Plymouth Rock, an idea will upheave the continent.
WENDELL PHILLIPS, *Speech* in New York City, Jan. 21, 1863.

6
When idiots ask where ideas come from, I reply: "It's inexplicable." When clever laymen ask, I discuss the mechanics. But when artists ask, I answer: "Ideas? I steal them." And they understand. Sometimes I rob myself.
NED ROREM, *Paris Diary.*

7
The French have an idea, the English give a guess, the Germans have a conviction, the Americans have a reaction.
LINCOLN STEFFENS, *Autobiography.*

8
A nice man is a man of nasty ideas.
JONATHAN SWIFT, *Thoughts on Various Subjects.*

9
The slowness of one section of the world about adopting the valuable ideas of another section of it is a curious thing and unaccountable. This form of stupidity is confined to no community, to no nation; it is universal.
MARK TWAIN, *Essays: Some National Stupidities.*

10
Ideas are like beards; men do not have them until they grow up.
VOLTAIRE.

IDLENESS

See also Leisure

11
Every once in a while it is important to do nothing. . . . Nothing is harder to do. Some puritan perversity in the American character makes us hate the nothing-doers of the world. A man quietly doing nothing is a challenge to the American system. He must be cajoled, badgered and, if necessary, blackguarded into purposeful living.
RUSSELL BAKER, "Observer" Column; *The New York Times,* June 29, 1965.

12
I feel like a locomotive hitched to a boy's express wagon.
GROVER CLEVELAND, when asked in 1897 how he felt with no Senate to fight and no official responsibility to bear. (MC-ELROY, *Grover Cleveland.*)

13
Sloth is an inlet to disorder, and makes way for licentiousness. People that have nothing to do are quickly tired of their own company.
JEREMY COLLIER. (*Classic Quotations,* ed. by JAMES ELMES.)

14
To be a nobody, do nothing.
B. C. FORBES, *Epigrams.*

15
The best time to loaf is after you're dead.
B. C. FORBES, *Epigrams.*

16
Idleness is the sepulchre of a living man.
J. G. HOLLAND, *Gold-Foil: Indolence and Industry.*

17
It is impossible to enjoy idling thoroughly unless one has plenty of work to do.
JEROME K. JEROME, *Idle Thoughts of an Idle Fellow: On Being Idle.*

18
The frivolous works of polished idleness.
SIR JAMES MACKINTOSH, *Dissertation on Ethical Philosophy: Remarks on Thomas Brown.*

19
For Satan finds some mischief still
For idle hands to do.
ISAAC WATTS, *Divine Songs for Children.* Song 20, *Against Idleness and Mischief.*

IGNORANCE

See also Stupidity

20
To be ignorant of one's ignorance is the malady of the ignorant.
AMOS BRONSON ALCOTT, *Table Talk: Discourse.*

21
Gross Ignorance—144 times worse than ordinary ignorance.
BENNETT CERF, *The Laugh's on Me.*

1
Ignorance is the mother of admiration.
GEORGE CHAPMAN, *Widow's Tears.*

2
He was distinguished for ignorance; for he had only one idea and that was wrong.
BENJAMIN DISRAELI.

3
If ignorance is bliss, why aren't there more happy people?
Farmer's Almanac, 1966.

4
There are no limits to invincible ignorance.
BARON VON HUEGEL, *Letters.*

5
Ignorance, Madam, pure ignorance.
SAMUEL JOHNSON, when a lady asked him why he defined pastern as the knee of a horse. Boswell's *Life,* 1775.

6
It is amazing how little Goldsmith knows. He seldom comes where he is not more ignorant than anyone else.
SAMUEL JOHNSON, Boswell's *Life,* Apr. 30, 1773.

7
A man must have a certain amount of intelligent ignorance to get anywhere.
CHARLES F. KETTERING, *Remark* on his 70th birthday, Aug. 29, 1946.

8
Even his ignorance is encyclopedic.
STANISLAW J. LEC, *Unkempt Thoughts,* tr. by JACEK GALASKA.

9
A Smattering of Ignorance.
OSCAR LEVANT, *Title* of book.

10
Everybody is ignorant, only on different subjects.
WILL ROGERS.

11
The road to ignorance is paved with good editions.
BERNARD SHAW, quoted in *Days with Bernard Shaw* by STEPHEN WINSTEN.

12
Nothing is so ignorant as a man's left hand, except a lady's watch.
MARK TWAIN.

13
Presently Mr. Bixby turned on me and said: "What is the name of the first point above New Orleans?"
I was gratified to be able to answer promptly and I did. I said I didn't know.
MARK TWAIN, *Life on the Mississippi.*

IMAGINATION

14
He was an absent-minded person with a mathematical imagination.
JOSEPH CONRAD, *A Personal Record.* Referring to Archimedes.

15
To make a mountain out of a mole-hill.
HENRY ELLIS, *Original Letters.* See also HARVEY in this section.

16
I say the very things that make the greatest stir
An' the most interestin' things, are things that didn't occur.
SAM WALTER FOSS, *Things That Didn't Occur.*

17
To make huge mountains out of small mole-hills.
GABRIEL HARVEY, *Letter-Book* (1573).

18
He who has imagination without learning, has wings and no feet.
JOSEPH JOUBERT, *Pensées,* No. 53.

19
Whene'er my maiden kisses me,
I'll think that I the Sultan be;
And when my cherry glass I tope,
I'll fancy then that I'm the Pope.
CHARLES LEVER, *Harry Lorrequer.*

20
Has your imagination the gout, that it limps so?
EDMOND ROSTAND, *Cyrano de Bergerac,* Act 3.

21
Don't part with your illusions. When they are gone you may still exist but you have ceased to live.
MARK TWAIN.

22
You can't depend on your eyes when your imagination is out of focus.
MARK TWAIN.

23
Against a diseased imagination demonstration goes for nothing.
MARK TWAIN.

IMITATION

24
None but blockheads copy each other.
WILLIAM BLAKE, quoted in GILCHRIST, *Life.*

25
When people are free to do as they please, they usually imitate each other.
ERIC HOFFER, *The Passionate State of Mind.*

1

Immature artists imitate. Mature artists steal.

LIONEL TRILLING, *Esquire,* Sept., 1962.

2

My greatest thrill has been surviving my imitators.

WALTER WINCHELL, in *Let's Go to Press* by ED WEINER.

IMMORTALITY

3

Millions long for immortality who do not know what to do with themselves on a rainy Sunday afternoon.

SUSAN ERTZ.

4

One world at a time.

HENRY D. THOREAU, *Remark,* shortly before his death in 1862, to PARKER PILLSBURY, who "would fain talk with Thoreau in this last winter concerning the next world."

5

The monuments of the nations are all protests against nothingness after death; so are statues and inscriptions; so is history.

LEW WALLACE, *Ben-Hur.* Bk. vii, ch. 3.

6

All men think all men mortal but themelves.

EDWARD YOUNG, *Night Thoughts.*

INDECISION

See also Doubt, Procrastination

7

Hesitation: the thief of good times.

OLIVER HERFORD, *Cupid's Cyclopedia.*

8

And while I at length debate and beat the bush,

There shall step in other men, and catch the birds.

JOHN HEYWOOD, *Proverbs,* pt. 1.

9

Suspense, that toothache of the mind.

FRANCIS E. SMEDLEY, *Frank Fairleigh,* ch. 31.

INDEPENDENCE

10

Colonies do not cease being colonies because they are independent.

BENJAMIN DISRAELI, *Speech,* House of Commons, Feb. 5, 1863.

11

For years I have been known for saying "Include me out."

SAMUEL GOLDWYN, *Address* to students of Balliol College, Oxford, Mar. 1, 1945.

12

Independence, like honor, is a rocky island without a beach.

NAPOLEON BONAPARTE, from *Sayings of Napoleon.*

13

Being grown up means we can have our own way—at our own expense.

HAL ROGERS, *Good Housekeeping.*

14

This patriotic business is always the Big Brother is helping the Weak Sister. But I don't care how poor and inefficient little Weak Sister is, they like to run their own business. Sure, Japan and America and England can run countries perhaps better than China, or Korea, or India, or the Philippines, but that don't mean they ought to. I know men that would make my wife a better husband than I am, but, darn it, I am not going to give her to 'em.

WILL ROGERS, *Autobiography.*

15

I would rather sit on a pumpkin and have it all to myself than be crowded on a velvet cushion.

HENRY D. THOREAU, *Walden,* ch. 1.

16

Some of the new nations are discovering that a country is like a children's birthday party. It's easier to get one started than to keep it going peacefully.

BILL VAUGHAN, *Kansas City Star.*

INDIVIDUALITY

17

I'm a ragged individualist.

JANE ACE, quoted in *The Fine Art of Hypochondria,* by GOODMAN ACE.

18

George Washington set many precedents, which, as the first President, he was in a good position to do.

RICHARD ARMOUR, *American Lit Relit.*

19

The Transcendentalists were a group of New Englanders who looked upon themselves as mystics and were looked upon by others as queer.

RICHARD ARMOUR, *American Lit Relit.*

20

What is not good for the swarm is not good for the bee.

MARCUS AURELIUS, *Meditations.*

21

Away he went, to live in a tent;

Over in France with his regiment.

Were you there, and tell me, did you notice?

They were all out of step but Jim.

IRVING BERLIN, *They Were All Out of Step But Jim* (1918).

1
You and I know that there is a correlation between the creative and the screwball. So we must suffer the screwball gladly.
> KINGMAN BREWSTER, JR., *Speech* in Hartford, Conn., Oct. 29, 1964.

2
Conventionality has slain the souls of more men and women than drink or immorality.
> G. B. BURGIN, *Which Woman?*

3
Conform and be dull.
> J. FRANK DOBIE, *The Voice of the Coyote:* introduction.

4
There is a certain type of human who is a radical when among conservatives, and a republican when living under a monarchy; who despises the forms and ceremonies of the Old World until he finds himself where they don't exist and becomes a loyal and ardent royalist when outside the domain of kingship.
> STEPHEN LEACOCK, *Charles Dickens.*

5
"Be yourself" is the worst advice you can give to some people.
> TOM MASSON.

6
Bah! The main thing is one's self.
> NAPOLEON BONAPARTE. (*The Mind of Napoleon*, ed. by J. CHRISTOPHER HEROLD.)

7
At bottom every man knows well enough that he is a unique being, only once on this earth; and by no extraordinary chance will such a marvelously picturesque piece of diversity in unity as he is, ever be put together a second time.
> FRIEDRICH WILHELM NIETZSCHE, *Thoughts out of Season*, vol. 2, tr. by ADRIAN COLLINS.

8
Our Unabashed Dictionary defines:
Individualist as a man who lives in the city and commutes to the suburbs.
> *More Playboy's Party Jokes* (1965).

9
All men are forced into one of two categories: those with eleven fingers and those without.
> NED ROREM, *Paris Diary.*

10
Men like conventions because men make them.
> BERNARD SHAW, *Misalliance.*

11
A square person has squeezed himself into the round hole.
> SYDNEY SMITH, *Elementary Sketches of Moral Philosophy*, lecture 9. See also MARK TWAIN in this section.

12
Curtius Rufus seems to me to be descended from himself.
> TIBERIUS. (TACITUS, *Annals.* Bk. xi, ch. 21.)

13
A round man cannot be expected to fit a square hole right away. He must have time to modify his shape.
> MARK TWAIN, *More Tramps Abroad*, ch. 71.

14
The race of men, while sheep in credulity, are wolves for conformity.
> CARL VAN DOREN, *Why I Am an Unbeliever.*

15
What would the world be without variety?
Soon all would die of sameness or satiety.
> Slogan of the newspaper *Varieties*, published in San Francisco in the 1860's. Probably written by J. WALTER WALSH.

INDUSTRY

See also Work

16
The beaver is very industrious but he is still a beaver.
> WILL CUPPY, *How to Tell Your Friends from the Apes: The Beaver.*

17
Everything comes to him who hustles while he waits.
> THOMAS A. EDISON, quoted in *Golden Book*, Apr., 1931

18
No one is so busy as the man who has nothing to do.
> Old French Proverb.

19
From beavers, bees should learn to mend their ways;
A bee just works; a beaver works and plays.
> ARTHUR GUITERMAN, *A Poet's Proverbs.*

20
As busy as a one-armed man with the nettle-rash pasting on wall-paper.
> O. HENRY, *Gentle Grafter: The Ethics of Pig.*

21
Goin' to work will be found twice as profitable as knockin' th' rich.
> FRANK McKINNEY (KIN) HUBBARD, *Abe Martin's Primer.*

22
What's become o' th' feller who used t' be willin' t' work at anything till somethin' better come along?
> FRANK McKINNEY (KIN) HUBBARD, *Abe Martin's Primer.*

1

He that looks after dead men's shoes, may chance go barefoot.

JAMES MABBE, *Celestina.*

2

The head of the most successful employment agency in America.

ADLAI E. STEVENSON, referring to Mrs. Joseph P. Kennedy, mother of the late President. (*Mother of a Dynasty; The New York Times,* Feb. 15, 1965, p. 16.)

3

We live in the age of the over-worked, and the under-educated; the age in which people are so industrious that they become absolutely stupid.

OSCAR WILDE, *The Critic as Artist.*

4

All work and no play makes—Jack.

DOUGLAS YATES, *Works.*

INHERITANCE

5

A Legacy

You told me, Maro, whilst you live
You'd not a single penny give.
But that, whene'er you chanct to die,
You'd leave a handsome legacy;
You must be mad beyond redress,
If my next wish you cannot guess!

MARTIAL (tr. by SAMUEL JOHNSON).

6

He that waits for dead men's shoes may go long enough barefoot.

JOHN RAY, *English Proverbs.*

7

Shall we sell our birthrite for a mess of potash?

ARTEMUS WARD, *Lecture.*

INTEGRITY

8

I should not like to think that integrity once lost is, like a maidenhead, irrecoverable.

ROBERT GRAVES, *The Crowning Privilege.*

9

Integrity is a lofty attitude assumed by someone who is unemployed.

OSCAR LEVANT, *Memoirs of an Amnesiac.*

10

Some people are likeable in spite of their unswerving integrity.

DON MARQUIS, *New York Sun.*

INTELLECTUAL

See also Mind

11

To the man-in-the-street who, I'm sorry to say
Is a keen observer of life,

The word Intellectual suggests straight away
A man who's untrue to his wife.

W. H. AUDEN, *Note on Intellectuals.*

12

For a long time I have hunted for a good definition of an intellectual. I wanted something simple and inclusive, not just an indirect way of bestowing my approval. But the more I tried to be fair, the more the exceptions and qualifications swamped the idea beneath them. Then one day while strap-hanging and scanning my homeward-bound fellow workers, it came over me in a flash: an intellectual is a man who carries a briefcase.

JACQUES BARZUN, *God's Country and Mine.*

13

No one is satisfied with his fortune, nor dissatisfied with his intellect. (Nul n'est content de sa fortune; Ni mécontent de son esprit.)

DESHOULIÈRES, *Epigram.*

14

Making political hay of the fact that Adlai [Stevenson] had a special appeal to the intellectuals, Eisenhower came up with one of his rare witticisms when he told a rally: "An intellectual is a man who takes more words than necessary to tell more than he knows."

PAUL STEINER, *The Stevenson Wit & Wisdom.*

15

An "egghead" is a person who stands firmly on both feet in mid-air on both sides of an issue.

SENATOR HOMER FERGUSON, *News summaries,* May 28, 1954.

16

A highbrow is the kind of person who looks at a sausage and thinks of Picasso.

A. P. HERBERT, *The Highbrow.*

17

It is easier to fake intellect than virginity.

ALEXANDER KING, *Rich Man, Poor Man, Freud and Fruit,* ch. 3.

18

. . . Swollen in head, weak in legs, sharp in tongue but empty in belly.

MAO TSE-TUNG, *Description* of intellectuals. From *The Wilting of the Hundred Flowers* (1963).

19

Eggheads, unite! You have nothing to lose but your yolks.

ADLAI E. STEVENSON, *Remark,* during the 1952 presidential campaign, in reply to the Republican taunt of "egghead."

20

On one occasion in a speech at Yale University, Adlai [Stevenson] talked about eggheads, saying: "Some people think it means that you have nothing on your head. In the latter respect I qualify as an egghead for obvious reasons. But it is when I am deemed to qualify in the former that I am happiest."

PAUL STEINER, *The Stevenson Wit & Wisdom.*

1

What is a highbrow? He is a man who has found something more interesting than women.

EDGAR WALLACE, *Interview* in Hollywood, Dec., 1931.

IRELAND AND THE IRISH

2

Oh! St. Patrick was a gentleman
  Who came of decent people;
He built a church in Dublin town,
  And on it put a steeple.

HENRY BENNETT, *Saint Patrick.*

3

She is not a distant, somewhat abstract goddess like those huge entities, America, Germany, France; she is a familiar acquaintance like Scotland or Venice, or those ancient lands, Britanny, Provence, Auvergne, which finally flocked under the fleurs-de-lis but whose hearts, if you only cock your ear, can still be heard beating distinctly.

ROGER CHAUVIRE, *A Short History of Ireland.*

4

My lips are sealed, and that is a pretty hard position to put an Irishman in.

MATTHEW J. CULLIGAN, *Reply* to inquiring reporters just after he had been removed from his post as president of the Curtis Publishing Company at a meeting of the firm's board of directors in Philadelphia, Oct. 19, 1964. He explained that he was bound by an agreement not to discuss proceedings of the meeting.

5

Their treason is a fairy tale, and their sedition is a child talking in its sleep.

BENJAMIN DISRAELI, *Lothair.*

6

It's so wonderful of all you people to come in wearing green ties and green scarves and shamrocks. How did you know I was Irish? ... Oh I am! The minute my mother heard the Irish had something called a Free State, we went! ... And after Alabama, it had to be.

DICK GREGORY, *From the Back of the Bus.*

7

Every Irishman, the saying goes, has a potato in his head.

J. C. AND A. W. HARE, *Guesses at Truth.*

8

The Irish are a fair people; they never speak well of one another.

SAMUEL JOHNSON, Boswell's *Life,* 1775.

9

The Irishman as a lover can be very charming provided he doesn't fall too frequently under the influence of his tipple.

ALEXANDER KING, *Rich Man, Poor Man, Freud and Fruit,* ch. 24.

10

The bravest toreador in Spain would be nonplused by an Irish bull.

MARY WILSON LITTLE.

11

In some parts of Ireland the sleep which knows no waking is always followed by a wake which knows no sleeping.

MARY WILSON LITTLE.

12

It was Whewell who asserted that all the Irish bulls had been calves in Greece; and it was Professor Tyrrell who neatly explained that the Irish bull differed from the bull of all other islands in that "it was always pregnant."

BRANDER MATTHEWS, *Recreations of an Anthologist.*

13

Nothing in Ireland lasts long except the miles.

GEORGE MOORE, *Ave.*

14

An Irishman's heart is nothing but his imagination.

BERNARD SHAW, *John Bull's Other Island,* Act 1.

15

The only way to deal with such a man as O'Connell is to hang him up and erect a statue to him under the gallows.

SYDNEY SMITH. (H. PEARSON, *The Smith of Smiths,* p. 272.)

16

Erin go bragh! A far better anthem would be, Erin go bread and cheese.

SYDNEY SMITH, *Fragment on the Irish Roman Catholic Church.*

17

In all other nations that are not absolutely barbarous, parents think themselves bound by the law of nature and reason to make some provision for their children; but the reason offered by the inhabitants of Ireland for marrying is, that they may have children to maintain them when they grow old and unable to work.

JONATHAN SWIFT, *Badges to Beggars.*

1
A servile race in folly nursed,
Who truckle most when treated worse.
JONATHAN SWIFT, *On the Death of Dr.
Swift.*

2
Give an Irishman lager for a month, and
he's a dead man. An Irishman is lined with
copper, and the beer corrodes it. But whiskey
polishes the copper and is the saving of him.
MARK TWAIN, *Life on the Mississippi,* ch.
23.

ITALY AND THE ITALIANS
3
We shall continue to operate on the Italian
donkey at both ends, with a carrot and with
a stick.
SIR WINSTON CHURCHILL, *Press Conference,* May 25, 1943.

4
Italy is only a geographical expression.
PRINCE METTERNICH, *Memorandum to
the Great Powers,* Aug. 2, 1814.

5
All Italians are plunderers. (Gli Italiani
tutti ladroni.)
NAPOLEON BONAPARTE, *Remark,* in a loud

voice, in public. To which a lady replied,
"Non tutti, ma buona parte" ("Not all,
but a good part"), a play upon Napoleon's name. (COLERIDGE, *Biographia
Literaria: Satyrane's Letters,* No. 2.)

6
The Italian seems wise, and is wise; the
Spaniard seems wise, and is a fool; the
French seems a fool, and is wise; and the
English seems a fool and is a fool.
THOMAS SCOTT, *The Highwaies of God
and the King.*

7
In Italy, the whole country is a theatre and
the worst actors are on the stage.
BERNARD SHAW.

8
Lump the whole thing! Say that the Creator
made Italy from designs by Michael Angelo!
MARK TWAIN, *The Innocents Abroad.*

9
They spell it Vinci and pronounce it Vinchy;
foreigners always spell better than they pronounce.
MARK TWAIN, *The Innocents Abroad.*

10
A paradise inhabited with devils.
SIR HENRY WOTTON, *Letters from Italy.*

J

JAPAN AND THE JAPANESE
11
Sometimes it looks as if Japan were created
as a satire on and for Western civilization.
LINCOLN STEFFENS, *Autobiography.*

12
The actual people who live in Japan are not
unlike the general run of English people;
that is to say, they are extremely commonplace, and have nothing curious or extraordinary about them. In fact the whole of
Japan is a pure invention.
OSCAR WILDE, *The Decay of Lying.*

13
The bomb is accorded by all Japan as a
power akin to legendary instruments—Thor's
hammer, David's slingshot, Arthur's Excali-
bur. For who can resist that which is mag-
ically irresistible? No one—not even the
Japanese! A beaten nation never had a better out, and the hue and cry raised in Japan
today over radioactive tuna, the radiation
sickness of the crew of the *Lucky Dragon*
and the fall-out from subsequent experiments, reflects in part an unconscious will

to sustain the idea that the war was lost
owing to magic.
PHILIP WYLIE, *The Innocent Ambassadors.*

JEALOUSY

See also Envy
14
The poison of the honey-bee
Is the artist's jealousy.
WILLIAM BLAKE, *Ideas of Good and Evil.*

15
Like Aesop's fox, when he had lost his tail,
would have all his fellow foxes cut off theirs.
ROBERT BURTON, *The Anatomy of Melancholy: Democritus to the Reader.*

16
All jealous women are mad.
SIR ARTHUR WING PINERO, *The Second
Mrs Tanqueray,* Act 2.

17
Is it for your honour, or mine, to have me
jealous? That he makes love to you, is a
sign you are handsome; and that I am not

jealous, is a sign you are virtuous.
> WILLIAM WYCHERLEY, *The Country Wife,*
> Act 3.

JEW

See also Prejudice

1
In Israel, in order to be a realist you must believe in miracles.
> DAVID BEN-GURION, *Comment* on CBS-TV, Oct. 5, 1956.

2
The gentleman will please remember that when his half-civilized ancestors were hunting the wild boar in Silesia, mine were princes of the earth.
> JUDAH BENJAMIN, *Reply* to a taunt by a Senator of German descent. (MOORE, *Reminiscences of Sixty Years in the National Metropolis.*)

3
. . . I don't mind saying it was a pretty big shake-up that after I decided to become a Jew only *then* did I learn the Jews don't really have all the money. When I found out Rockefeller and Ford were *goyim* I almost resigned.
> SAMMY DAVIS, JR., *Yes I Can.*

4
If my theory of relativity is proven successful, Germany will claim me as a German and France will declare that I am a citizen of the world. Should my theory prove untrue, France will say that I am a German and Germany will declare that I am a Jew.
> ALBERT EINSTEIN, *Address,* Sorbonne, Paris.

JUSTICE

See also Retribution

5
When men are friends there is no need of justice; but when they are just, they still need friendship.
> ARISTOTLE, *Ethics,* Bk. viii, ch. 1.

6
The price of justice is eternal publicity.
> ARNOLD BENNETT, *Things That Have Interested Me.*

7
The rain it raineth on the just
And also on the unjust fella:
But chiefly on the just, because
The unjust steals the just's umbrella.
> WALTER SICHEL (CHARLES BARON BOWEN), *Sands of Time.*

8
Justice is my being allowed to do whatever I like. Injustice is whatever prevents my doing so.
> SAMUEL BUTLER, *Notebooks.*

9
In a court of the fowls the cockroach never wins his case.
> SELWYN CHAMPION, *Racial Proverbs.*

10
Law and equity are two things which God hath joined, but which man has put asunder.
> CHARLES CALEB COLTON.

11
Justice is too good for some people and not good enough for the rest.
> NORMAN DOUGLAS, *Good-bye to Western Civilization.*

12
Justice is blind. Blind she is, an' deef an' dumb an' has a wooden leg.
> FINLEY PETER DUNNE, *Cross-Examinations.*

13
We may think we want justice. What we want is mercy. We need it.
> B. C. FORBES, *Epigrams.*

14
Indeed, I tremble for my country when I reflect that God is just.
> THOMAS JEFFERSON, *Notes on Virginia.*

15
McClellan complained to Lincoln, who remarked to Hay that "he seemed to think, in defiance of Scripture, that Heaven sent its rain only on the just and not on the unjust."
> CARL SANDBURG, *Abraham Lincoln: The Prairie Years and the War Years,* ch. 24.

16
Injustice is relatively easy to bear; what stings is justice.
> H. L. MENCKEN, *Prejudices,* ser. 3.

17
As to capital punishment: If it was good enough for my father, it's good enough for me.
> Line spoken by VICTOR MOORE in *Anything Goes.* Quoted by MAX EASTMAN in *Enjoyment of Laughter.*

18
A just man is not one who does no ill,
But he, who with the power, has not the will.
> PHILEMON, *Sententiae.*

19
We love justice greatly, and just men but little.
> JOSEPH ROUX, *Meditations of a Parish Priest.* Pt. iv, No. 10.

K

KINDNESS

1
The cheerful clatter of Sir James Barrie's cans as he went round with the milk of human kindness.
PHILIP GUEDALLA, *Some Critics.*

2
The traditional man from Mars, if he knew nothing of the American Republic except the so called "mass communications," would certainly be justified in thinking that there is not enough loving-kindness afloat in the contemporary United States to see a crippled old lady across an Indian trail.
MARGARET HALSEY, *The Folks at Home,* ch. 1.

3
He was so benevolent, so merciful a man that he would have held an umbrella over a duck in a shower of rain.
DOUGLAS JERROLD.

4
He's the kind man and generous, God bliss him! He never breaks his wife's head but he buys a plaster for it.
SEUMAS MACMANUS, *Heavy Hangs the Golden Grain.*

5
The founder of the Christian Religion was a good judge of character, wasn't he? It's so much harder to resist kindness than brute force.
W. SOMERSET MAUGHAM, *The Breadwinner,* Act 2.

6
Kind words will never die—neither will they buy groceries.
BILL NYE. (*Civil War Humor,* ed. by DORIS BERNADETE.)

7
And where does she find them?
DOROTHY PARKER, when informed that Clare Boothe Luce was kind to her inferiors. Quoted in Miss Parker's obituary in *Publishers' Weekly,* June 19, 1967.

8
Kindness is very indigestible. It disagrees with very proud stomachs.
WILLIAM MAKEPEACE THACKERAY, *Adventures of Philip,* bk. 2.

KINGS

9
Throughout the greater part of his life George III was a kind of "consecrated obstruction."
WALTER BAGEHOT, *The Monarchy.*

10
George the Third
Ought never to have occurred.
One can only wonder
At so grotesque a blunder.
EDMUND CLERIHEW BENTLEY, *Biography for Beginners.*

11
King George does not reign—he only sprinkles.
JOSEPH HODGES CHOATE, quoted by CLEVELAND AMORY, *The Last Resorts.* See also HOOD in this section.

12
We now come to King Henry the Eighth whom it has been too much the fashion to call "Bluff King Hal" and "Burly King Harry" and other fine names, but whom I shall take the liberty to call plainly one of the most detestable villains that ever drew breath.
CHARLES DICKENS, *A Child's History of England.*

13
It was said of Louis the Fourteenth that his gait was becoming enough in a king, but in a private man would have been an insufferable strut.
RALPH WALDO EMERSON, *Lectures: Public and Private Education.*

14
In a few years there will be only five kings in the world—the King of England and the four kings in a pack of cards.
KING FAROUK of Egypt, quoted in *Life,* Apr. 10, 1950.

15
I desire what is good; therefore, everyone who does not agree with me is a traitor.
GEORGE III, King of England.

16
. . . the first time a king got shot at he was a romantic, but the fifth time he was a comedian.
LILLIAN HELLMAN, *Watch on the Rhine,* Act 1.

17
How Monarchs die is easily explain'd,
    And thus it might upon the Tomb be chisell'd,
"As long as George the Fourth could *reign* he reign'd,
    And then he mizzled."
THOMAS HOOD, *On a Royal Demise.*

18
If any of our countrymen wish for a king, give them Aesop's fable of the frogs who

asked a King; if this does not cure them, send them to Europe. They will go back republicans.

THOMAS JEFFERSON, *Writings*. Vol. vi, p. 225.

1
George the First was always reckoned
Vile but viler George the Second;
And what mortal ever heard
Any good of George the Third?
When from earth the Fourth descended
God be praised, the Georges ended!

WALTER SAVAGE LANDOR, *The Georges*.

2
Some Queens can't marry Kings so they arrange to have Concerts.

ART LINKLETTER, *A Child's Garden of Misinformation*.

3
A king of France dies, but ought never to be ill.

LOUIS XVIII, *Comment*, Aug. 25, 1824, when urged not to hold his usual reception to celebrate the anniversary of St. Louis.

4
This hath not offended the king.

SIR THOMAS MORE, drawing his beard aside as he placed his head upon the block. (BACON, *Apothegms*, No. 22.)

5
A piece of lumber covered by a velvet rug.

NAPOLEON BONAPARTE, description of a throne. (*The Mind of Napoleon*, ed. by J. CHRISTOPHER HEROLD.)

6
But methought it lessened my esteem of a king, that he should not be able to command the rain.

SAMUEL PEPYS, *Diary*, July 19, 1662.

7
He that eats the king's goose shall be choked with his feathers.

SAMUEL RICHARDSON, *Clarissa Harlowe*, iv.

8
I guess the King of Spain will be buying a ranch in Canada or Mexico or someplace. Spain just pulled off a bloodless revolution. You know those bloodless revolutions are the ones that hurt the King business worse than a fighting one does. A king can stand people fighting but he can't last long if people start thinking.

WILL ROGERS, *Autobiography*.

9
I never heard of a king being drowned. Make haste, loose your cables, you will see the elements join to obey me.

WILLIAM RUFUS, from FREEMAN, *Life of William Rufus*.

10
Kings are not born: they are made by artificial hallucination. When the process is interrupted by adversity at a critical age, as in the case of Charles II, the subject becomes sane and never completely recovers his kingliness.

BERNARD SHAW, *Man and Superman*, preface: *Maxims for Revolutionists*.

11
Divine right of kings means the divine right of anyone who can get uppermost.

HERBERT SPENCER, *Social Statics*. Pt. ii, ch. 6, sec. 3.

12
All kings is mostly rapscallions.

MARK TWAIN, *Huckleberry Finn*, ch. 23.

13
Hark! The herald angels sing—
Mrs. Simpson pinched our king.

UNKNOWN, quoted in *Who Killed Society?* by CLEVELAND AMORY.

14
During the Napoleonic wars crowned heads were trembling in their shoes.

LOUIS UNTERMEYER, *A Treasury of Laughter*. Quoted as a student boner.

15
Here lies our Sovereign Lord, the King,
Whose word no man relies on:
He never says a foolsh thing,
Nor ever does a wise one.

JOHN WILMOT, EARL OF ROCHESTER, *Epitaph on Charles II*. These lines are said to have been written by Rochester on the door of the king's bedchamber. The first line is sometimes quoted: "Here lies our mutton-eating king."

KISS, KISSING

16
Kiss till the cow comes home.

BEAUMONT AND FLETCHER, *Scornful Lady*, Act 3.

17
When a piqued hostess chided actor David Niven for failing to greet her with a kiss at a Hollywood dinner party, he explained, "I was waiting for the interest to accrue."

Boston Globe, quoted in *Reader's Digest*, Feb., 1967.

18
Her eyes had languorously opened, and then the lids had fallen, about half way, just as the eyelids of a woman ought to do when she is being kissed properly.

JAMES BRANCH CABELL, *Jurgen*.

19
An old Spanish saying is that "a kiss without a mustache is like an egg without salt."

MADISON CAWEIN, *Nature-Notes*.

1
Love's great artillery.
RICHARD CRASHAW, *On a Prayer Book.*

2
Nobody wants to kiss when they are hungry.
DOROTHY DIX.

3
The anatomical juxtaposition of two orbicularis oris muscles is a state of contraction.
DR. HENRY GIBBONS, *Definition of a kiss.*

4
Never a lip is curved with pain
That can't be kissed into smiles again.
BRET HARTE, *The Lost Galleon.*

5
Osculation: A game of chance.
OLIVER HERFORD, *Cupid's Cyclopedia.*

6
What is a kiss? Why this, as some approve:
The sure sweet cement, glue, and lime of
    love.
ROBERT HERRICK, *A Kiss.*

7
Kisses and favors are sweet things,
But those have thorns and these have stings.
ROBERT HERRICK, *The Shower of Blossoms.*

8
The sound of a kiss is not so loud as that of
a cannon, but its echo lasts a great deal
longer.
OLIVER WENDELL HOLMES, *The Professor
    at the Breakfast-Table,* ch. 11.

9
People who throw kisses are mighty hopelessly lazy.
BOB HOPE.

10
A kiss on the lips does not always touch the
heart. (Bacio di bocca spesso cuor non
tocca.)
Old Italian Proverb.

11
You say, when I kissed you, you are sure
    I must quite
Have forgotten myself. So I did; you are
    right.
No, I'm not such an egoist, dear, it is true,
As to think of myself when I'm looking
    at you.
WALTER LEARNED, *Humility.*

12
"May I print a kiss on your lips?" I said,
And she nodded her full permission;
So we went to press and I rather guess
We printed a full edition.
JOSEPH LILIENTHAL, *A Full Edition.*

13
The kiss in which he half forgets even such
a yoke as yours.
THOMAS BABINGTON MACAULAY, *Lays of
    Ancient Rome.*

14
And she gave me a sisterly kiss. Older
sister.
NORMAN MAILER, *The Deer Park.*

15
Mayhem, death and arson
Have followed many a thoughtless kiss
Not sanctioned by a parson.
DON MARQUIS, *On Kissing.*

16
A legal kiss is never as good as a stolen one.
GUY DE MAUPASSANT, *A Wife's Confession.*

17
When women kiss it always reminds one of
prize-fighters shaking hands.
H. L. MENCKEN, *A Mencken Chrestomathy.*

18
How should great Jove himself do less than
    miss
To win the woman he forgets to kiss.
COVENTRY PATMORE, *De Natura Decorum.*

19
You can't always tell how much a girl wants
you to kiss her by the way she objects to it.
Reflections of a Bachelor.

20
Kissed lips tell no tales.
Reflections of a Bachelor.

21
Yet whoop, Jack! kiss Gillian the quicker,
'Till she bloom like a rose, and a fig for
    the vicar!
SIR WALTER SCOTT, *The Lady of the Lake,*
    canto 6.

22
Lord! I wonder what fool it was that first
invented kissing.
JONATHAN SWIFT, *Polite Conversation.*

KNOWLEDGE

See also Wisdom

23
I am the great Professor Jowett:
    What there is to know, I know it.
I am the Master of Balliol College,
    And what I don't know isn't knowledge.
ANONYMOUS.

24
The fox knows many things, but the hedgehog knows one big thing.
ARCHILOCHUS, *Fragment 103.*

25
What is all our knowledge? We do not even
know what weather it will be to-morrow.
BERTHOLD AUERBACH, *On the Heights.*

26
I am not young enough to know everything.
JAMES M. BARRIE.

1
I honestly believe it iz better tew know nothing than tew know what ain't so.
JOSH BILLINGS, *Encyclopedia of Proverbial Philosophy.*

2
The eagle never lost so much time as when he submitted to learn of the crow.
WILLIAM BLAKE, *Proverbs of Hell.*

3
I love the man who knows it all,
From east to west, from north to south,
Who knows all things, both great and small,
And tells it with his tiresome mouth.
ROBERT JONES BURDETTE, *He Knows It All.*

4
This devil of a man [Raymond Poincaré] is the opposite of Briand: The latter knows nothing and understands everything; the other knows everything and understands nothing.
GEORGES CLEMENCEAU, *Conversation* with friends, reported in *Les Annales.*

5
The whale is a mammal because we know so much nowadays. If we did not he would still be a fish. At the age of eighteen months our children are taught to say "The whale is a mammal."
WILL CUPPY, *How to Tell Your Friends from the Apes: The Whale.*

6
A man should keep his little brain attic stocked with all the furniture that he is likely to use, and the rest he can put away in the lumber-room of his library, where he can get it if he wants it.
SIR ARTHUR CONAN DOYLE, *The Adventures of Sherlock Holmes: The Five Orange Pips.*

7
Never try to tell everything you know. It may take too short a time.
NORMAN FORD, *Headmasters Courageous.*

8
It isn't only the things he doesn't know, it's the things he does know that aren't true.
SIGMUND FREUD, reference to Havelock Ellis.

9
A man of vast and varied misinformation.
WILLIAM GAYNOR, while mayor of New York. Describing Rabbi Stephen S. Wise.

10
Tell me what you *Know* is True;
I can *Guess* as well as you.
ARTHUR GUITERMAN, *A Poet's Proverbs.*

11
Who Knows what he is Told, must know
A Lot of Things that Are Not So.
ARTHUR GUITERMAN, *A Poet's Proverbs.*

12
Not All his Stock the Merchant's Window shows;
One should not make Display of All he knows.
ARTHUR GUITERMAN, *A Poet's Proverbs.*

13
It's what a feller thinks he knows that hurts him.
FRANK MCKINNEY (KIN) HUBBARD, *Abe Martin's Primer.*

14
If a little knowledge is dangerous, where is a man who has so much as to be out of danger?
THOMAS H. HUXLEY, *Science and Culture.*

15
I think this is the most extraordinary collection of talent, of human knowledge, that has ever been gathered together at the White House—with the possible exception of when Thomas Jefferson dined alone.
JOHN F. KENNEDY, *Greeting* to guests at White House dinner honoring Nobel Prize winners, Apr. 29, 1962.

16
A newly elected Congressman came in, Lincoln knowing him to have a sense of humor, for the gay greeting was: "Come in here and tell me what you know. It won't take long."
CARL SANDBURG, *Abraham Lincoln: The Prairie Years and the War Years,* ch. 50.

17
A dumb live man is a whole lot better than a dead smart man.
HUEY LONG, Senator from Louisiana.

18
"Where there is the tree of knowledge, there is always Paradise": so say the most ancient and the most modern serpents.
FRIEDRICH WILHELM NIETZSCHE, *Beyond Good and Evil,* tr. by HELEN ZIMMERN.

19
Learned men are the cisterns of knowledge, not the fountain-heads.
JAMES NORTHCOTE, *Table-Talk.*

20
There isn't much that you can teach the man who knows enough to know that he doesn't know much.
Reflections of a Bachelor.

21
We know lots of things we didn't use to

know but we don't know any way to prevent
'em happening.
WILL ROGERS, *Autobiography.*

1
It is better, of course, to know useless things
than to know nothing. (Satius est super-
vacua scire quam nihil.)
SENECA, *Epistulae ad Lucilium.* Epis.
LXXXVIII, sec. 45.

2
Thus men catch knowledge by throwing
their wit into the posteriors of a book, as
boys do sparrows with flinging salt on their
tails.
JONATHAN SWIFT, *A Tale of a Tub.*

3
How haughtily he cocks his nose to tell
what every schoolboy knows.
JONATHAN SWIFT, *The Country Life.*

4
He is a stranger to me but he is a most
remarkable man—and I am the other one.
Between us, we cover all knowledge; he
knows all that can be known and I know
the rest.
MARK TWAIN, *Autobiography,* ch. 59. Referring to Rudyard Kipling.

5
He was not made for climbing the tree of
knowledge.
SIGRID UNDSET.

6
It is a very sad thing that nowadays there
is so little useless information.
OSCAR WILDE, *Saturday Review,* Nov. 17,
1894.

L

LABOR

See also Industry, Work

7
I have known people to stop and buy an
apple on the corner and then walk away as
if they had solved the whole unemployment
problem.
HEYWOOD BROUN, *It Seems to Me.*

8
When a great many people are unable to find
work, unemployment results.
CALVIN COOLIDGE, *Syndicated newspaper
article.* Quoted in STANLEY WALKER,
City Editor.

9
They draw fat women for the *Masses,*
Denuded, fat, ungainly lasses—
How does that help the working classes?
BOBBY EDWARDS, quoted in *The Improper
Bohemians* by ALLEN CHURCHILL.

10
It is one of the comic delusions of the sentimental American working middle-class male
that he does it for the wife and kiddies. If
he cared to poke about in his unconscious
he might often discover that he acquired
the wife and kiddies so that he might have
a socially respectable excuse for acquiring
the jobs.
CLIFTON FADIMAN, *The Selected Writings
of Clifton Fadiman* (1955).

11
Is your boss entitled to regard you as an
ass or an asset?
B. C. FORBES, *Epigrams.*

12
There's more credit and satisfaction in being a first-rate truck-driver than a tenth-
rate executive.
B. C. FORBES, *Epigrams.*

13
He beats the bush and another catches the
bird. (Il bat le buisson sans prendre l'oiseau.)
Old French Proverb.

14
There are only three ways by which any individual can get wealth—by work, by gift,
or by theft. And, clearly, the reason why the
workers get so little is that the beggars and
thieves get so much.
HENRY GEORGE, *Social Problems.*

15
We're overpaying him but he's worth it.
SAMUEL GOLDWYN.

16
You better be nice to me. Chock Full O'
Nuts opens forty more stores—we're gonna
be at a premium!
DICK GREGORY, *From the Back of the Bus.*

17
But you gotta admit we're ahead of the Rus-
sians in one thing—strikes. . . . I haven't
seen so many people walking off their jobs
since I asked for a menu in Little Rock.
DICK GREGORY, *From the Back of the Bus.*

18
A newspaper editor friend of mine once told
me that he thought most people fell into
their occupations by chance, but the men

choose to join a circus, work on a railroad or enter newspapering.

THOMAS GRIFFITH, *The Waist-High Culture.*

1
We all belong t' th' union when it comes t' wantin' more money and less work.

FRANK MCKINNEY (KIN) HUBBARD, *Abe Martin's Primer.*

2
The ugliest of trades have their moments of pleasure. Now, if I were a grave-digger, or even a hangman, there are some people I could work for with a great deal of enjoyment.

DOUGLAS JERROLD, *Jerrold's Wit: Ugly Trades.*

3
In the old days . . . any woman who wanted to show her independent spirit and force of character took in washing. It was the last resort of a noble mind.

STEPHEN LEACOCK, *Laugh with Leacock.*

4
I hold that if the Almighty had ever made a set of men that should do all the eating and none of the work, He would have made them with mouths only and no hands; and if He had ever made another class that He intended should do all the work and no eating, He would have made them with hands only and no mouths.

ABRAHAM LINCOLN, *Mud-Sill Theory of Labor.*

5
For labor a short day is better than a short dollar.

WILLIAM MCKINLEY, *Letter* to Henry Cabot Lodge, Sept. 8, 1900.

6
Anybody who has any doubts about the ingenuity or the resourcefulness of a plumber never got a bill from one.

GEORGE MEANY, president, American Federation of Labor, a former plumber. CBS-TV, Jan. 8, 1954.

7
Since the people eats every day, it should be allowed to work every day.

NAPOLEON BONAPARTE, Decision on the right to work on Sundays and holidays. (*The Mind of Napoleon,* ed. by J. CHRISTOPHER HEROLD.)

8
Some are bent with toil, and some get crooked trying to avoid it.

The Public Speaker's Treasure Chest, ed. by HERBERT PROCHNOW.

9
The tons of soil.

WILLIAM A. SPOONER, warden of New College, Oxford, who transposed the sound of words. (The sons of toil.)

10
It is not necessary that a man should earn his living by the sweat of his brow, unless he sweats easier than I do.

HENRY D. THOREAU, *Walden.*

11
One employee to another: "My mistake was buying stock in the company. Now I worry about the lousy work I'm turning out."

MARVIN TOWNSEND, *The American Citizen.*

12
Let us be grateful to Adam, our benefactor. He cut us out of the "blessing" of idleness and won for us the "curse" of labor.

MARK TWAIN, *Pudd'nhead Wilson's Calendar.*

13
I was told by a person who said that he was studying for the ministry that even Noah got no salary for the first six months— partly on account of the weather and partly because he was learning navigation.

MARK TWAIN, *Autobiography,* ch. 46.

14
The law of work does seem utterly unfair; but there it is, and nothing can change it: the higher the pay in enjoyment the worker gets out of it, the higher shall be his pay in cash also.

MARK TWAIN, *A Connecticut Yankee in King Arthur's Court.*

15
I never fire an employee. They go from Maxim's to the cemetery.

LOUIS VAUDABLE, quoted in *Life,* Jan. 7, 1966. Vaudable was commenting as the owner of the famous French restaurant Maxim's.

LANGUAGE

See also Speech, Words

16
He [P. G. Wodehouse] is, I believe, the only man living who speaks with equal fluency the American and English languages.

MAX EASTMAN, *Enjoyment of Laughter.*

17
Language is fossil poetry.

RALPH WALDO EMERSON, *Essays: The Poet.*

18
Clearly spoken, Mr. Fogg; you explain English by Greek.

BENJAMIN FRANKLIN.

19
Language is the dress of thought.

SAMUEL JOHNSON, *Works.*

1
Comment allez-vous? . . . My wife speaks good French, I understand only one out of every five words, but always "de Gaulle."
  JOHN F. KENNEDY, on greeting Madame Hervé Alphand, wife of the French Ambassador, at a White House dinner, Jan., 1961.

2
I never went to bed before dawn in those days. One of the people I hung out with in the small hours was Walter Winchell. He'd often print remarks of mine. One that he paraphrased years later was my comment on the composer Vernon Duke, with his English accent: "You speak with a monocle in your throat."
  OSCAR LEVANT, Memoirs of an Amnesiac.

3
For more than forty years I have been speaking prose without knowing it.
  MOLIÈRE, Le Bourgeois Gentilhomme.

4
I must needs acknowledge that the Greek and Latin tongues are great ornaments in a gentleman, but they are purchased at overhigh a rate.
  MICHEL DE MONTAIGNE, Essays, tr. by JOHN FLORIO.

5
When Abraham Lincoln was murdered
The one thing that interested Matthew Arnold
Was that the assassin shouted in Latin
As he leapt from the stage.
This convinced Matthew
There was still hope for America.
  CHRISTOPHER MORLEY, Point of View.

6
It is a curious thing that God learned Greek when he wished to turn author—and that he did not learn it better.
  FRIEDRICH WILHELM NIETZSCHE, Beyond Good and Evil, tr. by HELEN ZIMMERN.

7
It doesn't really matter. But it would be better to send a bowler-hatted man speaking Spanish, than a man wearing a sombrero who could only speak English.
  PRINCE PHILIP, Comment, when asked whether businessmen visiting Spanish-speaking countries should wear bowlers or sombreros, Apr., 1962.

8
Slang is a language that rolls up its sleeves, spits on its hands and goes to work.
  CARL SANDBURG. (The New York Times, Feb. 13, 1959.)

9
You taught me language, and my profit on't Is, I know how to curse; the red plague rid you,

For learning me your language!
  WILLIAM SHAKESPEARE, The Tempest, Act i, sc. 2.

10
It is the true and native language of insincerity.
  ALFRED SUTRO, A Marriage Has Been Arranged. Referring to the French language.

11
My philological studies have satisfied me that a gifted person ought to learn English (barring spelling and pronouncing) in thirty hours, French in thirty days, and German in thirty years.
  MARK TWAIN, A Tramp Abroad.

12
Wilde came to the conclusion that "the English have really everything in common with the Americans, except of course language."
  HESKETH PEARSON, Lives of the Wits.

LATENESS

13
A Man consumes the Time you make him Wait
In thinking of your Faults—so don't be late!
  ARTHUR GUITERMAN, A Poet's Proverbs.

14
Unfaithfulness in the keeping of an appointment is an act of clear dishonesty. You may as well borrow a person's money as his time.
  HORACE MANN.

15
Punctuality is one of the cardinal virtues. Always insist on it in your subordinates and dependents.
  DON MARQUIS, Parody of Dale Carnegie. From O Rare Don Marquis by EDWARD ANTHONY.

16
I've been on a calendar, but never on time.
  MARILYN MONROE. (Look, Jan. 16, 1962.)

17
I cannot cure myself of punctuality.
  SYDNEY SMITH, from Bon-Mots of Sydney Smith, ed. by JERROLD.

18
Better late than never, as Noah remarked to the Zebra, which had understood that passengers arrived in alphabetical order.
  BERT LESTON TAYLOR, The So-Called Human Race.

19
If you're there before it's over, you're on time.
  JAMES J. WALKER, Remark to reporters on arriving at a dinner, Oct., 1931.

1

He was always late on principle, his principle being that punctuality is the thief of time.

OSCAR WILDE, *The Picture of Dorian Gray*, ch. 3.

LAUGHTER

2

In the language of screen comedians four of the main grades of laugh are the titter, the yowl, the belly laugh and the boffo. The titter is just a titter. The yowl is a runaway titter. Anyone who has ever had the pleasure knows all about a belly laugh. The boffo is the laugh that kills.

JAMES AGEE, *Comedy's Greatest Era; Life*, Sept. 5, 1949.

3

For what do we live, but to make sport for our neighbors, and laugh at them in our turn?

JANE AUSTEN, *Pride and Prejudice*, ch. 57.

4

Mirth is God's medicine.

HENRY WARD BEECHER, *Proverbs from Plymouth Pulpit*.

5

Strange, when you come to think of it, that of all the countless folk who have lived before our time on this planet not one is known in history or in legend as having died of laughter.

MAX BEERBOHM, *Laughter*.

6

Laughter is the sensation of feeling good all over, and showing it principally in one spot.

JOSH BILLINGS, *Laffing*.

7

The laughter of the soul at itself is a laughter from which it cannot flee.

JOSEPH COOK, *Boston Monday Lectures*.

8

Never make people laugh. If you would succeed in life, you must be solemn, solemn as an ass. All the great monuments are built over solemn asses.

THOMAS CORWIN, *Advice* to a young speaker, based upon his own experience.

9

As the crackling of thorns under a pot, so is the laughter of a fool.

Ecclesiastes, vii.

10

Then I commended mirth, because a man hath no better thing under the sun, than to eat, and to drink, and to be merry.

Ecclesiastes, viii.

11

"A man isn't poor if he can still laugh," declared Raymond Hitchcock when haled into the bankruptcy court. Said Carnegie: "Millionaires seldom laugh." Do your own moralizing.

B. C. FORBES, *Epigrams*.

12

The only way to make the English laugh, as laughter is understood in the United States, is to jab them with your elbow and say out of the corner of your mouth, "That's funny." Then they all look nervously around at each other and allow you two decibels of politely acquiescent mirth.

MARGARET HALSEY, *With Malice Toward Some*.

13

What provokes you to risibility, sir? Have I said anything that you understand? Then I ask the pardon of the rest of the company.

SAMUEL JOHNSON, *Remark*. (RICHARD CUMBERLAND, *Recollections*.)

14

Men have been wise in many different modes; but they have always laughed the same way.

SAMUEL JOHNSON, *Works*, VII (Oxford Edition, 1825).

15

We must laugh before we are happy, for fear we die before we laugh at all.

JEAN DE LA BRUYÈRE, *Les Caractères*, ch. 4.

16

Anything awful makes me laugh. I misbehaved once at a funeral.

CHARLES LAMB, *Letter to Southey* (1815).

17

Even Olympus needed the corrective of laughter. When they kicked Momus out, the deities degenerated into sots and jades.

DON MARQUIS, *New York Sun*.

18

No one is more profoundly sad than he who laughs too much.

J. P. F. RICHTER, *Hesperus*, 19.

19

Born with a gift of laughter and the sense that the world was mad, and that was his only patrimony.

RAFAEL SABATINI, *Scaramouche*, ch. 1.

20

There are few who would not rather be hated than laughed at.

SYDNEY SMITH, *Sketches of Moral Philosophy*, lecture 2.

21

An onion can make people cry, but there

has never been a vegetable invented to make them laugh.
> UNKNOWN, May Irwin's favorite quotation. In *Saturday Evening Post*, Apr. 25, 1931.

1
Laughter is not a bad beginning for a friendship, and it is the best ending for one.
> OSCAR WILDE.

LAW

2
Father protested vehemently, waving a volume of Blackstone under the justice's nose to emphasize his outrage.
"Sit down, Mr. Allen!" the judge shouted. "I know the law."
"Of course you do, Your Honor," Father replied. "I just wanted to read this to you to show you what a damned fool Blackstone was."
> GEORGE E. ALLEN, *Presidents Who Have Known Me.*

3
Wise men plead causes, but fools decide them.
> ANACHARSIS, from PLUTARCH'S *Lives: Solon*, sec. 5.

4
Laws are like spider's webs, that will catch flies, but not wasps and hornets.
> ANACHARSIS. (*Classic Quotations*, ed. by JAMES ELMES.)

5
Silence, here! We have decided half a dozen cases this morning, and I have not heard a word of one of them.
> Attributed to an old-time judge in Sullivan County, N.Y., who was irritated by the excessive amount of talking in his courtroom.

6
If you laid all our laws end to end, there would be no end.
> ARTHUR (BUGS) BAER.

7
Kings, that made laws, first broke them.
> APHRA BEHN, *The Golden Age*, st. 4.

8
Court fool: the plaintiff.
> AMBROSE BIERCE, *The Devil's Dictionary.*

9
One law for the Lion & Ox is oppression.
> WILLIAM BLAKE, *The Marriage of Heaven and Hell.*

10
I will tell you about judges. You can take the most mild-mannered and tender-hearted man you ever saw, make him a judge for life, and his disposition to tyrannize over

people will grow with what he feeds on.
> REPRESENTATIVE CHAMP CLARK of Missouri, 1919.

11
Out of the 93 persons who have sat on the Supreme Court, not one has been a woman. Too bad, for they always have the last word, except here, where the last word really counts.
> TOM CLARK, Associate Justice, Supreme Court. (*McCall's*, Sept., 1963.)

12
No man has ever yet been hanged for breaking the spirit of a law.
> GROVER CLEVELAND. (RHODES, *History of the United States*, vol. viii, p. 403. HIBBEN, *Peerless Leader*, p. 155.)

13
The law [is] a horrible business.
> CLARENCE DARROW, *Interview, The New York Times*, Apr. 19, 1936.

14
All laws are useless, for good men do not need them and bad men are made no better by them.
> DEMONAX, quoted in PLUTARCH'S *Apothegms.*

15
No matter whether th' Constitution follows th' flag or not, th' Supreme Coort follows th' iliction returns.
> FINLEY PETER DUNNE, *Mr. Dooley's Opinions: The Supreme Court Decisions.*

16
I care not who makes the laws of the nation if I can get out an injunction.
> FINLEY PETER DUNNE, *Mr. Dooley Remembers.*

17
An appeal, Hennessy, is when ye ask wan court to show its contempt for another court.
> FINLEY PETER DUNNE, *Mr. Dooley.*

18
The law, in its majestic equality, forbids the rich as well as the poor to sleep under bridges, to beg in the streets, and to steal bread.
> ANATOLE FRANCE.

19
Laws like to cobwebs, catch small flies,
Great ones break them before your eyes.
> BENJAMIN FRANKLIN, *Poor Richard*, 1734.

20
When constabulary duty's to be done,
The policeman's lot is not a happy one.
> SIR WILLIAM SCHWENCK GILBERT, *Pirates of Penzance*, Act 2.

21
The Law is the true embodiment

Of everything that's excellent.
It has no kind of fault or flaw,
And I, my Lords, embody the law.
>   SIR WILLIAM SCHWENCK GILBERT, *Iolanthe*, Act 1.

1
Lem Grainger's trial fer hoss stealin' is set
fer next week, and Attorney Tell Brinkley
is rehearsin' his wife an' baby on how t' cry
in court.
>   FRANK MCKINNEY (KIN) HUBBARD, *Abe Martin's Primer*.

2
You kin never tell what a woman or a country jury is goin' t' do.
>   FRANK MCKINNEY (KIN) HUBBARD, *Abe Martin's Broadcast*.

3
We prefer world law, in the age of self-determination, to world war in the age of mass extermination.
>   JOHN F. KENNEDY, *Address* to the United Nations General Assembly, Sept. 25, 1961.

4
Madison proposed a toast to the Federal judiciary in 1798: "May it remember that it is the Expositor of the laws, not the Trumpeter of politics."
>   JOHN C. MILLER, *Crisis in Freedom*.

5
Someone has tabulated that we have 35 million laws on the books to enforce the ten commandments.
>   BERT MASTERSON, *Wall Street Journal*.

6
A magistrate asked him [Wilson Mizner] if he was trying to show contempt of court. "No, I'm trying to conceal it," muttered Mizner.
>   ALVA JOHNSTON, *Legend of a Sport; The New Yorker*.

7
The people have nothing to do with the laws but obey them.
>   EDGAR ALLAN POE.

8
As in the case of Prof. Wubb, or whatever his name was, the ignorant of one generation set out to make laws, and gullible children next try to obey them.
>   EZRA POUND, *ABC of Reading*.

9
We are always saying let the law take its course, but what we mean is "Let the law take our course."
>   WILL ROGERS, *Autobiography*.

10
Many a good hanging prevents a bad marriage.
>   WILLIAM SHAKESPEARE, *Twelfth Night*. Act i, sc. 5.

11
Still you keep o' the windy side of the law.
>   WILLIAM SHAKESPEARE, *Twelfth Night*. Act iii, sc. 4.

12
Trying a case a second time is like eating yesterday morning's oatmeal.
>   LLOYD PAUL STRYKER, quoted in reports of his death, June 22, 1955.

13
"My Lord," said the foreman of an Irish jury when giving in his verdict, "we find the man who stole the mare not guilty."
>   *The Pun Book* by T.B. and T.C. (c. 1906).

14
Some circumstantial evidence is very strong, as when you find a trout in the milk.
>   HENRY DAVID THOREAU, *Unpublished Mss. in Miscellanies, Biographical Sketch* (1918). Vol. x, p. 30.

15
It can't be done because I've tried it and it doesn't work. Whenever you put a man on the Supreme Court, he ceases to be your friend. I'm sure of that.
>   HARRY S TRUMAN. (*New York Herald Tribune*, Apr. 29, 1959.)

16
Even the clearest and most perfect circumstantial evidence is likely to be at fault, after all, and therefore ought to be received with great caution. Take the case of any pencil, sharpened by any woman: if you have witnesses, you will find she did it with a knife; but if you take simply the aspect of the pencil, you will say she did it with her teeth.
>   MARK TWAIN, *Pudd'nhead Wilson's Calendar*.

17
To succeed in the other trades, capacity must be shown; in the law, concealment of it will do.
>   MARK TWAIN.

18
We have a criminal jury system which is superior to any in the world and its efficiency is only marred by the difficulty of finding twelve men every day who don't know anything and can't read.
>   MARK TWAIN.

19
[Laws] take a *meaning*, and get to be very vivid, when you come to apply them to yourself.
>   MARK TWAIN, *A Connecticut Yankee in King Arthur's Court*, ch. 34.

20
The departmental *interpreters* of the laws, in Washington . . . can always be depended

on to take a reasonably good law and interpret the common sense all out of it.
> MARK TWAIN, *Letter* to H. C. Christiancy, Dec. 18, 1887.

1
Are you going to hang him *anyhow*—and try him afterward?
> MARK TWAIN, *Innocents at Home*, ch. 5.

2
Man is without any doubt the most interesting fool there is. Also the most eccentric. He hasn't a single written law, in his Bible or out of it, which has any but just one purpose and intention—to limit or defeat a law of God.
> MARK TWAIN, *Letters from the Earth.*

3
There is plenty of law at the end of a nightstick.
> GROVER WHALEN.

4
Hanging was the worst use a man could be put to.
> SIR HENRY WOTTON, *The Disparity Between Buckingham and Essex.*

LAWYERS

5
Lawyers' gowns are lined with the wilfulness of their clients.
> H. G. BOHN, *Handbook of Proverbs*, 439.

6
A lawyer starts life giving $500 worth of law for $5, and ends giving $5 worth for $500.
> Attributed to BENJAMIN H. BREWSTER.

7
It is hard to say whether the doctors of law or divinity have made the greater advances in the lucrative business of mystery.
> EDMUND BURKE, *A Vindication of Natural Society.*

8
"In my youth," said his father, "I took to the law,
And argued each case with my wife;
And the muscular strength, which it gave to my jaw,
Has lasted the rest of my life."
> LEWIS CARROLL, *Alice in Wonderland*, ch. 5.

9
If there were no bad people there would be no good lawyers.
> CHARLES DICKENS, *The Old Curiosity Shop*, ch. 56.

10
God works wonders, now and then;
Behold! A lawyer, and an honest man.
> BENJAMIN FRANKLIN, *Poor Richard*, 1733.

11
A good lawyer, a bad neighbor.
> BENJAMIN FRANKLIN, *Poor Richard*, 1737.

12
Lawyers and soldiers are the devil's playmates.
> Old German Proverb.

13
Lawyers' houses are built on the heads of fools.
> GEORGE HERBERT, *Jacula Prudentum.*

14
It is a horrible demoralizing thing to be a lawyer. You look for such low motives in everyone and everything.
> KATHERINE T. HINKSON, *The Love of Sisters.*

15
When lawyers take what they would give
And doctors give what they would take.
> OLIVER WENDELL HOLMES, *Latterday Warnings.*

16
A man may as well open an oyster without a knife, as a lawyer's mouth without a fee.
> BARTEN HOLYDAY, *Technogamia*, ii, 5.

17
Johnson observed that he did not care to speak ill of any man behind his back, but he believed the gentleman was an attorney.
> BOSWELL'S *Life of Dr. Johnson.*

18
There is a general prejudice to the effect that lawyers are more honorable than politicians but less honorable than prostitutes. This is an exaggeration.
> ALEXANDER KING, *Rich Man, Poor Man, Freud and Fruit*, ch. 5.

19
It took man thousands of years to put words down on paper, and his lawyers still wish he wouldn't.
> MIGNON McLAUGHLIN, *The Saturday Review.*

20
I wanted to make it a law that only those lawyers and attorneys should receive fees who had won their cases. How much litigation would have been prevented by such a measure!
> NAPOLEON BONAPARTE. (*The Mind of Napoleon*, ed. by J. CHRISTOPHER HEROLD.)

21
Ignorance of the law does not prevent the losing lawyer from collecting his bill.
> *Puck.*

22
Personally I don't think you can make a lawyer honest by an act of legislature. You've got to work on his conscience. And

his lack of conscience is what makes him a lawyer.
> WILL ROGERS, *Autobiography*.

1
'Tis like the breath of an unfee'd lawyer; you gave me nothing for 't.
> WILLIAM SHAKESPEARE, *King Lear*. Act i, sc. 4.

2
Why may not that be the skull of a lawyer? Where be his quiddities now, his quillets, his cases, his tenures, and his tricks?
> WILLIAM SHAKESPEARE, *Hamlet*. Act v, sc. 1.

3
The first thing we do, let's kill all the lawyers.
> WILLIAM SHAKESPEARE, *Henry VI, Pt. 2*. Act iv, sc. 2.

4
I regret that I have but one law firm to give to my country.
> ADLAI STEVENSON, on the Kennedy administration's use of lawyers from his Chicago office.

5
Always remember that when you go into an attorney's office, you will have to pay for it, first or last.
> ANTHONY TROLLOPE, *The Last Chronicle of Barset*. Vol. i, ch. 20.

6
The New England folks have a saying that three Philadelphia lawyers are a match for the very devil himself.
> UNKNOWN, *Salem Observer*, Mar. 13, 1824.

LEADERSHIP

7
We all understand his position. "I am their leader, I must follow them."
> SIR WINSTON CHURCHILL, *Speech*, in House of Commons. Comment on CLEMENT ATTLEE.

8
The question, "Who ought to be boss?" is like asking "Who ought to be the tenor in the quartet?" Obviously, the man who can sing tenor.
> HENRY FORD, quoted in *Forbes Magazine*.

9
The crude ideals advanced by many of the successful mass movement leaders of our time incline one to assume that a certain coarseness and immaturity of mind is an asset to leadership.
> ERIC HOFFER, *The True Believer*.

10
Charlatanism of some degree is indispensable to effective leadership.
> ERIC HOFFER, *The True Believer*.

11
We don't want to be like the leader in the French Revolution who said, "There go my people. I must find out where they are going so I can lead them."
> JOHN F. KENNEDY, *Comment* in Sioux Falls, S. Dak., Sept. 22, 1960.

12
If the blind lead the blind, both shall fall into the ditch.
> *Matthew*, XV, 14.

13
If Voltaire ruled contemporary opinion, if he was the hero of his age, this was only because it was an age of dwarfs.
> NAPOLEON BONAPARTE. (*The Mind of Napoleon*, ed. by J. CHRISTOPHER HEROLD.)

LEISURE

See also Movies, Stage, Television

14
Why should I go to a night club? I can get better air in a closet. I can cook better food myself. I can hear better music on a portable phonograph, and I can meet a better class of people on the subway.
> FRED ALLEN, from *Fred Allen's Letters*, ed. by JOE McCARTHY.

15
We are all, it seems, saving ourselves for the Senior Prom. But many of us forget that somewhere along the way we must learn to dance.
> ALAN HARRINGTON, *Life in the Crystal Palace*. Referring to preparation to enjoy retirement.

16
All work and no play makes Jack a dull boy.
> JAMES HOWELL, *Proverbs* (1659).
> THOMAS FULLER, *Gnomologia* (1732).

17
Life would be tolerable if it were not for its amusements.
> SIR GEORGE CORNWALL LEWIS, on the authority of LORD GREY of Falladon.

18
For a territory the size of the United States, five millions of people would be about right . . . The human population of the entire world should be kept well under a hundred millions . . . If the world were not so full of people, and most of them did not have to work so hard, there would be more time for them to get out and lie on the grass, and there would be more grass to lie on.
> DON MARQUIS, *The Almost Perfect State*.

19
Amusement is the happiness of those who cannot think.
> ALEXANDER POPE, *Thoughts on Various Subjects*.

1

The secret of being miserable is to have leisure to bother about whether you are happy or not.

BERNARD SHAW, *Parents and Children.*

2

A perpetual holiday is a good working definition of hell.

BERNARD SHAW, *Parents and Children.*

3

One little chore to do, one little commission to fulfill, one message to carry, would spoil heaven itself.

HENRY D. THOREAU, *Journal,* July 21, 1851.

4

When we get to be our own hobby, riding the thing presents great difficulties.

UNKNOWN, *Meditations in Wall Street.*

5

There's a lot of good, clean entertainment around . . . the reason we don't hear much about it is, nobody's looking for it.

EARL WILSON. *New York Post,* Aug. 12, 1965.

LENDING, see Borrowing

LETTERS

6

One of the pleasures of reading old letters is the knowledge that they need no answer.

LORD BYRON.

7

His sayings are usually like women's letters: all the pith is in the postscript.

WILLIAM HAZLITT, *Boswell Redivivus.* Reference is to CHARLES LAMB.

8

A strange volume of real life in the daily packet of the postman. Eternal love and instant payment!

DOUGLAS JERROLD, *The Postman's Budget.*

9

Female friendships formed no particular part of his life. One might think perhaps of his long connection with Miss Coutts (the Baroness Burdett-Coutts) to whom he is said to have written over six hundred letters. But then Miss Coutts was a multi-millionaire giving away money. Any of us would have written six hundred letters to her.

STEPHEN LEACOCK, *Charles Dickens.*

10

An official letter on one desk had the signature of John Wintrup, operator at Wilmington, written with extraordinary and sweeping flourishes; Lincoln's eye caught it. "That reminds me of a short-legged man in a big overcoat, the tail of which was so long that it wiped out his footprints in the snow."

CARL SANDBURG, *Abraham Lincoln: The Prairie Years and the War Years,* ch. 34.

11

Do right and fear no man; don't write and fear no woman.

LUKE MCLUKE, *Epigram.*

12

A letter is an announced visit, and the postman is the intermediary of impolite surprises. Every week we ought to have one hour for receiving letters, and then go and take a bath.

FRIEDRICH WILHELM NIETZSCHE, *Human, All Too Human,* vol. 2, tr. by PAUL V. COHN.

13

Dear Mrs Jones:
Thank you for your letter.
I shall try to do better.

CARL SANDBURG, *Form letter* used for replying to "hate" letters or letters strongly critical. From *Carl Sandburg,* by HARRY GOLDEN.

14

A woman seldom writes her Mind, but in her postscript.

SIR RICHARD STEELE, *The Spectator.*

15

One man was so mad at me that he ended his letter: "Beware. You will never get out of this world alive."

JOHN STEINBECK, *The Mail I've Seen; The Saturday Review,* Aug. 3, 1956.

16

For my part, I could easily do without the post-office . . . I never received more than one or two letters in my life that were worth the postage.

HENRY D. THOREAU, *Walden,* ch. 2.

17

I was reminded many times of what Captain Thornton Wilder, the playwright, had written Woollcott from his army post: "Nothing so lifts a soldier's morale as getting a letter from home, and nothing so depresses him as reading it."

HARPO MARX, *Harpo Speaks!*

LIBERALISM

18

A liberal is a man who leaves the room when the fight begins.

HEYWOOD BROUN. (GEORGE SELDES, *The Great Quotations.*)

19

A liberal is a man who is willing to spend somebody else's money.

SENATOR CARTER GLASS.

1
In order to qualify as an American liberal a man had to favor compulsory FEPC, regard Taft-Hartley as completely evil, believe in the total wickedness of Generalissimo Chiang Kai-shek, take his political economics from John Maynard Keynes, and look to Washington for the answers to all problems.
>JOSEPH C. HARSCH, *The Reporter*, Sept., 1952.

2
He's a working liberal and not a talking liberal.
>LYNDON B. JOHNSON, speaking admiringly of a member of his staff. (MARQUIS W. CHILDS, Column, *St. Louis Post-Dispatch*, Mar. 31, 1964.)

3
A liberal is a person whose interests aren't at stake at the moment.
>WILLIS PLAYER, quoted by NEILL MORGAN in the *San Diego Tribune*.

4
A liberal is a man who wants to use his own idea on things in preference to generations who, he knows, know more than he does.
>WILL ROGERS, *Autobiography*.

5
A radical is a man with both feet firmly planted in the air.
>FRANKLIN DELANO ROOSEVELT.

6
Liberalism is the first refuge of political indifference and the last refuge of Leftists.
>HARRY ROSKOLENKO, *When I Was Last on Cherry Street*.

7
English Liberal
"I think" thought Sam Butler,
"Truth ever lies
In mean compromise."
What could be subtler
Than the thought of Sam Butler?
>GEOFFREY TAYLOR.

8
The radical of one century is the conservative of the next. The radical invents the views. When he has worn them out the conservative adopts them.
>MARK TWAIN, *Notebook*, ch. 31.

9
By a progressive I do not mean a man who is ready to move, but a man who knows where he is going when he moves.
>WOODROW WILSON, *Speech* in St. Paul, Minn., Sept. 9, 1919.

LIBERTY

See also Freedom

10
Liberty, n. One of Imagination's most precious possessions.
>AMBROSE BIERCE, *The Devil's Dictionary*.

11
The difference between liberty and liberties is as great as between God and Gods.
>LUDWIG BOURNE, *Fragments and Aphorisms*.

12
Liberty is always dangerous, but it is the safest thing we have.
>HARRY EMERSON FOSDICK, *Liberty*.

13
Liberty is from God, liberties from the devil. (Freiheit ist von Gott, Freiheiten von Teufel.)
>Old German Proverb.

14
We are not to expect to be translated from despotism to liberty in a feather bed.
>THOMAS JEFFERSON, *Writings*, vol. viii, p. 13.

15
The tree of liberty must be refreshed from time to time with the blood of patriots and tyrants. It is its natural manure.
>THOMAS JEFFERSON, *Letter* to William S. Smith, Paris, Nov. 13, 1787. (*Writings*, iv, 467.)

16
Liberty in the lowest rank of every nation is little more than the choice of working or starving.
>SAMUEL JOHNSON, *Works*, vi.

17
When we demand liberty of person as a constitutional right, we are taking away from the officials their liberty to chop off people's heads. The two kinds of liberties are diametrically opposed to each other. It cannot be helped.
>LIN YUTANG, *With Love and Irony*.

18
Liberty means responsibility. That is why most men dread it.
>BERNARD SHAW, *Maxims for Revolutionists*.

19
Liberty is the right of any person to stand up anywhere and say anything whatsoever that everybody thinks.
>LINCOLN STEFFENS, *Autobiography*.

20
Liberty is the only thing you cannot have

unless you are willing to give it to others.
WILLIAM ALLEN WHITE, *Address: A Free Press in a Machine Age,* University of Pennsylvania, May 2, 1938.

1
Wine gives you liberty, love takes it away.
WILLIAM WYCHERLEY, *The Country Wife,* Act 1.

LIBRARY

See also Books

2
On another table stood Zuleika's library. Both books were in covers of dull gold.
MAX BEERBOHM, *Zuleika Dobson.*

3
A man's library is a sort of harem, and tender readers have a great pudency in showing their books to a stranger.
RALPH WALDO EMERSON, *Society and Solitude: Books.*

4
He that revels in a well-chosen library, has innumerable dishes, and all of admirable flavor.
WILLIAM GODWIN, *The Enquirer.*

5
Every library should try to be complete on something, if it were only the history of pinheads.
OLIVER WENDELL HOLMES, *The Poet at the Breakfast Table,* ch. 8.

6
A circulating library in a town is an evergreen tree of diabolical knowledge.
RICHARD BRINSLEY SHERIDAN, *The Rivals.* Act I, sc. 2. Mrs. Malaprop speaking.

7
If there is an Unexpurgated in the Children's Department won't you please help that young woman remove Huck from that questionable companionship?
MARK TWAIN, *Letter* to a librarian. The reference is to Huckleberry Finn, and the "questionable companionship" refers to Biblical characters.

8
Unlearned men of books assume the care,
As Eunuchs are the guardians of the fair.
EDWARD YOUNG, *Love of Fame.* Sat. ii, l. 83.

LIES AND LYING

See also Deceit

9
A little inaccuracy saves a world of explanation.
C. E. AYRES, *Science, the False Messiah.*

10
None speaks false, when there is none to hear.
JAMES BEATTIE, *The Minstrel,* bk. 2.

11
Calumniate, calumniate, calumniate; there will always be something which will stick.
PIERRE DE BEAUMARCHAIS, *The Barber of Seville.*

12
A lie always needs a truth for a handle to it. The worst lies are those whose blade is false, but whose handle is true.
HENRY WARD BEECHER, *Proverbs from Plymouth Pulpit.*

13
Even a liar tells a hundred truths to one lie; he has to, to make the lie good for anything.
HENRY WARD BEECHER, *Proverbs from Plymouth Pulpit.*

14
I never knew an auctioneer to lie, unless it was absolutely necessary.
JOSH BILLINGS.

15
Travellers, poets and liars are three words all of one signification.
RICHARD BRATHWAITE, *English Gentleman.*

16
Falsehood has a perennial spring.
EDMUND BURKE, *A Vindication of Natural Society.*

17
Any fool can tell the truth, but it requires a man of some sense to know how to lie well.
SAMUEL BUTLER (1835–1902).

18
The best liar is he who makes the smallest amount of lying go the longest way—who husbands it too carefully to waste it where it can be dispensed with.
SAMUEL BUTLER, *The Way of All Flesh,* ch. 39.

19
With death doomed to grapple
  Beneath this cold slab, he
Who lied in the chapel
  Now lies in the abbey.
LORD BYRON, *Epitaph for William Pitt.*

20
And after all what is a lie? 'Tis but
The truth in masquerade.
LORD BYRON, *Don Juan,* canto 9.

21
In all matters which concern my daughter I would have you lie like a gentleman.
JAMES BRANCH CABELL, *Jurgen.*

1
The fun of talk is to find out what a man really thinks, and then contrast it with the enormous lies he has been telling all dinner, and, perhaps, all his life.
BENJAMIN DISRAELI, *Lothair.*

2
Sure men were born to lie, and women to believe them.
JOHN GAY, *The Beggar's Opera.* Act ii, sc. 2.

3
According to that old verse . . . Astronomers, painters and poets may lie by authority.
SIR JOHN HARINGTON, *Apologie of Poetry.*

4
A big lie is more plausible than truth. People who write fiction, if they had not taken it up, might have become very successful liars.
ERNEST HÉMINGWAY, *This Week,* Oct. 18, 1959.

5
Sin has many tools, but a lie is the handle that fits them all.
OLIVER WENDELL HOLMES, *The Autocrat of the Breakfast Table,* ch. 6.

6
If I accustom a servant to tell a lie for me, have I not reason to apprehend that he will tell many lies for himself?
SAMUEL JOHNSON, Boswell's *Life,* July 18, 1763.

7
Foote [the comedian] is quite impartial, for he tells lies of everyone.
SAMUEL JOHNSON, Boswell's *Life,* Mar. 16, 1776.

8
Lilac: She is very pretty but she can lilac anything.
Judge.

9
There is nothing so pathetic as a forgetful liar.
F. M. KNOWLES, *A Cheerful Year Book.*

10
Society can exist only on the basis that there is some amount of polished lying and that no one says exactly what he thinks.
LIN YUTANG, *With Love and Irony.*

11
Propaganda, ventured Walter Lippmann at a banquet in Washington, is that branch of lying which often deceives your friends without ever deceiving your enemies.
BENNETT CERF, *The Laugh's on Me.*

12
A man who won't lie to a woman has very little consideration for her feelings.
OLIN MILLER.

13
If one is to be called a liar, one may as well make an effort to deserve the name.
A. A. MILNE, *The Sunny Side.*

14
One may indeed lie with the mouth; but with the accompanying grimace one nevertheless tells the truth.
FRIEDRICH WILHELM NIETZSCHE, *Beyond Good and Evil,* tr. by HELEN ZIMMERN.

15
The perjurer's mother told white lies.
AUSTIN O'MALLEY.

16
Some lie beneath the churchyard stone,
And some before the speaker.
WINTHROP M. PRAED, *School and Schoolfellows.*

17
Be sure not to tell the first falsehood, and you needn't fear being detected in any subsequent ones.
GEORGE D. PRENTICE.

18
I said in my haste, All men are liars.
Psalms, CXVI, 11.

19
A liar needs a good memory. (Mendacem memorem esse oportere.)
QUINTILIAN, *De Institutione Oratoria.* Bk. iv, ch. 2, sec. 91.

20
He will lie, sir, with such volubility, that you would think truth were a fool.
WILLIAM SHAKESPEARE, *All's Well That Ends Well,* Act iv, sc. 3.

21
I am not a professional liar; I am even ashamed of the extent to which in my human infirmity I have been an amateur one.
BERNARD SHAW, *Love Among the Artists.*

22
There is no lie that many men will not believe; there is no man who does not believe many lies; and there is no man who believes only lies.
JOHN STERLING, *Essays and Tales.*

23
If it be possible, never tell a lie to your master or lady, unless you have some hopes that they cannot find it out in less than half an hour.
JONATHAN SWIFT, *Directions to Servants.*

24
But although the devil be the father of lies, he seems, like the great inventors, to have lost much of his reputation by the continual improvements that have been made upon him.
JONATHAN SWIFT, *The Examiner,* No. 15 (1710).

1
The superiority of his genius consists in nothing else but an inexhaustible fund of political lies, which he plentifully distributes every minute he speaks, and by an unparalleled generosity forgets, and consequently contradicts, the next half hour.
JONATHAN SWIFT, *The Examiner*, No. 15 (1710). Referring to the Earl of Wharton.

2
Few lies carry the inventor's mark, and the most prostitute enemy to truth may spread a thousand without being known for the author: besides, as the vilest writer has his readers, so the greatest liar has his believers: and it often happens that, if a lie be believed only for an hour, it has done its work, and there is no further occasion for it.
JONATHAN SWIFT, *The Examiner*, No. 15 (1710).

3
Falsehood flies, and truth comes limping after it, so that when men come to be undeceived it is too late; the jest is over, and the tale has had its effect: like a man who has thought of a good repartee when the discourse is changed or the company parted; or like a physician who has found out an infallible medicine after the patient is dead.
JONATHAN SWIFT, *The Examiner*, No. 15 (1710).

4
It is often the case that the man who can't tell a lie thinks he is the best judge of one.
MARK TWAIN, *Pudd'nhead Wilson's Calendar*.

5
The principal difference between a cat and a lie is that a cat has only nine lives.
MARK TWAIN.

6
I am different from Washington; I have a higher and grander standard of principle. Washington could not lie. I *can* lie, but I *won't*.
MARK TWAIN, from *Chicago Tribune*, Dec. 20, 1871 (quoted).

7
He was ignorant of the commonest accomplishments of youth. He could not even lie.
MARK TWAIN, *Brief Biographical Sketch of George Washington*.

8
Some authorities hold that the young ought not to lie at all. That, of course, is putting it rather stronger than necessary; still, while I cannot go quite so far as that, I do maintain, and I believe I am right, that the young ought to be temperate in the use of this great art until practice shall give them that

confidence, elegance, and precision which alone can make the accomplishment graceful and profitable.
MARK TWAIN, *Essays: Advice to Youth*.

9
An awkward, feeble, leaky lie is a thing which you ought to make it your unceasing study to avoid; such a lie as that has no more permanence than average truth.
MARK TWAIN, *Essays: Advice to Youth*.

10
An experienced, industrious, ambitious, and often quite picturesque liar.
MARK TWAIN, *My Military Campaign*.

11
The only form of lying that is absolutely beyond reproach is lying for its own sake.
OSCAR WILDE, *The Decay of Lying*.

LIFE

12
I look forward to playing Las Vegas every year or so. It's the last place in the world where it isn't against the law to live. Furthermore, it's the only city in America where you can get tan and faded at the same time.
JOEY ADAMS, *Cindy and I*, ch. 23.

13
There is no living with thee, or without thee.
JOSEPH ADDISON, translation of Martial, *The Spectator*, No. 68.

14
The less of routine, the more of life.
A. BRONSON ALCOTT, Table-Talk.

15
Now I am beginning to live a little, and feel less like a sick oyster at low tide.
LOUISA M. ALCOTT, quoted in EDNAH D. CHENEY, *Louisa May Alcott, Her Life, Letters and Journals*.

16
Every man's life is a fairy-tale written by God's fingers.
HANS CHRISTIAN ANDERSEN.

17
"Learn while you're young," he often said, "There is much to enjoy down here below; Life for the living, and the rest for the dead!"
Said the jolly old pedagogue, long ago.
GEORGE ARNOLD, *The Jolly Old Pedagogue*.

18
Throw theory into the fire; it only spoils life.
MIKHAIL BAKUNIN, *Letter* to sisters, November 4, 1842.

19
  To take things as they be—
  That's my philosophy.
No use to holler, mope, or cuss—

If they was changed they might be wuss.
JOHN KENDRICK BANGS, *A Philosopher.*

1
Man always knows his life will shortly cease,
Yet madly lives as if he knew it not.
RICHARD BAXTER, *Hypocrisy.*

2
Life is a one way street.
BERNARD BERENSON, *Notes* (1950).

3
The world is like a board with holes in it,
and the square men have got into the round
holes, and the round into the square.
BISHOP GEORGE BERKELEY, attributed to
him by *Punch* but not found in his
works.

4
Her whole Life is an Epigram, smart, smooth
& neatly pen'd,
Platted quite neat to catch applause with a
sliding noose at the end.
WILLIAM BLAKE, *Epigram.*

5
Life is a copycat and can be bullied into
following the master artist who bids it come
to heel.
HEYWOOD BROUN, *It Seems to Me* (1935).

6
We have too many people who live without
working, and altogether too many who work
without living.
CHARLES R. BROWN, quoted in *Case and
Comment.*

7
Grave-stones tell truth scarce forty years.
Generations pass while families last not three
oaks.
SIR THOMAS BROWNE, *Hydriotaphia: Urn
Burial.*

8
Most men's lives are so full of purple patches
that they merge into one another and become a mantle with which they cover themselves.
G. B. BURGIN, *Which Woman?*

9
All of the animals excepting man know that
the principal business of life is to enjoy it.
SAMUEL BUTLER, *Notebooks.*

10
As large as life, and twice as natural.
LEWIS CARROLL, *Through the Looking-
Glass,* ch. 7.

11
If life had a second edition, how I would
correct the proofs!
JOHN CLARE, *Letter.*

12
A man must take the fat with the lean;

that's what he must make up his mind to in
this life.
CHARLES DICKENS, *David Copperfield,*
ch. 51.

13
Life's a tumble-about thing of ups and
downs.
BENJAMIN DISRAELI, *Sybil,* Bk. i, ch. 8.

14
Life is like a B-picture script. It is that
corny. If I had my life story offered to me
to film, I'd turn it down.
KIRK DOUGLAS. (*Look,* Oct. 4, 1955.)

15
Life ain't all beer and skittles, and more's
the pity; but what's the odds, so long as
you're happy?
GEORGE DU MAURIER, *Trilby.*

16
If ye live enough befure thirty ye won't care
to live at all afther fifty.
FINLEY PETER DUNNE, *Mr. Dooley's Philosophy: Casual Observations.*

17
Things are in the saddle,
And ride mankind.
RALPH WALDO EMERSON, *Ode,* inscribed to
W. H. Channing.

18
Life is a boundless privilege, and when you
pay for your ticket, and get into the car,
you have no guess what good company you
will find there.
RALPH WALDO EMERSON, *Conduct of Life:
Considerations by the Way.*

19
If this world be a stage, what hours we give
to tedious make-up in the tiring room.
JOHN ERSKINE, *All the Front,* sonnet 3.

20
For most men life is a search for the proper
manila envelope in which to get themselves
filed.
CLIFTON FADIMAN. (*International Celebrity Register,* 1960.)

21
Life isn't complex if we walk straight.
B. C. FORBES, *Epigrams.*

22
In the sea of life it is the lightweights who
sink and the heavyweights who rise.
B. C. FORBES, *Epigrams.*

23
"Life is a gamble." Yes, but at least you
play your own cards.
B. C. FORBES, *Epigrams.*

24
I should have no objection to a repetition
of the same life from its beginning, only
asking the advantages authors have in a

second edition to correct some faults of the first.

BENJAMIN FRANKLIN, *Autobiography.*

1

We live merely on the crust or rind of things.

ANTHONY FROUDE, *Short Studies on Great Subjects.*

2

Life is a jest, and all things show it:
I thought so once, but now I know it.

JOHN GAY, *My Own Epitaph.*

3

Isn't your life extremely flat with nothing whatever to grumble at?

WILLIAM SCHWENCK GILBERT.

4

Life is a game of whist. From unseen sources
The cards are shuffled, and the hands are dealt.

EUGENE HARE, *Whist.*

5

He was as in love with life as an ant on a summer blade of grass.

BEN HECHT, *Gaily, Gaily.* Referring to himself as a young reporter in Chicago.

6

Life is made up of sobs, sniffles, and smiles, with sniffles predominating.

O. HENRY, *Gifts of the Magi.*

7

Life is a fatal complaint, and an eminently contagious one.

OLIVER WENDELL HOLMES, *The Poet at the Breakfast Table,* ch. 12.

8

Life is like an onion: you peel off layer after layer and then you find there is nothing in it.

JAMES G. HUNEKER.

9

Cats and monkeys, monkeys and cats—all human life is there.

HENRY JAMES, *The Madonna of the Future.*

10

Life is a predicament which precedes death.

HENRY JAMES.

11

We are but tenants, and . . . shortly the great Landlord will give us notice that our lease has expired.

JOSEPH JEFFERSON, *Inscription* on his monument at Sandwich, Cape Cod, Mass.

12

Life can only be understood backwards; but it must be lived forwards.

SÖREN KIERKEGAARD, *Life.*

13

Life is short; live it up.

NIKITA KHRUSHCHEV, quoted in *The New York Times Magazine,* Aug. 3, 1958.

14

What a rotten writer of detective stories life is.

NATHAN LEOPOLD, *Life Plus 99 Years.*

15

Someone has said that the ideal life is to live in an English country home, engage a Chinese cook, marry a Japanese wife, and take a French mistress.

LIN YUTANG, *With Love and Irony.*

16

Life is like a scrambled egg.

DON MARQUIS, *Frustration.*

17

Alex King didn't write a great autobiography; he lived one.

OTTO MEIDLIN, quoted by ALEXANDER KING in *I Should Have Kissed Her More.*

18

I know of no existing nation that deserves to live, and I know of very few individuals.

H. L. MENCKEN, *Prejudices.*

19

The basic fact about human existence is not that it is a tragedy, but that it is a bore.

H. L. MENCKEN, *Prejudices.*

20

It is not true that life is one damn thing after another—it's one damn thing over and over.

EDNA ST. VINCENT MILLAY. (*Letters of Edna St. Vincent Millay,* ed. by ALLEN R. MACDOUGALL.)

21

Life's a tough proposition, and the first hundred years are the hardest.

WILSON MIZNER, quoted by LOUIS UNTERMEYER in *A Treasury of Laughter.*

22

The great business of life is, to be, to do, to do without, and to depart.

JOHN MORLEY, *Address on Aphorisms,* Edinburgh, 1887.

23

Being both viable and friable I wish to prolong my existence . . .

OGDEN NASH, *Saturday Evening Post.*

24

In all ages the wisest have always agreed in their judgment of life: *it is no good.*

FRIEDRICH WILHELM NIETZSCHE, *The Twilight of the Idols.*

25

Drink, and dance and laugh and lie,
Love, the reeling midnight through,

For tomorrow we shall die!
(But, alas, we never do.)
> DOROTHY PARKER, *The Flaw in Paganism.*

1
Life is a stream upon which drift flowers
in spring, and blocks of ice in winter.
> JOSEPH ROUX, *Meditations of a Parish Priest,* tr. by HAPGOOD.

2
What good are vitamins? Eat four lobsters,
eat a pound of caviar—live! If you are in
love with a beautiful blonde with an empty
face and no brain at all, don't be afraid,
marry her—live!
> ARTUR RUBINSTEIN. (*The New York Times,* June 13, 1958.)

3
Life is not a spectacle or a feast; it is a
predicament.
> GEORGE SANTAYANA, *Articles and Essays.*

4
There is no cure for birth and death save to
enjoy the interval.
> GEORGE SANTAYANA, *Soliloquies in England.*

5
Born for a very brief space of time, we
regard this life as an inn which we are
soon to quit that it may be made ready for
the coming guest.
> SENECA, *Minor Dialogues.* Bk. vi, ch. 21.

6
We break up life into little bits and fritter
it away. (Diducimus illam in particulas
aclancinamus.)
> SENECA, *Epistulae ad Lucilium.*

7
I wish either my father or my mother, or
indeed both of them, as they were in duty
both equally bound to it, had minded what
they were about when they begot me.
> LAURENCE STERNE, *Tristram Shandy,* Bk. i, ch. 1.

8
The wise man warns me that life is but a
dew-drop on the lotus leaf.
> SIR RABINDRANATH TAGORE, *The Gardener,* No. 46.

9
Folks are better than angels.
> EDWARD THOMPSON TAYLOR, minister of the Seamen's Bethel, North Square, Boston. This remark was in reply to friends who sought to comfort him, as he lay dying in 1871, by assuring him that he would soon be among the angels.

10
Is life worth living? It depends on the liver.
> SIR HERBERT BEERBOHM TREE, quoted by HESKETH PEARSON in *Lives of the Wits.*

11
There is only the difference of a letter between the beginning and the end of life—creation and cremation.
> SIR HERBERT BEERBOHM TREE, quoted by HESKETH PEARSON in *Lives of the Wits.*

12
Keep breathing.
> SOPHIE TUCKER, on the secret of achieving a long life. Spoken Jan. 13, 1964, her 80th birthday anniversary.

13
Each person is born to one possession which
outvalues all the others—his last breath.
> MARK TWAIN, *Pudd'nhead Wilson's Calendar.*

14
All say, "How hard it is that we have to
die."—a strange complaint to come from
the mouths of people who have had to live.
> MARK TWAIN, *Pudd'nhead Wilson's Calendar.*

15
It is a pity that we cannot escape from life
when we are young.
> MARK TWAIN, *Autobiography,* ch. 24.

16
I advise you to go on living solely to enrage
those who are paying your annuities. It is
the only pleasure I have left.
> VOLTAIRE, *Letter* to Madame du Deffand.

17
Little wonder that the last years of his life
had become so precious to him that, as he
said, he would willingly stand at "street corners
hat in hand begging passers-by to drop
their unused minutes into it."
> JOHN WALKER, *Introduction* to *The Bernard Berenson Treasury,* ed. by HANNA KIEL.

18
One should absorb the colour of life, but one
should never remember its details. Details
are always vulgar.
> OSCAR WILDE, *The Picture of Dorian Gray,* ch. 8.

19
Life is far too important a thing ever to
talk seriously about.
> OSCAR WILDE, *Lady Windermere's Fan.* Act 1.

20
Lord Illingworth: The Book of Life begins
with a man and a woman in a garden.
Mrs. Allonby: It ends with Revelations.
> OSCAR WILDE, *A Woman of No Importance,* Act 1.

LITERATURE

See also Poetry, Writing

1
Autobiography is now as common as adultery, and hardly less reprehensible.
LORD ALTRINCHAM, *Sunday Times*, London, Feb. 28, 1962.

2
The naturalistic literature of this country has reached such a state that no family of characters is considered true to life which does not include at least two hypochondriacs, one sadist, and one old man who spills food down the front of his vest.
ROBERT BENCHLEY, *Family Life in America*. (*The Benchley Roundup*, ed. by NATHANIEL BENCHLEY.)

3
Literature is always a good card to play for honors. It makes people think that cabinet ministers are educated.
ARNOLD BENNETT, *The Title*, Act 3.

4
The problem of the historical novel is how to keep the old wineskin from bursting while you are pouring new wine into it.
BERNARD BERENSON, *Diaries* (1948).

5
The Fox knows many things but the Hedgehog knows one big thing.
ISAIAH BERLIN, on the difference between Dostoyevsky and Tolstoi. Columbia University Forum, summer, 1966. See also ARCHILOCHUS in section headed "Knowledge."

6
Realism is simply romanticism that has lost its reason.
G. K. CHESTERTON, *Alarms and Discursions*.

7
The Art of Biography
Is different from Geography.
Geography is about maps,
But Biography is about chaps.
G. K. CHESTERTON.

8
A savage is, after all, simply a human organism that has not received enough news from the human race. Literature is one most fundamental part of that news.
JOHN CIARDI, *Saturday Review*, Jan. 31, 1959.

9
Alas! for the South, her books have grown fewer;
She was never much given to literature.
J. GORDON COOGLER, *Purely Original Verse*.

10
The truth is a tough boss in literature. He don't even pay board wages, and if you go to work for him you want to have a job on the side.
FINLEY PETER DUNNE, *Mr. Dooley Remembers*.

11
On Waterloo's ensanguined plain
Lie tens of thousands of the slain;
But none by sabre or by shot
Fell half so flat as Walter Scott.
LORD ERSKINE, *Epigram*, on Scott's *Field of Waterloo*.

12
Science fiction is a kind of archaeology of the future.
CLIFTON FADIMAN, *The Selected Writings of Clifton Fadiman: The Reading Lamp* (1955).

13
I found nothing really wrong with this autobiography except poor choice of subject.
CLIFTON FADIMAN, *The Selected Writings of Clifton Fadiman: Puzzlements* (1955). Comment on *Everybody's Autobiography* by GERTRUDE STEIN.

14
Another odd thing about classics is that when their authors are writing them, they don't know what they're doing.
CLIFTON FADIMAN, *The Selected Writings of Clifton Fadiman* (1955).

15
Here lies Nolly Goldsmith, for shortness call'd Noll,
Who wrote like an angel, but talk'd like poor Poll.
DAVID GARRICK, *Impromptu Epitaph*.

16
He cannot die—though here's an end to strife—
Who hacked his way through literature to life.
KENSAL GREEN, *Premature Epitaphs*. On Theodore Dreiser.

17
Henry James had three reigns: James I, James II, and the Old Pretender.
PHILIP GUEDALLA.

18
Literature, like nobility, runs in the blood.
WILLIAM HAZLITT, *Table-Talk: Second Series*, pt. 2.

19
Literary history is the great *morgue* where all seek the dead ones whom they love or to whom they are related.
HEINRICH HEINE, *Excerpts: Art, Literature, and Criticism*.

1
Literature, like a gypsy, to be picturesque, should be a little ragged.
DOUGLAS JERROLD, *Literary Men.*

2
Classical quotation is the parole of literary men all over the world.
SAMUEL JOHNSON, Boswell's *Life,* May 8, 1781.

3
I have met with women whom I really think would like to be married to a Poem, and to be given away by a Novel.
JOHN KEATS, *Letters to Fanny Brawne,* letter 2.

4
An archangel a little damaged.
CHARLES LAMB, *Letter* to Wordsworth, 1816. Referring to Coleridge.

5
Literature is a very bad crutch, but a very good walking-stick.
CHARLES LAMB, *Letter* to Bernard Barton.

6
My friend the professor of Greek tells me that he truly believes the classics made him what he is. This is a very grave statement, if well founded.
STEPHEN LEACOCK, *Laugh with Leacock: Homer and Humbug, an Academic Discussion.*

7
"Then he too Ajax on the one hand leaped (or possibly jumped) into the fight wearing on the other hand, yes certainly a steel corselet (or possibly a bronze under tunic) and on his head of course, yes without doubt he had a helmet with a tossing plume taken from the mane (or perhaps extracted from the tail) of some horse which once fed along the banks of the Scamander (and it sees the herd and raises its head and paws the ground) and in his hand a shield worth a hundred oxen and on his knees too especially in particular greaves made by some cunning artificer (or perhaps blacksmith) and he blows the fire and it is hot. Thus Ajax leapt (or, better, was propelled from behind), into the fight."
STEPHEN LEACOCK, in a mock translation. *Homer and Humbug, an Academic Discussion.*

8
The classics are only primitive literature. They belong to the same class as primitive machinery and primitive music and primitive medicine.
STEPHEN LEACOCK, *Beyond the Beyond: Homer and the Humbug.*

9
Milton seems to the colleges profound be- cause he wrote of hell, a great place, and is dead.
STEPHEN LEACOCK, *Charles Dickens.*

10
But it so happened that Hugo's bottle of ink, a large one, with which he had begun the opening page of the story [*Les Travailleurs de la Mer,* tr. as *Toilers of the Sea*], ran out just as he wrote the concluding page. Nothing would do but he must re-name his book, *A Bottle of Ink and Its Contents.* Hugo, with the egotism of authorship, could not see the trivial vanity of such a title.
STEPHEN LEACOCK, *What's in a Name?*

11
Absurdly improbable things happen in real life as well as in weak literature.
ADA LEVERSON, *The Twelfth Hour.*

12
Our American professors like their literature clear and cold and pure and very dead.
SINCLAIR LEWIS, *Address,* on receiving the Nobel Prize for Literature, Dec. 12, 1930.

13
There comes Poe, with his raven, like Barnaby Rudge,
Three-fifths of him genius and two-fifths sheer fudge.
JAMES RUSSELL LOWELL, *A Fable for Critics.*

14
In literature as in love, we are astonished at what is chosen by others.
ANDRÉ MAUROIS, quoted in *The New York Times,* Apr. 14, 1963.

15
Literature is news that STAYS news.
EZRA POUND, *ABC of Reading.*

16
Literature was formerly an art and finance a trade: today it is the reverse.
JOSEPH ROUX, *Meditations of a Parish Priest.* Pt. i, No. 65.

17
Literature is the daughter of heaven, who has descended upon earth to soften and charm all human ills.
BERNARDIN ST. PIERRE, *Paul and Virginia.*

18
He was a man of the nineteenth century who took himself for Victor Hugo, as did so many others, including Victor Hugo himself.
JEAN-PAUL SARTRE, *The Words.*

19
The highest form of literature is the tragedy, a play in which everybody is murdered at the end.
BERNARD SHAW, *Don Juan in Hell.*

1
James felt buried in America; but he came here [England] only to be embalmed.
BERNARD SHAW, *Letter* to Molly Tompkins. Referring to HENRY JAMES.

2
With the single exception of Homer there is no eminent writer, not even Sir Walter Scott, whom I despise so entirely as I despise Shakespeare when I measure my mind against his.
BERNARD SHAW, quoted in *Bernard Shaw* by ERIC BENTLEY.

3
We cultivate literature on a little oatmeal.
SYDNEY SMITH, from LADY HOLLAND, *Memoir*.

4
On the day that God made Carl He didn't do anything else that day but sit around and feel good.
EDWARD STEICHEN, quoted in *Carl Sandburg* by HARRY GOLDEN.

5
When the Rudyards cease from Kipling
And the Haggards ride no more.
JAMES KENNETH STEPHENS, *Lapsus Calami*.

6
A classic is something that everybody wants to have read and nobody wants to read.
MARK TWAIN.

7
The two Great Unknowns, the two Illustrious Conjecturabilities! They are the best known unknown persons that have ever drawn breath upon the planet.
MARK TWAIN, *Shakespeare Dead?*, ch. 3. Referring to the Devil and Shakespeare.

8
A work of art? It has no invention; it has no order, system, sequence, or result; it has no lifelikeness, no thrill, no stir, no seeming of reality; its characters are confusedly drawn, and by their acts and words they prove that they are not the sort of people the author claims that they are; its humor is pathetic; its pathos is funny; its conversations are—oh! indescribable; its love-scenes odious, its English a crime against the language.
Counting these out, what is left is Art. I think we must all admit that.
MARK TWAIN, *Fenimore Cooper's Literary Offenses*. Referring to *The Deerslayer*.

9
He [Bernard Shaw] was the badman of letters. Though he took great pains to command respect, he took none at all to inspire affection. If Chaucer is the father of English literature, Shaw is the spinster aunt. By this I

do not mean to imply that he was sexless . . . It is only in his writing that the aunt in him rises up, full of warnings, wagged fingers, and brandished umbrellas . . . Shaw was unique. An Irish aunt so gorgeously drunk with wit is something English literature will never see again.
KENNETH TYNAN, on BERNARD SHAW. Quoted in *The New York Times*, Jan. 9, 1966.

10
Milton wrote "Paradise Lost"; then his wife died and he wrote "Paradise Regained."
LOUIS UNTERMEYER, *A Treasury of Laughter*. Quoted as a student boner.

11
There is so much nastiness in modern literature that I like to write stories which contain nothing worse than a little innocent murdering.
EDGAR WALLACE.

12
It is a pity that Chaucer, who had geneyus, was so unedicated; he's the wuss speller I know of.
ARTEMUS WARD.

13
Henry James writes fiction as if it were a painful duty.
OSCAR WILDE.

14
The difference between literature and journalism is that journalism is unreadable, and literature is not read.
OSCAR WILDE, *The Critic as Artist*.

15
Literature is the orchestration of platitudes.
THORNTON WILDER, *Literature*.

LOGIC

16
He was in Logic, a great critic,
Profoundly skill'd in Analytic;
He could distinguish, and divide
A hair 'twixt south and south-west side.
SAMUEL BUTLER, *Hudibras*.

17
We must beware of needless innovations, especially when guided by logic.
SIR WINSTON CHURCHILL, *Reply*, House of Commons, Dec. 17, 1942.

18
My regret is that Mencken does not contradict himself more. Logic is his sin.
BENJAMIN DE CASSERES, *Mencken and Shaw*.

19
Logical consequences are the scarecrows of fools and the beacons of wise men.
THOMAS H. HUXLEY, *Animal Automatism*.

1

Logic is the soul of wit, not of wisdom;
that's why wit is funny.
LINCOLN STEFFENS, *Autobiography*.

LOVE

See also Sex

2

In fool's paradise there is room for many
lovers.
SAMUEL HOPKINS ADAMS, *Tenderloin*.

3

The last time I saw Fay he was walking
down Lover's Lane, holding his own hand.
FRED ALLEN, *Much Ado About Me*. Reference to FRANK FAY.

4

Only little boys and old men sneer at love.
LOUIS AUCHINCLOSS, *The Rector of
Justin*.

5

'Tis impossible to love and be wise.
FRANCIS BACON, *Essays: Of Love*.

6

Men who do not make advances to women
are apt to become victims to women who
make advances to them.
WALTER BAGEHOT, *Biographical Studies*.

7

In love, one first deceives oneself and then
others—and that is what is called romance.
JOHN L. BALDERSTON, *Berkeley Square*.

8

The woman who has a lover becomes very
indulgent in judging others.
HONORÉ DE BALZAC, *The Physiology of
Marriage*.

9

Love is the poetry of the senses.
HONORÉ DE BALZAC, *The Physiology of
Marriage*.

10

It is as absurd to deny that it is possible
for a man always to love the same woman,
as it would be to affirm that some famous
musician needed several violins in order to
execute a piece of music or compose a
charming melody.
HONORÉ DE BALZAC, *The Physiology of
Marriage*.

11

Anything may be expected and anything
may be supposed of a woman who is in
love.
HONORÉ DE BALZAC, *The Physiology of
Marriage*.

12

To speak of love is to make love.
HONORÉ DE BALZAC, *The Physiology of
Marriage*.

13

The trouble with life is that there are so
many beautiful women—and so little time.
JOHN BARRYMORE.

14

I love you:
I'll cut your throat for your own sake.
BEAUMONT AND FLETCHER, *The Little
French Lawyer*. Act iv, sc. 1.

15

Love is the wine of existence.
HENRY WARD BEECHER, *Proverbs from
Plymouth Pulpit*.

16

Love ceases to be a pleasure when it ceases
to be a secret.
APHRA BEHN, *The Lover's Watch*.

17

Vows! dost think the gods regard the vows
of lovers? They are things made in necessity and ought not to be kept, nor punished
when broken.
APHRA BEHN, *The Dutch Lover*, Act 5.

18

Nobody in love has a sense of humor.
S. N. BEHRMAN, *The Second Man*.

19

Talking of love is making it.
W. G. BENHAM, *Proverbs*. See also BALZAC
in this section.

20

Make love to every woman you meet; if
you get five per cent on your outlay, it's a
good investment.
ARNOLD BENNETT.

21

Women in love are less ashamed than men.
They have less to be ashamed of.
AMBROSE BIERCE, *The Cynic's Word Book*.

22

Love is like the measles; we can have it
but once, and the later in life we have it,
the tougher it goes with us.
JOSH BILLINGS. (See also JEROME, JERROLD, AND KINGSLEY in this section.)

23

For he was a man of unwearied and prolific
conjugal fidelity.
VICENTE BLASCO Y IBÁÑEZ, *Blood and
Sand*.

24

The ability to make love frivolously is the
chief characteristic which distinguishes human beings from the beasts.
HEYWOOD BROUN.

25

If she had said "no" just once, I'd not have
said another word and left things there, but
as she said it more than a dozen times: "No,

no, no, ono, ono, noo, oono, nooono"—Right!
I said to myself; she wants it.
  GIORDANO BRUNO, *The Candle Bearer*. Act
   ii, sc. 5. English version by J. R. HALE.

1
She wants to dance on three legs, and as
she's only got two of her own, maybe I
ought to lend her one.
  GIORDANO BRUNO, *The Candle Bearer*. Act
   ii, sc. 5. English version by J. R. HALE.

2
Love is the business of the idle, but the
idleness of the busy.
  EDWARD GEORGE BULWER-LYTTON, *Rienzi*.

3
Leave the lady, Willy, let the racket rip,
She is going to fool you, you have lost your
  grip,
Your brain is in a muddle, and your heart
  is in a whirl,
Come along with me, Willy, never mind
  the girl!
  GELETT BURGESS, *Willy and the Lady*.

4
Jupiter himself was turned into a satyr, a
shepherd, a bull, a swan, a golden shower,
and what not for love.
  ROBERT BURTON, *The Anatomy of Melancholy*.

5
To enlarge or illustrate this power and effect
of love is to set a candle in the sun.
  ROBERT BURTON, *The Anatomy of Melancholy*.

6
Blessed is the wooing that is not long a-
doing.
  ROBERT BURTON, *The Anatomy of Melancholy*, pt. 3.

7
Love is a boy by poets styl'd;
Then spare the rod and spoil the child.
  SAMUEL BUTLER, *Hudibras*, pt. 2.

8
God is love, I dare say. But what a mischie-
vous devil love is.
  SAMUEL BUTLER, *Notebooks*.

9
For this is the sort of engagement, you see,
that is binding on you but not binding on
me.
  WILLIAM ALLEN BUTLER, *Nothing to
   Wear*.

10
In her first passion woman loves her lover;
In all the others, all she loves is love.
  LORD BYRON, *Don Juan*.

11
Love comes in at the window and goes out
at the door.
  WILLIAM CAMDEN, *Remains*.

12
Then crown my joys, or cure my pain:
Give me more love, or more disdain.
  THOMAS CAREW, *Mediocrity in Love Re-
   jected*.

13
Then fly betimes, for only they
Conquer love that run away.
  THOMAS CAREW, *Conquest by Flight*.

14
What a woman says to her lover should be
written in wind and running water. (Mulier
cupido quod dicit amanti In vento et rapida
scribere oportet aqua.)
  CATULLUS, *Odes*. No. lxx, l. 3.

15
Love lasteth as long as the money endureth.
  WILLIAM CAXTON, *The Game of Chesse*.

16
Many a man has fallen in love with a girl
in a light so dim he would not have chosen
a suit by it.
  MAURICE CHEVALIER, *News summaries*,
   July 7, 1955.

17
I have heard of reasons manifold
Why love must needs be blind,
But this is the best of all I hold
His eyes are in his mind.
  SAMUEL TAYLOR COLERIDGE, *To a Lady*.

18
Love, like death, a universal leveller of man-
kind.
  WILLIAM CONGREVE, *The Double-Dealer*,
   Act 2.

19
Would I were free from this restraint,
  Or else had hopes to win her:
Would she could make of me a saint,
  Or I of her a sinner.
  WILLIAM CONGREVE, *Pious Selinda*.

20
Pursued man loves to think himself pursuer.
  EDMUND VANCE COOKE, *The Book of
   Extenuations: Ruth*.

21
Him, who loves always one, why should they
  call
More constant, than the man loves always
  all.
  ABRAHAM COWLEY, *The Inconstant*.

22
Never was an owl more blind than a lover.
  DINAH M. M. CRAIK, *Magnus and Morna*.

23
When a man says he's willin', said Mr.
Barkis, it's as much as to say, that man's
a-waitin' for a answer.
  CHARLES DICKENS, *David Copperfield*, ch.
   8.

1

Love's a malady without a cure.

JOHN DRYDEN, *Palamon and Arcite,* bk. 2.

2

You men are like clocks; you never make love, but you clap your wings, and crow when you have done.

JOHN DRYDEN, *Marriage à lc Mode.* Act iii, sc. 1.

3

It sometimes takes a girl a long time to learn that a flirtation is attention without intention.

Toaster's Handbook, compiled by PEGGY EDMUND AND HENRY WORKMAN WILLIAMS. See also O'RELL in this section.

4

Is it what we love, or how we love,
That makes true good?

GEORGE ELIOT, *The Spanish Gypsy,* bk. 1.

5

All women know the value of love. But few will pay the price.

BETH ELLIS, *Blind Mouths.*

6

Let no man think that he is loved by any man when he loves no man.

EPICTETUS, *Fragments,* 156.

7

The girl with a future avoids the man with a past.

EVAN ESAR, *The Humor of Humor.*

8

Venus, thy eternal sway
All the race of men obey.

EURIPIDES, *Austice.*

9

He in a few minutes ravished this fair creature, or at least would have ravished her, if she had not, by a timely compliance, prevented him.

HENRY FIELDING, *Jonathan Wilde.* Bk. iii, ch. 7.

10

Love is like linen, often chang'd, the sweeter.

PHINEAS FLETCHER, *Sicelides,* Act 3.

11

Religion has done love a great service by making it a sin.

ANATOLE FRANCE.

12

Love often makes a fool of the cleverest men, and as often gives cleverness to the most foolish. (La passion fait souvent un fou du plus habile homme et rend souvent habiles les plus sots.)

Old French Proverb.

13

In the religion of love the courtesan is a heretic; but the nun is an atheist.

RICHARD GARNETT, quoted in *Cupid's Cyclopedia* by OLIVER HERFORD.

14

Once when George [Gershwin] was speaking about a girl he'd been in love with who'd just married someone else, he said, "If I wasn't so busy, I'd be upset."

OSCAR LEVANT, *Memoirs of an Amnesiac.*

15

Then a sentimental passion of a vegetable fashion must excite your languid spleen,
An attachment à la Plato for a bashful young potato, or a not too French French bean!
Though the Philistines may jostle, you will rank as an apostle in the high aesthetic band,
If you walk down Piccadilly with a poppy or a lily in your medieval hand.
And everyone will say,
As you walk your flowery way,
"If he's content with a vegetable love which would certainly not suit *me,*
Why, what a most particularly pure young man this pure young man must be!"

SIR WILLIAM SCHWENCK GILBERT, *Patience,* Act 1.

16

Or love me less, or love me more;
And play not with my liberty:
Either take all, or all restore;
Bind me at least, or set me free.

SIDNEY GODOLPHIN, *Song.*

17

Yes, indeed; all peoples recognize romantic love, but they recognize it for what it is—temporary insanity—and try to pay as little attention to it as possible . . .

JOHN GREENWAY, *The Inevitable Americans,* ch. 4.

18

A lover without indiscretion is no lover at all.

THOMAS HARDY, *The Hand of Ethelberta,* ch. 20.

19

It is better to love two too many than one too few.

SIR JOHN HARINGTON, *Epigrams.*

20

Diffidence and awkwardness are the two antidotes to love.

WILLIAM HAZLITT, *Sketches and Essays.*

21

A man in love like Romeo can no more join his beloved between the sheets than push his dear mother off a roof; at least, not for some time.

BEN HECHT, *Letters from Bohemia.*

22

A man of any age can persuade himself that a woman's thighs are altar rails, and that her passion is the hosanna of virtuous love rather than the wanton tumult of nerve endings.

BEN HECHT, *Gaily, Gaily.*

1
Here's to the love that lies in woman's eyes.
And lies, and lies, and lies.

Toasts for All Occasions, ed. by LEWIS C. HENRY.

2
True love: An old-fashioned sentiment.

OLIVER HERFORD, *Cupid's Cyclopedia.*

3
Love is a conflict between reflexes and reflections.

MAGNUS HIRSCHFELD, *Sex in Human Relationship.*

4
Do you realize what the word love means? It cannot be said at all. It is either a call or a curse—inexorable, unanswerable either way.

JOHN OLIVER HOBBES, *Life and Tomorrow.*

5
Love is sparingly soluble in the words of men, therefore they speak much of it; but one syllable of woman's speech can dissolve more of it than a man's heart can hold.

OLIVER WENDELL HOLMES, *The Autocrat of the Breakfast-Table,* ch. 2.

6
Lovers are fools, but nature makes them so.

ELBERT HUBBARD, *Epigrams.* A variation of a Latin proverb; see under UNKNOWN near the end of this section.

7
Mamie bloomed and bridled . . . "Any man's nice when he's in love."

HENRY JAMES, *The Ambassadors.*

8
Love is like the measles; we all have to go through it.

JEROME K. JEROME, *Idle Thoughts of an Idle Fellow: On Being in Love.*

9
Love's like the measles—all the worse when it comes late in life.

DOUGLAS JERROLD, *Wit and Opinions of Douglas Jerrold* (1859). See also BILLINGS in this section.

10
Many were in love with triflers like themselves, and many fancied that they were in love when in truth they were only idle.

SAMUEL JOHNSON, *Rasselas.*

11
Love has been in perpetual strife with monogamy.

ELLEN KEY, *Works.*

12
She never had a proposal, only propositions.

ALEXANDER KING, *Mine Enemy Grows Older.*

13
The truth has been staring us in the face for some twenty thousand years: Men are forever on the lookout to have *Affairs* . . . while the majority of women . . . even the seemingly most debauched of them . . . are . . . eternally . . . in search of love.

ALEXANDER KING, *Rich Man, Poor Man, Freud and Fruit,* ch. 1.

14
Athletes are the complete victims of their physical organisms. Their training tends to give them an exaggerated opinion of the value of their energy—hence they make bad lovers.

ALEXANDER KING, *Rich Man, Poor Man, Freud and Fruit,* ch. 12.

15
That gentlemen prefer blondes is due to the fact that, apparently, pale hair, delicate skin and an infantile expression represent the very apex of a frailty which every man longs to violate.

ALEXANDER KING, *Rich Man, Poor Man, Freud and Fruit,* ch. 17.

16
Love is sentimental measles.

CHARLES KINGSLEY.

17
Sudden love is the latest cured.

JEAN DE LA BRUYÈRE, *Les Caracteres.*

18
He gave her a look you could of poured on a waffle.

RING LARDNER, quoted in *I Wish I'd Said That,* by JACK GOODMAN AND ALBERT RICE.

19
True love is like seeing ghosts: we all talk about it, but few of us have ever seen one.

FRANÇOIS, DUC DE LA ROCHEFOUCAULD, *Maximes,* No. 76.

20
One can find women who have never had one love affair, but it is rare indeed to find any who have had only one.

FRANÇOIS, DUC DE LA ROCHEFOUCAULD, *Maximes,* No. 429.

21
If I am not worth the wooing, I surely am not worth the winning.

HENRY WADSWORTH LONGFELLOW, *The Courtship of Miles Standish.*

22
It is difficult to know at what moment love

begins; it is less difficult to know that it has begun.

> HENRY WADSWORTH LONGFELLOW, *Hyperion.* Bk. iii, ch. 6.

1

None without hope e'er loved the brightest fair,
But love can hope where reason would despair.

> GEORGE LYTTLETON, *Epigram.*

2

All the world loves a lover, but it shows more consideration toward the expectant father.

> J. P. McEVOY, *Charlie Would Have Loved This.*

3

In the arithmetic of love, one plus one equals everything and two minus one equals nothing.

> MIGNON McLAUGHLIN, *The Saturday Review.*

4

The art of flirtation is dying. A man and woman are either in love these days or just friends. In the realm of love, reticence and sophistication should go hand in hand, for one of the joys of life is discovery. Nowadays, instead of progressing from *vous* to *tu,* from Mister to Jim, it's "darling" and "come to my place" in the first hour.

> MARYA MANNES. (*New Bites by a Girl Gadfly; Life,* June 12, 1964.)

5

I love you as New Englanders love pie.

> DON MARQUIS, *Sonnets to a Red-Haired Lady.*

6

Coquetry is an art of the intellect; flirtation is a function of the senses.

> DON MARQUIS, *New York Herald.*

7

The new lust gives the lecher the new thrill.

> JOHN MASEFIELD, *Widow in the Bye Street.*

8

Love—The dirty trick nature played on us to achieve the continuation of the species.

> W. SOMERSET MAUGHAM.

9

When from time to time I have seen the persons with whom the great lovers satisfied their desires, I have often been more astonished by the robustness of their appetites than envious of their successes. It is obvious that you need not often go hungry if you are willing to dine off mutton hash and turnip tops.

> W. SOMERSET MAUGHAM, *The Summing Up.*

10

He's the sort of a fool who thinks a woman loves him just because he loves her.

> W. SOMERSET MAUGHAM, *The Constant Wife.*

11

Love is the delusion that one woman differs from another.

> H. L. MENCKEN, *A Mencken Chrestomathy.*

12

To be in love is merely to be in a state of perpetual anaesthesia—to mistake an ordinary young man for a Greek god or an ordinary woman for a goddess.

> H. L. MENCKEN, *Prejudices,* ser. 1.

13

Love is based upon a view of women that is impossible to any man who has had any experience of them.

> H. L. MENCKEN, *Prejudices,* ser. 4.

14

Love is the triumph of imagination over intelligence.

> H. L. MENCKEN.

15

One is easily fooled by that which one loves.

> MOLIÈRE, *Tartuffe.*

16

It takes time to make oneself loved, and even when I had nothing to do I always vaguely felt that I had no time to waste.

> NAPOLEON BONAPARTE. (*The Mind of Napoleon,* ed. by J. CHRISTOPHER HEROLD.)

17

The ivy clings to the first tree it meets. This in a few words is the story of love.

> NAPOLEON BONAPARTE. (*The Mind of Napoleon,* ed. by J. CHRISTOPHER HEROLD.)

18

Love should be a pleasure, not a torment.

> NAPOLEON BONAPARTE. (*The Mind of Napoleon,* ed. by J. CHRISTOPHER HEROLD.)

19

Romantic love is the privilege of emperors, kings, soldiers, and artists; it is the butt of democrats, traveling salesmen, magazine poets and the writers of American novels.

> GEORGE JEAN NATHAN, *Testament of a Critic.*

20

Discovering reciprocal love should really disenchant the lover with regard to the beloved. "What! *She* is modest enough to love even you? Or stupid enough? Or—or—."

> FRIEDRICH WILHELM NIETZSCHE, *Beyond Good and Evil,* tr. by HELEN ZIMMERN.

21

Flirtation, attention without intention.

> MAX O'RELL, *John Bull and His Island.*

1
When a man talks of love, with caution
  trust him;
But if he swears, he'll certainly deceive thee.
  THOMAS OTWAY, *The Orphan*. Act ii, sc. 1.

2
What is it that love does to a woman? Without it she only sleeps; with it alone, she
lives.
  OUIDA, *Wisdom, Wit, and Pathos*.

3
First let assurance come to your minds, that
all women can be caught; spread but your
nets and you will catch them.
  OVID, *The Art of Love*, bk. 1, tr. by J. H.
  MOZLEY.

4
Sooner would birds be silent in spring, or
grasshoppers in summer, or the hound of
Maenalus flee before the hare than a woman
persuasively wooed resist a lover: nay, even
she, whom you will think cruel, will be kind.
  OVID, *The Art of Love*, bk. 1, tr. by J. H.
  MOZLEY.

5
Did it suit us males not to ask any woman
first, the woman, already won, would play
the asker.
  OVID, *The Art of Love*, bk. 1, tr. by J. H.
  MOZLEY.

6
He who has taken kisses, if he take not the
rest beside, will deserve to lose even what
was granted.
  OVID, *The Art of Love*, bk. 1, tr. by J. H.
  MOZLEY.

7
For a woman to give herself to a man is no
more wasteful than taking a light from a
torch, or using water when it is needed. In
fact, not to do so is a waste.
  OVID, *The Art of Love*, bk. 3, tr. by J. H.
  MOZLEY.

8
Love may laugh at locksmiths, but he always
has a profound respect for money bags.
  G. SIDNEY PATERNOSTER, *The Folly of the
  Wise*.

9
Making love to a woman too many times is
like scratching a place that doesn't itch any
more.
  More Playboy's Party Jokes (1965).

10
A man will often take a girl to some retreat
in order to make advances.
  More Playboy's Party Jokes (1965).

11
Some girls are music lovers. Others can love
without music.
  More Playboy's Party Jokes (1965).

12
Girls who don't repulse men's advances ad-
vance men's pulses.
  More Playboy's Party Jokes (1965).

13
The man who can read women like a book
usually likes to read in bed.
  More Playboy's Party Jokes (1965).

14
You never know how a girl will turn out
until her folks turn in.
  More Playboy's Party Jokes (1965).

15
He offered her a scotch and sofa, and she
reclined.
  More Playboy's Party Jokes (1965).

16
These days, too many beautiful women are
spoiling their attractiveness by using four-
letter words—like don't, and can't, and
won't.
  More Playboy's Party Jokes (1965).

17
What then? what is love? what has love to
do with it? Did I marry her mother for love?
yet we were very happy together; at least I
can speak for myself. I was happy when I
married her—happy whilst she lived—happy
when she died: and I've been happy ever
since, and that's worth all the love in the
universe.
  JOHN POOLE, *Paul Pry*, Act. 1.

18
There goes a saying, and 'twas shrewdly
  said,
Old fish at table, young flesh in bed.
My soul abhors the tasteless dry embrace
Of a stale virgin with a winter face.
  ALEXANDER POPE, *January and May*.

19
Ye gods! annihilate but space and time,
And make two lovers happy.
  ALEXANDER POPE, *The Art of Sinking in
  Poetry*, ch. 11.

20
For, as our different ages move,
  'Tis so ordained (would fate but mend
    it!),
That I shall be past making love
  When she begins to comprehend it.
  MATTHEW PRIOR, *To a Child of Quality*.

21
He that would the daughter win,
Must with the mother first begin.
  JOHN RAY, *English Proverbs*, p. 49.

22
The garter has hanged more men than the
halter.
  Reflections of a Bachelor.

1
Loving a woman never satisfies her; you've got to make love to her.
Reflections of a Bachelor.

2
The people who are in dead earnest never make love; they just love.
Reflections of a Bachelor.

3
The man who wouldn't be a fool over the right woman doesn't deserve to have the right woman be a fool over him.
Reflections of a Bachelor.

4
Although it is idiotic to fall in love at first sight, it is not an unpleasant occurrence to be fallen in love with at first sight.
FRANK RICHARDSON, *2835 Mayfair.*

5
Any man worthy of the name is willing to make a fool of himself for the sake of a woman.
FRANK RICHARDSON, *Love, and All About It.*

6
"A jug and a book and a dame,
And a nice shady nook for the same,"
Said Omar Khayyám,
"And I don't give a darn
What you say, it's a great little game!"
E. M. ROBINSON, *Limericised Classics.*

7
Quarrels in France strengthen a love affair, in America they end it.
NED ROREM, *Paris Diary.*

8
The great lovers of history, observes Bertrand Russell, would be looked upon as juvenile delinquents today. Helen of Troy, for instance, was exactly twelve years old when Paris carried her off to Sparta.
BENNETT CERF, *The Laugh's on Me.*

9
Love is an egotism of two. (L'Amour est un égoisme à deux.)
ANTOINE DE SALLE.

10
A man fifty-four years old who in his heart does not really believe he is too old to fall in love needs all the help a tailor can give him.
ALLAN SEAGER, *Introduction* to Stendhal, *Memoirs of a Tourist.*

11
He was incessantly in love, and he tinkered away at a logical method for the seduction of women, but it seemed usually to develop bugs at crucial moments. However, when he did succeed, he wrote the date on his suspenders.
ALLAN SEAGER, *Introduction* to Stendhal, *Memoirs of a Tourist.*

12
She deceiving, I believing,
What can lovers wish for more?
SIR CHARLES SEDLEY, *Song.*

13
We, that are true lovers, run into strange capers; but as all is mortal in nature, so is all nature in love mortal in folly.
WILLIAM SHAKESPEARE, *As You Like It.* Act ii, sc. 4.

14
And then the lover,
Sighing like a furnace, with a woeful ballad
Made to his mistress' eyebrow.
WILLIAM SHAKESPEARE, *As You Like It.* Act ii, sc. 7.

15
It is as easy to count atomies, as to resolve the propositions of a lover.
WILLIAM SHAKESPEARE, *As You Like It.* Act iii, sc. 2.

16
Love is a familiar. Love is a devil. There is no evil angel but love.
WILLIAM SHAKESPEARE, *Love's Labour's Lost.* Act i, sc. 2.

17
By heaven, I do love: and it hath taught me to rhyme, and to be melancholy.
WILLIAM SHAKESPEARE, *Love's Labour's Lost.* Act iv, sc. 3.

18
All lovers swear more performance than they are able, and yet reserve an ability that they never perform; vowing more than the perfection of ten, and discharging less than the tenth part of one.
WILLIAM SHAKESPEARE, *Troilus and Cressida.* Act iii, sc. 2.

19
Your colt's-tooth is not cast yet.
WILLIAM SHAKESPEARE, *Henry VIII.* Act i, sc. 3.

20
Ham.: Is this the prologue or the posy of a ring?
Oph.: 'Tis brief, my lord.
Ham.: As woman's love.
WILLIAM SHAKESPEARE, *Hamlet.* Act iii, sc. 2.

21
At lovers' perjuries,
They say, Jove laughs.
WILLIAM SHAKESPEARE, *Romeo and Juliet.* Act ii, sc. 2.

22
He plough'd her, and she cropp'd.
WILLIAM SHAKESPEARE, *Antony and Cleopatra.* Act ii, sc. 2.

1
He was more than over shoes in love.
WILLIAM SHAKESPEARE, *The Two Gentlemen of Verona*. Act i, sc. 2.

2
Sigh no more, ladies, sigh no more,
Men were deceivers ever,
One foot in sea and one on shore,
To one thing constant never.
WILLIAM SHAKESPEARE, *Much Ado About Nothing*. Act ii, sc. 3.

3
No, Stella, I will not play horse to your Lady Godiva.
BERNARD SHAW, to Mrs Patrick Campbell. Quoted in *While Rome Burns* by ALEXANDER WOOLLCOTT.

4
First love is only a little foolishness and a lot of curiosity: no really self-respecting woman would take advantage of it.
BERNARD SHAW, *John Bull's Other Island*, Act 4.

5
The fickleness of the women I love is only equalled by the infernal constancy of the women who love me.
BERNARD SHAW, *The Philanderer*, Act 2.

6
Love in a cottage, with a broken window to let in the rain, is not my idea of comfort.
ALEXANDER SMITH, *Dreamthorp: On the Writing of Essays*.

7
In fact, all loves but one's own have an element of the tiresome.
C. P. SNOW, *The New Men*.

8
Plough not the seas, sow not the sands,
Leave off your idle pain;
Seek other mistresses for your minds;
Love's service is in vain.
ROBERT SOUTHWELL, *Love's Servile Lot*.

9
Love is the history of a woman's life; it is an episode in man's. (L'amour est l'historie de la vie des femmes; c'est un épisode dans celle des hommes.)
MADAME DE STAËL, *De L'influence des Passions*.

10
The success of any man with any woman is apt to displease even his best friends.
MADAME DE STAËL, quoted in *The Book of Diversion*, ed. by FRANKLIN P. ADAMS.

11
Though her [Lady Elizabeth Hastings'] mien carries much more invitation than command, to behold her is an immediate check to loose behavior; to love her was a liberal education.
SIR RICHARD STEELE, *The Tatler*, No. 49.

12
Once, when I raptured in a violet glow given off by the Queen of the World, my father asked me why, and I thought he was crazy not to see. Of course I know now she was a mouse-haired, freckle-nosed, scabby-kneed little girl with a voice like a bat and the loving kindness of a gila monster, but then she lighted up the landscape and me.
JOHN STEINBECK, *Travels with Charley*, pt. 3.

13
The Lion is the King of Beasts, but he is scarcely suitable for a domestic pet. In the same way, I suspect love is rather too violent a passion to make, in all cases, a good domestic sentiment.
ROBERT LOUIS STEVENSON, *Virginibus Puerisque*.

14
A woman despises a man for loving her, unless she returns his love.
ELIZABETH STODDARD, *Two Men*, ch. 32.

15
For kings and lovers are alike in this,
That their chief art in reign dissembling is.
SIR JOHN SUCKLING, *Loving and Beloved*.

16
Werther had a love for Charlotte
Such as words could never utter;
Would you know how first he met her?
She was cutting bread and butter.
WILLIAM MAKEPEACE THACKERAY, *The Sorrows of Werther*.

17
Love is master of the wisest. It is only fools who defy him.
WILLIAM MAKEPEACE THACKERAY, *Miscellanies.*.

18
There is no remedy for love but to love more.
HENRY D. THOREAU, *Journal*, July 25, 1839.

19
Love is the strange bewilderment which overtakes one person on account of another person.
JAMES THURBER AND E. B. WHITE, *Is Sex Necessary?*

20
To say that you can love one person all your life is just like saying that one candle will continue burning as long as you live.
LEO TOLSTOY, *The Kreutzer Sonata*, ch. 2.

21
If I had had a pistol I would have shot him —either that or fallen at his feet. There is no middle way when one loves.
LADY TROUBRIDGE, *The Millionaire*.

1
It is far easier to love a woman in picturesque rags than in the commonplace garments of respectability.
LADY TROUBRIDGE, *The Millionaire.*

2
To couple is a custom,
All things thereto agree;
Why should not I then love,
Since love to all is free?
UNKNOWN, *Famous History of Friar Bacon.*

3
If men did not put their responsibilities above everything else, the bulk of lovemaking would not be done at night.
UNKNOWN, *Meditations in Wall Street.*

4
Love is a transitive verb.
UNKNOWN, *Meditations in Wall Street.*

5
There is nothing lovers so love to love as repenting.
UNKNOWN, *Meditations in Wall Street.*

6
Nobody loves me; I'm going into the garden and eat worms.
UNKNOWN, *A Valentine Greeting.*

7
Lovers are fools. (Amantes amentes.)
UNKNOWN. Latin proverb.

8
From now on we are opposed, a man and a woman in love . . . the greatest, the most exhausting struggle in the world. Two moths racing for the flame—two cannibals devouring each other.
PETER USTINOV, *Romanoff and Juliet,* Act 1.

9
I can see from your utter misery, from your eagerness to misunderstand each other, and from your thoroughly bad temper, that this is the real thing.
PETER USTINOV, *Romanoff and Juliet,* Act 1.

10
Sometimes I wish I could just fall in love. Then, at least, you know who your opponent is!
PETER USTINOV, *Romanoff and Juliet,* Act 2.

11
Human nature being what it is, legend and literature are full to overflowing with tragic lovers—there's hardly a couple who don't end up horizontal, bloody and fruitless. Tristan and Isolde, Paolo and Francesca—Romeo and Juliet—Why should that be?

What is the point of suffering if you can't survive to enjoy the relief?
PETER USTINOV, *Romanoff and Juliet,* Act 2.

12
Give me hopes of bliss or dig my grave;
More love or more disdain I crave.
CHARLES WEBBE, *Against Indifference.*

13
I like you. I love you. I want you all the time, so please wire me back that you'll be my valentine.
WESTERN UNION FORM No. 2.

14
A fox is a wolf who sends flowers.
RUTH WESTON, actress. Quoted in *New York Post,* Nov. 8, 1955.

15
Love is a human emotion that wisdom will never conquer.
PERCY WHITE, *Mr. Strudge.*

16
For everything created
In the bounds of earth and sky,
Hath such longing to be mated,
It must couple or must die.
G. J. WHYTE-MELVILLE, *Like to Like.*

17
Young men want to be faithful and are not; old men want to be faithless and are not.
OSCAR WILDE, *The Picture of Dorian Gray.*

18
Those who are faithful know only the trivial side of love: it is the faithless who know love's tragedies.
OSCAR WILDE, *The Picture of Dorian Gray.*

19
The only difference between a caprice and a life-long passion is that the caprice lasts a little longer.
OSCAR WILDE, *The Picture of Dorian Gray.*

20
When one is in love, one always begins by deceiving oneself, and one always ends by deceiving others. That is what the world calls a romance.
OSCAR WILDE, *The Picture of Dorian Gray.*

21
When one is in love one begins to deceive oneself. And one ends by deceiving others.
OSCAR WILDE, *A Woman of No Importance,* Act 3.

22
One should always be in love. That is the reason one should never marry.
OSCAR WILDE, *A Woman of No Importance,* Act 3.

1
Woman begins by resisting a man's advances and ends by blocking his retreat.
OSCAR WILDE.

2
Platonic love is love from the neck up.
THYRA SAMTER WINSLOW, *Interview* with James Simpson, Aug. 10, 1952.

3
No, mistresses are like books. If you pore upon them too much, they doze you, and make you unfit for company; but if used discreetly, you are the fitter for conversation by 'em.
WILLIAM WYCHERLEY, *The Country Wife*, Act 1.

4
I love to be envied, and would not marry a wife that I alone could love; loving alone is as dull as eating alone.
WILLIAM WYCHERLEY, *The Country Wife*, Act 3.

5
Why should women have more invention in love than men? It can only be, because they have more desires, more soliciting passions, more lust, and more of the devil.
WILLIAM WYCHERLEY, *The Country Wife*, Act 4.

6
To talk of honour in the mysteries of love, is like talking of Heaven or the Deity in an operation of witchcraft, just when you are employing the devil: it makes the charm impotent.
WILLIAM WYCHERLEY, *The Country Wife*, Act 4.

7
People who are sensible about love are incapable of it.
DOUGLAS YATES, *Works*.

8
She bid me take love easy, as the leaves
    grow on the tree;
But I, being young and foolish, with her
    would not agree.
WILLIAM BUTLER YEATS, *Down by the Salley Gardens*.

9
The only true love is love at first sight; second sight dispels it.
ISRAEL ZANGWILL.

10
In how many lives does Love really play a dominant part? The average tax payer is no more capable of a "grand passion" than of a grand opera.
ISRAEL ZANGWILL, *Romeo and Juliet and Other Love Stories*.

LOYALTY

11
He has every attribute of a dog except loyalty.
SENATOR THOMAS P. GORE, *Comment* on a colleague. (GEORGE E. ALLEN, *Presidents Who Have Known Me*.)

12
People don't mind if you betray humanity, but if you betray your club you are considered a renegade.
ARTHUR KOESTLER, *The Age of Longing*.

13
Later in a political matter Sherman refused to correct a policy of Grant when so requested, saying, "Grant stood by me when I was crazy, and I stood by him when he was drunk, and now we stand by each other."
CARL SANDBURG, *Abraham Lincoln: The Prairie Years and the War Years*, ch. 47.

14
Let fools the name of loyalty divide:
Wise men and gods are on the strongest side.
SIR CHARLES SEDLEY, *Death of Marc Antony*. Act iv, sc. 2.

15
Every despot must have one disloyal subject to keep him sane.
BERNARD SHAW, *Plays, Pleasant and Unpleasant:* preface.

16
When you are down and out, something always turns up—and it is usually the noses of your friends.
ORSON WELLES, quoted in *The New York Times*, Apr. 1, 1962.

17
Isn't he the damnedest simulacrum.
WALT WHITMAN, *Comment* on Swinburne, when the latter had turned viciously against him.

18
Some Americans need hyphens in their names because only part of them has come over.
WOODROW WILSON, *Address* in Washington, D.C., May 16, 1914.

LUCK

19
With luck on your side you can do without brains.
GIORDANO BRUNO, *The Candle Bearer*. Act iv, sc. 5. English version by J. R. HALE.

20
Just like my luck! If I had been bred a hatter, little boys would have come into the world without heads.
SIR EDWARD BULWER-LYTTON, *Money*, Act 2.

1
He forc'd his neck into a noose,
To show his play at fast and loose;
And, when he chanc'd t' escape, mistook
For art and subtlety, his luck.
> SAMUEL BUTLER, *Hudibras*. Pt. iii, canto
> 2.

2
We must believe in luck. For how else can
we explain the success of those we don't like.
> JEAN COCTEAU.

3
Luck, mere luck, may make even madness
wisdom.
> DOUGLAS JERROLD, *Specimens of Jerrold's
> Wit*.

4
Some people are so fond of ill-luck that they
run half-way to meet it.
> DOUGLAS JERROLD, *Jerrold's Wit: Meeting
> Trouble Half-way*.

5
Three unluckiest things to meet first thing
in the morning: a mad dog, a man who lent
you money, and a red-haired girl.
> SEUMAS MACMANUS, *Heavy Hangs the
> Golden Grain*.

6
I think we consider too much the good luck
of the early bird and not enough the bad
luck of the worm.
> FRANKLIN D. ROOSEVELT.

7
The dice of Zeus have ever lucky throws.
> SOPHOCLES, *Fragments*, No. 763.

8
Throw a lucky man into the sea and he will
come up with a fish in his mouth.
> UNKNOWN, an Arab proverb.

LUXURY

See also Comfort, Wealth

9
You can only drink thirty or forty glasses
of beer a day, no matter how rich you are.
> ADOLPHUS BUSCH, *Newspaper interview*.

10
Though luxury is a delightful adjunct to happiness it has never been able to create it.
> LUCAS CLEEVE, *The Mascot of Park Lane*.

11
Watermelons twelve months a year.
> IRVIN S. COBB, *Reply* to the question,
> What would you regard as heaven on
> earth? (FRED G. NEUMAN, *Irvin S.
> Cobb*.)

12
There is a point at which satisfaction almost
suffocates, like an excellent cigar which is
too strong.
> R. N. DICKINSON, *Keddie*.

13
Honest bread is very well—it's the butter
that makes the temptation.
> DOUGLAS JERROLD, *The Catspaw*, Act 3.

14
After all, what could I have bought with
more than enough money for food, clothing
and lodging? Cigars? I don't smoke. Champagne? I don't drink. Thirty suits of fashionable clothes? The people I most avoid would
ask me to dinner if I could be persuaded to
wear such things. By this time I can afford
them all; but I buy nothing I didn't buy
before. Besides, I have an imagination. Ever
since I can remember, I have only had to
shut my eyes to be and do whatever I
pleased. What are your trumpery Bond
Street luxuries to me, George Bernard
Sardanapalus?
> BERNARD SHAW, *Sixteen Self Sketches*.

15
My idea of heaven is eating *pâtés de fois
gras* to the sound of trumpets.
> SYDNEY SMITH.

16
The essential for good living is money. It
provides for a variety of pleasures—gastron-
omy that brings daily contentment; music
that provides intellectual escape; and beautiful women.
> LOUIS VAUDABLE, quoted in *Life*, Jan. 7,
> 1966.

M

MACHINES

See also Automobile

17
Secretary on telephone: "Our automatic
answering device is away for repair. This is
a person speaking."
> ERIC BURGIN, *Punch*.

18
Machines won't take over the world entirely
so long as we have the little thrill that comes
when we add a column of figures and get
the same total we did the first time.
> *Kodiak* (Alaska) *Mirror*, quoted by JOHN
> M. HENRY in *McCall's*.

19
Machinery is the sub-conscious mind of the
world.
> GERALD STANLEY LEE, *Crowds*. Pt. ii, ch.
> 8.

MADNESS

1
I suppose it is much more comfortable to be mad and not know it, than to be sane and have one's doubts.
G. B. BURGIN, *Which Woman?*

2
"You are old, Father William," the young
     man said,
"And your hair has become very white;
And yet you incessantly stand on your
     head—
     Do you think, at your age, it is right?"

"In my youth," Father William replied to
     his son,
"I feared it might injure the brain;
But, now that I'm perfectly sure I have
     none,
Why, I do it again and again."
LEWIS CARROLL, *Alice's Adventures in Wonderland*, ch. 5.

3
That's the first lunatic I've had for an engineer. He probably ought to be shot at sunrise, but I guess we'll let him off, because nobody was hurt.
THOMAS E. DEWEY, *Remark* during a whistle-stop speech in Beaucoup, Ill., Oct. 12, 1948, in the midst of the presidential campaign. His speech was suddenly interrupted when the railroad observation coach, from the back platform of which he was talking, lurched backward in the direction of the audience gathered along the tracks. The totally unexpected movement of the train in reverse prompted Dewey to make his impromptu and very unflattering comment about the engineer. It received national circulation over a period of several days, very likely to Dewey's disadvantage.

4
A little madness in the Spring
Is wholesome even for the King.
EMILY DICKINSON, *Poems.*

5
Insanity is hereditary. You can get it from your children.
SAM LEVENSON.

6
My dear Sir, take any road, you can't go amiss. The whole state is one vast insane asylum.
JAMES L. PETIGRU, *Reply*, in 1860, upon being asked directions for reaching the insane asylum in Charleston, S. C. The state was then preparing to secede from the Union.

7
What garlic is to salad, insanity is to art.
AUGUSTUS SAINT-GAUDENS.

8
Sanity is a madness put to good uses.
GEORGE SANTAYANA, *Little Essays*, p. 146.

9
One of the commonest forms of madness is the desire to be noticed, the pleasure derived from being noticed.
MARK TWAIN, *Essays: The Memorable Assassination.*

MAJORITY AND MINORITY

10
Because half-a-dozen grasshoppers under a fern make the field ring with their importunate chink, whilst thousands of great cattle, reposed beneath the shadow of the British oak, chew the cud and are silent, pray do not imagine that those who make the noise are the only inhabitants of the field; that of course they are many in number; or that, after all, they are other than the little shrivelled meagre, hopping, though loud and troublesome insects of the hour.
EDMUND BURKE, *Reflections on the Revolution in France.*

11
One of the great difficulties of being a member of a minority race is that so many kindhearted, well-meaning bores gather around to help. Usually, to tell the truth, they have nothing to help with, except their company —which is often appallingly dull.
LANGSTON HUGHES, *Laughing to Keep from Crying.*

12
One, with God, is always a majority, but many a martyr has been burned at the stake while the votes were being counted.
THOMAS B. REED. (W. A. ROBINSON, *Life.*)

13
The worst cliques are those which consist of one man.
BERNARD SHAW, *Back to Methuselah*, Part v: *As Far As Thought Can Reach.*

14
In any civic crisis of a great and dangerous sort the common herd is not privately anxious about the rights and wrongs of the matter, it is only anxious to be on the winning side.
MARK TWAIN, *Notebook*, ch. 35.

MAN

See also Woman

1
Eventually I have high hopes I'll be able to retire from the human race.
> FRED ALLEN, *Statement* to a researcher for *Time*, quoted by MAURICE ZOLOTOW in *No People Like Show People.*

2
Man is nothing but contradiction: the less he knows it the more dupe he is.
> AMIEL, *Journal*, May 3, 1860.

3
Mankind fell in Adam, and has been falling ever since, but it never touched bottom till it got to Henry Ward Beecher.
> TOM APPLETON, *More Uncensored Recollections.*

4
She had nagged him almost beyond the point of endurance. "Men always were fools," she thundered at him. "Yes," he replied quietly, "I know, but I wish to Heaven that Adam hadn't been fool enough to part with one of his ribs."
> W. BURTON BALDRY, *Stray Thoughts.*

5
A man, however malicious he may possibly be, can never say about women as much good or as much evil as they themselves think.
> HONORÉ DE BALZAC, *The Physiology of Marriage: Dedication.*

6
Men are nervous of remarkable women.
> JAMES M. BARRIE, *What Every Woman Knows.*

7
The monkey is an organized sarcasm upon the human race.
> HENRY WARD BEECHER.

8
Man is a noble animal, splendid in ashes and pompous in the grave.
> SIR THOMAS BROWNE, *Hydriotaphia: Urn Burial*, ch. 5.

9
Man is the only animal that can remain on friendly terms with the victims he intends to eat until he eats them.
> SAMUEL BUTLER.

10
The more we really look at man as an animal, the less he will look like one.
> G. K. CHESTERTON, *The Everlasting Man.*

11
Man is a biped, but fifty men are not a centipede.
> G. K. CHESTERTON. (HESKETH PEARSON, *Lives of the Wits.*)

12
I would tell a man who was drinking too much "Be a man," but I would not tell a crocodile who was eating too many explorers "Be a crocodile."
> G. K. CHESTERTON. (HESKETH PEARSON, *Lives of the Wits.*)

13
The Peking Man was fond of overpopulation. We do not know whether he was religious or promiscuous or both. He did not have love as we understand it because he had no gin.
> WILL CUPPY, *How to Tell Your Friends from the Apes.*

14
A wonderful fact to reflect upon, that every human creature is constituted to be that profound secret and mystery to every other.
> CHARLES DICKENS, *A Tale of Two Cities.* Bk. i, ch. 1.

15
Man is the most intelligent of animals—and the most silly.
> DIOGENES. (DIOGENES LAERTIUS, *Diogenes*. Bk. vi, sec. 24.)

16
I tell you there isn't a thing under the sun that needs to be done at all, but what a man can do better than a woman, unless it's bearing children, and they do that in a poor makeshift way; it had better ha' been left to the men.
> GEORGE ELIOT, *Adam Bede.*

17
We are the hollow men
We are the stuffed men
Leaning together.
> T. S. ELIOT, *The Hollow Men.*

18
If you ride a horse, sit close and tight,
If you ride a man, sit easy and light.
> BENJAMIN FRANKLIN, *Poor Richard*, 1734.

19
Man is Creation's masterpiece. But who says so?—Man!
> PAUL GAVARNI, *Apothegms.*

20
Man is nature's sole mistake.
> W. S. GILBERT, *Princess Ida.*

21
Breathes there a man with hide so tough
Who says two sexes aren't enough?
> SAMUEL HOFFENSTEIN, *The Sexes.*

22
Man is a machine into which we put what we call food and produce what we call thought.
> ROBERT G. INGERSOLL, *The Gods.*

1
Man that is born of woman is small potatoes and few in the hill.
> RUDYARD KIPLING, *The Head of the District.*

2
To God what is God's, to Caesar what is Caesar's. To humans—what?
> STANISLAW J. LEC, *Unkempt Thoughts,* tr. by JACEK GALASKA.

3
If a man is only a little lower than the angels, the angels should reform.
> MARY WILSON LITTLE.

4
In this world a man must either be anvil or hammer.
> HENRY WADSWORTH LONGFELLOW, *Hyperion.* Bk. iv, ch. 7.

5
Women want mediocre men, and men are working hard to be as mediocre as possible.
> MARGARET MEAD. (*Quote,* May 15, 1958.)

6
Man, an ingenious assembly of portable plumbing.
> CHRISTOPHER MORLEY.

7
Let us confess it: the human situation is always desperate.
> LEWIS MUMFORD, *In the Name of Sanity.*

8
It is not true that men never change. They change for the worse—and even for the better.
> NAPOLEON BONAPARTE. (*The Mind of Napoleon,* ed. by J. CHRISTOPHER HEROLD.)

9
Men are like ciphers: they acquire their value merely from their position.
> NAPOLEON BONAPARTE. (*The Mind of Napoleon,* ed. by J. CHRISTOPHER HEROLD.)

10
Man is a rope stretched between the animal and the Superman—a rope over an abyss.
> FRIEDRICH WILHELM NIETZSCHE, *Thus Spake Zarathustra:* prologue, pt. 4, tr. by THOMAS COMMON.

11
Man is a two-legged animal without feathers.
> PLATO.

12
To be human should be considered a privilege, not an excuse.
> *Putnam County* (Ind.) *Graphic.*

13
I wish I loved the human race;
I wish I loved its silly face;
I wish I liked the way it walks;
I wish I liked the way it talks;
And when I'm introduced to one
I wish I thought, *What Jolly Fun!*
> WALTER RALEIGH, *The Wishes of an Elderly Man: Wished at a Garden Party,* June, 1914.

14
You can't change a man, no-ways. By the time his mummy turns him loose and he takes up with some innocent woman and marries her, he's what he is.
> MARJORIE KINNAN RAWLINGS, *Benny and the Bird Dogs.*

15
Man is a wild animal, and woman a wild animal trainer.
> *Reflections of a Bachelor* (1903).

16
Very few men care to have the obvious pointed out to them by a woman.
> MRS. BAILLIE SAUNDERS, *A Shepherd of Kensington.*

17
"How poor a thing is man!" Alas 'tis true,
I'd half forgot it when I chanced on you.
> JOHANN VON SCHILLER, *The Moral Poet.*

18
'Tis the way of all flesh.
> THOMAS SHADWELL, *The Sullen Lovers.*

19
Lord, what fools these mortals be!
> WILLIAM SHAKESPEARE, *A Midsummer Night's Dream,* Act iii, sc. 2.

20
I have thought some of nature's journeymen had made men and not made them well; they imitated humanity so abominably.
> WILLIAM SHAKESPEARE, *Hamlet.* Act iii, sc. 2.

21
God made him, and therefore let him pass for a man.
> WILLIAM SHAKESPEARE, *The Merchant of Venice.* Act i, sc. 2.

22
A critic recently described me as having 'a kindly dislike of my fellow creatures.' Dread would have been nearer the mark than dislike, for man is the only animal of which I am thoroughly and cravenly afraid. I have never thought much of the courage of a lion tamer. Inside the cage he is at least safe from other men.
> BERNARD SHAW, *Sixteen Self Sketches.*

23
Give Man a chance and he will do everything to destroy himself and laugh at his own imbecility.
> BERNARD SHAW, quoted in *Days with Bernard Shaw* by STEPHEN WINSTEN.

1

The more I see of men, the more I like dogs.
MADAME DE STAËL. See also LAMARTINE
in section headed "Dog."

2

Man is a substance clad in shadows.
JOHN STERLING, *Essays and Tales.*

3

Mankind—The most pernicious race of little
odious vermin that nature ever suffered to
crawl on the face of the earth.
JONATHAN SWIFT, *Gulliver's Travels.*

4

When I beheld this I sighed, and said within
myself, Surely mortal man is a broomstick.
JONATHAN SWIFT, *A Meditation Upon a
Broomstick.*

5

We are all alike—on the inside.
MARK TWAIN, *In Eruption.*

6

All I care to know is that a man is a human
being—that is enough for me; he can't be
any worse.
MARK TWAIN, *Concerning the Jews.*

7

Man seems to be a rickety sort of thing, any
way you take him; a kind of British Museum of infirmities and inferiorities. He is
always undergoing repairs. A machine that
was as unreliable as he is would have no
market.
MARK TWAIN, *Letters from the Earth.*

8

Man is a museum of diseases, a home of
impurities; he comes today and is gone tomorrow; he begins as dirt and departs as
stench.
MARK TWAIN.

9

Man—A creature made at the end of the
week's work when God was tired.
MARK TWAIN.

10

Of all created creatures man is the most detestable. Of the entire brood he is the only
one . . . that possesses malice. . . . Also
. . . he is the only creature that has a nasty
mind.
MARK TWAIN, *The Character of Man.*

11

No one knows the age of the human race,
but all agree that it is old enough to know
better.
UNKNOWN.

12

Man is the only animal that eats when he is
not hungry, drinks when he is not thirsty,
and makes love at all seasons.
UNKNOWN.

13

The Duke [of Wellington] said the natural
state of man was plunder. Society was based
on security of property alone. It was for
that object men associated; and he thought
we were coming to the natural state of society very fast.
BENJAMIN ROBERT HAYDON, *Memoirs,*
1839, ed. by TOM TAYLOR.

MANNERS

See also Behavior, Feeling, Gentleman

14

Miss Blachford is agreeable enough. I do not
want people to be very agreeable, as it saves
me the trouble of liking them a great deal.
JANE AUSTEN, *Letter* to her sister Cassandra, Dec. 24, 1798.

15

Mrs. Bennet was restored to her usual
querulous serenity.
JANE AUSTEN, *Pride and Prejudice,* ch. 42.

16

The guy is so smooth he could slide on sand-
paper.
W. T. BALLARD, *Say Yes to Murder.*

17

Of our spoken manners, the European would
say that we have none. By his standards,
we are rude or uncouth when we are not
downright impudent. Americans who have
lived even a short time abroad notice this
on their return—as did the young lady who
wrote to the papers of her experience at the
airport. She somehow got separated from her
husband and, looking bewildered, was asked
by an attendant what the matter was. She
said, "I've lost my husband." To which his
rejoinder was: "Don't worry, baby, we'll
get you another."
JACQUES BARZUN, *God's Country and
Mine.*

18

The cabdriver and his fare don't know each
other, and as often as not the driver feels
that he must reaffirm Liberty, Equality, and
Fraternity the moment a stranger enters his
territory. He calls me Big Boy, asks personal questions, turns the radio on for the
track results, and blows cigar smoke into my
compartment, all with the best humor and
fullest indifference to my comfort.
JACQUES BARZUN, *God's Country and
Mine.*

19

When they are at Rome, they do there as
they see done.
ROBERT BURTON, *The Anatomy of Melancholy.* Pt. iii, sec. 4.

1
Silence is not always tact and it is tact that is golden, not silence.
 SAMUEL BUTLER, *Notebooks.*

2
He was the mildest manner'd man
That ever scuttled ship or cut a throat.
 LORD BYRON, *Don Juan.* Canto iii, st. 3.

3
An almost spectral kind of phantasm of a man—nothing in him but forms and ceremonies and outside wrappings.
 THOMAS CARLYLE, *Letter,* Mar. 23, 1873, referring to Gladstone.

4
Curtsey while you're thinking of what to say. It saves time.
 LEWIS CARROLL, *Through the Looking-Glass,* ch. 2.

5
Don't go around with a chip on your shoulder, people might think it came off your head.
 CHANGING TIMES, *The Kiplinger Magazine.*

6
Abhor a knave and pity a fool in your heart, but let neither of them unnecessarily see that you do so.
 LORD CHESTERFIELD, *Letters,* Feb. 22, 1748.

7
You must embrace the man you hate if you cannot be justified in knocking him down.
 LORD CHESTERFIELD, *Letters,* Jan. 15, 1753.

8
It is true that there are many very polite men, but none that I ever heard of who were not either fascinating women or obeying them.
 G. K. CHESTERTON, *What's Wrong with the World.*

9
Pomposity is only the failure of pomp.
 G. K. CHESTERTON, *A Handful of Authors.*

10
After all, when you have to kill a man it costs nothing to be polite.
 SIR WINSTON CHURCHILL, *Reply,* in House of Commons, to criticism of letter he wrote to Japanese ambassador.

11
A want of tact is worse than a want of virtue.
 BENJAMIN DISRAELI, *The Young Duke.*

12
He that hath more manners than he ought,
Is more a fool than he thought.
 THOMAS D'URFEY, *Quixote.* Act ii, sc. 1.

13
If a man has good manners and is not afraid of other people, he will get by even if he is stupid.
 SIR DAVID ECCLES, *Look.*

14
Manners have been somewhat cynically defined to be a contrivance of wise men to keep fools at a distance.
 RALPH WALDO EMERSON, *Conduct of Life: Behavior.*

15
God may forgive sins, he said, but awkwardness has no forgiveness in heaven or earth.
 RALPH WALDO EMERSON, *Essays: Society and Solitude.*

16
He combines the manners of a marquis with the morals of a Methodist.
 W. S. GILBERT, *Ruddigore,* Act 1.

17
The good manners of educated Englishmen, which are the most exquisitely modulated attentions I have ever received. Such leaping to feet, such opening of doors, such lightening flourishes with matches and cigarettes—it is all so heroic, I never quite get over the feeling that someone has just said, "To the lifeboats!"
 MARGARET HALSEY, *With Malice Toward Some.*

18
Except in street cars one should never be unnecessarily rude to a lady.
 O. HENRY, *Strictly Business: The Gold That Glittered.*

19
A civil guest
Will no more talk, than eat all the feast.
 GEORGE HERBERT, *The Church-Porch,* st. 51.

20
I don't recall your name, but your manners are familiar.
 OLIVER HERFORD, to a back-slapping person who descended upon him one afternoon at the Players with a confident "You remember me?"

21
Rudeness is the weak man's imitation of strength.
 ERIC HOFFER, *The Passionate State of Mind,* p. 138.

22
The first quality of a good education is good manners—and some people flunk the course.
 HUBERT HUMPHREY, *Remark* to hecklers at San Fernando Valley State College. (*Connecticut Sunday Herald,* Jan. 1, 1967.)

1
They teach the morals of a harlot and the manners of a dancing-master.
SAMUEL JOHNSON, on Chesterfield's *Letters*.

2
You may observe that I am well-bred to a degree of needless scrupulosity.
SAMUEL JOHNSON, *Miscellanies*, vol. 1.

3
If there is one beast in all the loathsome fauna of civilization I hate and despise, it is a man of the world.
HENRY ARTHUR JONES, *The Liars*.

4
He spoke beautiful French and had a warm, sympathetic heart despite his good manners.
ALEXANDER KING, *Mine Enemy Grows Older*. Reference to Donald Friede.

5
I'm greatly attached
To Barbara Frietchie.
I bet she scratched
When she was itchy.
OGDEN NASH, *Taboo to Boot*.

6
I . . . couldn't drink a cup of tea without using the saucer.
WILL ROGERS, *The Illiterate Digest*.

7
What were once vices are now the manners of the day.
SENECA, *Epistulae ad Lucilium*.

8
The Retort Courteous . . . the Quip Modest; . . . the Reply Churlish; . . . the Reproof Valiant; . . . the Countercheck Quarrelsome; . . . the Lie with Circumstance; . . . the Lie Direct.
WILLIAM SHAKESPEARE, *As You Like It*. Act v, sc. 4.

9
I have the most perfect confidence in your indiscretion.
SYDNEY SMITH.

10
Politeness is excellent but it does not pay the bill.
CHARLES HADDON SPURGEON, *Salt-Cellars*.

11
Philistine—A term of contempt applied by prigs to the rest of their species.
LESLIE STEPHEN.

12
Politeness is the art of choosing among one's real thoughts.
ABEL STEVENS, *Life of Mme. de Staël*, ch. 4.

13
He is a barbarian, Scythian, yahoo, a gorilla, in respect of outward polish, but a most sensible, straightforward old codger.
GEORGE TEMPLETON STRONG, *Diary*. Referring to Abraham Lincoln.

14
Fingers were made before forks, and hands before knives.
JONATHAN SWIFT, *Polite Conversation*.

15
Truth is good manners; manners are a fiction.
MARK TWAIN.

16
Good breeding consists in concealing how much we think of ourselves and how little we think of the other person.
MARK TWAIN, *Unpublished Diaries*.

17
Preserve a respectful demeanor
When you are brought into the room;
Don't stare at the guests while they are eating,
No matter how much they consume.
CAROLYN WELLS, *To a Baked Fish*.

18
A little murder now and then,
A little bit of burglarizing,
Won't earn the hate of fellow-men
As much as being patronizing.
R. T. WOMBAT, *Quatrains*.

MARRIAGE

See also Divorce, Husband, Mother-in-Law, Widow, Wife

19
I let a couple of intimate friends know that I was thinking of getting married. Intimate friends have learned that generally an inquiry about marriage is followed by the act, no matter what advice they give, and that if they voice an adverse opinion they only gain the animosity of the new bride and lose the friendship of the couple. I received guarded answers.
GEORGE ABBOTT, *Mister Abbott*.

20
Accident counts for as much in companionship as in marriage.
HENRY ADAMS, *The Education of Henry Adams*, ch. 4.

21
Nowadays two can live as cheaply as one large family used to!
JOEY ADAMS, *Cindy and I*, ch. 3.

22
Marriage is give and take. You'd better give it to her or she'll take it anyway.
JOEY ADAMS, *Cindy and I*, ch. 3.

23
"Give 'em anything they want, but never marry 'em," has always been my credo. As a

charter member of the Bachelor's Club, I had been preaching this gospel since the day I issued my first alimony check.

JOEY ADAMS, *Cindy and I,* ch. 3.

1
Honey, a swinging signorina to a happily married man is like a plate of ravioli to a guy who's just eaten. Sure it's tasty, but who needs it?

JOEY ADAMS, *Cindy and I,* ch. 10.

2
I have a wife, you have a wife, we all have wives, we've had a taste of paradise, we know what it means to be married.

SHOLOM ALEICHEM, *On Account of a Hat.*

3
Relations between the sexes are so complicated that the only way you can tell if members of the set are "going together" is if they're married. Then, almost certainly, they are not.

CLEVELAND AMORY, *Who Killed Society?*

4
Marriage is a romance in which the hero dies in the first chapter.

ANONYMOUS.

5
As bad as marrying the devil's daughter and living with the old folks.

G. L. APPERSON, *English Proverbs and Proverbial Phrases.*

6
A sad barnyard where the hen crows louder than the cock.

G. L. APPERSON, *English Proverbs and Proverbial Phrases.*

7
In order to be happy in wedlock, you must either be a man of genius married to an affectionate and intellectual woman, or, by a chance which is not as common as might be supposed, you must both of you be exceedingly stupid.

HONORÉ DE BALZAC, *Petty Troubles of Married Life.*

8
In a husband, there is only a man; in a married woman, there is a man, a father, a mother, and a woman.

HONORÉ DE BALZAC, *Petty Troubles of Married Life.*

9
Putting yourself in the wrong with your lawful wife is solving the problem of Perpetual Motion.

HONORÉ DE BALZAC, *Petty Troubles of Married Life.*

10
We have come to our last observation. Doubtless this work is beginning to tire you quite as much as its subject does, if you are married.

HONORÉ DE BALZAC, *Petty Troubles of Married Life.*

11
When a husband and wife have got each other, the devil only knows which has got the other.

HONORÉ DE BALZAC, *Petty Troubles of Married Life.*

12
Marriage must incessantly contend with a monster which devours everything, that is, familiarity.

HONORÉ DE BALZAC, *The Physiology of Marriage.*

13
If a man cannot distinguish the difference between the pleasures of two consecutive nights, he has married too early.

HONORÉ DE BALZAC, *The Physiology of Marriage.*

14
The man who enters his wife's dressing room is either a philosopher or an imbecile.

HONORÉ DE BALZAC, *The Physiology of Marriage.*

15
A man ought not to marry without having studied anatomy, and dissected at least one woman.

HONORÉ DE BALZAC, *The Physiology of Marriage.*

16
When, after remaining a long time aloof from her husband, a woman makes overtures of a very marked character in order to attract his love, she acts in accordance with the axiom of maritime law, which says: *The flag protects the cargo.*

HONORÉ DE BALZAC, *The Physiology of Marriage.*

17
The woman who allows herself to be found out deserves her fate.

HONORÉ DE BALZAC, *The Physiology of Marriage.*

18
Marriage always demands the greatest understanding of the art of insincerity possible between two human beings.

VICKI BAUM, *And Life Goes On.*

19
Women, deceived by men, want to marry them; it is a kind of revenge as good as any other.

PHILLIPPE DE REMI BEAUMANOIR (1246?–1296).

1
Well-married a man is winged: ill-matched, he is shackled.
> HENRY WARD BEECHER, *Proverbs from Plymouth Pulpit.*

2
Even if a man was delightful, no woman would marry him if she knew what he was like.
> E. F. BENSON, *Paul.*

3
Marriage—A community consisting of a master, a mistress, and two slaves—making in all two.
> AMBROSE BIERCE.

4
Some husbands are born optimists. They go through life believing that somehow, somewhere, they eventually will arrive someplace on time—with their wife. It never happens.
> HAL BOYLE, *Column,* Associated Press, June 16, 1964.

5
Earning a living for a wife, a fellow finds out, is one of the easier things about marriage. It takes only about eight hours a day. This leaves a man sixteen full hours for wife-waiting and other such essential chores as sleeping, shaving, eating, walking the dog and obeying his children.
> HAL BOYLE, *Column,* Associated Press, June 16, 1964.

6
He that marries a widow with two daughters has three back doors to his house.
> FRANK C. BROWN, *Collection of North Carolina Folklore.*

7
won 1880. one 1884. . . .
> WILLIAM JENNINGS BRYAN, Inscription of wedding ring given to his wife. (PAXTON HIBBEN, *Life.*)

8
One was never married, and that's his hell; another is, and that's his plague.
> ROBERT BURTON, *The Anatomy of Melancholy.* Pt. i, sec. 2.

9
Marriage is distinctly and repeatedly excluded from heaven. Is this because it is thought likely to mar the general felicity?
> SAMUEL BUTLER, *Notebooks.*

10
Marriage, from love, like vinegar from wine—
A sad, sour, sober beverage—by time
Is sharpen'd from its high celestial flavour
Down to a very homely household savour.
> LORD BYRON, *Don Juan.*

11
Polygamy may well be held in dread,
Not only as a sin, but as a bore.
> LORD BYRON, *Don Juan.*

12
For talk six times with the same single lady,
And you may get the wedding dress ready.
> LORD BYRON, *Don Juan.*

13
Though women are angels, yet wedlock's the devil.
> LORD BYRON, *To Eliza.*

14
I shall marry in haste and repeat at leisure.
> JAMES BRANCH CABELL, *Jurgen,* ch. 38 (1919). A variation of the familiar "Marry in haste, repent at leisure." See also CONGREVE in this section.

15
Two dollars will buy all the happiness or all the misery in the world. At least that used to be the price of a marriage license.
> EDDIE CANTOR, *The Way I See It.*

16
I think people should finish school before marriage and acquire some direction in life. And I am all for retreat before weddings, nuptial masses, the replacement of Mendelssohn by Purcell, receptions with decent menus, and starting out without contraception. I am against double-ring ceremonies, twin beds, Schubert's *Ave Maria,* short bridal gowns, cheap champagne, looped bridegrooms, most receptions and weddings held in church for no Christian reason.
> FATHER ROBERT CAPON, *Bed and Board.*

17
The vow of fidelity is an absurd commitment, but it is the heart of marriage.
> FATHER ROBERT CAPON, *Bed and Board.*

18
There are but two objects in marriage, love or money. If you marry for love, you will certainly have some very happy days, and probably many uneasy ones; if you marry for money, you will have no happy days and probably no uneasy ones.
> LORD CHESTERFIELD, *Letters.* (To be delivered posthumously.)

19
The sane marriage is an untheatrical thing; it is therefore not surprising that most modern dramatists have devoted themselves to insane marriage.
> G. K. CHESTERTON, *George Bernard Shaw.*

20
Man and wife,
Coupled together for the sake of strife.
> CHARLES CHURCHILL (1731–1764), *The Rosciad.*

21
Oh! how many torments lie in the small circle of a wedding ring.
> COLLEY CIBBER, *The Double Gallant: or, The Sick Lady's Cure.* Act i, sc. 2.

1
There can be only one end to marriage without love, and that is love without marriage.
JOHN CHURTON COLLINS.

2
Marriage is a feast where the grace is sometimes better than the dinner.
CHARLES CALEB COLTON.

3
Thus grief still treads upon the heels of pleasure,
Marry'd in haste, we may repent at leisure.
WILLIAM CONGREVE, *The Old Bachelor.*

4
When singleness is bliss, it's folly to be wives.
BILL COUNSELMAN, *Ella Cinders.*

5
I've sometimes thought of marrying—and then I've thought again.
NOEL COWARD. (Ward Morehouse, *Dear Noel on Love and Marriage; Theatre Arts,* Nov., 1956.)

6
If a man stay away from his wife for seven years, the law presumes the separation to have killed him; yet, according to our daily experience, it might well prolong his life.
CHARLES JOHN DARLING, *Scintilae Juris.*

7
Wedlock indeed hath oft compared been
To public feasts, where meet a public rout;
Where they that are without would fain go in,
And they that are within would fain go out.
SIR JOHN DAVIES, *A Contention betwixt a Wife, a Widow, and a Maid.*

8
The wictim o' connubiality, as Blue Beard's domestic chaplain said, with a tear of pity, ven he buried him.
CHARLES DICKENS, *Pickwick Papers,* ch. 20.

9
Wen you're a married man, Samivel, you'll understand a good many things as you don't understand now; but vether it's worth while goin' through so much to learn so little, as the charity boy said ven he got to the end of the alphabet, is a matter o' taste.
CHARLES DICKENS, *Pickwick Papers,* ch. 27.

10
Never go to bed mad. Stay up and fight.
PHYLLIS DILLER, *Phyllis Diller's Housekeeping Hints.*

11
For a young man not yet; for an old man never at all.
DIOGENES, when asked the proper time to marry. (DIOGENES LAERTIUS, *Diogenes,* sec. 54.)

12
Every woman should marry—and no man.
BENJAMIN DISRAELI, *Lothair,* ch. 20.

13
The reason that husbands and wives do not understand each other is because they belong to different sexes.
DOROTHY DIX, *Syndicated Column.*

14
John Donne, Anne Donne, Un-done.
JOHN DONNE, *Letter* to his wife.

15
And sure all marriage in repentance ends.
JOHN DRYDEN, *Don Sebastian:* epilogue.

16
Falsely your Church seven sacraments does frame:
Penance and Matrimony are the same.
RICHARD DUKE, *To a Roman Catholic Friend Upon Marriage.*

17
Marriage must be a relation either of sympathy or of conquest.
GEORGE ELIOT, *Romola.* Bk. iii, ch. 48.

18
Is not marriage an open question, when it is alleged, from the beginning of the world, that such as are in the institution wish to get out; and such as are out wish to get in.
RALPH WALDO EMERSON, *Representative Men: Montaigne.* See also DAVIES in this section.

19
It is one of the boldest actions of a man's life to marry. Whoever passes that Rubicon has need of the fortune of Caesar to make him happy.
SIR GEORGE ETHEREGE. (JOHN HAROLD WILSON, *The Wits of the Restoration.*)

20
He who gets a dowry with his wife, sells himself for it.
EURIPIDES, *Phaeton: Fragment.*

21
All marriages are happy. It's the living together afterward that causes all the trouble.
Farmer's Almanac, 1966.

22
When the blind lead the blind, no wonder they both fall into—matrimony.
GEORGE FARQUHAR, *Love and a Bottle.* Act v, sc. 1.

23
His designs were strictly honorable, as the phrase is; that is, to rob a lady of her fortune by way of marriage.
HENRY FIELDING, *Tom Jones.* Bk. xi, ch. 4.

24
One fool in at least every married couple.
HENRY FIELDING, *Amelia.* Bk. ix, ch. 4.

1
A good husband should be deaf and a good wife blind.
> FRENCH PROVERB. See also MONTAIGNE in this section.

2
When the husband is fire and the wife tow, the devil easily sets all in a flame.
> THOMAS FULLER, *Gnomologia*, No. 5594.

3
Be not hasty to marry; it's better to have one plough going than two cradles; and more profit to have a barn filled than a bed.
> THOMAS FULLER, *Introductio ad Prudentiam*.

4
A man in love is incomplete until he has married. Then he's finished.
> ZSA ZSA GABOR, quoted in *Newsweek*, Mar. 28, 1960.

5
Women marry because they don't want to work.
> MARY GARDEN, *Newspaper Interview*.

6
The old man who is married bids death to the feast.
> OLD GERMAN PROVERB.

7
My wife and I made a bargain many years ago that in order to live harmoniously, I would decide all the major problems and she would decide all the unimportant problems. So far, in our twenty-five years of matrimony, we have never had any major problems.
> JUDGE JONAH GOLDSTEIN, quoted by JOEY ADAMS in *Cindy and I*, ch. 3.

8
At Ft. Vancouver on the West Coast in 1854 no works or projects challenged him. He was homesick, carried in his inside pocket a worn pack of letters from his wife. Grant had married her without a regular proposal; they were buggy-driving across a flooded bridge when she cried, "I'm going to cling to you no matter what happens," and safely over, he asked, "How would you like to cling to me for the rest of your life?"
> CARL SANDBURG, *Abraham Lincoln: The Prairie Years and the War Years*, ch. 24. Referring to Ulysses S. Grant.

9
How To Be Happy Though Married.
> REV. E. J. HARDY, *Title* of book (1910).

10
Residents of the East like to point out that people in the West fall in love and then get married, whereas Orientals get married and then fall in love. The Eastern order of things seems to have worked better than most Westerners realize.
> ERNEST HAVEMANN, *Men, Women, and Marriage*, p. 189.

11
Married folk frequently raise their voices, unfortunately.
> LILLIAN HELLMAN, *The Little Foxes*, Act 2.

12
Bond: There are two kinds. The United States bonds and Cupid's bonds of the united state.
> OLIVER HERFORD, *Cupid's Cyclopedia*.

13
Girls engaged write Sonnets from the Portuguese—married women never.
> ELBERT HUBBARD, *The Philistine*, vol. 5.

14
Keepin' a marriage a secret must be a good deal like hidin' a bass drum.
> FRANK McKINNEY (KIN) HUBBARD, *Abe Martin's Primer*.

15
There'll allus be somethin' funny about a weddin' write-up no matter how seriously it's written.
> FRANK McKINNEY (KIN) HUBBARD, *Abe Martin's Primer*.

16
Th' ole time father who used t' go home at noon an' eat a hearty dinner now has a married son who refuses t' take any chances.
> FRANK McKINNEY (KIN) HUBBARD, *Abe Martin's Primer*.

17
Marriage is a mistake every man should make.
> GEORGE JESSEL, quoted in *Treadmill to Oblivion* by FRED ALLEN.

18
Alas! Another instance of the triumph of hope over experience.
> SAMUEL JOHNSON, referring to the second marriage of a friend who had been unhappy with his first wife. BOSWELL's *Life*, 1770.

19
Marriage is the best state for man in general; and every man is a worse man, in proportion as he is unfit for the married state.
> SAMUEL JOHNSON, BOSWELL's *Life*, Mar. 22, 1776.

20
It is commonly a weak man who marries for love.
> SAMUEL JOHNSON, BOSWELL's *Life*, Mar. 28, 1776.

21
Sir, it is a very foolish resolution to resolve not to marry a pretty woman. Beauty is of

itself very estimable. No, Sir, I would prefer a pretty woman, unless there are objections to her. A pretty woman may be foolish; a pretty woman may be wicked; a pretty woman may not like me. But there is no such danger in marrying a pretty woman as is apprehended; she will not be persecuted if she does not invite persecution. A pretty woman, if she has a mind to be wicked, can find a readier way than another and that is all.

SAMUEL JOHNSON, BOSWELL's *Life,* June 5, 1781.

1
The world must be peopled by marriage or peopled without it.

SAMUEL JOHNSON, *Rasselas,* ch. 28.

2
At length he stretches out his foolish head to the conjugal halter.

JUVENAL, *Satires.*

3
I was never married less than five years to anybody, which proves that there was nothing trivial or temporary about my love affairs.

ALEXANDER KING, *Mine Enemy Grows Older.*

4
If he proposes marriage to you, it is wisest to accept him immediately, but grant him no undue concessions on the strength of this commitment.

ALEXANDER KING, *Rich Man, Poor Man, Freud and Fruit,* ch. 2.

5
Today, he admits, he gave his sons just one piece of advice. "Never confuse," he told them, "I love you," with "I want to marry you."

CLEVELAND AMORY, *The Last Resorts.* Quoting LE ROY KING.

6
For of all wise words of tongue or pen
The wisest are these: "Leave pants to men."

SAMUEL E. KISER, *Maud Muller A-Wheel.*

7
Marriage is a lottery, but you can't tear up your ticket if you lose.

F. M. KNOWLES, *A Cheerful Year Book.*

8
Matrimony is something that the bachelor misses and the widower escapes.

F. M. KNOWLES, *A Cheerful Year Book.*

9
I lost a good secretary and found a lousy cook.

FIORELLO H. LA GUARDIA. The reference is to Mrs. La Guardia, who had been his secretary. (JOEY ADAMS, *Cindy and I,* ch. 6.)

10
Nothing is more distasteful to me than that entire complacency and satisfaction which beam in the countenances of a new-married couple.

CHARLES LAMB, *Essays of Elia: The Behaviour of Married People.*

11
Many a man in love with a dimple makes the mistake of marrying the whole girl.

STEPHEN LEACOCK.

12
"Ma," I said, "I just got married." "That's nice," she said. "Did you practice the piano today?"

OSCAR LEVANT, *Memoirs of an Amnesiac.*

13
Marriage is a triumph of habit over hate.

OSCAR LEVANT, *Memoirs of an Amnesiac.*

14
I have now come to the conclusion never again to think of marrying, and for this reason: I can never be satisfied with anyone who would be blockhead enough to have me.

ABRAHAM LINCOLN, *Letter* to Mrs. Browning, Apr. 1, 1838, after he was rejected by Mary Owens.

15
We might knit that knot with our tongues, that we shall never undo with our teeth.

JOHN LYLY, *Euphues.*

16
When an American heiress wants to buy a man, she at once crosses the Atlantic.

MARY MCCARTHY, *On the Contrary.*

17
The Japanese have a word for it. It's judo —the art of conquering by yielding. The Western equivalent of judo is "Yes, dear."

J. P. MCEVOY, *Charlie Would Have Loved This.*

18
Marry a mountain woman and you marry the mountain.

SEUMAS MACMANUS, *Heavy Hangs the Golden Grain.*

19
A caress is better than a career.

ELISABETH MARBURY, *Interview.* Referring to careers for women.

20
Marriage . . . is a damnably serious business, particularly around Boston.

JOHN P. MARQUAND, *The Late George Apley,* ch. 2.

21
I have been called a monster. But I am not. No bigamist is. Nor yet a woman hater. The man who marries just once proves only his ignorance of women. The man who marries

many times proves, in spite of his disillusionments, his faith in women . . .
DON MARQUIS, *Reveries of a Bigamist.*

1
After a few years of marriage a man and his wife are apt to be, if nothing else, at least the sort of enemies who respect each other.
DON MARQUIS, *New York Herald.*

2
You wish to marry Priscus, Paula?
Very wise of you!
Priscus, though, declines, you tell me?
He's wise, too.
MARTIAL, *Epigrams.* From *Roman Culture,* ed. by GARRY WILLS.

3
You're so alike, you're matched for life:
A nitwit man, his nitwit wife.
(I wonder then why it should be
That such a pair cannot agree?)
MARTIAL, *Epigrams.* From *Roman Culture,* ed. by GARRY WILLS.

4
A man marries to have a home, but also because he doesn't want to be bothered with sex and all that sort of thing.
W. SOMERSET MAUGHAM, *The Circle.*

5
Marriage, to tell the truth, is an evil, but a necessary evil.
MENANDER.

6
Who are happy in marriage? Those with so little imagination that they cannot picture a better state, and those so shrewd that they prefer quiet slavery to a hopeless rebellion.
H. L. MENCKEN, *Prejudices,* ser. 2.

7
Marriage, as everyone knows, is chiefly an economic matter. But too often it is assumed that its economy concerns only the wife's hats; it also concerns, and perhaps more importantly, the husband's cigars. No man is genuinely happy, married, who has to drink worse whiskey than he used to drink when he was single.
H. L. MENCKEN, *Prejudices,* ser. 4.

8
I see no mariages faile or more troubled than such as are concluded for beauties sake, and hudled up for amorous desires . . .
MICHEL DE MONTAIGNE, *Essays,* tr. by JOHN FLORIO.

9
A good marriage would be between a blind wife and a deaf husband.
MICHEL DE MONTAIGNE. See also TAVERNER and TORRIANO in this section.

10
In Texas when a girl marries well, the well is usually oil.
JAN MURRAY, quoted by JOEY ADAMS in *Cindy and I,* ch. 4.

11
I generally had to give in.
NAPOLEON BONAPARTE, speaking of his relation with the Empress Josephine, on St. Helena, May 19, 1816.

12
Marriage—A book of which the first chapter is written in poetry and the remaining chapters in prose.
BEVERLEY NICHOLS.

13
Marriage is a meal where the soup is better than the dessert.
AUSTIN O'MALLEY.

14
Any woman will marry any man that bothers her enough.
HENRY WALLACE PHILLIPS, *Mr. Scroggs.*

15
Marriage is a good deal like taking a bath—not so hot once you get accustomed to it.
More Playboy's Party Jokes (1965).

16
Our Unabashed Dictionary defines:
Shotgun wedding as a case of wife or death.
More Playboy's Party Jokes (1965).

17
Our Unabashed Dictionary defines:
Vicious circle as a wedding ring.
More Playboy's Party Jokes (1965).

18
Marriage starts with billing and cooing, but only the billing lasts.
More Playboy's Party Jokes (1965).

19
They dream in courtship, but in wedlock wake.
ALEXANDER POPE, *The Wife of Bath.*

20
Don't.
PUNCH, *Advice* to those about to marry.

21
Marry in Lent, live to repent.
JOHN RAY, *English Proverbs.*

22
The more times a man has been married the less faith he has in the male judgment.
Reflections of a Bachelor.

23
A reasonable man can get out of most any trouble, except marriage, without going to law.
Reflections of a Bachelor.

24
A married man no sooner gets out of his

trouble by becoming a widower than he wants to go and do it all over again.
Reflections of a Bachelor.

1
It's easier most always to marry the person you love than to love the person you marry.
Reflections of a Bachelor.

2
The only cheap thing about getting married is the price of the marriage license.
Reflections of a Bachelor.

3
Some vinegar is spilled into the sweetest marriage honey.
Reflections of a Bachelor.

4
Getting engaged is like running to a fire; after they are married they walk back.
Reflections of a Bachelor.

5
When a girl proposes to a man she isn't any more comfortable about it than a man is when he does.
Reflections of a Bachelor.

6
The man who marries for money may lack sentiment, but he has a large stock of horse sense.
Reflections of a Bachelor.

7
Marriage is a lottery in which men stake their liberty and women their happiness.
MADAME DE RIEUX, *Epigram.*

8
Marriage is the Keeley cure for love's intoxication.
HELEN ROWLAND, *Love Letters of a Cynic.*
Referring to a treatment for alcoholism.

9
But who ever heard of marriage deterred
Or even deferred
By any contrivance so very absurd
As scolding the boy, and caging his bird?
JOHN GODFREY SAXE, *Pyramus and Thisbe.*

10
I have wedded her, not bedded her, and sworn to make the "not" eternal.
WILLIAM SHAKESPEARE, *All's Well That Ends Well.* Act iii, sc. 2.

11
Men are April when they woo, December when they wed: Maids are May when they are maids, but the sky changes when they are wives.
WILLIAM SHAKESPEARE, *As You Like It.* Act iv, sc. 1.

12
What God hath joined together no man shall ever put asunder: God will take care of that.
BERNARD SHAW, *Getting Married.*

13
Marriage is popular because it combines the maximum of temptation with the maximum of opportunity.
BERNARD SHAW, *Maxims for Revolutionists.*

14
It is most unwise for people in love to marry.
BERNARD SHAW, quoted in *Days with Bernard Shaw* by STEPHEN WINSTEN.

15
It resembles a pair of shears, so joined that they cannot be separated, often moving in opposite directions, yet always punishing anyone who comes between them.
SYDNEY SMITH.

16
By all means marry; if you get a good wife, you'll become happy; if you get a bad one, you'll become a philosopher.
SOCRATES.

17
Marriage: a ceremony in which rings are put on the finger of the lady and through the nose of the gentleman.
HERBERT SPENCER.

18
One is almost tempted to hint that it does not much matter whom you marry; that, in fact, marriage is a subjective affection, and if you have made up your mind to it, and once talked yourself fairly over, you could "pull it through" with anybody.
ROBERT LOUIS STEVENSON, *Virginibus Puerisque.*

19
In marriage, a man becomes slack and selfish, and undergoes a fatty degeneration of his moral being.
ROBERT LOUIS STEVENSON, *Virginibus Puerisque.*

20
A certain sort of talent is almost indispensable for people who would spend years together and not bore themselves to death.
ROBERT LOUIS STEVENSON, *Virginibus Puerisque.*

21
Marriage is terrifying, but so is a cold and forlorn old age.
ROBERT LOUIS STEVENSON, *Virginibus Puerisque.*

22
No woman should marry a teetotaler or a man who does not smoke.
ROBERT LOUIS STEVENSON, *Virginibus Puerisque.*

23
Marriage is a step so grave and decisive that

it attracts light-headed men by its very awfulness.
ROBERT LOUIS STEVENSON, *Virginibus Puerisque.*

1
Marriage is like life in this—that it is a field of battle, and not a bed of roses.
ROBERT LOUIS STEVENSON, *Virginibus Puerisque.*

2
Marriage is one long conversation, chequered by disputes.
ROBERT LOUIS STEVENSON, *Memories and Portraits.*

3
Some pray to marry the man they love,
My prayer will somewhat vary;
I humbly pray to heaven above
That I love the man I marry.
ROSE PASTOR STOKES, *My Prayer.*

4
The reason why so few marriages are happy is because young ladies spend their time in making nets, not in making cages.
JONATHAN SWIFT, *Thoughts on Various Subjects.*

5
I must caution you particularly against my lord's eldest son; if you are dextrous enough it is odds that you may draw him in to marry you, and make you a lady; if he is a common rake, or a fool, (and he must be one or the other) but, if the former, avoid him like Satan, for he stands in less awe of a mother, than my lord doth of a wife; and, after ten thousand promises, you will get nothing from him, but a big belly, or a clap, and probably both together.
JONATHAN SWIFT, *Directions to Servants: Directions to the Waiting-Maid.*

6
Wedded persons may thus pass over their lives quietly . . . if the husband becomes deaf and the wife blind.
RICHARD TAVERNER, *Garden of Wisdom.* See also MONTAIGNE in this section.

7
Better to sit up all night than to go to bed with a dragon.
JEREMY TAYLOR, *Holy Living.*

8
Some fellows marry poor girls to settle down and others rich ones to settle up.
The Pun Book by T. B. and T. C. (1906).

9
Remember, it is as easy to marry a rich woman as a poor woman.
WILLIAM MAKEPEACE THACKERAY, *Pendennis.* Bk. i, ch. 28.

10
A ring on the finger is worth two on the phone.
HAROLD THOMPSON, *Body, Books and Britches.*

11
American girls often marry someone they can't stand to spite someone they can.
JAMES THURBER, *Credos and Curios.*

12
A husband must be deaf, and a wife blind, to have quietness.
TORRIANO, *Piazza Universale: Wife.* See also MONTAIGNE and TAVERNER in this section.

13
A girl can't analyze marriage, and a woman —daren't.
LADY TROUBRIDGE, *The Millionaire.*

14
Monday for wealth, Tuesday for health,
Wednesday the best day of all:
Thursday for crosses, Friday for losses,
Saturday no luck at all.
UNKNOWN, in HALLIWELL, *Nursery Rhymes.*

15
In every marriage two things are allowed,
A wife in wedding-sheets and in a shroud;
How can a marriage state then be accurst,
Since the last day's as happy as the first?
UNKNOWN, *Agreeable Companion*, 44 (1745).

16
A rich man's wooing is seldom long of doing.
UNKNOWN, Scotch saying, quoted in *Marriage in Epigrams* by FREDERICK W. MORTON.

17
If you want peace in the home, do what your wife wants.
UNKNOWN, an African proverb.

18
I never married, and I wish my father never had.
UNKNOWN, *Epigram.* From *Greek Anthology.* Bk. vii, No. 309.

19
As she is going to be married next month, she is very busy getting her torso ready.
LOUIS UNTERMEYER, *A Treasury of Laughter.* Quoted as a student boner.

20
Nowadays marriage like everything else is strictly business, and business is pressure.
PETER USTINOV, *Romanoff and Juliet*, Act 2.

21
What cloying meat is love, when matrimony's the sauce to it!
SIR JOHN VANBRUGH, *The Provoked Wife*, Act 1.

1
Marriage is the only adventure open to the cowardly.
VOLTAIRE, *Pensées d'un Philosophe.*

2
He is dreadfully married. He's the most married man I ever saw in my life.
ARTEMUS WARD, *A Morman Romance.*

3
If you mean gettin' hitched, I'm in!
ARTEMUS WARD, *Artemus Ward, His Book: The Showman's Courtship.*

4
Alas, she married another. They frequently do. I hope she is happy—because I am.
ARTEMUS WARD, *Lecture.*

5
Twenty years of romance make a woman look like a ruin; but twenty years of marriage make her something like a public building.
OSCAR WILDE, *A Woman of No Importance,* Act 1.

6
Men marry because they are tired; women because they are curious. Both are disappointed.
OSCAR WILDE, *A Woman of No Importance,* Act 3.

7
The one charm of marriage is that it makes a life of deception absolutely necessary for both parties.
OSCAR WILDE, *The Picture of Dorian Gray.*

8
In married life three is company and two none.
OSCAR WILDE, *The Importance of Being Earnest,* Act 1.

9
The London season is entirely matrimonial; people are either hunting for husbands or hiding from them.
OSCAR WILDE.

10
Marriage is a status of antagonistic co-operation. In such a status, necessarily, centripetal and centrifugal forces are continuously at work, and the measure of its success obviously depends on the extent to which the centripetal forces are predominant.
FEDERAL JUDGE JOHN M. WOOLSEY, *Decision* rendered Apr. 6, 1931, in which he held that Marie Stopes's *Married Love* was not obscene.

11
To get married is to tie a knot with the tongue that you cannot undo with your teeth.
E. M. WRIGHT, *Rustic Speech.*

12
Marriage is rather a sign of interest than love; and he that marries a fortune covets a mistress, not loves her.
WILLIAM WYCHERLEY, *The Country Wife,* Act 2.

13
Married women show all their modesty the first day, because married men show all their love the first day.
WILLIAM WYCHERLEY, *The Country Wife,* Act 4.

14
Marrying to increase love is like gaming to become rich; alas! you only lose what little stock you had before.
WILLIAM WYCHERLEY, *The Country Wife,* Act 4.

15
She didn't think he was good enough for her, but she married him because she thought he was too good for any other woman.
DOUGLAS YATES, *Works.*

16
Some ladies are too beauteous to be wed,
For where's the man that's worthy of their bed?
EDWARD YOUNG, *Love of Fame,* Satire vi, l. 83.

MEDICINE

See also Doctors

17
A rule of thumb in the matter of medical advice is to take everything any doctor says with a grain of aspirin.
GOODMAN ACE, *The Fine Art of Hypochondria.*

18
If you're a hypochondriac, first class, you awaken each morning with the firm resolve not to worry; everything is going to turn out all wrong.
GOODMAN ACE, *The Fine Art of Hypochondria.*

19
An ounce of prevention is worth a pound of cure and costs more.
GEORGE ADE, *Fables.*

20
The remedy is worse than the disease.
FRANCIS BACON, *Essays: Of Seditions.*

21
I find the medicine worse than the malady.
BEAUMONT AND FLETCHER, *Love's Cure,* Act 3.

22
Medicine, the only profession that labours

incessantly to destroy the reason for its own existence.
> JOHN BRYCE, *Address,* at dinner for General Gorgas, Mar. 23, 1914.

1
"In my youth," said the sage, as he shook his gray locks,
"I kept all my limbs very supple
By the use of this ointment—one shilling the box—
    Allow me to sell you a couple."
> LEWIS CARROLL, *Alice in Wonderland,* ch. 5.

2
Every other day
    Take a drop in water,
You'll be better soon
    Or at least you oughter.
> GEORGE WASHINGTON DOANE, *Lines on Homeopathy.*

3
"I think," said Mr. Dooley, "that if the Christian Scientists had some science and the doctors more Christianity, it wouldn't make any difference which you called in—if you had a good nurse."
> FINLEY PETER DUNNE, *Christian Science and the Doctors.*

4
Dead flies cause the ointment of the apothecary to send forth a stinking savour.
> *Ecclesiastes,* X, 1.

5
For that tired, run-down feeling, try jay-walking.
> FARMER'S ALMANAC, 1966.

6
Mrs. X had bosom trouble,
    She was flat across the bow;
Then she took three bottles of Compound,
    Now they milk her like a cow!
Oh we sing, we sing, we sing
    Of Lydia Pinkham, Pinkham, Pinkham
And her love for the human race!
> Song, quoted in *The Life and Times of the Late Demon Rum* by J. C. FURNAS, 1965.

7
Some fell by laudanum, and some by steel,
And death in ambush lay in every pill.
> ROMAIN GARTH, *The Dispensary,* canto 4.

8
I firmly believe that if the whole *materia medica* could be sunk to the bottom of the sea, it would be all the better for mankind and all the worse for the fishes.
> OLIVER WENDELL HOLMES, *Lecture,* Harvard Medical School.

9
The worst about medicine is that one kind makes another necessary.
> ELBERT HUBBARD, *The Philistine,* vol. 27.

10
He gobbled pills like a famished chicken pecking up corn.
> DALE KRAMER, *Ross and the New Yorker.* On Harold Ross.

11
The cure is worse than the disease.
> PHILIP MASSINGER, *The Bondman.* Act i, sc. 1. See also BACON and BEAUMONT AND FLETCHER in this section.

12
If physic do not work, prepare for the kirk.
> JOHN RAY, *English Proverbs.*

13
It is all right to talk about practicing what you preach, but doctors prescribe lots of medicine that they don't have to take themselves.
> *Reflections of a Bachelor* (1903).

14
By medicine life may be prolonged, yet death
    Will seize the doctor too.
> WILLIAM SHAKESPEARE, *Cymbeline,* Act v, sc. 5.

15
A quack is as fit for a pimp, as a midwife for a bawd: they are still but in their way, both helpers of nature.
> WILLIAM WYCHERLEY, *The Country Wife,* Act 1.

MEEKNESS

See also Fear, Timidity

16
Don't make yourself a mouse or the cat will eat you.
> A. B. CHEALES, *Proverbial Folk-lore.*

17
Moses was a merciful, meek man, and yet with what fury did he run through the camp, and cut the throats of three-and-thirty thousand of his dear Israelites that were fallen into idolatry.
> DANIEL DEFOE, *The Shortest Way with the Dissenters.*

18
It's goin' t' be fun t' watch an' see how long th' meek kin keep th' earth after they inherit it.
> FRANK McKINNEY (KIN) HUBBARD, *Sayings.*

19
Turning the other cheek is a kind of moral jiu-jitsu.
> GERALD STANLEY LEE, *Crowds.* Bk. iv, ch. 9.

1
Pity the meek, for they shall inherit the earth.
  DON MARQUIS, *New York Sun.*

2
Let the meek inherit the earth—they have it coming to them.
  JAMES THURBER, quoted in *Life,* Mar. 14, 1960.

MEMORY

3
It's a poor sort of memory that only works backwards.
  LEWIS CARROLL (CHARLES LUTWIDGE DODGSON).

4
A good storyteller is a person who has a good memory and hopes other people haven't.
  IRVIN S. COBB.

5
A good memory is one trained to forget the trivial.
  CLIFTON FADIMAN, *The Selected Writings of Clifton Fadiman* (1955).

6
If knaves had not foolish memories, they would not trust one another as often as they do.
  LORD HALIFAX, *Works.*

7
You can close your eyes to reality but not to memories.
  STANISLAW J. LEC, *Unkempt Thoughts,* tr. from the Polish by JACEK GALASKA.

8
There is nothing like an odour to stir memories.
  WILLIAM McFEE, *The Market.*

9
A strong memory is commonly coupled with infirm judgment.
  MICHEL DE MONTAIGNE, *Essays.* Bk. i, ch. 9.

10
Women and elephants never forget an injury.
  HECTOR HUGH MUNRO (SAKI), *Reginald on Besetting Sins.* See also DOROTHY PARKER in this section.

11
A great memory does not make a philosopher, any more than a dictionary can be called a grammar.
  CARDINAL JOHN HENRY NEWMAN, *Knowledge in Relation to Culture.*

12
The advantage of a bad memory is that one enjoys several times the same good things for the first time.
  FRIEDRICH WILHELM NIETZSCHE, *Human, All Too Human,* vol. 1, tr. by HELEN ZIMMERN.

13
Prince, a precept I'd leave for you,
  Coined in Eden, existing yet;
Skirt the parlor, and shun the zoo—
  Women and elephants never forget.
  DOROTHY PARKER, *Ballade of Unfortunate Mammals.*

14
No memory is short enough ever to forget a fancied wrong.
  Reflections of a Bachelor (1903).

15
If a young man when leaving a company does not recollect where he laid his hat, it is nothing; but if the same forgetfulness is discovered in an old man, people will shrug up their shoulders and say his memory is going.
  BERNARD SHAW, quoted in *Days with Bernard Shaw* by STEPHEN WINSTEN.

16
The Right Honorable gentleman is indebted to his memory for his jests and to his imagination for his facts.
  RICHARD BRINSLEY SHERIDAN, *Speech* in reply to Mr. Dundas.

17
Illiterate him, I say, quite from your memory.
  RICHARD BRINSLEY SHERIDAN, *The Rivals.* Act i, sc. 2. Mrs. Malaprop speaking.

MIND

See also Intellectual, Thought

18
Sumner's mind had reached the calm of water which receives and reflects images without absorbing them; it contained nothing but itself.
  HENRY ADAMS, *The Education of Henry Adams.*

19
She was short on intellect but long on shape.
  GEORGE ADE.

20
I had a pleasant time with my mind, for it was happy.
  LOUISA M. ALCOTT, quoted in EDNAH D. CHENEY: *Louisa May Alcott, Her Life, Letters and Journals.*

21
Fat heads, lean brains.
  ANONYMOUS, Italian proverb.

22
My Lord St. Albans said that nature did

never put her precious jewels into a garret
four stories high, and therefore that exceeding tall men had very empty heads.
> FRANCIS BACON, *Apothegms*, No. 17.

1
Little minds that have nothing to confer
Find little to perceive.
> PHILIP JAMES BAILEY, *Festus*.

2
I'm not smart. I try to observe. Millions
saw the apple fall but Newton was the one
who asked why.
> BERNARD BARUCH, quoted by LEONARD
> LYONS, *New York Post*, June 24, 1965.

3
His [Lincoln's] mind works in the right
directions but seldom works clearly and
cleanly. His bread is of unbolted flour, and
much straw, too, mixes in the bran, and
sometimes gravel stones.
> HENRY WARD BEECHER, *Letter*, to Salmon
> Chase.

4
Some men are like pyramids, which are very
broad where they touch the ground, but
grow narrow as they reach the sky.
> HENRY WARD BEECHER, *Life Thoughts*.

5
His mind is open; yes, it is so open that
nothing is retained; ideas simply pass
through him.
> FRANCIS HERBERT BRADLEY.

6
His brains were only candle-grease, and
wasted down like tallow.
> ROBERT BUCHANAN, *City of the Saints*,
> pt. 1.

7
Such as take lodgings in a head
That's to be let, unfurnished.
> SAMUEL BUTLER, *Hudibras*, pt. 1.

8
The Modern Man's highly developed brain
has made him what he is and you know
what he is.
> WILL CUPPY, *How to Tell Your Friends
> from the Apes*.

9
His [Shaw's] brain is a half-inch layer of
champagne poured over a bucket of Methodist near-beer.
> BENJAMIN DE CASSERES, *Mencken and
> Shaw*.

10
Certain it is that minds, like bodies, will
often fall into a pimpled, ill-conditioned
state from mere excess of comfort.
> CHARLES DICKENS, *Barnaby Rudge*, ch. 7.

11
Little things affect little minds.
> BENJAMIN DISRAELI, *Sybil*. Bk. iii, ch. 2.

12
The brain is as strong as its weakest think.
> *Speaker's Sourcebook*, Ed. by ELEANOR
> DOAN.

13
If you want to change a woman's mind, agree
with her.
> *Speaker's Sourcebook*, Ed. by ELEANOR
> DOAN.

14
A mind without occupation is like a cat
without a ball of yarn.
> SAMUEL WILLOUGHBY DUFFIELD, *Eric, or,
> The Fall of a Crown*. Act i, sc. 1.

15
A liberal mind is a mind that is able to imagine itself believing anything.
> MAX EASTMAN, *Masses*, Sept., 1917.

16
Men are seldom in the right when they guess
at a woman's mind.
> SIR GEORGE ETHEREGE, *The Man of Mode*.

17
When Harry Lehr suffered a nervous breakdown she wrote to him that she wished
him to come down to Newport immediately.
"You know quite well, sweet lamb," she
wrote, "that you won't need any mind to go
with the people here."
> CLEVELAND AMORY, *The Last Resorts*.
> Reference to Mrs. Stuyvesant Fish.

18
Cultivate your brain, not your brayin'.
> B. C. FORBES, *Epigrams*.

19
An empty head leads to an empty pocket.
> B. C. FORBES, *Epigrams*.

20
It is better to understand little than to misunderstand a lot.
> ANATOLE FRANCE, *Revolt of the Angels*,
> ch. 1.

21
Both Minds and Fountain Pens will work
    when willed,
But Minds, like Fountain Pens, must first
    be Filled.
> ARTHUR GUITERMAN, *A Poet's Proverbs*.

22
The mind is like a sheet of white paper in
this, that the impressions it receives the
oftenest, and retains the longest, are black
ones.
> J. C. AND A. W. HARE, *Guesses at Truth*.

23
There is an unseemly exposure of the mind,
as well as of the body.
> WILLIAM HAZLITT, *Sketches and Essays:
> On Disagreeable People*.

24
The mind of man is like a clock that is al-

ways running down and requires to be as constantly wound up.
WILLIAM HAZLITT, *Sketches and Essays.*

1
Our brains are seventy-year clocks. The Angel of Life winds them up once for all, then closes the case, and gives the key into the hand of the Angel of the Resurrection.
OLIVER WENDELL HOLMES, *The Autocrat of the Breakfast-Table,* ch. 8.

2
Little minds are interested in the extraordinary; great minds in the commonplace.
ELBERT HUBBARD, *Epigrams.*

3
He was worse than provincial—he was parochial.
HENRY JAMES, on Thoreau.

4
To be bored by essentials is characteristic of small minds.
R. U. JOHNSON, *Poems of Fifty Years:* preface.

5
What is mind? No matter. What is matter? Never mind.
T. H. KEY.

6
Since he has for years practiced an open mind, it is now so well ventilated that very few notions of his own have remained.
ALEXANDER KING, *Rich Man, Poor Man, Freud and Fruit,* ch. 8.

7
Your absence of mind we have borne, till your presence of body came to be called in question by it.
CHARLES LAMB, *Last Essays of Elia.*

8
When a girl says she can't make up her mind, it shows they's nothing to make up.
RING LARDNER, *The Big Town: Shut Up, He Explained.*

9
We must view with profound respect the infinite capacity of the human mind to resist the introduction of useful knowledge.
THOMAS R. LOUNSBURY. (LOCKWOOD, *The Freshman and His College.*)

10
Most brains reflect but the crown of a hat.
JAMES RUSSELL LOWELL, *A Fable for Critics.*

11
The defect in his brain was just absence of mind.
JAMES RUSSELL LOWELL, *A Fable for Critics.*

12
A friend argued that a certain Broadway producer "must have a head" to be so successful. "They put better heads on umbrellas," said Mizner.
ALVA JOHNSTON, *Legend of a Sport; The New Yorker.* Referring to Wilson Mizner.

13
At a certain age some people's minds close up; they live on their intellectual fat.
WILLIAM LYON PHELPS.

14
What is Matter?—Never mind.
What is Mind?—No matter.
Punch, Vol. xxix, p. 19 (1855). See also KEY in this section.

15
Lincoln heard from Alexander Stephens when they were in congress, and may have retailed the incident of an undersized lawyer in an acrimonious stump debate with the massive Robert Toombs. Toombs called out, "Why, I could button your ears back and swallow you whole." The little fellow retorted, "And if you did, you would have more brains in your stomach than you have in your head."
CARL SANDBURG, *Abraham Lincoln: The Prairie Years and the War Years,* ch. 50.

16
Not Hercules
Could have knocked out his brains, for he had none.
WILLIAM SHAKESPEARE, *Cymbeline.* Act iv, sc. 2.

17
An improper mind is a perpetual feast.
LOGAN PEARSALL SMITH, *Afterthoughts.*

18
Not body enough to cover his mind decently with; his intellect is improperly exposed.
SYDNEY SMITH, quoted in LADY HOLLAND, *Memoir (1st ed.* 1855). Vol. i, ch. 9, p. 258.

19
The clothing of our minds certainly ought to be regarded before that of our bodies.
SIR RICHARD STEELE, *The Spectator,* No. 75.

20
Instinct is intelligence incapable of self-consciousness.
JOHN STERLING, *Essays and Tales.*

21
A man's body and his mind, with the utmost reverence to both, I speak it, are exactly like a jerkin and a jerkin's lining;—rumple the one,—you rumple the other.
LAURENCE STERNE, *Tristram Shandy,* bk. 3.

1
The mind that becomes soiled in youth can never again be washed clean.
MARK TWAIN, *Letter,* 1905.

2
Great minds discuss ideas, average minds discuss events, small minds discuss people.
UNKNOWN, *Minds.*

3
The mind that is unfed is also unstored.
E. P. WHIPPLE, *Success and Its Conditions.*

4
He has a bungalow mind.
WOODROW WILSON, speaking of President Harding. Quoted in THOMPSON, *Presidents I've Known,* p. 334.

MIRACLE

5
Miracles are laughed at by a nation that reads thirty million newspapers a day and supports Wall Street.
FINLEY PETER DUNNE, *Mr. Dooley Remembers.*

6
Miracles are the swaddling clothes of infant churches.
THOMAS FULLER, *Church History,* vol. 2.

7
A Miracle: An event told by those to whom it was told by men who did not see it.
ELBERT HUBBARD, *Epigrams.*

8
It would have approached nearer to the idea of miracle if Jonah had swallowed the whale.
THOMAS PAINE.

9
There has never been a miracle that noticeably resembled a fact.
MARK TWAIN, *Letters from the Earth.*

10
By order of the King: "It is forbidden for God to work miracles here." (De par de roi: Defense à Dieu De faire des miracles en ce lieu.)
UNKNOWN, *Epigram,* written by a wit on gates of St. Médard when closed by Louis XV, because of reputed miracles worked by relics of La Diacre Paris.

11
The wonder would be if the water did not fall.
OSCAR WILDE, *Comment* on observing Niagara Falls. (HESKETH PEARSON, *Lives of the Wits.*)

MIRROR

12
What your glass tells you will not be told by counsel.
GEORGE HERBERT, *Jacula Prudentum.*

13
The best mirror is an old friend.
GEORGE HERBERT, *Jacula Prudentum.*

14
You, lady, certainly don't dye your hair to deceive others or even yourself. You only deceive—and ever so little at that—your own image in the glass.
LUIGI PIRANDELLO, *The Emperor,* Act 1. English version by ERIC BENTLEY.

15
Venus, take my votive glass;
  Since I am not what I was,
What from this day I shall be,
  Venus, let me never see.
MATTHEW PRIOR, *The Lady who Offers her Looking-Glass to Venus.*

16
If you wish to avoid seeing a fool you must first break your mirror.
FRANÇOIS RABELAIS.

17
The mirror had taught me what I had always known: I was horribly natural. I have never got over that.
JEAN-PAUL SARTRE, *The Words.*

18
There was never yet fair woman but she made mouths in a glass.
WILLIAM SHAKESPEARE, *King Lear.* Act iii, sc. 2.

19
Mirrors reflect without speaking and women often speak without reflecting.
The Pun Book by T. B. and T. C.

20
The devil's behind the glass.
J. C. WALL, *Devils.*

MODERATION

21
Subdue your appetites, my dears, and you've conquered human natur'.
CHARLES DICKENS, *Nicholas Nickleby,* ch. 5.

22
A middle-of-the-roader is one who's apt to have trouble on the one hand and also on the other.
FRANKLIN P. JONES, *The Saturday Evening Post.*

MODESTY

See also Humility

23
Modesty is a relative virtue; there is the modesty of the woman of twenty, the woman of thirty, the woman of forty-five.
HONORÉ DE BALZAC, *Petty Troubles of Married Life.*

1
Modesty . . . is a prime virtue when nobody is looking.
JIM BISHOP, *Some of My Very Best: The Love Story That Cannot Be.*

2
Modesty is the only sure bait when you angle for praise.
LORD CHESTERFIELD, *Letters to His Son,* May 17, 1750.

3
Hide not your talents, they for use were made.
What's a Sun-Dial in the Shade?
BENJAMIN FRANKLIN, *Poor Richard,* 1750.

4
An impudent fellow may counterfeit modesty; but I'll be hanged if a modest man can ever counterfeit impudence.
OLIVER GOLDSMITH, *She Stoops to Conquer,* Act 2.

5
You may praise, you may flatter, I. Cobb as you will
But the band of his derby will fit round him still
JULIAN STREET.

6
Modesty antedates clothes and will be resumed when clothes are no more.
MARK TWAIN, *Following the Equator.*

7
The granddaughter of the girl who wouldn't show her instep now shows her step-ins.
ALICE VAN RENSSELAER, on why flirting is extinct. Quoted in *The Last Resorts* by CLEVELAND AMORY.

MONEY

See also Finance, Wealth

8
What this country needs is a good five-cent nickel.
FRANKLIN P. ADAMS, *The Sun Dial,* 1932.

9
Never pretend to have money except when you are in straits. The poor man who pretends to have a bank account betters his credit and takes no risk. But the prosperous individual who counts his money in the street, forthwith will be invited to attend a charity bazaar.
GEORGE ADE, *The Fable of the Old Fox and the Young Fox.*

10
Money is round. It rolls away.
SHOLOM ALEICHEM, *The Enchanted Tailor.*

11
Money talks, and it is the only conversation worth hearing when times are bad.
FRED ALLEN, *Much Ado About Me.*

12
A man who is paid in the dark can't make light of his salary.
FRED ALLEN, *Treadmill to Oblivion.*

13
Next time the government announces that personal income is at an all-time high, do a little figuring and you'll discover that so is personal outgo.
ROGER ALLEN, *Grand Rapids Press.*

14
If you want to know what God thinks of money, look at the people he gives it to.
ANONYMOUS, New England saying.

15
To bring owls to Athens.
ARISTOPHANES, *Aves,* 1. The Athenian coins were stamped with an owl. Equivalent to bringing coals to New Castle.

16
What *Babbitt* did for the American businessman, *Arrowsmith* did for the American doctor. The main theme of both novels is that money does not pay.
RICHARD ARMOUR, *American Lit Relit.*

17
Money is like muck, not good except it be spread.
FRANCIS BACON, *Essays: Of Seditions.*

18
A tip is a small sum of money you give to somebody because you're afraid he won't like not being paid for something you haven't asked him to do.
The Baile, Glasgow, c. 1913.

19
I'm tired of love; I'm still more tired of rhyme;
But money gives me pleasure all the time.
HILAIRE BELLOC, *Fatigued.*

20
Live within your income, even if you have to borrow money to do so.
JOSH BILLINGS.

21
Money is honey, my little sonny,
And a rich man's joke is always funny.
T. E. BROWN, *The Doctor.*

22
There is no fortress so strong that money cannot take it.
MARCUS TULLIUS CICERO, *In Verrem.*

23
Money is so unlike every other article that I believe a man has neither a legal or a moral right to take all that he can get.
PETER COOPER, quoted by A. J. CUMMINGS, U.S. Attorney General, in a letter to Samuel Gompers, read at A.F.L. convention, Philadelphia, Dec., 1892.

1
Money, Paul, can do anything.
  CHARLES DICKENS, *Dombey and Son*, ch.
    8.

2
The reason you have no money is because
you don't love it for itself alone. Money
won't ever surrender to such a flirt.
  FINLEY PETER DUNNE, *Mr. Dooley Remembers.*

3
A feast is made for laughter, and wine
maketh merry: but money answereth all
things.
  Ecclesiastes, X, 19.

4
You know a dollar would go much farther in
those days.
  WILLIAM M. EVARTS, *Remark* to Lord
    Coleridge, at Mount Vernon. This was
    in response to the latter's observation
    that he had heard that Washington was
    able to throw a dollar across the Poto-
    mac. (LUCY, *Diary of Two Parlia-
    ments.*) Later, Evarts was quoted thus:
    "But I met a journalist just afterwards
    who said, 'Oh, Mr. Evarts, you should
    have said that it was a small matter to
    throw a dollar across the Potomac for
    a man who had chucked a Sovereign
    across the Atlantic.' " (*Collections and
    Recollections*, p. 181.)

5
Money is the sinews of love, as of war.
  GEORGE FARQUHAR, *Love and a Bottle.*

6
As James T. Hill used to say: "There'll be
no pockets in your shroud."
  B. C. FORBES, *Epigrams.*

7
There's more lying about money than about
any other one thing in the world. Money
isn't half the curse it's often painted—nor
half the blessing. It all depends on who
owns it.
  B. C. FORBES, *Epigrams.*

8
Money is like honey: a little of it is sweet,
but a superabundance cloys.
  B. C. FORBES, *Epigrams.*

9
Money is like an arm or a leg—use it or
lose it.
  HENRY FORD, *Interview, The New York
    Times*, Nov. 8, 1931.

10
Never ask of money spent
Where the spender thinks it went.
Nobody was ever meant
To remember or invent

What he did with every cent.
  ROBERT FROST, *The Hardship of Accounting.*

11
People never discuss their salaries publicly,
or their income, or their patrimony. People
make a successful effort never to discuss
money in front of friends or relatives, because money in our society is the ultimate
reality and to discuss it is to reveal oneself.
  HARRY GOLDEN, *For 2¢ Plain.*

12
What I know about money, I learned the
hard way—by having had it.
  MARGARET HALSEY, *The Folks at Home.*

13
You Can't Take It with You.
  MOSS HART AND GEORGE S. KAUFMAN,
    Title of comedy (1937).

14
Here's to our town—a place where people
spend money they haven't earned to buy
things they don't need to impress people
they don't like.
  Toasts for All Occasions, ed. by LEWIS C.
    HENRY.

15
When a man says money can do anything,
that settles it; he hasn't any.
  E. W. HOWE.

16
M stands fer money, root of evil an' vice,
However, nothin' succeeds like havin' th'
    price.
  FRANK McKINNEY (KIN) HUBBARD, *Abe
    Martin's Primer.*

17
Nobody works as hard for his money as the
man who marries it.
  FRANK McKINNEY (KIN) HUBBARD.

18
Never spend your money before you have
it.
  THOMAS JEFFERSON, *Letter* to Thomas
    Jefferson Smith, Feb. 21, 1825.

19
There are few ways in which a man can be
more innocently employed than in getting
money.
  SAMUEL JOHNSON, Boswell's *Life.*

20
I'm Captain Jinks of the Horse Marines,
I often live beyond my means;
I sport young ladies in their teens,
  To cut a swell in the army.
  WILLIAM LINGARD, *Captain Jinks of the
    Horse Marines* (1869).

21
It is extraordinary how many emotional
storms one may weather in safety if one is
ballasted with ever so little gold.
  WILLIAM McFEE, *Casuals of the Sea.*

1

Money is like a sixth sense—and you can't make use of the other five without it.

W. SOMERSET MAUGHAM, in *The New York Times*, Oct. 18, 1958.

2

Money may not buy friends, but it certainly gives you a better class of enemies.

Metropolis (Ill.) *News.*

3

Money is like manure. If you spread it around, it does a lot of good. But if you pile it up in one place it stinks like hell.

CLINT MURCHISON, JR., Texas financier. Quoting his father's advice.

4

Men with money to burn have started many a girl playing with fire.

More Playboy's Party Jokes (1965).

5

Our Unabashed Dictionary defines *money* as the poor man's credit card.

More Playboy's Party Jokes (1965).

6

He was subject to a kind of disease which at that time they called lack of money.

FRANÇOIS RABELAIS.

7

Beauty is potent, but money is omnipotent.

JOHN RAY, *English Proverbs*, No. 122.

8

The way some people talk you might think a rich man couldn't be happy unless he made some happy poor man unhappy by giving him all his money.

Reflections of a Bachelor.

9

Money makes a man laugh.

JOHN SELDEN, *Table Talk.*

10

Chief Justice: Your means are very slender and your waste is great.

Falstaff: I would it were otherwise. I would my means were greater and my waist slenderer.

WILLIAM SHAKESPEARE, *Henry IV, Part 2.* Act i, sc. 2.

11

Cokane: Ah, my dear fellow, the love of money is the root of all evil.

Lickcheese: Yes, Sir; and we'd all like to have the tree growing in our garden.

BERNARD SHAW, *Widower's Houses*, Act 2.

12

Solvency is entirely a matter of temperament and not of income.

LOGAN PEARSALL SMITH, *Afterthoughts.*

13

I make good the old saying, we sailors get money like horses, and spend it like asses.

TOBIAS SMOLLETT, *Peregrine Pickle*, ch. 2.

14

Let all the learned say what they can,
'Tis ready money makes the man.

WILLIAM SOMERVILLE, *Ready Money.*

15

A fool may make money, but it needs a wise man to spend it.

CHARLES HADDON SPURGEON, *John Ploughman*, ch. 19.

16

Doant thou marry for munny, but goa wheer munny is!

ALFRED LORD TENNYSON, *Northern Farmer, New Style*, st. 5.

17

Remarking to old Mr. B.—the other day on the abundance of apples, "Yes," says he, "and fair as dollars too." That's the kind of beauty they see in apples.

HENRY D. THOREAU, *Journal*, Oct. 7, 1860.

18

Britain Friday withdrew the farthing from circulation as a coin of the realm because after 800 years it isn't worth a farthing any more.

UNITED PRESS INTERNATIONAL dispatch, *Chicago Sun-Times*, July 30, 1960.

19

The only thing that can console one for being poor is extravagance. The only thing that can console one for being rich is economy.

OSCAR WILDE, *Saturday Review*, Nov. 17, 1894.

20

. . . nothing more demoralizing than a small but adequate income.

EDMUND WILSON, *Memoirs of Hecate County.*

MORALITY

See also Chastity, Goodness, Virtue

21

Morality is a private and costly luxury.

HENRY ADAMS, *The Education of Henry Adams.*

22

A puritan is a person who pours righteous indignation into the wrong things.

GILBERT KEITH CHESTERTON, quoted in *The New York Times*, Nov. 21, 1936.

23

Men talk of "mere morality," which is much as if one should say "Poor God, with nobody to help him."

RALPH WALDO EMERSON, *Conduct of Life: Worship.*

1
A woman can look both moral and exciting
—if she also looks as if it was quite a struggle.
> EDNA FERBER, quoted in *Reader's Digest,*
> Dec., 1954.

2
More tears have been shed over men's lack
of manners than their lack of morals.
> HELEN HATHAWAY, *Manners for Men.*

3
Dr. Johnson's morality was as English an
article as a beefsteak.
> NATHANIEL HAWTHORNE, *Our Old Home.*

4
The crab, more than any of God's creatures,
has formulated the perfect philosophy of
life. Whenever he is confronted by a great
moral crisis in life, he first makes up his
mind what is right, and then goes sideways
as fast as he can.
> OLIVER HERFORD, quoted by FRANK
> CROWNINSHIELD, *A Wit with a Whim
> of Iron.*

5
Ain't chamberin' a worse sin than drunkenness? You think you can put a stop to
drunkenness by pullin' up all the grapes. I
suppose you can put a stop to chamberin'
by pulling up all the women!
> SIDNEY HOWARD, *They Knew What They
> Wanted.*

6
Be not too hasty . . . to trust or admire the
teachers of morality: they discourse like
angels, but they live like men.
> SAMUEL JOHNSON, *Rasselas.*

7
Whatever spiteful fools may say,
Each jealous, ranting yelper,
    No woman ever went astray
Without a man to help her.
> UNKNOWN, recited by ABRAHAM LINCOLN
> and quoted by CARL SANDBURG in *Abra-
> ham Lincoln: The Prairie Years and the
> War Years,* ch. 5.

8
Remember the end never really justifies the
meanness.
> *Longview* (Wash.) *News.* Quoted by *Read-
> er's Digest,* Sept., 1966.

9
We know of no spectacle so ridiculous as
the British public in one of its periodical
fits of morality.
> THOMAS BABINGTON MACAULAY, *Essays:
> Moore's Life of Lord Byron.*

10
The difference between a moral man and a
man of honor is that the latter regrets a

discreditable act even when it has worked.
> H. L. MENCKEN, *Prejudices,* ser. 4.

11
Dispatch from Reno: The rich leap from
the bed to the altar; the poor leap from the
altar to the bed.
> H. L. MENCKEN, *A Mencken Chresto-
> mathy.*

12
Corruption and golf is two things we might
just as well make up our minds to take up,
for they are both going to be with us.
> WILL ROGERS, *Autobiography.*

13
If you're going to pick and choose your ac-
quaintans on moral principles, you'd better
clear out of this country, unless you want
to cut yourself out of all decent society.
> BERNARD SHAW, *Mrs. Warren's Profes-
> sion,* Act 3.

14
Women may, as Napoleon once said, be the
occupation of the idle man, just as men are
the preoccupation of the idle woman; but
the mass of mankind is too busy and too
poor for the long and expensive sieges
which the professed libertine lays to virtue.
> BERNARD SHAW, *Overruled:* preface.

15
We are told by Moralists with the plainest
faces that immorality will spoil our looks.
> LOGAN PEARSALL SMITH, *Afterthoughts.*

16
Some men like to ponder over the moral
conclusions they have drawn from a fact,
but they are so unlucky as to be unable to
remember any figures or proper names. Men
like this are apt to be brought up short in
the midst of a lively discussion by some idiot
who knows a date.
> STENDHAL (MARIE HENRI BEYLE). *Mem-
> oirs of a Tourist,* tr. by ALLAN SEAGER.

17
Thus the Philadelphia of Fields' youth—a
city then, as now, of high moral indignation
and average morals.
> ROBERT LEWIS TAYLOR, *W. C. Fields.*

18
There are two kinds of Christian morals,
one private and the other public.
> MARK TWAIN, *Essays: Taxes and Morals.
> Address,* New York, Jan. 22, 1906.

19
Morals are an acquirement—like music, like
a foreign language, like piety, poker, paraly-
sis—no man is born with them.
> MARK TWAIN, *Essays: Seventieth Birth-
> day.*

20
Morals are of inestimable value, for every
man is born crammed with sin microbes,

and the only thing that can extirpate these sin microbes is morals. Now you take a sterilized Christian—I mean, you take *the* sterilized Christian, for there's only one. Dear sir, I wish you wouldn't look at me like that.
> MARK TWAIN, *Essays: Seventieth Birthday.*

1
Cats are loose in their morals, but not consciously so. Man, in his descent from the cat, has brought the cat's looseness with him but has left the unconsciousness behind—the saving grace which excuses the cat. The cat is innocent, man is not.
> MARK TWAIN, *Letters from the Earth.*

2
Since the Moral Sense has but the one office, the one capacity—to enable man to do wrong—it is plainly without value to him.
> MARK TWAIN, *Letters from the Earth.*

3
Moral indignation is jealousy with a halo.
> H. G. WELLS, *The Wife of Sir Isaac Harman.* Ch. ix, sec. 2.

4
Morality is simply the attitude we adopt towards people we personally dislike.
> OSCAR WILDE, *An Ideal Husband,* Act 2.

5
They were really prudish to the verge of indecency.
> CURTIS YORKE, *The World and Delia.*

MOTHER

6
A mother is not a dust rag.
> SHOLOM ALEICHEM, *Modern Children.*

7
It's a wise child that knows its own mother in a bathing suit.
> G. L. APPERSON, *English Proverbs and Proverbial Phrases.*

8
My wife is the kind of girl who'll not go anywhere without her mother, and her mother will go anywhere.
> JOHN BARRYMORE.

9
The mother's heart is the child's schoolroom.
> HENRY WARD BEECHER, *Proverbs from Plymouth Pulpit.*

10
Children love fat mothers, because while any mother is a diagram of *place,* a picture of *home* . . . a fat one is more *there.*
> FATHER ROBERT CAPON, *Bed and Board.*

11
The old-time mother who used to wonder where her boy was now has a grandson who wonders where his mother is.
> FRANK MCKINNEY (KIN) HUBBARD.

12
They're very age-conscious, those Kennedys. They don't want me around because I don't look enough like Whistler's mother.
> LADY LAWFORD, mother of Peter Lawford. (VICTOR LASKY, *J.F.K.: The Man and the Myth.*)

13
I did not throw myself into the struggle for life: I threw my mother into it.
> BERNARD SHAW, *The Irrational Knot:* preface.

14
All women become like their mothers. That is their tragedy. No man does. That's his.
> OSCAR WILDE, *The Importance of Being Earnest,* Act 1.

15
Motherhood is sacred in America. Even New Yorkers want their mothers to have every attention.
> REX YEAGER, quoted by GENE FOWLER in *Skyline,* ch. 2.

MOTHER-IN-LAW

16
When you bury a rich mother-in-law you can afford to spend a few extra *groschen.*
> SHOLOM ALEICHEM, *Eternal Life.*

17
Peter remained on friendly terms with Christ notwithstanding Christ's having healed his mother-in-law.
> SAMUEL BUTLER.

18
Behind every successful man stands a surprised mother-in-law.
> HUBERT HUMPHREY, *Speech* during the 1964 presidential campaign.

19
Give up all hope of peace so long as your mother-in-law is alive.
> JUVENAL, *Satires,* sat. 6.

MOUTH

See also Speech, Teeth

20
You love your automatic mouth;
  You love its giddy whirl;
You love its fluent flow;
  You love to wind your mouth up;
You love to hear it go!
> REPRESENTATIVE MARRIOT BROSIUS of Pennsylvania to Representative John A. Pickler of South Dakota.

21
To this nation I've made this bequest
  So spread the word North and South

Some folks leave their brains to science
But when I go I'm leaving my mouth.
   It's the greatest!
   CASSIUS CLAY. (LANGSTON HUGHES, *The Book of Negro Humor.*)

1
The opening in his face was too small for the size of his stomach.
   FREDERICK LAING, *The Giant's House.*

2
I know some o' you has berry brig mout, brigger dan oders; but then de brig mouts sometimes has de small bellies . . .
   HERMAN MELVILLE, *Moby Dick*, ch. 64.

3
If you keep your mouth shut, you will never put your foot in it.
   AUSTIN O'MALLEY.

MOVIES

See also Acting

4
Hollywood is a place where people from Iowa mistake each other for stars.
   FRED ALLEN, quoted in *No People Like Show People*, by MAURICE ZOLOTOW.

5
Hollywood is like Picasso's bathroom.
   CANDICE BERGEN, quoted by syndicated columnist SHEILAH GRAHAM. (*New York Post*, Feb. 14, 1967.)

6
American motion pictures are written by the half-educated for the half-witted.
   ST. JOHN ERVINE, quoted in *New York Mirror*, June 6, 1963.

7
Of course, since the natives are zombies, there were no rest rooms in the Hollywood restaurants. (They drink formaldehyde instead of coffee, and have no sex organs.) In Hollywood, you can always recognize the out-of-towners . . . they carry their chamber-pots with them.
   ARTHUR FELLIG (WEEGEE). *An Autobiography.*

8
He had a sort of copyright on the Bible.
   ROBERT FONTAINE, *That's a Good Question.* Reference to Cecil B. de Mille.

9
Hollywood is a place where your best friend will plunge a knife in your back and then call the police to tell them that you are carrying a concealed weapon.
   GEORGE FRAZIER, quoted by ART MOGER in *Some Of My Best Friends Are People.*

10
Too caustic? To hell with the cost; we'll make the picture anyway.
   SAMUEL GOLDWYN.

11
A wide screen just makes a bad film twice as bad.
   SAMUEL GOLDWYN. (*Quote,* Sept. 9, 1956.)

12
His footprints were never asked for, yet no one has ever filled his shoes.
   HEDDA HOPPER, *From Under My Hat.* Reference to D. W. Griffith, and the fact that he was not asked to contribute an impression of his footprints at Grauman's Chinese Theatre.

13
In Hollywood gratitude is Public Enemy Number One.
   HEDDA HOPPER, *From Under My Hat.*

14
If your lover returns from a stint in Hollywood, remember the pungent analysis given by a young poet of the state of mind that permeates the authors in the capital of filmdom. "The films take our best ideas," he said. "We work like slaves, inventing, devising, changing, to please the morons who run this game. We spend endless hours in search of novel ideas, and in the end, what do we get for it? . . . A lousy fortune!"
   ALEXANDER KING, *Rich Man, Poor Man, Freud and Fruit,* ch. 3.

15
Strip away the phony tinsel of Hollywood and you find the real tinsel underneath.
   OSCAR LEVANT.

16
Garbo, Greta—A deer, in the body of a woman, living resentfully in the Hollywood zoo.
   CLARE BOOTHE LUCE.

17
Hollywood is the town where inferior people have a way of making superior people feel inferior.
   DUDLEY FIELD MALONE.

18
It's a trip through a sewer in a glass-bottomed boat.
   WILSON MIZNER, referring to Hollywood. Quoted by ALVA JOHNSTON in *Legend of a Sport; The New Yorker.*

19
Hollywood impresses me as being ten million dollars' worth of intricate and ingenious machinery functioning elaborately to put skin on baloney.
   GEORGE JEAN NATHAN.

20
My interest in the cinema has lapsed since women began to talk.
   GEORGE JEAN NATHAN, *Letter* to James Agate.

1
Rare is the literary dog who leaves Hollywood without biting the hand that fed him.
Time.

2
What, when drunk, one sees in other women, one sees in Garbo sober.
KENNETH TYNAN, quoted in *The New York Times*, Jan. 9, 1966.

3
In some respects the film business is rather like that prehistoric animal the dinosaur, which apparently had two brains, one in its head and one in its rear.
LORD WILLIS, quoted in *The New York Times*, Feb. 13, 1966.

MULE, see Ass

MUSIC

See also Opera, Song

4
The music teacher came twice each week to bridge the awful gap between Dorothy and Chopin.
GEORGE ADE.

5
Beethoven can write music, thank God—but he can do nothing else on earth.
LUDWIG VAN BEETHOVEN, *Letter* to Ferdinand Reis.

6
He could fiddle all the bugs off a sweet-potato-vine.
STEPHEN VINCENT BENÉT, *The Mountain Whippoorwill.*

7
The fiddle: An instrument to tickle human ears by friction of a horse's tail on the entrails of a cat.
AMBROSE BIERCE, *The Devil's Dictionary.*

8
It's a pity to shoot the pianist when the piano is out of tune.
RENÉ COTY, President of French Republic, *Remark*, referring to confusion of French politics. (*Time,* Jan. 4, 1957.) See also WILDE in this section.

9
I think popular music in this country is one of the few things in the 20th century that have made giant strides in reverse.
BING CROSBY, *This Week Magazine.*

10
Music is the poor man's Parnassus.
RALPH WALDO EMERSON, *Letters and Social Aims.*

11
You make as good music as a wheelbarrow.
THOMAS FULLER, *Gnomologia,* No. 5938.

12
I know only two tunes; one of them is "Yankee Doodle," and the other isn't.
ULYSSES S. GRANT.

13
[Bernard Shaw] persisted in regarding the fortissimos of Paderewski, then just sensationally "arriving" in England, as brutal contests between the piano and the pianist to settle the question of survival of the fittest.
ARCHIBALD HENDERSON, *George Bernard Shaw: Man of the Century.*

14
Music helps not the toothache.
GEORGE HERBERT, *Jacula Prudentum.*

15
Miss Truman is a unique American phenomenon with a pleasant voice of little size and fair quality . . . There are few moments during her recital when one can relax and feel confident that she will make her goal, which is the end of the song.
PAUL HUME, music critic, *Washington Post.* On a concert by President Truman's daughter Margaret. Quoted in *Time,* Dec. 18, 1950. See also TRUMAN in section headed "Criticism."

16
Of all the noises I think music the least disagreeable.
SAMUEL JOHNSON.

17
Difficult—I wish it had been impossible.
SAMUEL JOHNSON, about a violinist who had exhibited his virtuosity.

18
Last year, more Americans went to symphonies than went to baseball games. This may be viewed as an alarming statistic, but I think that both baseball and the country will endure.
JOHN F. KENNEDY, *Remark* at White House youth concert, Aug. 6, 1962.

19
The conductor has the advantage of not seeing the audience.
ANDRE KOSTELANETZ.

20
When Frank Sinatra, Jr. was kidnapped, I said, "It must have been done by music critics."
OSCAR LEVANT, *Memoirs of an Amnesiac.*

21
At that time Lennie [Leonard Bernstein] was in an agitated embryonic state. His conducting had a masturbatory, oppressive and febrile zeal, even for the most tranquil passages. (Today he uses music as an accompaniment to his conducting.)
OSCAR LEVANT, *Memoirs of an Amnesiac.*

1
Leonard Bernstein has been disclosing musical secrets that have been well known for over four hundred years.
OSCAR LEVANT, *Memoirs of an Amnesiac.*

2
A materialist asks of a concert audience, "What are you crying about with your Wagner and your Brahms? It is only horsehair scraping on catgut."
SIR OLIVER LODGE, *Reason and Belief,* p. 78. See also BIERCE in this section.

3
I never use a score when conducting my orchestra . . . Does a lion tamer enter a cage with a book on how to tame a lion?
DIMITRI MITROPOULOS, *News Reports,* Feb. 19, 1956.

4
When a musician can no longer count up to three, he becomes "dramatic," he becomes "Wagnerian."
FRIEDRICH WILHELM NIETZSCHE, *The Case of Wagner,* tr. by A. M. LUDOVICI.

5
Epitaph for the tombstone of a cool musician: "Man, this cat is really gone."
More Playboy's Party Jokes (1965).

6
Composition is notation of distortion of what composers think they've heard before. Masterpieces are marvelous misquotations.
NED ROREM, *Paris Diary.*

7
Wagner is a composer who has beautiful moments but awful quarter hours.
GIOACCHINO ANTONIO ROSSINI.

8
Don't tell Mr. Hurok, but I love playing the piano so much I would do it for nothing.
ARTUR RUBINSTEIN. (*Rubinstein Speaking; The New York Times Magazine,* Jan. 26, 1964.) "Mr. Hurok" is Sol Hurok, the noted impresario.

9
Music is essentially useless, as life is.
GEORGE SANTAYANA, *The Life of Reason.*

10
Hell is full of musical amateurs: music is the brandy of the damned.
BERNARD SHAW, *Man and Superman,* Act 3.

11
A painter paints his pictures on canvas. But musicians paint their pictures on silence. We provide the music, and you provide the silence.
LEOPOLD STOKOWSKI, to an audience at a Carnegie Hall concert.

12
To listen is an effort, and just to hear is no merit. A duck hears also.
IGOR STRAVINSKY, *News summaries,* June 24, 1957.

13
After I die I shall return to earth as the doorkeeper of a bordello, and I won't let a one of you in.
ARTURO TOSCANINI, *Threat* to members of orchestra, recalled in reports of his death, Jan. 17, 1957.

14
I don't give a damn about *The Missouri Waltz* but I can't say it out loud because it's the song of Missouri. It's as bad as *The Star-Spangled Banner* so far as music is concerned.
HARRY S TRUMAN, quoted in *Time,* Feb. 10, 1958.

15
Jazz—Music invented by demons for the torture of imbeciles.
HENRY VAN DYKE.

16
Over the piano was printed a notice: "Please do not shoot the pianist. He is doing his best."
OSCAR WILDE, *Impressions of America: Leadville.*

17
After playing Chopin, I feel as if I had been weeping over sins that I had never committed.
OSCAR WILDE, *The Critic as Artist.*

MUSTACHE

18
My dear madam, pray do not disturb yourself. You are not likely to come in contact with either.
Attributed to WINSTON S. CHURCHILL, *Reply* to a young woman who said she didn't like his politics or his mustache. On the authority of Gertrude Atherton.

19
Strange that pre-eminence in Germany has more than once been indicated by an eccentric pattern in the hair upon the upper lip.
PHILIP GUEDALLA, *The Hundred Years.*

20
Being kissed by a man who didn't wax his moustache was like eating an egg without salt.
RUDYARD KIPLING, *Soldiers Three: The Gadsbys. Poor Dear Mamma.*

N

NAME

1
There is everything in a name. A rose by any other name would smell as sweet, but would not cost half as much during the winter months.
GEORGE ADE, *Fables.*

2
The Ancient Mariner would not have taken so well if it had been called *The Old Sailor.*
SAMUEL BUTLER, *The Way of All Flesh.*

3
What good can it do an ass to be called a lion?
THOMAS FULLER, *Gnomologia,* No. 5490.

4
I'm called Little Buttercup—dear Little Buttercup,
Though I could never tell why.
SIR WILLIAM SCHWENCK GILBERT, *H.M.S. Pinafore,* Act 1.

5
There, I guess King George will be able to read that.
JOHN HANCOCK, *Remark,* on signing the Declaration of Independence, July 4, 1776. His was the first signature, and in so bold a handwriting that "John Hancock" became a synonym for signature.

6
A self-made man may prefer a self-made name.
JUDGE LEARNED HAND, on granting permission for Samuel Goldfish to change his name to Samuel Goldwyn. (BOSLEY CROWTHER, *The Lion's Share.*)

7
A nickname is the hardest stone that the devil can throw at a man.
Quoted by WILLIAM HAZLITT.

8
Bee to the blossom, moth to the flame;
Each to his passion; what's in a name?
HELEN HUNT JACKSON, *Variety of Vanities.*

9
The ancient Athenians used to cover up the ugliness of things with auspicious and kindly terms, giving them polite and endearing names. Thus they called harlots "companions," taxes "contributions," and the prison a "chamber."
PLUTARCH, *Lives: Solon,* sec. 15.

10
He who pronounces Saxe as Saxy

Would surely call an axe an axy.
JOHN GODFREY SAXE, *Epigram,* upon being asked the correct pronunciation of his name.

11
No family has a better right to an *O* than our family, for in truth we owe everybody.
RICHARD BRINSLEY SHERIDAN, when asked why his name was not preceded by an *O.*

12
Her name is Susanna, I assume?
SYDNEY SMITH, on seeing a lady seated between two Bishops. (*Bon-Mots of Sydney Smith.*)

13
Sticks and stones
Will break your bones
But names will never hurt you.
UNKNOWN.

NATURE

14
Do not get your nose into an artificial manure heap and think you are studying nature.
JOHN OLIVER HOBBES, *Life and Tomorrow.*

15
Art may make a suit of clothes: but nature must produce a man.
DAVID HUME, *Essays:* No. 15, *The Epicurean.*

16
The whole of nature, as has been said, is a conjugation of the verb to eat, in the active and passive.
DEAN W. R. INGE, *Outspoken Essays.*

17
Nature is proving that she can't be beaten—not by the likes of us. She's taking the world away from the intellectuals and giving it back to the apes.
ROBERT E. SHERWOOD, *The Petrified Forest.*

18
Your salvation is in your own hands . . . Nature is indifferent to the survival of the human species, including Americans. She does not weep over those who fall by the way.
ADLAI STEVENSON, *Speech,* Chicago, Sept. 29, 1952.

19
The great secretary of Nature,—Sir Francis Bacon.
IZAAK WALTON, *Life of Herbert.*

1
Nature is usually wrong.
JAMES MCNEILL WHISTLER, *Ten O'Clock*.

2
Like most artificial people he [Thomas Griffiths Wainewright] had a great love of nature.
OSCAR WILDE, *Pen, Pencil and Poison*.

3
Nature has good intentions, of course, but, as Aristotle once said, she cannot carry them out.
OSCAR WILDE, *The Decay of Lying*.

NECESSITY

4
Without fingers you can't even thumb your nose.
SHOLOM ALEICHEM, *The Enchanted Tailor*. Quoting an old saying.

5
Invention is the mother of necessity.
SAMUEL BUTLER.

6
Liquor is not a necessity. It is a means of momentarily side-stepping necessity.
CLIFTON FADIMAN, *The Selected Writings of Clifton Fadiman* (1955).

7
Necessity is the argument of tyrants; it is the creed of slaves.
WILLIAM PITT, *Speech* on the India Bill, Nov., 1783.

8
Necessity, my friend, is the mother of courage, as of invention.
SIR WALTER SCOTT, *Quentin Durward*, ch. 23.

NEGRO

See also Majority and Minority, Prejudice, Tolerance

9
I was offered the ambassadorship of Liberia once, when that post was earmarked for a Negro. I told them I wouldn't take a Jim Crow job.
RALPH BUNCHE, after becoming United Nations Under Secretary. (*Think*, Jan. 1961.)

10
I am beset by a lingering suspicion that Negroes were originally born Black, Broke, Baptist, Republican, $600.00 in Debt, and on the short ends of bets that they'd never make it.
DAN BURLEY, *New York Citizen-Call*, Aug. 13, 1960. (*The Book of Negro Humor*, by LANGSTON HUGHES.)

11
Cassius [Clay] treats the fact of color—but not race—casually. Sometimes, when he is into his act, he will look at somebody and say, "You know, man, you lucky, you seen me here in living color."
TOM WOLFE, *The Kandy-Colored Tangerine-Flake Streamline Baby*.

12
She thinks that even up in heaven
Her class lies late and snores,
While poor black cherubs rise at seven,
To do celestial chores.
COUNTEE CULLEN, *Epitaph: A Lady I Know*.

13
Some of my best friends are white boys.
When I meet 'em
I treat 'em
Just the same as if
They was people.
RAY DUREM, *Friends*. (LANGSTON HUGHES, *The Book of Negro Humor*.)

14
Doctor, doctor, hear me beg:
I want a *black* artificial leg.
RAY DUREM. (LANGSTON HUGHES, *The Book of Negro Humor*.)

15
What a ball going through one of those Indian reservations. Where else could I ever get to be called a paleface?
DICK GREGORY, *From the Back of the Bus*.

16
I know my wife wondered if she was doing the right thing when I made her give up her job. She still figures the boys in white are gonna get me. Sheets or coats, take your pick.
DICK GREGORY, *From the Back of the Bus*.

17
You gotta realize, my people have never known what job security is. For instance, comes another recession and the economy has to tighten its belt—who do you think's gonna be the first notch?
DICK GREGORY, *From the Back of the Bus*.

18
People keep talking about the white race and the black race—and it really doesn't make sense. I played Miami last week—met a fella two shades darker than me—and his name was Ginsberg! . . . Took my place in two sit-in demonstrations—nobody knew the difference. . . . Then he tried for a third lunch counter and blew the whole bit. Asked for blintzes.
DICK GREGORY, *From the Back of the Bus*.

19
This book is dedicated to Abraham Lincoln

—if it wasn't for Abe, I'd still be on the open market.

DICK GREGORY, *From the Back of the Bus:* dedication.

1

Last year I got to stay at the same hotel as the President. Who knows? Maybe next year I'll be a guest at their Virginia estate —riding behind hounds instead of running in front of them.

DICK GREGORY, *From the Back of the Bus.*

2

Man, we're making it. Even the phone company's coming out with colored phones.

DICK GREGORY, *From the Back of the Bus.*

3

Some people have a wonderful way of looking at things. Like the ones who hire one of us to baby sit—so they can go to a Ku Klux Klan meeting.

DICK GREGORY. (LANGSTON HUGHES, *The Book of Negro Humor.*)

4

Lost in the shuffle during the filibuster concerning the 1964 Civil Rights Bill in the Senate, and therefore probably not to be found in the *Congressional Record,* was this shouted remark from the floor by a southern senator, "Gentlemen, Ah, believe in segregated integration, *not* integrated segregation."

LANGSTON HUGHES, *The Book of Negro Humor: Segregated Integration.*

5

Black is fine!
And, God knows,
It's mine!

LANGSTON HUGHES, *Argument, The Langston Hughes Reader.*

6

I want to be the white man's brother, not his brother-in-law.

MARTIN LUTHER KING, JR. (*New York Journal-American,* Sept. 10, 1962.)

7

I personally wish Jacob Freese, of New Jersey, to be appointed colonel of a colored regiment, and this regardless of whether he can tell the exact shade of Julius Caesar's hair.

ABRAHAM LINCOLN, *Letter* to Secretary of War Stanton.

8

The black man in this country has been sitting on the hot stove for nearly 400 years. And no matter how fast the brainwashers and the brainwashed think they are helping him advance, it's still too slow for the man whose behind is burning on that hot stove!

MALCOLM X. (GORDON PARKS, *What Their Cry Means to Me; Life,* May 31, 1963.)

9

Beware of Greeks bearing gifts, colored men looking for loans, and whites who understand the Negro.

ADAM CLAYTON POWELL, quoted in *Dominion,* Nov., 1966.

10

Never forget that two blacks do not make a white.

BERNARD SHAW, *The Adventures of the Black Girl in Her Search for God.*

NEIGHBOR

11

It's other folks' dogs and children that make most of the bad feelin's between neighbors.

ELLIS PARKER BUTLER, *The Confessions of a Daddy,* ch. 1.

12

That man should be taught to love his neighbor as himself is both admirable and inspiring, and yet no one who respects his banking account could ever seriously accept so unbusinesslike a theory.

WARWICK DEEPING, *A Woman's War.*

13

Christianity teaches us to love our neighbor as ourself; modern society acknowledges no neighbor.

BENJAMIN DISRAELI, *Sybil.* Bk. ii, ch. 5.

14

Here's talk of the Turk and the Pope, but it's my next door neighbor that does me harm.

THOMAS FULLER, *Gnomologia,* No. 2497.

15

Love your Neighbor, yet respect him, too;
Don't pull down the Fence 'twixt him and you.

ARTHUR GUITERMAN, *A Poet's Proverbs.*

16

Love your neighbor, yet pull not down your hedge.

GEORGE HERBERT, *Jacula Prudentum.*

17

Don't shout for help at night. You may wake your neighbors.

STANISLAW J. LEC, *Unkempt Thoughts,* tr. from the Polish by JACEK GALASKA.

18

There are 869 different forms of lying, but only one of them has been squarely forbidden. Thou shalt not bear false witness against thy neighbor.

MARK TWAIN, *Pudd'nhead Wilson's New Calendar.*

19

A neighborhood is where, when you go out of it, you get beat up.

UNKNOWN, quoted by MURRAY KEMPTON in the *New York Post,* Dec. 3, 1957.

NERVES

1
He was so high-strung that he could have gone to a masquerade as a tennis racket.
FRED ALLEN, *Treadmill to Oblivion.*

2
The person who is "on pins and needles" usually is a pin-head.
B. C. FORBES, *Epigrams.*

3
He who lost his head has many headaches.
STANISLAW J. LEC, *Unkempt Thoughts,* tr. from the Polish by JACEK GALASKA.

4
In moments of crisis my nerves act in the most extraordinary way. When utter disaster seems imminent my whole being is instantaneously braced to avoid it: I size up the situation in a flash, set my teeth, contract my muscles, take a firm grip of myself, and without a tremor, always do the wrong thing.
BERNARD SHAW, quoted by HESKETH PEARSON in *Lives of the Wits.*

5
The impotence of the intellectuals is nature hitting back. Not with the old weapons— floods, plagues, holocausts. We can neutralize them. She's fighting back with strange instruments called neuroses. She's deliberately afflicting mankind with the jitters.
ROBERT E. SHERWOOD, *The Petrified Forest.*

NEWS

See also Press

6
Tell those guys out there to get the smell of warm blood into their copy.
HUGH BAILLIE, *Instruction* to United Press war correspondents during World War II, while he was president of that news agency.

7
News is news only when you've heard it before.
JACQUES BARZUN, *God's Country and Mine.*

8
Harmony seldom makes a headline.
SILAS BENT, *Strange Bedfellows.*

9
All I have to do to get a story on the front page of every one of the AP's 2,000 clients is to mention in the lead a treatment for piles, ulcers, or sexual impotence—three conditions that every telegraph editor has, or is worried about.
ALTON BLAKESLEE, science editor, The Associated Press. (*Newsweek,* Oct. 21, 1957.)

10
When a dog bites a man that is not news, but when a man bites a dog that is news.
JOHN B. BOGART, about 1880, when he was city editor of the New York *Sun.* F. M. MOTT, in *American Journalism,* and Frank M. O'Brien, a later editor of the *Sun,* are authorities for this attribution, though the classic definition is also credited to CHARLES A. DANA, most famous of *Sun* editors; and STANLEY WALKER, in *City Editor,* attributes it to a Dana assistant, AMOS CUMMINGS.

11
Except the Flood, nothing was ever as bad as reported.
E. W. HOWE.

12
News—Anything that makes a woman say: "For heaven's sake!"
E. W. HOWE.

13
No normally constituted feller kin read a daily newspaper without congratulatin' himself that he haint in jail or a candidate fer office.
FRANK MCKINNEY (KIN) HUBBARD, *Abe Martin's Primer.*

14
People everywhere confuse
What they read in newspapers with news.
A. J. LIEBLING, *A Talkative Something or Other; The New Yorker,* Apr. 7, 1956.

15
Writing for a newspaper is like running a revolutionary war; you go into battle not when you are ready but when action offers itself.
NORMAN MAILER, *The Presidential Papers.*

16
No news, good news. (Pas de nouvelles, bonnes nouvelles.)
MEILHAC AND HALEVY, *La Belle Hélène,* Act 2.

17
I like to get where the cabbage is cooking and catch the scents.
RED SMITH, explaining his travels in the course of covering major sports events. (*Newsweek,* Apr. 21, 1958.)

18
An editor is a person who separates the wheat from the chaff and prints the chaff.
ADLAI STEVENSON.

19
Nothing in the world affords a newspaper reporter so much satisfaction as gathering up the details of a bloody and mysterious murder and writing them up with aggravating circumstantiality.
MARK TWAIN, *The Killing of Julius Caesar "Localized."*

1
Women, wampum and wrongdoing are always news.
STANLEY WALKER, *City Editor.*

2
News is as hard to hold as quicksilver, and it fades more rapidly than any morning-glory.
STANLEY WALKER, *City Editor.*

NEW YORK

3
No king, no clown, to rule this town!
WILLIAM O. BARTLETT, in the *New York Sun,* about 1870, referring to "Boss" Tweed and Peter B. Sweeney, mastermind of the Tweed ring.

4
New York, the hussy, was taken in sin again!
THOMAS BEER, *The Mauve Decade.*

5
London is a wide flat pie of redbrick suburbs with the West End stuck in the middle like a currant. New York is a huge rich raisin, and is the biggest city I can imagine.
BRENDAN BEHAN, *Where We All Came into Town; Evergreen Review.* Vol. v, No. 18.

6
Everyone in New York knows that he is an important person living among other important persons.
BRENDAN BEHAN, *Where We All Came into Town; Evergreen Review.* Vol. v, No. 18.

7
"When I first went to New York," said Robert Benchley, "I was warned to look out for the pitfalls, and I did. But it was Sunday, and they were all closed."
EARL WILSON, *New York Post.*

8
Proposed name for a subway in the Bronx: "The Bronchial Tube."
DR. L. BINDER, *Catholic Digest.* (*Reader's Digest,* Nov., 1966.)

9
Greenwich Village is the Coney Island of the soul.
MAXWELL BODENHEIM. (ALLEN CHURCHILL, *The Improper Bohemians.*)

10
The City of Dreadful Height.
JAMES BONE, *Description of New York,* in the *Guardian,* Manchester.

11
New Yorkers are nice about giving you street directions; in fact, they seem quite proud of knowing where they are themselves.
KATHARINE BRUSH.

12
New York is a sucked orange.
RALPH WALDO EMERSON, *Conduct of Life: Culture.*

13
Personally, I've always favored New York 'cause this is one city where you don't have to ride in the back of the bus. Not that they're so liberal—it's just that in New York, *nobody* moves to the back of the bus!
DICK GREGORY, *From the Back of the Bus.*

14
New York is the greatest city in the world—especially for my people. Where else, in this grand and glorious land of ours, can I get on a subway, sit in any part of the train I please, get off at any station above 110th Street, and know I'll be welcome?
DICK GREGORY, *From the Back of the Bus.*

15
Rudeness is the privacy of New Yorkers.
THOMAS GRIFFITH, *The Waist-High Culture.*

16
In my youth not much was known in our Chicago newspaper circles about fairies, except that they existed—chiefly in New York.
BEN HECHT, *Gaily, Gaily.*

17
If there ever was an aviary overstocked with jays it is that Yaptown-on-the-Hudson, called New York. . . . "Little ole New York's good enough for us"—that's what they sing.
O. HENRY, *Gentle Grafter: A Tempered Wind.*

18
What else can you expect from a town that's shut off from the world by the ocean on one side and New Jersey on the other?
O. HENRY, *Gentle Grafter: A Tempered Wind.*

19
Well, little old Noisyville-on-the-Subway is good enough for me.
O. HENRY, *Strictly Business: The Duel.*

20
It's a city where everyone mutinies but no one deserts.
HARRY HERSHFIELD, *Interview, The New York Times,* Dec. 5, 1965.

21
New York attracts the most talented people in the world in the arts and professions. It also attracts them in other fields. Even the bums are talented.
EDMUND LOVE, *Subways Are for Sleeping:* introduction.

22
Most of the people living in New York have

come here from the farm to try to make enough money to go back to the farm.
DON MARQUIS.

1
New York, the nation's thyroid gland.
CHRISTOPHER MORLEY, *Shore Leave.*

2
The Bronx?
No thonx.
OGDEN NASH, These lines originally appeared in *The New Yorker* in 1931.

3
Vulgar of manner, overfed,
Overdressed and underbred.
B. R. NEWTON, *Owed to New York.*

4
Crazed with avarice, lust and rum,
New York, thy name's Delirium.
B. R. NEWTON, *Owed to New York.*

5
New York—A city of 7,000,000, so decadent that when I leave it I never dare look back lest I turn into salt and the conductor throw me over his left shoulder for good luck.
FRANK SULLIVAN.

6
It can destroy an individual, or it can fulfill him, depending a good deal on luck. No one should come to New York to live unless he is willing to be lucky.
E. B. WHITE, *Here Is New York.*

7
A little strip of an island with a row of well-fed folks up and down the middle, and a lot of hungry folks on each side.
HARRY LEON WILSON, *The Spenders.*

NOISE

8
Here we go like three tin kettles at the tail of a mad cougar!
HERMAN MELVILLE, *Moby Dick*, ch. 81.

9
It is with narrow-souled people as with narrow-necked bottles: the less they have in them the more noise they make in pouring it out.
ALEXANDER POPE, *Thoughts on Various Subjects.*

10
Noise is louder than anything.
STOOPNAGLE AND BUDD, *Radio broadcast*, quoted by MAX EASTMAN in *Enjoyment of Laughter.*

11
A whistling woman and a crowing hen
Is neither fit for God nor men.
UNKNOWN.

12
The audience strummed their catarrhs.
ALEXANDER WOOLLCOTT.

NONSENSE

See also Humor

13
A little nonsense now and then
Is relished by the best of men.
ANONYMOUS, old nursery rhyme.

14
As I was laying on the green
A small English book I seen
Carlyle's Essay on Burns was the edition,
So I left it laying in the same position.
ANONYMOUS.

15
'Twas brillig and the slithy toves
  Did gyre and gimble in the wabe;
All mimsy were borogoves,
  And the mome raths outgrabe.
LEWIS CARROLL, *Jabberwocky.* (*Through the Looking-Glass*, ch. 1.)

16
"And hast thou slain the Jabberwock?
  Come to my arms, my beamish boy!
O frabjous day! Callooh! Callay!"
  He chortled in his joy.
LEWIS CARROLL, *Jabberwocky.* (*Through the Looking-Glass.*)

17
He left it dead, and with its head
He went galumphing back.
LEWIS CARROLL, *Jabberwocky.* (*Through the Looking-Glass.*)

18
The sun was shining on the sea,
  Shining with all his might:
He did his very best to make
  The billows smooth and bright—
And this was odd, because it was
  The middle of the night.
LEWIS CARROLL, *Through the Looking-Glass*, ch. 4.

19
He thought he saw an Elephant,
  That practiced on a fife:
He looked again, and found it was
  A letter from his wife.
"At length I realize," he said,
  "The bitterness of Life!"
LEWIS CARROLL, *The Gardener's Song.* (*Sylvie and Bruno.*)

20
They told me you had been to her,
  And mentioned me to him:
She gave me a good character,
  But said I could not swim.
LEWIS CARROLL, *Alice's Adventures in Wonderland*, ch. 12.

21
To die for faction is a common evil,
But to be hang'd for nonsense is the devil.
JOHN DRYDEN, *Absalom and Achitophel.*

1

So she went into the garden to cut a cabbage leaf to make an apple pie; and at the same time a great she-bear, coming up the street, pops its head into the shop. "What! no soap?" So he died, and she very imprudently married the barber; and there were present the Picninnies, and the Joblillies, and the Garyulies, and the Grand Panjandrum himself, with the little round button at top, and they fell to playing the game of catch as catch can, till the gunpowder ran out at the heels of their boots.

SAMUEL FOOTE, nonsense written to test the boasted memory of Charles Macklin. *The Quarterly Review*, 1854.

2

If the man who turnips cries,
Cry not when his father dies,
'Tis proof that he had rather
Have a turnip than his father.

SAMUEL JOHNSON, *Burlesque of Lope de Vega.*

3

I'm the Prophet of the Utterly Absurd,
Of the Patently Impossible and Vain.

RUDYARD KIPLING, *Song of Banjo.*

4

There was an old man with a beard,
Who said: "It's just as I feared—
Two Owls and a Hen,
Four Larks and a Wren
Have all built their nests in my beard."

EDWARD LEAR, *Book of Nonsense*

5

Bunk is mental junk.

GEORGE W. LYON AND O. F. PAGE, *Definition* submitted simultaneously by these two men, strangers to each other, in a contest sponsored by *The Forum*, Sept., 1927.

6

Don't talk to me about a man's being able to talk sense; everyone can talk sense—can he talk nonsense?

WILLIAM PITT (1759–1806).

7

No matter how thin you slice it, it's still baloney.

ALFRED E. SMITH, *Speech*, 1936.

8

Transcendental moonshine.

JOHN STERLING, reference to Coleridge. (*Life*, p. 84.)

9

Madam, I'm Adam. (Adam to Eve)
Able was I ere I saw Elba. (Napoleon loq.)
Name no one man.
Red root put up to order.
No, it is opposition.
No, it is opposed; art sees trade's opposition.

Examples of Palindromes. From *The*

Home Book of Quotations by BURTON STEVENSON.

10

One, whom we see not, is; and one, who is not, we see;
Fiddle, we know, is diddle; and diddle, we take it, is dee.

ALGERNON CHARLES SWINBURNE, *The Higher Pantheism in a Nutshell.*

11

Peter Piper picked a peck of pickled peppers,
A peck of pickled peppers did Peter Piper pick;
If Peter Piper picked a peck of pickled peppers,
Where's the peck of pickled peppers that Peter Piper picked?

UNKNOWN. Old nursery rhyme.

NOSE

12

A red nose is caused by sunshine or moonshine.

EVAN ESAR, *The Humor of Humor.*

13

He that has a great nose thinks everybody is speaking of it.

THOMAS FULLER, *Gnomologia*, No. 2129.

14

Morgan's ruby nose added to his personal fame and with some humor he once said it "would be impossible for me to appear on the streets without it." His nose, he remarked on another occasion, "was part of the American business structure."

STEWART HOLBROOK, *The Age of the Moguls.*

15

If Cleopatra's nose had been flat, the face of the world would have been changed.

BRANDER MATTHEWS, *Cleopatra's Nose.* See also PASCAL in this section.

16

Lo, I spy Nikon's hooked nose, Menippos, and the face itself cannot be far removed.
Be patient, friend, and let us wait,
for it stands no more than half a mile behind:
the parabolic snout leads the way
and if we climb a high hill we may catch a glimpse of the face.

NIKARCHOS, *On Nikon's Nose*, tr. by WILLIAM BARNSTONE.

17

Cleopatra's nose: had it been shorter, the whole aspect
of the world would have been altered.

BLAISE PASCAL, *Pensées.* Sec. II, No. 162, tr. by W. F. TROTTER.

18

To cut off one's nose to spite one's face.

PUBLILIUS SYRUS, *Sententiae.*

1
Thou canst tell why one's nose stands i' the middle on's face? . . . Why, to keep one's eyes of either side's nose; that what a man cannot smell out, he may spy into.
WILLIAM SHAKESPEARE, *King Lear.* Act i, sc. 5.

2
Take my advice and seek no further than the end of your nose. You will always know that there is something beyond that; and in that knowledge you will be hopeful and happy.
BERNARD SHAW, *The Adventures of the Black Girl in Her Search for God.*

3
If you point your big nose sunward
and open your gaping
                    mouth,
                        all who pass by
will know the time of day.
THE EMPEROR TRAJAN, *A Natural Sundial,* tr. by WILLIAM BARNSTONE.

NUDITY

See also Dress

4
. . . world understanding depends upon peo-ple of all nations looking alike, which they cannot do with their clothes on.
ALOIS KLAPP, speaking as President of the American Sunbathing Association.

5
He felt as naked as a peeled banana.
FREDERICK LAING, *The Giant's House.*

6
If you want to hide your face, walk naked.
STANISLAW J. LEC, *Unkempt Thoughts,* tr. from the Polish by JACEK GALASKA.

7
I am sure that, in a world where nudism has become conventionally respectable, almost all women will long for a rag to cover up the persistent forgetfulness of their Maker. After all the downfall of man and the coquetry of women began with a fig leaf.
LIN YUTANG, *With Love and Irony.*

8
A reporter who visited a nudist camp asked one of the campers, "How did you get to be a nudist?" The camper replied: "I was born that way."
LEONARD LYONS, *New York Post,* Aug. 12, 1965.

O

OPERA

9
No good opera can be sensible, for people do not sing when they are feeling sensible.
W. H. AUDEN, quoted in *Time,* Dec. 29, 1961.

10
I look upon opera as a magic scene contrived to please the eyes and the ears at the expense of the understanding.
LORD CHESTERFIELD.

11
Sleep is an excellent way of listening to an opera.
JAMES STEPHENS.

12
This present opera was "Parsifal". Madame Wagner does not permit its representation anywhere but in Bayreuth. The first act of the three occupied two hours, and I enjoyed that in spite of the singing.
MARK TWAIN, *Essays: At the Shrine of St. Wagner.*

OPINION

13
His opinion, having once risen, remained at "set fair."
ARNOLD BENNETT, *Denry the Audacious.*

14
Every man has a perfect right to his opinion, provided it agrees with ours.
JOSH BILLINGS.

15
The man who never alters his opinion is like standing water, and breeds reptiles of the mind.
WILLIAM BLAKE, *Proverbs of Hell.*

16
The public buys its opinions as it buys its meat, or takes its milk, on the principle that it is cheaper to do this than to keep a cow. So it is, but the milk is more likely to be watered.
SAMUEL BUTLER, *The Way of All Flesh.*

17
Popular opinion is the greatest lie in the world.
THOMAS CARLYLE.

18
The reader deserves an honest opinion. If he doesn't deserve it, give it to him anyhow.
JOHN CIARDI, *Saturday Review,* Feb. 16, 1957.

19
I am always of the opinion with the learned, if they speak first.
WILLIAM CONGREVE.

1
"My idea of an agreeable person", said Hugo Bohun, "is a person who agrees with me."
BENJAMIN DISRAELI, *Lothair*, ch. 41.

2
"I never offered an opinion till I was sixty," said the old Turk, "and then it was one which had been in our family for a century."
BENJAMIN DISRAELI, *Iskander*, ch. 8.

3
Stay at home in your mind. Don't recite other people's opinions.
RALPH WALDO EMERSON, *Letters and Social Aims: Social Aims*.

4
Your opinion of others is apt to be their opinion of you.
B. C. FORBES, *Epigrams*.

5
Any stigma will do to beat a dogma.
PHILIP GUEDALLA.

6
It seems to me one of the principal differences in the feeling-tone of English and American life comes from the fact that Americans are prone to favor you with their opinions and to do it, moreover, in the manner of an office boy favoring letters with stamps at five minutes to five, whereas the English think of an opinion as something which a decent person, if he has the misfortune to have one, does all he can to hide.
MARGARET HALSEY, *With Malice Toward Some*.

7
With effervescing opinions, as with the not yet forgotten champagne, the quickest way to let them get flat is to let them get exposed to the air.
JUSTICE OLIVER WENDELL HOLMES, *Opinion*, U.S. Supreme Court, 1920.

8
Next t' a fourteen-year-ole boy ther hain't nothin' as worthless as th' average opinion.
FRANK MCKINNEY (KIN) HUBBARD, *Abe Martin's Primer*.

9
Dogmatism is puppyism come to its full growth.
DOUGLAS JERROLD, *Man Made of Money*.

10
"He's a great man," the President [Lyndon B. Johnson] once said, "because he agrees with me."
PHILIP GEYELIN, *Lyndon B. Johnson and the World*. The reference is to Walter Lippmann.

11
One man's Mede is another man's Persian.
GEORGE S. KAUFMAN.

12
Unless they share our opinions, we seldom find people sensible.
FRANÇOIS, DUC DE LA ROCHEFOUCAULD, *Maximes*, No. 347.

13
The pressure of public opinion is like the pressure of the atmosphere; you can't see it—but, all the same, it is sixteen pounds to the square inch.
JAMES RUSSELL LOWELL, *Interview* with Julian Hawthorne.

14
In conversation we are sometimes confused by the tone of our own voice, and misled into making assertions that do not at all correspond to our opinions.
FRIEDRICH WILHELM NIETZSCHE, *Human, All Too Human*, vol. 1, tr. by HELEN ZIMMERN.

15
To seduce their neighbor to a favorable opinion, and afterwards to believe implicitly in this opinion of their neighbor—who can do this conjuring trick so well as women?
FRIEDRICH WILHELM NIETZSCHE, *Beyond Good and Evil*, tr. by HELEN ZIMMERN.

16
A difference of opinion is what makes horse-racing and missionaries.
WILL ROGERS, quoted in *One Man's America* by ALISTAIR COOKE. See also MARK TWAIN in this section.

17
A plague of opinion! A man may wear it on both sides, like a leather jerkin.
WILLIAM SHAKESPEARE, *Troilus and Cressida*. Act iii, sc. 3.

18
Opinion's but a fool, that makes us scan The outward habit by the inward man.
WILLIAM SHAKESPEARE, *Pericles*. Act ii, sc. 2.

19
It were not best that we should all think alike; it is difference of opinion that makes horse-races.
MARK TWAIN, *Pudd'nhead Wilson's Calendar*.

20
Loyalty to petrified opinion never yet broke a chain or freed a human soul.
MARK TWAIN, *Inscription* beneath his bust in the Hall of Fame.

21
Oscar . . . has the courage of the opinions . . . of others.
JAMES MCNEILL WHISTLER, quoted in *The World*, London, Nov. 17, 1886. Comment on Oscar Wilde.

1
It is only about things that do not interest one that one can give a really unbiassed opinion, which is no doubt the reason why an unbiassed opinion is always absolutely valueless.
OSCAR WILDE, *The Critic as Artist.*

2
Public opinion exists only where there are no ideas.
OSCAR WILDE, *Saturday Review,* Nov. 17, 1894.

OPPORTUNITY

3
Opportunity is whoredom's bawd.
WILLIAM CAMDEN, *Remains* (1605).

4
It should be spelled Hop-portunity.
B. C. FORBES, *Epigrams.*

5
Makes you wonder. When I left St. Louis, I was making five dollars a night. Now I'm getting $5,000 a week—for saying the same things out loud I used to say under my breath.
DICK GREGORY, *From the Back of the Bus.*

6
The actual fact is that in this day Opportunity not only knocks at your door but is playing an anvil chorus on every man's door, and then lays for the owner around the corner with a club.
ELBERT HUBBARD, *The Philistine.*

7
Then, like an old-time orator
    Impressively he rose;
"I make the most of all that comes
And the least of all that goes."
SARA TEASDALE, *The Philosopher.*

OPTIMISM

8
I hate the Pollyanna pest
Who says that All is for the Best.
FRANKLIN P. ADAMS, *Thoughts on the Cosmos.*

9
Every cloud has a silver lining—but that is small consolation when you cannot see through the cloud.
W. BURTON BALDRY, *Stray Thoughts.*

10
When the outlook is steeped in pessimism, I remind myself, "Two and two still make four, and you can't keep mankind down for long."
BERNARD BARUCH. (*Time,* Aug. 19, 1957.)

11
The optimist proclaims that we live in the best of all possible worlds; and the pessimist fears this is true.
JAMES BRANCH CABELL, *The Silver Stallion,* p. 112.

12
I am an optimist. It does not seem too much use being anything else.
SIR WINSTON CHURCHILL, *News reports* of Nov. 10, 1954.

13
The place where optimism most flourishes is the lunatic asylum.
HAVELOCK ELLIS, *The Dance of Life.*

14
Optimism is a kind of heart stimulant—the digitalis of failure.
ELBERT HUBBARD, *A Thousand and One Epigrams.*

15
There's just as much bunk among the busters as among the boosters.
KEITH PRESTON, *Pot Shots from Pegasus.*

16
No optimist tries to capitalize rainbows.
Reflections of a Bachelor (1903).

17
An optimist is a person who sees a green light everywhere, while the pessimist sees only the red stop light . . . But the truly wise person is color-blind.
ALBERT SCHWEITZER, *News summaries,* Jan. 14, 1955.

18
'Twixt optimist and pessimist
    The difference is droll;
The optimist sees the doughnut,
    The pessimist, the hole.
McLANDBURGH WILSON, *Optimist and Pessimist.*

19
Optimist—A man who gets treed by a lion but enjoys the scenery.
WALTER WINCHELL.

20
Two knights contended in the list—
An optimist, a pessimist;
But each by mist was blinded so
That neither struck a single blow.
R. T. WOMBAT, *Quatrains.*

ORATOR, ORATORY

21
The best audience is one that is intelligent, well-educated—and a little drunk.
ALBEN W. BARKLEY, quoted by ADLAI E. STEVENSON in *The New York Times,* Feb. 15, 1965.

1
You call that a maiden speech? It was a brazen hussy of a speech.
> SIR WINSTON CHURCHILL, *Remark*, to A. P. Herbert, quoted in *The New York Times*, June 25, 1965.

2
I can't think of an extemporaneous comment. As soon as I prepare one, I'll let you know.
> MIKE DiSALLE, *Comment* on "extemporaneous" speech to be delivered by an assistant director.

3
A sophisticated rhetorician, inebriated with the exuberance of his own verbosity.
> BENJAMIN DISRAELI, *Speech*, 1878. On W. E. Gladstone.

4
Ye could waltz to it.
> FINLEY PETER DUNNE, referring to the oratory of Senator Albert J. Beveridge.

5
I guess a man never becomes an orator if he has anything to say.
> FINLEY PETER DUNNE. (WALTER BLAIR, *Horse Sense in American Humor*.)

6
One of our statesmen said, "The curse of this country is eloquent men."
> RALPH WALDO EMERSON, *Society and Solitude: Eloquence*.

7
WHEREAS, it has become obvious that three minutes is ample time for any member to speak to the record to impress the Folks Back Home, and
WHEREAS, it is equally obvious that no member of this House can speak for longer than three minutes without repeating himself,
ORDERED, that any member who speaks at any one time for longer than three minutes shall, at the sole discretion of the Speaker, be shot, stuffed and displayed in a glass case in the State Museum—bearing around his neck the legend—
> Here am I, for E'er enshrined,
> My mouth is open, teeth are shined;
> My colleagues' treatment less than kind,
> I talked them all deaf, dumb and blind.
> JAMES S. ERWIN of the Maine House of Representatives, *Legislative Order* proposed in that assembly, May 19, 1965. It was read and "indefinitely postponed." The order and poem, both original, were inspired by one of Rep. Erwin's long-winded colleagues.

8
True he can talk, and yet he is no speaker.
> EUPOLIS, *Demes*. (PLUTARCH'S *Lives: Alcibiades*.)

9
You'd scarce expect one of my age
To speak in public on the stage;
And if I chance to fall below
Demosthenes or Cicero,
> Don't view me with a critic's eye,
> But pass my imperfections by.
Large streams from little fountains flow,
Tall oaks from little acorns grow.
> DAVID EVERETT, *Lines Written for a School Declamation by a Little Boy of Seven*. (*Columbian Orator*, Boston, 1797.)

10
When a man gets up to speak, people listen, then look. When a woman gets up, people *look;* then, if they like what they see, they listen.
> PAULINE FREDERICK, quoted by GAY TALESE in *The Saturday Evening Post*.

11
I am not fond of uttering platitudes
In stained-glass attitudes.
> W. S. GILBERT, *Patience*, Act 1.

12
Here comes another of the spellbinders!
> WILLIAM CASSIUS GOODLOE. The reference is to the Republican stump-speakers in the campaign of 1888.

13
He rose without a friend, and sat down without an enemy.
> HENRY GRATTAN, of Dr. Lucas after a speech in the Irish Parliament.

14
Fill your mouth with marbles and make a speech. Every day, reduce the number of marbles in your mouth and make a speech. You will soon become an accredited public speaker—as soon as you have lost all your marbles.
> Former Rep. BROOKS HAYS. (*Poor H. Allen Smith's Almanac*, 1965.)

15
When a speaker begins his remarks by sayin', "I'm not goin' t' take up th' valuable time o' this convention," you kin git ready t' be bored.
> FRANK McKINNEY (KIN) HUBBARD, *Abe Martin's Primer*.

16
Why don't th' feller who says, "I'm not a speechmaker," let it go at that instead o' givin' a demonstration?
> FRANK McKINNEY (KIN) HUBBARD, *Abe Martin's Primer*.

17
You people always write that I talk on every subject. I do—I *like* every subject. I can't help it—it's just glands.
> HUBERT HUMPHREY. (MICHAEL AMRINE, *This Is Humphrey*.)

1
Amplification is the vice of the modern orator . . . Speeches measured by the hour die with the hour.
THOMAS JEFFERSON, *Writings,* vol. 16.

2
A man whose eloquence has power
To clear the fullest house in half an hour.
SOAME JENYNS, *Imitations of Horace.* Bk. ii, epis. 1.

3
If you haven't struck oil in your first three minutes, *stop boring!*
GEORGE JESSEL, *Dais Without End.*

4
Hot air has thawed out many a cold reception.
F. M. KNOWLES, *A Cheerful Year Book.*

5
The politicians were talking themselves red, white, and blue in the face.
CLARE BOOTHE LUCE.

6
A speech is like a love affair. Any fool can start it, but to end it requires considerable skill.
LORD MANCROFT, quoted in *Reader's Digest,* Feb., 1967.

7
Plainly on furlough from some home for extinct volcanoes.
H. L. MENCKEN, quoted in *Hats in the Ring* by MOOS AND HESS. The reference is to convention orators.

8
What orators lack in depth they make up to you in length. (Ce qui manque aux orateurs en profondeur ils vous le donnent en longuer.)
CHARLES LOUIS DE SECONDAT DE MONTESQUIEU, *Lettres.*

9
I never failed to convince an audience that the best thing they could do was to go away.
THOMAS LOVE PEACOCK, *Crochet Castle,* ch. 18.

10
A speech is like an airplane engine. It may sound like hell but you've got to go on.
WILLIAM THOMPSON PIPER, quoted in *Time,* Jan. 13, 1961.

11
Few speeches which have produced an electrical effect on an audience can bear the colorless photography of a printed record.
ARCHIBALD PRIMROSE, *Life of Pitt.*

12
He is like a carving knife whetted on a brickbat.
JOHN RANDOLPH of Roanoke, on Ben Hardin of Kentucky, powerful back-

woods orator. From *The Wit and Wisdom of Congress,* ed. by EDWARD BOYKIN.

13
Our public men are speaking every day on something, but they ain't saying anything.
WILL ROGERS, *The Illiterate Digest.*

14
He draweth out the thread of his verbosity finer than the staple of his argument.
WILLIAM SHAKESPEARE, *Love's Labour's Lost.* Act v, sc. 1.

15
I sometimes marvel at the extraordinary docility with which Americans submit to speeches.
ADLAI STEVENSON, from *Adlai's Almanac,* ed. by BESSIE R. JAMES AND MARY WATERSTREET.

16
When I was a boy I never had much sympathy for a holiday speaker. He was just a kind of interruption between the hot dogs, a fly in the lemonade.
ADLAI E. STEVENSON, *Speech* in Flint, Mich., 1952.

17
Oratory is the art of making pleasant sounds, which cause the hearers to say "Yes, yes" in sympathy with the performer, without inquiring too closely exactly what he means.
SAM TUCKER, *Decatur* (Ill.) *Herald.*

18
Let him never make a speech until he has something to say. This last is about the hardest advice to follow that could be offered to a Senator, perhaps.
MARK TWAIN, to Senator Casserly of California, Feb. 11, 1868.

19
It usually takes me more than three weeks to prepare a good impromptu speech.
MARK TWAIN.

20
My dear friends—I will not call you ladies and gentlemen, since I know you too well.
UNKNOWN, attributed to a curate addressing his congregation. From *Among the Humorists* by WILLIAM PATTEN.

21
The reason there are so few women afterdinner speakers is because few can wait that long.
UNKNOWN.

22
Abraham Lincoln wrote the Gettysburg Address while traveling from Washington to Gettysburg on the back of an envelope.
LOUIS UNTERMEYER, *A Treasury of Laughter.* Quoted as a student boner.

P

PAIN

See also Suffering

1
TV program director to announcer: "And keep running the aspirin commercials right after the school-closing bulletins!"
CHON DAY, *TV Guide*, Cartoon Caption.

2
Oh, what a bellyache!
DWIGHT D. EISENHOWER, at the time he underwent surgery, in 1956, for removal of an intestinal obstruction.

3
And he, whom in itching no scratching will forbear,
He must bear the smarting that shall follow there.
THOMAS FULLER, *Gnomologia*, No. 2449.

4
Do you think that I, then, am taking pleasure in my bath?
GAUTEMOZIN, successor to Montezuma. To his companion, the cacique of Tacuba, while being tortured by Cortez. (PRESCOTT, *Conquest of Mexico*. Bk. vii, ch. 1.)

5
"Who's got some paregoric?" said Stubb, "he has the stomach-ache, I'm afraid. Lord, think of having half an acre of stomach-ache!"
HERMAN MELVILLE, *Moby Dick*, ch. 81.

6
To a person with a toothache, even if the world is tottering, there is nothing more important than a visit to a dentist.
BERNARD SHAW, quoted in *Days with Bernard Shaw* by STEPHEN WINSTEN.

PAINTING

7
When a man sits for a portrait he is seldom satisfied because he has a preconception of how he looks, a certain angle, and of course the most flattering one, which he has decided is *him*.
GEORGE ABBOTT, *Mister Abbott*.

8
The love of gain never made a painter, but it has marred many.
WASHINGTON ALLSTON, *Lectures on Art: Aphorisms*.

9
A product of the untalented, sold by the unprincipled to the utterly bewildered.
AL CAPP, *Comment* on abstract art. (*National Observer*, July 1, 1963.)

10
Modern art is what happens when painters stop looking at girls and persuade themselves that they have a better idea.
JOHN CIARDI, *Saturday Review*.

11
There are only two styles of portrait painting, the serious and the smirk.
CHARLES DICKENS, *Nicholas Nickleby*, ch. 10.

12
Pictures must not be too picturesque.
RALPH WALDO EMERSON, *Essays, First Series: Art*.

13
When they talk'd of their Raphaels, Correggios, and stuff,
He shifted his trumpet, and only took snuff.
OLIVER GOLDSMITH, *Retaliation*.

14
Indifferent pictures, like dull people, must absolutely be moral.
WILLIAM HAZLITT, *Criticisms on Art*.

15
I would rather see the portrait of a dog that I know, than all the allegorical paintings they can shew me in the world.
SAMUEL JOHNSON, Boswell's *Life of Johnson*.

16
I think it will be wise for you never to pose for your artist lover for more than fifteen minutes. No one can afford a prolonged inventory of her charms and if you can possibly avoid it you ought not to sit for him at all. But, if you do, you are easily fatigued . . . and remember to make no comments on his work while it is still in progress.
ALEXANDER KING, *Rich Man, Poor Man, Freud and Fruit*, ch. 3.

17
Only God Almighty makes painters.
SIR GODFREY KNELLER, *Reply* to his tailor, who requested that his son be taken as a pupil.

18
I like Eyck.
London Sun, Headline for an article on Flemish painter Jan van Eyck. Quoted in *Reader's Digest*, Feb., 1967.

19
Eutychos the portrait painter got twenty sons, but even among his children—never one likeness.
LUCILIUS (LOUKILLIOS), *Fidelity in the Arts*, tr. by WILLIAM BARNSTONE.

1
I have seen, and heard, much of Cockney impudence before now; but never expected to hear a coxcomb ask two hundred guineas for flinging a pot of paint in the public's face.
JOHN RUSKIN, *Fors Clavigera,* letter 79, June 18, 1877. On Whistler's "Nocturne in Black and Gold."

2
Every time I paint a portrait I lose a friend.
JOHN SINGER SARGENT.

3
Van Gogh's contemporaries objected to his modus operandi: he would actually smear colors on with his thumbs! ("Even with my heels, if necessary," he would answer.) But that is what Vincent's art is: all thumbs and genius.
JOHN SIMON, *Acid Test.*

4
To sit for one's portrait is like being present at one's own creation.
ALEXANDER SMITH, *Dreamthorp.*

5
What sight is sadder than the sight of a lady we admire admiring a nauseating picture?
LOGAN PEARSALL SMITH, *All Trivia.*

6
A tortoise-shell having a fit in a platter of tomatoes.
MARK TWAIN, *Description* of Turner's "The Slave Ship."

7
When a painter was looked upon as a vagabond and you always counted the spoons as soon as he had left your house, it meant that no one was going to choose painting for a profession unless he had it in him and it just *had* to come out. But nowadays, when it has become one of the respectable professions, every kind of ass crowds into it on the chance of ending up with a peerage. So, of course, the average level is bound to go down.
JANE WARDLE, *The Artistic Temperament.*

8
Ah! but the shock will come when you see what you paint.
JAMES MCNEILL WHISTLER, *Comment* to a student who asserted that he painted what he saw. (HESKETH PEARSON, *Lives of the Wits.*)

PARTING

9
Some weep because they part,
And languish broken-hearted,
And others—O my heart!—
Because they never parted.
THOMAS BAILEY ALDRICH, *The Difference.*

10
And he turned away with a heart full sore,
And he never was seen, not none no more.
ROBERT J. BURDETTE, *Romance of the Carpet.*

11
I now bid a welcome adoo.
ARTEMUS WARD, *The Shakers.*

PAST

See also History

12
The past invariably strangles a woman, but makes the man. The men with a past are the only men with a future.
WYMOND CAREY, *Love the Judge.*

13
The past always looks better than it was. It's only pleasant because it isn't here.
FINLEY PETER DUNNE, *Mr. Dooley Remembers.*

14
Why should we grope among the dry bones of the past, or put the living generation into masquerade out of its faded wardrobe?
RALPH WALDO EMERSON, *Essays, Second Series: Lecture.*

15
Past: Something to be forgotten.
OLIVER HERFORD, *Cupid's Cyclopedia.*

16
Th' nearest some fellers ever come t' gardenin' is diggin' up the past.
FRANK MCKINNEY (KIN) HUBBARD, *Abe Martin's Primer.*

17
Nobody can live in the past or the future without being something of a nut.
EVELYN NESBIT, *News summaries,* Sept. 26, 1955.

18
Miniver loved the Medici,
Albeit he had never seen one;
He would have sinned incessantly
Could he have been one.
EDWIN ARLINGTON ROBINSON, *Miniver Cheevy.*

19
The past at least is secure.
DANIEL WEBSTER, *Speech* on Foote's Resolution, U.S. Senate, Jan. 26, 1830.

20
It's futile to talk too much about the past—something like trying to make birth control retroactive.
CHARLES E. WILSON, Secretary of Defense. *News summaries,* May 22, 1955.

PATIENCE

21
Patience is a flatterer, sir—and an ass, sir.
APHRA BEHN, *Feigned Courtezans,* Act 3.

1
There are two kinds of people in one's life
—people whom one keeps waiting—and the
people for whom one waits . . .
    S. N. BEHRMAN, *Biography*.

2
Beware the fury of a patient man.
    JOHN DRYDEN, *Absalom and Achitophel*,
    pt. 1.

3
Patience is not only a virtue, but it pays.
    B. C. FORBES, *Epigrams*.

4
Many a man thinks he is patient when, in
reality, he is indifferent.
    B. C. FORBES, *Epigrams*.

5
There was a time when Patience ceased to
be a virtue. It was long ago.
    CHARLOTTE PERKINS GILMAN, *The Fore-
    runner*.

6
Patience is the virtue of an ass,
That trots beneath his burthen, and is quiet.
    GEORGE GRANVILLE, *Heroic Love*.

7
Be plastered with patience.
    WILLIAM LANGLAND, *Piers Plowman*, pas-
    sus 20.

8
I have no more patience than anyone else.
It's just that I use mine.
    IGNACE JAN PADEREWSKI, *Reply* to a
    woman who had remarked that learning
    to play the piano with his skill must
    require great patience.

9
I am as poor as Job, my Lord, but not so
patient.
    WILLIAM SHAKESPEARE, *Henry IV, Pt. 2*.
    Act i, sc. 2.

10
That's the advantage of having lived 65
years. You don't feel the need to be impatient any longer.
    THORNTON WILDER. (FLORA LEWIS, *Thorn-
    ton Wilder at 65; The New York Times
    Magazine*, Apr. 15, 1962, p. 28.)

PATRIOTISM

11
In time of war the loudest patriots are the
greatest profiteers.
    AUGUST BEBEL, *Speech*, Reichstag, Nov.,
    1870.

12
No man can be a patriot on an empty
stomach.
    WILLIAM C. BRANN, *The Iconoclast: Old
    Glory*.

13
"My country right or wrong," is a thing that
no patriot would think of saying except in a
desperate case. It is like saying, "My mother,
drunk or sober."
    G. K. CHESTERTON, *The Defendant*.

14
Many a bum show has been saved by the
flag.
    GEORGE M. COHAN, quoted in LA FOL-
    LETTE'S *Progressive*.

15
True patriots all; for be it understood
We left our country for our country's good.
    GEORGE CRABBE, *Prologue Written for the
    Opening of the Play-House at New
    South Wales, Jan. 16, 1796*.

16
Thomas Dixon, Jr., of the People's Church
of New York, told his congregation that
Bryan was "a mouthing, slobbering demagogue whose patriotism was all in his jaw-
bone."
    IRVING STONE, *They Also Ran*. Remark
    was made during the presidential cam-
    paign of 1896.

17
Nationalism is an infantile disease. It is the
measles of mankind.
    ALBERT EINSTEIN, *The World As I See It*.

18
It seems like th' less a statesman amounts
to th' more he loves th' flag.
    FRANK MCKINNEY (KIN) HUBBARD, *Abe
    Martin's Primer*.

19
I think patriotism is like charity—it begins
at home.
    HENRY JAMES, *The Portrait of a Lady*, ch.
    10.

20
Patriotism is the last refuge of a scoundrel.
    SAMUEL JOHNSON, BOSWELL'S *Life*, Apr.
    7, 1775.

21
Among really small nations, patriotism has
a tendency to become a disease, and for lack
of genuine heroes, the natives will worship
brigands, thieves, and even fabulous animals.
    ALEXANDER KING, *Rich Man, Poor Man,
    Freud and Fruit*, ch. 24.

22
Charles Dickens shared with all his race
that peculiar and almost insulting insular
smugness which deplores the sins of other
nations, forgetting the recentness of their
own conversion.
    STEPHEN LEACOCK, *Charles Dickens*.

23
Whenever you hear a man speak of his love

of his country it is a sign that he expects to be paid for it.
> H. L. MENCKEN, *A Mencken Chrestomathy.*

1

Our country is wherever we are well off.
> JOHN MILTON, *Letter* to P. Heinbach, Aug. 15, 1666.

2

Patriotism is often an arbitrary veneration of real estate above principles.
> GEORGE JEAN NATHAN, *Testament of a Critic.*

3

Don't spread patriotism too thin.
> THEODORE ROOSEVELT, quoted in *Metropolitan Magazine*, July, 1918.

4

You'll never have a quiet world until you knock the patriotism out of the human race.
> BERNARD SHAW, *O'Flaherty, V.C.*

5

The national anthem belongs to the eighteenth century. In it you find us ordering God about to do our political dirty work.
> BERNARD SHAW, *The Adventures of the Black Girl in Her Search for God.*

6

What they called patriotism was a conviction that because they were born in Tooting or Camberwell, they were the natural superiors of Beethoven, of Rodin, of Ibsen, of Tolstoy and all other benighted foreigners.
> BERNARD SHAW, *Getting Married:* preface.

7

Do not . . . regard the critics as questionable patriots. What were Washington and Jefferson and Adams but profound critics of the colonial status quo?
> ADLAI E. STEVENSON, *The Hard Kind of Patriotism; Harper's Magazine*, July, 1963.

8

Patriotism knows neither latitude nor longitude. It is not climatic.
> EMERY A. STORRS, *Political Oratory*, ch. 2.

9

July 4. Statistics show that we lose more fools on this day than in all the other days of the year put together. This proves, by the number left in stock, that one Fourth of July per year is now inadequate, the country has grown so.
> MARK TWAIN, *Pudd'nhead Wilson's Calendar.*

PEACE

10

A conqueror is always a lover of peace.
> KARL VON CLAUSEWITZ, copied by LENIN

in his notebook, with notation, "Ah! Ah! Witty."

11

If you wish to avoid foreign collision, you had better abandon the ocean.
> HENRY CLAY, *Speech,* House of Representatives, Jan. 22, 1812.

12

Peace is better than war, because in peace the sons bury their fathers, but in war the fathers bury their sons.
> CROESUS, to Cambyses. (BACON, *Apothegms,* No. 149.)

13

If man does find the solution for world peace it will be the most revolutionary reversal of his record we have ever known.
> GEORGE C. MARSHALL, *Report of Chief of Staff*, U.S. Army, Sept. 1, 1945.

14

What a beautiful fix we are in now; peace has been declared.
> NAPOLEON BONAPARTE, spoken Mar. 7, 1802, about the Treaty of Amiens.

15

Professional pacifists, the peace-at-any-price, non-resistance, universal arbitration people, are seeking to Chinafy this country.
> THEODORE ROOSEVELT, *Speech* in San Francisco.

16

It's co-existence
Or no existence.
> BERTRAND RUSSELL.

PERFECTION

17

Were it not for the presence of the unwashed and the half-educated, the formless, queer and incomplete, the unreasonable and absurd, the infinite shapes of the delightful human tadpole, the horizon would not wear so wide a grin.
> FRANK MOORE COLBY, *Imaginary Obligations.*

18

The very pink of perfection.
> OLIVER GOLDSMITH, *She Stoops to Conquer.*

19

In life nothing below one hundred percent is passing.
> J. P. McEVOY, *Charlie Would Have Loved This.*

20

Trifles make perfection, and perfection is no trifle.
> MICHELANGELO, quoted by C. C. COLTON, *Lacon.*

21

Whoever thinks a faultless piece to see,

Thinks what ne'er was, not is, nor e'er shall
be.
ALEXANDER POPE, *Essay on Criticism*.

1
The impossible is the perfect woman.
FRANK RICHARDSON, *2835 Mayfair*.

PERSEVERANCE

2
Consider the postage stamp: its usefulness
consists in the ability to stick to one thing
till it gets there.
JOSH BILLINGS.

3
Even the woodpecker owes his success to the
fact that he uses his head and keeps pecking
away until he finishes the job he starts.
COLEMAN COX, *Perseverance*.

4
Are you a thoroughbred? It has been well
said that the cart horse goes until he can't
go another inch and then gives up; that the
thoroughbred goes until he can't go another
inch—and then goes the other inch.
B. C. FORBES, *Epigrams*.

5
It's dogged as does it. It ain't thinking about
it.
ANTHONY TROLLOPE, *The Last Chronicle
of Barset*, vol. 1.

6
When the going gets tough, the tough get
going.
UNKNOWN, *Maxim* adopted by Joseph P.
Kennedy as a motto for his sons. (WIL-
LIAM V. SHANNON, *The Emergence of
Senator Kennedy; The New York Times
Magazine*, Aug. 22, 1965, p. 64.)

PERSONALITY

7
Personal magnetism is that quality in human
nature which enables a feller t' git by with
a red carnation in his lapel an' little ability.
FRANK MCKINNEY (KIN) HUBBARD, *Abe
Martin's Primer*.

8
I don't think being well-rounded is particularly important. I would like to see people with a cutting edge on them.
BARNABY KEENEY, *Life*.

9
Personality is to a man what perfume is to a
flower.
CHARLES SCHWAB, *Ten Commandments
of Success*.

10
Everyone is a moon, and has a dark side
which he never shows to anybody.
MARK TWAIN, *Pudd'nhead Wilson's New
Calendar*.

11
Either heaven or hell will have continuous
background music piped in. Which one you
think it is tells a lot about your personality.
BILL VAUGHAN, *Kansas City Star*.

12
Mrs. Akemit was not only like St. Paul, "all
things to all men," but she had gone a step
beyond that excellent theologue. She could
be all things to one man.
HARRY LEON WILSON, *The Spenders*.

PESSIMISM

See also Optimism

13
Pessimism, when you get used to it, is just
as agreeable as optimism.
ARNOLD BENNETT, *Things That Have Interested Me*.

14
Cops never begin by suspecting the best in
anyone . . .
THOMAS GRIFFITH, *The Waist-High Culture*.

15
A pessimist is one who has been intimately
acquainted with an optimist.
ELBERT HUBBARD, *A Thousand and One
Epigrams*, p. 121.

16
Nothing to do but work,
   Nothing to eat but food,
Nothing to wear but clothes,
   To keep one from going nude.
BEN KING, *The Pessimist*.

17
Do you know what a pessimist is? A man
who thinks everybody as nasty as himself,
and hates them for it.
BERNARD SHAW, *An Unsocial Socialist*, ch.
5.

18
The man who is a pessimist before forty-
eight knows too much; the man who is an
optimist after forty-eight knows too little.
MARK TWAIN.

PHILOSOPHY

19
Philosophy: unintelligible answers to insolu-
ble problems.
HENRY ADAMS.

20
My definition [of a philosopher] is of a man
up in a balloon, with his family and friends
holding the ropes which confine him to
earth and trying to haul him down.
LOUISA M. ALCOTT, quoted in EDNAH D.
CHENEY, *Louisa May Alcott, Her Life,
Letters and Journals*.

1
Philosophers sit in their sylvan hall
And talk of the duties of man,
Of Chaos and Cosmos, Hegel and Kant,
With the Oversoul well in the van;
All on their hobbies they amble away
And a terrible dust they make;
Disciples devout both gaze and adore,
As daily they listen and bake.
LOUISA M. ALCOTT.

2
The philosophy of one century is the common sense of the next.
HENRY WARD BEECHER, *Life Thoughts.*

3
O reader behold the philosopher's grave!
He was born quite a fool but he died quite a knave.
WILLIAM BLAKE, *On Sir Joshua Reynolds.*

4
Metaphysics is the finding of bad reasons for what we believe on instinct.
FRANCIS HERBERT BRADLEY, *Appearance and Reality,* ch. 14.

5
Philosophy is common-sense in a dress suit.
OLIVER S. BRASTON, *Philosophy.*

6
Not to be a metaphysician is no sin; it is only an inconvenience when one insists on talking about metaphysics.
ORESTES BROWNSON, quoted in H. BROWNSON, *O. H. Brownson: Middle Life.*

7
But all be that he was a philosopher,
Yet had he but little gold in coffer..
GEOFFREY CHAUCER, *Canterbury Tales:* prologue.

8
Old men [reference to Tolstoy] have always been prone to see the end of the world. The hell with the philosophy of the great of this world.
ANTON CHEKHOV, *The Selected Letters of Anton Chekhov* (1955).

9
Philosophy is the home made medicine those take who have not the courage to meet life as it is.
LUCAS CLEEVE, *The Rose Geranium.*

10
You are a philosopher, Dr. Johnson. I have tried, too, in my time to be a philosopher; but, I don't know how, cheerfulness was always breaking in.
OLIVER EDWARDS, the schoolmate of Dr. Johnson at Pembroke. (JAMES BOSWELL, *The Life of Samuel Johnson, LL.D.:* Apr. 17, 1778.)

11
The Arabians say that Abul Khain, the mystic, and Abu Ali Seena, the philosopher, conferred together; and, on parting, the philosopher said, "All that he sees I know"; and the mystic said, "All that he knows I see."
RALPH WALDO EMERSON, *Representative Men: Swedenborg.*

12
The society which scorns excellence in plumbing because plumbing is a humble activity and tolerates shoddiness in philosophy because it is an exalted activity will have neither good plumbing nor good philosophy. Neither its pipes nor its theories will hold water.
JOHN W. GARDNER, *Excellence: Can We Be Equal and Excellent Too?* When Gardner was named Secretary of Health, Education and Welfare in the cabinet of Lyndon B. Johnson, July 27, 1965, Mr. Johnson quoted this passage at the White House ceremony.

13
Society can overlook murder, adultery or swindling; it never forgives the preaching of a new gospel.
FREDERICK HARRISON, English philosopher (1831–1923).

14
A modest confession of ignorance is the ripest and last attainment of philosophy.
ROSWELL D. HITCHCOCK, *Eternal Atonement: Secret Things of God.*

15
Be a philosopher, but amidst all your philosophy, be still a man.
DAVID HUME, *An Enquiry Concerning Human Understanding.*

16
A bilious philosopher's opinion of the world can only be accepted with a pinch of salt, of Epsom salt by preference.
ALDOUS HUXLEY, *Proper Studies.*

17
Thank God I am a man,
Not a philosopher!
Oriental Romances, ed. by MANUEL KOMROFF: *The Vampire's Stories,* told to Raja Vikram.

18
Metaphysics may be, after all, only the art of being sure of something that is not so, and logic only the art of going wrong with confidence.
JOSEPH WOOD KRUTCH, *The Modern Temper,* p. 228.

19
Be quiet and people will think you are a philosopher.
Old Latin Proverb.

1
Many tried to create the philosopher's stone by petrifying thoughts.
> STANISLAW J. LEC, *Unkempt Thoughts,* tr. from the Polish by JACEK GALASKA.

2
Language originated before philosophy, and that's what's wrong with philosophy.
> GEORG C. LICHTENBERG.

3
There is no record in human history of a happy philosopher.
> H. L. MENCKEN, *Prejudices.*

4
Philosophy drips gently from his tongue
Who hath three meals a day in guarantee.
> CHRISTOPHER MORLEY, *So This Is Arden.*

5
Socrates was a clown who succeeded in making men take him seriously: what then was the matter?
> FRIEDRICH WILHELM NIETZSCHE, *The Twilight of the Idols,* tr. by A. M. LUDOVICI.

6
It is a great advantage for a system of philosophy to be substantially true.
> GEORGE SANTAYANA, *The Unknowable.*

7
Philosophy is nothing but Discretion.
> JOHN SELDEN, *Table Talk.*

8
For there was never yet philosopher
That could endure the toothache patiently.
> WILLIAM SHAKESPEARE, *Much Ado About Nothing.* Act v, sc. 1.

9
Socrates died from an overdose of wedlock.
> LOUIS UNTERMEYER, *A Treasury of Laughter.* Quoted as a student boner.

PITY

10
Compassion will cure more sins than condemnation.
> HENRY WARD BEECHER, *Proverbs from Plymouth Pulpit.*

11
Everybody in the world ought to be sorry for everybody else. We all have our little private hell.
> BARONESS VON HUTTEN, *The Halo.*

12
In the gilded sheath of pity is sometimes hidden the dagger of envy.
> FRIEDRICH WILHELM NIETZSCHE, *Human, All Too Human,* vol. 2, tr. by PAUL V. COHN.

PLAGIARISM

13
Every generation has the privilege of standing on the shoulders of the generation that went before; but it has no right to pick the pockets of the first-comer.
> BRANDER MATTHEWS, *Recreations of an Anthologist,* p. 20.

14
For such kind of borrowing as this, if it be not bettered by the borrower, among good authors is accounted Plagiary.
> JOHN MILTON, *Eikonoklastes,* ch. 23.

15
If you steal from one author it's plagiarism; if you steal from many, it's research.
> WILSON MIZNER.

16
The only "ism" she believes in is plagiarism.
> DOROTHY PARKER, speaking of a well-known author. Quoted in Miss Parker's obituary in *Publishers' Weekly,* June 19, 1967.

17
Adam was the only man who, when he said a good thing, knew that nobody had said it before him.
> MARK TWAIN.

18
Call them, if you please, bookmakers, not authors; range them rather among second-hand dealers than plagiarists.
> VOLTAIRE, *Plagiarism.*

PLEASURE

19
He more had pleased us had he pleased us less.
> JOSEPH ADDISON, *English Poets.* Referring to Cowley.

20
The great pleasure in life is doing what people say you cannot do.
> WALTER BAGEHOT, *Literary Studies,* vol. 1.

21
The rule of my life is to make business a pleasure, and pleasure my business.
> AARON BURR, *Letter* to Pichon.

22
Pleasure's a sin and sometimes sin's a pleasure.
> LORD BYRON, *Don Juan.* Canto i, st. 133.

23
Let us have wine and women, mirth and laughter,
Sermons and soda-water the day after.
> LORD BYRON, *Don Juan.* Canto ii, st. 178.

24
It is the part of a wise man to resist pleasures, but of a foolish one to be a slave to them.
> EPICTETUS, *Fragments,* III.

1
A life of pleasure is . . . the most unpleasing life in the world.
> OLIVER GOLDSMITH, *The Citizen of the World*, letter 44.

2
Follow pleasure, and then will pleasure flee,
Flee pleasure, and pleasure will follow thee.
> JOHN HEYWOOD, *Proverbs*.

3
The liberty of using harmless pleasures . . . will not be disputed; but it is still to be examined what pleasures are harmless.
> SAMUEL JOHNSON, *Rasselas*, ch. 47.

4
The public pleasures of far the greater part of mankind are counterfeit.
> SAMUEL JOHNSON, *The Idler*, No. 18.

5
The roses of pleasure seldom last long enough to adorn the brow of him who plucks them; for they are the only roses which do not retain their sweetness after they have lost their beauty.
> HANNAH MORE, *Essays on Various Subjects*.

6
Pleasure is nothing but the intermission of pain, the enjoying of something I am in great trouble for till I have it.
> JOHN SELDEN, *Table Talk*.

7
Pleasure is frail like a dewdrop, while it laughs it dies.
> SIR RABINDRANATH TAGORE, *The Gardener*, No. 27.

8
Then sing as Martin Luther sang,
As Doctor Martin Luther sang,
"Who loves not wine, woman and song,
He is a fool his whole life long."
> WILLIAM MAKEPEACE THACKERAY, *A Credo*.

9
All human race, from China to Peru,
Pleasure, howe'er disguis'd by art, pursue.
> THOMAS WARTON, *Universal Love of Pleasure*.

10
Pleasure that most enchants us
  Seems the soonest done;
What is life with all it grants us,
  But a hunting run?
> G. J. WHYTE-MELVILLE, *A Lay of the Ranston Bloodhounds*.

POETRY

11
I agree with one of your reputable critics that a taste for drawing-rooms has spoiled more poets' than ever did a taste for the gutter.
> THOMAS BEER, *The Mauve Decade*, p. 235.

12
But those that write in rhyme still make
The one verse for the other's sake;
For one for sense, and one for rhyme,
I think's sufficient for one time.
> SAMUEL BUTLER, *Hudibras*, Pt. 1.

13
Poetry therefore we will call musical thought.
> THOMAS CARLYLE, *Heroes and Hero Worship*.

14
It is the supreme proof of a man being prosaic that he always insists on poetry being poetical.
> G. K. CHESTERTON, *The Everlasting Man*.

15
Swans sing before they die—'twere no bad thing
Did certain persons die before they sing.
> SAMUEL TAYLOR COLERIDGE, *Epigram*.

16
Of those few fools, who with ill stars are curst,
Sure scribbling fools, called poets, fare the worst:
For they're a sort of fools which Fortune makes,
And after she has made 'em fools, forsakes.
> WILLIAM CONGREVE, *The Way of the World*, prologue.

17
To him [H. L. Mencken] Pegasus is just a runaway horse.
> BENJAMIN DE CASSERES, *Mencken and Shaw*.

18
When Robert Frost was asked to explain one of his poems, he replied, "What do you want me to do—say it over again in worser English?"
> H. E. F. DONOHUE, *New York Herald Tribune Book Week*.

19
Poets, like disputants, when reasons fail,
Have one sure refuge left, and that's to rail.
> JOHN DRYDEN, *All for Love*: epilogue.

20
I knew a very wise man that believed that if a man were permitted to make all the ballads, he need not care who should make the laws of a nation.
> ANDREW FLETCHER, *Letter*, to the Marquis of Montrose, the Earl of Rothes.

21
What are our poets, take them as they fall,
Good, bad, rich, poor, much read, not read at all?

Them and their works in the same class
   you'll find—
They are the mere wastepaper of mankind.
   BENJAMIN FRANKLIN, *Paper*.

1
I don't call myself a poet yet. It's for the
world to say whether you're a poet or not.
I'm one-half teacher, one-half poet, and one-
half farmer. That's three halves.
   ROBERT FROST, commenting on his 80th
   birthday, in Mar., 1954.

2
I'd just as soon play tennis with the net
down.
   ROBERT FROST, *Comment* on the writing
   of "free" verse. (*Newsweek*, Jan. 30,
   1956.)

3
By the way, I heard an answer today to the
platitude: "There's no money in poetry." It
was: "There's no poetry in money, either."
   ROBERT GRAVES, *The Crowning Privilege*.

4
Then he asked the question that you are
all itching to ask me: "How can you tell
good poetry from bad?"
   I answered: "How does one tell good fish
from bad? Surely by the smell? Use your
nose."
   ROBERT GRAVES, *The Crowning Privilege:
   The Poet and His Public*.

5
A poet like Homer seems to me worth a
dozen such fellows as Achilles and Alexander.
   OLIVER WENDELL HOLMES. (*Wit and Wisdom of Oliver Wendell Holmes, father
   and son*, ed. by LESTER E. DENONN.)

6
What is a modern poet's fate?
To write his thoughts upon a slate;
The critic spits on what is done,
Gives it a wipe—and all is gone.
   THOMAS HOOD, *The Poet's Fate*.

7
The man is mad, or else he's writing verses.
(Aut insanit homo aut versus facit.)
   HORACE, *Satires*. Bk. ii, sat. 7, l. 117. The
   line is spoken by Davus, Horace's slave,
   referring to his master's eccentric
   habits.

8
Poetry is the bill and coo of sex.
   ELBERT HUBBARD, *Epigrams*.

9
I never knowed a successful man that could
quote poetry.
   FRANK MCKINNEY (KIN) HUBBARD, *Abe
   Martin's Primer*.

10
Poetry is evidently a contagious complaint.
   WASHINGTON IRVING, *Tales of a Traveller*
   (1824).

11
Dr. Donne's verses are like the peace of
God; they pass all understanding.
   JAMES I OF ENGLAND AND VI OF SCOT-
   LAND, *Saying* recorded by Archdeacon
   Plume (1630–1704).

12
Was ever poet so trusted before?
   SAMUEL JOHNSON, *Letter to Boswell*, July
   4, 1774. Referring to Goldsmith's debts
   at his death.

13
He is upbraidingly called a poet, as if it
were a most contemptible nickname.
   BEN JONSON, *Explorata: Jam Literae
   Sordent*.

14
From a review: The poet showed a noble
poverty of thought.
   STANISLAW J. LEC, *Unkempt Thoughts*, tr.
   from the Polish by JACEK GALASKA.

15
It is a better and a wiser thing to be a
starved apothecary than a starved poet; so
back to the shop, Mr. John, back to "plas-
ters, pills, and ointment boxes."
   J. G. LOCKHART, *Review* of Keats's *Endymion* in *Blackwood's Magazine*.

16
I shall never be a poet till I get out of the
pulpit, and New England was all meeting-
house when I was growing up.
   JAMES RUSSELL LOWELL, *Letter to Nor-
   ton*, Aug. 28, 1865.

17
Publishing a volume of verse is like dropping a rose petal down the Grand Canyon
and waiting for the echo.
   DON MARQUIS, *The Sun Dial*.

18
gods i am pent in a cockroach
i with the soul of a dante
am mate and companion of fleas
i with the gift of a homer
must smile when a mouse calls me pal
tumble bugs are my familiars
this is the punishment meted
because i have written vers libre
   DON MARQUIS, *the wail of archy*.

19
Poetry is what Milton saw when he went
blind.
   DON MARQUIS, quoted in *O Rare Don
   Marquis* by EDWARD ANTHONY.

20
The pearl is a disease of the oyster.
A poem is a disease of the spirit

Caused by the irritation
Of a granule of Truth
Fallen into that soft gray bivalve
We call the mind.
CHRISTOPHER MORLEY, *Bivalves.*

1
Poets are sultans, if they had their will;
For every author would his brother kill.
ROGER ORRERY, *Prologues.*

2
I was following in the exquisite footsteps of
Miss Edna St. Vincent Millay, unhappily in
my own horrible sneakers.
DOROTHY PARKER, quoted in Miss Park-
er's obituary in *Publishers' Weekly,*
June 19, 1967.

3
Fiction is the privilege of poets.
PLINY THE YOUNGER, *Letters,* bk. 6.

4
I had rather be a kitten and cry mew,
Than one of those same metre ballad-mon-
gers:
I had rather hear a brazen canstick turn'd,
Or a dry wheel grate on the axle-tree;
And that would set my teeth nothing on
edge,
Nothing so much as mincing poetry.
WILLIAM SHAKESPEARE, *Henry IV.* Act
iii, sc. 1.

5
Robert Creeley's poems have two main characteristics: (1) they are short; (2) they
are not short enough.
JOHN SIMON, *Acid Test.*

6
We should nourish our souls on the dew of
Poesy, and manure them as well.
LOGAN PEARSALL SMITH.

7
Poetry is nothing but healthy speech.
HENRY D. THOREAU, *Journal,* Sept. 4,
1841.

8
Mr. Swinburne is already the Poet Laureate
of England. The fact that his appointment
to this high post has not been degraded by
official confirmation renders his position all
the more unassailable.
OSCAR WILDE, *The Idler,* Apr., 1895.
Written when Wilde was asked who he
thought should be the next Poet Laureate.

POLITICS

See also Conservatism; Government;
Liberalism; Reform, Reformers; Voting

9
I will undoubtedly have to seek what is
happily known as gainful employment, which
I am glad to say does not describe holding
public office.
DEAN ACHESON, on leaving his position
as Secretary of State. Quoted in *Time,*
Dec. 22, 1952.

10
Practical politics consists in ignoring facts.
HENRY ADAMS, *The Education of Henry
Adams.*

11
Although the Senate is much given to admiring in its members a superiority less obvious or quite invisible to outsiders, one
Senator seldom proclaims his own inferiority
to another, and still more seldom likes to be
told of it.
HENRY ADAMS, *The Education of Henry
Adams.*

12
"My country," wrote our first vice-president,
John Adams, "has contrived for me the most
insignificant office that ever the invention of
man contrived or his imagination conceived."
MOOS AND HESS, *Hats in the Ring.* See
also JOHN NANCE GARNER and THOMAS
R. MARSHALL in this section.

13
His face is livid; gaunt his whole body,
His breath is green with gall; his tongue
drips poison.
JOHN QUINCY ADAMS on John Randolph
of Virginia. (*The Wit and Wisdom of
Congress,* ed. by EDWARD BOYKIN.)

14
The Senate finally approved Charles E. Wilson. The Senators were suspicious of any
man who had two million dollars when he
arrived in Washington.
FRED ALLEN, *Comment* on Senate confirmation of Wilson as Secretary of
Defense in 1953. (*Fred Allen's Letters,*
ed. by JOE MCCARTHY.)

15
Truman . . . seemed to stand for nothing
more spectacular than honesty in war con-
tracting, which was like standing for virtue
in Hollywood or adequate rainfall in the
Middle West.
GEORGE E. ALLEN, *Presidents Who Have
Known Me.*

16
In politics one frequently hears it said that
so-and-so may be an s.o.b. but he is our
s.o.b. and therefore deserving of our support.
GEORGE E. ALLEN, *Presidents Who Have
Known Me.*

17
Gallup was only 4.7 per cent pregnant.
GEORGE E. ALLEN, *Presidents Who Have
Known Me.* Reference to Gallup poll
on 1948 elections.

1
More recently one United States Senator said of another: "There's no use telling that fellow anything. It just goes in one head and out the other."
GEORGE E. ALLEN, *Presidents Who Have Known Me.*

2
He's certain to get the divorce vote, and remember that's one in four these days.
CLEVELAND AMORY, NBC-TV, April 6, 1962.

3
The presidential campaign speech is, like jazz, one of the few truly American art forms. It is not, of course, unknown in other democratic countries, but nowhere else has it achieved the same degree of virtuosity; nowhere else is it so accurate a reflection of national character: by turns solemn or witty, pompous or deeply moving, full of sense or full of wind.
ANONYMOUS, *American Heritage,* Aug., 1964.

4
As Maine goes, so goes the nation.
ANONYMOUS, political saying that gained currency after Benjamin Harrison's victory in 1888. See also FARLEY in this section.

5
All political parties die at last of swallowing their own lies.
JOHN ARBUTHNOT, quoted by RICHARD GARNETT, *Life of Emerson.*

6
Esthetically speaking, Presidential Inaugurations have begun to go the way of the Hollywood biblical epic. Both are afflicted by the national passion for overproducing the simplest of dramas.
RUSSELL BAKER, *The New York Times,* Jan. 21, 1965.

7
I defined a bureaucrat as "a Democrat who holds some office that a Republican wants."
ALBEN W. BARKLEY, *That Reminds Me.*

8
When I was in the House, I was told that the difference between the House Foreign Affairs Committee and the Senate Foreign Relations Committee was that the Senators were too old to have affairs. They only have relations.
ALBEN W. BARKLEY, quoted by PEGGY McEVOY, *Reader's Digest,* Feb., 1951.

9
A political leader must keep looking over his shoulder all the time to see if the boys are still there. If they aren't still there, he's no longer a political leader.
BERNARD M. BARUCH, quoted in his obituary, *The New York Times,* June 21, 1965.

10
Vote for the man who promises least. He'll be the least disappointing.
BERNARD M. BARUCH, quoted in *Meyer Berger's New York.*

11
The Payne tariff bill has also shown that the Republicans are expert mathematicians. They can add, subtract, multiply, and divide all in one operation. They can add to the wealth of the rich, subtract from the substance of the poor, multiply millionaires, and divide themselves—all in one bill.
REPRESENTATIVE JACK BEALL OF TEXAS, 1910.

12
Let the hand of discipline smite the leprous lips which utter the profane heresy, *All is fair in politics.*
HENRY WARD BEECHER, quoted in *Henry Ward Beecher: An American Portrait,* by PAXTON HIBBEN.

13
Dr. Beer . . . had distinguished himself for having described the Eisenhower era as a period of "glacial immobility—the Ike age."
VICTOR LASKY, *J.F.K.: The Man and the Myth.*

14
Disraeli cynically expressed the dilemma when he said: "I must follow the people. Am I not their leader?" He might have added: "I *must* lead the people. Am I not their servant?"
EDWARD L. BERNAYS, *Propaganda.*

15
Politics is the art of the next best.
OTTO VON BISMARCK, quoted in *The New York Times,* Aug. 11, 1957.

16
Mr. Lincoln is like a waiter in a large eating house where all the bells are ringing at once; he cannot serve them all at once, and so some grumblers are to be expected.
JOHN BRIGHT, *Cincinnati Gazette,* 1864.

17
In several ways, the [political] convention is a peculiar institution. Like an impatient Brigadoon, it comes to life every four years; it is master of its own rules, and its decisions are as irrevocable as a haircut. Yet, the convention isn't even mentioned in the Constitution or in any law ever passed by Congress. In this sense, it might be described as the most unofficial official (or most official unofficial) gathering in politics.
DAVID BRINKLEY, *The Way It's Been; The New York Times,* July 12, 1964, sec. 11, p. 3.

1

Open each session with a prayer and close it with a probe.

CLARENCE BROWN, *Statement* after Republican victory, Nov., 1946. (*Time*, Aug. 4, 1947.)

2

"All Coolidge had to do in 1924," he was to say, "was to keep his mean trap shut, to be elected. All Harding had to do in 1920 was repeat 'avoid foreign entanglements.' All Hoover had to do in 1928 was to endorse Coolidge. All Roosevelt had to do in 1932 was to point to Hoover."

JOHN MASON BROWN, *The Worlds of Robert E. Sherwood.*

3

The more I observed Washington, the more frequently I visited it, and the more I interviewed there, the more I understood how prophetic L'Enfant was when he laid it out as a city that goes around in circles.

JOHN MASON BROWN, *Through These Men.*

4

An honest politician is one who when he is bought will stay bought.

SIMON CAMERON.

5

Blaine, Blaine, Blaine,
The continental liar from the State of Maine.
Burn this letter!

Campaign jingle used by Democrats during Blaine-Cleveland campaign, referring to the incriminating letter written by Blaine to a business associate named Warren G. Fisher, which he had endorsed on the back, "Burn this letter." (ALLAN NEVINS, *Grover Cleveland.*)

6

A president without both Houses of Congress back of him doesn't amount to much more than a cat without claws in that place that burneth with fire and brimstone.

REPRESENTATIVE JOSEPH G. CANNON OF ILLINOIS, from *The Wit and Wisdom of Congress,* ed. by EDWARD BOYKIN.

7

As soon as you get into politics words go completely crazy. Would you believe that "politic" means wise and prudent?

EDDIE CANTOR, *The Way I See It.*

8

Vain hope to make man happy by politics!

THOMAS CARLYLE, *Journal,* Oct. 10, 1831. (FROUDE, *Thomas Carlyle, First Forty Years.*)

9

The only difference, after all their rout,
Is that one is *in,* the other *out.*

CHARLES CHURCHILL, *The Conference.*

10

It is an error to believe that the world began when any particular party or statesmen got into office. It has all been going on quite a long time.

SIR WINSTON CHURCHILL, *Guildhall Speech,* Nov. 9, 1951.

11

The difference between a politician and a statesman is: a politician thinks of the next election and a statesman thinks of the next generation.

JAMES FREEMAN CLARKE, *Unitarian Minister.*

12

This office-seeking is a disease. It is even catching.

GROVER CLEVELAND, *Interview* in 1885. (NEVINS, *Grover Cleveland,* p. 235.)

13

Party honesty is party expediency.

GROVER CLEVELAND, *Interview, New York Commercial Advertiser,* Sept. 19, 1889.

14

The Forgotten Man was never more completely forgotten than he is now. Congress does not know that he exists. The President [Warren G. Harding] suspects that there is such a person, who may turn up at the polls in November, but he is not quite sure.

FRANK I. COBB, *Editorial, New York World,* Sept., 1922.

15

Moreover, when Cobbett [William Cobbett, publisher of *Porcupine's Gazette,* 1798] warned the young women of America that it was "better to be married to a felon or a hangman than to a Democrat," thousands of Federalist fathers approved the sentiment. "No bundling with Democrats" might well have been the motto hung in pious New England households.

JOHN C. MILLER, *Crisis in Freedom,* ch. 8.

16

An upright minister asks, *what* recommends a man; a corrupt minister, *who.*

C. C. COLTON, *Lacon: Reflections,* No. 9.

17

A chess tournament disguised as a circus.

ALISTAIR COOKE. The reference is to political conventions. (MOOS AND HESS, *Hats in the Ring.*)

18

A fairground smile painted on a cardboard cut-out.

ALISTAIR COOKE. The reference is to a political candidate. (MOOS AND HESS, *Hats in the Ring.*)

19

Perhaps one of the most important accomplishments of my administration has been minding my own business.

> CALVIN COOLIDGE, *News Conference*, Mar. 1, 1929.

1
I think the American people wants a solemn ass as a President. And I think I'll go along with them.

> CALVIN COOLIDGE, to Ethel Barrymore. (*Time*, May 16, 1955.)

2
Cromwell looked to the Lord—had great confidence in the Great Ruler of the universe—but he had a certain confidence in charcoal and saltpetre when it was kept dry.

> REPRESENTATIVE THOMAS CORWIN of Ohio, 1861.

3
I do not engage in criminal practice.

> GEORGE WILLIAM CURTIS, when asked why he did not speak for Blaine during the Blaine-Cleveland campaign of 1884. (NEVINS, *Grover Cleveland*.) MUZZEY (*Life of Blaine*) attributes this phrase to ROSCOE CONKLING.

4
Now, Mr. Speaker, is the Democratic party as we see it represented here in the Congress run by the horse or the jackass? Or is it a composite of the horse and jackass, a sterile coalition for power?

> REPRESENTATIVE THOMAS B. CURTIS of Missouri (1957).

5
A third-rate county politician [Franklin Pierce] President of the United States!

> R. H. DANA, quoted by IRVING STONE in *They Also Ran*.

6
I will issue such a stamp if you will develop a glue to put on the back that tastes like beer.

> J. EDWARD DAY, when Postmaster General. *Response* to pretzel interests who wanted their product honored by a commemorative stamp. (MYRA MACPHERSON, Washington *Evening Star*, Mar. 29, 1963.)

7
The foreign policy of the noble Earl . . . may be summed up in two truly expressive words: "meddle" and "muddle."

> LORD DERBY, *Speech*, House of Lords, Feb., 1864. Reference to Lord Russell.

8
I'll wage a campaign that's hard and tough, As only Dick Nixon can really get rough. I'll smear and slander, vilify, attack, For of guts and spirit I sure have no lack.

> Read by Tammany boss CARMINE DE-SAPIO during 1960 campaign.

9
Di-plomacy has become a philanthropic pursoot like shop-keepin', but politics, me lords, is still th' same ol' spoort iv highway robb'ry.

> FINLEY PETER DUNNE, *Observations by Mr. Dooley: International Amenities.*

10
"I don't like a rayformer," said Mr. Hennessy.
"Or anny other raypublican," said Mr. Dooley.

> FINLEY PETER DUNNE, *Observations by Mr. Dooley: Reform Administration.*

11
Th' prisidincy is th' highest office in th' gift iv th' people. Th' vice-prisidincy is th' next highest an' th' lowest. It isn't a crime exactly. Ye can't be sint to jail f'r it, but it's a kind iv a disgrace. It's like writin' anonymous letters.

> FINLEY PETER DUNNE, *Dissertations by Mr. Dooley: The Vice President.*

12
Sure, politics ain't bean bags. 'Tis a man's game, an' women, childher, and pro-hybitionists do well to keep out iv it.

> FINLEY PETER DUNNE, *Mr. Dooley on Ward Leaders.*

13
The Democratic party is never so good as when it's broke, when respectable people speak of it in whispers, and when it has no leaders and only one principle, to go in and take it away from the other fellows.

> FINLEY PETER DUNNE, *Mr. Dooley Remembers.*

14
The Democratic party ain't on speaking terms with itself.

> FINLEY PETER DUNNE, *Mr. Dooley Remembers.*

15
A reformer tries to get into office on a flying machine. He succeeds now and then, but the odds are a hundred to one on the lad that tunnels through.

> FINLEY PETER DUNNE, *Mr. Dooley Remembers.*

16
The man who goes into politics as a business has no business to go into politics.

> *Toaster's Handbook*, compiled by PEGGY EDMUND AND HENRY WORKMAN WILLIAMS.

17
Politicians always belong to the opposite party.

> *Toaster's Handbook*, compiled by PEGGY EDMUND AND HENRY WORKMAN WILLIAMS.

1
I feel almost like bawling on my own shoulder.
> DWIGHT D. EISENHOWER, on the first anniversary of his election to the presidency. (*New York World-Telegram and Sun,* Nov. 5, 1953.)

2
I feel like the fellow in jail who is watching his scaffold being built.
> DWIGHT D. EISENHOWER, Comment on construction of reviewing stands for President-elect John F. Kennedy's inauguration. (*The New York Times,* Dec. 6, 1960.)

3
Each of us has his portion of ego. At least one night I dreamed that the 22nd amendment [limiting a president to two terms] had been repealed—and it wasn't wholly a nightmare.
> DWIGHT D. EISENHOWER, when asked if he would like to be back in the White House. (*The New York Times,* May 13, 1962.)

4
The Democratic party is the party of the Poor marshalled against the Rich. . . . But they are always officered by a few self-seeking deserters from the Rich or Whig party.
> RALPH WALDO EMERSON, *Journals,* 1857.

5
Politics is a deleterious profession, like some poisonous handicrafts.
> RALPH WALDO EMERSON, *Conduct of Life: Power.*

6
In politics and in trade, bruisers and pirates are of better promise than talkers and clerks.
> RALPH WALDO EMERSON, *Essays, Second Series: Manners.*

7
A mugwump is one of those boys who always has his mug on one side of the political fence and his wump on the other.
> ALBERT J. ENGEL, *Speech,* House of Representatives, Apr. 23, 1936. Also credited to Harold W. Dodds.

8
We are fortunate to have inherited an institution [the House of Lords] which we certainly should never have had the intelligence to create. We might have been landed with something like the American Senate.
> LORD ESHER (OLIVER S. B. BRETT, 3RD VISCOUNT ESHER), quoted in *Wall Street Journal,* May 2, 1963.

9
At twenty-three Charles Dickens had already made a reputation for himself as a transcriber of the words of others, being probably the fastest and most accurate shorthand reporter ever to take down the inanities of the House of Commons. Politicians have their uses: their dullness may have driven Dickens to original composition.
> CLIFTON FADIMAN, *The Selected Writings of Clifton Fadiman: Pickwick and Dickens* (1955).

10
As Maine goes, so goes Vermont.
> JAMES A. FARLEY, *Interview,* Nov. 4, 1936, after the 46 other states had just landed in the Democratic column in the reelection of Franklin D. Roosevelt. A paraphrase of an anonymous saying appearing earlier in this section.

11
What are we here for, except the offices?
> WEBSTER FLANAGAN, leader of the Republican party in Texas, at the Republican national convention in 1880. (*The Nation,* June 10, 1880.)

12
The middle of the road is where the white line is—and that's the worst place to drive.
> ROBERT FROST, *Interview. Collier's,* 27 Apr., 1956, p. 42. The Eisenhower administration of that period was frequently described as "middle of the road."

13
That was the Kennedy way. You bit off more than you could chew. And then you chewed it.
> GERALD GARDNER, *Robert Kennedy in New York.* Reference to Robert Kennedy's campaign against Senator Kenneth Keating in New York.

14
Whatever I may believe in theology, I do not believe in the doctrine of vicarious atonement in politics.
> JAMES A. GARFIELD, *Speech,* House of Representatives, Jan. 12, 1876.

15
[The President] is the last person in the world to know what the people really want and think.
> JAMES A. GARFIELD.

16
My God! What is there in this place that a man should ever want to get into it?
> JAMES A. GARFIELD, Reference to the Presidency. (*Time,* Apr. 24, 1950.)

17
Worst damfool mistake I ever made was letting myself be elected Vice-President of the United States. Should have stuck with my old chores as Speaker of the House. I gave up the second most important job in the Government for one that didn't amount

to a hill of beans. I spent eight long years as Mr. Roosevelt's spare tire. I might still be Speaker if I hadn't let them elect me Vice-President.

> JOHN NANCE GARNER. (FRANK X. TOL-BERT, *What Is Cactus Jack Up to Now?;* *Saturday Evening Post,* Nov. 2, 1963.)

1

Since a politician never believes what he says, he is surprised when others believe him.

> CHARLES DE GAULLE, quoted in *Newsweek,* Oct. 1, 1962.

2

We cannot safely leave politics to politicians, or political economy to college professors.

> HENRY GEORGE, *Social Problems.*

3

I always voted at my party's call,
And never thought of thinking for myself at all!
I thought so little, they rewarded me
By making me the ruler of the Queen's navee!

> W. S. GILBERT, *H.M.S. Pinafore,* Act 1.

4

"Lyndon has always been acrobatically inclined," smiled Goldwater.

> VICTOR LASKY, *J.F.K.: The Man and the Myth.* Senator Barry Goldwater on Lyndon B. Johnson.

5

I never said all Democrats were saloon-keepers. What I said was that all saloon-keepers are Democrats.

> HORACE GREELEY.

6

I can't remember a time when a President had prosperity and poverty going for him at the same time.

> LEONARD HALL, commenting, as former chairman of the Republican National Committee, on Lyndon B. Johnson's "war on poverty" during a time of general prosperity. (*Time,* May 15, 1964, p. 31.)

7

Don't any of you realize that there's only one life between this madman and the White House?

> MARK HANNA. The reference is to Theodore Roosevelt's nomination for the vice-presidency. (MOOS AND HESS, *Hats in the Ring.*)

8

Now look, that damned cowboy is President of the United States.

> MARK HANNA. Reference to Theodore Roosevelt.

9

Timely political squib, from the files of the

immortal Will Rogers: "They took me in to meet President Harding, and I said, 'Mr. President, I would like to tell you all the latest jokes.' 'You don't have to, Will,' he answered. 'I appointed them.' "

> BENNETT CERF, *The Laugh's on Me.*

10

We drew a pair of deuces and filled.

> WARREN G. HARDING, describing his nomination for the presidency in 1920 to a group of reporters just after he was selected. He was employing poker terms: to "fill" is to get a "full house," a pair and three of a kind.

11

One thing, if no more, I have gained by my custom-house experience—to know a politician. It is a knowledge which no previous thought, or power of sympathy, could have taught me, because the animal, or the machine rather, is not in nature.

> NATHANIEL HAWTHORNE, *Note-Books,* Mar. 15, 1840. This is said to be the origin of the term "machine politics."

12

A politician will do anything to keep his job —even become a patriot.

> WILLIAM RANDOLPH HEARST, *Editorial,* Aug. 28, 1933.

13

The Kansas-Nebraska bill was not the product of one of the South's best minds. Stephen Arnold Douglas, its author, was what was known in that day as a Northern man with Southern principles—that is to say, a practical politician.

> PAXTON HIBBEN, *Henry Ward Beecher: An American Portrait,* ch. 15.

14

I am a Democrat still—very still.

> DAVID B. HILL, after the nomination of William Jennings Bryan in 1896. (NEVINS, *Grover Cleveland.*)

15

A statesman makes the occasion, but the occasion makes the politician.

> GEORGE S. HILLARD, *The Life and Services of Daniel Webster.*

16

In the Middle Ages it was the fashion to wear hair shirts to remind one's self of trouble and sin. Many years ago I concluded that a few hair shirts were part of the mental wardrobe of every man. The President differs only from other men in that he has a more extensive wardrobe.

> HERBERT HOOVER, *Speech* in Washington, D.C., Dec. 14, 1929.

17

I was in favor of giving former Presidents a seat in the Senate until I passed 75 years.

Since then I have less taste for sitting on hard-bottomed chairs during long addresses.
> HERBERT HOOVER, quoted in *This Week*, Feb. 7, 1960.

1
It is a curious fact that when we get sick we want an uncommon doctor. If we have a construction job, we want an uncommon engineer. When we get into a war, we dreadfully want an uncommon admiral and an uncommon general. Only when we get into politics are we content with the common man.
> HERBERT HOOVER, quoted in *The New York Times* obituary of Hoover, Oct. 21, 1964, p. 40.

2
"I think we should all snip out the picture and paste it on the wall," commented *San Francisco Chronicle* columnist Art Hoppe. "Then when people imply reverently that we should all have blind faith in The President, we could all look at it. For there is nothing that renews one's belief in political equality and the fallibility of any leadership better than contemplating the Presidential navel. After all, I've got one myself."
> VICTOR LASKY, *J.F.K.: The Man and the Myth*. The reference is to a picture of John F. Kennedy in swim trunks.

3
There's some folks standing behind the President that ought to get around where he can watch 'em.
> FRANK MCKINNEY (KIN) HUBBARD.

4
We'd all like t' vote fer th' best man, but he's never a candidate.
> FRANK MCKINNEY (KIN) HUBBARD, *Abe Martin's Primer*.

5
C stands for candidate, with a smile an' a smirk,
He's out fer an office so he won't have t' work.
> FRANK MCKINNEY (KIN) HUBBARD, *Abe Martin's Primer*.

6
Some defeated candidates go back t' work an' others say th' fight has jest begun.
> FRANK MCKINNEY (KIN) HUBBARD, *Abe Martin's Primer*.

7
Politics makes strange pustmasters.
> FRANK MCKINNEY (KIN) HUBBARD, *Abe Martin's Primer*.

8
Th' election hain't very fer off when a candidate kin recognize you across the street.
> FRANK MCKINNEY (KIN) HUBBARD, *Abe Martin's Primer*.

9
Jest because a candidate kin place you while he's runnin' fer office it's no sign he kin do it after he's elected.
> FRANK MCKINNEY (KIN) HUBBARD, *Abe Martin's Primer*.

10
Ever' once in a while we miss a nuisance, an' then find out he's got a political job.
> FRANK MCKINNEY (KIN) HUBBARD, *Abe Martin's Primer*.

11
Of all sciences, there is none where first appearances are more deceitful than in politics.
> DAVID HUME, *Essays, 33.*

12
Barry is so handsome that I understand he's been offered a movie contract—with 18th Century Fox.
> HUBERT HUMPHREY, *Comment* on Senator Goldwater at banquet of Women's National Press Club. (*Time*, Jan. 27, 1961.)

13
The purification of politics is an iridescent dream.
> JOHN JAMES INGALLS, *Epigram.*

14
Gag popular in the South, about Alabama Governor Wallace's putting his wife up for governor: "Bedfellows make strange politics."
> *The Insider's Newsletter.* Quoted in *Reader's Digest*, Sept., 1966. See WARNER in this section.

15
The Constitution rides behind
  And Big Stick rides before,
(Which is the rule of precedent
  In the reign of Theodore.)
> WALLACE IRWIN, *The Ballad of Grizzly Gulch.*

16
If I could not go to heaven but with a party, I would not go there at all.
> THOMAS JEFFERSON, *Letter* to Francis Hopkinson, 1789.

17
Whenever a man has cast a longing eye on offices, a rottenness begins in his conduct.
> THOMAS JEFFERSON, *Letter* to T. Coxe, 1799.

18
Few die and none resign.
> THOMAS JEFFERSON, *Letter* to a Committee of Merchants of New Haven, July 12, 1801. Reference to office holders.

19
If you're in politics and you can't tell when you walk into a room who's for you and

who's against you, then you're in the wrong line of work.

LYNDON B. JOHNSON, quoted by BOOTH MOONEY in *The Lyndon Johnson Story.*

1
I seldom think of politics more than eighteen hours a day.

LYNDON B. JOHNSON, *Speech* to a Texas audience, 1958. (HENRY A. ZEIGER, *Lyndon B. Johnson: Man and President,* p. 68.)

2
Good-by, Culpeper. God bless you, Culpeper! What did Dick Nixon ever do for Culpeper?

LYNDON B. JOHNSON, *Speech* (conclusion) in Culpeper, Va., during the 1960 campaign. This is the best-remembered example of Johnson's whistle-stop technique during an intensive tour of the South in behalf of the Kennedy-Johnson ticket.

3
Jack was out kissing babies when I was passing bills.

LYNDON B. JOHNSON. The reference is to John F. Kennedy.

4
They've been peddling eyewash about themselves and hogwash about Democrats. What they need is a good mouthwash.

LYNDON B. JOHNSON, charging his opponents with slurring John F. Kennedy's patriotism, Oct. 23, 1960.

5
I want to be progressive without getting both feet off the ground at the same time. . . . If I had to place a label on myself, I would want to be a progressive who is prudent.

LYNDON B. JOHNSON, *Interview* televised nationally from Washington, D.C., Mar. 15, 1964.

6
I think that it is very important that we have a two-party country. I am a fellow that likes small parties, and the Republican party is about the size I like.

LYNDON B. JOHNSON, *Press Conference,* Washington, D.C., Apr. 21, 1964.

7
Talking to Democrats about the qualities of our party—and the shortcomings of the opposition—is like the preacher telling the people who are already in their pews what a sin is not to come to church.

LYNDON B. JOHNSON, *Speech,* Jefferson-Jackson Day Dinner.

8
The irresponsibles win elections—but always for the other party.

LYNDON B. JOHNSON, commenting on his

role as Senate majority leader during the Eisenhower Administration, when he was frequently criticized by fellow Democrats for not following a more aggressively partisan course. (HENRY A. ZEIGER, *Lyndon B. Johnson: Man and President,* p. 61.)

9
"In politics," he drummed into his protégé's [John F. Kennedy] head, "you have no friends, only co-conspirators."

JOSEPH KANE, quoted by VICTOR LASKY in *J.F.K.: The Man and the Myth.*

10
"I have always found Roosevelt [Franklin Delano Roosevelt, Jr.] an amusing fellow," commented the irrepressible Murray Kempton, "but I would not employ him, except for reasons of personal friendship, as a geek in a common carnival."

VICTOR LASKY, *J.F.K.: The Man and the Myth.*

11
There is one piece about how I felt when Eisenhower beat Stevenson which I have kept because I feel the same way even now. I quit voting after 1956, the second time Stevenson lost; I could not think of a better time to stop.

MURRAY KEMPTON, *America Comes of Middle Age.*

12
A political convention is just not a place where you can come away with any trace of faith in human nature.

MURRAY KEMPTON, *America Comes of Middle Age.*

13
Jack and Bob will run the show,
While Ted's in charge of hiding Joe.

Couplet in reference to John F. Kennedy, Robert Kennedy, and Ted Kennedy. Joe is Joseph Kennedy, their father. The accusation had been made that Kennedy senior was kept under wraps during J.F.K.'s campaign because he had views different from those of the presidential candidate.

14
This district [Brooklyn] was the first district to endorse me as a candidate for President . . . My own family had not even endorsed me when you endorsed me.

JOHN F. KENNEDY, from *The Quotable Mr. Kennedy,* ed. by GERALD C. GARDNER.

15
Mr. Nixon, like the rest of us, has had his troubles in this campaign. At one point even the Wall Street Journal was criticizing his

tactics. That is like the Observatore Romano criticizing the Pope.

JOHN F. KENNEDY, from *The Quotable Mr. Kennedy,* ed. by GERALD GARDNER.

1

Whenever, he said, a politician means to give you the knife at a convention, the last thing he'll say to you, as he leaves the room, is: "Now look, Jack, if there's *anything* I can do for you, you just let me know!" That's the euphemism for "You're dead."

JOHN F. KENNEDY, quoted by GORE VIDAL in *Rocking the Boat: Politics,* 1962.

2

Mr. Nixon may be very experienced in kitchen debates. So are a great many other married men I know.

JOHN F. KENNEDY, *Speech* in Alexandria, Va., Aug. 24, 1960. The reference is to Richard Nixon's debate with Khrushchev.

3

In the Soviet Union he [Richard Nixon] argued with Mr. Khrushchev in the kitchen, it is true, pointing out that while we may be behind in space, we were ahead in color television.

JOHN F. KENNEDY, *Speech* in Alexandria, Va., Aug. 24, 1960.

4

It is, I think, a source of concern to us all that the first dogs carried around in outer space were not named Rover and Fido but instead were named Belka and Strelka. It was not named Checkers either.

JOHN F. KENNEDY, *Speech* in Muskegon, Mich., Sept. 5, 1960. Checkers was the dog owned by Kennedy's opponent, Richard M. Nixon.

5

Question: Senator, when does the moratorium end on Nixon's hospitalization and your ability to attack him?

Mr. Kennedy: Well, I said I would not mention him unless I could praise him until he got out of the hospital, and I have not mentioned him.

JOHN F. KENNEDY, *Speech* in Burbank, Calif., Sept. 9, 1960, during the presidential campaign.

6

Ladies and Gentlemen, it is my understanding that the last candidate for the presidency to visit this community in a presidential year was Herbert Hoover in 1928. President Hoover initiated on the occasion of his visit the slogan "Two chickens for every pot," and it is no accident that no presidential candidate has ever dared come back to this community since.

JOHN F. KENNEDY, *Speech* in Bristol, Tenn., Sept. 21, 1960.

7

What are we going to do with the Republicans? They can point to Benjamin Harrison, who according to legend saw a man forced by the depression to eat grass on the White House lawn and had only one suggestion for him—that he go around to the back where the grass was longer.

JOHN F. KENNEDY, *Speech* in Springfield, Ill., Oct. 3, 1960.

8

I want to express my great appreciation to all of you for your kindness in coming out and giving us a warm Hoosier welcome. I understand that this town suffered a misfortune this morning when the bank was robbed. I am confident that the *Indianapolis Star* will say, "Democrats Arrive and Bank Robbed." But we don't believe that.

JOHN F. KENNEDY, *Campaign speech* in Anderson, Ind., Oct. 5, 1960.

9

Mr. [Harold] Stassen announces he will run for Governor of Pennsylvania. He has already been Governor of Minnesota. That leaves only forty-six states still in jeopardy.

JOHN F. KENNEDY, *Speech* in San Francisco, Nov. 2, 1960.

10

I understand Tom Dewey has just joined Dick Nixon out on the Coast, to give him some last-minute strategy on how to win an election.

JOHN F. KENNEDY, *Speech* in New York City, Nov. 5, 1960.

11

Mr. Nixon in the last seven days has called me an economic ignoramus, a Pied Piper, and all the rest. I've just confined myself to calling him a Republican, but he says that is getting low.

JOHN F. KENNEDY, *Speech* in New York City, Nov. 5, 1960.

12

It's a big job. It isn't going to be so bad. You've got time to think. You don't have all those people bothering you that you had in the Senate—besides, the pay is pretty good.

JOHN F. KENNEDY, *Statement* about the presidency, Georgetown, Dec., 1960.

13

What a lousy, fouled-up job this has turned out to be.

JOHN F. KENNEDY to Senator Barry Goldwater after Kennedy's election as President. Quoted by VICTOR LASKY in *J.F.K.: The Man and the Myth.*

14

I know that when things don't go well they like to blame the Presidents, and that is one

of the things which Presidents are paid for.
JOHN F. KENNEDY, *News conference,* June
14, 1962.

1
When we got into office, the thing that surprised me most was to find that things were just as bad as we'd been saying they were.
JOHN F. KENNEDY, *Speech* at dinner in
Washington, D.C., May 27, 1961.

2
I can't see that it's wrong to give him a little legal experience before he goes out to practice law.
JOHN F. KENNEDY. The reference is to
Robert Kennedy's appointment as Attorney General. (VICTOR LASKY, *J.F.K.: The Man and the Myth.*)

3
It is my pleasure to be back from whence I came. Many people are under the impression that all the Kennedys are in Washington, but I am happy to see so many present who have missed the boat.
JOHN F. KENNEDY, *Address* to a gathering of friends and relatives in Wexford, Ireland, June 28, 1963.

4
The only other president to have visited Ashland was Calvin Coolidge, who never said a word. I was here for only one night and spoke all the time.
JOHN F. KENNEDY, *Speech* in Ashland, Wis., Sept. 24, 1963.

5
Politics is like football. If you see daylight, go through the hole.
JOHN F. KENNEDY, on the authority of Pierre Salinger, Kennedy's press secretary. (JOSEPH ALSOP, Syndicated Column, Apr. 3, 1964.)

6
We concentrated on women because they could do the work in a campaign, said Bobby Kennedy. Men just talk.
VICTOR LASKY, *J.F.K.: The Man and the Myth.* The reference is to John F. Kennedy's first campaign for the U.S. Senate.

7
The Catskills, Kennedy observed to the diners in the Concord's cavernous dining room, were immortalized by Washington Irving. He wrote of a man who fell asleep and awoke in another era. The only other area that can boast such a man is Phoenix, Arizona.
GERALD GARDNER, quoting Robert Kennedy's speech at the Concord during Kennedy's 1964 campaign for the U.S. Senate. Reference is to Senator Barry Goldwater. From *Robert Kennedy in New York.*

8
Our President, my boy, has a tail for every emergency, as a rat-trap has an emergency for every tail.
ORPHEUS C. KERR, quoted by CARL SANDBURG in *Abraham Lincoln: The Prairie Years and the War Years,* ch. 50.

9
Politicians are the same all over. They promise to build a bridge even where there is no river.
NIKITA KHRUSHCHEV, quoted in *New York Herald Tribune,* Aug. 22, 1963.

10
He [the politician] is willing to embrace any issue, however idiotic, that will get him votes, and he is willing to sacrifice any principle, however sound, that will lose them for him.
ALEXANDER KING, *Rich Man, Poor Man, Freud and Fruit,* ch. 13.

11
The Democrats have been hogging the administration at Washington for twenty years, and it's about time the people began to squeal.
HENRY B. KRAJEWSKI, Secaucus, N.J., explaining why he chose the pig as a symbol of his presidential candidacy. (*Time,* Mar. 17, 1952.)

12
The most political animal to occupy the White House since Andrew Jackson, if not since the creation of the Federal Government, has just completed the first six months of his Presidency.
ARTHUR KROCK, *Washington Column, The New York Times,* May 24, 1964. Referring to Lyndon B. Johnson.

13
I am not in favor of turning out the lights at City Hall. We operate enough in the dark as it is.
THEODORE R. KUPFERMAN, *Comment,* as a New York City Councilman, on economy in government, May, 1964. The observation was spurred by President Lyndon B. Johnson's campaign against wasted electric light at the White House.

14
"Mr. Speaker, can there be anything brought into this House that will not be repealed sooner or later?" asked Representative John F. Potter of Wisconsin during the Thirty-seventh Congress. "Yes," replied Representative William E. Lansing of New York, "a skinned orange."
The Wit and Wisdom of Congress, ed. by EDWARD BOYKIN.

15
I once said cynically of a politician, "He'll

doublecross that bridge when he comes to it."

OSCAR LEVANT, *Memoirs of an Amnesiac.*

1

No man knows, when the presidential grub gets to gnawing at him, just how deep it will get until he has tried it.

ABRAHAM LINCOLN, from CARL SANDBURG, *Abraham Lincoln: The Prairie Years and the War Years,* ch. 40.

2

I'm the longest but he's better looking.

ABRAHAM LINCOLN, *Statement* of the difference between him and General McClellan as candidates for the Presidency. (*The Humorous Mr. Lincoln* by KEITH W. JENNISON.)

3

A headless torso that must find a central nervous system.

JOHN V. LINDSAY, defining the Republican party after its decisive defeat in the 1964 presidential election, in a speech to the Women's National Press Club, Washington, D.C., Dec. 15, 1964.

4

It is impossible to rock a boat resting at the bottom of an ocean. The thing to do is get it back to the top.

JOHN V. LINDSAY, *Speech* to the Women's National Press Club, Washington, D.C., Dec. 15, 1964. This was shortly after he had won re-election to the U.S. House of Representatives, as a Republican from New York, in the face of a strong Democratic trend nationally. It was his reply to those in his party who claimed that change in the top structure of the G.O.P. amounted to rocking the boat.

5

Senatorial courtesy means to stop calling the other senators names after the election.

ART LINKLETTER, *A Child's Garden of Misinformation.*

6

A public servant is one who serves the public for his own good.

ART LINKLETTER, *A Child's Garden of Misinformation.*

7

NRA—Nuts Running America.

HUEY LONG, Description of the National Recovery Act.

8

I expect to fight that proposition until hell freezes over. Then I propose to start fighting on the ice.

SENATOR RUSSELL LONG of Louisiana. *Comment* on President Kennedy's request for a cutoff of federal funds to areas practicing segregation. (*The New York Times,* July 14, 1963.)

9

He looks as if he had been weaned on a pickle.

ALICE ROOSEVELT LONGWORTH, describing Calvin Coolidge by quoting her physician. (*Crowded Hours,* p. 337.)

10

Ez to my princerples, I glory
 In hevin' nothin' o' the sort;
I aint a Whig, I aint a Tory,
 I'm jest a canderdate, in short.

JAMES RUSSELL LOWELL, *The Biglow Papers.* Ser. i, No. 7.

11

A ginooine statesman should be on his guard,
Ef he *must hev* beliefs, not to b'lieve 'em tu hard.

JAMES RUSSELL LOWELL, *The Biglow Papers.* Ser. ii, No. 5.

12

Skilled to pull wires, he baffles Nature's hope,
Who sure intended him to stretch a rope.

JAMES RUSSELL LOWELL, *The Boss.* Probably referring to Boss Tweed of New York.

13

Much of what Mr. [Henry] Wallace calls his global thinking is, no matter how you slice it, still Globaloney.

CLARE BOOTHE LUCE, *Speech* in the House of Representatives, Feb. 9, 1943.

14

I am grateful for the overwhelming vote of confirmation in the Senate. We must now wait until the dirt settles. My difficulties, of course, go some years back when Senator Wayne Morse was kicked in the head by a horse.

CLARE BOOTHE LUCE, *Statement* to newsmen a half hour after Senate confirmation of her appointment as ambassador to Brazil; her comment started another controversy and she resigned the post. *News Reports* of Apr. 29, 1959.

15

There is always some principle that will ultimately get the Republican party together. If my observations are worth anything, that basic principle is the cohesive power of public plunder.

A. J. MCLAURIN, *Speech,* U.S. Senate, May, 1906.

16

When we've been there ten thousand years,
 And sucked from sun to sun,

'Tis just as hard to quit the teat
  As when we first begun.
    REPRESENTATIVE JOHN MCSWEENEY of
    Ohio. Describing the length of time the
    Republican party had been "sucking at
    the public teat."

1
A demagogue is a person with whom we
disagree as to which gang should mismanage
the country.
    DON MARQUIS, *New York Sun.*

2
Once there were two brothers. One ran away
to sea, the other was elected Vice-President,
and nothing was heard of either of them
again.
    THOMAS R. MARSHALL, *Recollections.*

3
The Vice President is like a man in a cata-
leptic state; he cannot speak; he cannot
move; he suffers no pain; and yet he is
perfectly conscious of everything that is going on around him.
    THOMAS R. MARSHALL, quoted by ALBEN
    W. BARKLEY in *That Reminds Me.*

4
One reporter remembered the joke of the
child who asked her parent: "If McKinley
should die, will Hanna still be President?"
    RALPH G. MARTIN, *Ballots & Band-*
    wagons: Republican National Conven-
    tion of 1900 (1964).

5
Franklin D. and Alfred E.
One for each and each for one.
Till the presidential run;
Franklin D. and Alfred E.
Love no longer—Hope is stronger
Each for ME.
    Poem on program of Albany Legislative
    Correspondents Dinner in 1931. From
    Ballots & Bandwagons by RALPH G.
    MARTIN (1964).

6
If you are Wet, vote for Smith,
If you are Dry, vote for Garner,
—If you don't know what you are,
Vote for Roosevelt.
    Circulated at the Democratic national
    convention of 1932. From *Ballots &*
    Bandwagons by RALPH G. MARTIN.

7
The statesman throws his shoulders back,
  and straightens out his tie,
And says, "My friends, unless it rains, the
  weather will be dry."
And when this thought into our brains has
  percolated through,
We common people nod our heads and
  loudly cry, "How true!"
    WALT MASON, *The Statesman.*

8
It's very unfair to expect a politician to
live in private up to the statements he
makes in public.
    W. SOMERSET MAUGHAM, *The Circle.*

9
They [politicians] are men who, at some
time or other, have compromised with their
honor, either by swallowing their convictions
or by whooping for what they believe to be
untrue. They are in the position of the
chorus girl who, in order to get her humble
job, has had to admit the manager to her
person.
    H. L. MENCKEN, *The Politician Under*
    Democracy.

10
When an excited man rushed up to Wilson
Mizner and said, "Coolidge is dead," Mizner
asked, "How do they know?"
    ALVA JOHNSTON, *Legend of a Sport; The*
    New Yorker. A variant of this is at-
    tributed to DOROTHY PARKER, who is
    said to have reacted to the news by
    asking: "How can they tell?"

11
Toward the end of the century, a Cook
County, Illinois, political convention was
made up of 723 delegates, of whom 17 had
been tried for homicide, 46 had been in penitentiaries for homicide or other felonies, 84
were known to have criminal records, one-
third were saloon-keepers, and several others
were identified as gamblers or operators of
houses of prostitution.
    MOOS AND HESS, *Hats in the Ring* (1960).

12
. . . the humorless calculation of a certified
public accountant in pursuit of the Holy
Grail.
    ANONYMOUS English newspaperman,
    quoted in *Hats in the Ring* by MOOS
    AND HESS (1960). The reference is to
    candidates for presidential nomination
    who pretend they are not candidates.

13
When the prohibition issue threatened the
harmony of the 1928 Democratic convention,
the party attempted to compose its policy
difference by forming an Al Smith-Joe Robinson ticket, which prompted one writer to
say that the Democratic donkey left its
Houston site "with a *wet* head and wagging
a *dry* tail."
    MOOS AND HESS, *Hats in the Ring.*

14
Politics is the science of the second-best.
    JOHN MORLEY, quoted in *Ballots & Band-*
    wagons by RALPH G. MARTIN.

15
Any party which takes credit for the rain

must not be surprised if its opponents blame it for the drought.

DWIGHT W. MORROW, *Speech,* Oct., 1930.

1

I considered the case of corn, and I pointed out that the corn tassel is the male part of the flower and is not the full flower. The Senator [Senator Paul Douglas of Illinois] will find Susan B. Anthony rolling over in her grave, should he make the fight for the corn tassel.

SENATOR THRUSTON MORTON of Kentucky, *Comment* during debate on the question of a national flower. See also NEUBERGER in this section.

2

In parliamentary life, he was never to be one who stayed to get his feet wet before deciding that a ship was sinking.

LEONARD MOSLEY, *The Glorious Fault.* Reference to LORD CURZON.

3

The conspirators got, instead of him [Lord Curzon], Stanley Baldwin, the Prime Minister they preferred. And that might have been possible to bear, had it not been for the fact that the people—who had played no part in this squalid comedy—got Stanley Baldwin too.

LEONARD MOSLEY, *The Glorious Fault.* The reference is to the passing over of Curzon for Prime Minister when he was the logical choice.

4

In a political campaign, the most important thing is the ability to turn lemons into lemonade—to make the potentially damaging issues work for you, not against you.

DEBS MYERS. (*The New York Times,* Feb. 3, 1965.)

5

Monsieur Lafayette is a political monomaniac, a mule.

NAPOLEON BONAPARTE. (*The Mind of Napoleon,* ed. by J. CHRISTOPHER HEROLD.)

6

Democrats are to the manna born.

OGDEN NASH, *Vive le Postmaster General.*

7

Politics is the diversion of trivial men who, when they succeed at it, become important in the eyes of more trivial men.

GEORGE JEAN NATHAN, *News summaries,* July 9, 1954.

8

I should like to point out to my colleagues on the other side of the aisle that more roses grow in Oregon than in any other state, and that, unlike the corn tassel, the rose does not need price supports to enable it to flourish.

SENATOR RICHARD NEUBERGER of Oregon,

1959. *Debate* on the question of a national flower.

9

You won't have Nixon to kick around any more.

RICHARD M. NIXON, *Statement* to the press, Nov. 7, 1962, the day after the California election in which he unsuccessfully tried to unseat Governor Edmund G. (Pat) Brown.

10

I never wear a hat, so it must always be in the ring.

RICHARD M. NIXON, *Radio interview* in New York City, Jan. 20, 1964.

11

Nikita Khrushchev thought so too. Returning from Moscow, labor leader Joseph Curran reported that the Soviet ruler had told him that Kennedy "made sense" while Nixon was "not a politician but a grocery clerk." To which Nixon replied he'd rather be a grocery clerk in the U.S. than a politician in the U.S.S.R.

VICTOR LASKY, *J.F.K.: The Man and the Myth.*

12

Overnominated and underelected.

RICHARD M. NIXON, describing his plight to a dinner audience in Washington, D.C., in 1965. (ROBERT J. DONOVAN, *The New York Times Magazine,* Apr. 25, 1965, p. 14.)

13

A dropout from the Electoral College.

RICHARD NIXON, referring to himself. (*The Wall Street Journal,* Dec. 27, 1966.)

14

People keep asking me, why can't you do something about your face? Well, if I grew a beard they'd say I was trying to look like Lincoln. A mustache might make me look like Dewey. And if I let my hair grow they'd say I was trying to look like Bobby.

RICHARD NIXON, quoted in *The Wall Street Journal,* Dec. 27, 1966.

15

The statesman shears the sheep, the politician skins them.

AUSTIN O'MALLEY.

16

He thinks like Nixon, talks like Eisenhower, goofs like Goldwater.

NOEL PARMENTEL, JR., *Esquire,* Oct., 1965. Referring to John V. Lindsay.

17

Public office is the last refuge of a scoundrel.

BOIES PENROSE, *Colliers' Weekly,* Feb. 14, 1931.

1
Perhaps it is the expediency in the political eye that blinds it.
VIRGILIA PETERSON, *A Matter of Life and Death.*

2
You can always get the truth from an American statesman after he has turned seventy or given up all hope of the Presidency.
WENDELL PHILLIPS.

3
President Lincoln selected Hale [John Parker Hale, appointed minister to Spain] out of general kindness and good-will to the lame ducks.
E. L. PIERCE. (*Memoir and Letters of Charles Sumner,* vol. 4.)

4
In politics you've got to have a sense of humor. If you don't have humor you'll end up in a nuthouse with a lot of paper dolls.
MICHAEL PRENDERGAST, speaking from a background of long experience as chairman of the Democratic party in New York State. (*The New York Times,* May 17, 1964.)

5
There lies beneath this mossy stone
A politician who
Touched a live issue without gloves,
And never did come to.
KEITH PRESTON, *Epitaph.*

6
There's not a particle of doubt
We've turned a bunch of rascals out,
And put a nice clean aggregation
In very serious temptation.
KEITH PRESTON, *Post-Election Misgivings.*

7
That most delicious of all privileges—spending other people's money.
JOHN RANDOLPH OF ROANOKE, from *The Wit and Wisdom of Congress,* ed. by EDWARD BOYKIN.

8
Clay's eye is on the presidency; and my eye is on him.
JOHN RANDOLPH OF ROANOKE, referring to Henry Clay. From *The Wit and Wisdom of Congress,* ed. by EDWARD BOYKIN.

9
Never were abilities so much below mediocrity so well rewarded; no, not since Caligula's horse was made Consul.
JOHN RANDOLPH OF ROANOKE, on the appointment of Richard Rush to be Secretary of the Treasury. From *The Wit and Wisdom of Congress,* ed. by EDWARD BOYKIN.

10
He rowed to his object with muffled oars.
JOHN RANDOLPH OF ROANOKE, on Martin Van Buren. From *The Wit and Wisdom of Congress,* ed. by EDWARD BOYKIN.

11
The Democratic party is like a man riding backward in a railroad car; it never sees anything until it has got past it.
THOMAS B. REED. (W. A. ROBINSON, *Life of Reed.*)

12
The Senate is a nice, quiet sort of place where good Representatives go when they die.
THOMAS B. REED, from *The Wit and Wisdom of Congress,* ed. by EDWARD BOYKIN.

13
Theodore, if there is one thing more than another for which I admire you, it is your original discovery of the ten commandments.
THOMAS B. REED, referring to Theodore Roosevelt.

14
A statesman is a successful politician who is dead.
THOMAS B. REED. (LODGE, *The Democracy of the Constitution.*) Senator Henry Cabot Lodge, in a magazine article, told the story of the editor who thereupon telegraphed Reed, "Why don't you die and become a statesman?" To which Reed wired back, "No, fame is the last infirmity of a noble mind."

15
Everybody is in doubt about whether President Johnson is a conservative progressive or a progressive conservative, and he is in clover.
JAMES RESTON, *Washington Column, The New York Times,* Jan. 20, 1964.

16
H.S.T. "gave 'em hell" then [1948], but L.B.J. has turned it around. He's now giving them heaven.
JAMES RESTON, *Washington Column, The New York Times,* Sept. 9, 1964. Contrasting Harry S Truman's aggressive campaign tactics with the "Great Society" approach of Lyndon B. Johnson in the campaign of 1964.

17
Political campaigns are designedly made into emotional orgies which endeavor to distract attention from the real issues involved, and they actually paralyze what slight powers of cerebration man can normally muster.
JAMES H. ROBINSON, *The Human Comedy,* ch. 9.

1
Our policy is "Nothing is no good."
WILL ROGERS, *The Illiterate Digest*.

2
Politics has got so expensive that it takes
lots of money to even get beat with.
WILL ROGERS, *Newspaper column,* June
28, 1931.

3
I could study all my life and not think up
half the amount of funny things they can
think of in one session of Congress.
WILL ROGERS, *Autobiography*.

4
All you would have to do to make some men
atheists is just to tell them the Lord belonged to the opposition political party. After
that they could never see any good in him.
WILL ROGERS, *Autobiography*.

5
A politician is just like a necktie salesman
in a big department store. If he decides to
give all the ties away, or decides to pocket
all the receipts, it don't affect the store. It
don't close. He closes, as soon as he is found
out.
WILL ROGERS, *Autobiography*.

6
We got wind in the Senate where we paid to
get wisdom.
WILL ROGERS, *Autobiography*.

7
Now about politicians. The least said about
them the best. They haven't the social standing of the diplomats. All of their damage
is internal. Where the ambassador generally
winds up with a decoration of red ribbon,
the politician generally winds up with an
indictment staring him in the face.
WILL ROGERS, *Autobiography*.

8
He [Franklin D. Roosevelt] is a Roosevelt
by blood, but a namesake politically. If he
had retained his splendid qualities and stayed
with the Republican end of the family, he
would have been President. But I doubt if
he could have retained those qualities and
been Republican.
WILL ROGERS, *Autobiography*. (This comment was made in 1928.)

9
England elects a Labor government. When a
man goes in for politics over here, he has no
time to labor, and any man that labors has
no time to fool with politics. Over there
politics is an obligation; over here it's a
business.
WILL ROGERS, *Autobiography*.

10
I am glad Chicago's children didn't come by
on their way to school that morning and see
how this wonderful system of choosing our
country's leaders was conducted. They would
never again have asked, "What's the matter
with the country?"
WILL ROGERS, *Autobiography*. Remark
made at the Republican national convention in 1932.

11
A newspaper man spoiled my whole convention by asking me if "I was an alternate."
Now a delegate is bad enough, but an alternate is just a spare tire for a delegate.
An alternate is the lowest form of political life there is. He is the parachute on a
plane that never leaves the ground.
WILL ROGERS, *Autobiography*. The remark was made at the Republican national convention in Chicago in 1932.

12
You are not going to get people's votes
nowadays by calling them common. Lincoln
might have said it but I bet you it was not
until after he was elected.
WILL ROGERS, *The Illiterate Digest*.

13
Senate—A club which a hundred men belong
to but pay no dues.
WILL ROGERS.

14
If we can boondoggle our way out of the
depression, that word is going to be en-
shrined in the hearts of the American people
for years to come.
FRANKLIN D. ROOSEVELT, *Speech* in Newark N.J., Jan. 18, 1936. The word
"boondoggle" (noun), said to have been
coined about 1926 by Robert H. Link, a
Rochester, N.Y. Scoutmaster, originally
was applied to leather neckwear made
and worn by Boy Scouts. When it was
disclosed that New Deal work-relief
projects in New York included a class
in making boondoggles, critics soon used
the word in the general sense of any
wasteful and useless project.

15
Franklin D. Roosevelt told this story on
himself at many a dinner party: A son introduced the new deacon to his father, who
was both slightly deaf and a staunch Republican. "Pa," said the son, "here's our new
deacon." "New Dealer," echoed Pa. "No,
new deacon," repeated the son. "He's a son
of a bishop." That pleased Pa, who agreed
happily, "They all are."
BENNETT CERF, *The Laugh's on Me*.

16
Take it to the Vice-President; he needs
something to keep him awake.
THEODORE ROOSEVELT, to a White House
butler who was puzzled about the best

procedure for disposing of a chandelier in the Treaty Room of the White House. In the era before air conditioning, breeze through the open windows caused the chandelier to tinkle at night, and so disturb the President's sleep until Roosevelt ordered its removal. Lyndon B. Johnson quoted these words, and recalled the background of the story, during a tour of the White House, Jan. 22, 1964.

1

I am as strong as a bull moose and you can use me to the limit.

THEODORE ROOSEVELT, *Speech,* Milwaukee, Wisc., on the evening of the attempt to assassinate him, Oct. 14, 1912.

2

At three O'Clock
Thursday afternoon
Theodore ROOSEVELT
WILL WALK
on the
WATERS OF LAKE MICHIGAN

Handbill printed by opponents of Theodore Roosevelt during Republican national convention of 1912. (RALPH G. MARTIN, *Ballots & Bandwagons.*)

3

Mort Sahl described the arrivals of the Presidential hopefuls [at the 1960 Democratic national convention] for his Los Angeles audiences: "Jack Kennedy got off the plane and said, 'I came here to accept the nomination.' Lyndon Johnson got off the plane and said, 'I'm sorry I'm late, but I've been busy running the country,' and Adlai Stevenson said, 'I don't want the nomination and I'm not here.' "

VICTOR LASKY, *J.F.K.: The Man and the Myth.*

4

I could tell you that I have succumbed to the urging of my many friends. But the truth is that this candidacy is a genuine draft—a draft inspired by the candidate himself.

PIERRE SALINGER, announcing his candidacy for the Democratic nomination for Senator from California, Mar. 21, 1964. He won the nomination but lost to his Republican opponent, George Murphy, in the November election.

5

Whatever President Truman does is wrong somewhere among 160,000,000 people. That is 130,000,000 more than Lincoln had to handle.

CARL SANDBURG, in 1946. Quoted by HARRY GOLDEN in *Carl Sandburg.*

6

The cut of the clothes may change, but that's it. If you look at a cage of monkeys today, or ten years from today, they'll act the same. They never change. Believe me, that's the way human beings are.

LOUIS SAXE, *Interview* with Bernard Weinraub, *The New York Times,* Oct. 26, 1964, p. 27. Saxe, a prominent New York lawyer and lifelong Republican, was commenting, at age 91, on the similarity of politicians through the years.

7

I myself have denounced the John Birch Society, and will probably get some more letters because I say this, but we have a saying in the Republican Party that it was born under the oaks and I don't want it to founder under the "birches."

HUGH SCOTT, Republican Senator of Pennsylvania.

8

If Webster from his grave
Could to this place repair
And hear the constitution thus explained,
Great God! how he would swear!

Quoted by REP. GEORGE E. SENEY OF OHIO, speaking on a direct tax-refunding bill, 1888.

9

A politician, . . . one that would circumvent God.

WILLIAM SHAKESPEARE, *Hamlet.* Act v, sc. 1.

10

When I first came into Parliament, Mr. Tierney, a great Whig authority, used always to say that the duty of an Opposition was very simple—it was to oppose everything and propose nothing.

LORD STANLEY, *Debate,* June 4, 1841.

11

Politics is nothing but good manners in public.

LINCOLN STEFFENS, *Autobiography.*

12

Better to speak above people's heads than behind their backs.

ADLAI STEVENSON.

13

You learn more about yourself while campaigning for just one week than in six months spent with a psychoanalyst.

ADLAI STEVENSON.

14

. . . a candidate has a hard life—he has to shave twice a day.

ADLAI STEVENSON.

15

I have read Governor Green's speech when he opened the Republican campaign. He damns me with being on leave from the "striped pants brigade to the Roosevelt-

Truman State Department." Damned or striped—I will keep my pants on!

ADLAI STEVENSON, during his campaign against Governor Green of Illinois in 1948.

1
The Republicans have a "me too" candidate running on a "yes but" platform, advised by a "has been" staff.

ADLAI STEVENSON, *Speech,* Fort Dodge, Ia., 1952.

2
When I practiced law we looked for jokers in a contract. In the Republican farm platform it is not a question of finding the loopholes in the contract. It is a question of finding a contract in the loopholes.

ADLAI STEVENSON, *Speech,* Fort Dodge, Ia., 1952.

3
They pick a President and then for four years they pick on him.

ADLAI STEVENSON, *Speech,* Aug. 28, 1952.

4
This is the first time I have ever heard of a party going into battle under the slogan, "Throw the rascals in."

ADLAI STEVENSON, *Speech* in Phoenix, Ariz., Sept. 12, 1952.

5
It is a tragedy that the Old Guard has succeeded in doing what Hitler's best general could never do: they have captured Eisenhower.

ADLAI STEVENSON, *Speech,* Nov. 3, 1952.

6
He [Adlai Stevenson] referred to Senator Robert A. Taft of Ohio (who had strongly contested General Eisenhower at the Republican convention, but later became his staunch champion) as "the greatest living authority on what General Eisenhower thinks."

PAUL STEINER, *The Stevenson Wit & Wisdom.*

7
Someone asked . . . how I felt, and I was reminded of a story that a fellow townsman of ours used to tell—Abraham Lincoln. They asked him how he felt once after an unsuccessful election. He said he felt like a little boy who has stubbed his toe in the dark. He said that he was too old to cry, but it hurt too much to laugh.

ADLAI E. STEVENSON, *Speech* on election night, Nov. 5, 1952. See also LINCOLN in the section headed "Disappointment."

8
Liberal Republicans are like opera singers; when they are stabbed they don't die; they sing.

ADLAI STEVENSON, *Speech,* New York, Sept. 11, 1956. Referring to Harold Stassen.

9
Well, when someone says to me that the two parties' programs are just about the same I say that so are two checks, signed by different people. The question is which one can be cashed and which one will bounce.

ADLAI STEVENSON, *Campaign speech* in Harrisburg, Pa., 1956.

10
I have finally figured out what the Republican orators mean by what they call "moderate progressivism." All they mean is: "Don't do something. Stand there."

ADLAI STEVENSON, about his opponents in 1956.

11
A funny thing happened to me on the way to the White House.

ADLAI STEVENSON, following his defeat for the presidency. Quoted in *The Wall Street Journal,* Dec. 27, 1966.

12
I was touched and flattered but I confess the thought occurred to me that a little x in the right place on the ballot would have been so much easier than a long thoughtful letter.

ADLAI STEVENSON, *Comment* on letters from people who had not voted for him. Quoted in *The Wall Street Journal,* Dec. 27, 1966.

13
I shall not argue that it is necessarily fatal to change horses in mid-stream. But I doubt if it is wise to jump on a struggling two-headed elephant trying to swim in both directions at the same time in very rough water.

ADLAI STEVENSON, quoted by PAUL STEINER in *The Stevenson Wit & Wisdom.* See also LINCOLN in section headed "Change."

14
An independent is a person who wants to take the politics out of politics.

ADLAI STEVENSON, quoted by PAUL STEINER in *The Stevenson Wit & Wisdom.*

15
Politics is perhaps the only profession for which no preparation is thought necessary.

ROBERT LOUIS STEVENSON, *Yoshida-Torajiro.*

16
Henry Clay said, "I would rather be right than be president." This was the sourest grape since Aesop originated his fable.

IRVING STONE, *They Also Ran.*

1
He [Henry Clay] was a chameleon: he could turn any color that might be useful to him. To read of his career one must have corkscrew eyes.
IRVING STONE, *They Also Ran.*

2
No one knew better than the Cock of Kentucky [Henry Clay] which side his bread was buttered on: and he liked butter. A considerable portion of his public life was spent in trying to find butter for both sides of the slice.
IRVING STONE, *They Also Ran.*

3
His mind was like a soup dish, wide and shallow; it could hold a small amount of nearly anything, but the slightest jarring spilled the soup into somebody's lap.
IRVING STONE, *They Also Ran.* The reference is to William Jennings Bryan.

4
He [Stephen Douglas] appears to have been called the Little Giant more because he was little than because he was a giant.
IRVING STONE, *They Also Ran.*

5
The better man was elected by the worst possible methods.
IRVING STONE, *They Also Ran.* The reference is to the presidential campaign of 1896.

6
The only crack that got under his skin was Secretary of the Interior Ickes' comment that "Wendell Willkie is just a simple barefoot Wall Street lawyer."
IRVING STONE, *They Also Ran.* Reference to Willkie in the presidential campaign of 1940.

7
The Democratic party is like a mule—without pride of ancestry or hope of posterity.
EMERY A. STORRS, *Speech,* during campaign of 1888.

8
You can't beat somebody with nobody.
MARK SULLIVAN, *Our Times.*

9
Congressmen? In Washington they hitch horses to them.
TIMOTHY D. (BIG TIM) SULLIVAN, of New York City. Upon announcing his decision to retire from the House of Representatives and return to the New York State Senate.

10
When the water reaches the upper deck, follow the rats.
CLAUDE SWANSON, on the authority of Joseph Alsop: Column, *New York Herald*

Tribune, Feb. 5, 1964. Quoted as "one of the basic rules of American politics."

11
Never wait till the train leaves the station before climbing aboard.
CLAUDE SWANSON, quoted in *Hats in the Ring* by MOOS AND HESS. The reference is to presidential campaigns.

12
When quacks with pills political would dope us,
  When politics absorbs the livelong day,
I like to think about the star Canopus,
  So far, so far away!
BERT LESTON TAYLOR, *Canopus.*

13
Politics . . . are but the cigar-smoke of a man.
HENRY D. THOREAU, *Walking.*

14
Greater love hath no man than this, that he lay down his friends for his life.
JEREMY THORPE, member of Parliament. On changes in the cabinet. Quoted in *The Wall Street Journal,* Aug. 20, 1962.

15
First in war, first in peace, and first in the pockets of its countrymen.
Time. Referring to Tammany Hall.

16
If you don't like the heat, get out of the kitchen.
HARRY S TRUMAN, on the rigors of practical politics. Also attributed to Major General Harry Vaughan, Truman's military aide.

17
Polls are like sleeping pills designed to lull the voters into sleeping on election day. You might call them "sleeping polls."
HARRY S TRUMAN, *Speech* in Cleveland, Oct. 26, 1948, during the presidential campaign. On election day Truman upset the pollsters' predictions by defeating Thomas E. Dewey.

18
If I'd known how much packing I'd have to do, I'd run again.
HARRY S TRUMAN, on leaving the White House. (*Time,* Jan. 26, 1953.)

19
I never give them hell. I just tell the truth and they think it's hell.
HARRY S TRUMAN, quoted in *Look,* Apr. 3, 1956.

20
When a leader is in the Democratic Party he's a boss; when he's in the Republican Party he's a leader.
HARRY S TRUMAN, *Lecture,* Columbia University, Apr. 28, 1959.

1
You don't set a fox to watching the chickens just because he has a lot of experience in the hen house.
> HARRY S TRUMAN, *Comment* on Vice President Nixon's seeking the presidency, Oct. 30, 1960.

2
Grand Old Platitudes.
> HARRY S TRUMAN, *Description* of G.O.P. (*Time,* Apr. 30, 1961.)

3
Whenever a fellow tells me he's bipartisan, I know he's going to vote against me.
> HARRY S TRUMAN, *Comment,* Jan. 21, 1962.

4
I never had any falling out with him. The only trouble was, he had a lot of damn fool Republicans around him. He's a good man.
> HARRY S TRUMAN, on Dwight D. Eisenhower. (*The New York Times,* "Ideas and Men," Dec. 29, 1963.)

5
If you want to get on the front page of a newspaper you should attack someone, especially when you're in politics.
> HARRY S TRUMAN, *News Conference* in New York City, Jan. 9, 1964.

6
An appropriation was a tangible thing, if you got hold of it, and it made little difference what it was appropriated for, so long as you got hold of it.
> MARK TWAIN, *The Gilded Age,* ch. 22.

7
Political parties who accuse the one in power of gobbling the spoils etc. are like the wolf who looked in at the door and saw the shepherds eating mutton, and said: "Oh, certainly—it's all right as long as it's you—but there'd be hell to pay if I was to do that."
> MARK TWAIN, *Notebook,* ch. 12.

8
. . . If we were sane, we should all see a political or religious doctrine alike . . .
> MARK TWAIN, *Christian Science,* Bk. i, ch. 4.

9
When the votes are all in a public man's favor the verdict is against him. It is sand, and history will wash it away.
> MARK TWAIN, *Letter* to Grover Cleveland, Mar. 6, 1906.

10
It could probably be shown by facts and figures that there is no distinctly native American criminal class except Congress.
> MARK TWAIN, *Following the Equator.*

11
. . . those burglars that broke into my house recently . . . are in jail, and if they keep on they will go to Congress. When a person starts downhill you can never tell where he's going to stop.
> MARK TWAIN, *Address* to Redding, Conn., Library Association, at the opening of the Mark Twain Library, Oct. 28, 1908.

12
To my mind Judas Iscariot was nothing but a low, mean, premature Congressman.
> MARK TWAIN, quoted in *New York Tribune,* Mar. 7, 1873.

13
Fleas can be taught nearly anything that a Congressman can.
> MARK TWAIN.

14
The chameleon . . . whirls one eye rearwards and the other forwards—which gives him a most Congressional expression (one eye on the constituency and one on the swag).
> MARK TWAIN, *Following the Equator,* ch. 65.

15
The political and commercial morals of the United States are not merely food for laughter, they are an entire banquet.
> MARK TWAIN, from *Mark Twain in Eruption,* Jan. 30, 1907.

16
The New Political Gospel: Public office is private graft.
> MARK TWAIN, *More Maxims of Mark.*

17
Public Servant: Persons chosen by the people to distribute the graft.
> MARK TWAIN, *More Maxims of Mark.*

18
An honest man in politics shines more than he would elsewhere.
> MARK TWAIN, *A Tramp Abroad,* ch. 9.

19
"Senator" is not a legitimate title. A Senator has no more right to be addressed by it than have you or I; but, in the several state capitals and in Washington, there are five thousand Senators who take very kindly to that fiction, and who purr gratefully when you call them by it—which you may do quite unrebuked.
> MARK TWAIN, *Does the Race of Man Love a Lord?*

20
We Polked you in 1844 and we shall Pierce you in 1852.
> UNKNOWN, Democratic slogan in the 1852 presidential electon. The reference is to the comparative anonymity of the two men who were elected.

1
Hurrah for Maria,
Hurrah for the kid,
I voted for Grover
And am damn glad I did.
UNKNOWN, *Campaign song,* Blaine-Cleve-
land campaign, 1884. The reference is
to Maria Halpin of Buffalo; according
to campaign rumor, her child had been
fathered by Cleveland, a bachelor.

2
What have you done? cried Christine.
You've wrecked the whole party machine.
To lie in the nude may be rude,
But to lie in the House is obscene.
UNKNOWN, quoted widely in England dur-
ing the Profumo affair after Profumo
admitted he lied to the House of Com-
mons in March, 1963 concerning his
relations with Miss Christine Keeler.

3
A Senator is half horse and half man.
LOUIS UNTERMEYER, *A Treasury of Laugh-
ter.* Quoted as a student boner.

4
The people trust you rich boys, figurin' since
you got a lot of money of your own you
won't go stealin' theirs.
GORE VIDAL, *The Best Man.*

5
Because he's a bastard don't mean he
wouldn't make a good candidate. Or even a
good President.
GORE VIDAL, *The Best Man.*

6
A candidate should not mean but be.
GORE VIDAL, *The Best Man.*

7
I would say that he had better start running
faster than he has to catch up with where
he was.
ROBERT F. WAGNER, JR., former mayor of
New York. Speaking of Mayor Lindsay.
Quoted in *The New York Times,* May
22, 1966.

8
My pollertics, like my religion, bein of a
exceedin accommodatin character.
ARTEMUS WARD, *The Crisis.*

9
I am not a politician and my other habits
are good.
ARTEMUS WARD.

10
Truth is that politics makes strange bedfellows.
CHARLES DUDLEY WARNER, *My Summer
in a Garden.*

11
No thank you, I do not propose to be buried
until I am really dead and in my coffin.
DANIEL WEBSTER, quoted in *Hats in the
Ring* by MOOS AND HESS. Webster's remark was in reply to Thurlow Weed,
who suggested that Webster run for the
vice-presidency.

12
Tin-horn politicians.
WILLIAM ALLEN WHITE, *Editorial, Empo-
ria* (Kan.) *Gazette,* Oct. 25, 1901.

13
William Allen White had a Kansan's suspicion of anyone with a handshake "like a
ten-cent pickled mackerel in brown paper."
WALTER LORD, *The Good Years.* Referring
to Woodrow Wilson.

14
Senator Tom Heflin: At least I am in com-
plete command of my faculties.
Senator John Sharp Williams: What differ-
ence does that make?
Quoted in *Presidents Who Have Known
Me* by GEORGE E. ALLEN.

15
Roosevelt and I took office at the same time,
only my company is running at a profit while
his company is running at a loss.
WENDELL WILLKIE, quoted by IRVING
STONE in *They Also Ran.* The reference
is to Willkie's becoming head of Commonwealth and Southern at the same
time Franklin D. Roosevelt was elected
President of the United States.

16
A good catchword can obscure analysis for
fifty years.
WENDELL WILLKIE, *Town Hall Debate,*
1938.

17
Fastest way for a politician to become an
elder statesman is to lose an election.
EARL WILSON, *New York Post.*

18
I believe if we introduced the Lord's Prayer
here, Senators would propose a large number
of amendments to it.
SENATOR HENRY WILSON of Massachusetts.

19
Every man who takes office in Washington
either grows or swells.
WOODROW WILSON.

20
The Great Inevitable.
WOODROW WILSON, *Description* of William
Jennings Bryan. From *The Good Years*
by WALTER LORD.

21
When politics are in, the truth is out.
HAROLD WINTLE, *A Mirror of Folly.*

POPULARITY

1
Popularity is a crime from the moment it is sought; it is only a virtue when men have it whether they will or no.
LORD HALIFAX, *Works*, p. 232.

2
When one has a good table, one is always in the right. (Quand on a bonne table on a toujours raison.)
COLLIN D'HARLEVILLE, *M. de Crac*, sc. 4.

3
Popularity? It is glory's small change.
VICTOR HUGO, *Ruy Blas*, Act iii, sc. 5.

4
Have I inadvertently said some evil thing?
PHOCION, when one of his sentences in a public debate was universally applauded. (PLUTARCH, *Lives: Phocion*, ch. x, sec. 3.)

5
The popular girl is the one who has been weighed in the balance and found wanton.
More Playboy's Party Jokes (1965).

6
About the only person we ever heard of that wasn't spoiled by being lionized was a Jew named Daniel.
GEORGE D. PRENTICE.

7
Even popularity can be overdone. In Rome, alone at first, you are full of regrets that Michelangelo died; but by and by you only regret that you didn't see him do it.
MARK TWAIN, *Pudd'nhead Wilson's Calendar*.

8
Everybody's private motto: It's better to be popular than right.
MARK TWAIN, from *More Maxims of Mark*.

9
These heroes—erst extolling—
A fickle public drops;
Folks chase a ball that's rolling,
And kick it when it stops.
UNKNOWN, *Popularity*. Quoted in *Life*, Apr., 1900.

POSSESSION

10
Possession is eleven points of the law.
COLLEY CIBBER, *Woman's Wit*, Act 1.

11
The accepted and betrothed lover has lost the wildest charm of his maiden in her acceptance of him.
RALPH WALDO EMERSON, *Essays, Second Series: Nature*.

12
"Why isn't your wife riding the burro?" asked the indignant white man of the mountain Indian whose wife trudged behind, her head buried beneath a huge bundle of household goods. "Ain't her burro," was the sensible reply.
JOHN GREENWAY, *The Inevitable Americans*, ch. 4.

13
As soon as women belong to us, we no longer belong to them. (Soudain qu'elles sont a nous, nous ne sommes plus a elles.)
MICHEL DE MONTAIGNE, *Essays*. Bk. iii, ch. 5.

14
He who says, what is mine is yours and what is yours is yours, is a saint. He who says, what is yours is mine and what is mine is mine, is a wicked man.
BABYLONIAN TALMUD, *Aboth*, V.

15
It is a comfortable feeling to know that you stand on your own ground. Land is about the only thing that can't fly away.
ANTHONY TROLLOPE, *The Last Chronicle of Barset*. Vol. ii, ch. 58.

16
Papa's having and mama's having is not like having one's self.
UNKNOWN, Chinese proverb.

17
No man can lose what he never had.
IZAAK WALTON, *The Compleat Angler*. Pt. i, ch. 5.

18
It [land] gives one position, and prevents one from keeping it up.
OSCAR WILDE, *The Importance of Being Earnest*, Act 1.

POSTERITY

19
We are always doing, says he, something for posterity, but I would fain see posterity do something for us.
JOSEPH ADDISON, *The Spectator*, No. 583.

20
After being turned down by numerous publishers, he decided to write for posterity.
GEORGE ADE.

21
General Alexander Smyth, a tedious speaker in Congress, observed: "You, sir, speak for the present generation; but I speak for posterity."
"Yes," said Mr. Clay, "and you seem resolved to speak until the arrival of your audience."
HENRY CLAY. (EPES SARGENT, *Life of Henry Clay*.)

1
He seems to think that posterity is a pack-horse, always ready to be loaded.
> BENJAMIN DISRAELI, *Speech*, House of Commons, June 3, 1862.

2
To evoke posterity
Is to weep on your own grave . . .
> ROBERT GRAVES, *The Crowning Privilege.*

3
As to posterity, I may ask what has it ever done to oblige me?
> THOMAS GRAY, *Letter* to Dr. Wharton.

4
The love of posterity is the consequence of the necessity of death. If a man were sure of living forever here, he would not care about his off-spring.
> NATHANIEL HAWTHORNE, *American Note-Books.*

5
I do not give you to posterity as a pattern to imitate, but as an example to deter.
> JUNIUS, *To the Duke of Grafton.*

6
Posterity? Why posterity is just around the corner.
> GEORGE S. KAUFMAN AND MORRIE RYSKIND, *Of Thee I Sing*, Act ii, sc. 3.

7
Few can be induced to labor exclusively for posterity. Posterity has done nothing for us.
> ABRAHAM LINCOLN, *Speech*, Feb. 22, 1842.

8
Posterity is the patriotic name for grandchildren.
> ART LINKLETTER, *A Child's Garden of Misinformation.*

9
We used to do things for posterity, now we do things for ourselves and leave the bill to posterity.
> *Lutheran Education.*

POVERTY

10
Poverty is very good in poems, but it is very bad in a house.
> HENRY WARD BEECHER, *Proverbs from Plymouth Pulpit.*

11
Remember the poor—it costs nothing.
> JOSH BILLINGS.

12
Squeamishness was never yet bred in an empty pocket.
> JAMES BRANCH CABELL, *The Cream of the Jest*, p. 86.

13
Poverty, the reward of honest fools.
> COLLY CIBBER, *Richard III.*

14
One of the strangest things about life is that the poor, who need money the most, are the very ones that never have it.
> FINLEY PETER DUNNE.

15
Poverty is no vice, but an inconvenience.
> JOHN FLORIO, *Second Frutes*, Fo. 105.

16
When poverty comes in at the door, love creeps out at the window.
> THOMAS FULLER, *Gnomologia*, No. 5565.

17
The loss of wealth is loss of dirt,
As sages in all times assert;
The happy man's without a shirt.
> JOHN HEYWOOD, *Be Merry, Friends.*

18
There is nothing perfectly secure but poverty.
> HENRY WADSWORTH LONGFELLOW, *Final Memorials: Letter*, Nov. 13, 1872, to G. W. Green.

19
We shall never solve the paradox of want in the midst of plenty by doing away with plenty.
> OGDEN MILLS, *Speech*, New York, Mar. 21, 1934.

20
Poverty of course is no disgrace, but it is damned annoying.
> WILLIAM PITT.

21
Poverty is the only load which is the heavier the more loved ones there are to assist in supporting it.
> J. P. F. RICHTER, *Flower, Fruit, Thorn Pieces*, ch. 10.

22
No wonder that his soul was sad,
When not one penny piece he had.
> CHRISTINA ROSSETTI, *Johnny.*

23
Do not waste your time on Social Questions. What is the matter with the poor is Poverty: what is the matter with the rich is Uselessness.
> BERNARD SHAW, *Maxims for Revolutionists.*

24
Very few people can afford to be poor.
> BERNARD SHAW, quoted by STEPHEN WINSTEN in *Days with Bernard Shaw.*

25
Hark ye, Clinker, you are a most notorious offender. You stand convicted of sickness, hunger, wretchedness and want.
> TOBIAS SMOLLETT, *Humphrey Clinker.*

26
I have been assured by a very knowing

American of my acquaintance in London, that a young healthy child well nursed is at a year old a most delicious, nourishing, and wholesome food, whether stewed, roasted, baked, or broiled; and I make no doubt that it will equally serve in a fricassee or a ragout.

> JONATHAN SWIFT, *A Modest Proposal*. In which he proposed, ironically, that the children of the Irish poor be used for food.

1

James Peterson was the son of a common weaver, who was so miraculously poor that his friends were encouraged to believe that in case the Scriptures were carried out he would "inherit the earth". He never got his property.

> MARK TWAIN, *Origin of Illustrious Men*.

2

A nice wife and a back door
Maketh ofttimes a rich man poor.

> UNKNOWN, *Proverbs of Good Counsel*.

3

No naked man ever lost anything.

> UNKNOWN, Japanese proverb, in *Oriental Humor*, ed. by R. H. BLYTH.

4

I know how to be rich and still enjoy all the little comforts of poverty.

> HARRY LEON WILSON, *The Spenders*, p. 24.

POWER

5

The more you are talked about, the less powerful you are.

> BENJAMIN DISRAELI, *Endymion*, ch. 36.

6

We have the power to do any damn fool thing we want to do, and we seem to do it about every ten minutes.

> SENATOR J. WILLIAM FULBRIGHT, quoted in *Time*, Feb. 4, 1952.

7

I feel like a lion in a den of Daniels.

> W. S. GILBERT, quoted by HESKETH PEARSON in *Lives of the Wits*.

8

What's the use of wasting dynamite when insect-powder will do?

> CARTER GLASS, *Speech* (unpublished), Democratic caucus, 1913.

9

In the past, those who foolishly sought power by riding the back of the tiger ended up inside.

> JOHN F. KENNEDY, *Inaugural Address*, Jan. 20, 1961.

10

I have sat at the sumptuous tables of power, but I have not run away with the silverware.

> DIOSDADO MACAPAGAL, President of the Philippines. On his career. (*Time*, Nov. 24, 1961.)

11

The whale, like all things that are mighty, wears a false brow to the common world.

> HERMAN MELVILLE, *Moby Dick*, ch. 80.

12

No man was ever satisfied to be half a king.

> JOHN RANDOLPH of Roanoke. From *The Wit and Wisdom of Congress*, ed. by EDWARD BOYKIN.

13

I am only an historical telephone operator.

> ARTHUR SEYSS-INQUART, quoted in *The Netherlands at War* by WALTER B. MAASS. The reference is to Seyss-Inquart's appointment as Chancellor of Austria by Adolf Hitler.

14

Thou hast seen a farmer's dog bark at a beggar? . . . And the creature run from the cur? There thou might'st behold the great image of authority: a dog's obeyed in office.

> WILLIAM SHAKESPEARE, *King Lear*. Act iv, sc. 6.

15

It is not necessary to light a candle to the sun.

> ALGERNON SYDNEY, *Discourses on Government*.

16

All the human race loves a lord—that is, it loves to look upon or be noticed by the possessor of Power or Conspicuousness; and sometimes animals, born to better things and higher ideals, descend to man's level in this matter. In the Jardin des Plantes I have seen a cat that was so vain of being the personal friend of an elephant that I was ashamed of her.

> MARK TWAIN, *Does the Race of Man Love a Lord?*

PRAISE

17

There is not a more unhappy being than a superannuated idol.

> JOSEPH ADDISON, *The Spectator*, No. 73.

18

Praise yourself daringly, something always sticks.

> FRANCIS BACON, *Apothegms*.

19

Fan Mail—A sort of hippopotamus that, having pushed one's front door open with his nose, squats with a dripping smile in a pool on one's hearthrug. Its impulse is charming, but one doesn't quite know what the devil to do with him.

> JOHN BARRYMORE.

1
Be quick to praise. People like to praise those who praise them.
> BERNARD M. BARUCH, quoted in *St. Louis Post-Dispatch*, 21 June, 1965.

2
Applause: the echo of a platitude.
> AMBROSE BIERCE, *The Devil's Dictionary*.

3
The advantage of doing one's praising for oneself is that one can lay it on so thick and exactly in the right places.
> SAMUEL BUTLER, *The Way of All Flesh*, ch. 34.

4
I studied the *Divine Comedy* for two months this year and thought I knew quite a lot. After reading your article, I knew nothing. It is a splendid article.
> Letter received by JOHN CIARDI, *The Saturday Review*. (Aug. 14, 1965.)

5
Is it not possible to eat me up without insisting that I sing the praises of my devourer?
> FYODOR DOSTOEVSKY, quoted by BEN HECHT, *Letters from Bohemia*.

6
The idiot who praises, with enthusiastic tone,
All centuries but this and every country but his own.
> W. S. GILBERT, *The Mikado*, Act 1.

7
If a girl was with us, I was sure to hear Swatty open up as a searcher for deep truths. You could tell how smitten he was with a girl by how ardently he started praising himself. He called it "self-revelation."
> BEN HECHT, *Letters from Bohemia*. Reference to SHERWOOD ANDERSON.

8
He who praises everybody praises nobody.
> SAMUEL JOHNSON, BOSWELL'S *Life*.

9
What are compliments . . . they are things you say to people when you don't know what else to say.
> CONSTANCE JONES, *The Ten Years' Agreement*.

10
In their very praise of one another women are slanderous.
> JOSEPH KLING, *Echoes*.

11
To refuse praise is to seek praise twice.
> FRANÇOIS, DUC DE LA ROCHEFOUCAULD.

12
We run ourselves down so as to be praised by others.
> FRANÇOIS, DUC DE LA ROCHEFOUCAULD, *Maximes*, No. 554.

13
The Disappointed One Speaks.—"I listen for the echo and I hear only praise."
> FRIEDRICH WILHELM NIETZSCHE, *Beyond Good and Evil*, tr. by HELEN ZIMMERN.

14
Praise, the fine diet which we're apt to love,
If given to excess, does hurtful prove.
> JOHN OLDHAM, *A Letter From the Country to an Old Friend in Town*.

15
I much prefer a compliment, insincere or not, to sincere criticism. (Equidem pol vel falso tamen laudari multo malo.)
> PLAUTUS, *Mostellaria*.

16
Praise is like ambergris: a little whiff of it, and by snatches, is very agreeable; but when a man holds a whole lump of it up to your nose, it is a stink, and strikes you down.
> ALEXANDER POPE, *Thoughts on Various Subjects*.

17
Try praising your wife even if it does frighten her at first.
> BILLY SUNDAY, *Sermon*.

18
I can live for two months on a good compliment.
> MARK TWAIN, quoted in PAINE, *Mark Twain*.

19
A man's praises may have very musical and charming accents in another's mouth; but very flat and untuneable in his own.
> XENOPHON, quoted in *Classic Quotations*, ed. by JAMES ELMES.

PRAYER

20
Prayers come from the same mouth as oaths.
> FRANK C. BROWN, *Collection of North Carolina Folklore*.

21
"As for that," said Aldegonde, "I am not clear we ought to pray at all, either in public or private. It seems very arrogant in us to dictate to an all-wise Creator what we desire."
> BENJAMIN DISRAELI, *Lothair*.

22
A suggestion: Pray more and prey less.
> B. C. FORBES, *Epigrams*.

23
It is proper to pray on your knees but not to work.
> POPE JOHN XXIII. (*Wit and Wisdom of Good Pope John*, collected by HENRI FESQUET.)

1
O God, assist our side: at least avoid assisting the enemy, and leave the rest to me.
> PRINCE LEOPOLD of Anhalt-Dessau, before his last battle. (CARLYLE, *Life of Frederick the Great*. Bk. xv, ch. 14.)

2
O Lord—if there is a Lord; save my soul—if I have a soul.
> JOSEPH ERNEST RENAN, *Prayer of a Skeptic*.

3
Common people do not pray, my lord: they only beg.
> BERNARD SHAW, *Misalliance*.

4
God bless mother and daddy, my brother and sister, and save the King. And, oh God, do take care of yourself, because if anything happens to you we're all sunk.
> ADLAI STEVENSON, *Speech* at Harvard Business School, June 6, 1959.

5
" 'Twas then belike," Honorious cried,
"When you the public fast defied,
Refused to heav'n to raise a prayer,
Because you'd no connections there."
> JOHN TRUMBULL, *McFingal*, canto 1.

6
To pray for something one doesn't understand is to be an idolater.
> SUTTON VANE, *Outward Bound*. Act iii, sc. 1.

7
I have never made but one prayer to God, a very short one: "O Lord, make my enemies ridiculous." And God granted it.
> VOLTAIRE, *Letter* to M. Damiliville, May 16, 1767.

8
Prayer must never be answered: if it is, it ceases to be prayer and becomes a correspondence.
> OSCAR WILDE, *Remark* to LAURENCE HOUSMAN.

9
When the gods wish to punish us they answer our prayers.
> OSCAR WILDE, *An Ideal Husband*, Act 2.

10
Some people will say anything except their prayers.
> HORACE WYNDHAM, *The Flare of the Footlights*.

PREJUDICE

See also Jew, Negro

11
A prejudice is a vagrant opinion without visible means of support.
> AMBROSE BIERCE, *The Devil's Dictionary*.

12
. . . being a star has made it possible for me to get insulted in places where the average Negro could never *hope* to go and get insulted.
> SAMMY DAVIS, JR., *Yes I Can*.

13
I read a joke in one of the columns that said you were playing golf on Long Island and the pro asked you for your handicap and you told him, "I'm a colored, one-eyed Jew—do I need anything else?"
> SAMMY DAVIS, JR., *Yes I Can*.

14
I am free of all prejudice. I hate everyone equally.
> W. C. FIELDS, quoted in column by JEROME BEATTY, JR., *The Saturday Review*, Jan. 28, 1967.

15
But I'm only half-Jewish. Can't I play nine holes?
> BARRY GOLDWATER, *Response*, when told he could not play at a restricted golf club. (CLEVELAND AMORY, *Who Killed Society?*)

16
You'd be amazed the places segregation pops up in. I went out to the racetrack last week—every horse I bet on was shuffled to the rear.
> DICK GREGORY, *From the Back of the Bus*.

17
Without the aid of prejudice and custom, I should not be able to find my way across the room.
> WILLIAM HAZLITT, *Sketches and Essays: On Prejudice*.

18
Prejudice is never easy unless it can pass itself off for reason.
> WILLIAM HAZLITT, *Sketches and Essays: On Prejudice*.

19
Prejudice is a raft onto which the shipwrecked mind clambers and paddles to safety.
> BEN HECHT, *A Guide for the Bedevilled*.

20
A great many people think they are thinking when they are merely rearranging their prejudices.
> WILLIAM JAMES.

21
It is usual for people to defend their prejudices by calling them instincts.
> JOSEPH KLING, *Echoes*.

22
A prejudiced person is one who doesn't believe in the same things we do.
> ART LINKLETTER, *A Child's Garden of Misinformation*.

1
One may no more live in the world without picking up the moral prejudices of the world than one will be able to go to hell without perspiring.
H. L. MENCKEN, *Prejudices*, ser. 2.

2
The latter part of a wise man's life is taken up in curing the follies, prejudices, and false opinions he had contracted in the former.
JONATHAN SWIFT, *Thoughts on Various Subjects*.

PREPAREDNESS

3
An infallible method of conciliating a tiger is to allow oneself to be devoured.
KONRAD ADENAUER, quoted by BENNETT CERF in *The Laugh's on Me*.

4
We can't cross a bridge until we come to it; but I always like to lay down a pontoon ahead of time.
BERNARD M. BARUCH.

5
An appeaser is one who feeds a crocodile—hoping it will eat him last.
SIR WINSTON CHURCHILL, quoted in *Reader's Digest*, Dec. 1954.

6
I see the doctrine of non-resistance is never practiced thoroughly, but when a man can't help himself.
JOHN DRYDEN, *Don Sebastian*. Act i, sc. 1.

7
Khrushchev reminds me of the tiger hunter who has picked a place on the wall to hang the tiger's skin long before he has caught the tiger. This tiger has other ideas.
JOHN F. KENNEDY, *State of the Union Address*, Jan. 11, 1962.

8
If men can't look after themselves, they deserve what they get. If a woman can, she deserves the same.
RONALD MACDONALD, *A Human Trinity*.

9
Considering the alternative, it is better to eat than be eaten.
NAPOLEON BONAPARTE, to his brother in 1793. Quoted in *The Mind of Napoleon*, ed. by CHRISTOPHER HEROLD.

10
What things we see when we don't have a gun!
UNKNOWN, *Troy* (N.Y.) *Times*, Dec. 26, 1883.

11
Our hero is a man of peace,
Prepardness he implores;
His sword within his scabbard sleeps,

But mercy, how it snores!
McLANDBURGH WILSON, *A Man of Peace*.
The reference is to THEODORE ROOSEVELT.

PRESS, THE

See also News

12
I keep reading between the lies.
GOODMAN ACE, *The Fine Art of Hypochondria*.

13
The focus of Tenderloin night life was Clark's restaurant. . . . Its clientele were ten- and twenty-dollar girls, half price to newspapermen, a concession which Selah Merril Clarke, the acid-tongue cynic of the *Sun's* night desk, characterized as "commercial courtesy to an allied profession."
SAMUEL HOPKINS ADAMS, *Tenderloin*.

14
He had been kicked in the head by a mule when young, and believed everything he read in the Sunday papers.
GEORGE ADE.

15
Newspapers are the schoolmasters of the common people. That endless book, the newspaper, is our national glory.
HENRY WARD BEECHER, *Proverbs from Plymouth Pulpit*.

16
Journalists say a thing that they know isn't true, in the hope that if they keep on saying it long enough it *will* be true.
ARNOLD BENNETT, *The Title*.

17
I tell the honest truth in my paper, and leave the consequences to God. Could I leave them in better hands?
JAMES GORDON BENNETT, *Editorial, New York Morning Herald*, May 10, 1836.

18
The best description of the *Mirror* in those days was devised by its own staff: a quail and crime sheet (although the original word was not quail.)
JIM BISHOP, *The Mark Hellinger Story*.

19
New York, the Jerusalem of journalism.
JIM BISHOP, *New York Journal-American*, Apr. 30, 1961.

20
He makes righteousness readable.
JAMES BONE, of C. P. SCOTT, editor of the *Guardian*, Manchester.

21
What is the newspaper but a sponge or invention for oblivion?
RALPH WALDO EMERSON, *Natural History of Intellect: Memory*.

1
The newspaper, which does its best to make every square acre of land and sea give an account of itself at your breakfast table.
RALPH WALDO EMERSON, *Society and Solitude: Works and Days.*

2
. . . We thought a journalist was a newspaperman who wore spats and took on airs.
THOMAS GRIFFITH, *The Waist-High Culture.*

3
Journalism is in fact history on the run.
THOMAS GRIFFITH, *The Waist-High Culture.*

4
"I'm Ernie Hemorrhoid, the poor man's Pyle," Hemingway announced when he put on his war correspondent's uniform.
ROBERT MACERVING, *Hemingway in Cuba.*

5
Ther hain't much in th' newspapers these days cept motions fer new trials an hints fer women.
FRANK MCKINNEY (KIN) HUBBARD, *Abe Martin's Primer.*

6
The man who never looks into a newspaper is better informed than he who reads them, inasmuch as he who knows nothing is nearer the truth than he whose mind is filled with falsehoods and errors.
THOMAS JEFFERSON, *Writings,* vol. xi, p. 224.

7
I do not take a single newspaper, nor read one a month, and I feel myself infinitely the happier for it.
THOMAS JEFFERSON, *Letter* to Madison.

8
Karl Marx used to write for the *Herald Tribune* but that isn't why I cancelled my subscription.
JOHN F. KENNEDY, *Press Conference,* Nov. 18, 1962. Referring to the *New York Herald Tribune.*

9
I notice that nowadays *Holiday* magazine claims to be devoting itself to promoting "Active Leisure." On that basis, sloganwise, *Life* magazine was certainly dedicated to "Informed Stupidity."
ALEXANDER KING, *Mine Enemy Grows Older.*

10
. . . Most *Time* and *Life* employees loathe their unknown readers with a passion that is matched only by their loathing for themselves.
ALEXANDER KING, *Rich Man, Poor Man, Freud and Fruit,* ch. 8.

11
Just remember that to the majority of them [newspapermen] a woman is either somebody's mother or a whore.
ALEXANDER KING, *Rich Man, Poor Man, Freud and Fruit,* ch. 10.

12
Newspapers always excite curiosity. No one ever lays one down without a feeling of disappointment.
CHARLES LAMB, *Last Essays of Elia.*

13
"The papers are not always reliable," Lincoln interjected, "That is to say, Mr. Welles, they lie and then they *re-lie.*"
CARL SANDBURG, *Abraham Lincoln: The Prairie Years and the War Years,* ch. 34.

14
Sam reads the paper as if he were peeling an enormous banana.
NORMAN MAILER, *Advertisements for Myself.*

15
Once a newspaper touches a story, the facts are lost forever, even to the protagonists.
NORMAN MAILER, *The Presidential Papers.*

16
The mass media know their reports are worth nothing compared to the eye and voice of a serious writer. Like cowardly bulls, people in the mass media paw the ground when one comes near.
NORMAN MAILER, *The Presidential Papers.*

17
The art of newspaper paragraphing is to stroke a platitude until it purrs like an epigram.
DON MARQUIS, *New York Sun.*

18
The press is not our daily bread but our daily sugar pill.
T. S. MATHEWS, *The Sugar Pill.*

19
All successful newspapers are ceaselessly querulous and bellicose. They never defend anyone or anything if they can help it; if the job is forced upon them, they tackle it by denouncing someone or something else.
H. L. MENCKEN, *Prejudices.* Ser. i, ch. 13.

20
I have always thought that I would like to be a newspaperman myself, because I love the classics and I love good literature.
JOHN P. O'BRIEN, *Speech* to a group of journalists, in 1933, when he was mayor of New York City.

21
We live under a government of men and morning newspapers.
WENDELL PHILLIPS, *Address: The Press.*

1
The press is like the air; a chartered libertine.
> WILLIAM PITT, *Letter* to Lord Grenville, 1757.

2
I hope we never live to see the day when a thing is as bad as some of our newspapers make it.
> WILL ROGERS.

3
Journalists are too poorly paid in this country [England] to know anything that is fit for publication.
> BERNARD SHAW, *Getting Married:* preface.

4
The newspapers! Sir, they are the most villainous—licentious—abominable—infernal —Not that I ever read them—no—I make it a rule never to look into a newspaper.
> RICHARD BRINSLEY SHERIDAN, *The Critic.*

5
I am convinced that nearly all publishers are doing their honest best, according to their lights—even if I must confess that sometimes their lights seem to me a little dim.
> ADLAI STEVENSON, *Speech,* Portland, Ore., Sept. 8, 1952.

6
I am considerably concerned when I see the extent to which we are developing a one-party press in a two-party country.
> ADLAI STEVENSON, *Speech* during the 1952 presidential campaign.

7
Accuracy is to newspapers what virtue is to a lady, except that a newspaper can always print a retraction.
> ADLAI STEVENSON, quoted from *Joseph Pulitzer* in *Portrait: Adlai E. Stevenson* by ALDEN WHITMAN.

8
We tell the public which way the cat is jumping. The public will take care of the cat.
> ARTHUR HAYS SULZBURGER, of *The New York Times.* Quoted in *Time,* May 8, 1950.

9
The *liberty* of the Press is called the Palladium of Freedom, which means, in these days, the liberty of being deceived, swindled, and humbugged by the Press and paying hugely for the deception.
> MARK TWAIN, *Comment,* Nov., 1870.

10
There are laws to protect the freedom of the press's speech, but none that are worth anything to protect the people from the press.
> MARK TWAIN, *Talk* before the Monday Evening Club, Hartford, Conn., 1873.

11
There are two forces that carry light to all corners of the globe—the sun in the heavens and the Associated Press down here.
> MARK TWAIN, *Speech,* New York City, Sept. 19, 1906.

12
Often his editorial policy was a nice compromise between blackmail and begging.
> WILLIAM ALLEN WHITE, *Address: A Free Press in a Machine Age,* at University of Pennsylvania.

13
Modern journalism justifies its own existence by the great Darwinian principle of the survival of the vulgarist.
> OSCAR WILDE, *The Critic as Artist.*

14
They [newspapers] give us the bald, sordid, disgusting facts of life. They chronicle, with degrading avidity, the sins of the second-rate, and with the conscientiousness of the illiterate give us accurate and prosaic details of the doings of people of absolutely no interest whatsoever.
> OSCAR WILDE, *The Critic as Artist.*

15
For forty years he has carried out, rather literally, the dictum of Mr. Dooley that the mission of a modern newspaper is to "comfort the afflicted and afflict the comfortable."
> JOHN K. WINKLER, *W. R. Hearst.*

16
A totem newspaper is the kind people don't really have to buy to read but just to *have,* physically, because they know it supports their own outlook on life.
> TOM WOLFE, *The Kandy-Kolored Tangerine-Flake Streamline Baby.*

17
An ambassador is a man of virtue sent to lie abroad for his country; a news-writer is a man without virtue who lies at home for himself.
> SIR HENRY WOTTON, when twitted on his famous definition of an ambassador by a newspaperman. See WOTTON in section headed "Diplomacy."

PRICE

18
Still as of old, men by themselves are priced—
For thirty pieces Judas sold himself, not Christ.
> HESTER H. CHOLMODELEY, quoted in *Diana Tempest.*

19
On a good bargain think twice.
> GEORGE HERBERT, *Jacula Prudentum.*

1
A good bargain is a pick-purse.
    GEORGE HERBERT, *Jacula Prudentum.*

2
Ther kin never be anything in common between plain people an' fancy prices.
    FRANK MCKINNEY (KIN) HUBBARD, *Abe Martin's Primer.*

3
Never buy what you do not want because it is cheap; it will be dear to you.
    THOMAS JEFFERSON, *Writings,* vol. 16.

4
The highest price we can pay for anything, is to ask it.
    W. S. LANDOR, *Imaginary Conversations: Eschines and Phocion.*

5
Zeus bought Danae with golden rain and I purchase you with a gold coin. I can't, after all, pay more than Zeus.
    PARMENION, *A Discreet Purchase,* tr. from the Greek by WILLIAM BARNSTONE.

6
A dear bargain is always disagreeable, because it is a reflection upon the judgment of the buyer. (Nam mala emptio semper ingrata est eo maxime, quod exprobrare stultitiam domino videtur.)
    PLINY THE YOUNGER, *Epistles.* Bk. i, 24.

7
Men are gradually realizing that a thing that is free is of no earthly importance.
    WILL ROGERS, *Autobiography.*

8
Lest the bargain should catch cold and starve.
    WILLIAM SHAKESPEARE, *Cymbeline,* Act i, sc. 4.

9
Every man has his price, and every woman her figure.
    UNKNOWN.

10
I'd like to buy him at my price and sell him at his.
    UNKNOWN.

11
Nowadays people know the price of everything and the value of nothing.
    OSCAR WILDE, *The Picture of Dorian Gray,* ch. 4. See also WILDE in section headed "Cynicism."

12
I have heard that great ladies, like great merchants, set but the higher prices upon what they have, because they are not in necessity of taking the first offer.
    WILLIAM WYCHERLEY, *The Country Wife,* Act 5.

PRIDE

See also Vanity

13
'Tis pride, rank pride, and haughtiness of soul;
I think the Romans call it stoicism.
    JOSEPH ADDISON, *Cato,* Act 1.

14
A man never feels more important than when he receives a telegram containing more than ten words.
    GEORGE ADE, *Fables.*

15
No one in the world except a mortified saint is actually displeased at the fact of becoming rather important.
    R. H. BENSON, *An Average Man.*

16
One of the best temporary cures for pride and affectation is seasickness: a man who wants to vomit never puts on airs.
    JOSH BILLINGS (HENRY WHEELER SHAW). From *Civil War Humor,* ed. by DORIS BENADETE.

17
Of all the lunatics earth can boast,
The one that must please the devil most
Is pride reduced to the whimsical terms
Of causing the slugs to despise the worms.
    ROBERT BROUGH, *The Tent-Maker's Song.*

18
Too proud to beg, too honest to steal,
I know what it is to be wanting a meal;
My tatters and rags I try to conceal,
I'm one of the shabby genteel.
    HARRY CLIFTON, *Shabby Genteel.*

19
And the Devil did grin, for his darling sin
  Is pride that apes humility.
    SAMUEL TAYLOR COLERIDGE, *The Devil's Thoughts.*

20
There is a paradox in pride: it makes some men ridiculous, but prevents others from becoming so.
    C. C. COLTON, *Lacon.*

21
For whatsoe'er the sages charge on pride,
The angels' fall, and twenty faults beside,
On earth, I'm sure, 'mong us of mortal calling,
Pride saves man oft, and woman too, from falling.
    GEORGE FARQUHAR, *The Beaux' Stratagem,* Act 2.

22
A man has jest naturally got to have something to cuss and boss, so's to keep himself from finding out he don't amount to nothing.
    DON MARQUIS, *Danny's Own Story.*

1
"I did that," says my memory. "I could not have done that," says my pride, and remains inexorable. Eventually—the memory yields.
FRIEDRICH WILHELM NIETZSCHE, *Beyond Good and Evil,* tr. by HELEN ZIMMERN.

2
Pride is at the bottom of all great mistakes.
JOHN RUSKIN, *Modern Painters,* vol. 1.

3
Pride is pleasure springing from a man thinking too highly of himself.
BENEDICT DE SPINOZA, *Ethics.* Pt. iii, def. 28.

4
She is a peacock in everything but beauty.
OSCAR WILDE, *The Picture of Dorian Gray,* ch. 1.

PRINCIPLE

5
It is easier to fight for one's principles than to live up to them.
ALFRED ADLER.

6
Some things pay in the long run and for a little while, but honesty and truth and diligence pay in the long run, and that is the run we have to die by.
BILL ARP. (*Horse Sense in American Humor,* by WALTER BLAIR, JR.)

7
A man should *be* upright, not be *kept* upright.
MARCUS AURELIUS, *Meditations.*

8
Gladstone: "Mr. Disraeli, you will probably die by the hangman's noose or a vile disease."
Disraeli: "Sir, that depends upon whether I embrace your principles or your mistress."
Quoted in *Presidents Who Have Known Me,* by GEORGE E. ALLEN. See also PEARSON in this section.

9
Like the British constitution, she owes her success in practice to her inconsistencies in principle.
THOMAS HARDY, *Hand of Ethelberta,* ch. 9.

10
It doesn't pay well to fight for what we believe in.
LILLIAN HELLMAN, *Watch on the Rhine,* Act 1.

11
A marciful Providence fashioned us holler,
O' purpose thet we might our princerples swaller.
JAMES RUSSELL LOWELL, *The Biglow Papers.* Ser. i, No. 4.

12
I *don't* believe in princerple,
But O, I *du* in interest.
JAMES RUSSELL LOWELL, *The Biglow Papers.* Ser. i, No. 6.

13
Our differences are politics. Our agreements, principles.
WILLIAM MCKINLEY, *Speech* in Des Moines, Ia., 1901.

14
You can't learn too soon that the most useful thing about a principle is that it can always be sacrificed to expediency.
W. SOMERSET MAUGHAM, *The Circle.*

15
He is so stuffed with principles that there is no room left for a little Christian tolerance . . .
LORD MORAN, *Diaries,* Jan. 22, 1943. Referring to Charles de Gaulle.

16
It is often easier to fight for principles than to live up to them.
ADLAI E. STEVENSON, *Speech* in New York City, Aug. 27, 1952. See also ADLER in this section.

17
When his friend Lord Sandwich told him [John Wilkes] that he would die either of the pox or on the gallows, he saw the possibilities: "That depends, my Lord, on whether I embrace your mistress or your principles."
HESKETH PEARSON, *Lives of the Wits.*

PRIVACY

18
As lacking in privacy as a goldfish.
ANONYMOUS.

19
Poor people are not fussy about privacy; they have other problems.
ARTHUR FELLIG (WEEGEE), *An Autobiography.*

20
An age of publicity cannot but make privacy first difficult and at length undesirable: eventually people, if they can feel sure that everyone will know their address, will cheerfully live in glass houses.
LOUIS KRONENBERGER, *Company Manners,* p. 130.

21
Everyone heard that I'd written the book and got it in the press. After that, I might have been a gold-fish in a glass bowl for all the privacy I got.
H. H. MUNRO (SAKI), *The Innocence of Reginald* (1904). Irvin S. Cobb used the phrase "No more privacy than a goldfish" in describing his sojourn in a

hospital, and is often credited with its invention. See also ANONYMOUS entry in this section.

PROCRASTINATION

1
He slept beneath the moon,
  He basked beneath the sun;
He lived a life of going-to-do,
  And died with nothing done.
  JAMES ALBERY, *Epitaph*, written for himself.

2
Procrastination—The art of keeping up with yesterday.
  DON MARQUIS.

3
Never put off till to-morrow what you can do day after to-morrow just as well.
  MARK TWAIN, *The Late Benjamin Franklin.*

PROFANITY

4
Why are the fingers tapered like pegs? So that when one hears improper language he may insert them in his ears.
  BABYLONIAN TALMUD, *Kethuboth.*

5
Take not God's name in vain; select
A time when it will have effect.
  AMBROSE BIERCE, *The Devil's Dictionary: The Decalogue Revised.*

6
The man who first abused his fellows with swear words instead of bashing their brains out with a club should be counted among those who laid the foundations of civilization.
  JOHN COHEN, quoted in *The New York Times.*

7
Th' best thing about a little judicyous swearin' is that it keeps th' temper. 'Twas intinded as a compromise between runnin' away an' fightin'.
  FINLEY PETER DUNNE, *Observations by Mr. Dooley: Swearing.*

8
When he's excited he uses language that would make your hair curl.
  SIR WILLIAM SCHWENCK GILBERT, *Ruddigore.*

9
The good, upright, usually well-tempered Fessenden, it was told over Washington, in a rage over some unjust distribution of patronage turned loose a flow of "intemperate language" on Lincoln one morning. Lincoln kept cool. The fury of his Maine friend spent itself. Lincoln inquired gently, "You are an Episcopalian, aren't you, Senator?" "Yes, sir. I belong to that church." "I thought so. You Episcopalians all swear alike. Seward is an Episcopalian. But Stanton is a Presbyterian. You ought to hear him swear." Then Lincoln went on telling about several varieties of profanity, and he and Fessenden settled down to an even-toned conversation.
  CARL SANDBURG, *Abraham Lincoln: The Prairie Years and the War Years*, ch. 50.

10
If God listened to every shepherd's curse, our sheep would all be dead.
  OLD RUSSIAN PROVERB.

11
You do not swear at your serious troubles. One only swears at trifling annoyances.
  G. F. TURNER, *The Conversion of Claude.*

12
Sometimes an ordained minister sets out to be blasphemous. When this happens, the layman is out of the running; he stands no chance.
  MARK TWAIN, *Essays: To the Person Sitting in Darkness.*

PROGRESS

13
All progress is based upon a universal innate desire on the part of every organism to live beyond its income.
  SAMUEL BUTLER, *The Way of All Flesh.*

14
The way to resumption is to resume.
  SALMON P. CHASE, *Letter* to Horace Greeley, May 17, 1866.

15
Behold the turtle. He makes progress only when he sticks his neck out.
  JAMES BRYANT CONANT.

16
What we call "progress" is the exchange of one nuisance for another nuisance.
  HAVELOCK ELLIS, *Impressions and Comments.*

17
To make headway, improve your head.
  B. C. FORBES, *Epigrams.*

18
Stand still and you'll fall down.
  B. C. FORBES, *Epigrams.*

19
We ain't what we oughta be,
we ain't what we wanta be,
we ain't what we gonna be,
but thank God we ain't what we was.
  MARTIN LUTHER KING, JR., quoted by SAMMY DAVIS, JR., *Yes I Can.*

1

Is it progress if a cannibal uses knife and fork?

STANISLAW J. LEC, *Unkempt Thoughts*, tr. from the Polish by JACEK GALASKA.

2

Two hundred years from now history will record: America, a nation that flourished from 1900 to 1942, conceived many odd inventions for getting somewhere, but could think of nothing to do when they got there.

WILL ROGERS, *Autobiography*.

3

Too many apples from the tree of systematized knowledge lead to the fall of progress.

ALFRED NORTH WHITEHEAD.

PROHIBITION

4

Prohibition has made nothing but trouble.

ALPHONSE (AL) CAPONE, *Newspaper Interview*.

5

Water flowed like wine.

WILLIAM M. EVARTS, describing a dinner at the White House in 1877 during the administration of Rutherford B. Hayes, whose wife was a prohibitionist.

6

Some love strong beer, and the maniac's cheer,

And the bacchanalian's glee;

But the gurgling rill, from the rock-bound hill

And a peaceful home for me!

The Temperance Musician, quoted in *The Life and Times of the Late Demon Rum* by J. C. FURNAS.

7

I could suggest something that might make the law more drastic. Just two hundred years ago this year Sultan Amurath of Turkey issued an edict which provided that the nose of any person who smoked tobacco could be cut off. If you want to enact these provisions, go ahead. There's a suggestion.

REPRESENTATIVE JOHN D. MCCRATE of Maine, *Remark*, 1919, during a debate on prohibition.

8

O' water for me! bright water for me,

And wine for the tremulous debauchee.

McGuffey's New Eclectic Speaker (1858).

9

There is some sneaking Temperance Society movement about this business!

HERMAN MELVILLE, *Moby Dick*, ch. 72.

10

Of old, all invitations ended

With the well-known *R.S.V.P.*,

But now our laws have been amended

The hostess writes *B.Y.O.B.*

CHRISTOPHER MORLEY, *Thoughts on Being Invited to Dinner*. "B.Y.O.B." meant "Bring your own booze."

11

"I see," said he, speaking to some American friends, "that you, too, put up monuments to your great dead."

RALPH NEVILL, *Paris of Today*. A distinguished Frenchman speaking to American friends as he viewed the Statue of Liberty during the prohibition era.

12

The South is dry and will vote dry. That is, everybody that is sober enough to stagger to the polls will.

WILL ROGERS, *Saturday Evening Post*, Oct. 29, 1926.

13

Noah was told to collect two of every variety of animals and take them on board . . . I defy any man to show me where he took a prohibitionist and his wife aboard.

WILL ROGERS, quoted by DONALD DAY in *Will Rogers: A Biography*.

14

The prohibition law, written for weaklings and derelicts, has divided the nation, like Gaul, into three parts—wets, drys and hypocrites.

MRS. CHARLES H. SABIN, *Address*, Feb. 9, 1931.

15

Good-bye, John. You were God's worst enemy. You were Hell's best friend. I hate you with a perfect hatred.

BILLY SUNDAY, *Funeral Oration* over John Barleycorn, Norfolk, Va., Jan. 16, 1920.

16

I prefer temperance hotels—although they sell worse liquor than any other kind of hotels.

ARTEMUS WARD, *Temperance*.

PROMISE

17

More chorus girls are kept than promises.

FRED ALLEN, *Treadmill to Oblivion*. Reference to show business.

18

For this you've my word, and I've never yet broke it.

So put that in your pipe, my Lord Otto, and smoke it.

R. H. BARHAM, *The Lay of St. Odille*.

19

This is the first convention of the space age

—when a candidate can promise the moon
and mean it.
> DAVID BRINKLEY, NBC commentator.
> Quoted in *Newsweek,* Mar. 13, 1961.

1
He that imposes an oath makes it,
Not he that for convenience takes it;
Then how can any man be said
To break an oath he never made?
> SAMUEL BUTLER, *Hudibras,* pt. 2.

2
A woman's oaths are wafers, break with
making.
> JOHN FLETCHER, *The Chances.* Act ii, sc.
> 1.

3
A man apt to promise is apt to forget.
> THOMAS FULLER, *Gnomologia,* No. 2007.

4
Count not his broken pledges as a crime
He *meant* them, HOW he meant them—at
> the time.
> KENSAL GREEN, *Premature Epitaphs.* On
> Lloyd George.

5
Promise is a promise, dough you make it in
de dark er de moon.
> JOEL CHANDLER HARRIS, *Nights with Un-
> cle Remus,* ch. 39.

6
And they all had trust in his cussedness,
And knowed he would keep his word.
> JOHN HAY, *Jim Bludso.*

7
Some persons make promises for the pleasure
of breaking them.
> WILLIAM HAZLITT, *Characteristics.*

8
Half the promises people say were never
kept were never made.
> E. W. HOWE, *Howe's Monthly.*

9
Once you pledge, don't hedge.
> NIKITA KHRUSHCHEV, quoted by JOHN
> GUNTHER in *Inside Russia Today.*

10
He who breaks a resolution is a weakling;
He who makes one is a fool.
> F. M. KNOWLES, *A Cheerful Year Book.*

11
He's as good as his word—and his word is
no good.
> SEUMAS MACMANUS, *Heavy Hangs the
> Golden Grain.*

12
Promises don't fill the belly.
> CHARLES HADDON SPURGEON, *Ploughman's
> Pictures.*

13
The two maxims of any great man at court

are, always to keep his countenance, and
never to keep his word.
> JONATHAN SWIFT, *Thoughts on Various
> Subjects.*

14
Promises and pie-crust are made to be
broken.
> JONATHAN SWIFT, *Polite Conversation,*
> Dial. 1. See also WARD in this section.

15
. . . prophecies which promise valuable
things, desirable things, good things, worthy
things, never come true. Prophecies of this
kind are like wars fought in a good cause—
they are so rare that they don't count.
> MARK TWAIN, *Autobiography.*

16
Fair promises avail but little,
Like so much pie crust, they're so brittle.
> EDWARD WARD, *Hudibras Redivivus.* Pt. V,
> canto 7.

PROSPERITY

17
In the Western World the idea still lingers
that the wages of righteousness is prosperity.
> WALTER FREEMAN, *Morning in an Empty
> Room.*

18
The human race has had long experience and
a fine tradition in surviving adversity. But
now we face a task for which we have little
experience, the task of surviving prosperity.
> ALAN GREGG, quoted in *The New York
> Times,* Nov. 4, 1956.

19
I don't think you can spend yourself rich.
> GEORGE HUMPHREY, Secretary of the
> Treasury, *News summaries,* Jan. 28,
> 1957. On compensatory spending during
> business declines.

20
Era of wonderful nonsense.
> WESTBROOK PEGLER, *Newspaper Column.*
> The reference is to the wild stock-
> market speculation of 1929.

21
It costs most men a good deal more to live
up to their prosperity than they get out of
it.
> *Reflections of a Bachelor.*

22
Every official in the government and every
prominent manufacturer is forever bragging
about our "high standard of living." Why,
we could always have lived this high if we
had wanted to live on the installment plan.
> WILL ROGERS, *Autobiography.*

23
We all know that you [President Herbert
Hoover] was handed a balloon that was

blowed up to the utmost, you held it as carefully as anyone could, but the thing "busted" right in your hands.
WILL ROGERS, *Autobiography.*

1
Prosperity is the surest breeder of insolence I know.
MARK TWAIN.

2
A man is never so on trial as in the moment of excessive good-fortune.
LEW WALLACE, *Ben-Hur.* Bk. v, ch. 7.

PRUDENCE

3
He bade me have a care for the future, to make sure of the bear before I sell his skin.
AESOP. See also LYLY in this section.

4
Do not count your chickens before they are hatched.
AESOP, *The Milkmaid and Her Pail.*

5
Discretion, the best part of valour.
BEAUMONT AND FLETCHER, *A King and No King.* Act iv, sc. 3.

6
For those that fly may fight again,
Which he can never do that's slain.
SAMUEL BUTLER, *Hudibras,* pt. 3.

7
It is always wise to look ahead, but difficult to look further than you can see.
WINSTON CHURCHILL, *Speech,* House of Commons, Jan. 30, 1952.

8
Tho' the bear be gentle, don't bite him by the nose.
THOMAS D'URFEY, *Quixote,* pt. 3.

9
That same man that runneth away
May fight again on another day.
GERARD DIDIER ERASMUS, *Adagia,* No. 372.

10
More trouble is caused in the world by indiscreet answers than by indiscreet questions.
SYDNEY J. HARRIS, *Chicago Daily News,* Mar. 27, 1958.

11
He that goes barefoot must not plant thorns.
GEORGE HERBERT, *Jacula Prudentum.*

12
Who lets his wife go to every feast, and his horse drink at every water, shall have neither good wife nor good horse.
GEORGE HERBERT, *Jacula Prudentum.*

13
When you have got an elephant by the hind leg, and he is trying to run away, it's best to let him run.
ABRAHAM LINCOLN, *Remark,* to Charles A. Dana, Apr. 14, 1865, just before his death. Lincoln had been urged to arrest Jacob Thompson, a Confederate commissioner who was trying to flee to Europe. (WILSON, *Life of Charles A. Dana,* p. 358; MITCHELL, *Memoirs of an Editor,* p. 35.)

14
My gran'ther's rule was safer 'n 'tis to crow:
Don't never prophesy—onless ye know.
JAMES RUSSELL LOWELL, *Mason and Slidell.*

15
I trusted so much that I sold the skin before the bear was taken.
JOHN LYLY, *Mother Bombie.*

16
In baiting a mouse-trap with cheese, always leave room for the mouse.
HECTOR HUGH MUNRO (SAKI), *The Square Egg: The Infernal Parliament.*

17
He that fights and runs away
May live to fight and run away.
Musarum Deliciae, a collection made by Sir John Mennes and Dr. James Smith, and published in 1656. No author was given. The lines were attributed to Sir John Suckling, but no confirmation was ever recorded.

18
He can return who flies:
Not so with him who dies.
(Qui fuit peut revenir aussi:
Qui meurt, il n'en est pas ainsi.)
PAUL SCARRON, *Epigram.*

PSYCHIATRY

19
They say a psychiatrist is a fellow who asks you a lot of expensive questions your wife asks for nothing.
JOEY ADAMS, *Cindy and I,* ch. 3.

20
When I talk about food and sex with psychologists, and wonder about other equivalent basic human drives, they almost always bring up aggression. I am beginning to wonder about psychologists, since they seem to see aggression everywhere. It is difficult to argue with them about it though, because if you disagree you are simply being hostile.
MARSTON BATES, *On Being Mean; The American Scholar,* winter 1966–67.

21
A neurotic does well to be either rich or a poet: In one case he can support his neurosis; in the other he can employ it.
JOHN CIARDI, *The Saturday Review,* Sept. 24, 1966.

1
I didn't know the full facts of life until I
was seventeen. My father never talked about
his work.
>MARTIN FREUD, *News summaries,* Nov.
15, 1957.

2
Neurosis seems to be a human privilege.
>SIGMUND FREUD, *Moses and Monotheism.*

3
During his start in analysis I said to him,
"Does it help your constipation, George
[George Gershwin]?" (I used to make fun
of analysis.)
He answered, "No, but now I understand
why I have constipation."
>OSCAR LEVANT, *Memoirs of an Amnesiac.*

4
The alienist is not a joke;
He finds you cracked and leaves you broke.
>KEITH PRESTON, *The Alienist.*

5
A lot of people, especially this one psychoanalyst guy they have here, keeps asking me
if I'm going to apply myself when I go back
to school in September. It's such a stupid
question, in my opinion. I mean, how do you
know what you're going to do till you do it?
>J. D. SALINGER, *The Catcher in the Rye.*

6
I do not have a psychiatrist and I do not
want one, for the simple reason that if he
listened to me long enough, he might become disturbed.
>JAMES THURBER, *Credos and Curios.*

7
A neurotic is a man who builds a castle in
the air. A psychotic is the man who lives
in it. And a psychiatrist is the man who
collects the rent.
>LORD WEBB-JOHNSON, British surgeon. In
Look, Oct. 4, 1955.

PUBLIC, THE
8
The trouble with the public is that there is
too much of it.
>DON MARQUIS, *Letter* to Lyman Beecher
Stowe.

9
The masses gladly take revenge for the
honors they render us.
>NAPOLEON BONAPARTE. (*The Mind of Na-
poleon,* ed. by J. CHRISTOPHER HER-
OLD.)

10
The Mob destroys spiritual values by ac-
cepting them; it destroys great men by
adopting their principles.
>FRANK K. NOTCH, *King Mob.*

11
Marie Antoinette made only one mistake.
She should have said, "Let them eat hokum."
>WESTBROOK PEGLER, *Fair Enough,* Dec.
5, 1934.

12
I am a member of the rabble in good standing.
>WESTBROOK PEGLER, *The Lynching Story.*

13
Admitting to be a fool doesn't keep one
from being a fool. The public is lazy, likes
only lies. From the minute they sense the
truth they lose interest.
>NED ROREM, *Paris Diary.*

14
The angry Buzz of a multitude is one of
the bloodiest noises in the world.
>GEORGE SAVILE, Marquis of Halifax. *The
Complete Works of George Savile.*

PUBLICITY
See also Advertising
15
All press agents belong to a club of which
Ananias is the honorary president.
>JOHN KENDRICK BANGS.

16
Ordeal by Publicity is the legitimate grand-
child of Ordeal by Fire, Water and Battle.
>GEORGE H. BOLDT, *Address,* American Bar
Association, Aug., 1954.

17
The fellow is blowing his own strumpet.
>W. S. GILBERT, of a theatrical manager
who was puffing an actress who was
also his mistress. (PEARSON, *Gilbert
and Sullivan,* pt. 3.)

18
Public relations specialists make flower ar-
rangements of the facts, placing them so
that the wilted and less attractive petals
are hidden by sturdy blooms.
>ALAN HARRINGTON, *Life in the Crystal
Palace.*

19
We know that there are a number of what
are known as image-producing organizations.
They produce marvelous images, but no one
believes them.
>PRINCE PHILIP, from *The Wit of Prince
Philip,* compiled by PETER BUTLER.

20
Man is a creature who lives not upon bread
alone, but principally by catchwords . . .
>ROBERT LOUIS STEVENSON, *Virginibus
Puerisque.*

21
What rage for fame attends both great and
small!

Better be d—d than mentioned not at all.
JOHN WOLCOT, *To the Royal Academicians.*

PURITANS

1
Shaw is a Puritan who missed the Mayflower by five minutes.
BENJAMIN DE CASSERES, *Mencken and Shaw.*

2
"Whin I was a young man," said Mr. Dooley, "I often heerd Thanksgivin' day alooded to fr'm th' altar as a pagan fistival. Father Kelly don't think so. He says 't was founded by th' Puritans to give thanks f'r bein' presarved fr'm th' Indyans, an' that we keep it to give thanks we are presarved fr'm the Puritans."
FINLEY PETER DUNNE, *Mr. Dooley's Opinions: Thanksgiving.*

3
Puritans should wear fig leaves on their eyes.
STANISLAW J. LEC, *Unkempt Thoughts,* tr. from the Polish by JACEK GALASKA.

4
He had stiff knees, the Puritan,
That were not good at bending.
JAMES RUSSELL LOWELL, *An Interview with Miles Standish,* st. 12.

5
Puritanism, believing itself quick with the seed of religious liberty, laid, without knowing it, the egg of democracy.
JAMES RUSSELL LOWELL, *Among My Books.*

6
The Puritan hated bear-baiting not because it gave pain to the bear but because it gave pleasure to the spectators.
THOMAS BABINGTON MACAULAY.

7
The objection to Puritans is not that they try to make us think as they do, but that they try to make us do as they think.
H. L. MENCKEN.

8
A puritan is a fanatical idealist to whom all the stimulations of the sense are abhorred; a philistine is a prosaic person who has no ideals.
BERNARD SHAW, *Dramatic Opinions.*

PURPOSE

9
"They were obliged to have him with them," the Mock Turtle said: "no wise fish would go anywhere without a porpoise."
"Wouldn't it really?" said Alice in a tone of great surprise.
"Of course not," said the Mock Turtle; "why if a fish came to *me,* and told me he was going on a journey, I should say, 'With what porpoise?'"
LEWIS CARROLL, *Alice in Wonderland,* ch. 10.

10
If your life isn't planned you'll end by being panned.
B. C. FORBES, *Epigrams.*

11
The trouble with our age is all signposts and no destination.
LOUIS KRONENBERGER, *Look,* May 17, 1954.

12
Men are not flattered by being shown that there has been a difference of purpose between the Almighty and them.
ABRAHAM LINCOLN, *Letter* to Thurlow Weed, Mar. 14, 1865.

13
With the supermarket as our temple and the singing commercial as our litany, are we likely to fire the world with an irresistible vision of America's exalted purposes and inspiring way of life?
ADLAI STEVENSON.

Q

QUARRELING

See also Fighting

14
Just then flew down a monstrous crow,
As black as a tar-barrel;
Which frightened both the heroes so,
They quite forgot their quarrel.
LEWIS CARROLL, *Through the Looking-Glass,* ch. 4.

15
A quarrel between man and wife is like cutting water with a sword.
Chinese Proverb, from *Oriental Humor,* ed. by R. H. BLYTH.

16
In all private quarrels the duller nature is triumphant by reason of dullness.
GEORGE ELIOT, *Felix Holt,* ch. 9.

17
A chip on the shoulder is too heavy a piece of baggage to carry through life.
B. C. FORBES, *Epigrams.*

1
The world is too narrow for two fools a quarrelling.
THOMAS FULLER, *Gnomologia*, No. 4844.

2
Those who in quarrels interpose,
Must often wipe a bloody nose.
JOHN GAY, *Fables*. Pt. i, No. 34.

3
Thrice is he armed that hath his quarrel just—and four times he who gets his fist in fust.
ARTEMUS WARD.

4
Do unto the other feller the way he'd like to do unto you, an' do it fust.
EDWARD NOYES WESTCOTT, *David Harum*.

QUESTION

See also Curiosity

5
Avoid a questioner, for such a man is also a tattler. (Preconctatorem fugito; nam garrulus idem est.)
HORACE, *Epistles*. Bk. i, epis. 18.

6
I will not be baited with *what* and *why*.

What is this? What is that? Why is a cow's tail long? Why is a fox's tail bushy?
SAMUEL JOHNSON, BOSWELL'S *Life*, Apr. 10, 1778.

7
He's been that way for years—a born questioner but he hates answers.
RING LARDNER, *Dinner Bridge*.

8
He had a way of meeting a simple question with a compound answer—you could take the part you wanted, and leave the rest.
EVA LATHBURY, *Mr. Meyer's Pupil*.

9
Where is everybody?
CARL SANDBURG, *Answer* to the question, "What was it the last man on earth said?" From *Carl Sandburg*, by HARRY GOLDEN.

10
Do we now?
JAMES J. WALKER, *Reply* when asked by Franklin D. Roosevelt why the Irish always answer a question with a question.

11
Questions are never indiscreet. Answers sometimes are.
OSCAR WILDE, *An Ideal Husband*, Act 1.

R

READING

12
If the Man in the Grey Flannel Suit married Marjorie Morningstar on my front porch at high noon, I wouldn't bother to go to the wedding.
NELSON ALGREN, on novelists Sloan Wilson and Herman Wouk. (MYRICK LAND, *The Fine Art of Literary Criticism*.)

13
Thoreau's quality is very penetrating and contagious; reading him is like eating onions —one must look out or the flavor will reach his own page.
JOHN BURROUGHS, *Journal*, 1878.

14
There is a great deal of difference between the eager man who wants to read a book and the tired man who wants a book to read.
G. K. CHESTERTON.

15
What a glorious garden of wonders this world would be to anyone who was lucky enough to be unable to read.
G. K. CHESTERTON, *What I Saw in America*. Describing the lights of Broadway.

16
Reading without thinking is worse than no reading at all.
HARRY GOLDEN, *For 2¢ Plain*.

17
Reading is sometimes an ingenious device for avoiding thought.
SIR ARTHUR HELPS, *Friends in Council*. Bk. ii, ch. 1.

18
He [Hobbes] had read much, but his contemplation was much more than his reading. He was wont to say that if he had read as much as other men, he should have known no more than other men.
JOHN AUBREY, *Brief Lives*.

19
I never desire to converse with a man who has written more than he has read.
SAMUEL JOHNSON, *Miscellanies*, vol. 2.

20
He has left off reading altogether, to the great improvement of his originality.
CHARLES LAMB, *Last Essays of Elia: Detached Thoughts on Books and Reading*.

1

I can remember no time at which a page of print was not intelligible to me, and can only suppose that I was born literate.

BERNARD SHAW, quoted by ARCHIBALD HENDERSON in *George Bernard Shaw: Man of the Century.*

2

The eminent critic Lionel Trilling once observed that Shelley should not be read, but inhaled through a gas pipe.

CLIFTON FADIMAN, *Enter, Conversing.*

3

The man who does not read good books has no advantage over the man who can't read them.

MARK TWAIN.

4

A book worm is a person who would rather read than eat, or it is a worm that would rather eat than read.

UNKNOWN.

REASON

5

Every man's reason is every man's oracle.

LORD BOLINGBROKE, *Of the True Use of Retirement and Study,* letter 2.

6

Nothing pleases an impulsive, featherbrained woman so much as to prove to her that she always acts with logical deliberation.

G. B. BURGIN, *Which Woman?*

7

May I know your reasons? . . . I am a woman, I haven't any.

WYMOND CAREY, *Love the Judge.*

8

Most people have ears, but few have judgment; tickle those ears, and, depend upon it, you will catch their judgments, such as they are.

LORD CHESTERFIELD, *Letters,* Dec. 9, 1749.

9

Her reasoning is full of tricks
  And butterfly suggestions,
I know no point to which she sticks;
  She begs the simplest questions,
And, when her premises are strong
She always draws her inference wrong.

ALFRED COCHRANE, *Upon Lesbia Arguing.*

10

The lower your senses are kept, the better you may govern them. Appetite and Reason are commonly like two buckets; when one is at the top, the other is at the bottom. Now of the two, I had rather the Reasonbucket be uppermost.

JEREMY COLLIER. (*Classic Quotations,* ed. by JAMES ELMES.)

11

Reasons are not like garments, the worse for wearing.

ROBERT DEVEREUX, Earl of Essex. *Letter to Lord Willoughby.*

12

I'm not one o' those as can see the cat i' the dairy an' wonder what she's come after.

GEORGE ELIOT, *Adam Bede,* ch. 52.

13

Reason always means what someone else has got to say.

MRS. (ELIZABETH CLEGHORN) GASKELL, *Cranford.*

14

I don't care anything about reasons, but I know what I like.

HENRY JAMES, *The Portrait of a Lady,* ch. 24.

15

As thin as the homoeopathic soup that was made by boiling the shadow of a pigeon that had been starved to death.

ABRAHAM LINCOLN, on the reasoning of STEPHEN DOUGLAS. (*The Humorous Mr. Lincoln* by KEITH W. JENNISON.)

16

Some folks dey would 'a' beat him:
Now, dat would only heat him;
I know jes' how to treat him:
  You mus' *reason* wid a mule.

IRWIN RUSSELL, *Nebuchadnezzar.*

17

When they wished to justify their actions, they gave reasons which were so dull that they could not fail to be true.

JEAN-PAUL SARTRE, *The Words.*

18

I have no other but a woman's reason.
I think him so because I think him so.

WILLIAM SHAKESPEARE, *Two Gentlemen of Verona.* Act i, sc. 2.

19

I was promised on a time
To have reason for my rhyme;
From that time unto this season,
I received neither rhyme nor reason.

EDMUND SPENSER, *Lines on His Promised Pension.*

20

I can stand brute force, but brute reason is quite unbearable. There is something unfair about its use. It is hitting below the intellect.

OSCAR WILDE, *The Picture of Dorian Gray,* ch. 3.

REFORM, REFORMERS

21

In uplifting, get underneath.

GEORGE ADE, *Fables.*

1
A man that'd expict to thrain lobsters to fly in a year is called a loonytic; but a man that thinks men can be tu-rrned into angels be an illiction is called a rayformer an remains at large.
> FINLEY PETER DUNNE, *Mr. Dooley's Philosophy.*

2
No true reform has ever come to pass
Unchallenged by a lion and an ass.
> ARTHUR GUITERMAN, *A Poet's Proverbs.*

3
The role of a do-gooder is not what actors call a fat part.
> MARGARET HALSEY, *The Folks at Home.*

4
A bishopric conferred on Luther at the right moment might have cooled his ardor for a Reformation.
> ERIC HOFFER, *The True Believer.*

5
Both claim the legal right to the pursuit of other people's happiness.
> ELBERT HUBBARD, *The Philistine,* vol. 25.

6
Becomin' a reformer after th' joys o' youth have fled don't count.
> FRANK McKINNEY (KIN) HUBBARD, *Abe Martin's Primer.*

7
. . . his sister was Harriet Beecher Stowe, whose *Uncle Tom's Cabin* was the first evidence to America that no hurricane can be so disastrous to a country as a ruthlessly humanitarian woman.
> SINCLAIR LEWIS, *Introduction* to *Henry Ward Beecher: An American Portrait* by PAXTON HIBBEN.

8
Few friends he has that please his mind.
  His marriage failed when it began,
Who worked unceasing for mankind
  But loathed his fellowman.
> PHYLLIS McGINLEY, *The Old Reformer.*

9
A party doesn't reform; it is reformed.
> MOOS AND HESS, *Hats in the Ring.*

10
The race would save one half its wasted labor
Would each reform himself and spare his neighbor.
> FRANK PUTNAM, *Reform.*

11
God did not make man a hound-dog to scent out evil.
> JOHN TIMOTHY STONE, *Everyday Religion.*

12
If anything ail a man so that he does not perform his functions, if he have a pain in his bowels even . . . he forthwith sets about reforming—the world.
> HENRY D. THOREAU, *Walden.*

13
A reformer is a guy who rides through a sewer in a glass-bottomed boat.
> JAMES J. WALKER, *Newspaper Interview.*

REGRET

14
It's no use crying over spilt milk: it only makes it salty for the cat.
> ANONYMOUS. (See also GILBERT in this section.)

15
Regrets are the natural property of gray hairs.
> CHARLES DICKENS, *Martin Chuzzlewit,* ch. 10.

16
That vague kind of penitence which holidays awaken next morning.
> CHARLES DICKENS, *The Old Curiosity Shop,* ch. 40.

17
Too late repents the rat when caught by the cat.
> JOHN FLORIO, *Second Fruites,* 165.

18
However, it's no use crying over spilt milk.
> W. S. GILBERT, *Foggarty's Fairy,* Act 1.

19
Regret is a woman's natural food—she thrives upon it.
> SIR ARTHUR WING PINERO, *Sweet Lavender,* Act 3.

20
The dream is short, repentance long. (Der Wahn ist kurtz, die Reu ist lang.)
> JOHANN VON SCHILLER, *Lied von der Glocke.*

21
For of all sad words of tongue or pen,
The saddest are these: "It might have been."
> JOHN GREENLEAF WHITTIER, *Maud Muller,* l. 105.

RELIGION

**See also Atheism, Church, Clergy,
Faith, Prayer, Saints**

22
True, you might say that these modern irreligious people nowadays are no better and may even be worse than the old-timers with their false piety. But they're not so revolting. At least they don't pretend to be on speaking terms with God.
> SHOLOM ALEICHEM, *Eternal Life.*

1
Next Sunday the Reverend Dr. Jones will preach on "Skiing on the Sabbath" or "Are Our Young Women Backsliding on Their Week-Ends?"
FRED ALLEN, *Radio Broadcast.*

2
You generally notice that when the devil has tired of a man he will turn to religion.
W. BURTON BALDRY, *Stray Thoughts.*

3
Being an Episcopalian interferes neither with my business nor my religion.
JOHN KENDRICK BANGS.

4
There are many people who think that Sunday is a sponge to wipe out all the sins of the week.
HENRY WARD BEECHER, *Life Thoughts.*

5
If a man cannot be a Christian in the place where he is, he cannot be a Christian anywhere.
HENRY WARD BEECHER, *Life Thoughts.*

6
Christians and camels receive their burdens kneeling.
AMBROSE BIERCE, *The Devil's Dictionary.*

7
Orthodox, n. An ox wearing the popular religious yoke.
AMBROSE BIERCE, *The Devil's Dictionary.*

8
More Catholic than the pope.
OTTO VON BISMARCK (1887).

9
. . . I saw a Puritane one
Hanging of his cat on Monday,
For killing of a mouse on Sunday.
R. BRATHWAITE, *Barnabee's Journal.*

10
We have all known . . .
Good popes who brought all good to jeopardy,
Good Christians who sat still in easy chairs
And damned the general world for standing up.
E. B. BROWNING, *Aurora Leigh,* bk. 4.

11
      Mothers, wives and maids,
These be the tools wherewith priests manage fools.
ROBERT BROWNING, *The Ring and The Book,* iv.

12
Some of the most beautiful passages in the apostolic writings are quotations from pagan authors.
HENRY T. BUCKLE, *Introduction to the History of Civilization in England.*

13
Nothing is so fatal to religion as indifference, which is, at least, half infidelity.
EDMUND BURKE, *Letter,* to WILLIAM SMITH, Jan. 9, 1795.

14
'Twas Presbyterian true blue.
SAMUEL BUTLER, *Hudibras,* pt. 1.

15
And prove their doctrine orthodox,
By apostolic blows and knocks.
SAMUEL BUTLER, *Hudibras,* pt. 1.

16
With crosses, relics, crucifixes,
Beads, pictures, rosaries, and pixies,—
The tools of working our salvation
By mere mechanic operation.
SAMUEL BUTLER, *Hudibras,* pt. 3.

17
Christians have burnt each other, quite persuaded
That all the Apostles would have done as they did.
LORD BYRON, *Don Juan,* Canto i, st. 83.

18
His religion is at best an anxious wish,—
like that of Rabelais, a great Perhaps.
THOMAS CARLYLE, *Burns.*

19
No truly great man, from Jesus Christ down, ever founded a sect.
THOMAS CARLYLE, *Journal.*

20
A machine for converting the heathen.
THOMAS CARLYLE, *Signs of the Times.*
Reference to the Bible Society.

21
Men will wrangle for religion; write for it; fight for it; die for it; anything but—*live* for it.
C. C. COLTON, *Lacon: Reflections,* No. 25.

22
Steele observed that there is this difference between the Church of Rome and the Church of England—that the one professes to be infallible, the other never to be in the wrong.
C. C. COLTON.

23
Some keep the Sabbath going to church;
I keep it staying at home,
With a bobolink for a chorister,
And an orchard for a dome.
EMILY DICKINSON, *Poems,* Pt. ii, No. 57.

24
"As for that," said Waldershare, "sensible men are all of the same religion." "And pray, what is that?" "Sensible men never tell."
BENJAMIN DISRAELI, *Endymion,* ch. 81.

1
You can and you can't,
You will and you won't;
You'll be damned if you do,
You'll be damned if you don't.
    LORENZO DOW, *Chain*. Definition of Cal-
    vinism.

2
Once when he was asked if he was a Roman
Catholic, he answered, "No, I'm a Chicago
Catholic."
    FINLEY PETER DUNNE, *Mr. Dooley Re-
    members*.

3
Every Stoic was a Stoic; but in Christiandom, where is the Christian?
    RALPH WALDO EMERSON, *Essays, First
    Series: Self Reliance*.

4
I knew a witty man who used to affirm that
if there was a disease in the liver, the man
became a Calvinist, and if that organ was
sound, he became a Unitarian.
    RALPH WALDO EMERSON, *Essays, Second
    Series: Experience*.

5
Luther was guilty of two great crimes—
he struck the Pope in his crown, and the
monks in their belly.
    GERARD DIDIER ERASMUS, *Colloquies*.

6
Dear me, how strange it would be to have
someone guessing infallibly.
    CARDINAL GASQUET, *Reply* to an English
    lady who asked him whether the next
    pope would be an American (1914).

7
He advised that Methodists be accepted as
jurymen because their religious emotions
can be transmuted into love and charity;
but warned against taking Presbyterians because they know right from wrong.
    HARRY GOLDEN, *For 2¢ Plain*. Reference
    to Clarence Darrow.

8
I do not love the Sabbath,
    The soapsuds and the starch,
The troop of solemn people
    Who to Salvation march.
    ROBERT GRAVES, *The Boy Out of Church*.

9
Most men's anger against religion is as if
two men should quarrel for a lady they
neither of them care for.
    LORD HALIFAX, *Works*.

10
Some persons are so devotional that they
have not one bit of true religion in them.
    B. R. HAYDON, *Table Talk*.

11
Religion, credit and the eye are not to be
touched.
    GEORGE HERBERT, *Jacula Prudentum*.

12
He [Theodore Tilton] had no sense of
humor and was incapable of achieving that
practical separation of Christianity from
daily life that enabled the brethren of Plymouth Church to sob over their souls on
Sunday and go about gouging their fellow
men the rest of the week with a clear conscience.
    PAXTON HIBBEN, *Henry Ward Beecher:
    An American Portrait*.

13
The sedate, sober, silent, serious, sad-col-
oured sect [Quakers].
    THOMAS HOOD, *The Doves and the Crows*.

14
Theology is an attempt to explain a subject
by men who do not understand it. The intent is not to tell the truth but to satisfy
the questioner.
    ELBERT HUBBARD, *The Philistine*.

15.
I have noticed all my life that many people
think they have religion when they are
troubled with dyspepsia.
    ROBERT G. INGERSOLL, *Liberty of Man,
    Woman and Child*.

16
Millions of innocent men, women and children, since the introduction of Christianity,
have been burned, tortured, fined and im-
prisoned, yet we have not advanced one
inch toward uniformity. What has been the
effect of coercion? To make one-half of the
world fools and the other half hypocrites.
    THOMAS JEFFERSON, *Notes on Virginia*.

17
Not versions, but perversions.
    ST. JEROME, of the versions of the Bible
    current in his day.

18
At night Mrs. Heron read the Evening Service to us, and I beheld with delight so fine
a Creature employed in adoring her Creator.
    SAMUEL JOHNSON, reported by Boswell.

19
Christiandom has done away with Christianity without being quite aware of it.
    SÖREN KIERKEGAARD, quoted in *Time*,
    Dec. 16, 1946.

20
Theology is an exact science often misin-
terpreted as a sentimental opinion just as
geology is often a sentimental opinion mis-
interpreted as an exact science.
    BRUCE MARSHALL, *Father Malachy's Mir-
    acle*.

21
Christian endeavor is notoriously hard on
female pulchritude.
    H. L. MENCKEN, *The Aesthetic Recoil;
    American Mercury*, July, 1931.

1
Religion is the vaccine of the imagination.
NAPOLEON BONAPARTE. (*The Mind of Napoleon,* ed. by J. CHRISTOPHER HEROLD.)

2
The religion of Jesus is a threat, that of Mohammed is a promise.
NAPOLEON BONAPARTE. (O'MEARA, *Napoleon in Exile.*)

3
And when religious sects ran mad,
  He held, in spite of all his learning,
That if a man's belief is bad,
  It will not be improved by burning.
WINTHROP M. PRAED, *The Vicar,* st. 9.

4
A modernist married a fundamentalist wife,
And she led him a catechism and dogma life.
KEITH PRESTON, *Marital Tragedy.*

5
Oaths are the fossils of piety.
GEORGE SANTAYANA, *Interpretations of Poetry.*

6
Many Christians are like chestnuts—very pleasant nuts, but enclosed in very prickly burrs, which need various dealings of Nature and her grip of frost before the kernel is disclosed.
HORACE SMITH, *The Tin Trumpet: Christians.*

7
The observances of the church concerning feasts and fasts are tolerably well kept since the rich keep the feasts and the poor the fasts.
SYDNEY SMITH.

8
Piety, stretched beyond a certain point, is the parent of impiety.
SYDNEY SMITH. (LADY HOLLAND, *Memoir,* ch. 3.)

9
No man should write on such subjects unless he is prepared to go the whole lamb.
SYDNEY SMITH, *Comment* on Milman's *History of Christianity.*

10
Volumes might be written upon the impiety of the pious.
HERBERT SPENCER, *First Principles.*

11
What religion is he of? Why, he is an Anythingarian.
JONATHAN SWIFT.

12
But mark me well; Religion is my name;
An angel once, but now a fury grown,

Too often talked of, but too little known.
JONATHAN SWIFT, *The Swan Tripe Club in Dublin.*

13
Religion seems to have grown an infant with age, and requires miracles to nurse it, as it had in its infancy.
JONATHAN SWIFT, *Thoughts on Various Subjects.*

14
If there is a famine, if there is a plague, the cry is at once: "The Christians to the lion." What! all of them to one lion?
Q. S. TERTULLIAN, *Apology,* 40.

15
Even in the valley of the shadow of death, two and two do not make six.
LEO TOLSTOY, when, as he was dying, he was urged to return to the fold of the Russian Orthodox Church.

16
Man is the religious animal. He is the only religious animal. He is the only animal that has the True Religion—several of them.
MARK TWAIN, *Letters from the Earth.*

17
Martin Luther died a horrible death. He was excommunicated by a bull.
LOUIS UNTERMEYER, *A Treasury of Laughter.* Quoted as a student boner.

18
My parents were religious people in a rather devil-may-care fashion. But aha, you moderns, the Devil does care!
IRA WALLACH, *Hopalong Freud.*

19
Orthodoxy is my doxy—heterodoxy is another man's doxy.
WILLIAM WARBURTON, Bishop of Gloucester. Quoted by JOSEPH PRIESTLY, *Memoirs* (1733–1804).

20
Artemus Ward's best joke, in the opinion of Josh Billings, was his remark when talking of Brigham Young and the Mormons that, "the pretty girls in Utah mostly marry Young."
MAX EASTMAN, *Enjoyment of Laughter.*

21
If I were a Cassowary
  On the plains of Timbuctoo,
I would eat a missionary,
  Coats, and bands, and hymn-book too.
BISHOP WILBERFORCE, *Epigram.*

22
The growth of common sense in the English Church is a thing very much to be regretted. It is really a degrading concession to a low form of reality.
OSCAR WILDE, *The Decay of Lying.*

1
You say that you believe the Gospel: you
live as if you were sure not one word of it
is true.
> THOMAS WILSON, *Maxims of Piety.*

2
I would rather think of my religion as a
gamble than to think of it as an insurance
premium.
> STEPHEN S. WISE, *Religion.*

3
To all things clergic
I am allergic.
> ALEXANDER WOOLLCOTT. (Quoted by SAM-
> UEL HOPKINS ADAMS, *A. Woollcott, His
> Life and His World.*)

4
A Christian is a man who feels
Repentance on a Sunday
For what he did on Saturday
And is going to do on Monday.
> THOMAS R. YBARRA, in *The Christian.*

5
Scratch the Christian and you find the pagan
—spoiled.
> ISRAEL ZANGWILL, *Children of the Ghetto.*

REPUTATION

See also Fame

6
You can leave a will directing how to handle
your money but not your reputation. The
public will attend to that.
> B. C. FORBES, *Epigrams.*

7
Any victim whose posthumous good name
can survive a long murder trial is a noble
specimen indeed.
> MURRAY KEMPTON, *America Comes of
> Middle Age.*

8
Popularity is when people like you; and
reputation is when they ought to but really
can't.
> FRANK RICHARDSON. (*Toaster's Hand-
> book*, compiled by PEGGY EDMUND and
> HENRY WORKMAN WILLIAMS.)

9
After your death you were better have a
bad epitaph than their ill report while you
lived.
> WILLIAM SHAKESPEARE, *Hamlet.* Act ii,
> sc. 2.

10
Better to be thought a scoundrel than a
clown.
> BERNARD SHAW, quoted in *Days with
> Bernard Shaw* by STEPHEN WINSTEN.

11
It is a maxim, that those to whom everybody allows the second place have an un-
doubted title to the first.
> JONATHAN SWIFT, *A Tale of a Tub:* dedi-
> cation.

12
Our great Dryden has long carried it as far
as it would go, and with incredible success.
He has often said to me in confidence, that
the world would have never suspected him
to be so great a poet, if he had not assured
them so frequently in his prefaces that it
was impossible they could either doubt or
forget it.
> JONATHAN SWIFT, *A Tale of a Tub.*

13
Never speak ill of yourself; your friends
will always say enough on that subject.
> CHARLES MAURICE DE TALLEYRAND.

14
One man lies in his words and gets a bad
reputation; another in his manners, and enjoys a good one.
> HENRY D. THOREAU, *Journal*, June 25,
> 1852.

15
A woman with a past has no future.
> OSCAR WILDE.

16
Every great man nowadays has his disciples,
and it is always Judas who writes the biography.
> OSCAR WILDE, *The Critic as Artist.*

17
Everything I know about her is merely dare-
say.
> ALEXANDER WOOLLCOTT.

RESPECT

18
To be capable of respect is almost as rare as
to be worthy of it. (Être capable de respect
est aujourd'hui presque aussi rare qu'en être
digne.)
> JOSEPH JOUBERT, *Pensées*, No. 247.

19
In a village a rich man is respected, a great
man suspected.
> BERNARD SHAW, quoted in *Days with Ber-
> nard Shaw* by STEPHEN WINSTEN.

20
Good little girls always show marked deference for the aged. You ought never to
"sass" old people unless they "sass" you
first.
> MARK TWAIN, *Advice to Little Girls.*

RESPECTABILITY

21
Respectability is the dickey on the bosom of
civilization.
> ELBERT HUBBARD, *A Thousand and One
> Epigrams.*

1
To be respectable implies a multitude of little observances, from the strict keeping of Sunday, down to the careful tying of a cravat.
> VICTOR HUGO, *Toilers of the Sea*. Pt. i, bk. 3, ch. 12.

2
The great artists of the world are never Puritans, and seldom even ordinarily respectable.
> H. L. MENCKEN, *Prejudices*. Ser. i, ch. 16.

3
Respectable means rich, and decent means poor. I should die if I heard my family called decent.
> THOMAS LOVE PEACOCK, *Crochet Castle*, ch. 3.

4
I have always thought respectable people scoundrels and I look anxiously at my face every morning for signs of my becoming a scoundrel.
> BERTRAND RUSSELL, quoted in *The Passionate Skeptic* by ALAN WOOD.

5
Well, dearie, men have to do some awfully mean things to keep up their respectability.
> BERNARD SHAW, *Fanny's First Play*.

6
To equip a dull, respectable person with wings would be but to make a parody of an angel.
> ROBERT LOUIS STEVENSON, *Virginibus Puerisque: Crabbed Age and Youth*.

RETRIBUTION

7
Once in an age the biter should be bit.
> THOMAS D'URFEY, *Richmond Heiress:* epilogue.

8
As they bake they shall brew,
Old Nick and his crew.
> DAVID GARRICK, *May-Day*, sc. 2.

9
Although starlets and models are not popular in the ordinary household, everyone feels a delightful glow of pleasure when one of these ladies succeeds in milking some lecherous tycoon of some of his boodle.
> ALEXANDER KING, *Rich Man, Poor Man, Freud and Fruit*, ch. 15.

10
I shot a rocket in the air
It fell to earth I knew not where
Until next day, with rage profound,
The man it fell on came around.
> TOM MASSON, *Enough*.

11
He that plants thorns must never expect to gather roses.
> PILPAY, *Fables: The Ignorant Physician*.

12
Use every man after his desert, and who should 'scape whipping?
> WILLIAM SHAKESPEARE, *Hamlet*. Act ii, sc. 2.

REVOLUTION

13
I'm strong for any revolution that isn't going to happen in my day.
> FINLEY PETER DUNNE, *Mr. Dooley Remembers*.

14
The effect of every revolt is merely to make the bonds galling.
> H. L. MENCKEN, *Prejudices*, ser. 2.

15
Women hate revolutions and revolutionists. They like men who are docile, and well-regarded at the bank, and never late at meals.
> H. L. MENCKEN, *Prejudices*, ser. 4.

16
One revolution is just like one cocktail; it just gets you organized for the next.
> WILL ROGERS, quoted in *One Man's America* by ALISTAIR COOKE.

17
Revolutions have never lightened the burden of tyranny: they have only shifted it to another shoulder.
> BERNARD SHAW, *Revolutionist's Handbook:* preface.

REWARD

18
Perhaps the reward of the spirit who tries
Is not the goal but the exercise.
> EDMUND VANCE COOKE, *Prayer*.

19
It may be that a willing horse gets the heaviest load. But once in a while he also gets the most oats.
> B. C. FORBES, *Epigrams*.

20
The Reverend Henry Ward Beecher
Called a hen a most elegant creature.
    The hen, pleased with that,
    Laid two eggs in his hat.
And thus did the hen reward Beecher.
> OLIVER WENDELL HOLMES, *An Eggstravagance*. Attributed but questioned.

21
There is no reward for lost love, because nobody wants its return.
> *Reflections of a Bachelor*.

1
The reward of great men is that, long after they have died, one is not quite sure that they are dead.
JULES RENARD, *Journal.*

2
I miss a good many faces. They have gone—gone to the tomb, to the gallows, or to the White House. All of us are entitled to at least one of these distinctions, and it behooves us to be wise and prepare for all.
> MARK TWAIN, *Remark* to a lecture audience in Buffalo shortly after Grover Cleveland's first election to the presidency, 1884.

3
I hate to be a kicker, I always long for peace,
But the wheel that does the squeaking
Is the one that gets the grease.
UNKNOWN, *The Kicker.*

RIGHT

4
Altogether they puzzle me quite,
They all seem wrong and they all seem right.
ROBERT BUCHANAN, *Fine Weather on the Digentia,* st. 6.

5
If ever the multitude deviate into the right, it is always for the wrong reason.
LORD CHESTERFIELD, *The Letters of Lord Chesterfield.*

6
Everyone is looked upon as a fool who does right.
LUCAS CLEEVE, *The Rose Geranium.*

7
We are not satisfied to be right, unless we can prove others to be wrong.
WILLIAM HAZLITT, *Note-Books.*

8
It is not that you do wrong by design, but that you should never do right by mistake.
JUNIUS, *Letters: To the Duke of Grafton.* Letter xii, May 30, 1769.

9
He came out for the right side of every question—always a little too late.
> SINCLAIR LEWIS, *Introduction* to *Henry Ward Beecher: An American Portrait* by PAXTON HIBBEN.

10
Always do right; this will gratify some people and astonish the rest.
MARK TWAIN.

RISING

11
You rose on the wrong side of the bed today.
RICHARD BROME, *Court-Beggar,* Act 2.

12
What can you expect of a day that begins with getting up in the morning?
Farmer's Almanac, 1966.

13
He who has the reputation of rising early may sleep till noon.
OLD FRENCH PROVERB.

14
In every country the sun rises in the morning.
GEORGE HERBERT, *Jacula Prudentum.*

15
Dawn: A term for early morning used by people who don't have to get up.
OLIVER HERFORD, *Cupid's Cyclopedia.*

16
Many a good man has caught his death of cold getting up in the middle of the night to go home.
LUKE McLUKE, *Epigram.*

17
I forgot who it was that recommended men for their soul's good to do each day two things they disliked: . . . it is a precept that I have followed scrupulously, for every day I have got up and I have gone to bed.
> W. SOMERSET MAUGHAM, *The Moon and Sixpence.*

18
There is nothing like getting up early in the morning to teach one the beauty of sleeping late.
Reflections of a Bachelor.

19
The people who like to get up early in the morning must have uncomfortable beds or disagreeable bedfellows.
Reflections of a Bachelor.

20
Yes; bless the man who first invented sleep,
. . .
But blast the man with curses loud and deep, . . .
Who first invented, and went round advertising,
That artificial cut-off—Early Rising.
JOHN GODFREY SAXE, *Early Rising.*

21
It is true, I never assisted the sun materially in his rising: but, doubt not, it was of the last importance only to be present at it.
HENRY D. THOREAU, *Walden.*

22
Early to rise and early to bed makes a male healthy and wealthy and dead.
JAMES THURBER, *Fables for Our Time.*

23
Go to bed early, get up early—this is wise.
Some authorities say get up with one thing, some with another. But a lark is really the

best thing to get up with. It gives you a
splendid reputation with everybody to know
that you get up with the lark; and if you get
the right kind of a lark, and work at him
right, you can easily train him to get up
at half past nine, every time—it is no trick
at all.

MARK TWAIN, *Essays: Advice to Youth.*

1
We prefer the old-fashioned alarm clock to
the kind that awakens you with soft music
or a gentle whisper. If there's one thing we
can't stand early in the morning, it's hypocrisy.

BILL VAUGHAN, *Kansas City Star.*

RIVER

2
It fills me full of joie de viver
To look across the Hudson River.

FRANKLIN P. ADAMS, *Diary of Our Own
Samuel Pepys,* Mar. 22, 1924.

3
The St. Lawrence is water, and the Mississippi is muddy water; but that, sir, is liquid
history.

JOHN BURNS, said on the terrace of the
House of Commons, to transatlantic
visitors who belittled the size of the
Thames.

4
A popular description of the old Colorado
River was, "It's too thick to drink and not
thick enough to plow."

HARRY OLIVER, *The Desert Rat Scrap
Book.*

5
    I like rivers
Better than oceans, for we see both sides.

EDWIN ARLINGTON ROBINSON, *Roman
Bartholow,* pt. 3.

6
It is with rivers as it is with people: the
greatest are not always the most agreeable
nor the best to live with.

HENRY VAN DYKE, *Little Rivers,* ch. 2.

RUSSIA AND THE RUSSIANS

See also Communism

7
Russia—A riddle wrapped in a mystery inside an enigma.

SIR WINSTON CHURCHILL, *Broadcast,* Oct.
1, 1939.

8
Their [the Russian people's] worst mis-

fortune was his birth, the next worst—his
death.

SIR WINSTON CHURCHILL, *The World
Crisis.* Reference to Lenin.

9
Moscow is the city where, if Marilyn Monroe should walk down the street with nothing
on but shoes, people would stare at her feet
first.

JOHN GUNTHER, *Inside Russia Today.*

10
Make ye no truce with Adam-zad—the Bear
that walks like a Man!

RUDYARD KIPLING, *The Truce of the Bear.*
Referring to Russia.

11
It did look like the other side of the moon
should look—gray, flat, and spooky.

HARPO MARX, *Harpo Speaks!* Reference
to Moscow.

12
Everybody in Moscow seemed to be concen-
trating on what he was doing, even when he
was doing nothing.

HARPO MARX, *Harpo Speaks!*

13
I bought me a fur hat, fur coat, and fur-
lined galoshes, all for forty dollars. Back on
the street, wearing my new outfit, it came
to me why the bear was the symbol of Russia. The only way a Russian could survive
the winter was to dress like a bear.

HARPO MARX, *Harpo Speaks!*

14
One time here in New York I played at a
big benefit to get a statue of liberty for
Russia. Now can you imagine Russia with a
statue of liberty? We don't even know if
they want one or not. If they do want one,
we will loan them ours. Ours has got its back
turned on us at the present time, showing
us that our liberty is behind us.

WILL ROGERS, *Autobiography.*

15
Russia is a country that buries its troubles.
Your criticism is your epitaph. You simply
say your say and then you're through.

WILL ROGERS, quoted in *One Man's America* by ALISTAIR COOKE.

16
. . . you will still come up against it if you
accuse any Russian of being a lady or gentleman.

BERNARD SHAW, *On the Rocks:* preface.

17
The juggernaut just doesn't jug.

ADLAI STEVENSON, *Comment* on Russia,
1962.

S

SAINTS

1
Ordinary saints grow faint to posterity; whilst ordinary sinners pass vividly down the ages.
> MAX BEERBOHM, *Zuleika Dobson,* ch. 6.

2
Saint: a dead sinner revised and edited.
> AMBROSE BIERCE, *The Devil's Dictionary.*

3
The saints engage in fierce contests
About their carnal interests.
> SAMUEL BUTLER, *Hudibras,* pt. 3.

4
Saints are all right in heaven but they're hell on earth.
> RICHARD CARDINAL CUSHING, quoted by OSCAR LEVANT in *Memoirs of an Amnesiac.*

5
The way of the world is to praise dead saints and to persecute living ones.
> NATHANIEL HOWE, *Sermon.*

6
A young Saint is an old Devil, (mark this, an old saying and as true a one, as a young Whore an old Saint).
> FRANÇOIS RABELAIS, *Works.* Bk. iv, ch. 64.

7
There never was a saint with red hair.
> RUSSIAN PROVERB.

8
It is easier to make a saint out of a libertine than out of a prig.
> GEORGE SANTAYANA, *Little Essays,* p. 253.

9
Martyrdom, sir, is what these people like: it is the only way in which a man can become famous without ability.
> BERNARD SHAW, *The Devil's Disciple,* Act 3.

SATIRE

10
Satire is a lonely and introspective occupation, for nobody can describe a fool to the life without much patient self-inspection.
> FRANK MOORE COLBY, *Simple Simon.*

11
His foe was folly and his weapon wit.
> ANTHONY HOPE (SIR ANTHONY HOPE HAWKINS), *Inscription* on the tablet to W. S. Gilbert, Victoria Embankment, London (1915).

12
Satire is a sort of glass wherein beholders do generally discover everybody's face but their own . . .
> JONATHAN SWIFT, *The Battle of the Books.*

13
On me, when dunces are satiric
I take it for a panegyric.
> JONATHAN SWIFT, quoted in *Classic Quotations,* ed. by JAMES ELMES.

14
Satire lies about literary men while they live, and eulogy lies about them when they die.
> VOLTAIRE.

SCIENCE

15
Every great scientific truth goes through three stages. First, people say it conflicts with the Bible. Next, they say it has been discovered before. Lastly, they say they have always believed it.
> LOUIS AGASSIZ, quoted by BENNETT CERF in *The Laugh's on Me.*

16
Has it ever occurred to anyone that *space* may eventually conquer *man?*
> MARK BELTAIRE, Detroit *Free Press.*

17
Art is I; science is we.
> CLAUDE BERNARD.

18
If we continue at this leisurely pace, we will have to pass Russian customs when we land on the moon.
> WERNHER VON BRAUN. (United Press International compilation of outstanding quotations of 1959, datelined London, Dec. 29, 1959; in New York *Times* of Dec. 30, 1959.)

19
When science finishes getting man up to the moon, maybe it can have another try at getting pigeons down from public buildings.
> CHANGING TIMES, *The Kiplinger Mazazine.*

20
To a chemist nothing on earth is unclean.
> ANTON CHEKHOV, *The Personal Papers of Anton Chekhov.*

21
I love fools' experiments. I am always making them.
> CHARLES DARWIN, *Life.*

22
Scientists could study the independent existence of a plum pudding for one thousand

years before they discovered it had been steamed in a towel.
HARRY GOLDEN, *Carl Sandburg.*

1
A lot of people have been asking why there are no Negro astronauts. Well I got a surprise for you. One of those seven boys is. He's just *looked* this way since they told him what he volunteered for.
DICK GREGORY, *From the Back of the Bus.*

2
"What Fruits," the Speaker jeered, "can Science show?"
And Science brought his words by Radio.
ARTHUR GUITERMAN, *A Poet's Proverbs.*

3
Science is a first-rate piece of furniture for a man's upper-chamber, if he has common-sense on the ground floor.
OLIVER WENDELL HOLMES, *The Poet at the Breakfast-Table,* ch. 5.

4
A beautiful theory killed by a nasty, ugly little fact.
THOMAS H. HUXLEY. (FRANCIS GALTON, *The Practical Cogitator.*)

5
Ten years ago the moon was an inspiration to poets and young sweethearts; ten years from now it will be just another airport.
REP. CARROLL KEARNS. (*Washington Humor,* ed. by PHILIP FRIEDMAN.)

6
In everything that relates to science, I am a whole encyclopedia behind the rest of the world.
CHARLES LAMB.

7
Some people think that physics was invented by Sir Francis Bacon, who was hit by an apple when he was sitting under a tree one day writing Shakespeare.
ERIC LARRABEE, in *Humor from Harper's.*

8
Research is something that tells you that a jackass has two ears.
ALBERT D. LASKER, quoted by JOHN GUNTHER in *Taken at the Flood: The Story of Albert D. Lasker.*

9
Science has always been too dignified to invent a good back-scratcher.
DON MARQUIS, *New York Sun.*

10
Geometry is the art of correct reasoning on incorrect figures.
G. POLYA, *How to Solve It.*

11
Nature and Nature's laws lay hid in Night:
God said, Let Newton be! and all was Light.
ALEXANDER POPE, *Epitaph for Sir Isaac Newton.*

12
Of science and logic he chatters,
  As fine and as fast as he can;
Though I am no judge of such matters,
  I'm sure he's a talented man.
WINTHROP M. PRAED, *The Talented Man.*

13
Our investigations have always contributed more to our amusement than they have to knowledge.
WILL ROGERS, *Autobiography.*

14
Extracting sunbeams out of cucumbers.
JONATHAN SWIFT, *Gulliver's Travels.* Pt. iii, ch. 5.

15
Scientists have odious manners, except when you prop up their theory; then you can borrow money of them.
MARK TWAIN, *Essays: The Bee.*

16
The higher we soar on the wings of science, the worse our feet seem to get entangled in the wires.
UNKNOWN, *The New Yorker,* Feb. 7, 1931.

17
To define it rudely but not inaptly, engineering is the art of doing that well with one dollar which any bungler can do with two after a fashion.
ARTHUR M. WELLINGTON, *The Economic Theory of Railway Location:* introduction.

18
Mathematics—A wonderful science, but it hasn't yet come up with a way to divide one tricycle between three small boys.
EARL WILSON.

19
No scientific theory achieves public acceptance until it has been thoroughly discredited.
DOUGLAS YATES.

SCOTLAND AND THE SCOTS

20
But all Scotchmen are not religious . . . some are theologians.
GERALD BENDALL, *Mrs. Jones' Bonnet.*

21
Oats—a grain which is generally given to horses, but in Scotland supports the people.
SAMUEL JOHNSON, *Dictionary.*

22
And now, let us consider the Scotsman. (You will note that he *is* a Scotsman and that he must never be referred to as Scotch. Scotch is a *drink.*)
ALEXANDER KING, *Rich Man, Poor Man, Freud and Fruit,* ch. 24.

1

It requires a surgical operation to get a joke well into a Scotch understanding.

SYDNEY SMITH, quoted in *A Memoir of the Rev. Sydney Smith,* by LADY HOLLAND, ch. 2.

2

That knuckle-end of England,—that land of Calvin, oat-cakes, and sulphur.

SYDNEY SMITH, quoted in Lady Holland's *Memoir.*

SEA

See also Ship

3

But the principal failing occurred in the sailing,
And the Bellman, perplexed and distressed,
Said he *had* hoped, at least, when the wind blew due East,
  That the ship would *not* travel due West!

LEWIS CARROLL, *The Hunting of the Snark.*

4

The sea was wet as wet could be,
  The sands were dry as dry.
You could not see a cloud, because
  No cloud was in the sky:
No birds were flying overhead—
  There were no birds to fly.

LEWIS CARROLL, *Through the Looking-Glass,* ch. 4.

5

The wonder is always new that any sane man can be a sailor.

RALPH WALDO EMERSON, *English Traits,* p. 36.

6

When I was a lad I served a term
As office boy to an Attorney's firm.
I cleaned the windows and I swept the floor,
And I polished up the handle of the big front door.
  I polished up that handle so carefullee
  That now I am the Ruler of the Queen's Navee!

SIR WILLIAM SCHWENCK GILBERT, *H.M.S. Pinafore,* Act 1.

7

Now landsmen all, whoever you may be,
If you want to rise to the top of the tree
If your soul isn't fettered to an office stool
Be careful to be guided by this golden rule:
Stick close to your desks and *never go to sea*
And you all may be Rulers of the Queen's Navee.

SIR WILLIAM SCHWENCK GILBERT, *H.M.S. Pinafore,* Act 1.

8

Love the sea? I dote upon it—from the beach.

DOUGLAS JERROLD, *Specimens of Jerrold's Wit.*

9

Any port in a storm.

JOHN POOLE, *Paul Pry,* Act 2.

10

Dame Partington . . . was seen . . . with mop and pattens . . . vigorously pushing away the Atlantic Ocean. The Atlantic Ocean beat Mrs. Partington.

REVEREND SYDNEY SMITH, *Peter Plymely's Letters, Persecuting Bishops,* p. 228.

11

We all like to see people sea-sick when we are not ourselves.

MARK TWAIN, *The Innocents Abroad,* ch. 3.

12

She: Have you known many women?
He: I am a sailor by profession.
She: Thank you for your honesty.

PETER USTINOV, *Romanoff and Juliet,* Act 1.

SECRET

13

  A secret's safe
'Twixt you, me, and the gate-post!

ROBERT BROWNING, *The Inn Album.*

14

Oil and water—woman and a secret—
Are hostile properties.

SIR EDWARD BULWER-LYTTON, *Richelieu.* Act i, sc. 1.

15

None are so fond of secrets as those who do not mean to keep them; such persons covet secrets as a spendthrift covets money, for the purpose of circulation.

C. C. COLTON, *Lacon,* No. 40.

16

Thus through a woman was the secret known;
Tell us, and in effect you tell the town.

JOHN DRYDEN, *The Wife of Bath, Her Tale.*

17

Three may keep a secret if two of them are dead.

BENJAMIN FRANKLIN.

18

Three may keep counsel if two be away.

JOHN HEYWOOD, *Proverbs.* Pt. ii, ch. 5.

19

A man can keep another person's secret better than his own: a woman, on the contrary, keeps her secret though she blabs all others.

JEAN DE LA BRUYÈRE, *Les Caracteres*, pt. 5.

1
I have many secrets from myself. Will I manage to keep them?

STANISLAW J. LEC, *Unkempt Thoughts*, tr. from the Polish by JACEK GALASKA.

2
You are in a pitiable condition when you have to conceal what you wish to tell. (Miserum est tacere cogi, quod cupias loqui.)

PUBLILIUS SYRUS, *Sententiae*, No. 348.

3
If you wish to preserve your secret, wrap it up in frankness.

ALEXANDER SMITH, *Dreamthorp: On the Writing of Essays*.

4
A woman can keep one secret—the secret of her age.

VOLTAIRE.

5
Is there whom you detest, and seek his life?
Trust no soul with the secret—but his wife.

EDWARD YOUNG, *Love of Fame*. Satire vi, l. 389.

SELFISHNESS

6
I never look a gift horse in the mouth but I am not averse to looking an organization in the motive.

FRED ALLEN, from *Fred Allen's Letters*, ed. by JOE MCCARTHY.

7
Let me have my own way exactly in everything, and a sunnier and pleasanter creature does not exist.

THOMAS CARLYLE.

8
Men are not against you; they are merely for themselves.

GENE FOWLER, *Skyline*.

9
The same people who can deny others everything are famous for refusing themselves nothing.

LEIGH HUNT, *Table Talk: Catherine II*, note.

10
It ain't by princerples nor men
My preudunt course is steadied:
I scent wich pays the best, an' then
Go into it baldheaded.

JAMES RUSSELL LOWELL, *The Biglow Papers*. Ser. i, No. 6.

11
The man who lives for himself alone

Lives for the meanest mortal known.

JOAQUIN MILLER (CINCINNATUS HINER MILLER), *Walker in Nicaragua*.

12
. . . the coat of arms of the human race ought to consist of a man with an ax on his shoulder proceeding toward a grindstone, or it ought to represent the several members of the human race holding out the hat to one another; for we are all beggars, each in his own way.

MARK TWAIN.

SELF-KNOWLEDGE

13
The fox condemns the trap, not himself.

WILLIAM BLAKE, *Proverbs of Hell*.

14
To know oneself is to misunderstand everyone else.

G. B. BURGIN, *Which Woman?*

15
Oh wad some Power the giftie gie us to see oursels as ithers see us!

ROBERT BURNS, *To a Louse*, st. 8.

16
Just stand aside and watch yourself go by,
Think of yourself as "he" instead of "I."

STRICKLAND GILLILAN, *Watch Yourself Go By*.

17
Until the donkey tried to clear
The Fence, he thought himself a deer.

ARTHUR GUITERMAN, *A Poet's Proverbs*.

18
I have the greatest contempt for women who keep diaries. They are such liars.

COSMO HAMILTON, *Adam's Clay*.

19
In running away from ourselves we either fall on our neighbor's shoulder or fly at his throat.

ERIC HOFFER, *The True Believer*.

20
Sir, he must be very singular in his opinion if he thinks himself one of the best of men, for none of his friends think him so.

SAMUEL JOHNSON, when told by Boswell that a friend of his had said: "I hate mankind, for I think myself one of the best of them, and I know how bad I am." (BOSWELL's *Life*, Feb., 1776.)

21
He doesn't know what he means, and doesn't know he doesn't.

F. R. LEAVIS, *Two Cultures?: The Significance of C. P. Snow*.

22
The losing horse blames the saddle.

SAMUEL LOVER, *Handy Andy*, ch. 34.

1
I have had more trouble with myself than any other person I know.
> DWIGHT L. MOODY.

2
He who despises himself, nevertheless esteems himself thereby, as a despiser.
> FRIEDRICH WILHELM NIETZSCHE, *Beyond Good and Evil,* tr. by HELEN ZIMMERN.

3
However un-Christian it may seem, I do not even bear any ill-feeling toward myself.
> FRIEDRICH WILHELM NIETZSCHE, *Ecce Homo,* tr. by A. M. LUDOVICI.

4
I should not talk so much about myself if there were anybody else whom I knew as well.
> HENRY D. THOREAU, *Walden,* ch. 1.

SELF-RELIANCE

5
The gods help them that help themselves.
> AESOP, *Hercules and the Waggoner.*

6
Men are made stronger on realization that the helping hand they need is at the end of their own right arm.
> SIDNEY PHILLIPS, *Address* at dedication of Booker T. Washington Memorial Highway in Virginia, July, 1953.

7
For an impenetrable shield, stand inside yourself.
> HENRY D. THOREAU, *Journal,* June 27, 1840.

8
"Let God do it all," someone will say; but if man folds his arms, God will go to sleep.
> MIGUEL DE UNAMUNO, *The Tragic-Sense of Life.*

9
There are three things in life you must do alone: be born, die, and testify.
> JAMES J. WALKER, quoted in *For 2¢ Plain* by HARRY GOLDEN.

10
There was never a nation great until it came to the knowledge that it had nowhere in the world to go for help.
> CHARLES DUDLEY WARNER, *Studies: Comments on Canada,* ch. 3.

11
I have always liked bird dogs better than kennel-fed dogs myself—you know, one that will get out and hunt for food rather than sit on his fanny and yell.
> CHARLES E. WILSON, Secretary of Defense. On unemployment, a comment that became known as "Secretary Wilson's bird dog statement." *News reports,* Oct. 11, 1954.

SENSE

12
Even the devil hadn't sufficient common sense to stay in heaven.
> ANONYMOUS.

13
Take care of the sense and the sounds will take care of themselves.
> LEWIS CARROLL, *Alice in Wonderland,* ch. 9.

14
When I can't talk sense, I talk metaphor.
> JOHN PHILPOT CURRAN, quoted in MOORE, *Life of Sheridan.*

15
Nothing astonishes men so much as common sense and plain dealing.
> RALPH WALDO EMERSON, *Essays, First Series: Art.*

16
Ther hain't nothin' as uncommon as common sense.
> FRANK MCKINNEY (KIN) HUBBARD, *Abe Martin's Primer.*

17
Nay, sir, it was not the wine that made your head ache but the sense that I put into it.
> SAMUEL JOHNSON, BOSWELL's *Life,* Apr. 7, 1779.

18
I know a hawk from a handsaw.
> WILLIAM SHAKESPEARE, *Hamlet.* Act ii, sc. 2.

19
Common sense is not so common. (Le sens commun n'est pas si commun.)
> VOLTAIRE, *Philosophical Dictionary: Self-Love.*

SEX

20
Sex is the great amateur art. The professional, male or female, is frowned on; he or she misses the whole point and spoils the show.
> DAVID CORT, *Social Astonishments.*

21
I discarded a whole book because the leading character wasn't on my wavelength. She was a lesbian with doubts about her masculinity.
> PETER DE VRIES, quoted by LEWIS NICHOLS in *The New York Times,* Jan. 15, 1967.

22
Little Willie wrote a book.
Woman was the only theme he took.
Woman was his only text.
Ain't he cute? He's oversexed.
> HARRY GRAHAM, *Little Willie.*

1
I had to admit that in his old-fashioned way O'Hara was still romantic about sex; like Scott Fitzgerald, he thought of it as an upper-class prerogative.
> ALFRED KAZIN, *Contemporaries: Lady Chatterley in America.*

2
To Thurber and White it seemed that, the way things were going, sex as nature intended it was on the way out. After a while people would just sit around and read sex books. Boldly they undertook to save the human race from extinction. They also hoped to make some money.
> DALE KRAMER, *Ross and the New Yorker.* Referring to JAMES THURBER and E. B. WHITE.

3
Some sexes change their sexes now and make a mere man wonder how.
> ALFRED KREYMBORG, *Outmoded.*

4
Europeans used to say Americans were puritanical. Then they discovered that we were not puritans. So now they say that we are obsessed with sex.
> MARY MCCARTHY. (*Lady with a Switchblade; Life,* Sept. 20, 1963.)

5
This world consists of men, women, and Hervey's.
> LADY MARY WORTLEY MONTAGU, *Letters,* vol. 1. Reference is to JOHN HERVEY, whom POPE attacked in *The Dunciad* as "Lord Fanny."

6
A lady, that is an enlightened, cultivated, liberal lady—the only kind to be in a time of increasing classlessness—could espouse any cause: wayward girls, social diseases, unmarried mothers, and/or birth control with impunity. But never by so much as the shadow of a look should she acknowledge her own experience with the Facts of Life.
> VIRGILIA PETERSON, *A Matter of Life and Death.*

7
Our Unabashed Dictionary defines:
Suburban husband as a gardener with sex privileges.
> *More Playboy's Party Jokes* (1965).

8
All biological necessities have to be made respectable whether we like it or not . . .
> BERNARD SHAW, *Back to Methuselah,* pt. 2: *The Gospel of the Brothers Barnabas.*

9
Late every night in Connecticut, lights go out in the cities and towns, and citizens by tens of thousands proceed zestfully to break the law . . . And, of course, there is always a witness to the crime—but as though to make the law completely unenforceable, Connecticut forbids spouses from testifying against one another.
> *Time,* Mar. 10, 1961, on the Connecticut law on birth control.

10
Sex is too often not only Topic A, but also Topics B and C as well.
> *Time,* June 7, 1963, on works of JOHN O'HARA.

11
The sexual revolution began with Man's discovery that he was not attractive to Woman, as such. The lion had his mane, the peacock his gorgeous plumage, but Man found himself in a three-button sack suit.
> E. B. WHITE, quoted by MAX EASTMAN in *Enjoyment of Laughter.*

12
Sex is the tabasco sauce which an adolescent national palate sprinkles on every course in the menu.
> MARY DAY WINN, *Adam's Rib,* p. 8.

13
The reputation of impotency is as hardly recovered again in the world as that of cowardice, dear madam.
> WILLIAM WYCHERLEY, *The Country Wife,* Act 2.

14
And here's the happy bounding flea—
You can not tell the he from she.
The sexes look alike, you see;
But she can tell and so can he.
> ROLAND YOUNG, *The Flea.*

SHAME

15
What is shame?
Shame is the feeling you have when you agree with the woman who loves you that you are the man she thinks you are . . .
> CARL SANDBURG, *Incidentals.*

16
The more things a man is ashamed of, the more respectable he is.
> BERNARD SHAW, *Man and Superman,* Act 1.

SHIP

17
Water can both float and sink a ship.
> CHINESE PROVERB, from *Oriental Humor,* ed. by R. H. BLYTH.

18
A ship under sail, a man in complete armour, and a woman with a big belly, are the three handsomest sights in the world.
> JAMES HOWELL, *Proverbs.*

1
A ship is always referred to as "she" because it costs so much to keep one in paint and powder.
>   ADMIRAL CHESTER W. NIMITZ, *Address* before the Society of Sponsors of the U. S. Navy, Feb. 13, 1940.

2
Women are jealous of ships. They always suspect the sea. They know they're three of a kind when it comes to a man.
>   EUGENE O'NEILL, *Mourning Becomes Electra*, Act 1.

3
A ship in harbor is safe, but that is not what ships are built for.
>   JOHN A. SHEDD, *Salt from My Attic*, p. 20.

4
It would have been as though he were in a boat of stone with masts of steel, sails of lead, ropes of iron, the devil at the helm, the wrath of God for a breeze, and hell for his destination.
>   EMERY A. STORRS, *Speech* in Chicago, 1866, referring to President Andrew Johnson, who had threatened to use troops to force Congress to adjourn.

5
Noah would not be allowed to sail from Bremen in our day. The inspectors would come and examine the Ark, and make all sorts of objections. A person who knows Germany can imagine the scene and conversation without difficulty and without missing a detail.
>   MARK TWAIN, *About All Kinds of Ships*.

6
Between Noah's time and the time of Columbus naval architecture underwent some changes, and from being unspeakably bad was improved to a point which may be described as less unspeakably bad.
>   MARK TWAIN, *About All Kinds of Ships*.

SHOES

7
None of you can tell where it [the shoe] pinches me.
>   From a conversation quoted and applied by PLUTARCH in his *Life of Aemilius Paulus*.

8
A man's shoes get tight by imbibing water, but he doesn't.
>   GEORGE D. PRENTICE.

9
When during his [Adlai Stevenson's] first presidential try a photographer caught a picture of him with a large hole in his shoe, it became the trademark of the 1952 cam-paign. His followers wore silver lapel pins showing the famous shoe sole.
"Better a hole in the shoe, than a hole in the head," remarked Governor Stevenson drily.
>   PAUL STEINER, *The Stevenson Wit & Wisdom*.

SILENCE

See also Mouth, Speech

10
A husband never loses anything by appearing to believe in the fidelity of his wife, by preserving an air of patience and by keeping silence. Silence especially troubles a woman amazingly.
>   HONORÉ DE BALZAC, *The Physiology of Marriage*.

11
For six years profound silence was mistaken for profound wisdom.
>   ALBEN W. BARKLEY, *That Reminds Me*. Comment on Coolidge administration. Made at Democratic national convention in 1932, in keynote address.

12
If people would only hold their tongues on unpleasant topics, how the things themselves would improve.
>   E. F. BENSON, *The House of Defense*.

13
Silence is one of the hardest arguments to refute.
>   JOSH BILLINGS.

14
When you are climbing a mountain, don't talk; silence gives ascent.
>   ROBERT JONES BURDETTE.

15
Beware of a man who does not talk, and a dog that does not bark.
>   JACOB CATS, *Moral Emblems*.

16
Silence—The unbearable repartee.
>   G. K. CHESTERTON.

17
I have noticed that nothing I never said ever did me any harm.
>   CALVIN COOLIDGE. (*Congressional Record*, Mar. 22, 1945.)

18
Persons in public positions—including me—miss too many chances to keep their mouths shut. I'm not passing up my chance tonight.
>   DWIGHT D. EISENHOWER, on refusing to state publicly his preference for the Republican presidential nomination in advance of the 1964 national convention. This comment was made at the com-

mencement exercises of George Washington University, Washington, D.C., June 7, 1964.

1
Blessed is the man who, having nothing to say, abstains from giving us wordy evidence of the fact.
GEORGE ELIOT, *Theophrastus Such,* ch. 4.

2
There is nothing so like a wise man as a fool who holds his tongue.
ST. FRANCIS DE SALES.

3
Silence is become his mother tongue.
OLIVER GOLDSMITH, *The Good-Natured Man.*

4
I never discuss discussions.
DAG HAMMARSKJÖLD, after talks with Russian leaders. (*Look,* Sept. 19, 1956.)

5
That man's silence is wonderful to listen to.
THOMAS HARDY.

6
A man is known by the silence he keeps.
OLIVER HERFORD.

7
You've got to know when to keep your mouth shut. The Senate's the cruelest judge in the world. A man's a fool to talk to other fellows about any subject unless he knows more about that subject than they do.
LYNDON B. JOHNSON. (HENRY A. ZEIGER, *Lyndon B. Johnson: Man and President,* p. 67.)

8
Sometimes you have to be silent to be heard.
STANISLAW J. LEC, *Unkempt Thoughts,* tr. from the Polish by JACEK GALASKA.

9
Better to remain silent and be thought a fool than to speak out and remove all doubt.
ABRAHAM LINCOLN. (*Golden Book,* Nov., 1931.)

10
Blessed are they who have nothing to say, and who cannot be persuaded to say it.
JAMES RUSSELL LOWELL.

11
. . . My father used to say to me: "Son, you do all right in this world if you just remember that when you talk you are only repeating what you already know—but if you listen you may learn something."
J. P. McEVOY, *Charlie Would Have Loved This.*

12
Carlyle finally compressed his Gospel of Silence into thirty handsome octavos.
JOHN MORLEY.

13
Even a fool, when he holdeth his peace, is counted wise.
OLD TESTAMENT, *Proverbs:* XVII, 28.

14
A silent tongue makes sweet music for the soul.
Reflections of a Bachelor.

15
Silence—The most perfect expression of scorn.
BERNARD SHAW, *Back to Methuselah, Pt. V: As Far as Thought Can Reach.*

16
You ain't learnin' nothing when you're talking.
UNKNOWN. *Motto* that hung in the office of Lyndon B. Johnson during his years in the U.S. Senate. (HENRY A. ZEIGER, *Lyndon B. Johnson: Man and President,* p. 67.)

17
He knew the precise psychological moment when to say nothing.
OSCAR WILDE, *The Picture of Dorian Gray,* ch. 2.

SIMPLICITY

18
Simplicity is the most deceitful mistress that ever betrayed a man.
HENRY ADAMS, *The Education of Henry Adams.*

19
Unless one is a genius, it is best to aim at being intelligible.
ANTHONY HOPE, *The Dolly Dialogues,* No. 15.

20
To be natural is such a very difficult pose to keep up.
OSCAR WILDE, *An Ideal Husband.*

SIN

See also Vice

21
Hawthorne was against sin. Without it, though, he would never have become a great author.
RICHARD ARMOUR, *American Lit Relit.*

22
The sin is not in the sinning, but in the being found out.
W. G. BENHAM, *Proverbs.*

23
The sins that tarnish whore and thief
  Beset me every day.
My most ethereal belief
  Inhabits common clay.
GAMALIEL BRADFORD, *Rousseau.*

1

Frenchmen sin in lechery,
English in ennui.
  ROBERT DE BRUNNE, *Handlyng Synne*, l. 4156.

2

Compound for sins they are inclined to,
By damning those they have no mind to.
  SAMUEL BUTLER, *Hudibras*, pt. 1.

3

Keep yourself from opportunity and God will keep you from sins.
  JACOB CATS, *Moral Emblems*.

4

Now who that runs can read it,
The riddle that I write
Of why this poor old sinner
Should sin without delight?
But I, I cannot read it
(Although I run and run)
Of them that do not have the faith
And will not have the fun.
  G. K. CHESTERTON, *The Song of the Strange Ascetic*.

5

Every sin is the result of a collaboration.
  STEPHEN CRANE.

6

I am the worst man in the world at repenting, till a sin be thoroughly done.
  JOHN DRYDEN, *Marriage à la Mode*. Act iv, sc. 5.

7

Oh, Lord, it is not the sins I have committed that I regret, but those which I have had no opportunity to commit.
  SHEYKH GHALIB, *Prayer* (c. 1800). Last of the great poets of the old Turkish school.

8

Sin writes histories, goodness is silent.
  JOHANN WOLFGANG VON GOETHE, *Table-Talk*, 1810.

9

Don't tell my mother I'm living in sin,
  Don't let the old folks know:
Don't tell my twin that I breakfast on gin,
  He'd never survive the blow.
  A. P. HERBERT, *Don't Tell My Mother*.

10

Sin: What other people do and we talk about.
  OLIVER HERFORD, *Cupid's Cyclopedia*.

11

The longer thread of life we spin,
The more occasion still to sin.
  ROBERT HERRICK, *Long Life*.

12

Men are punished by their sins, not for them.
  ELBERT HUBBARD, *The Philistine*, vol. 11.

13

No matter how hard th' times git th' wages o' sin are allus liberal an' on th' dot.
  FRANK McKINNEY (KIN) HUBBARD, *Abe Martin's Primer*.

14

You put me in mind of Dr. Barrowly, the physician, who was very fond of swine's flesh. One day, when he was eating it, he said, "I wish I was a Jew."—Why so? (said somebody) the Jews are not allowed to eat your favorite meat.—"Because (said he) I should then have the gust of eating it, with the pleasure of sinning!"
  SAMUEL JOHNSON, BOSWELL'S *Life*, June 9, 1784.

15

Sin has always been an ugly word, but it has been made so in a new sense over the last half-century. It has been made not only ugly but passé. People are no longer sinful, they are only immature or underprivileged or frightened or, more particularly, sick.
  PHYLLIS McGINLEY, *The Province of the Heart: In Defense of Sin*.

16

What a dull world it would be for us honest men if it weren't for its sinners.
  H. L. MENCKEN, quoted by BEN HECHT in *Gaily, Gaily*.

17

The sins they sinned in Eden, boys,
Are bad enough for me.
  CHRISTOPHER MORLEY, *A Glee Upon Cider*.

18

It makes a great difference whether a person is unwilling to sin, or does not know how. (Multum interest utrum peccare aliquis nolit an nesciat.)
  SENECA, *Epistulae ad Lucilium*, Epis. 90.

19

Commit the oldest sins the newest kind of ways.
  WILLIAM SHAKESPEARE, *Henry IV, Pt. 2*. Act iv, sc. 5.

20

To call themselves "miserable sinners" is with many people a kind of religious good manners, just as a man inscribes himself "your humble servant."
  J. A. SPENDER, *The Comments of Bagshot*.

21

He could dress up a sin so religiously that hardly the devil himself would know it to be of his own manufacture.
  J. M. STUART YOUNG, *Passion's Peril*.

22

A sin takes on new and real terrors when

there seems a chance that it is going to be found out.

MARK TWAIN.

1

We condemn a sin before we have even tried it.

UNKNOWN, *Meditations in Wall Street.*

2

Sin, every day, takes out a new patent for some new invention.

E. P. WHIPPLE, *Essays: Romance of Rascality.*

SINCERITY

3

You can be sincere and still be stupid.

CHARLES KETTERING, quoted in *Professional Amateur* by T. A. BOYD. See also SHAW in this section.

4

By virtue of that candid confession he takes his place with the shining company of simple souls, the hierarchy of the ingenuous.

E. V. LUCAS.

5

It is dangerous to be sincere unless you are also stupid.

BERNARD SHAW, *Maxims for Revolutionists.*

6

In religion, as in friendship, they who profess most are the least sincere.

RICHARD BRINSLEY SHERIDAN, *The Duenna.* Act iii, sc. 3.

7

A little sincerity is a dangerous thing, and a great deal of it is absolutely fatal.

OSCAR WILDE, *The Critic as Artist.*

8

What people call insincerity is simply a method by which we can multiply our personalities.

OSCAR WILDE, *The Critic as Artist.*

SIZE

9

Well, I'm about as tall as a shotgun, and just as noisy.

TRUMAN CAPOTE, quoted in *Time,* Mar. 3, 1952.

10

Big men are always trying to be practical, like Sir Isaac Newton when he ordered a good sized hole to be cut in his barn door for the cat, and a little one next it for the kitten.

F. MARION CRAWFORD, *The Little City of House.*

11

Sometimes two are better than an army

. . . at least they make less noise and attract less attention.

W. T. ELDRIDGE, *Hilma.*

12

The bigger they come the harder they fall.

BOB FITZSIMMONS, just before he was beaten in a heavyweight boxing match by James J. Jeffries, July 25, 1902.

13

A dwarf on a giant's shoulders sees farther of the two.

GEORGE HERBERT, *Jacula Prudentum.*

14

Tall men are like houses of four stories, wherein commonly the uppermost room is worst furnished.

JAMES HOWELL, *Letters.* Bk. i, sec. 2.

15

Small town, great renown. (Petite ville, grand renom.)

FRANÇOIS RABELAIS, *Works.* Bk. v, ch. 35. Of Chinon, Rabelais' native town.

16

Like a barber's chair, that fits all buttocks.

WILLIAM SHAKESPEARE, *All's Well That Ends Well.* Act II, sc. 2.

17

Elephants are always drawn smaller than life, but a flea always larger.

JONATHAN SWIFT, *Thoughts on Various Subjects.*

SLANDER

See also Gossip

18

A slander is like a hornet; if you cannot kill it dead at the first blow, better not strike at it.

JOSH BILLINGS, *The Kicker.*

19

One half the world takes a pleasure in slander, the other half in believing the slanderers. (La moitié du monde prend plaisir a medire el l'autre moitie croire les medisantes.)

OLD FRENCH PROVERB.

20

I don't care what is written about me so long as it isn't true.

KATHARINE HEPBURN, *News summaries,* May 24, 1954.

21

Who by aspersions throw a stone
At th' head of others, hit their own.

GEORGE HERBERT, *Charms and Knots.*

22

Make not thy sport abuses; for the fly
That feeds on dung is colored thereby.

GEORGE HERBERT, *The Church-Porch,* st. 39.

1
Defamation is becoming a necessity of life; insomuch that a dish of tea in the morning or evening cannot be digested without this stimulant.
THOMAS JEFFERSON, *Writings*. Vol. xi, p. 224.

2
If slander be a snake, it is a winged one— it flies as well as creeps.
DOUGLAS JERROLD, *Slander*.

3
Cut men's throats with whisperings.
BEN JONSON, *Sejanus*. Act i, sc. 1.

4
Knowing, what all experience serves to show, No mud can soil us but the mud we throw.
JAMES RUSSELL LOWELL, *Epistle to George William Curtis*.

5
He who slings mud generally loses ground.
ADLAI STEVENSON, *News summaries*, Jan. 11, 1954.

6
There is never wanting in this town a tribe of bold, swaggering, rattling ladies, whose talents pass among coxcombs for wit and humor; their excellency lies in rude, shocking expressions, and what they call running a man down. If a gentleman in their company happens to have any blemish in his birth or person, if any misfortune has befallen his family or himself for which he is ashamed, they will be sure to give him broad hints of it without any provocation. I would recommend you to the acquaintance of a common prostitute rather than to that of such termagants as these. I have often thought that no man is obliged to suppose such creatures to be women, but to treat them like insolent rascals disguised in female habits, who ought to be stripped and kicked downstairs.
JONATHAN SWIFT, *A Letter, to a Very Young Lady on Her Marriage*.

SLAVERY

7
The most successful slave trader operating out of Liverpool was Sir John Hawkins. He kidnapped some 75,000 natives from their homes in West Africa. The name of his slave ship was "The Jesus."
McNEIL DIXON, quoted by BEN HECHT in *Letters from Bohemia*.

8
Whenever I hear anyone arguing for slavery, I feel a strong impulse to see it tried on him personally.
ABRAHAM LINCOLN, *Address*, Mar. 17, 1865.

9
Who ain't a slave? Tell me that. Well, then, however the old sea captains may order me about—however they may thump and punch me about, I have the satisfaction of knowing that it is all right; that everybody else is one way or other served in much the same way—either in a physical or metaphysical point of view, that is; and so the universal thump is passed round, and all hands should rub each other's shoulder-blades, and be content.
HERMAN MELVILLE, *Moby Dick*, ch. 1.

10
I am against slavery simply because I dislike slaves.
H. L. MENCKEN, *A Mencken Chrestomathy*.

SLEEP

See also Bed, Dreams, Rising, Snoring

11
Most people spend their lives going to bed when they're not sleepy and getting up when they are!
CINDY ADAMS, quoted by JOEY ADAMS in *Cindy and I*, ch. 1.

12
Early to bed and early to rise is a bad rule for any one who wishes to become acquainted with our most prominent and influential people.
GEORGE ADE, *Fables*.

13
. . . a man is almost always ridiculous when he is asleep.
HONORÉ DE BALZAC, *The Physiology of Marriage*.

14
No civilized person ever goes to bed the same day he gets up.
RICHARD HARDING DAVIS, *Gallagher*.

15
Was it true, as legend had it, that Mr. Edison, like Napoleon, slept but four hours? Yes, said Mr. Ford, but Mr. Edison slept twice and sometimes *three times* a day!
GENE FOWLER, *Skyline*.

16
Insomnia never comes to a man who has to get up at exactly six o'clock. Insomnia troubles only those who can sleep any time.
ELBERT HUBBARD, *The Philistine*. Vol. xxv, p. 78.

17
"A man ought to have more than just two sides to sleep on," declared Simple. "Now if I get tired of sleeping on my left side, I have nothing to turn over on but my right side."
LANGSTON HUGHES, *Two Sides Not*

Enough. From *The Langston Hughes Reader.*

1
I'd really hate to go to bed
Just swinging from some wall.
But bats, they say, do just that way.
I'd not wish to at all.
I'd hate to swing down from my toes
All up-side-down—and try to doze.
  MARY EFFIE LEE NEWSOME, from *The Book of Negro Humor* by LANGSTON HUGHES.

2
Early to bed and you'll wish you were dead.
Bed before eleven, nuts before seven.
  DOROTHY PARKER, *The Little House.*

3
I never sleep comfortably except when I am at a sermon or when I pray to God.
  FRANÇOIS RABELAIS, *Gargantua.*

4
Maybe it's because I sleep slow.
  JACK TEAGARDEN, explaining why he liked to sleep for long periods.

5
He slept the deep sleep of the unjust.
  SIR HERBERT BEERBOHM TREE, quoted by HESKETH PEARSON in *Lives of the Wits.*

SMELL

6
He who smells good always does not smell good. (Non bene olet qui bene semper olet.)
  PETRONIUS, *Fragments,* No. 24.

7
And all your courtly civet-cats can vent,
Perfume to you, to me it's excrement.
  ALEXANDER POPE, *Epilogue to the Satires,* dial. 2.

SMILE

8
Simple and faithless as a smile and shake of the hand.
  T. S. ELIOT, *La Figlia Che Piange.*

9
A stale article, if you dip it in a good, warm, sunny smile, will go off better than a fresh one that you've scowled upon.
  NATHANIEL HAWTHORNE, *The House of the Seven Gables,* ch. 4.

10
There are a good many real miseries in life that we cannot help smiling at, but they are the smiles that make wrinkles and not dimples.
  OLIVER WENDELL HOLMES, *The Poet at the Breakfast Table.*

11
Show me a smile that won't come off an' I'll show you a cheerful idiot.
  FRANK McKINNEY (KIN) HUBBARD, *Abe Martin's Primer.*

12
When Milly smiled it was a public event— when she didn't it was a chapter of history.
  HENRY JAMES, *The Wings of the Dove.*

13
I smile so seldom that I wonder at Arlene Francis who smiles persistently. Like the Sorcerer's Apprentice, once she turns it on, can she turn it off?
  OSCAR LEVANT, *Memoirs of an Amnesiac.*

14
He's a man way out there in the blue, riding on a smile and a shoeshine. And when they start not smiling back—that's an earthquake.
  ARTHUR MILLER, *Death of a Salesman:* requiem. Referring to a salesman— specifically to Willy Loman, the protagonist of the play.

15
One may smile, and smile, and be a villain.
  WILLIAM SHAKESPEARE, *Hamlet.* Act i, sc. 5.

16
When you call me that, *smile!*
  OWEN WISTER, *The Virginian: A Horseman of the Plains,* ch. 2.

SMOKING

17
To smoke a cigar through a mouthpiece is equivalent to kissing a lady through a respirator.
  ANONYMOUS, *A Veteran of Smokedom; The Smoker's Guide.*

18
John Barrymore . . . came up with his own ingenious theory to explain why women are pushovers for the cigarette habit. "They have no pockets," said Barrymore, "so they have to find something to do with their hands."
  J. P. McEVOY, *Charlie Would Have Loved This: You Can Stop Smoking.*

19
It [tobacco] smells like Saturday, and consequently puts me in a chronic holiday mood.
  ROBERT BENCHLEY, *Saturday's Smells.* (*The Benchley Roundup,* ed. by NATHANIEL BENCHLEY.)

20
Those who give up cigarette smoking aren't the heroes. The real heroes are the rest of us—who have to listen to them. Sometimes they make me feel so sad I have to light up

a big fat cigar to keep from breaking into tears.

> HAL BOYLE, *Column,* Associated Press, 21 Jan., 1964.

1

The sweet post-prandial cigar.

> ROBERT BUCHANAN, *De Berny.*

2

Sublime tobacco! which from East to West Cheers the tar's labour or the Turkman's rest.

> LORD BYRON, *The Island,* canto 2.

3

The pipe with solemn interposing puff,
Makes half a sentence at a time enough;
The dozing sages drop the drowzy strain;
Then, pause and puff and speak, and pause again.

> WILLIAM COWPER, *Conversation.*

4

A cigarette . . . a man's refuge when he cannot face a woman's eyes.

> R. HALIFAX, *The Grip of Gold.*

5

Nobody can be so revoltingly smug as the man who has just given up smoking.

> SYDNEY J. HARRIS, *Strictly Personal.*

6

Tobacco is a dirty weed: I like it.
It satisfies no normal need: I like it.
It makes you thin, it makes you lean,
It takes the hair right off your bean;
It's the worst darn stuff I've ever seen:
I like it.

> GRAHAM HEMMINGER, *Tobacco; Penn State Froth,* Nov., 1915, p. 19.

7

A custom loathsome to the eye, hateful to the nose, harmful to the brain, dangerous to the lungs, and in the black, stinking fume thereof, nearest resembling the horrible Stygian smoke of the pit that is bottomless.

> JAMES I OF ENGLAND AND VI OF SCOTLAND, *A Counterblast to Tobacco* (1604).

8

A million surplus Maggies are willing to bear the yoke;
And a woman is only a woman, but a good cigar is a smoke.

> RUDYARD KIPLING, *The Betrothed.*

9

It is now proved beyond doubt that smoking is one of the leading causes of statistics.

> FLETCHER KNEBEL, quoted in *Reader's Digest,* Dec., 1961.

10

This very night I am going to leave off tobacco! Surely there must be some other

world in which this unconquerable purpose shall be realized.

> CHARLES LAMB, *Letter to Manning* (1815).

11

For thy sake, tobacco, I
Would do anything but die.

> CHARLES LAMB, *A Farewell to Tobacco.*

12

What this country needs is a good five cent cigar.

> THOMAS R. MARSHALL, *Remark,* while presiding over the U. S. Senate during a debate on the needs of the country. See also ROGERS in this section.

13

The light ones may be killers,
And the dark ones may be mild;
Not the wrappers, but the fillers,
Make cigars or women wild.

> KEITH PRESTON, *Popular Fallacies.*

14

Man has as much trouble with his first cigar as woman with her first baby.

> *Reflections of a Bachelor.*

15

The woman who smokes does it as naturally as the man who bathes the baby.

> *Reflections of a Bachelor.*

16

Our country has plenty of good five-cent cigars, but the trouble is they charge fifteen cents for them.

> WILL ROGERS.

17

A straw with a light on one end and a fool on the other, that's what he called a cigarette.

> SIR VIRGIL SCOTT, *The Dead Tree Gives No Shelter.*

18

Bernard Shaw made the pertinent inquiry: "How can the smoker and the nonsmoker be equally free in the same railway car?" This is one of the fundamental problems—that of special and conflicting interests—in this heterogeneous railway car we call a nation.

> SYDNEY J. HARRIS, Publishers Newspaper Syndicate.

19

More than one cigar at a time is excessive smoking.

> MARK TWAIN.

20

I will grant, here, that I have stopped smoking now and then, for a few months at a time, but it was not on principle, it was only to show off; it was to pulverize those critics who said I was a slave to my habits and couldn't break my bonds.

MARK TWAIN, *Essays: Seventieth Birthday.*

1
Children of twenty-five, who have seven years of experience, try to tell me what is a good cigar and what isn't. Me, who never learned to smoke, but always smoked; me, who came into the world asking for a light.

MARK TWAIN, *Essays: Concerning Tobacco.*

2
To cease smoking is the easiest thing I ever did; I ought to know because I've done it a thousand times.

MARK TWAIN.

3
With a soft sigh such as might have proceeded from some loving father on the steppes of Russia when compelled, in order to insure his own safety, to throw his children out of the back of the sleigh to the pursuing wolf pack, he took the pipe from his mouth, collected his other pipes, his tobacco and his cigars, wrapped them in a neat parcel and, summoning the charwoman who cleaned his studio, gave her the consignment to take home to her husband.

P. G. WODEHOUSE.

4
Cheap, foul-smelling cigars burn much more evenly than expensive cigars. That's life.

DOUGLAS YATES, *Works.*

SNEEZING

5
Everyone sneezes as God pleases.

JACOB CATS, *Moral Emblems.*

6
Do you know how helpless you feel if you have a full cup of coffee in your hand and you start to sneeze?

JEAN KERR, *Mary, Mary*, Act 2.

7
I am just here reminded that the only way whereby you may pronounce the Shah's title correctly is by taking a pinch of snuff. The result will be "t-Shah!"

MARK TWAIN, *O'Shah.*

SNOB

8
Snobbishness is a cancer in America because we pretend it is not there and let it grow until it's inoperable.

LOUIS AUCHINCLOSS, *The Rector of Justin.*

9
Snobbery sometimes is thought to be a prerogative of the rich. But no man is so

poverty-stricken he can't afford to be a snob.

HAL BOYLE, *Column,* Associated Press, datelined Jan. 27, 1966.

10
His grandmother Mews was a snob who took her exercise picking up celebrities and dropping their names. Her life (really an interesting one) was a string of diamonds which she managed to turn into costume jewelry.

JOHN MASON BROWN, *The Worlds of Robert E. Sherwood.*

11
Snobbery is but a point in time. Let us have patience with our inferiors. They are ourselves of yesterday.

ISAAC GOLDBERG, *Tin Pan Alley.*

12
"Which is superior to which?"
    Asked the snob when she came to the city.
"I want to know people to kick,
    I want to know people to pity."

VACHEL LINDSAY, *The Village Magazine.*

13
The most extreme example of this type of snobbism I have heard of is credited to the family of the Duc de Levis-Mirepoix, one of the oldest important French titles that dates back to the ninth century. The family is purported to be descended from the sister of the Virgin Mary, and when the members of the Levis-Mirepoix family pray, they are said to say: *"Ave Maria, ma Cousine . . ."*

RUSSELL LYNES, *Snobs:* footnote.

14
I am sure that there is no greater snob than a snob who thinks he can define a snob.

RUSSELL LYNES, *Snobs.*

15
Now she is dead she greets Christ with a nod,—
(He was a carpenter)—*but she knows God.*

VIRGINIA McCORMICK, *The Snob.*

16
It is impossible, in our condition of Society, not to be sometimes a Snob.

WILLIAM MAKEPEACE THACKERAY, *The Book of Snobs.*

17
He who meanly admires mean things is a Snob.

WILLIAM MAKEPEACE THACKERAY, *The Book of Snobs.*

SNORING

18
Snoring—The tuneful serenade of that wakeful nightingale, the nose.

GEORGE FARQUHAR.

1
O the pleasure of counting the melancholy clock by a snoring husband!
  GEORGE FARQUHAR, *The Beaux' Stratagem*, Act 2.

2
There ain't no way to find out why a snorer can't hear himself snore.
  MARK TWAIN, *Tom Sawyer Abroad*, ch. 1.

SOCIETY

3
The Hostess with the Mostes' on the Ball.
  IRVING BERLIN, *Title* of song from the musical comedy *Call Me Madam* (1950), sung by Ethel Merman.

4
Men ain't apt to get kicked out of good society for being rich.
  JOSH BILLINGS (HENRY WHEELER SHAW).

5
Oh, give me a home
Where the millionaires roam,
And the dear little glamour girls play—
Where seldom is heard
An intelligent word,
And we round up the dollars all day.
  JOHNNY BOYLE, Palm Springs theme song. Quoted by CLEVELAND AMORY in *The Last Resorts*.

6
American social fences have to be continually repaired; in England they are like wild hedges; they grow if left alone.
  D. W. BROGAN, *The English People*.

7
The would-be wits and can't-be gentlemen,
I leave them to their daily "tea is ready,"
Smug coterie, and literary lady.
  LORD BYRON, *Beppo*, st. 76.

8
Thus does society naturally divide itself into four classes: Noblemen, Gentlemen, Gigmen and Men.
  THOMAS CARLYLE, *Essays: Boswell*, note.

9
Society, to be permanently interesting, must be made up of idle professionals, not of professional idlers.
  PRICE COLLIER, quoted by CLEVELAND AMORY in *The Last Resorts*.

10
It's true, a great many more accepted
Than we thought would want to come. But what can you do?
There's usually a lot who don't want to come
But all the same would be bitterly offended
To hear we'd given a party without asking them.
  T. S. ELIOT, *The Cocktail Party*, Act 2.

11
And everyone likes to be seen at a party
Where everybody else is, to show they've been invited.
  T. S. ELIOT, *The Cocktail Party*, Act 2.

12
Society is a masked ball, where every one hides his real character, and reveals it by hiding.
  RALPH WALDO EMERSON, *Conduct of Life: Worship*.

13
Society is a hospital of incurables.
  RALPH WALDO EMERSON, *New England Reformers*.

14
Society is a joint stock company, in which the members agree, for the better securing of his bread to each shareholder, to surrender the liberty and culture of the eater.
  RALPH WALDO EMERSON, *Essays, First Series: Self-Reliance*.

15
Those who didn't show [referring to the Inauguration ceremonies for President-elect Kennedy in 1960] included William Faulkner, Ernest Hemingway, and Thornton Wilder. Shortly before his death, Faulkner was invited to a White House soiree. "Why should I go?" responded Faulkner. "I don't know any of those people."
  VICTOR LASKY, *J.F.K.: The Man and the Myth*.

16
Debut: the first time a young girl is seen drunk in public.
  F. SCOTT FITZGERALD, *The Crack-up*.

17
Society is a Nineteenth Century word in a Twentieth Century world.
  MRS. AUGUSTUS HEMENWAY, quoted by CLEVELAND AMORY in *Who Killed Society?*

18
Ermined and minked and Persian-lambed,
  Be-puffed (be-painted, too, alas!)
Be-decked, be-diamonded—be-damned!
  The Women of the Better Class.
  OLIVER HERFORD, *The Women of the Better Class*.

19
Mrs. Montagu has dropt me. Now, Sir, there are people whom one should like very well to drop, but you would not wish to be dropt by.
  SAMUEL JOHNSON, BOSWELL's *Life*.

20
I live in the crowds of jollity, not so much to enjoy company as to shun myself.
  SAMUEL JOHNSON, *Rasselas*, ch. 16.

1
Doorman—A genius who can open the door of your car with one hand, help you in with the other, and still have one left for the tip.
DOROTHY KILGALLEN.

2
In general, American social life constitutes an evasion of talking to people. Most Americans don't, in any vital sense, get together; they only do things together.
LOUIS KRONENBERGER, *Company Manners*, p. 148.

3
Hans Breitmann gife a barty—
Where ish dat barty now?
CHARLES GODFREY LELAND, *Hans Breitmann's Party*.

4
A cocktail party is a place where you talk with a person you do not know about a subject you have no interest in.
LIN YUTANG, *With Love and Irony*.

5
A town that boasts inhabitants like me
Can have no lack of good society!
HENRY WADSWORTH LONGFELLOW, *The Birds of Killingworth*.

6
W. Somerset Maugham prefers small parties. "Four is a wonderful number," he decrees. "Six is all right, and eight will do in a pinch. After that, it's not a party: it's a rabble."
BENNETT CERF, *The Laugh's on Me*.

7
Social Research Center Off To Prying Start.
New York University Alumni News. Headline, quoted in *Reader's Digest*, Feb., 1967.

8
European society (society, that is, in its narrowest sense) automatically assumes its superiority to Americans whether they have money or not, but money tends to blur the sharpness of the distinction.
VIRGILIA PETERSON, *A Matter of Life and Death*.

9
The "400," he said, has been marked down to $3.98.
ALEXANDER PHILLIPS, quoted by CLEVELAND AMORY in *The Last Resorts*.

10
A switch on the oldest Party Joke in the world goes like so: Who was that lady I saw you outwit last night?
More Playboy's Party Jokes (1965).

11
Advice to the exhausted: When wine, women and song become too much for you, give up singing.
More Playboy's Party Jokes (1965).

12
A . . . brief version of the F.F.V. story is credited to the late Will Rogers, who was once accosted by a lady who boasted lengthily of being an F.F.V. "I, madam," he said, "am an L.F.A." What on earth, the lady wanted to know, was that? Replied Rogers, "A Last Family of Arkansas."
CLEVELAND AMORY, *Who Killed Society?*

13
Society is like the air, necessary to breathe, but insufficient to live on.
GEORGE SANTAYANA, *Little Essays*.

14
When many people are together, they must be separated by rites; otherwise, they slaughter each other.
JEAN-PAUL SARTRE, *The Words*.

15
There are only two classes in good society in England: the equestrian classes and the neurotic classes.
BERNARD SHAW, *Heartbreak House*, Act 3.

16
Society ladies are the most notable works of art in our modern galleries—they are painted well.
J. M. STUART-YOUNG, *Passion's Peril*.

17
My wife had the last word. "Well, I'll say one thing for you," she remarked. "When you throw a party, it *always* hits *somebody.*"
JAMES THURBER, *Credos and Curios*.

18
Regard the society of women as a necessary unpleasantness of social life, and avoid it as much as possible.
LEO TOLSTOY, *Diary*.

19
People whose parents came over in steerage
Here entertain only the peerage.
UNKNOWN. Old Palm Beach poem. Quoted in *The Last Resorts* by CLEVELAND AMORY.

20
Other people are quite dreadful. The only possible society is one's self.
OSCAR WILDE, *An Ideal Husband*, Act 3.

21
She tried to found a salon, but only succeeded in opening a restaurant.
OSCAR WILDE, *The Picture of Dorian Gray*, ch. 1.

22
I must decline your invitation owing to a subsequent engagement.
OSCAR WILDE.

23
Frank Harris is invited to all the great houses in England—once.
OSCAR WILDE.

1

To get into the best society nowadays, one has either to feed people, amuse people, or shock people.

OSCAR WILDE, *A Woman of No Importance*.

2

The security of society lies in custom and unconscious instinct, and the basis of the stability of society, as a healthy organism, is the complete absence of any intelligence amongst its members.

OSCAR WILDE, *The Critic as Artist*.

SOLITUDE

3

He that is pleased with solitude must be either a wild beast or a god.

ARISTOTLE. (*Classic Quotations*, ed. by JAMES ELMES.)

4

In Genesis it says that it is not good for a man to be alone, but sometimes it is a great relief.

JOHN BARRYMORE.

5

Many people live alone and like it, but most of them live alone and look it.

GELETT BURGESS.

6

Secret, and self-contained, and solitary as an oyster.

CHARLES DICKENS, *A Christmas Carol*.

7

Anythin' for a quiet life, as the man said wen he took the sitivation at the lighthouse.

CHARLES DICKENS, *Pickwick Papers*, ch. 43.

8

The owl is not considered the wiser for living retiredly.

THOMAS FULLER, *Gnomologia*, No. 4697.

9

In solitude the lonely man is eaten up by himself, among crowds by the many. Choose which you prefer.

FRIEDRICH WILHELM NIETZSCHE, *Human, All Too Human*, vol. 2, tr. by PAUL V. COHN.

10

Devote six years to your work but in the seventh go into solitude or among strangers so that your friends, by remembering what you were, do not prevent you from being what you have become.

LEO SZILARD, *Harper's*, July, 1960.

11

Why should I feel lonely? is not our planet in the Milky Way?

HENRY D. THOREAU, *Walden: Solitude*.

12

Girls who wear zippers shouldn't live alone.

JOHN VAN DRUTEN, *The Voice of the Turtle*.

SONG

13

She was a town-and-country soprano of the kind often used for augmenting grief at a funeral.

GEORGE ADE.

14

If you can't say just what you mean, in words and all other efforts at precise meaning, then sing it.

BERNARD BERENSON, *Diaries* (1957).

15

A nightingale dies for shame if another bird sings better.

ROBERT BURTON, *The Anatomy of Melancholy*.

16

I'll never forget a certain charity affair. For a $500 contribution, I offered to sing a song. Without a moment's hesitation, philanthropist Harry Gould offered $1,000 if I *didn't* sing. That would have been bad enough— but how that audience *applauded!* I ask you, how far would I get with a fragile ego?

EDDIE CANTOR, *The Way I See It*.

17

A robin's song is not pretty to the worm.

SELWYN CHAMPION, *Racial Proverbs*.

18

All singers have this fault: if asked to sing among friends they are never so inclined; if unasked, they never leave off.

HORACE, *Satires*, I, 3.

19

Musicians have the reputation of being not overly bright. This happens to be only too fatally true in the case of singers.

ALEXANDER KING, *Rich Man, Poor Man, Freud and Fruit*, ch. 3.

20

As a singer you're a great dancer.

AMY LESLIE, to George Primrose. (MARKS, *They All Sang*, p. 67.)

21

Minnesingers traveled from town to town. They didn't really sing too good, which is the main reason they kept moving.

ART LINKLETTER, *A Child's Garden of Misinformation*.

22

They tune like bells, and want but hanging.

GEORGE MERITON, *Yorkshire Ale*, 83.

23

I claim that it [*Yes, We Have No Bananas*] is the greatest document that has been

penned in the entire history of American
literature.
>   WILL ROGERS, *The Illiterate Digest.* See
>   below.

1
Mrs. Jones sat on her bed a-sighin',
Just received a message that Casey was
>   dyin';
Said, "Go to bed, children, and hush your
>   cryin'
'Cause you've got another pappa on the Salt
>   Lake Line."
>   T. LAWRENCE SEIBERT, *Casey Jones*
>   (1909). See also THURBER in this sec-
>   tion.

2
I can suck melancholy out of a song, as a
weasel sucks eggs.
>   WILLIAM SHAKESPEARE, *As You Like It.*
>   Act ii, sc. 5.

3
Yes, we have no bananas,
We have no bananas today.
>   FRANK SILVER AND IRVING COHN, *Yes,
>   We Have No Bananas* (1923).

4
Where was Moses when the light went out?
>   JOHN STAMFORD, *Where Was Moses When
>   the Light Went Out?* (c. 1880)

5
Singing is sweet, but be sure of this,
Lips only sing when they cannot kiss.
>   JAMES THOMSON (B.V.), *Sunday up the
>   River.*

6
Casey Jones was a son of a bitch.
He went through Toledo on an open switch,
Dropstitch stockings and low cut shoes,
A pack of Fatimas and a bottle of booze.
>   JAMES THURBER, quoted by HARRY GOLD-
>   EN in *Carl Sandburg.*

7
I can't sing. As a singist I am not a success.
I am saddest when I sing. So are those who
hear me. They are sadder even than I am.
>   ARTEMUS WARD, *Lecture.*

SORROW

See also Grief

8
Hang sorrow, care'll kill a cat.
>   BEN JONSON, *Every Man in His Humour.*

9
every cloud
has its silver
lining but it is
sometimes a little
difficult to get it to
the mint
>   DON MARQUIS, *certain maxims of archy.*

10
There are few sorrows, however poignant,
in which a good income is of no avail.
>   LOGAN PEARSALL SMITH, *Afterthoughts.*

11
Who flies afar from the sphere of our sorrow is here today and here tomorrow.
>   JAMES THURBER, *Fables for Our Time.*

12
Hang sorrow! care will kill a cat,
And therefore let's be merry.
>   GEORGE WITHER, *Christmas.* See also
>   JONSON in this section.

SOUL

13
I have too great a soul to die like a criminal.
>   JOHN WILKES BOOTH.

14
The souls of women are so small,
That some believe they've none at all;
Or if they have, like cripples, still
They've but one faculty, the will.
>   SAMUEL BUTLER, *Miscellaneous Thoughts,*
>   l. 386.

15
Strange that the soul, that very fiery particle,
Should let itself be snuffed out by an article.
>   LORD BYRON, *Comment on the Death of
>   Keats.*

16
Beneath this stone OWEN LOVEJOY lies,
Little in everything—except in size;
What though his burly body fills this hole,
Yet through hell's keyhole crept his little
>   soul.
>   REPRESENTATIVE SAM COX of Ohio about
>   Representative Owen Lovejoy of Illi-
>   nois.

17
Said Descartes, "I extoll
Myself because I have a soul
And beasts do not." (Of course
He *had* to put Descartes before the horse.)
>   CLIFTON FADIMAN, *Theological.*

18
No soul is bad enough for a fixed "hell," or
good enough for a fixed "heaven," however
useful the words may be as pointing to opposite states.
>   HUGH R. HAWEIS, *Speech in Season,* bk.
>   2.

19
Do I have no soul as a punishment for not
believing in the soul?
>   STANISLAW J. LEC, *Unkempt Thoughts,* tr.
>   from the Polish by JACEK GALASKA.

20
It's prudent to gain the whole world and lose
your own soul.
>   BERNARD SHAW, *Heartbreak House,* Act
>   2.

1
Most people sell their souls and live with good conscience on the proceeds.
LOGAN PEARSALL SMITH, *Afterthoughts.*

2
The lusts and greeds of the Body scandalize the Soul; but it has come to heel.
LOGAN PEARSALL SMITH, *Afterthoughts.*

3
Be careless in your dress if you must, but keep a tidy soul.
MARK TWAIN, *Pudd'nhead Wilson's Calendar.*

4
Nobody knows how the idea of a soul or the supernatural started. It probably had its origin in the natural laziness of mankind.
JOHN B. WATSON, *Behaviorism,* p. 3.

SPEECH

See also Conversation; Orator, Oratory; Silence

5
If you take care to pronounce correctly the words usually mispronounced, you may have the self-love of the purist, but you will not sell any goods.
GEORGE ADE, *Fables.*

6
The American must go to London in order to learn for a dead certainty that he does not speak the English language. On the Continent if he kicks on the charges and carries a great deal of hand luggage and his clothes do not fit him any too well, he may be mistaken for an Englishman. This great joy never awaits him in London.
GEORGE ADE, *In Pastures New.*

7
But since he was still in the midst of his prayers and did not want to interrupt them with secular discourse, he spoke to me in the holy tongue, that is, in a language that consisted of gestures of the hands, winks of the eye, shrugs and motions of the head and even the nose, with a few Hebrew words thrown in.
SHOLOM ALEICHEM, *Eternal Life.*

8
Public lecturing in America is the perfect vehicle for that rich compound of vanity and greed which makes up the literary character.
KINGSLEY AMIS, *Who Needs No Introduction.*

9
I don't let my mouth say nothing my head can't stand.
LOUIS ARMSTRONG, quoted by RICHARD MERYMAN in *Life.*

10
Ten measures of speech descended on the world; women took nine and men one.
Babylonian Talmud: Kiddushim.

11
As men do walk a mile, women should talk an hour, after supper: 'tis their exercise.
BEAUMONT AND FLETCHER, *Philaster.* Act ii, sc. 4.

12
It would talk; Lord, how it talked!
BEAUMONT AND FLETCHER, *The Scornful Lady.* Act iv.

13
No one in America will deny that many of the beautiful young gentlemen and ladies of Hollywood should never have been called upon to talk. Neither will anyone deny that a large number of American actresses and actors who go to London in the spoken drama might well offend the sensitive British ear. They have offended even the cauliflower ear of New York.
ROBERT BENCHLEY, *The King's English.* (*The Benchley Roundup,* ed. by NATHANIEL BENCHLEY.)

14
Drawing on my fine command of language, I said nothing.
ROBERT BENCHLEY.

15
The sound of his own voice will often give a man consolation where all other things would fail.
GERALD BENDALL, *Mrs. Jones' Bonnet.*

16
Even the damned may salute the eloquence of Mr. Webster.
STEPHEN VINCENT BENÉT, *The Devil and Daniel Webster.*

17
Speaking without thinking is shooting without aiming.
W. G. BENHAM, *Proverbs.*

18
Lecturer: one with his hand in your pocket, his tongue in your ear, and his faith in your patience.
AMBROSE BIERCE.

19
I don't care how much a man talks, if he only says it in a few words.
JOSH BILLINGS. (*Work of the Wits,* by A. CRAIG.)

20
"Correct my manners or my waggeries,
But though my accent's not the berries,
Spare my pronunciation's vagaries . . ."
To that she merely said, "Vagaries!"
MORRIS BISHOP, *Why and How I Killed My Wife.*

1
Two great talkers will not travel far together.
GEORGE BORROW, *Lavengro,* ch. 35.

2
If a thing goes without saying, let it.
JACOB M. BRAUDE, *Treasury of Wit and Humor.*

3
The best way to get a woman to listen is to whisper.
STAN BURNS, *Parade Magazine,* Apr. 9, 1967.

4
He is considered the most graceful speaker who can say nothing in most words.
SAMUEL BUTLER.

5
Speak in French when you can't think of the English for a thing.
LEWIS CARROLL, *Through the Looking-Glass,* ch. 2.

6
"The time has come," the Walrus said,
"To talk of many things:
Of shoes—and ships—and sealing-wax—
Of cabbages—and kings—
And why the sea is boiling hot—
And whether pigs have wings."
LEWIS CARROLL, *Through the Looking-Glass,* ch. 3.

7
Don't grunt, said Alice: that's not a proper way of expressing yourself.
LEWIS CARROLL, *Alice in Wonderland,* ch. 6.

8
"Then you should say what you mean," the March Hare went on.
"I do," Alice hastily replied; "at least—at least I mean what I say—that's the same thing, you know."
"Not the same thing a bit!" said the Hatter. "Why, you might as well say 'I see what I eat' is the same thing as 'I eat what I see'!"
LEWIS CARROLL, *Alice in Wonderland,* ch. 7.

9
Birds are entangled by their feet, and men by their tongues.
JACOB CATS, *Moral Emblems.*

10
When a man dies, the last thing that moves is his heart; in a woman her tongue.
GEORGE CHAPMAN, *Widow's Tears.* Act iv, sc. 2.

11
He mouths a sentence as curs mouth a bone.
CHARLES CHURCHILL (1731–1764), *The Rosciad.*

12
The United States is a land of free speech. Nowhere is speech freer—not even here where we sedulously cultivate it even in its most repulsive form.
SIR WINSTON CHURCHILL, *Address* in the House of Commons, Sept. 28, 1944.

13
You cannot believe, unless you pay close attention, how many devices nature has wrought for us to use in speech. For in the first place an artery stretches from the lungs to the inner part of the mouth, whereby the voice, starting from the mind, is caught up and uttered. Then the tongue is situated in the mouth and fenced about with teeth; it shapes and limits unduly loud sounds, and when it strikes the teeth and other parts of the mouth makes the sound of the voice distinct and clipped; and so we Stoics usually compare the tongue to the pick, the teeth to the strings, the nostrils to the sounding board which echoes to the string in music.
CICERO, *On the Nature of the Gods.* From *Roman Culture,* ed. by GARRY WILLS.

14
If you don't say anything, you won't be called on to repeat it.
CALVIN COOLIDGE.

15
"You must talk to me, Mr. Coolidge. I made a bet today that I could get more than two words out of you."
"You lose," said the Vice-President with a poker face, and let it go at that.
ISHBEL ROSS, *Grace Coolidge and Her Era,* ch. 3.

16
But far more numerous was the herd of such,
Who think too little, and who talk too much.
JOHN DRYDEN, *Absalom and Achitophel.*

17
Nature has given men one tongue, but two ears, that we may hear from others twice as much as we speak.
EPICTETUS, *Fragments,* 142.

18
The tongue offends and the ears get the cuffing.
BENJAMIN FRANKLIN, *Poor Richard,* 1757.

19
You may talk too much on the best of subjects.
BENJAMIN FRANKLIN, *Poor Richard.*

20
Men who have little business are great talkers. The less one thinks, the more one speaks. (Les gens qui ont peu d'affaires sont de tres grands parleurs. Moins on pense, plus on parle.)
OLD FRENCH PROVERB.

1
A slip of the foot may be soon recovered;
but that of the tongue perhaps never.
THOMAS FULLER, *Gnomologia*, No. 403.

2
Unto those who talk and talk,
    This proverb should appeal:
The steam that blows the whistle
    Will never turn the wheel.
REPRESENTATIVE GALLAGHER of Illinois.

3
He who talks much cannot always talk well.
(Chi parla troppo non puo parlar sempre
bene.)
CARLO GOLDONI, *Pamela*. Act i, sc. 6.

4
A blockhead is as ridiculous when he talketh,
as is a goose when it flieth.
LORD HALIFAX, *Works*.

5
The wise hand does not all that the foolish
mouth speaks.
GEORGE HERBERT, *Jacula Prudentum*.

6
The tongue is not steel, yet it cuts.
GEORGE HERBERT, *Jacula Prudentum*.

7
The tongue is no edge-tool, but yet it will
cut.
JOHN HEYWOOD, *Proverbs*, pt. 1.

8
Speak clearly, if you speak at all;
Carve every word before you let it fall.
OLIVER WENDELL HOLMES, *A Rhymed
    Lesson*, l. 408.

9
Talking is like playing on the harp; there is
as much in laying the hands on the strings
to stop their vibration as in twanging them
to bring out their music.
OLIVER WENDELL HOLMES, *The Autocrat
    of the Breakfast Table*, ch. 1.

10
The man that often speaks, but never talks.
OLIVER WENDELL HOLMES, *The Banker's
    Secret*.

11
A word once let out of the cage cannot be
whistled back again.
HORACE, *Epistles*, xviii.

12
Think twice before you speak and then say
it to yourself.
ELBERT HUBBARD, *The Philistine*, Cover
    No. 4.

13
She was a professional athlete—of the
tongue.
ALDOUS HUXLEY.

14
A sharp tongue is the only edged tool that
grows keener with constant use.
WASHINGTON IRVING, *Rip van Winkle*.

15
The worst of Warburton is that he has a
rage for saying something when there's
nothing to be said.
SAMUEL JOHNSON, Boswell's *Life of John-
    son*.

16
Talking and eloquence are not the same: to
speak, and to speak well are two things. A
fool may talk, but a wise man speaks.
BEN JONSON, *Timber; or, Discoveries
    Made Upon Men and Matter*.

17
Men of your kidney talk little; they glory
in taciturnity and cut their hair shorter than
their eyebrows. (Rarus sermo illis et magna
libido tacendi Atque supercilio brevior
coma.)
JUVENAL, *Satires*, sat. 2.

18
It is a great misfortune neither to have
enough wit to talk well nor enough judgment
to be silent.
JEAN DE LA BRUYÈRE.

19
Most people tire of a lecture in ten minutes;
clever people can do it in five. Sensible
people never go to lectures at all.
STEPHEN LEACOCK, *Laugh with Leacock:
    We Have with Us Tonight*.

20
Then he will talk—good gods, how he will
talk!
NATHANIEL LEE, *Alexander the Great*,
    Act 1.

21
I was asked some years ago to speak to the
China League for Civil Rights on freedom
of speech. It is a great topic, and I was
going to make my speech as free as possible.
But this can never be done, for when anyone announces that he is going to speak his
mind freely, everyone is frightened. This
shows that there is no such thing as true
freedom of speech. No one can afford to let
his neighbors know what he is thinking about
them.
LIN YUTANG, *With Love and Irony*.

22
And though the tongue has no bones, it can
sometimes break millions of them.
F. L. LUCAS, *What Is Style?; Holiday*,
    Mar., 1960.

23
Ladies may take infinite pains about having
style in their clothes, but how many of us
remain curiously indifferent about having

it in our words? How many women would
dream of polishing not only their nails but
also their tongues?

F. L. LUCAS, *What Is Style?; Holiday*,
Mar., 1960.

1

Some men are like bagpipes—they can't
speak till their belly's filled.

SEUMAS MACMANUS, *Heavy Hangs the
Golden Grain.*

2

Many a man's tongue broke his nose.

SEUMAS MACMANUS, *Heavy Hangs the
Golden Grain.*

3

Why is the word "tongue" feminine in
Greek, Latin, Italian, Spanish, French and
German?

AUSTIN O'MALLEY.

4

Generally speaking, women are.

More Playboy's Party Jokes (1965).

5

He sometimes draws out the thread of his
verbosity finer than the staple of his argument.

RICHARD PORSON, *Of Gibbon's Decline
and Fall: Letters to Travis* (1790),
preface, p. 29.

6

If a woman could talk out of the two sides
of her mouth at the same time, a great deal
would be said on both sides.

GEORGE D. PRENTICE.

7

And 'tis remarkable that they
Talk most who have the least to say.

MATTHEW PRIOR, *Alma.*

8

He replies nothing but monosyllables. I believe he would make three bites of a cherry.

FRANÇOIS RABELAIS, *Pantagruel.*

9

Annoyed one day by the persistent chatter
of two members, Reed [Thomas B. Reed of
Maine] turned to the nearby Sergeant-at-
Arms and remarked in a tone so loud that
all could hear, "They never open their
mouths without subtracting from the sum
of human knowledge."

The Wit and Wisdom of Congress, ed. by
EDWARD BOYKIN.

10

Talkative rather than eloquent. (Loquax
magis quam facundus.)

SALLUST, *History*, bk. 4.

11

What cracker is this same that deafs our
ears
With this abundance of superfluous breath?

WILLIAM SHAKESPEARE, *King John*. Act
ii, sc. 1.

12

My method is to take the utmost trouble
to find the right thing to say, and then to
say it with the utmost levity.

BERNARD SHAW, *Answers to Nine Questions.*

13

They only babble who praise not reflection.

ROBERT BRINSLEY SHERIDAN, *Pizarro*, Act
1.

14

There, Sir, an attack upon my language!
What do you think of that:—an aspersion
upon my parts of speech! Was ever such a
brute! Sure, if I reprehend anything in this
world, it is the use of my oracular tongue,
and a nice derangement of epitaphs.

RICHARD BRINSLEY SHERIDAN, *The Rivals.*
Act iii, sc. 3. Mrs. Malaprop speaking.

15

He said enough, Enough said.

GERTRUDE STEIN, *Enough Said*. The poem
consists of these words, five times repeated.

16

There are few wild beasts more to be
dreaded than a talking man having nothing
to say.

JONATHAN SWIFT.

17

Did you say that in the asphalt or the concrete?

SIR HERBERT BEERBOHM TREE, quoted by
HESKETH PEARSON in *Lives of the Wits.*

18

Often a quite assified remark becomes sanc-
tified by use and petrified by custom; it is
then a permanency, its term of activity a
geologic period.

MARK TWAIN, *Does the Race of Man
Love a Lord?*

19

He [Gladstone] speaks to me as if I was
a public meeting.

QUEEN VICTORIA, quoted by G. W. E.
RUSSELL, *Collections and Recollections*,
ch. 14.

20

I like the way you always manage to state
the obvious with a sense of real discovery.

GORE VIDAL, *The Best Man.*

21

Free speech is like garlic. If you are perfectly sure of yourself, you enjoy it and
your friends tolerate it.

LYNN WHITE, *Look*, Apr. 17, 1956.

SPORTS

22

These are the saddest of possible words:
"Tinker to Evers to Chance."

Trio of bear cubs, and fleeter than birds,
  Tinker and Evers and Chance.
Ruthlessly pricking our gonfalon bubble,
Making a Giant hit into a double—
Words that are heavy with nothing but trouble:
  "Tinker to Evers to Chance."
  FRANKLIN P. ADAMS, *Baseball's Sad Lexicon,* referring to the famed double-play combination of the Chicago Cubs in the early 1900's: Joe Tinker, Johnny Evers, and Frank Chance.

1
Rockne wanted nothing but "bad losers."
Good losers get into the habit of losing.
  GEORGE E. ALLEN, *Presidents Who Have Known Me.* Referring to Knute Rockne, football coach at Notre Dame.

2
My riding career was fired with an ambition to be on the front end as often as possible.
  EDDIE ARCARO, *Foreword, The Fireside Book of Horse Racing.*

3
Sittin' in the catbird seat.
  UNKNOWN, signifying a favorable position in general, but best known to baseball fans through its use by Red Barber, the broadcaster.

4
If the people don't want to come out to the park, nobody's gonna stop 'em.
  LAWRENCE PETER (YOGI) BERRA, a familiar example of his malapropism. He was referring to lagging baseball attendance in Kansas City, and the impossibility of forcing fans to attend games.

5
Who can think and hit at the same time?
  LAWRENCE PETER (YOGI) BERRA.

6
I want to thank everyone who made this day necessary.
  LAWRENCE PETER (YOGI) BERRA. This was his public acknowledgment of an honor paid him by admiring baseball followers who staged a "day" in his name. A favorite example of Berra's malapropism.

7
When I was 40, my doctor advised me that a man in his forties shouldn't play tennis. I heeded his advice carefully and could hardly wait until I reached 50 to start again.
  HUGO BLACK, quoted in *Think,* Feb., 1963.

8
Cow-pasture pool.
  O. K. BOVARD, *Description* of golf, when he was managing editor of the *St. Louis Post-Dispatch.*

9
A noted psychologist's wife asked him why he never let her play golf with him. "My dear," he admonished her, "there are three things a man must do alone: testify, die, and putt."
  BENNETT CERF, *The Laugh's on Me.*

10
The golf links lie so near the mill
  That almost any day
The laboring children can look out
  And see the men at play.
  SARAH N. CLEGHORN, *The Conning Tower; New York Tribune,* Jan. 1, 1915.

11
As I understand it, sport is hard work for which you do not get paid.
  IRVIN S. COBB, *Sports and Pastimes; The Saturday Evening Post,* 1912.

12
Baseball must be a great game to survive the people who run it.
  UNKNOWN, quoted by ARTHUR DALEY in "Sports of the Times," *The New York Times,* Nov. 10, 1964.

13
In my younger days it was not considered respectable to be an athlete. An athlete was always a man that was not strong enough to work.
  FINLEY PETER DUNNE, *Mr. Dooley's Opinions.*

14
You don't save a pitcher for tomorrow. Tomorrow it may rain.
  LEO DUROCHER.

15
Camp life is just one canned thing after another.
  Toaster's Handbook, compiled by PEGGY EDMUND AND HENRY WORKMAN WILLIAMS.

16
If you can't break 85 you have no business on the golf course. If you can break 85 you probably have no business.
  Farmer's Almanac, 1966.

17
The biggest fish I caught got away.
  EUGENE FIELD, *Our Biggest Fish,* st. 2.

18
Boxing is definitely here to stay, no matter what the general attitude of those male grandmothers and young men of the nincompoop class who want to see its demise.
  NAT FLEISCHER, veteran boxing authority. *Interview, The New York Times,* Jan. 3, 1965.

1
Golf is an ideal diversion, but a ruinous disease.
    B. C. FORBES, *Epigrams*.

2
I occasionally get birthday cards from fans. But it's often the same message: they hope it's my last.
    AL FORMAN, National League baseball umpire. Quoted in *Time,* Aug. 25, 1961.

3
Pro football is like nuclear warfare. There are no winners, only survivors.
    FRANK GIFFORD, quoted in *Sports Illustrated,* July 4, 1960.

4
In a way an umpire is like a woman. He makes quick decisions, never reverses them, and doesn't think you're safe when you're out.
    LARRY GOETZ, baseball umpire. *News summaries,* Apr. 17, 1955.

5
Men like to win; but women hate to lose. The difference can be summed up in one word: bridgemanship.
    CHARLES GOREN, *McCall's,* Aug., 1961.

6
Baseball is very big with my people. It figures. It's the only time we can get to shake a bat at a white man without starting a riot.
    DICK GREGORY, *From the Back of the Bus.*

7
Every New England deacon ought to see Derby day to learn what sort of a world he lives in. Man is a sporting as well as a praying animal.
    OLIVER WENDELL HOLMES. (*Wit and Wisdom of Oliver Wendell Holmes,* ed. by LESTER E. DENONN.)

8
What he hit is history,
What he missed is mystery.
    THOMAS HOOD, *Impromptu.* In reference to a guest's hunting stories.

9
There are only two occasions when Americans respect privacy, especially in Presidents. Those are prayer and fishing. So that some have taken to fishing.
    HERBERT HOOVER, 1944.

10
All men are equal before fish.
    HERBERT HOOVER, *Comment,* 1951.

11
If you watch a game, it's fun. If you play it, it's recreation. If you work at it, it's golf.
    BOB HOPE, quoted in *Reader's Digest,* Oct., 1958.

12
Football—A sport that bears the same relation to education that bullfighting does to agriculture.
    ELBERT HUBBARD.

13
Knowin' all about baseball is just about as profitable as bein' a good whittler.
    FRANK McKINNEY (KIN) HUBBARD.

14
I'll bet th' hardest thing about prize fightin' is pickin' up yer teeth with a boxin' glove on.
    FRANK McKINNEY (KIN) HUBBARD.

15
Why do I like baseball? The pay is good, it keeps you out in the fresh air and sunshine, and you can't beat them hours.
    TIM HURST. It should be pointed out that the veteran umpire's classic words applied to the early 1900's—an era of daytime baseball and rapid play.

16
I do not see the relationship of these highly industrialized affairs on Saturday afternoons to higher learning in America.
    ROBERT MAYNARD HUTCHINS, referring to college football.

17
I should of stood in bed.
    JOE JACOBS, a widely quoted saying that applies to any exercise in frustration, though Jacobs, a boxing manager, coined it after an experience in baseball. He had been bedridden just prior to the 1935 World Series, and the only reward he got for journeying to the Series was picking the wrong team (Chicago) to back.

18
We cheer for the [Washington] Senators, we pray for the Senators, and we hope that the Supreme Court doesn't declare that unconstitutional.
    LYNDON B. JOHNSON, *Speech* at a luncheon given in connection with the 1962 All-Star baseball game in Washington, D.C., July 9, 1962.

19
Angling—I can only compare to a stick and a string, with a worm at one end and a fool at the other.
    SAMUEL JOHNSON, in *Hebrides Tour.*

20
Hockey players are like mules. They have no fear of punishment and no hope of reward.
    EMORY JONES, general manager of the St. Louis Arena. (BOB BROEG, "Sports Comment," *St. Louis Post-Dispatch,* Dec. 26, 1963.)

1
A couple of years ago they told me I was too young to be President and you were too old to be playing baseball. But we fooled them.
> JOHN F. KENNEDY, to Stan Musial, of the St. Louis Cardinals, at the 1962 All-Star game in Washington, D.C. Kennedy was forty-five at the time, and Musial was three years younger.

2
He did not know that a keeper is only a poacher turned outside in, and a poacher a keeper turned inside out.
> CHARLES KINGSLEY, *The Water Babies*, ch. 1.

3
Golf may be played on Sunday, not being a game within view of the law, but being a form of moral effort.
> STEPHEN LEACOCK, *Why I Refuse to Play Golf*.

4
I know a little boy who told me the other day that he could easily have won a race at his school except that there was another boy who could run faster.
> STEPHEN LEACOCK, *Who Canonizes the Classics*.

5
A sportsman is a man who, every now and then, simply has to get out and kill something.
> STEPHEN LEACOCK, *What Is a Sport?*

6
Let it be understood right away that real fishermen don't go fishing for the sake of the fish. They pretend they do. It is a good excuse for paying ten dollars for a new rod and five dollars for a new reel to say that after all fishing cuts down housekeeping bills. Not at all. No true fisherman ever wants to eat the darned things.
> STEPHEN LEACOCK, *Why Do We Fish?*

7
It is to be observed that "angling" is the name given to fishing by people who can't fish.
> STEPHEN LEACOCK, *When Fellers Go Fishing*.

8
There are only two kinds of coaches—those who have been fired and those who will be fired.
> KEN LOEFFLER, a veteran and highly successful basketball coach on the hazards involved in coaching or managing in any sport.

9
Rodeoing is about the only sport you can't fix. You'd have to talk to the bulls and horses, and they wouldn't understand you.
> BILL LUNDERMAN, holder of title "All-Around Cowboy of the U.S." *News summaries*, Mar. 8, 1954.

10
Fishing is a delusion entirely surrounded by liars in old clothes.
> DON MARQUIS.

11
It is necessary to relax your muscles when you can. Relaxing your brain is fatal.
> STIRLING MOSS, British racing-car driver. (*Newsweek*, May 16, 1955.)

12
Golf is essentially an exercise in masochism conducted out of doors; it affords opportunity for a certain swank, it induces a sense of kinship in its victims, and it forces them to breathe fresh air, but it is, at bottom, an elaborate and addictive rite calculated to drive them crazy for hours on end and send them straight to the whisky bottle after that.
> PAUL O'NEIL, *Palmer Tightens His Grip on Golf; Life*, June 15, 1962, p. 103.

13
Competition makes a horse-race.
> OVID, *Ars Amatoria*, bk. 3, tr. by YOUNG.

14
I am convinced that the greatest contribution Britain has made to the national life of Uruguay was teaching the people football.
> PRINCE PHILIP, *Comment* in Montevideo, Mar., 1962.

15
Lincoln went down in history as "Honest Abe," but he never was a jockey. If he had been a jockey he might have gone down as just "Abe."
> WILL ROGERS, *The Illiterate Digest*.

16
Gregory [Prof. Paul Gregory, University of Alabama] reminds us that some sportswriter or other was disturbed because Babe Ruth made more money than Herbert Hoover. "What the hell has Hoover got to do with it?" said Ruth. "Besides, I had a better year than he did."
> MURRAY KEMPTON, *New York Post*, Aug. 10, 1956.

17
It was the last game of the year, and you were supposed to commit suicide or something if old Pencey didn't win.
> J. D. SALINGER, *The Catcher in the Rye*.

18
A successful coach is one who is still coaching.
> BEN SCHWARTZWALDER, himself a successful football coach, to a gathering of coaches in San Francisco, Dec. 19, 1963.

1

Knowing he [Bernard Shaw] hated blood-sports and would agree with the sentiment, Lady Astor remarked, "I hate killing for pleasure." As he said nothing, one of her children probed: "Do you hate killing for pleasure?" "It depends upon whom you kill," he answered.

HESKETH PEARSON, *Lives of the Wits.*

2

He had splendid conformation—broad shoulders, white hair and erect carriage—and was beautifully turned out in an ensemble of rich brown. One was inclined to hope he would, in the end, award first prize to himself.

RED SMITH, *Description* of a judge at a dog show. (*Newsweek,* Apr. 21, 1958.)

3

It was an ideal day for football—too cold for the spectators and too cold for the players.

RED SMITH, quoting a classic line and applying it to the 1963 National Football League championship game between New York and Chicago, played in Chicago, Dec. 29, 1963.

4

To play billiards well is a sign of a misspent youth.

HERBERT SPENCER, quoted in DUNCAN, *Life of Spencer.*

5

The old pitcher went to the well once too often, but I'm glad the championship remains in America.

JOHN L. SULLIVAN, after his defeat by the heavyweight boxer James J. Corbett, Sept. 7, 1892.

6

Oh, somewhere in this favored land the sun is shining bright;
The band is playing somewhere, and somewhere hearts are light,
And somewhere men are laughing, and little children shout;
But there is no joy in Mudville—mighty Casey has struck out.

ERNEST LAWRENCE THAYER, *Casey at the Bat,* st. 13.

7

It's a lot tougher to be a football coach than a President. You've got four years as a President, and they guard you. A coach doesn't have anyone to protect him when things go wrong.

HARRY S TRUMAN, quoted in *Sports Illustrated,* Mar. 17, 1958.

8

I have never taken any exercise, except for sleeping and resting, and I never intend to take any. Exercise is loathsome.

MARK TWAIN, *Essays: Seventieth Birthday.*

9

This is a sport which makes the body's very liver curl with enjoyment.

MARK TWAIN, *Life on the Mississippi,* referring to piloting.

10

As a nation we are dedicated to keeping physically fit—and parking as close to the stadium as possible.

BILL VAUGHAN, *Kansas City Star.*

11

No man is born an Artist nor an Angler.

IZAAK WALTON, *The Compleat Angler: To the Reader.*

12

The English country gentleman galloping after a fox—the unspeakable in full pursuit of the uneatable.

OSCAR WILDE, *A Woman of No Importance,* Act 1.

13

The fascination of shooting as a sport depends almost wholly on whether you are at the right or wrong end of the gun.

P. G. WODEHOUSE.

SPRING

14

Spring beckons! All things to the call respond,
The trees are leaving and cashiers abscond.

AMBROSE BIERCE, *The Devil's Dictionary.*

15

June Is Bustin' Out All Over.

OSCAR HAMMERSTEIN II, *Title* of song, from the musical play *Carousel* (1945), with music by Richard Rodgers.

16

Like the month of March, in like a lion, he purposed to go out like a lamb.

ROGER NORTH, *Lives of the Norths.*

17

Spring makes everything young again except man.

JEAN PAUL RICHTER.

18

Sweet April's tears,
Dead on the hem of May.

ALEXANDER SMITH, *A Life Drama,* sc. 8.

19

April, April, laugh thy girlish laughter.

SIR WILLIAM WATSON, *Song,* l. 1.

20

It is the month of June,
The month of leaves and roses,
When pleasant sights salute the eyes,
And pleasant scents the noses.

NATHANIEL PARKER WILLIS, *The Month of June.*

STAGE

See also Acting, Opera

1
Forty years ago there was a young Jewish entertainer named Al Jolson who was trying to pass as Negro. Today there is a young Negro entertainer named Sammy Davis who is trying to pass as Jewish.
GOODMAN ACE, *The Fine Art of Hypochondria* (1966).

2
In the caste system of show business along Broadway there are two kinds of nobility—Celebrities and Owls. An owl is an accomplished actor not too widely known. When his name is mentioned to prospective producers they ask, "Who? Who? Who?"
GOODMAN ACE, *The Fine Art of Hypochondria.*

3
I played a suburban theatre that was so far back in the woods the manager was a bear.
FRED ALLEN.

4
It was the kind of flop that even made the audience look bad.
FRED ASTAIRE, *Steps in Time.*

5
Good plays drive bad playgoers crazy.
BROOKS ATKINSON, *Column, The New York Times*, 1956, on the perversity of the handful who wrote in to criticize such widely acclaimed shows as *My Fair Lady.*

6
Shake was a dramatist of note;
He lived by writing things to quote.
H. C. BUNNER, *Shake, Mulleary and Goethe.*

7
Lord Bacon could as easily have created the planets as he could have written *Hamlet.*
THOMAS CARLYLE.

8
When he saw *All God's Chillun Got Wings,* Irvin S. Cobb is supposed to have said, "If they play Paducah, they'll need 'em."
JOHN MASON BROWN, *Seeing Things.*

9
His plays are magnificently dressed show-windows with no store behind them.
BENJAMIN DE CASSERES, *Mencken and Shaw,* on Shaw.

10
Theater people are always pining and agonizing because they're afraid that they'll be forgotten. And in America they're quite right. They will be.
AGNES DE MILLE. (*The Grande Dame of Dance; Life,* Nov. 15, 1963.)

11
I never saw such sad faces or such gay behinds.
MARSHAL FERDINAND FOCH, *Remark* when he first went to the Folies-Bergère. (MAX EASTMAN, *Enjoyment of Laughter.*)

12
Generally speaking, the American theatre is the aspirin of the middle classes.
WOLCOTT GIBBS, *Shakespeare, Here's Your Hat.*

13
Do you know how they are going to decide the Shakespeare-Bacon dispute? They are going to dig up Shakespeare and dig up Bacon; they are going to get Tree [the actor Beerbohm Tree] to recite Hamlet to them. And the one who turns in his coffin will be the author of the play.
W. S. GILBERT, *Letters.*

14
Everybody has his own theatre, in which he is manager, actor, prompter, playwright, sceneshifter, boxkeeper, doorkeeper, all in one, and audience into the bargain.
J. C. AND A. W. HARE, *Guesses at Truth.*

15
The Fabulous Invalid.
MOSS HART AND GEORGE S. KAUFMAN, *Title* of play (1938). The term has become synonymous with the American theater in general.

16
It has not vitality enough to preserve it from putrefaction.
SAMUEL JOHNSON, talking of the comedy *The Rehearsal.* BOSWELL'S *Life,* June 15, 1784.

17
The most alarming thing about the contemporary American theater is the absolute regularity of its march toward extinction.
WALTER KERR, *How Not to Write a Play* (1955): introduction, p. 1.

18
The sort of play that gives failures a bad name.
WALTER KERR, *Review* of *Hook 'n' Ladder,* a short-lived Broadway production of the 1950's, in the *New York Herald Tribune.*

19
And Hamlet, how boring, how boring to live with,
So mean and self-conscious, blowing and snoring
His wonderful speeches, full of other folks' whoring!
D. H. LAWRENCE, *When I Read Shakespeare.*

1
The structure of a play is always the story of how the birds came home to roost.
> ARTHUR MILLER, *The Shadows of the Gods; Harper's Magazine*, Aug., 1958.

2
A stage meal is popular, because it proves to the audience that the actors, even when called Charles Hawtrey or Owen Nares, are real people, just like you and me.
> A. A. MILNE, *The Sunny Side*.

3
Tea is the most usual meal on the stage, for the reason that it is the least expensive, the property lump of sugar being dusted and used again on the next night.
> A. A. MILNE, *The Sunny Side*.

4
But it is the cigarette which chiefly has brought the modern drama to its present state of perfection. Without the stage cigarette many an epigram would pass unnoticed, many an actor's hands would be much more noticeable . . .
> A. A. MILNE, *The Sunny Side*.

5
I was supposed to be writing a Revue at this time for a certain impresario. I wasn't getting on very fast, because whenever I suggested a scene to him, he either said, "Oh, that's been done," which killed it, or else he said, "Oh, but that's never been done," which killed it even more completely.
> A. A. MILNE, *The Sunny Side*.

6
The stage can be defined as a place where Shakespeare murdered Hamlet and a great many Hamlets murdered Shakespeare.
> ROBERT MORSE.

7
Drama—what literature does at night.
> GEORGE JEAN NATHAN, *Testament of a Critic*.

8
So long as there is one pretty girl left on the stage, the professional undertakers may hold up their burial of the theatre.
> GEORGE JEAN NATHAN, *Theatre Arts*, July, 1958.

9
Where certain other quondam distinguished valetudinarians have, like M. Maeterlinck, run off with a young girl, Shaw, being a vegetarian, has run off with an old joke.
> GEORGE JEAN NATHAN, *Back to Methuselah*.

10
The House Beautiful is the play lousy.
> DOROTHY PARKER, *Review* of a stage work. Quoted by ALEXANDER WOOLLCOTT in *While Rome Burns*.

11
[His] father, having failed in business, took to drinking; [his] mother, having failed in matrimony, took to singing.
> HESKETH PEARSON, *Lives of the Wits*. Referring to Bernard Shaw.

12
Shakespeare is the only author that can play to losing business for hundreds of years and still be known as an author.
> WILL ROGERS, *Autobiography*.

13
I quite agree with you, my friend, but what can we two do against a whole houseful of the opposite opinion?
> BERNARD SHAW, when confronted with a "boo" after the first performance of *Arms and the Man* (1894).

14
There is a simple law governing the dramatization of novels: if it is worth doing, it can't be done; if it can be done, it isn't worth it.
> JOHN SIMON, *Acid Test: Novels into Plays*.

15
By increasing the size of the keyhole, today's playwrights are in danger of doing away with the door.
> PETER USTINOV, quoted in *Christian Science Monitor*, Nov. 14, 1962.

16
Ladies and Gentlemen: I have enjoyed this evening immensely. The actors have given us a charming rendering of a delightful play, and your appreciation has been most intelligent. I congratulate you on the success of your performance, which persuades me that you think almost as highly of the play as I do myself.
> OSCAR WILDE, *Curtain speech* to audience of his first comedy, Feb. 20, 1892.

17
. . . the play was a great success. But the audience was a failure.
> OSCAR WILDE, *Comment* when asked about the reception of one of his least successful plays.

18
The only link between Literature and Drama left to us in England at the present moment is the bill of the play.
> OSCAR WILDE, *Saturday Review*, Nov. 17, 1894.

19
It is written by a butterfly for butterflies.
> OSCAR WILDE, to Arthur Humphreys, Feb., 1895. Reference to *The Importance of Being Earnest*.

STATISTICS

1
There are three kinds of lies: lies, damned lies, and statistics.
> BENJAMIN DISRAELI.

2
Figures won't lie, but liars will figure.
> GENERAL CHARLES H. GROSVENOR, Representative from Ohio, who for many years was famous for his prognostications of the vote in presidential elections.

3
Statistics are like alienists—they will testify for either side.
> FIORELLO H. LA GUARDIA, *The Banking Investigation; Liberty,* May 13, 1933.

4
He uses statistics as a drunken man uses lampposts—for support rather than for illumination.
> ANDREW LANG.

STEALING, see Thieving

STRENGTH

See also Power

5
And the Texas Rangers—they grow big, too. Seems there was a riot or something in one of the towns and the mayor wired for a company of Rangers to come and disperse the mob. Pretty soon a lone Ranger showed up. "Hey," said the mayor, "it's a tough mob—I wired for a company of Rangers, not just one Ranger!" "Well," drawled the Ranger, "you ain't got but one mob, ain't you?"
> MAX ADELER (CHARLES HEBER CLARK), *Ten Tall Tales.*

6
Samson with his strong body had a weak head, or he would not have laid it in a Harlot's lap.
> BENJAMIN FRANKLIN, *Poor Richard,* 1756.

7
The tusks that clashed in mighty brawls of mastodons are billiard balls.
> ARTHUR GUITERMAN, *On the Vanity of Earthly Greatness.*

8
Set an ass to carry an elephant's burden, and his back will be broken.
> J. G. HOLLAND, *Plain Talks on Familiar Subjects.*

9
I would rather have a big burden and a strong back, than a weak back and a caddy to carry life's luggage.
> ELBERT HUBBARD, *The Philistine.* Vol. xx, p. 26.

10
I never saw an athletic girl that thought she was strong enough to do indoor work.
> FRANK McKINNEY (KIN) HUBBARD.

11
The weakest link in the chain is also the strongest. It can break the chain.
> STANISLAW J. LEC, *Unkempt Thoughts,* tr. from the Polish by JACEK GALASKA.

12
Let Hercules himself do what he may,
The cat will mew and dog will have his day.
> WILLIAM SHAKESPEARE, *Hamlet.* Act v, sc. 1.

STUPIDITY

See also Ignorance

13
Only the stupidest calves chose their own butcher.
> KONRAD ADENAUER, opposing wheat shipments to Russia. (*New York Herald Tribune,* Oct. 6, 1963.)

14
A thick head can do as much damage as a hard heart.
> HAROLD WILLIS DODDS.

15
I don't know what a moron is,
And I don't give a damn.
I'm thankful that I'm not one—
My God! Perhaps I am.
> HENRY PRATT FAIRCHILD, *The Great Economic Paradox; Harper's Magazine,* May, 1932.

16
It is occasionally possible to charge Hell with a bucket of water but against stupidity the gods themselves struggle in vain.
> DORIS FLEESON, *Syndicated Column,* Feb. 17, 1964. See SCHILLER in this section.

17
Why, Sir, Sherry [Thomas Sheridan] is dull, naturally dull; but it must have taken him a great deal of pains to become what we now see him. Such an excess of stupidity, Sir, is not in Nature.
> SAMUEL JOHNSON, Boswell's *Life,* July 26, 1763.

18
Stupidity is no excuse for not thinking.
> STANISLAW J. LEC, *Unkempt Thoughts,* tr. from the Polish by JACEK GALASKA.

19
Nobody is so stupid as not to be good for something.
> NAPOLEON BONAPARTE. (*The Mind of Napoleon,* ed. by J. CHRISTOPHER HEROLD.)

1
Nothing in the world's smarter than one Chinaman and nothing dumber than two.
WILL ROGERS, *Autobiography*.

2
Against stupidity the very gods
Themselves contend in vain.
JOHANN VON SCHILLER, *The Maid of Orleans*. Act iii, sc. 6.

3
This lord . . . who wears his wit in his belly and his guts in his head.
WILLIAM SHAKESPEARE, *Troilus and Cressida*. Act ii, sc. 1.

4
Dumb enough to chew on the stick instead of sucking the lollipop.
REX STOUT, *The Broken Vase*.

5
He was good-natured, obliging, and immensely ignorant and was endowed with a stupidity which by the least little stretch would go around the globe four times and tie.
MARK TWAIN.

6
See the happy moron,
He doesn't give a damn.
I wish I were a moron;
My God, perhaps I am!
UNKNOWN, quoted in *Journal of Heredity* by its editor, ROBERT COOK. See also FAIRCHILD in this section.

7
It's not that I mind your bein' a bastard, don't get me wrong there . . . It's your bein' such a *stupid* bastard I object to.
GORE VIDAL, *The Best Man*.

8
I want to be a moron,
Because you see, gee whiz!
I like congenial spirits,
I'm lonely as it is.
CAROLYN WELLS, *A Longing*.

9
Statesmanship should quickly learn the lesson of biology as stated by Conklin, that "Wooden legs are not inherited, but wooden heads are."
ALBERT EDWARD WIGGAM, *The New Decalogue of Science*.

10
Whenever a man does a thoroughly stupid thing, it is always from the noblest motives.
OSCAR WILDE, *The Picture of Dorian Gray*, ch. 6.

11
That man is so stupid it sits on him like a halo.
EMLYN WILLIAMS, *The Corn Is Green*. Act ii, sc. 1.

SUCCESS

12
Success has made failures of many men.
CINDY ADAMS, quoted by JOEY ADAMS, *Cindy and I*, ch. 6.

13
Good luck is a lazy man's estimate of a worker's success.
ANONYMOUS.

14
Be commonplace and creeping, and you will be a success.
PIERRE DE BEAUMARCHAIS, *The Barber of Seville*.

15
The toughest thing about success is that you've got to keep on being a success.
IRVING BERLIN, *Interview* with Ward Morehouse, *Theatre Arts*, Feb., 1958.

16
The dictionary is the only place where success comes before work.
ARTHUR BRISBANE, quoted by BENNETT CERF.

17
It takes twenty years to make an overnight success.
Attributed to EDDIE CANTOR, quoted in *The New York Times Magazine*, Oct. 20, 1963.

18
Everyone has his day, and some days last longer than others.
SIR WINSTON CHURCHILL, *Speech*, House of Commons, July 23, 1952.

19
In public we say the race is to the strongest; in private we know that a lopsided man runs the fastest along the little side-hills of success.
FRANK MOORE COLBY, *Constrained Attitudes*.

20
The road to success is filled with women pushing their husbands along.
LORD THOMAS ROBERT DEWAR, *Epigram*.

21
Yes, I have climbed to the top of the greasy pole.
BENJAMIN DISRAELI, *Reply* to an admirer who congratulated him upon his appointment as prime minister.

22
Nothing succeeds like success.
ALEXANDRE DUMAS, *père*, *Ange Pitou*, vol. 1.

23
Nothing succeeds like excess.
Toaster's Handbook, compiled by PEGGY EDMUND AND HENRY WORKMAN WILLIAMS.

1
Born in a log cabin, he defied Alger's law
and did not become President.
> CLIFTON FADIMAN, *The Selected Writings
> of Clifton Fadiman: Portrait of a Mis-
> anthrope* (1955). Reference to Ambrose
> Bierce.

2
I quote the words of your great general,
Nathan Bedford Forrest, the eminently successful Confederate leader. Asked the secret
of his victories, Forrest said, "I git thar
fustest with the mostest men."
> WINSTON CHURCHILL, *Press Conference*,
> Washington, D.C., May 25, 1943.

3
If you wish in this world to advance
Your merits you're bound to enhance;
You must stir it and stump it,
And blow your own trumpet.
Or, trust me, you haven't a chance.
> W. S. GILBERT, *Ruddigore*, Act. 1.

4
Of course everybody likes and respects self-
made men. It is a great deal better to be
made in that way than not to be made at
all.
> OLIVER WENDELL HOLMES, *The Autocrat
> of the Breakfast-Table*, ch. 1.

5
It seems like they pile all th' crushed stone
on th' road t' success.
> FRANK McKINNEY (KIN) HUBBARD, *Abe
> Martin's Primer*.

6
Ther's no secret about success. Did you ever
know a successful man that didn't tell you
all about it?
> FRANK McKINNEY (KIN) HUBBARD, *Abe
> Martin's Primer*.

7
Everything bows to success, even grammar.
> VICTOR HUGO, *Les Misérables*.

8
There is an old motto that runs, "If at first
you don't succeed, try, try again." This is
nonsense. It ought to read—"If at first you
don't succeed, quit, quit at once."
> STEPHEN LEACOCK, *Laugh with Leacock*.

9
Nothing fails like success; nothing is so defeated as yesterday's triumphant Cause.
> PHYLLIS McGINLEY, *The Province of the
> Heart: How to Get Along with Men*, p.
> 71.

10
In the game of success a level head is the
trump and a silent tongue the joker.
> *Reflections of a Bachelor*.

11
Take care to get what you like or you will be
forced to like what you get.
> BERNARD SHAW, *Maxims for Revolution-
> ists*.

12
I dread success. To have succeeded is to
have finished one's business on earth, like
the male spider, who is killed by the female
the moment he has succeeded in his courtship.
> BERNARD SHAW, *Letter* to Ellen Terry.

13
. . . the secret of success is to offend the
greatest number of people.
> BERNARD SHAW, quoted in *Days with Ber-
> nard Shaw* by STEPHEN WINSTEN.

14
I don't feel like a gift from Providence, and
I really don't believe I am. I feel very much
like a corn-fed Illinois lawyer who has gotten
into the big time unintentionally.
> ADLAI E. STEVENSON, *Speech* in Denver,
> 1952.

15
Success to me is having ten honeydew
melons and eating only the top half of each
one.
> BARBRA STREISAND, quoted in *Life*, Sept.
> 20, 1963, p. 112.

16
All you need in this life is ignorance and
confidence, and then success is sure.
> MARK TWAIN, *Letter* to Mrs. Foote, Dec.
> 2, 1878.

17
Success is just a matter of luck. Ask any
failure.
> EARL WILSON, *Syndicated column*.

SUFFERING

See also Pain

18
In his owen grese I made him frie.
> GEOFFREY CHAUCER, *The Reves Tale*.

19
If you suffer, thank God!—it is a sure sign
that you are alive.
> ELBERT HUBBARD, *Epigrams*.

20
He wears a hair shirt but is fussy about its
cut.
> STANISLAW J. LEC, *Unkempt Thoughts*, tr.
> from the Polish by JACEK GALASKA.

21
Who breathes must suffer, and who thinks
      must mourn;
And he alone is blessed who ne'er was born.
> MATTHEW PRIOR, *Solomon on the Vanity
> of the World*, bk. 3.

1
When a wicked married man dies he gets out of the frying pan and into the fire.
Reflections of a Bachelor (1903).

2
I would thou didst itch from head to foot and I had the scratching of thee.
WILLIAM SHAKESPEARE, *Troilus and Cressida.* Act ii, sc. 1.

3
The vermin only tease and pinch
Their foes superior by an inch.
So, naturalists observe, a flea
Hath smaller fleas that on him prey;
And these have smaller still to bite 'em,
And so proceed *ad infinitum.*
JONATHAN SWIFT, *A Rhapsody on Poetry.*

4
If misery loves company, misery has company enough.
HENRY D. THOREAU, *Journal,* Sept. 1, 1851.

5
The mass of men lead lives of quiet desperation.
HENRY D. THOREAU, *Walden.*

SUICIDE

6
Suicide is a belated acquiescence in the opinion of one's wife's relatives.
H. L. MENCKEN, *A Mencken Chrestomathy.*

7
The relatives of a suicide always take it in bad part that he did not remain alive out of consideration for the family dignity.
FRIEDRICH WILHELM NIETZSCHE, *Human, All Too Human.*

8
In church your grandsire cut his throat;
To do the job too long he tarried:
He should have had my hearty vote
To cut his throat before he married.
JONATHAN SWIFT, *On an Upright Judge.*

SUMMER

9
Ah, summer, what power you have to make us suffer and like it.
RUSSELL BAKER, "Observer" Column, *The New York Times,* June 27, 1965.

10
An English summer, two fine days and a thunderstorm.
MICHAEL DENHAM, *Proverbs and Popular Sayings.*

11
Do what we can, summer will have its flies.
RALPH WALDO EMERSON.

12
I have a lot of fun in the summer time. People come up, slap me on the back and I say: "Watch it! My sunburn!"—And you'd be surprised how many apologies I get!
DICK GREGORY, *From the Back of the Bus.*

SUPERSTITION

13
Superstition is the religion of feeble minds.
EDMUND BURKE, *Reflections on the Revolution in France.*

14
A superstition is a premature explanation that overstays its time.
GEORGE ILES, *Jottings.*

15
You know, Tolstoy, like myself, wasn't taken in by superstitions like science and medicine.
BERNARD SHAW, quoted in *Days with Bernard Shaw* by STEPHEN WINSTEN.

16
One may as well preach a respectable mythology as anything else.
MRS. HUMPHRY WARD, *Robert Elsmere.*

SYMPATHY

17
A sympathizer is a fellow who is for you as long as it doesn't cost anything.
Toaster's Handbook, compiled by PEGGY EDMUND AND HENRY WORKMAN WILLIAMS.

18
Since they started this Civil War Centennial, they're showing a lot of those old movies on TV again. The ones where, at the end, all the slaves are weeping and wailing, cause the South lost. Now ain't that somethin'? That's like Jimmie Hoffa pulling for Bobby Kennedy.
DICK GREGORY, *From the Back of the Bus.*

19
No man can hold out for long against another man's helplessness.
MURRAY KEMPTON, *New York Review of Books.*

20
I never knew any man in my life who could not bear another's misfortune perfectly like a Christian.
JONATHAN SWIFT.

21
My nose bleeds for you.
SIR HERBERT BEERBOHM TREE, quoted by HESKETH PEARSON in *Lives of the Wits.*

T

TASTE

1
There's no accounting for tastes, as the woman said when somebody told her her son was wanted by the police.
FRANKLIN P. ADAMS.

2
Each one carries his own inch-rule of taste, and amuses himself by applying it, triumphantly, whenever he travels.
HENRY ADAMS, *The Education of Henry Adams.*

3
For those who like this sort of thing, this is the sort of thing they like.
MAX BEERBOHM, *Zuleika Dobson.* The remark has been attributed to Abraham Lincoln and to Dr. Johnson. See LINCOLN in this section.

4
People care more about being thought to have taste than about being thought either good, clever, or amiable.
SAMUEL BUTLER, *Notebooks.*

5
Tolstoy is like Homer: he does not fear banalities because he is not aware that they are banalities.
CLIFTON FADIMAN, *The Selected Writings of Clifton Fadiman* (1955).

6
You can't get high esthetic tastes like trousers, ready made.
W. S. GILBERT, *Patience,* Act 2.

7
Taste is the literary conscience of the soul.
JOSEPH JOUBERT, *Pensees,* No. 366.

8
Well, for those who like that sort of thing I should think that is just about the sort of thing they would like.
ABRAHAM LINCOLN, to Robert Dale Owen, the spiritualist, when the latter asked for Lincoln's opinion of a long article on spiritualism that Owen had just read. (GROSS, *Lincoln's Own Stories,* p. 96.)

9
Anybody who doesn't like this book is healthy.
GROUCHO MARX, *Comment* on *Memoirs of an Amnesiac* by OSCAR LEVANT.

10
But different taste in different men prevails,
And one is fired by heads, and one by tails.
ALEXANDER POPE, *A Sermon Against Adultery.*

11
Every one to his taste, as the woman said when she kissed her cow.
FRANÇOIS RABELAIS, *Pantagruel.*

12
An ass is beautiful to an ass, and a pig to a pig.
JOHN RAY, *English Proverbs.*

13
Sir, I have read your letter, and I see that to the brazen everything is brass.
OSCAR WILDE, to R. GOLDING BRIGHT, Jan. 14, 1895. Bright (1874–1941) was a newspaperman who wrote to playwrights and actors, criticizing their work.

TAXES

14
Count that day won when, turning on its axis, this earth imposes no additional taxes.
FRANKLIN P. ADAMS.

15
There is something wrong with any law that causes that many people to have to take a whole day off from their jobs to find out how to comply.
T. COLEMAN ANDREWS, Reaction to report that twelve million people in 1954 sought aid from the Internal Revenue service in filling out tax forms.

16
We are not the bosses of taxpapers; they are ours.
T. COLEMAN ANDREWS, on changing name of his department from Internal Revenue Bureau to Internal Revenue Service. *News reports,* Oct. 24, 1955.

17
Governments last as long as the under-taxed can defend themselves against the over-taxed.
BERNARD BERENSON, *Rumor and Reflection.*

18
To tax and to please, no more than to love and to be wise, is not given to men.
EDMUND BURKE, *Speech,* 1774.

19
What's it to us if taxes rise or fall?
Thanks to our fortune, we pay none at all.
CHARLES CHURCHILL (1731–1764), *Night.*

20
The art of taxation consists in so plucking the goose as to obtain the largest amount of feathers with the least amount of hissing.
JEAN BAPTISTE COLBERT.

1
Collecting more taxes than is absolutely necessary is legalized robbery.
CALVIN COOLIDGE, quoted in *The New York Times,* Mar. 6, 1955.

2
The only thing that hurts more than paying an income tax is not having to pay an income tax.
LORD THOMAS R. DEWAR.

3
"It was as true," said Mr. Barkis, ". . . as taxes is. And nothing's truer than them."
CHARLES DICKENS, *David Copperfield,* ch. 21.

4
The war is over—the part you see in the picture papers. But the tax collector will continue his part with relentless fury. Cavalry charges are not the only ones in a real war.
FINLEY PETER DUNNE, *Mr. Dooley Remembers.*

5
If Patrick Henry thought that taxation without representation was bad, he should see how bad it is with representation.
Farmer's Almanac, 1966.

6
In this world, nothing is certain but death and taxes.
BENJAMIN FRANKLIN, *Letter* to M. Leroy, 1789.

7
Worker, examining his paycheck: "Well, I see the government got another raise."
DAVE GERARD, *Register and Tribune* Syndicate.

8
Where is the politician who has not promised to fight to the death for lower taxes—and who has not proceeded to vote for the very spending projects that make tax cuts impossible?
BARRY M. GOLDWATER, *Article, The Reader's Digest,* Jan., 1961.

9
The young century wore a merry, untaxed look. People could get rich without cheating the government.
BEN HECHT, *Gaily, Gaily.*

10
The reason some folks don't understand th' income tax is because they can't beat it.
FRANK MCKINNEY (KIN) HUBBARD, *Abe Martin's Primer.*

11
Taxed on the coffin, taxed on the crib,
On the old man's shroud, on the young babe's bib,
To fatten the bigot and pamper the knave

We are taxed from the cradle plumb into the grave.
REPRESENTATIVE THOMAS R. HUDD of Wisconsin, 1888.

12
The purse of the people is the real seat of sensibility. Let it be drawn upon largely, and they will then listen to truths which could not excite them through any other organ.
THOMAS JEFFERSON, *Writings,* vol. 10.

13
Excise: a hateful tax levied upon commodities.
SAMUEL JOHNSON, *Dictionary.*

14
Taxes milks dry, but, neighbor, you'll allow
Thet havin' things onsettled kills the cow.
JAMES RUSSELL LOWELL, *The Biglow Papers: Mason and Slidell.*

15
O that there might in England be
A duty on hypocrisy,
A tax on humbug, an excise
On solemn plausibilities.
HENRY LUTTRELL, *An Aspiration.*

16
The man who never has a word to say about the excise tax will go wild when he gets his water-tax bill of $2.
Reflections of a Bachelor.

17
I figured why Uncle Sam wears such a tall hat. It comes in handy when he passes it around.
SOUPY SALES, *Parade,* June 11, 1967.

18
"I would," says Fox, "a tax devise
That shall not fall on me."
"Then tax receipts," Lord North replies,
"For those you never see."
RICHARD BRINSLEY SHERIDAN, *Epigram.*

19
The schoolboy whips his taxed top—the beardless youth manages his taxed horse, with a taxed bridle, on a taxed road;—and the dying Englishman, pouring his medicine, which has paid seven per cent., into a spoon that has paid fifteen per cent.—flings himself back upon his chintz bed, which has paid twenty-two per cent.—and expires in the arms of an apothecary who has paid a licence of a hundred pounds for the privilege of putting him to death.
SYDNEY SMITH, *Works,* vol. 1: *Review of Seyber's Statistical Annal of the United States,* p. 291.

20
Men who prefer any load of infamy, how-

ever great, to any pressure of taxation, however light.

> SYDNEY SMITH, *Letters on American Debts.*

1

It is the part of the good shepherd to shear his flock, not flay it. (Boni pastoris esse tondere pecus, non degludere.)

> TIBERIUS CAESAR, to certain governors who recommended heavy taxes. (SUETONIUS, *Lives.*)

2

What is the difference between a taxidermist and a tax collector? The taxidermist takes only your skin.

> MARK TWAIN, *Notebook,* ch. 33.

3

You approach men through taxes, you touch men through the purse, but you reach women through the heart.

> MARK TWAIN, *Address* to members of the Hebrew Technical School for Girls, in Temple Emanu-El, New York, Jan. 20, 1901.

4

This talk 'bout the Revenoo is of the bosh, boshy.

> ARTEMUS WARD, *Things in New York.*

5

The thing that is most generally raised on city land is taxes.

> CHARLES DUDLEY WARNER, *My Summer in a Garden.*

TEACHING

See also Education

6

She used to be a schoolteacher but she has no class now.

> FRED ALLEN, *Much Ado About Me.*

7

Even the Concord ice had bubbles in it. As wood and grass were its only staples, Emerson advised his fellow townsmen to manufacture schoolteachers and make them the best in the world.

> VAN WYCK BROOKS, *The Flowering of New England,* ch. 13.

8

It is always safe to learn, even from our enemies; seldom safe to venture to instruct, even our friends.

> C. C. COLTON, *Lacon,* No. 286.

9

My teacher, Miss G., is very gifted. By that I mean she is young and beautiful.

> ROBERT FONTAINE, *That's a Good Question.*

10

It is a luxury to learn; but the luxury of learning is not to be compared with the luxury of teaching.

> R. D. HITCHCOCK, *Eternal Atonement: Receiving and Giving.*

11

For he that was only taught by himself had a fool to his master.

> BEN JONSON, *Explorata: Consilia.*

12

At this time it is still almost axiomatic that quite a number of pedagogues are inclined to consider the whole world as their classroom and will continue to examine and give homework to any casual strangers that happen to cross their paths.

> ALEXANDER KING, *Rich Man, Poor Man, Freud and Fruit,* ch. 8.

13

The average schoolmaster is and always must be essentially an ass, for how can one imagine an intelligent man engaging in so puerile an avocation?

> H. L. MENCKEN, *Prejudices,* ser. 3.

14

You don't have to think too hard when you talk to a teacher.

> J. D. SALINGER, *The Catcher in the Rye.*

15

He who can, does. He who cannot, teaches.

> BERNARD SHAW, *Maxims for Revolutionists.*

16

The same persons telling to the same people the same things about the same things.

> UNKNOWN. A Greek proverb, quoted by ISAAC LE GRANGE, apropos of teaching.

17

Seven pupils in the class
Of Professor Callias,
Listen silent while he drawls,—
Three are benches, four are walls.

> HENRY VAN DYKE, *The Professor.*

18

Everybody who is incapable of learning has taken to teaching.

> OSCAR WILDE, *The Decay of Lying.*

19

He is either dead or teaching school.

> ZENOBIUS, quoted by ERASMUS in *Adagia.*

TEETH

20

But you're a Spaniard,
and we already know the Spanish custom:
  how Spaniards clean their teeth
and scour their gums with the same water
    that issues
from their bladders.
  So if your teeth are clean, my friend, we
    know how
you have used your urine.

> CATULLUS, *Poems,* tr. by HORACE GREGORY.

1
Do not leave your teeth at home when you attend a comic opera.
WALTER S. GRIFFIN, *Swatches.*

2
I begin to understand the unsavory reputation of English teeth, which—from the little bit I have seen so far—is lamentably well deserved. But one curious point remains unexplained—why are the false teeth so amateurish? They all look as if they had been filched from the Etruscan Room of a museum.
MARGARET HALSEY, *With Malice Toward Some.*

3
The best of friends fall out, and so—
His teeth had done some years ago.
THOMAS HOOD, *A True Story.*

4
Sit melancholy and pick you teeth when you cannot speak.
BEN JONSON, *Every Man in His Humor.* Act i, sc. 2.

5
Thais her teeth are black and nought,
    Lecania's white are grown:
But what's the reason? these are bought,
    The other wears her own.
MARTIAL, *Epigrams*, bk. 5.

6
Man calls from bathroom: "Who forgot to recharge the toothbrush?"
ROY MORIN, *Cartoon caption, The American Legion Magazine.*

7
A Westporter confided at Asti's: "I just bought my wife a dinner set for her birthday—32 teeth."
HARRY NEIGHER, *Connecticut Sunday Herald,* Feb. 19, 1967.

TELEVISION AND RADIO

8
Television—A device that permits people who haven't anything to do to watch people who can't do anything.
FRED ALLEN.

9
Television was . . . trying to get radio to pucker up for the kiss of death.
FRED ALLEN, *Treadmill to Oblivion.*

10
I think I can safely say my few appearances on those early Paar shows influenced his development. For instance, he was suddenly pro-Castro with more influence than I bargained for.
OSCAR LEVANT, *Memoirs of an Amnesiac.*

11
If you [a radio chatterer] don't get off the air, I'll stop breathing it.
WILSON MIZNER, quoted by LOUIS UNTERMEYER in *A Treasury of Laughter.*

12
Joyce Kilmer
I think that I shall never see
A snowless show on my TV,
Because of trees whose boughs impinge
Upon reception in this fringe.
JACK SHARKEY, *Playboy,* May, 1965.

13
Robert Burns
Oh wad some power the giftie gie us
To see oursels as others see us!
Thus all the TV stars lamented,
Till program taping was invented.
JACK SHARKEY, *Playboy,* May, 1965.

14
William Shakespeare
Friends, Romans, countrymen—We interrupt this telecast to bring you a special news bulletin—
JACK SHARKEY, *Playboy,* May, 1965.

15
But soft! What light through yonder window
    breaks?
Is Juliet watching the late-late show *again?*
JACK SHARKEY, *Playboy,* May, 1965.

16
Television is now so desperately hungry for material that they're scraping the top of the barrel.
GORE VIDAL, *Comment,* July 20, 1955.

17
It must have been two years ago that I attended a television demonstration at which it was shown beyond reasonable doubt that a person sitting in one room could observe the nonsense in another.
E. B. WHITE, from *The Selected Writings of Clifton Fadiman.*

TEMPTATION

18
The Devil, having nothing else to do,
Went off to tempt My Lady Poltagrue.
My Lady, tempted by a private whim,
To his extreme annoyance, tempted him.
HILAIRE BELLOC.

19
There is not any memory with less satisfaction than the memory of some temptation we resisted.
JAMES BRANCH CABELL, *Jurgen,* p. 39.

20
Temptations are like women: he who knows one has the key for understanding all.
DESMOND COKE, *The Call.*

1
The Woman tempted me—and tempts me still!
Lord God, I pray You that she ever will!
EDMUND VANCE COOKE, *Book of Extenuations: Adam.*

2
Don't worry about avoiding temptation—as you grow older, it starts avoiding you.
Farmer's Almanac, 1966.

3
It is easy to keep a castle that was never assaulted.
THOMAS FULLER, *Gnomologia,* No. 2924.

4
Like Children taking peeps at Pantry Shelves,
We think we're Tempted when we Tempt Ourselves.
ARTHUR GUITERMAN, *A Poet's Proverbs.*

5
There are temptations that require all of one's strength to yield to.
ELBERT HUBBARD, *The Philistine.* Vol. xx, p. 86.

6
We could all resist temptation if it was to do right.
Reflections of a Bachelor (1905).

7
Many men have too much will power. It's won't power they lack.
JOHN A. SHEDD, *Salt from My Attic,* p. 16.

8
The only way to get rid of a temptation is to yield to it.
OSCAR WILDE, *The Picture of Dorian Gray,* ch. 2.

9
I can resist everything except temptation.
OSCAR WILDE, *Lady Windermere's Fan.* Act 1.

THIEVING

10
He's a good boy—everything he steals he brings right home to his mother.
FRED ALLEN, *Much Ado About Me.*

11
You didn't expect strangers to steal your material; you depended on your friends.
FRED ALLEN, *Much Ado About Me.*

12
I'm for anything crooked but like to be approached as a fellow crook.
SHERWOOD ANDERSON, *Letter* to Ben Hecht.

13
Expense accounts are tax deductible. The swindle-sheet's a cheat right down the line.
It's stealing—but it's socially acceptable. In fact, it's now a mainstay of our economic life. Most restaurants and theatres would close down in a matter of weeks without it.
EDDIE CANTOR, *The Way I See It.*

14
The big thieves lead away the little one.
DIOGENES, when he saw the officials of a temple leading away a man who had stolen one of the sacred vessels. (DIOGENES LAERTIUS, *Diogenes,* sec. 45.)

15
Gold is pale because it has so many thieves plotting against it.
DIOGENES. (DIOGENES LAERTIUS, *Diogenes,* sec. 51.)

16
Old burglars never die, they just steal away.
GLEN GILHEATH, *Remark,* on facing his 13th robbery charge, at age 72. (Chicago *Sun-Times,* Apr. 26, 1958.)

17
Men are not hanged for stealing horses, but that horses may not be stolen.
LORD HALIFAX, *Works.*

18
If it wuzn' fer th' fellers who "intend to put it back t'morrow" who'd keep books in our penitentiaries?
FRANK MCKINNEY (KIN) HUBBARD, *Abe Martin's Primer.*

19
If you left a handful of money right on a table near him, with no one in sight, no one to find out, he wouldn't steal it. Of course not; it's not the kind of thing a gentleman does. But if you left it in a bank account, he might have a go at it; but, of course, that's not exactly stealing; that's embezzlement. Gentlemen embezzle but don't steal.
STEPHEN LEACOCK, *The Struggle to Make Us Gentlemen.*

20
STOLEN, A WATCH WORTH A HUNDRED DOLLARS. IF THE THIEF WILL RETURN IT, HE SHALL BE INFORMED, GRATIS, WHERE HE MAY STEAL ONE WORTH TWO OF IT, AND NO QUESTIONS ASKED.
ABRAHAM LINCOLN, *Advertisement* placed in the *New York Herald* by Lincoln when his watch was stolen on the occasion of his Cooper Union speech in New York. (*The Humorous Mr. Lincoln* by KEITH W. JENNISON.)

21
A little thieving is a dangerous art,
But thieving largely is a noble part;

'Tis vile to rob a henroost of a hen,
But stealing largely makes us gentlemen.
  REPRESENTATIVE SAMUEL S. MARSHALL
    of Illinois, *Speech*, 1868.

1
He'd steal a hot stove and come back for
the smoke.
  WILSON MIZNER, quoted by LOUIS UN-
    TERMEYER in *A Treasury of Laughter*.

2
For de little stealin' dey gits you in jail
soon or late. For de big stealin' dey makes
you emperor and puts you in de Hall o'
Fame when you croaks.
  EUGENE O'NEILL, *The Emperor Jones*.

3
The mountain sheep are sweeter,
But the valley sheep are fatter;
We therefore deemed it meeter
To carry off the latter.
  THOMAS LOVE PEACOCK, *War Song of
    Dinas Vawr*.

4
Thieves can't steal your money if you spend
it fast enough.
  Reflections of a Bachelor.

5
The early burglar catches the police.
  Reflections of a Bachelor.

6
If you give to a thief he cannot steal from
you, and he is then no longer a thief.
  WILLIAM SAROYAN, *The Human Comedy*,
    ch. 4.

7
A plague upon 't when thieves cannot be
true to one another.
  SHAKESPEARE, *King Henry IV, Pt. 1*. Act
    ii, sc. 2.

8
There was an old man of Nantucket
Who kept all his cash in a bucket;
    But his daughter named Nan,
    Ran away with a man—
And as for the bucket—Nantucket.
  DAYTON VOORHEES, *The Old Man of Nan-
    tucket*. First published in *The Prince-
    ton Tiger*, 1902.

9
He that prigs what isn't his'n,
When he's cotched 'll go to prison.
  "HOPPY" WEBB, on authority of Lord Wil-
    liam Lennox.

10
Except for a slight bias toward dishonesty
which led her to steal everything she could
lay her hands on which was not nailed down,
Aileen Peavey's was an admirable character.
  P. G. WODEHOUSE.

THOUGHT

See also Mind

11
I am no athlete—but at one sport I used
to be an expert. It was a dangerous game,
called "jumping to conclusions."
  EDDIE CANTOR, *The Way I See It*.

12
The times call for clear, lucid thinking rather
than Clare Luceish thought.
  BENNETT CERF, *Speech*, 1943.

13
But my thoughts ran a wool-gathering; and
I did like the countryman, who looked for
his ass while he was mounted on his back.
  MIGUEL DE CERVANTES, *Don Quixote*. Pt.
    ii, ch. 57.

14
For God's sake don't let us think. If we did
there would be an end to society.
  LUCAS CLEEVE, *Selma*.

15
There is no expedient to which a man will
not go to avoid the real labor of thinking.
  THOMAS A. EDISON, *Motto*, posted
    throughout his laboratories.

16
All the thoughts of a turtle are turtle.
  RALPH WALDO EMERSON, *Journal*, Sept.
    5, 1855.

17
Beware when the great God lets loose a
thinker on this planet.
  RALPH WALDO EMERSON, *Essays, First
    Series: Circles*.

18
Think and you won't sink.
  B. C. FORBES, *Epigrams*.

19
Thinking is the hardest work there is, which
is the probable reason why so few engage
in it.
  HENRY FORD, *Interview*, Feb., 1929.

20
In much of your talking, thinking is half
murdered.
  KAHLIL GIBRAN, *The Prophet*.

21
Just get up enough courage to say to your
wife, "Honey, please don't bother me for a
few hours. I want to do some thinking."
First your wife will split her sides laughing;
then she'll reach for a broom handle.
  HARRY GOLDEN, *For 2¢ Plain*.

22
I was down in Little Rock last week—which
is the only safe position for me to assume
in Little Rock. . . . And they won't even
allow vanilla-fudge ice cream. Call it Integrated Vanilla. . . . I'm not knocking any-

body, you understand—but I'd hate to be the one who sells THINK signs down there.
DICK GREGORY, *From the Back of the Bus.*

1
All fools think. Wise men just live, and let it go at that.
COSMO HAMILTON, *Adam's Clay.*

2
Ours is an age which is proud of machines that think, and suspicious of any man who tries to.
HOWARD MUMFORD JONES, quoted in *Reader's Digest,* Feb., 1966.

3
Western thought was invented by the Greeks, who were the first people to realize they were thinking.
ERIC LARRABEE, in *Humor from Harper's.*

4
Think before you think!
STANISLAW J. LEC, *Unkempt Thoughts,* tr. from the Polish by JACEK GALASKA.

5
Whether a thought is a dud depends also on the head it hits.
STANISLAW J. LEC, *Unkempt Thoughts,* tr. from the Polish by JACEK GALASKA.

6
They never taste who always drink;
They always talk who never think.
MATTHEW PRIOR, *Upon a Passage in the Scaligeriana.*

7
One reason a woman has so much scorn for thinking is she has so little use for it among her friends.
Reflections of a Bachelor.

8
When humanity begins to think, it stops having fun.
Reflections of a Bachelor.

9
There is nothing either good or bad, but thinking makes it so: to me it is a prison.
WILLIAM SHAKESPEARE, *Hamlet,* Act ii, sc. 2.

10
Thinking is but an idle waste of thought
And nought is everything, and everything is nought.
HORACE SMITH, *Rejected Addresses: Cui Bono?,* st. 8.

11
What right have you to think? Haven't you been in the Police force long enough to know that?
J. C. SNAITH, *William Jordan, Junior.*

12
He thinks things through very carefully before going off half-cocked.
GENERAL CARL SPAATZ, *Comment* on Cal-

vin Coolidge. In *Presidents Who Have Known Me,* by GEORGE E. ALLEN.

13
Sixty minutes of thinking of any kind is bound to lead to confusion and unhappiness.
JAMES THURBER, quoted in *Horse Sense in American Humor.*

14
Thought depends absolutely on the stomach, but in spite of that, those who have the best stomachs are not the best thinkers.
VOLTAIRE, *Letter to d'Alembert,* Aug. 20, 1770.

15
Thinking is the most unhealthy thing in the world, and people die of it just as they die of any other disease.
OSCAR WILDE, *The Decay of Lying.*

TIME

See also Future, Past

16
Well, time wounds all heels.
JANE ACE, quoted by GOODMAN ACE in *The Fine Art of Hypochondria.*

17
Time is a dressmaker specializing in alterations.
FAITH BALDWIN, *Face Toward the Spring.*

18
I've stood upon Achilles' tomb,
And heard Troy doubted: time will doubt of Rome.
LORD BYRON, *Don Juan.*

19
As the Texas darky said: "Dinner-time fur some folks; but just twelve o'clock fur me!"
IRVIN S. COBB, *Paths of Glory.*

20
Old Time, that greatest and longest established spinner of all! . . . His factory is a secret place, his work is noiseless, and his Hands are mutes.
CHARLES DICKENS, *Hard Times.* Bk. i, ch. 14.

21
Father Time is not always a hard parent, and, though he tarries for none of his children, often lays his hand lightly on those who have used him well.
CHARLES DICKENS, *Barnaby Rudge,* ch. 2.

22
He who anticipates his century is generally persecuted when living, and is always pilfered when dead.
BENJAMIN DISRAELI, *Vivian Grey.*

23
Times goes, you say? Ah no!
Alas, Time stays, *we* go.
AUSTIN DOBSON, *The Paradox of Time.*

1
When a man sits with a pretty girl for an hour, it seems like a minute. But let him sit on a hot stove for a minute—and it's longer than any hour. That's relativity.
ALBERT EINSTEIN. (*The New York Times,* Apr. 19, 1955; quoted in his obituary.)

2
Kill time and you kill your career.
B. C. FORBES, *Epigrams.*

3
What's the use of watching? A watched pot never boils.
MRS. (ELIZABETH CLEGHORN) GASKELL, *Mary Barton,* ch. 31.

4
Time is . . . Time was . . . Time is past.
ROBERT GREENE, *The Honorable Historie of Friar Bacon.*

5
The twentieth century is only the nineteenth speaking with a slightly American accent.
PHILIP GUEDALLA.

6
"Man's Life is all-too-brief!" Man writes in sorrow;
Yet man will sigh, "I wish it were Tomorrow!"
ARTHUR GUITERMAN, *A Poet's Proverbs.*

7
Time is a circus always packing up and moving away.
BEN HECHT, *Charlie.*

8
Pick my left pocket of its silver dime,
But spare the right,—it holds my golden time!
OLIVER WENDELL HOLMES, *A Rhymed Lesson,* l. 324.

9
Old Time, in whose bank we deposit our notes,
Is a miser who always wants guineas for groats;
He keeps all his customers still in arrears
By lending them minutes and charging them years.
OLIVER WENDELL HOLMES, *Our Banker,* st. 1.

10
People find life entirely too time-consuming.
STANISLAW J. LEC, *Unkempt Thoughts,* tr. from the Polish by JACEK GALASKA.

11
Time is a great legalizer, even in the field of morals.
H. L. MENCKEN, *A Book of Prefaces.* Ch. iv, sec. 6.

12
Go, sir, gallop, and don't forget that the world was made in six days. You can ask me for anything you like, except time.
NAPOLEON BONAPARTE. (R. M. JOHNSTON, *The Corsican.*)

13
Poets and kings are but the clerks of Time.
EDWIN ARLINGTON ROBINSON, *The Clerks.*

14
The pace of events is so fast that unless we can find some way to keep our sights on tomorrow, we cannot expect to be in touch with today.
DEAN RUSK, quoted in *Time.*

15
In the posteriors of this day, which the rude multitude call the afternoon.
WILLIAM SHAKESPEARE, *Love's Labour's Lost.* Act v, sc. 1.

16
Time himself is bald and therefore to the world's end will have bald followers.
WILLIAM SHAKESPEARE, *The Comedy of Errors.* Act ii, sc. 2.

17
Time: That which man is always trying to kill, but which ends in killing him.
HERBERT SPENCER, *Definitions.*

18
Dollars cannot buy yesterday.
ADMIRAL HAROLD R. STARK, commenting, as Chief of Naval Operations, about a $300,000,000 appropriation for improving the protection of U.S. warships. (*Time,* Dec. 16, 1940, p. 26.)

TIMIDITY

See also Fear, Meekness

19
He that's afraid of every grass must not sleep in a meadow.
GABRIEL HARVEY, *Marginalia* (*1590*).

20
Faint heart never won fair lady or sold any life insurance.
FRANK MCKINNEY (KIN) HUBBARD, *Abe Martin's Primer.*

21
My dear McClellan:
If you don't want to use the army I should like to borrow it for a while.
Yours respectfully,
A. Lincoln.
ABRAHAM LINCOLN, *Letter* to General McClellan, hinting that the general was too inactive and reluctant to engage the enemy in combat.

TOLERANCE

22
Sir Roger told them, with the air of a man who would not give his judgment rashly,

that much might be said on both sides.
JOSEPH ADDISON, *The Spectator*, No. 122.

1
Bigotry murders religion to frighten fools
with her ghost.
C. C. COLTON, *Lacon*.

2
Wouldn't it be a helluva joke if all this were
really burnt cork and you people were being
tolerant for nuthin'?
DICK GREGORY, *From the Back of the Bus*.

3
A liberal Southerner is one who'll go to see
a performance of *Green Pastures,* providing
it has an all white cast.
DICK GREGORY, *From the Back of the Bus*.

4
I live in one of those inter-racial apartments.
In fact, I was the first one in. They don't
care *what* color you are, so long as your
money is green.
DICK GREGORY, *From the Back of the Bus*.

5
On the other hand, if you've liked the book
—don't tell your friends. Just take me to
lunch when it's *not* Brotherhood Week.
DICK GREGORY, *From the Back of the Bus*.

6
I play it cool
   And dig all jive.
That's the reason
   I stay alive.

My motto,
   As I live and learn,
      is:
*Dig and be Dug
   In return.*
LANGSTON HUGHES, *The Book of Negro
Humor.*

7
If we must disagree, let's disagree without
being disagreeable.
LYNDON B. JOHNSON, *Remark,* at the California State Democratic convention,
Aug., 1963. He was seeking to assuage
discord within the party. (*Time,* Aug.
23, 1963, p. 18.)

8
He admits that there are two sides to every
question—his own and the wrong side.
CHANNING POLLOCK.

9
We are in favor of tolerance, but it is a
very difficult thing to tolerate the intolerant
and impossible to tolerate the intolerable.
GEORGE D. PRENTICE.

10
You must never disagree with a man while
you are facing him. Go around behind him
and look the same way he is looking and
you will see that things look different from
what they do when you are facing him.
Look over his shoulder and get his view-
point, then go back and face him and you
will have a different idea.
WILL ROGERS, *Autobiography.*

TRADE

11
It takes two to make love and two partners
to make trade agreements work. Unrequited
trade or unrequited exports pay no better
than unrequited love.
R. A. BUTLER, Chancellor of the Exche-
quer. Comparison of affairs of state to
affairs of love. *News summaries,* Jan.
29, 1954.

12
The law has been a little slow in coming to
the protection of cheese—probably because
the many varieties of cheese have been
thoroughly able to take care of themselves.
It would seem, for example, that limburger
cheese is endowed by nature with means of
defense that requires very little assistance
from an act of Congress.
REPRESENTATIVE JONATHAN P. DOLLIVER
of Iowa.

13
What is more incongruous than the admin-
istering of custom-house oaths and the
searching of trunks and handbags under
the shadow of "Liberty, Enlightening the
World"?
HENRY GEORGE, *Protection or Free Trade,*
ch. 9.

14
The tariff is the Gulf Stream of politics. It
flows through both parties, and each is trying to catch the other in bathing and steal
his clothes.
PATRICK FRANCIS MURPHY, *Speech* at
Manhattan Club.

TRAVEL

15
A rolling stone gathers no moss and there-
fore will not be derided as a moss-back.
Roll as much as possible.
GEORGE ADE, *Fables.*

16
The penguin flies backwards because he
doesn't care to see where he's going, but
wants to see where he's been.
FRED ALLEN, *The Backward View.*

17
At Hot Springs the story is told of a Virginia lady who became extremely irritated
with the mass of tourists visiting her state;
she was promptly reminded of the fact that

those tourists brought more than one hundred million dollars a year to the state of Virginia. "But why," she protested, "couldn't they just *send* the money?"

CLEVELAND AMORY, *The Last Resorts.*

1
There was a young lady named Bright
Who traveled much faster than light,
    She started one day
    In the relative way,
And returned on the previous night.

ANONYMOUS.

2
In America there are two classes of travel
—first class and with children.

ROBERT BENCHLEY, *Kiddie-Kar Travel.*

3
The conductor when he receives a fare,
Must punch in the presence of the passen-
    jare;
    A blue trip slip for an 8-cent fare,
    A buff trip slip for a 6-cent fare,
    A pink trip slip for a 3-cent fare,
All in the presence of the passenjare.
Punch, boys, punch, punch with care,
All in the presence of the passenjare.

ISAAC H. BROMLEY, originally published
in the *New York Tribune,* Sept. 27,
1875. Erroneously attributed to Mark
Twain, because of his article, *A Literary
Nightmare,* in *The Atlantic Monthly,*
for February 1876 (p. 167), in which
he describes the sufferings inflicted upon
him by this jingle, which, as he states,
he "came across in a newspaper, a little
while ago," and which he quotes in-
exactly. The lines were based upon an
actual sign seen by Bromley in a street-
car. (From STEVENSON's *Home Book of
Quotations.*)

4
Airline clerk about child sitting in waiting
room: "He's waiting for a flight with an
all-cartoon movie."

JOE E. BURESCH, *Caption* for cartoon,
National Enquirer.

5
Travelling is the ruin of all happiness.
There's no looking at a building here, after
seeing Italy.

FANNY BURNEY, *Cecilia,* bk. 2.

6
The only way of catching a train I ever
discovered is to miss the train before.

GILBERT KEITH CHESTERTON.

7
How much a dunce, that has been sent to
    roam,
Excels a dunce that has been kept at home.

WILLIAM COWPER, *The Progress of Error.*

8
. . . English trains apparently make a habit
of always going toward London, and when
they get there, are taken apart and mailed
back to Land's End and Edinburgh.

MARGARET HALSEY, *With Malice Toward
Some.*

9
From a purely tourist standpoint, Oxford
is overpowering, being so replete with architecture and history and anecdote that
the visitor's mind feels dribbling and helpless, as with an over-large mouthful of
nougat.

MARGARET HALSEY, *With Malice Toward
Some.*

10
All of Stratford, in fact, suggests powdered
history—add hot water and stir and you
have a delicious, nourishing Shakespeare.

MARGARET HALSEY, *With Malice Toward
Some.*

11
Through all the shrines [at Stratford-on-
Avon] surge English and American tourists,
either people who have read too much
Shakespeare at the expense of good, healthy
detective stories or people who have never
read him at all and hope to get the same
results by bumping their heads on low
beams.

MARGARET HALSEY, *With Malice Toward
Some.*

12
Surely never did small hero experience
greater misadventures than I did on the first
two or three days of my travelling. Twice
did my horse run away with me, and greatly
endanger the breaking my neck on the first
day. On the second I drove two hours
through as copious a rain as ever I have
seen, without meeting with a single house
to which I could repair for shelter. On the
third, in going through Pamunkey, being
unacquainted with the ford I passed through
water so deep as to run over the cushion as
I sat on it, and, to add to the danger, at
that instant one wheel mounted a rock which
I am confident was as high as the axle, and
rendered it necessary for me to exercise all
my skill in the doctrine of gravity in order
to prevent the center of gravity from being
left unsupported, the consequence of which
would, according to Bob Carter's opinion,
have been the corruption of myself, chair
and all into the water. . . . I confess that
on this occasion I was seized with violent
hydrophobia. . . .

THOMAS JEFFERSON, *Letter* to John Page,
May 25, 1776.

1
Worth seeing? Yes; but not worth going to see.
> SAMUEL JOHNSON, in reference to the Giant's Causeway. BOSWELL's *Life*, Oct. 12, 1779.

2
Mother set facing the front end of the train, as it makes her giddy to ride backwards. I set facing her, which does not affect me.
> RING LARDNER, *The Golden Honeymoon.*

3
The traveller of today "sees France" by tearing through it in a closed car over a straight cement highway at the rate of sixty miles an hour; by stopping in "international" hotels run in imitation of American methods, where all the waiters talk English; and, as a diversion, playing bridge with other English-speaking tourists, and looking at American moving pictures and English newspapers.
> STEPHEN LEACOCK, *Charles Dickens.*

4
A man travels the world over in search of what he needs and returns home to find it.
> GEORGE MOORE, *The Brook Kerith.*

5
I have just arrived back home from Europe with 850,000 other half-wits who think that a summer not spent among the decay and mortification of the Old World is a summer squandered.
> WILL ROGERS, *Autobiography.*

6
There was a young lady of Spain
Who often got sick on a train,
Not once and again
But again and again
And again and again and again.
> Quoted by OSBERT SITWELL as a favorite of John Sargent.

7
When I was very young and the urge to be someplace else was on me, I was assured by mature people that maturity would cure this itch. When years described me as mature, the remedy prescribed was middle age. In middle age I was assured that greater age would calm my fever, and now that I am fifty-eight perhaps senility will do the job.
> JOHN STEINBECK, *Travels with Charley,* pt. 1.

8
It is not worth the while to go round the world to count the cats in Zanzibar.
> HENRY D. THOREAU, *Walden*, ch. 18.

9
Have you ever seen a family of geese just back from Europe—or Yurrup, as they pronounce it? They never talk *to* you, of course, being strangers, but they talk to each other

and *at* you till you are pretty nearly distracted with their clatter; till you are sick of their ocean experiences; their mispronounced foreign names; their dukes and emperors; their trivial adventures; their pointless reminiscences; till you are sick of their imbecile faces and their relentless clack, and wish it had pleased Providence to leave the clapper out of their empty skulls.
> MARK TWAIN, *Back From "Yurrup."*

10
Commuter—one who spends his life
In riding to and from his wife;
A man who shaves and takes a train
And then rides back to shave again.
> E. B. WHITE, *The Commuter.*

TREASON

11
Treason doth never prosper, what's the reason?
For if it prosper, none dare call it treason.
> SIR JOHN HARINGTON, *Of Treason. (Epigrams.* Bk. iv, epig. 259.)

12
Pension: An allowance made to anyone without an equivalent. In England it is generally understood to mean pay given to a state hireling for treason to his country.
> SAMUEL JOHNSON, *Dictionary.*

TREE

13
Why, out in the Paul Bunyan country—that's the country that runs from Michigan through Minnesota clear out to Oregon and the Pacific—they say the trees grow so high it takes a man a whole week to see the top of them.
> MAX ADELER (CHARLES HEBER CLARK), *Ten Tall Tales.*

14
Except during the nine months before he draws his first breath, no man manages his affairs as well as a tree does.
> BERNARD SHAW, *Maxims for Revolutionists.*

TRIFLES

15
Better a louse in the pot than no flesh at all.
> JOHN CLARKE, *Paroemiologia.*

16
And noting that both Lincoln and [Adlai E.] Stevenson came from Springfield, Illinois, Ike punned: "Adlai's no rail-splitter, just a hair-splitter."
> PAUL STEINER, *The Stevenson Wit & Wisdom.* Referring to Dwight D. Eisenhower.

1
He that despiseth small things will perish by
little and little.
> RALPH WALDO EMERSON, *Essays, First
> Series: Prudence.*

2
If we take a farthing from a thousand
pounds, it will be a thousand pounds no
longer.
> OLIVER GOLDSMITH, *The Citizen of the
> World*, No. 27.

3
No harm befalls the granary
If a poor ant obtains half a grain.
> *Oriental Romances*, ed. by MANUEL KOM-
> ROFF: *The Three Deceitful Women*,
> trans. from the Persian by EDWARD
> REHATSEK.

4
Little drops of water poured into the milk,
give the milkman's daughter lovely gowns of
silk. Little grains of sugar mingled with the
sand, make the grocer's assets swell to beat
the band.
> WALT MASON, *Little Things.*

5
A hole is nothing at all, but you can break
your neck in it.
> AUSTIN O'MALLEY.

TROUBLE

6
Perhaps statistics would show that most
calamities never happen.
> GEORGE ABBOTT, *Mister Abbott.*

7
Our disputants put me in mind of the
scuttlefish, that when he is unable to extri-
cate himself, blackens the water about him
till he becomes invisible.
> JOSEPH ADDISON, *The Spectator*, No. 476.

8
There is nothing in the world to which
God's creatures can't become accustomed.
Our prisoners had grown so used to their
troubles that they now thought things were
as they should be, just like the proverbial
worm that has made its home in horseradish
and thinks it sweet.
> SHOLOM ALEICHEM, *The Pair.*

9
Never play cards with a man called Doc.
Never eat at a place called Mom's. Never
sleep with a woman whose troubles are
worse than your own.
> NELSON ALGREN, quoted in *Newsweek*,
> July 2, 1956.

10
Misfortunes and twins never come singly.
> JOSH BILLINGS.

11
Misfortunes come on wings and depart on
foot.
> H. G. BOHN, *Handbook of Proverbs*, 452.

12
Afflictions induce callosities.
> SIR THOMAS BROWNE, *Hydriotaphia: Urn
> Burial.*

13
The biggest problem in the world
Could have been solved when it was small.
> WITTER BYNNER, *The Way of Life Ac-
> cording to Lao-tzu.*

14
Most of our misfortunes are more support-
able than the comments of our friends upon
them.
> C. C. COLTON, *Lacon*, vol. 1.

15
Oh, a trouble's a ton, or a trouble's an ounce,
Or a trouble is what you make it,
And it isn't the fact that you're hurt that
    counts,
But only how did you take it?
> EDMUND VANCE COOKE, *How Did You
> Die?*

16
Never go out to meet trouble. If you will
just sit still, nine times out of ten someone
will intercept it before it reaches you.
> CALVIN COOLIDGE.

17
In trouble to be troubled
Is to have your trouble doubled.
> DANIEL DEFOE, *Further Adventures of
> Robinson Crusoe.*

18
What is a romantic? One who, when life is
too banal or too lazy to manufacture tragedy
for him, creates it artificially, thus getting
himself into the hot water he himself has
boiled.
> CLIFTON FADIMAN, *The Selected Writings
> of Clifton Fadiman* (1955).

19
Big fleas have little fleas to plague, perplex
    and bite 'em,
Little fleas have lesser fleas, and so *ad
    infinitum.*
> R. R. FIEDLER, *Pulex Irritans.* Also in
> variant form by JONATHAN SWIFT AND
> AUGUSTUS DE MORGAN.

20
You have no idea how big the other fellow's
troubles are.
> B. C. FORBES, *Epigrams.*

21
W'en you see a man in woe,
Walk right up and say "hullo."
Say "hullo" and "how d'ye do,"
"How's the world a-usin' you?"
> SAM WALTER FOSS, *Hullo.*

1

To bear other people's afflictions, every one has courage enough to spare.

BENJAMIN FRANKLIN, *Poor Richard*, 1740.

2

I have had troubles in my life but the worst of them never came.

JAMES A. GARFIELD, *Remark*.

3

Women like to sit down with trouble as if it were knitting.

ELLEN GLASGOW, *The Sheltered Life*.

4

Ay, people are generally calm at the misfortunes of others.

OLIVER GOLDSMITH, *She Stoops to Conquer*, Act 3.

5

"Law, Brer Tarrypin," sez Brer Fox, sezee, "you ain't see no trouble yit. Ef you wanter see sho' nuff trouble, you des oughter go 'longer me; I'm de man w'at kin show yer trouble," sezee.

JOEL CHANDLER HARRIS, *Nights with Uncle Remus*, ch. 17.

6

If pleasures are greatest in anticipation, just remember that this is also true of trouble.

ELBERT HUBBARD, *Epigrams*.

7

No one has ever been turned down yit that started out t' borrow trouble.

FRANK MCKINNEY (KIN) HUBBARD, *Abe Martin's Primer*.

8

A man in trouble *must* be possessed, somehow, of a woman.

HENRY JAMES, *The Ambassadors*.

9

Too often our Washington reflex is to discover a problem and then throw money at it, hoping it will somehow go away.

SENATOR KENNETH KEATING, quoted in *The New York Times*, Dec. 24, 1961.

10

Better never trouble Trouble
Until Trouble troubles you;
For you only make your trouble
Double-trouble when you do.

DAVID KEPPEL, *Trouble*.

11

Hot and bothered.

RUDYARD KIPLING, *Rectorial Address*, St. Andrew's, Scotland, Oct. 10, 1923.

12

Borrow trouble for yourself, if that's your nature, but don't lend it to your neighbors.

RUDYARD KIPLING, *Rewards and Fairies: Cold Iron*.

13

When Prince de Joinville asked what was his policy, he replied: "I have none. I pass my life preventing the storm from blowing down the tent, and I drive in the pegs as fast as they are pulled up."

CARL SANDBURG, *Abraham Lincoln: The Prairie Years and the War Years*, ch. 34.

14

He can always be counted upon to make an impossible situation infinitely worse.

BRANCH RICKEY, on Leo Durocher as a baseball manager.

15

The whole of my life has passed like a razor—in hot water or a scrape.

SYDNEY SMITH.

16

Never answer a telephone that rings before breakfast. It is sure to be one of three types of persons that is calling: a strange man in Minneapolis who has been up all night and is phoning collect; a salesman who wants to come over and demonstrate a new, patented combination dictaphone and music box that also cleans rugs; or a woman out of one's past.

JAMES THURBER, *Lanterns and Lances*.

17

When a man fronts catastrophe on the road, he looks in his purse—but a woman looks in her mirror.

MARGARET TURNBULL, *The Left Lady*, p. 44.

18

I am an old man and have known a great many troubles, but most of them never happened.

MARK TWAIN.

TRUST

19

Where Mistrust now has sway, put Trust to dwell,
And where Trust is, Mistrust; and all is well.

ARISTOPHANES, *The Frogs*, tr. by GILBERT MURRAY.

20

Never trust a man who speaks well of everybody.

CHURTON COLLINS, *Aphorisms*.

21

Trust everybody—but cut the cards.

FINLEY PETER DUNNE, *Mr. Dooley Remembers*.

22

Trust him no further than you can throw him.

THOMAS FULLER, *Gnomologia*, No. 5286.

1
In choosing a wife and buying a sword we ought not to trust another.
  GEORGE HERBERT, *Jacula Prudentum*, No. 486.

2
He's mad that trusts in the tameness of a wolf, a horse's health, a boy's love, or a whore's oath.
  WILLIAM SHAKESPEARE, *King Lear*. Act iii, sc. 6.

3
IN GOD WE TRUST
Others pay cash.
  Sign frequently seen in restaurants and bars in the United States. It was probably first seen in the 18th century. It is also the title of a book by Jean Shepherd.

TRUTH

See also Lies and Lying

4
Yet the deepest truths are best read between the lines, and, for the most part, refuse to be written.
  AMOS BRONSON ALCOTT, *Concord Days: June.*

5
You can't make the Duchess of Windsor into Rebecca of Sunnybrook Farm. The facts of life are very stubborn things.
  CLEVELAND AMORY, on Duchess of Windsor's memoirs, news reports of Oct. 6, 1955.

6
A truth that's told with bad intent
Beats all the lies you can invent.
  WILLIAM BLAKE, *Auguries of Innocence.*

7
Truth has a way of shifting under pressure.
  CURTIS BOK, *Address*, National Book Awards. (*Saturday Review*, Feb. 13, 1954.)

8
Facts that are not frankly faced have a habit of stabbing us in the back.
  SIR HAROLD BOWDEN, quoted in *Reader's Digest*, Sept., 1966.

9
For truth there is no deadline.
  HEYWOOD BROUN, *The Nation*, Dec. 30, 1939.

10
What makes all doctrines plain and clear?
About two hundred pounds a year.
And that which was proved true before
  Prove false again? Two hundred more.
  SAMUEL BUTLER, *Hudibras*, pt. 3.

11
I don't believe it is possible to live with total truth. Imagine life *without* the little lies—the social fibs that save us so much pain. Truth or tact? You have to choose. Most times they're not compatible.
  EDDIE CANTOR, *The Way I See It.*

12
Can there be a more horrible object in existence than an eloquent man not speaking the truth?
  THOMAS CARLYLE, *Address*, University of Edinburgh, 1866.

13
In war-time . . . truth is so precious that she should always be attended by a bodyguard of lies.
  SIR WINSTON CHURCHILL, *The Second World War*, vol. 5: *Closing the Ring.*

14
They decided that all liars should be whipped.
And a man came along and told them the truth.
And they hanged him.
  T. W. H. CROSLAND, *Little Stories.*

15
Chase after the truth like all hell and you'll free yourself, even though you never touch its coat-tails.
  CLARENCE DARROW, *Writing on Voltaire.*

16
Truth is such a rare thing, it is delightful to tell it.
  EMILY DICKINSON, *Letter* to Thomas Wentworth Higginson, Aug., 1870.

17
Truth is beautiful. Without doubt; and so are lies.
  RALPH WALDO EMERSON, *Journals*. Vol. iii, p. 437.

18
No man speaks the truth or lives a true life two minutes together.
  RALPH WALDO EMERSON, *Journals*. Vol. iii, p. 455.

19
The truth doesn't hurt unless it ought to.
  B. C. FORBES, *Epigrams.*

20
Craft must have clothes, but truth loves to go naked.
  THOMAS FULLER, *Gnomologia.*

21
Truth always lags behind, limping along on the arm of time.
  BALTASAR GRACIAN, *The Art of Worldly Wisdom.*

22
The truth is so simple that it is regarded as pretentious banality.
  DAG HAMMARSKJÖLD, *Remark* in 1955.

1
Truth: A very painful irritant.
OLIVER HERFORD, *Cupid's Cyclopedia.*

2
Interesting things are never true . . . and the truth is only convincing when it is told by an experienced liar.
JOHN OLIVER HOBBES, *Life and Tomorrow.*

3
Truth is for other worlds, and hope for this;
The cheating future lends the present's bliss.
OLIVER WENDELL HOLMES, *The Old Player.*

4
No generalization is wholly true, not even this one.
Attributed to OLIVER WENDELL HOLMES, JR.

5
Telling the truth to people who misunderstand you is generally promoting falsehood.
ANTHONY HOPE, *The Dolly Dialogues,* No. 14.

6
Truth is always at the bottom of a grave.
JAMES G. HUNEKER, *Iconoclasts,* p. 63.

7
It is always the best policy to speak the truth, unless of course you are an exceptionally good liar.
JEROME K. JEROME, *The Idler,* Feb. 1892.

8
A man would rather have a hundred lies told of him than one truth which he does not wish should be told.
SAMUEL JOHNSON, BOSWELL'S *Life,* 1773.

9
Every man has a right to utter what he thinks truth, and every man has a right to knock him down for it.
SAMUEL JOHNSON, BOSWELL'S *Life.*

10
The greater the truth the greater the libel.
EDWARD LAW, 1st Baron Ellenborough.

11
Truth will always be naked, even when turned out in the latest fashion.
STANISLAW J. LEC, *Unkempt Thoughts,* tr. from the Polish by JACEK GALASKA.

12
Don't be a snob. Never lie when truth is more profitable.
STANISLAW J. LEC, *Unkempt Thoughts,* tr. from the Polish by JACEK GALASKA.

13
It is hard to believe that a man is telling the truth when you know you would lie if you were in his place.
H. L. MENCKEN.

14
Truth is not a diet But a condiment.
CHRISTOPHER MORLEY, *Veritas vos Damnabit.*

15
A bare assertion is not necessarily the naked truth.
GEORGE D. PRENTICE.

16
Truth consists of paradoxes and a paradox is two facts that stand on opposite hilltops and across the intervening valley call each other liars.
CARL SANDBURG, *Incidentals.*

17
Truth telling is not compatible with the defense of the realm.
BERNARD SHAW, *Heartbreak House:* preface.

18
The truth is the one thing nobody will believe.
BERNARD SHAW, *The Man of Destiny.*

19
My way of joking is to tell the truth. It's the funniest joke in the world.
BERNARD SHAW, *John Bull's Other Island,* Act 2.

20
Burgoyne: Is William—Maindeck and so on —a man of his word?
Richard: Is he selling you anything?
Burgoyne: No.
Richard: Then you may depend on him.
BERNARD SHAW, *The Devil's Disciple,* Act 3.

21
You can get away with anything nowadays except the truth. Dare to tell the truth and you are at once accused of being an outrageous liar.
BERNARD SHAW, quoted in *Days with Bernard Shaw* by STEPHEN WINSTEN.

22
If you want to be thought a liar always tell the truth.
LOGAN PEARSALL SMITH.

23
Considering that natural disposition in many men to lie, and in multitudes to believe, I have been perplexed what to do with that maxim so frequent in everybody's mouth, that truth will at last prevail.
JONATHAN SWIFT, *The Examiner,* No. 15 (1710).

24
In every generation there has to be some fool who will speak the truth as he sees it.
H. N. TAYLOR, *Interview, The New York Times,* Feb. 2, 1959.

1
Tell the truth or trump—but get the trick.
MARK TWAIN, *Pudd'nhead Wilson's Calendar*.

2
Truth is stranger than fiction—to some people, but I am measurably familiar with it.
MARK TWAIN, *Pudd'nhead Wilson's New Calendar*.

3
I don't mind what the opposition say of me, so long as they don't tell the truth about me; but when they descend to telling the truth about me, I consider that that is taking an unfair advantage.
MARK TWAIN, *Speech* in Hartford, Conn., Oct. 26, 1880.

4
Facts, or what a man believes to be facts, are delightful. . . . Get your facts first, and then you can distort them as much as you please.
MARK TWAIN. (KIPLING, *From Sea to Sea*, letter 37.)

5
The English are always degrading truth into facts. When a truth becomes a fact it loses all its intellectual value.
OSCAR WILDE, *Saturday Review*, Nov. 17, 1894.

6
Truth is a narrow lane all full of quags,
Leading to broken heads, abuse, and rags.
JOHN WOLCOT, *More Lyric Odes*, No. 9.

U

UMBRELLA

7
Umbrellas, like faces, acquire a certain sympathy with the individual who carries them.
J. W. FERRIER AND R. L. STEVENSON, *The Philosophy of Umbrellas*.

8
"Where is my toadstool?" loud he lamented.
And that's how umbrellas were first invented.
OLIVER HERFORD, *The Elf and the Dormouse*.

UNITY

9
Yes, we must, indeed, all hang together, or, most assuredly, we shall all hang separately.
BENJAMIN FRANKLIN, *Retort* to John Hancock, who, in his address to the Continental Congress, just previous to the signing of the Declaration of Independence, had said, "It is too late to pull different ways; the members of the Continental Congress must hang together."

10
We do not usually look for allies when we love. Indeed, we often look on those who love with us as rivals and trespassers. But we always look for allies when we hate.
ERIC HOFFER, *The True Believer*.

UNIVERSE

11
A man said to the universe:

"Sir, I exist!"
"However," replied the universe,
"The fact has not created in me
A sense of obligation."
STEPHEN CRANE, *War Is Kind*, pt. 4.

12
The universe is not composed of newts only; it has its Newtons.
HARRY EMERSON FOSDICK, *Easter Sermon*.

13
"I accept the universe" is reported to have been a favorite utterance of our New England transcendentalist, Margaret Fuller; and when some one repeated this phrase to Thomas Carlyle, his sardonic comment is said to have been, "Gad! she'd better."
WILLIAM JAMES, *The Varieties of Religious Experience*.

14
A handful of sand is an anthology of the universe.
DAVID MCCORD, *Once and for All:* introduction.

15
My theology, briefly, is that the universe was dictated but not signed.
CHRISTOPHER MORLEY.

16
But oh, those heavenly moments when I feel this three-dimensioned universe too small to contain my Attributes; when a sense of the divine Ipseity invades me; when I know that my voice is the voice of Truth, and my umbrella God's umbrella!
LOGAN PEARSALL SMITH.

V

VAGABOND

1
A hobo is a man who builds palaces and
lives in shacks,
He builds Pullmans and rides the rods . . .
He reaps the harvest and stands in the bread
line.
GODFREY IRWIN, *American Tramp and
Underworld Slang.*

2
The vagabond, when rich, is called a tourist.
PAUL RICHARD, *The Scourge of Christ*, p.
40.

3
Nature makes us vagabonds, the world
makes us respectable.
ALEXANDER SMITH, *Dreamthorp.*

4
Oh, why don't you work like other men do?
How the hell can I work when there's no
work to do?
Hallelujah, I'm a bum, hallelujah, bum again,
Hallelujah, give us a handout to revive us
again.
UNKNOWN, *Hallelujah, I'm a Bum.*

VANITY

See also Conceit, Egotism

5
It was prettily devised of Aesop: The fly
sat upon the axle-tree of the chariot-wheel
and said, what a dust I do raise!
FRANCIS BACON, *Essays: Of Vain Glory.*

6
Pampered vanity is a better thing, perhaps,
than starved pride.
JOANNA BAILLIE, *The Election.* Act ii, sc. 2.

7
To say that a man is vain means merely that
he is pleased with the effect he produces on
other people. A conceited man is satisfied
with the effect he produces on himself.
MAX BEERBOHM, *Quia Imperfectum.*

8
In heaven I yearn for knowledge, account all
else inanity;
On earth I confess an itch for the praise of
fools that's vanity.
ROBERT BROWNING, *Solomon and Balkis.*

9
The sixth insatiable sense.
THOMAS CARLYLE, *The French Revolution.*
Reference to vanity.

10
And by my grave you'd pray to have me
back

So I could see how well you looked in black.
MARCO CARSON, *To Any Woman.*

11
Vanity is the more odious and shocking to
everybody, because everybody, without exception, has vanity; and two vanities can
never love one another.
LORD CHESTERFIELD, *Letters*, Jan. 14,
1766.

12
Vanity, like murder, will out.
HANNAH COWLEY, *The Belle's Stratagem.*
Act I, sc. 4.

13
What dotage will not vanity maintain?
What web too weak to catch a modern
brain?
WILLIAM COWPER, *Expostulation.*

14
The fellow who fancies himself the "whole
cheese" is at least a piece of it.
B. C. FORBES, *Epigrams.*

15
Why does a blind man's wife paint herself?
BENJAMIN FRANKLIN, *Poor Richard*, 1736.

16
Virtue would not go so far if vanity did
not bear it company. (La vertu n'irait pas
si loin si la vanite ne lui tenait compagne.)
OLD FRENCH PROVERB.

17
Vanity is possible today only to those who
close their minds.
THOMAS GRIFFITH, *The Waist-High Culture.*

18
Vanity is the mother, and affectation is the
darling daughter; vanity is the sin, and affectation is the punishment; the first may
be called the root of self-love, the other the
fruit.
LORD HALIFAX, *Works.*

19
The dominating instincts in mankind are
fear and vanity, and many thoughtful people are of the opinion that greater accuracy
is served if they are mentioned in reverse
order.
ALEXANDER KING, *Rich Man, Poor Man,
Freud and Fruit*, ch. 14.

20
Every stink that fights the ventilator thinks
it is Don Quixote.
STANISLAW J. LEC, *Unkempt Thoughts*, tr.
from the Polish by JACEK GALASKA.

1
There are many spurs to a woman's vanity, but declared indifference is the sharpest of them all.
MAX PEMBERTON, *The Lodestar.*

2
Vanity dies hard; in some obstinate cases it outlives the man.
ROBERT LOUIS STEVENSON, *Prince Otto.*

3
To be vain is rather a mark of humility than pride . . . Whoever desires the character of a proud man ought to conceal his vanity.
JONATHAN SWIFT, *Works,* vol. 3.

4
Life without vanity is almost impossible.
LEO TOLSTOY, *The Kreutzer Sonata,* ch. 23.

5
He thinks only of his being a frog, and forgets his having once been a tadpole.
UNKNOWN, Korean proverb, in *Oriental Humor,* ed. by R. H. BLYTH.

VICE

See also Sin

6
It is good to be without vices, but it is not good to be without temptation.
WALTER BAGEHOT, *Biographical Studies.*

7
There is scarcely a social vice that does not produce good.
BERNARD BERENSON, *Diaries* (1956).

8
Virtue is dull and disappointing: vice—especially unimaginative vice—is disappointingly dull.
G. B. BURGIN, *Which Woman?*

9
It is the function of vice to keep virtue within reasonable bounds.
SAMUEL BUTLER, *Notebooks.*

10
"Vice," said Mr. Dooley, "is a creature of such heijous mien, as Hogan says, that th' more ye see it th' better ye like it."
FINLEY PETER DUNNE, *The Crusade Against Vice.*

11
A policeman goes after vice as an officer of the law and comes away as a philosopher.
FINLEY PETER DUNNE, *Mr. Dooley Remembers.*

12
Was it Bonaparte who said that he found vices very good patriots?—"he got five million from the love of brandy, and he should be glad to know which of the virtues would pay him as much." Tobacco and opium have broad backs, and will cheerfully carry the load of armies.
RALPH WALDO EMERSON, *Society and Solitude: Civilization.*

13
We do not despise all those who have vices; but we despise those who are without any virtue.
OLD FRENCH PROVERB.

14
I've always been given to understand that men only abandon their vices when advancing years have made them a burden rather than a pleasure.
W. SOMERSET MAUGHAM, *The Constant Wife.*

15
I prefer an accommodating vice to an obstinate virtue.
MOLIÈRE, *Amphitryon.*

16
To vice, innocence must always seem only a superior kind of chicanery.
OUIDA, *Wisdom, Wit, and Pathos.*

17
Our habit of disguising our vices by giving polite names to the offenses we intend to commit, does not, unfortunately for my own comfort, impose on me.
BERNARD SHAW, *The Doctor's Dilemma:* preface.

18
Men do not persevere with their vices because they admire them, but because they are weary.
J. M. STUART YOUNG, *Passion's Peril.*

19
Even vice, once a habit, is conventional and stupid.
UNKNOWN, *A Woman.*

VICTORY

20
Anybody can win, unless there happens to be a second entry.
GEORGE ADE.

21
If we win, nobody will care. If we lose, then there will be nobody to care.
SIR WINSTON CHURCHILL, *Speech,* House of Commons, June 25, 1941.

22
Our defeats are but stepping-stones to victory, and his victories are but stepping-stones to ruin.
SIR WINSTON CHURCHILL, *Speech* in Edinburgh, Oct. 12, 1942. The reference is to Adolf Hitler.

23
When 'tis an aven thing in the prayin', may

th' best man win . . . an' th' best man will win.
> FINLEY PETER DUNNE, *On Prayers for Victory.*

1
The victor belongs to the spoils.
> F. SCOTT FITZGERALD, *The Beautiful and the Damned.*

2
Truth is with the victor—who, as you know, also controls the historians.
> ROLF HOCHHUTH, *The Deputy.* Act i, sc. 3.

3
Victory is no longer a truth. It is only a word to describe who is left alive in the ruins.
> LYNDON B. JOHNSON, *Speech* in New York City, Feb. 6, 1964.

4
In human history a moral victory is always a disaster. . . .
> H. L. MENCKEN, *The Calamity of Appomattox; American Mercury,* Sept., 1930.

5
Madame Montholon having inquired what troops he considered the best, "Those which are victorious, Madame," replied the Emperor.
> NAPOLEON BONAPARTE. (BOUVIENNE, *Memoirs,* vol. 10.)

6
Another such victory over the Romans, and we are undone.
> PYRRHUS, King of Epirus. Referring to his dearly bought victory at Asculum, 280 B.C. (PLUTARCH, *Lives: Pyrrhus;* ch. 21.) Hence a "Pyrrhic victory," which means one gained at a too great cost.

7
I do not think that winning is the most important thing. I think winning is the only thing.
> BILL VEECK, *Comment* on his long career as a baseball executive.

VIRTUE

See also Chastity, Goodness, Morality

8
Curse on his virtues! They've undone his country.
> JOSEPH ADDISON, *Cato.* Act iv, sc. 4.

9
Virtues are merely bad traits in her character which have not been discovered by the world.
> W. BURTON BALDRY, *Stray Thoughts.*

10
Virtues are all very well so long as they are hidden from the world: but as soon as they become exposed they become merely habits.
> W. BURTON BALDRY, *Stray Thoughts.*

11
Virtue, perhaps, is nothing more than politeness of soul.
> HONORÉ DE BALZAC, *The Physiology of Marriage.*

12
A virtuous woman has in her heart one fibre less or one fibre more than other women; she is either stupid or sublime.
> HONORÉ DE BALZAC, *The Physiology of Marriage.*

13
I think mankind by thee would be less bored
If thou wert not thine own reward.
> JOHN KENDRICK BANGS, *A Hint to Virtue.*

14
Youth should heed the older-witted
When they say, don't go too far—
Now their sins are all committed,
Lord, how virtuous they are!
> WILLIAM BUSCH, *Pious Helen.*

15
Virtue has always been conceived of as victorious resistance to one's vital desire to do this, that or the other.
> JAMES BRANCH CABELL, *Beyond Life,* p. 114.

16
Two men of perfect virtue—the one dead, the other yet unborn.
> CHINESE PROVERB, from *Oriental Humor,* ed. by R. H. BLYTH.

17
Halifax's virtues have done more harm in the world than the vices of hundreds of other people.
> SIR WINSTON CHURCHILL, quoted in *Diaries* by LORD MORAN, Dec. 7, 1947.

18
And he by no uncommon lot
Was fam'd for virtues he had not.
> WILLIAM COWPER, *To the Rev. William Bull,* l. 19.

19
Virtue does not consist so much is abstaining from vice, as in not having an affection for it.
> W. T. ELDRIDGE, *Hilma.*

20
The formula for Utopia on earth remains always the same: to make a necessity of virtue.
> CLIFTON FADIMAN, *The Selected Writings of Clifton Fadiman* (1955).

21
He lives who lives to virtue; men who cast
Their ends for pleasure, do not live, but last.
> ROBERT HERRICK, *On Himself.*

1
Men are virtuous because women are;
women are virtuous from necessity.
E. W. HOWE, *A Letter from Mr. Biggs.*

2
Most virtuous women are like hidden treasures, only safe because nobody looks for them.
FRANÇOIS, DUC DE LA ROCHEFOUCAULD, *Maximes,* No. 368.

3
When we are planning for posterity, we ought to remember that virtue is not hereditary.
THOMAS PAINE, *Common Sense,* ch. 4.

4
Nice women shudder at chorus girls who get presents of valuable jewels, but they can't help thinking how lucky they are.
Reflections of a Bachelor.

5
In a world only peopled by virtues, it is difficult to initiate the possibility of trespass.
C. A. DAWSON SCOTT, *The Story of Anna Beames.*

6
. . . what is virtue but the trade unionism of the married?
BERNARD SHAW, *Don Juan in Hell.*

7
Woman's virtue is man's greatest invention.
CORNELIA OTIS SKINNER, *Paris '90.*

8
Downright virtue, we have all learned from experience, is uneasy. The eyes of the prude are seldom clear.
J. M. STUART YOUNG, *Passion's Peril.*

9
We are double-edged blades, and every time we whet our virtue the return stroke straps our vice.
HENRY D. THOREAU, *Journal,* Feb. 8, 1841.

10
Be good and you will be lonesome.
MARK TWAIN, *Following the Equator:* caption for author's photograph, which is used as a frontispiece.

11
Be virtuous and you will be eccentric.
MARK TWAIN, *Mental Photographs.*

12
When I see angels in pettycoats I'm always sorry they hain't got wings so they kin quietly fly off whare they will be appreshiated.
ARTEMUS WARD, *Piccolomini.*

13
To be good, according to the vulgar standard of goodness, is obviously quite easy. It merely requires a certain amount of

sordid terror, a certain lack of imaginative thought, and a certain low passion for middle class respectability.
OSCAR WILDE, *The Critic as Artist.*

14
How easy it is to be virtuous when we have no inclination to be otherwise.
DOLF WYLLARDE, *Mafoota.*

VOICE

15
The shadow of a sound—a voice without a mouth, and words without a tongue.
PAUL CHATFIELD, *The Tin Trumpet.*

16
There is a tremendous rush of voiceless voices.
NOBUSUKE KISHI, referring to the cancellation of President Eisenhower's visit to Japan. (*The New York Times,* June 17, 1960.)

17
I know a Jew fish crier down on Maxwell Street with a voice like a north wind blowing over corn stubble in January.
CARL SANDBURG, *Fish Crier.*

18
What is more enchanting than the voices of young people when you can't hear what they say?
LOGAN PEARSALL SMITH, *All Trivia.*

VOTING

See also Politics

19
Some women should be given the right to vote.
GEORGE ADE, *Fables.*

20
Susan Anthony was found speaking out for equal votes for women. [Horace] Greeley [editor of the *New York Tribune*] remarked that the ballot went with the bullet, and inquired of Miss Anthony whether she would be willing to have this right. She replied, "Yes, Mr. Greeley, just as you fought in the late [Civil] war, at the end of a goose quill."
KATHERINE ST. GEORGE, Representative from New York, on the 139th anniversary of the birth of Susan B. Anthony, pioneer for women's rights, in 1959.

21
Universal suffrage is the government of a house by its nursery.
OTTO VON BISMARCK.

22
A vote on th' tallysheet is worth two in the box.
FINLEY PETER DUNNE, *Mr. Dooley's Philosophy.*

1
Bad public officials are elected by good citizens who don't vote.
Farmer's Almanac, 1966. See also NATHAN in this section.

2
"Who are you going to vote for, Uncle Willie?" asked Fowler.
"Hell, I never vote *for* anybody," cried Fields, incensed, "I always vote *against.*"
ROBERT LEWIS TAYLOR, *W. C. Fields.*

3
A straw vote only shows which way the hot air blows.
O. HENRY. (*New American Literature*, p. 170.)

4
An unknown wit defined a suffragette as "one who has ceased to be a lady and not yet become a gentleman."
WALTER LORD, *The Good Years.*

5
"Vote early and vote often," advice openly displayed on the election banners in one of our northern cities.
W. P. MILES of South Carolina, *Speech*, House of Representatives, Mar. 31, 1858.

6
Bad officials are elected by good citizens who do not vote.
GEORGE JEAN NATHAN.

7
Washington was besieged by marching, picketing, highly vocal suffragettes . . . I remember the time . . . when they finally cornered one of their die-hard foes, Senator Boies Penrose, the political boss of Pennsylvania, in his office . . . "You might as well be for suffrage, because it's coming," one of them angrily called to him.
"Yes," said Senator Penrose. "So's death, but I don't have to go out to meet it halfway!"
ALBEN W. BARKLEY, *That Reminds Me.*

8
More men have been elected between Sundown and Sunup, than ever were elected between Sunup and Sundown.
WILL ROGERS, *The Illiterate Digest.*

9
. . . with all the mechanical improvements they have in the way of adding machines, and counting machines, they can't seem to invent anything to take the place of the old political mode of counting—two for me and one for you.
WILL ROGERS, *The Illiterate Digest.*

10
Vote: The only commodity that is peddleable without a license.
MARK TWAIN, *More Maxims of Mark.*

VULGARITY

11
Vulgarity is an inadequate conception of the art of living.
MANDELL CREIGHTON, *Life and Letters.*

12
Immodest words admit of no defense,
For want of decency is want of sense.
WENTWORTH DILLON, EARL OF ROSCOMMON, *Essay on Translated Verse*, l. 96.

13
The barbarism of our time is the more appalling because so many people are not really appalled by it.
HERBERT J. MULLER, *Freedom in the Modern World.*

14
Vulgarity in a king flatters the majority of the nation.
BERNARD SHAW, *Maxims for Revolutionists.*

15
Vulgarity is simply the conduct of other people.
OSCAR WILDE, *An Ideal Husband*, Act 3.

W

WANTING AND WANTS

16
Give the people what they think they want.
GEORGE ADE, *Fables.*

17
Much wanting makes many a maid a wanton.
MAXWELL ANDERSON, *Elizabeth the Queen*, Act 1.

18
I want what I want when I want it.
HENRY BLOSSOM, *Mlle. Modiste.* Title of Song (1905).

19
If wishes were horses, beggars would ride.
H. G. BOHN, *Handbook of Proverbs.*

20
If a woman has all she wants of a thing, she doesn't want it.
G. B. BURGIN, *Which Woman?*

1
I did not suffer from any desire to be relieved of my responsibilities. All I wanted was compliance with my wishes after reasonable discussion.
SIR WINSTON CHURCHILL, *The Second World War*, vol. 4: *The Hinge of Fate*.

2
"A man," said Mr. Dooley, "has more fun wishing for the things he hasn't got than enjoying the things he has got."
FINLEY PETER DUNNE, *The Pursuit of Riches*.

3
Some people want champagne and caviar when they should have beer and hot dogs.
DWIGHT D. EISENHOWER, *Speech* to St. Andrews Society, New York City, Nov. 30, 1949.

4
There are three wants which never can be satisfied: that of the rich, who wants something more; that of the sick, who wants something different; and that of the traveller, who says, "Anywhere but here."
RALPH WALDO EMERSON, *Conduct of Life: Considerations by the Way*.

5
Want is a growing giant whom the coat of Have was never large enough to cover.
RALPH WALDO EMERSON, *Conduct of Life: Wealth*.

6
No one should ever give the people what they want. What if the president of a college would say, "Give the students what they want"? He would be laughed out of existence.
MORRIS ERNST, *Address* in St. Louis, July 16, 1964. He was specifically deriding the television network owners who answer criticism of programming by saying they give the public what it wants.

7
Despite my 30 years of research into the feminine soul, I have not yet been able to answer . . . the great question that has never been answered: What does a woman want?
SIGMUND FREUD, quoted by ERNEST JONES, *The Life and Works of Sigmund Freud*, vol. 2.

8
What I most admire about Shakespeare is that he was a guy who said when he made enough he was going to quit, and when he made enough, he did quit.
HARRY GOLDEN, quoting a booking agent in *For 2¢ Plain*.

9
The true use of speech is not so much to express our wants as to conceal them.
OLIVER GOLDSMITH, *The Bee*, No. 3.

10
If mankind had wished for what is right they might have had it long ago.
WILLIAM HAZLITT, *Plain Speaker*.

11
God forgives those who invent what they need.
LILLIAN HELLMAN, *The Little Foxes*, Act 1.

12
What a woman wants is what you're out of.
O. HENRY, *Heart of the West: Cupid à la Carte*.

13
I wish I hadn't broke that dish,
I wish I was a movie-star,
I wish a lot of things, I wish
   That life was like the movies are.
A. P. HERBERT, *It May Be Life, But Ain't It Slow?*

14
Would'st thou both eat thy cake and have it?
GEORGE HERBERT, *The Size*.

15
There are three things which the public will always clamour for, sooner or later: namely, novelty, novelty, novelty.
THOMAS HOOD, *Announcement of Comic Annual for 1836*.

16
Ther's too many folks o' limited means who think that nothin's too good fer 'em.
FRANK MCKINNEY (KIN) HUBBARD, *Abe Martin's Primer*.

17
People who have what they want are very fond of telling people who haven't what they want that they really don't want it.
OGDEN NASH, *The Terrible People*.

18
Content is mostly due to sleepiness.
Reflections of a Bachelor.

19
As long as I have a want, I have a reason for living. Satisfaction is death.
BERNARD SHAW, *Overruled*.

20
All the things I really like to do are either immoral, illegal or fattening.
ALEXANDER WOOLLCOTT, *The Knock at the Stage-Door*.

WAR

See also Fighting

21
Two weeks later, on February 25, 1918, I arrived at the Poli Theatre in New Haven

to find, in with my mail, what the boys called a German Hunting License. It was a notice from the draft board.
FRED ALLEN, *Much Ado About Me.*

1
Well, if you knows of a better 'ole, go to it.
BRUCE BAIRNSFATHER, *Fragments From France.* Caption from cartoon, 1915.

2
When one animal kills another, it requires a few minutes and no money. When man kills his own in war, it costs fifty thousand dollars per death.
JIM BISHOP, *Some of My Very Best: Mankind—An Enigma.*

3
Better pointed bullets than pointed speeches. (Lieber Spitzkugeln als Spitzreden.)
OTTO VON BISMARCK, *Speech,* during the Hesse-Cassel insurrection of 1850.

4
It is magnificent, but it isn't war. (C'est magnifique, mais ce n'est pas la guerre.)
PIERRE FRANÇOIS BOSQUET, at the charge of the Light Brigade, 1854.

5
We don't want any more wars, but a man is a damn fool to think there won't be any more of them.
GEN. SMEDLEY BUTLER, quoted in *The New York Times,* Aug. 21, 1931.

6
We are waiting for the long-promised invasion. So are the fishes.
SIR WINSTON CHURCHILL, *Broadcast* to the French, October 21, 1940.

7
All his usual formalities of perfidy were observed with scrupulous technique.
SIR WINSTON CHURCHILL, *Radio Address,* June 21, 1941. The reference is to Germany's invasion of Russia.

8
The Japanese, whose game is what I may call to make hell while the sun shines.
SIR WINSTON CHURCHILL, *Speech,* House of Commons, Jan. 27, 1942.

9
I am too weak for that sort of thing [to paint] but I am still strong enough to wage war.
SIR WINSTON CHURCHILL, *Retort,* when General Charles de Gaulle, at their meeting at Marrakech, asked him if he was still painting. (*The New York Times,* Jan. 17, 1944, p. 3.)

10
War is much too important a matter to be left to the generals.
GEORGES CLEMENCEAU. See also TALLEYRAND in this section.

11
Rats and conquerors must expect no mercy in misfortune.
C. C. COLTON, *Lacon,* pt. 1.

12
I dare say, when Tamerlane descended from his throne built of seventy thousand skulls, and marched his ferocious battalions to further slaughter, I dare say he said, "I want room."
SENATOR THOMAS CORWIN of Ohio, *Speech* on the war with Mexico, Feb. 11, 1847.

13
My idea of anti-imperialism is opposition to the fashion of shooting everybody who doesn't speak English.
RICHARD CROKER, *Interview* during 1900 campaign.

14
His charge is resistless; but when he returns from the pursuit, he always finds his camp in possession of the enemy.
BENJAMIN DISRAELI, *Speech,* House of Commons. Apr., 1844. The reference is to Edward Geoffrey, Earl of Derby.

15
Scratch one flat-top.
LIEUTENANT COMMANDER ROBERT E. DIXON, *Radio Message* to his carrier after sinking Japanese carrier off Misima Island, May 7, 1942.

16
I can see in my mind the day when explosives will be so explosive and guns will shoot so far that only the folks that stay at home will be killed, and life insurance agents will be advising people to go into the army.
FINLEY PETER DUNNE, *Mr. Dooley Remembers.*

17
Oh yes, I studied dramatics under him for twelve years.
GENERAL DWIGHT D. EISENHOWER, quoted in *By Quentin Reynolds,* 1963, about GENERAL MACARTHUR.

18
Let me give you some advice, Lieutenant. Don't become a general. Don't ever become a general. If you become a general you just plain have too much to worry about.
GENERAL DWIGHT D. EISENHOWER, *Remark* to Lieutenant Andrew Wnukowski of the Army Reserve, when the latter was introduced to Eisenhower at the New York World's Fair, May 9, 1965.

19
War is delightful to those who have had no experience of it. (Dulce bellum inexpertis.)
GERARD DIDIER ERASMUS, *Adagia.* Chil. iv, cent. 1, No. 1.

1
We're ready for a fight or a frolic.
> REAR ADMIRAL R. D. EVANS, *Remark,*
> Dec. 16, 1907, as the American fleet
> under his command started on a world
> cruise, undertaken to impress Japan.

2
I've got nothing against the army, though.
I wouldn't even mind fighting to make
Berlin and Laos free. Alabama might be
next!
> DICK GREGORY, *From the Back of the Bus.*

3
Please remain. You furnish the pictures and
I'll furnish the war.
> WILLIAM RANDOLPH HEARST, *Telegram,*
> Mar., 1898. The message was sent to
> the artist Frederic Remington when the
> latter expressed a desire to return to the
> United States from Cuba, where he had
> been sent by Hearst to supply illustra-
> tions of the war with Spain for Hearst's
> newspapers. Remington complained that
> there was no war—and thus no material
> for him. (JOHN K. WINKLER, *W. R.*
> *Hearst.*)

4
War makes thieves, and peace hangs them.
> GEORGE HERBERT, *Jacula Prudentum.*

5
Ben Battle was a soldier bold,
  And used to war's alarms;
But a cannon-ball took off his legs,
  So he laid down his arms.
> THOMAS HOOD, *Faithless Nelly Gray.*

6
Napoleon was whipped because he carried a
chip on his shoulder: that is the one thing
that the gods who write the laws of nations
will not palliate nor excuse.
> ELBERT HUBBARD, *The Philistine,* vol. 20.

7
Army Food: The spoils of war.
> *Hudson Newsletter.*

8
Waterloo is a battle of the first rank won by
a captain of the second.
> VICTOR HUGO, *Les Misérables.*

9
A man may build himself a throne of bayonets, but he cannot sit on it.
> DEAN W. R. INGE. (MARCHANT, *Wit and*
> *Wisdom of Dean Inge.*)

10
We can't let Goldwater and Red China both
get the bomb at the same time.
> LYNDON B. JOHNSON, referring to Barry
> M. Goldwater, Johnson's opponent in
> the 1964 presidential campaign. (PHILIP
> GEYELIN, *Lyndon B. Johnson and the*
> *World.*)

11
Doughboys were paid a whole dollar a day
and received free burial under the clay.
And movie heroes are paid even more
shooting one another in a Hollywood war.
> ALFRED KREYMBORG, *What Price Glory?*

12
That expression "positive neutrality" is a
contradiction in terms. There can be no
more positive neutrality than there can be
a vegetarian tiger.
> V. K. KRISHNA MENON, Indian Defense
> Minister. *Address* to General Assembly
> of the United Nations, Oct., 1960.

13
In a war of ideas it is people who get killed.
> STANISLAW J. LEC, *Unkempt Thoughts,* tr.
> from the Polish by JACEK GALASKA.

14
I am sorry it was not a general—I could
make more of them.
> ABRAHAM LINCOLN, *Remark,* upon hearing
> of the death of a private.

15
Military glory—the attractive rainbow that
rises in showers of blood.
> ABRAHAM LINCOLN, *Speech,* House of
> Representatives. (GROSS, *Lincoln's Own*
> *Stories.*)

16
Sending men to that army is like shoveling
fleas across a barnyard—not half of them get
there.
> ABRAHAM LINCOLN, quoted by CARL
> SANDBURG in *Abraham Lincoln: The*
> *Prairie Years and the War Years,* ch.
> 24. The reference is to reinforcements
> for Gen. McClellan's army.

17
If I gave McClellan all the men he asks for
they could not find room to lie down. They'd
have to sleep standing up.
> ABRAHAM LINCOLN. (CARL SANDBURG,
> *Abraham Lincoln: The Prairie Years*
> *and the War Years,* ch. 24.)

18
I have just read your dispatch about sore
tongued and fatigued horses. Will you pardon me for asking what the horses of your
army have done since the battle of Antietam
that fatigues anything?
> ABRAHAM LINCOLN, *Message* to Gen. Mc-
> Clellan when the latter complained to
> him. (CARL SANDBURG, *Abraham Lin-*
> *coln: The Prairie Years and the War*
> *Years,* ch. 27.)

19
So McClellan sent a telegram to Lincoln
one day: "Have captured two cows. What

disposition should I make of them?" And Lincoln: "Milk 'em, George."

> CARL SANDBURG, *Abraham Lincoln: The Prairie Years and the War Years,* ch. 24.

1

Old Frank Blair argued with Lincoln against McClellan's removal. Monty Blair told of this interview: "Lincoln . . . at the end of the conference rose up and stretched his long arms almost to the ceiling above him, saying, 'I said I would remove him if he let Lee's army get away from him, and I must do so. He has got the slows, Mr. Blair.' "

> CARL SANDBURG, *Abraham Lincoln: The Prairie Years and the War Years,* ch. 27.

2

In time the new governor [Gen. Benjamin Butler, military governor of New Orleans during the Civil War] was to be known among Southerners as "Beast Butler" or "Butler the Beast," or in token of stolen silverware, "Spoons Butler."

> CARL SANDBURG, *Abraham Lincoln: The Prairie Years and the War Years,* ch. 24.

3

I can't spare this man—he fights.

> ABRAHAM LINCOLN, Reference to Ulysses S. Grant. (CARL SANDBURG, *Abraham Lincoln: The Prairie Years and the War Years,* ch. 24.)

4

One day a delegation headed by a distinguished doctor of divinity from New York, called on me and made a familiar . . . protest against Grant being retained in his command. After the clergyman had concluded his remarks, I asked if any others desired to add anything to what had already been said. They replied that they did not. Then looking serious as I could, I said: "Doctor, can you tell me where General Grant gets his liquor?" The doctor seemed quite nonplussed, but replied that he could not. I then said to him: "I am very sorry, for if you could tell me I would direct the Chief Quartermaster of the army to lay in a large stock of the same kind of liquor, and would also direct him to furnish a supply to some of my other generals who have never yet won a victory."

> ABRAHAM LINCOLN. (CARL SANDBURG, *Abraham Lincoln: The Prairie Years and the War Years,* ch. 32.)

5

The great difference between our staff corps and the staff corps of other armies is caused thus: you have to graduate a man at West Point to make him a quartermaster. Think of it! In order to make a man competent to issue shoes, boots, pork, sugar, coffee, and molasses, you have to educate him in engineering and in artillery, cavalry and infantry tactics, at West Point. What an absurdity!

> REPRESENTATIVE LOGAN of Illinois. From *The Wit and Wisdom of Congress,* ed. by EDWARD BOYKIN.

6

Ninepunce a day fer killin' folks comes kind o' low fer murder.

> JAMES RUSSELL LOWELL, *The Biglow Papers.*

7

Old soldiers never die; they just fade away.

> GENERAL DOUGLAS MACARTHUR, *Address* to joint session of U.S. Congress, Apr. 19, 1951. He was quoting an old army ballad with a double meaning.

8

Nuts!

> GENERAL ANTHONY C. MCAULIFFE, *Retort* to a German demand for surrender at Bastogne, Belgium, Dec. 22, 1944. In a letter to the compiler, General McAuliffe reported:
>
> " 'Nuts' was the reply. I received a surrender demand addressed to 'The American Commander' and signed 'The German Commander.' It threatened heavy shelling and bombing and suggested that I consider the effects on the Belgian civilians in the town. After reading it, I commented 'Nuts' and went out to visit the troops. Upon my return to the C.P., I was told that the German envoys still remained at the 327th Infantry regimental C.P., were still blindfolded and were asking for an official reply to their official communication. My staff suggested that my first crack would be appropriate, so I said: 'Write it up.' They typed: 'To the German Commander. Nuts. (signed) The American Commander.' The English-speaking German officer did not understand. Our Colonel Harpur said: 'It means the same as "Go to Hell." You understand that, don't you?' He did."

9

Sighted sub. Sank same.

> DONALD FRANCIS MASON, *Radio Message* to U.S. Navy Department, Feb. 26, 1942.

10

War is the only sport that is genuinely amusing. And it is the only sport that has any intelligible use.

> H. L. MENCKEN, *Prejudices,* ser. 5.

1

War hath no fury like a non-combatant.
C. E. MONTAGUE, *Disenchantment.*

2

When after many battles past,
Both tir'd with blows, make
    peace at last,
What is it, after all, the people
    get?
Why! taxes, widows, wooden legs,
    and debt.
FRANCIS MOORE, *Almanac.*

3

An army marches on its stomach.
Attributed to NAPOLEON BONAPARTE.

4

The ancients had a great advantage over us
in that their armies were not trailed by a
second army of pen-pushers.
NAPOLEON BONAPARTE. (*The Mind of Na-
    poleon,* ed. by J. CHRISTOPHER HER-
    OLD.)

5

Providence is always on the side of the last
reserve.
NAPOLEON BONAPARTE. (*Sayings of Napo-
    leon.*)

6

WAR—An evil and it is often the lesser
evil. Those who take the sword perish by the
sword, and those who don't take the sword
perish by smelly diseases.
GEORGE ORWELL (ERIC HUGH BLAIR).

7

Hell, Heaven or Hoboken by Christmas.
Attributed to GENERAL JOHN J. PER-
    SHING (1918).

8

I didn't particularly want to go into the
army—I didn't fancy walking much.
PRINCE PHILIP, *Comment,* Apr., 1965.

9

The bird of war is not the eagle but the
stork.
CHARLES FRANCIS POTTER, *Speech,* at
    Senate hearing on birth-control bill,
    1931.

10

Against eight hundred ships in commission
we enter the lists with a three-shilling pam-
phlet.
JOHN RANDOLPH of Roanoke. Referring
    to MADISON's pamphlet on neutral rights.
    From *The Wit and Wisdom of Con-
    gress,* ed. by EDWARD BOYKIN.

11

The Seabees are always happy to welcome
the Marines.
LIEUTENANT BOB RYAN, *Greeting* to Ma-
    rines as they landed at Segi, New

Georgia, Sept., 1943. Although the Seabees were supposed to land simultaneously with the Marines, or shortly
thereafter, they had arrived first.

12

Gay humor lighted grim incidents. General
O. O. Howard's right arm was shattered,
and when he met General Phil Kearny, who
had lost his left arm in Mexico, the two
men shook hands on Howard's saying, "Hereafter we buy our gloves together."
CARL SANDBURG, *Abraham Lincoln: The
    Prairie Years and the War Years,* ch.
    24.

13

This war was got up drunk but they will
have to settle it sober.
A Louisiana father to his son in the Con-
    federate army. (CARL SANDBURG, *Abra-
    ham Lincoln: The Prairie Years and
    the War Years,* ch. 37.)

14

Mother Goose

Jack and Jill went over the hill.
Universal military training will never be
    popular.
JACK SHARKEY, *Playboy,* May, 1965.

15

War fever is like any other epidemic, and
what the patients say or do in their delirium is no more to be counted against
them than if they were all in bed with
brain fever.
BERNARD SHAW, *Remark* to HESKETH
    PEARSON, quoted by PEARSON in *Lives
    of the Wits.*

16

Retreat, hell! We're just fighting in another
direction.
GENERAL O. P. SMITH, U.S. Marine Corps.
    Retort at Changjin Reservoir, North
    Korea, 1950. *Retreat, Hell* became the
    title of a film based on the Korean
    War.

17

War is much too serious a thing to be left
to military men.
CHARLES-MAURICE DE TALLEYRAND,
    quoted by BRIAND to LLOYD GEORGE
    during the First World War.

18

In June I joined the Confederates in Ralls
County, Missouri, as a second lieutenant
under General Tom Harris and came near
having the distinction of being captured by
Colonel Ulysses S. Grant. I resigned after
two weeks' service in the field, explaining
I was "incapacitated by fatigue" through
persistent retreating.
MARK TWAIN, *Autobiography,* ch. 21.

1
When you leave a battlefield, always leave it in good order. Remove the wreck and rubbish and tidy up the place. However, in the case of a drawn battle, it is neither party's business to tidy up anything—you can leave the field looking as if the city government of New York had bossed the fight.

> MARK TWAIN, *Essays: Instructing the Soldier.*

2
We'll hang out the washing on the Siegfried line.

> UNKNOWN, *Title* of British popular song in World War II.

3
Our ships have been salvaged and are retiring at high speed toward the Japanese fleet.

> UNKNOWN, *Radio message,* from an American ship, Oct., 1944, after Japanese claims that most of the American Third Fleet had been sunk or was retiring.

4
To my mind, every mother who has successfully borne five children should be given a free issue of toy bayonets by a grateful nation.

> PETER USTINOV, *Romanoff and Juliet,* Act 1.

5
There are no manifestoes like cannon and musketry.

> THE DUKE OF WELLINGTON, *Maxims and Table-talk.*

6
A conquerer, like a cannon-ball, must go on; if he rebounds, his career is over.

> THE DUKE OF WELLINGTON, to J. W. CROCKER, 1845.

7
I launched the phrase "The war to end war"—and that was not the least of my crimes.

> H. G. WELLS, quoted by GEOFFREY WEST in *H. G. Wells.*

8
As long as war is regarded as wicked it will always have its fascinations. When it is looked upon as vulgar, it will cease to be popular.

> OSCAR WILDE, *The Critic as Artist.*

9
I rose by sheer military ability to the rank of Corporal.

> THORNTON WILDER, on his World War I army career. *News summaries,* Jan. 12, 1953.

10
As one of our American humorists says, Germany couldn't understand how we could get men over there and get them trained so quick. They didn't know that in our manual there's nothing about retreating! And when you have only to teach an army to go one way, you can do it in half the time.

> WOODROW WILSON, quoting WILL ROGERS.

11
Our Jimmy has gone for to live in a tent,
  They have grafted him into the army;
He finally pucker'd up courage and went
  When they grafted him into the army.

> HENRY C. WORK, *Grafted into the Army* (1862).

WASHINGTON, D.C.

12
There are a number of things wrong with Washington. One of them is that everyone has been too long away from home.

> DWIGHT D. EISENHOWER, *Statement* at presidential press conference, May 11, 1955.

13
Washington is a city of Southern efficiency and Northern charm.

> JOHN F. KENNEDY, quoted by WILLIAM MANCHESTER in *Portrait of a President.*

14
People only leave by way of the box—ballot or coffin.

> SENATOR CLAIBORNE PELL, on Washington life. (*Vogue,* Aug. 1, 1963.)

15
The tendency to make the capital a catch-all for a variety of monuments to honor the immortals, the not-so-immortals, the greats, the near-greats, and the not-so-greats must stop. We must be on our guard lest the nation's capital come to resemble an unplanned cemetery.

> HUGH SCOTT, commenting as U.S. Senator from Pennsylvania, Sept. 10, 1960.

16
First in war, first in peace, and last in the American League.

> UNKNOWN, a paraphrase of COLONEL HENRY LEE's tribute to George Washington, plus a comment on the low (at times) estate of baseball in Washington, D.C.

17
Things get very lonely in Washington sometimes. The real voice of the great people of America sometimes sounds faint and distant in that strange city. You hear politics until you wish that both parties were smothered in their own gas.

> WOODROW WILSON, *Speech* in St. Louis, Sept. 5, 1919.

WEALTH

See also Money

1
"Silver and gold," said our wise men, "make even pigs clean."
> SHOLOM ALEICHEM, *The Enchanted Tailor.*

2
Rothschild . . . counted out three hundred *rubles,* one by one.

Our Kasrilevkite slipped the money into his pocket, and said to Rothschild: "If you want to live forever, my advice to you is to leave this noisy, busy Paris, and move to our town of Kasrilevka [a town where everyone is poor]. There you can never die, because since Kasrilevka has been a town, no rich man has ever died there."
> SHOLOM ALEICHEM, *The Town of The Little People.*

3
"A man who has a million dollars," old John Jacob Astor once told Julia Ward Howe, "is as well off as if he were rich."
> CLEVELAND AMORY, *The Last Resorts.*

4
He has not acquired a fortune; the fortune has acquired him.
> BION, of a miser. (DIOGENES LAERTES, *Bion,* bk. 4.)

5
They say that gold is the heaviest of metals, yet nothing else makes a man so agile, light-headed, and capricious.
> GIORDANO BRUNO, *The Candle Bearer.* Act iv, sc. 4. English version by J. R. HALE.

6
Rich men have no faults.
> JACOB CATS, *Moral Emblems.*

7
Gold begets in brethren hate;
Gold in families debate;
Gold does friendships separate;
Gold does civil wars create.
> ABRAHAM COWLEY, *Anacreontics.*

8
A rich man is an honest man, no thanks to him, for he would be a double knave to cheat mankind when he had no need of it.
> DANIEL DEFOE, *Serious Reflections.*

9
All heiresses are beautiful.
> JOHN DRYDEN, *King Arthur.*

10
'Tis as hard f'r a rich man to enther th' kingdom iv Hiven as it is f'r a poor man to get out iv Purgatory.
> FINLEY PETER DUNNE, *Mr. Dooley's Philosophy.*

11
A rich man is nothing but a poor man with money.
> W. C. FIELDS.

12
Fitzgerald: The rich are different from us.
Hemingway: Yes, they have more money.
> F. SCOTT FITZGERALD, *Note-Books,* quoted in a footnote by EDMUND WILSON.

13
A man that keeps riches and enjoys them not is like an ass that carries gold and eats thistles.
> THOMAS FULLER, *Gnomologia,* No. 312.

14
(Oh, death where is our Inge?)
Surely for him among the saints
  Will be a special niche
Who had the courage to espouse
  The causes of the rich.
> KENSAL GREEN, *Premature Epitaphs.* On Dean Inge.

15
Little, hobbling on his Crutch,
Hurries to the Side of Much.
> ARTHUR GUITERMAN, *A Poet's Proverbs.*

16
The English have refined upon our naive American way of judging people by how much money they happen to have at the moment. The subtler English criterion is how much expensive upper-class education they have been able to afford. Consequently, in England, having had money (provided it was not too mushroomy a phase) is just as acceptable as having it, since the upper-class mannerisms persist, even after the bankroll has disappeared. But never having had money is unforgivable, and can only be atoned for by never trying to get any.
> MARGARET HALSEY, *With Malice Toward Some.*

17
After the first million, it doesn't matter. You can only eat three meals a day—I tried eating four and I got sick. You can't sleep in more than one bed a night. Maybe I have twenty suits, but I can only wear one at a time, and I can't use more than two shirts a day.
> JOSEPH HIRSHHORN, American multimillionaire. Quoted in *Time,* July 25, 1955.

18
I can also tell you that he was one of the few rich people I have ever met who could tell a funny story with point and with grace. (Generally the rich don't bother, because people are going to laugh anyway.)
> ALEXANDER KING, *Mine Enemy Grows Older,* ch. 3.

1
Like most other rich men, he'd sent his sons and daughters to good, or at least expensive, schools all over the country, and this traditional piece of parental strategy had, naturally, come as an effective barrier between himself and his offspring.
ALEXANDER KING, *I Should Have Kissed Her More.*

2
During the Depression I made it a point to make friends with the rich. This was my way of combating hard times.
OSCAR LEVANT, *Memoirs of an Amnesiac.*

3
Our Lord commonly giveth Riches to such gross asses, to whom he affordeth nothing else that is good.
MARTIN LUTHER, *Colloquies.*

4
When a man tells you that he got rich through hard work, ask him: "Whose?"
DON MARQUIS, *New York Sun.*

5
The most valuable of all human possessions, next to a superior and disdainful air, is the reputation of being well to do.
H. L. MENCKEN, *Prejudices,* ser. 3.

6
God shows his contempt for wealth by the kind of person he selects to receive it.
AUSTIN O'MALLEY. See also LUTHER and SWIFT in this section.

7
The man who gets rich quickly must economize quickly, or he'll go hungry quickly. (Qui homo mature quaesivit pecuniam, Nisi eam mature parsit, mature esurit.)
PLAUTUS, *Curculio,* Act iii, sc. 1, l. 380.

8
The next hardest thing to getting rich is keeping from getting poor.
Reflections of a Bachelor.

9
Some people who get rich quick seem to be afraid nobody will know it unless they make fools of themselves.
Reflections of a Bachelor.

10
After a man gets rich his next ambition is to get richer.
Reflections of a Bachelor (1903).

11
Wealthy students often act as if ashamed of their wealth. I have sometimes been tempted to point out that the rich are a minority and have rights, too.
DAVID RIESMAN, *Individualism Reconsidered.*

12
It is an unfortunate human failing that a full pocketbook often groans more loudly than an empty stomach.
FRANKLIN D. ROOSEVELT, *Speech,* in Brooklyn, N.Y., Nov. 1, 1940.

13
Well, whiles I am a beggar I will not rail
And say there is no sin but to be rich;
And being rich, my virtue then shall be
To say there is no vice but beggary.
WILLIAM SHAKESPEARE, *King John.* Act ii, sc. 1.

14
. . . rich men without convictions are more dangerous in modern society than poor women without chastity.
BERNARD SHAW, *Plays Unpleasant:* preface.

15
Those who set out to serve both God and Mammon soon discover that there is no God.
LOGAN PEARSALL SMITH, *Afterthoughts.*

16
Everyone wants to make a fortune, an enormous fortune very quickly, and without working.
STENDHAL (MARIE HENRI BEYLE), *Memoirs of a Tourist,* tr. by ALLAN SEAGER.

17
If heaven had looked upon riches to be a valuable thing, it would not have given them to such a scoundrel.
JONATHAN SWIFT, *Letter to Miss Vanhomrigh,* Aug. 12, 1720.

18
He that is proud of riches is a fool. For if he be exalted above his neighbors because he hath more gold, how much inferior is he to a gold mine!
JEREMY TAYLOR, *Holy Living: Of Humility.*

19
The doctrine of the divine right of kings was bad enough, but not so intolerable as the doctrine of the divine right of plutocrats.
UNKNOWN, *Editorial, Boston Watchman,* July, 1902.

20
Them that has gits.
EDWARD NOYES WESTCOTT, *David Harum,* ch. 35.

WEATHER

21
We found Florida beautiful and balmy. I could say the same thing about my wife. The weather was sensational and so were the prices. It takes six days to get a tan; and then you get the bill and turn white.
JOEY ADAMS, *Cindy and I,* ch. 16.

1

Dorion, ridiculing the description of a tempest in the "Nautilus" of Timotheus, said that he had seen a more formidable storm in a boiling saucepan.

ATHENAEUS, *The Deipnosophists.*

2

What dreadful hot weather we have! It keeps me in a continual state of inelegance.

JANE AUSTEN, *Letter* to her sister Cassandra, Sept. 18, 1796.

3

There is no season such delight can bring,
As summer, autumn, winter, and the spring.

WILLIAM BROWNE, *Variety.*

4

I was born with a chronic anxiety about the weather.

JOHN BURROUGHS, *Is It Going to Rain?*

5

Though it rain daggers with their points down.

ROBERT BURTON, *The Anatomy of Melancholy.*

6

New England climate consists of nine months winter and three months late in the fall.

New England Joke Lore, Ed. by ARTHUR G. CRANDALL.

7

If the Scotch knew enough to go in when it rained, they would never get any outdoor exercise.

SIMEON FORD, *My Trip to Scotland.*

8

Some are weather-wise, some are otherwise.

BENJAMIN FRANKLIN, *Poor Richard's Almanac,* Feb., 1735.

9

No Weather is Bad
When you're Suitably Clad.

ARTHUR GUITERMAN, *A Poet's Proverbs.*

10

Oh, what a blamed uncertain thing
This pesky weather is!
It blew and snew and then it thew
And now, by jing, it's friz!

PHILANDER JOHNSON, *Shooting Stars.*

11

Bad weather always looks much worse through a window.

JOHN KIERAN, *Footnotes on Nature.*

12

The most serious charge which can be brought against New England is not Puritanism but February.

JOSEPH WOOD KRUTCH, *The Twelve Seasons.*

13

Thunder does all the barking, but it's lightning that bites.

ART LINKLETTER, *A Child's Garden of Misinformation.* See also MARK TWAIN in this section.

14

He Says It Never Will Be Mist.

New York Post, Headline on a report of a Russian professor's invention to prevent formation of fog at sea. Quoted by *Reader's Digest,* Feb., 1967.

15

The expression "as right as rain" must have been invented by an Englishman.

WILLIAM LYON PHELPS, *The Country or the City.*

16

This is Methodist weather—sprinkling. We Baptists prefer total immersion.

ADAM CLAYTON POWELL, JR., *Comment,* before the start of a parade in Harlem, New York City, staged in honor of him, Sept. 19, 1964. (*The New York Times,* Sept. 21, 1964.)

17

What in the dark I had taken to be a stump of a little tree appearing above the snow, to which I had tied my horse, proved to have been the weathercock of the church steeple.

RUDOLF E. RASPE, *Travels of Baron Munchausen.*

18

There must have been a charming climate in Paradise. The temperature was perfect; and connubial bliss, I allot, was real jam up.

SAM SLICK, *Human Nature.*

19

Heat, ma'am! It was so dreadful here that I found there was nothing left for it but to take off my flesh, and sit in my bones.

SYDNEY SMITH. (LADY HOLLAND, *Memoir,* ch. 9.)

20

I've lived in good climate, and it bores the hell out of me.

JOHN STEINBECK, *Travels with Charley,* pt. 2.

21

Thunder is good, thunder is impressive; but it is lightning that does the work.

MARK TWAIN.

22

If you don't like the weather in New England, just wait a few minutes.

MARK TWAIN.

23

Weather is a literary specialty, and no untrained hand can turn out a good article on it.

MARK TWAIN, *The American Claimant.*

1
Everybody talks about the weather, but nobody does anything about it.
> CHARLES DUDLEY WARNER, *Editorial,
> Hartford Courant* (c. 1890). This is
> often wrongly credited to Mark Twain.

2
The Weather Bureau has changed its name to Environmental Science Services Administration—and we still get six inches of snow when the forecast says partly cloudy.
> JACK WILSON, *Register and Tribune* Syndicate.

3
It was so cold I almost got married.
> SHELLEY WINTERS, quoted in *The New
> York Times,* Apr. 29, 1956.

WEEPING

4
"I weep for you," the Walrus said:
"I deeply sympathize."
With sobs and tears he sorted out
  Those of the largest size,
Holding his pocket-handkerchief
  Before his streaming eyes.
> LEWIS CARROLL, *Through the Looking-
> Glass,* ch. 4.

5
She would have made a splendid wife, for crying only made her eyes more bright and tender.
> O. HENRY, *Options.*

6
Tears are the noble language of the eye.
> ROBERT HERRICK, *Hesperides,* No. 150.

7
The most effective water power in the world —women's tears.
> WILSON MIZNER.

8
    The big round tears
Coursed one another down his innocent nose
  in piteous chase.
> WILLIAM SHAKESPEARE, *As You Like It.*
> Act ii, sc. 1.

9
Laugh and the world laughs with you
  Weep and you weep alone,
For the sad old earth must borrow its mirth,
  But has trouble enough of its own.
> ELLA WHEELER WILCOX, *Solitude.* This
> first appeared in the *New York Sun,*
> Feb. 25, 1883.

10
Crying is the refuge of plain women, but the ruin of pretty ones.
> OSCAR WILDE, *Lady Windermere's Fan,*
> Act 1.

WHORE

11
Venus, a notorious strumpet, as common as a barber's chair.
> ROBERT BURTON, *The Anatomy of Melancholy.*

12
A woman that paints puts up a bill that she is to let.
> THOMAS FULLER, *Gnomologia,* No. 481.

13
The puritan strain in our culture hounded the professional out of the brothel and forced her to move into the apartment next door, where she quickly became the best tenant.
> HARRY GOLDEN, *For 2¢ Plain.*

14
In calling a prostitute an "unfortunate" the Victorians wished to imply that a prostitute was someone who had invested in the wrong stock, in spite of the advice of more experienced investors.
> HUGH KINGSMILL, *Matthew Arnold.*

15
The only way for a woman to provide for herself decently is for her to be good to some man that can afford to be good to her.
> BERNARD SHAW, *Mrs. Warren's Profession,* Act 2.

16
Who drives an ass and leads a whore,
Hath pain and sorrow evermore.
> UNKNOWN, from *Poor Robin Almanac,*
> July, 1736.

17
The two oldest professions in the world ruined by amateurs.
> ALEXANDER WOOLLCOTT, *The Knock at the
> Stage-Door.* Referring to the professions of actor and streetwalker.

WIDOW

18
Be wery careful o' vidders all your life.
> CHARLES DICKENS, *Pickwick Papers,* ch.
> 20.

19
I have heerd how many ord'nary women one vidder's equal to, in pint o' comin' over you. I think it's five-and-twenty, but I don't rightly know vether it a'n't more.
> CHARLES DICKENS, *Pickwick Papers,* ch.
> 23.

20
Rich widows are the only secondhand goods that sell at first-class prices.
> BENJAMIN FRANKLIN.

1
My idea of walking into the jaws of death is marrying some woman who's lost three husbands.

FRANK MCKINNEY (KIN) HUBBARD.

2
It's bad manners to begin courting a widow before she gets home from the funeral.

SEUMAS MACMANUS, *Heavy Hangs the Golden Grain*.

3
Old maids are the toast and tea of life, widows the coffee and cheese.

Reflections of a Bachelor (1903).

4
Marilla W. Ricker has often told us that widows are divided into two classes—the bereaved and relieved. She forgot the deceived —the grass widows.

VICTOR ROBINSON, *William Godwin; The Truth Seeker*, Jan. 6, 1906.

5
Families, to be sure, prefer widows to unmarried mothers, but just about.

JEAN-PAUL SARTRE, *The Words*.

6
If you dance with a grass widow you will get hay fever.

The Pun Book by T.B. and T.C.

7
Never marry a widow unless her first husband was hanged.

UNKNOWN, Scotch saying, quoted in *Marriage in Epigrams* by FREDERICK W. MORTON.

WIFE

See also Husband, Marriage

8
The wife of Willis Anderson came again to petition for his pardon. She hinted that her husband did not wish to be discharged from prison himself, and that it would be no relaxation of his punishment to turn him over to her.

JOHN QUINCY ADAMS, *Diary*, June 19, 1828.

9
No matter how much she may be criticized by cynics, no matter how much the humorists may joke about her, a wife is still a wife.

SHOLOM ALEICHEM, *Two Dead Men*.

10
It did him no good to answer and explain. She buried him alive. Oh, well, that's what wives are for.

SHOLOM ALEICHEM, *On Account of a Hat*.

11
Wives are young men's mistresses, companions for middle age, and old men's nurses.

FRANCIS BACON, *Essays: Of Marriage and Single Life*. Quoted by BURTON, *Anatomy of Melancholy*, iii, 2, 5.

12
That a man of intellect has doubts about his mistress is conceivable, but about his wife!—that would be too stupid.

HONORÉ DE BALZAC, *The Physiology of Marriage*.

13
Your wife will defend you like the bear in the fable of La Fontaine; she will throw paving stones at your head to drive away the flies that alight on it.

HONORÉ DE BALZAC, *The Physiology of Marriage*.

14
The woman whose life is of the head will strive to inspire her husband with indifference; the woman whose life is of the heart, with hatred; the passionate woman, with disgust.

HONORÉ DE BALZAC, *The Physiology of Marriage*.

15
A lover teaches a wife all that her husband has concealed from her.

HONORÉ DE BALZAC, *The Physiology of Marriage*.

16
If a man strike his mistress it is a self-inflicted wound; but if he strike his wife it is suicide!

HONORÉ DE BALZAC, *The Physiology of Marriage*.

17
However careful a man is, his wife always finds out his failings.

JAMES M. BARRIE, *What Every Woman Knows*.

18
Matrimonial Thought

In the blithe days of honey-moon,
With Kate's allurements smitten,
I loved her late, I loved her soon,
And called her dearest kitten.

But now my kitten's grown a cat,
And cross like other wives,
Oh! by my soul, my honest Mat,
I fear she has nine lives.

JAMES BOSWELL, a convivial song composed and sung by him. (BOSWELL'S *Life*, Nov. 10, 1769.)

19
"And now, Madam," I addressed her, "we shall try who shall get the breeches."

ANTONIUS MUSA BRASSAVOLUS, *My Wife and I*.

1
His wife not only edited his works but edited him.

> VAN WYCK BROOKS, *The Ordeal of Mark Twain*, ch. 5.

2
Every man, as the saying is, can tame a shrew but he that hath her.

> ROBERT BURTON, *The Anatomy of Melancholy*.

3
Think you if Laura had been Petrarch's wife,
He would have written sonnets all his life?

> LORD BYRON, *Don Juan*.

4
To this burden women are born: they must obey their husbands if they are ever such blockheads.

> MIGUEL DE CERVANTES, *Don Quixote*. Pt. ii, ch. 5.

5
There is no hope for men who do not boast that their wives bully them.

> G. K. CHESTERTON, *Alarms and Discursions*.

6
But monogamy is not merely a good event; it is a good habit.

> G. K. CHESTERTON, *A Handful of Authors*.

7
". . . You were present on the occasion of the destruction of these trinkets, and indeed are the more guilty of the two, in the eye of the law; for the law supposes that your wife acts under your direction."

"If the law supposes that," said Mr. Bumble, squeezing his hat emphatically in both hands, "the law is a ass—a idiot."

> CHARLES DICKENS, *Oliver Twist*, ch. 51.

8
You dislike her for no other reason but because she's your wife.

> JOHN DRYDEN, *Marriage à la Mode*, Act 1.

9
A wife is only to have the ripe fruit, that falls of itself; but a wise man will always preserve a shaking for his mistress.

> JOHN DRYDEN, *Marriage à la Mode*. Act v, sc. 1.

10
Here lies my wife: here let her lie!
Now she's at rest, and so am I.

> JOHN DRYDEN, *Suggested Epitaph*.

11
'Tis a saying that there is only one good wife in the world, and every man enjoys her.

> JOHN DUNTON, *Athenian Sport*.

12
A man does not have to be a bigamist to have one wife too many.

> *Farmer's Almanac*, 1966.

13
Behind every man with pull is a woman with push.

> DEAN ROBERT H. FELIX, *Address* at a seminar of Metropolitan College, St. Louis University. (*St. Louis Post-Dispatch*, Nov. 23, 1965, p. 4-D.)

14
A fair wife without a fortune is a fine house without furniture.

> THOMAS FULLER, *Gnomologia*, No. 91.

15
A wife is not to be chosen by the eye only. Choose a wife rather by your ear than your eye.

> THOMAS FULLER, *Gnomologia*, No. 1107.

16
Next to no wife, a good wife is best.

> THOMAS FULLER, *The Holy State: Marriage*.

17
Wives are liars by law.

> JOHN GALSWORTHY, *Loyalties*. Act ii, sc. 2.

18
One wife is too much for most husbands to hear,
But two at a time there's no mortal can bear.

> JOHN GAY, *The Beggar's Opera*. Act iii, sc. 11.

19
Such a wife as I want . . . must be young, handsome (I lay most stress upon a good shape), sensible (a little learning will do), well bred, chaste, and tender. . . . As to religion a moderate stock will satisfy me. She must believe in God and hate a saint.

> ALEXANDER HAMILTON, *Letter* to John Laurens, Dec., 1779.

20
To our sweethearts and wives. May they never meet.

> *Toasts for All Occasions*, ed. by LEWIS C. HENRY.

21
Who will have a handsome wife, let him choose her upon Saturday, and not upon Sunday, viz. when she is in her fine clothes.

> JAMES HOWELL, *Proverbs: Span.-Eng.*, ii.

22
Th' only time some fellers are ever seen with their wives is after they've been indicted.

> FRANK McKINNEY (KIN) HUBBARD, *Abe Martin's Primer*.

23
Some women seem t' be able t' entertain ever'buddy but ther husbands.

> FRANK McKINNEY (KIN) HUBBARD, *Abe Martin's Primer*.

1
His wife "ruled the roast," and in governing the governor, governed the province, which might thus be said to be under petticoat government.

> WASHINGTON IRVING, *Knickerbocker's History of New York*. Bk. iv, ch. 4. See also JUVENAL in this section.

2
After all what does a strict guard avail, as a lewd wife cannot be watched and a chaste one does not have to be?

> JOHN of Salisbury, *Policraticus*, 8.

3
I have learned that only two things are necessary to keep one's wife happy. First, let her think she's having her way. And second, let her have it.

> LYNDON B. JOHNSON, to Lord Snowdon of Great Britain at a White House reception for Princess Margaret and Snowdon, Nov. 17, 1965.

4
A man is in general better pleased when he has a good dinner upon his table, than when his wife talks Greek.

> SAMUEL JOHNSON, *Miscellanies*, vol. 2.

5
The wife rules the roast. (Regnat poscitque maritum.)

> JUVENAL, *Satires*, sat. 6.

6
She had become so dully habituated to married life that in her full matronliness she was as sexless as an anemic nun.

> SINCLAIR LEWIS, *Babbitt*.

7
One day, when a grocer complained about Mrs. Lincoln's burst of temper, Mr. Lincoln laid a hand on the grocer's shoulder and murmured: "Can you not stand for fifteen minutes what I have stood for fifteen years?"

> JIM BISHOP, *Some of My Very Best: Some Famous—Some Infamous*.

8
Never make a toil of pleasure, as Billy Ban said when he dug his wife's grave only three feet deep.

> SEUMAS MACMANUS, *Heavy Hangs the Golden Grain*.

9
The wife should be inferior to the husband; that is the only way to insure equality between the two.

> MARTIAL.

10
When you go forth to find a wife, leave your eyes at home but take both ears with you.

> SEUMAS MACMANUS, *Heavy Hangs the Golden Grain*. See also FULLER in this section.

11
Constance: I'm tired of being the modern wife.
Martha: What do you mean by the modern wife?
Constance: A prostitute who doesn't deliver the goods.

> W. SOMERSET MAUGHAM, *The Constant Wife*.

12
I fear that in the election of a wife,
As in a project of war, to err but once
Is to be undone for ever.

> THOMAS MIDDLETON, *Anything for a Quiet Life*. Act i, sc. 1.

13
"Come, come," said Tom's father, "at your time of life,
There's no longer excuse for thus playing the rake—
It's time you should think, boy, of taking a wife."
"Why so it is, father—whose wife shall I take?"

> THOMAS MOORE, *Taking a Wife*.

14
Xantippe—Socrates found a wife such as he required—but he would not have sought her had he known her sufficiently well; even the heroism of his free spirit would not have gone so far.

> FRIEDRICH WILHELM NIETZSCHE, *Human, All Too Human*, tr. by HELEN ZIMMERN.

15
With quarrels let wives pursue husbands and husbands wives; this befits wives; the dowry of a wife is quarreling.

> OVID, *Ars Amatoria*, bk. 2.

16
Better be an old man's darling
Than become a young man's slave.

> JAMES ROBINSON PLANCHÉ, *Extravaganza*.

17
The difference between a wife and a mistress is night and day.

> *More Playboy's Party Jokes* (1965).

18
A bachelor friend defines the ideal wife as a beautiful, sex-starved deaf-mute who owns a liquor store.

> *More Playboy's Party Jokes* (1965).

19
A wife made to order can't compare with a ready maid.

> *More Playboy's Party Jokes* (1965).

20
Chaste to her husband, frank to all beside,
A teeming mistress, but a barren bride.

> ALEXANDER POPE, *Moral Essays*. III.

1

A virtuous wife rules her husband by obeying him. (Casta ad virum matrona parendo imperat.)
> PUBLILIUS SYRUS, *Sententiae*, No. 105.

2

Man has found remedies against all poisonous creatures, but none was yet found against a bad wife.
> FRANÇOIS RABELAIS, *Works*. Bk. iv, ch. 65. Quoting EURIPIDES.

3

Rely upon it that to love a woman as a mistress, although a delicious delirium, an intoxication far surpassing that of champagne, is altogether unessential, nay pernicious, in the choice of a wife, which a man ought to set about in his sober senses—choosing her, as Mrs. Primrose did her wedding gown, for qualities that wear well.
> JOHN RANDOLPH of Roanoke. From *The Wit and Wisdom of Congress*, ed. by EDWARD BOYKIN.

4

Every man can rule an ill wife but him that has her.
> JOHN RAY, *English Proverbs: Scottish.*

5

The cunning wife makes her husband her apron.
> JOHN RAY, *English Proverbs.*

6

Men, dying, make their will, but wives
Escape a task so sad;
Why should they make what all their lives
The gentle dames have had?
> JOHN GODFREY SAXE, *Woman's Will.*

7

She's not well married that lives married long
But she's best married that dies married young.
> WILLIAM SHAKESPEARE, *Romeo and Juliet.* Act iv, sc. 5.

8

Mother Goose
As I was going to St. Ives,
I met a man with seven wives,
So I figured I was pretty near Hollywood.
> JACK SHARKEY, *Playboy*, May, 1965.

9

The more a man knows, and the farther he travels, the more likely he is to marry a country girl afterwards.
> BERNARD SHAW, *John Bull's Other Island*, Act 2.

10

Married women are kept women and they are beginning to find it out.
> LOGAN PEARSALL SMITH, *Afterthoughts.*

11

God save us all from wives who are angels in the street, saints in the church, and devils at home.
> CHARLES HADDON SPURGEON, *John Ploughman*, ch. 13.

12

An ideal wife is any woman who has an ideal husband.
> BOOTH TARKINGTON, *Looking Forward*, p. 97.

13

A wife is one who stands by a man in all the trouble he wouldn't have had if he hadn't married her.
> UNKNOWN.

14

Break her betimes, and bring her under by force,
Or else the grey mare will be the better horse.
> UNKNOWN, *Marriage of Wit and Science* (1570).

15

Many a wife since Xanthippe has given her husband excuse for classing himself with Socrates.
> UNKNOWN, *Meditations in Wall Street.*

16

The uglier the woman, the better the housewife.
> UNKNOWN, German proverb.

17

My wife is one of the best wimin on this continent, altho' she isn't always gentle as a lamb, with mint sauce.
> ARTEMUS WARD, *A War Meeting.*

18

My wife's gone to the country,
Hurrah! Hurrah!
She thought it best; I need a rest,
That's why she went away.
> GEORGE WHITING AND IRVING BERLIN, *My Wife's Gone to the Country* (Song, 1909).

19

There's nothing in the world like the devotion of a married woman. It's a thing no married man knows anything about.
> OSCAR WILDE, *Lady Windermere's Fan*, Act 3.

20

The large-hearted wits found it quite within their powers to love their wives as well as their mistresses.
> JOHN HAROLD WILSON, *The Court Wits of the Restoration.*

21

Good wives and private soldiers should be ignorant.
> WILLIAM WYCHERLEY, *The Country Wife*, Act 1.

WINE

See also Drinking

1
In the order named these are the hardest to control: Wine, Women and Song.
> FRANKLIN P. ADAMS, *The Ancient Three.*

2
On one occasion some one put a very little wine into a wine-cooler, and said that it was sixteen years old. "It is very small for its age," said Gnathaena.
> ATHENAEUS, *The Deipnosophists.*

3
When wine is in the wit is out.
> THOMAS BECON, *Catechism.*

4
Wine is the drink of the gods, milk the drink of babies, tea the drink of women, and water the drink of beasts.
> JOHN STUART BLACKIE.

5
I may not here omit those two main plagues and common dotages of human kind, wine and women, which have infatuated and besotted myriad of people; they go commonly together.
> ROBERT BURTON, *The Anatomy of Melancholy.*

6
And Noah he often said to his wife when he sat down to dine,
"I don't care where the water goes if it doesn't get into the wine."
> GILBERT KEITH CHESTERTON, *The Flying Inn.*

7
Well, my dear fellow, what did you expect—champagne?
> GROVER CLEVELAND, to John Finley, who had complained that there was water in the cellar of a house he had rented from Cleveland. (FINLEY, *Cleveland; Scribner's Magazine*, Apr., 1927.)

8
"I rather like bad wine," said Mr. Mountchesney; "one gets so bored with good wine."
> BENJAMIN DISRAELI, *Sybil.* Bk. i, ch. 1.

9
God made the Vine,
  Was it a sin
That Man made Wine
  To drown trouble in?
> OLIVER HERFORD, *A Plea.*

10
You appear to have emptied your wine-cellar into your bookseller.
> THEODORE HOOK, to a friend who made his publisher drunk at dinner.

11
When you ask one friend to dine,
Give him your best wine!
When you ask two,
The second best will do!
> HENRY WADSWORTH LONGFELLOW, quoted in BRANDER MATTHEWS, *Recreations of an Anthologist*, p. 117.

12
If with water you fill up your glasses,
  You'll never write anything wise;
For wine is the horse of Parnassus,
  Which hurries a bard to the skies.
> THOMAS MOORE, *Anacreontic.*

13
One drink of wine, and you act like a monkey; two drinks and you strut like a peacock; three drinks and you roar like a lion; and four drinks—you behave like a pig.
> HENRY V. MORTON, *In the Steps of St. Paul.*

14
O thou invisible spirit of wine, if thou hast no name to be known by, let us call thee devil.
> WILLIAM SHAKESPEARE, *Othello.* Act ii, sc. 3.

15
A meal without wine is a day without sunshine.
> LOUIS VAUDABLE, quoted in *Life*, Jan. 7, 1966. Vaudable was speaking as owner of the French restaurant Maxim's.

16
If, when tasting wine, you close your eyes and flowers appear before your inner eye, then the wine has bouquet—the greater the wine the more concentrated its bouquet.
> LOUIS VAUDABLE, quoted in *Life*, Jan. 7, 1966.

17
Burgundy is for those with strong heads and constitutions.
> LOUIS VAUDABLE, quoted in *Life*, Jan. 7, 1966.

18
Wine gives you joy; love, grief and tortures, besides surgeons. Wine makes us witty; love, only sots. Wine makes us sleep; love breaks it.
> WILLIAM WYCHERLEY, *The Country Wife*, Act 1.

19
Wine and women, good apart, together are as nauseous as sack and sugar.
> WILLIAM WYCHERLEY, *The Country Wife*, Act 3.

WINTER

20
The tendinous part of the mind, so to speak,

is more developed in winter; the fleshly, in summer. I should say winter had given the bone and sinew to literature, summer the tissues and the blood.

JOHN BURROUGHS, *The Snow-Walkers*

1
Unwelcome Winter, that old Reprobate,
Is always Early; Spring is always late.
ARTHUR GUITERMAN, *A Poet's Proverbs.*

2
Th' poor we have allus with us, t'gether with th' feller who says, "You won't ketch me in this climate another winter."
FRANK McKINNEY (KIN) HUBBARD, *Abe Martin's Primer.*

3
I oft stand in the snow at dawn,
Harking the drear church chime,
Thinking long thoughts with arctics on,
And wailing: "Winter time."
DON MARQUIS, *To a Lost Sweetheart.*

4
Now fades the glossy, cherished anthracite;
The radiators lose their temperature:
How ill avail, on such a frosty night,
The "short and simple flannels of the poor."
CHRISTOPHER MORLEY, *Elegy Written in a Country Coal-Bin*, st. 2.

5
Despite March's windy reputation, winter isn't really blown away; it is washed away. It flows down all the hills, goes swirling down the valleys and spills out to sea. Like so many of this earth's elements, winter itself is soluble in water.
The New York Times. Editorial, Mar. 17, 1964.

6
Winter lingered so long in the lap of Spring, that it occasioned a great deal of talk.
BILL NYE, *Spring.*

7
Now is the winter of our discontent made glorious summer by central heating.
JACK SHARKEY, *Playboy*, May, 1965.

WISDOM

See also Knowledge

8
There was a *melamed*, a teacher, in that town, named Chaim-Chana the Wise (because he was such a fool) who had a wife named Tema-Gittel the Silent (because she was so talkative), and this Tema Gittel owned two goats, both giving milk.
SHOLOM ALEICHEM, *The Enchanted Tailor.*

9
A wise man knows everything; a shrewd one, everybody.
ANONYMOUS.

10
Some are wise, but most are other wise.
W. BURTON BALDRY, *Stray Thoughts.*

11
If a man had half as much foresight as he has twice as much hindsight, he'd be a lot better off.
ROBERT J. BURDETTE, *Hawkeyes.* Sometimes paraphrased: "If our foresight were as good as our hindsight, we'd be better off a damn sight."

12
God Almighty never created a man half as wise as he looks.
THOMAS CARLYLE, referring to Webster.

13
There is this difference between happiness and wisdom: he that thinks himself the happiest man, really is so; but he that thinks himself the wisest is generally the greatest fool.
C. C. COLTON, *Lacon*, vol. 1.

14
The wise make proverbs and fools repeat them.
ISAAC D'ISRAELI, *Curiosities of Literature.* Ser. ii, vol. 1, p. 449.

15
If a man is wise, he gets rich, an' if he gets rich, he gets foolish, or his wife does. That's what keeps the money movin' around.
FINLEY PETER DUNNE, *Observations by Mr. Dooley.*

16
The wise through excess of wisdom is made a fool.
RALPH WALDO EMERSON, *Experience.*

17
Wisdom is knowing when you can't be wise.
PAUL ENGLE, *Poems in Praise*, 1959.

18
The great wisdom in man consists in knowing his follies. (La grande sagesse de l'homme consiste a connaitre ses folies.)
Old French Proverb.

19
This idea of the wisdom of the taxi driver is one of America's greatest myths. It is utter nonsense. The taxi driver is universally a hanging juror.
HARRY GOLDEN, *For 2¢ Plain.*

20
Where ignorance is bliss
'Tis folly to be wise.
THOMAS GRAY, *Ode on a Distant Prospect of Eton College.*

21
No doubt but ye are the people, and wisdom shall die with you.
Job. XII, 2. Job's reply to Zophar, one of his comforters.

1

He may die of wind but he'll never die of wisdom.

SEUMAS MACMANUS, *Heavy Hangs the Golden Grain.*

2

A wise old owl sat on an oak,
The more he saw the less he spoke;
The less he spoke the more he heard;
Why aren't we like that wise old bird?

EDWARD HERSEY RICHARDS, *A Wise Old Owl.*

3

Two heads are better than one: but this refers only to asparagus.

W. PETT RIDGE, *Name of Garland.*

4

Nine-tenths of wisdom is being wise in time.

THEODORE ROOSEVELT, *Speech* in Lincoln, Neb., June 14, 1917.

5

A little group of wise hearts is better than a wilderness of fools.

JOHN RUSKIN, *Crown of Wild Olive: War*

6

         I do know of these
That therefore only are reputed wise
For saying nothing.

WILLIAM SHAKESPEARE, *The Merchant of Venice.* Act i, sc. 1.

7

Any fool can hang the wisest man in the country.

BERNARD SHAW, *The Shewing-up of Blanco Posnet.*

8

Wisdom is a hen, whose cackling we must value and consider because it is attended with an egg; but, then, lastly, it is a nut, which, unless you choose with judgment, may cost you a tooth, and pay you with nothing but a worm.

JONATHAN SWIFT, *The Tale of a Tub:* introduction.

9

He who thinks himself wise, O heavens! is a great fool.

VOLTAIRE, *Le Droit du Seigneur,* Act 2.

WIT

See also Humor, Laughter

10

We grant, although he had much wit,
He was very shy of using it.

SAMUEL BUTLER, *Hudibras,* pt. 1.

11

For daring nonsense seldom fails to hit,

Like scattered shot, and pass with some for wit.

SAMUEL BUTLER, *On Modern Critics.*

12

His wit ran him out of his money, and now his poverty has run him out of his wits.

WILLIAM CONGREVE, *Love for Love.* Act v, sc. 2.

13

Great Wits are sure to madness near allied.

JOHN DRYDEN, *Absalom and Achitophel.* Pt. i, l. 163.

14

Repartee is a duel fought with the points of jokes.

MAX EASTMAN.

15

Wit makes its own welcome, and levels all distinctions. No dignity, no learning, no force of character, can make any stand against good wit.

RALPH WALDO EMERSON, *Letters and Social Aims: The Comic.*

16

Of all wit's uses the main one
Is to live well with who has none.

RALPH WALDO EMERSON, *Life.*

17

Wit is the salt of conversation, not the food.

WILLIAM HAZLITT, *Lectures on English Comic Writers.*

18

A woman's wit is often better than a man's arm.

A. G. HOLES, *Maid Molly.*

19

The man [Chesterfield] I thought had been a Lord among wits; but I find he is only a wit among Lords.

SAMUEL JOHNSON, BOSWELL's *Life*, 1754.

20

Levity is the soul of wit.

MELVILLE D. LANDON (ELI PERKINS).

21

Endow me, if Thou grant me wit,
Likewise with sense to mellow it.

DON MARQUIS, *Prayer.*

22

Impropriety is the soul of wit.

W. SOMERSET MAUGHAM.

23

Novelty is the soul of wit. A jest shaken with the palsy of age amuses only children and drunkards.

G. SYDNEY PATERNOSTER, *The Folly of the Wise.*

24

Wits have one thing in common with bores: they recognize at sight and avoid one another, fearing competition.

HESKETH PEARSON, *Lives of the Wits.*

1
You beat your pate, and fancy wit will come:
Knock as you please, there's nobody at home.
>ALEXANDER POPE, *Epigram: An Empty House.*

2
Better a witty fool than a foolish wit.
>WILLIAM SHAKESPEARE, *Twelfth Night.* Act i, sc. 5.

3
Look, he's winding up the watch of his wit; by and by it will strike.
>WILLIAM SHAKESPEARE, *The Tempest.* Act ii, sc. 1.

4
It is with wits as with razors, which are never so apt to cut those they are employed on as when they have lost their edge.
>JONATHAN SWIFT, *Tale of a Tub:* preface.

WOMAN

See also Man

5
At any age the ladies *are* delightful, delectable and, most important, deductible.
>GOODMAN ACE, *The Fine Art of Hypochondria.*

6
Women like silent men. They think they are listening.
>MARCEL ACHARD. (*Quote,* Nov. 4, 1956.)

7
Women have, commonly, a very positive moral sense; that which they will, is right; that which they reject, is wrong; and their will, in most cases, ends by settling the moral.
>HENRY ADAMS, *The Education of Henry Adams,* ch. 6.

8
The woman who is known only through a man is known wrong.
>HENRY ADAMS, *The Education of Henry Adams,* ch. 23.

9
She looks too lovely to be quite a lady.
>SAMUEL HOPKINS ADAMS, *Tenderloin.*

10
The woman that deliberates is lost.
>JOSEPH ADDISON, *Cato,* Act 4.

11
Too lightly open are a woman's ears;
Her fence downtrod by many trespassers.
>AESCHYLUS, *Agamemnon.*

12
So I am, compared with her.
>THOMAS BAILEY ALDRICH, Comment to a friend when told that a certain woman

called him "effeminate." (WILLIAM PATTEN, *Among the Humorists.*)

13
If men are always more or less deceived on the subject of women, it is because they forget that they and women do not speak altogether the same language.
>AMIEL, *Journal,* Dec. 26, 1868.

14
Actually, the original meaning of "lady" was "bread kneader," and if the dictionary adds, "See dough," it refers, we add sternly, to bread only.
>CLEVELAND AMORY, *Who Killed Society?*

15
I change, and so do women too;
But I reflect, which women never do.
>ANONYMOUS, *Inscription* on a looking glass.

16
Women give themselves to God when the devil wants nothing more to do with them.
>SOPHIE ARNOULD, French opera star.

17
We women do talk too much, but even then we don't tell half we know.
>LADY NANCY ASTOR.

18
Women love the lie that saves their pride, but never an unflattering truth.
>GERTRUDE ATHERTON, *The Conqueror.* Bk. iii, ch. 6.

19
An honest woman is necessarily a married woman.
>HONORÉ DE BALZAC, *The Physiology of Marriage.*

20
Adolphe says to himself: "Women are children: offer them a lump of sugar, and you will easily get them to dance all the dances that greedy children dance; but you must always have a sugar plum in hand, hold it up pretty high, and—take care that their fancy for sweetmeats does not leave them."
>HONORÉ DE BALZAC, *Petty Troubles of Married Life.*

21
You see, dear, it is not true that woman was made from man's rib; she was really made from his funny bone.
>JAMES M. BARRIE, *What Every Woman Knows.*

22
There is no other purgatory but a woman.
>BEAUMONT AND FLETCHER, *Scornful Lady,* Act 3.

23
Most women are not as young as they are painted.
>MAX BEERBOHM, *A Defense of Cosmetics.*

1
Zuleika, on a desert island, would have spent most of her time in looking for a man's foot-print.
MAX BEERBOHM, *Zuleika Dobson,* ch. 2.

2
When a man starts worrying out loud about unprotected women you may know that he's a hypocritical sensualist.
S. N. BEHRMAN, *Biography.*

3
Here's to woman! Would that we could fall into her arms without falling into her hands.
AMBROSE BIERCE, his favorite toast. (GRATTAN, *Bitter Bierce.*)

4
The only people who understand women are women.
JIM BISHOP, *Some of My Very Best: It Takes One to Know One.*

5
What appears to be intuition in a woman—is often only transparency in a man.
JIM BISHOP, *Some of My Very Best: It Takes One to Know One.*

6
Women, who are, beyond all doubt, the mothers of all mischief, also nurse that babe to sleep when he is too noisy.
RICHARD BLACKMORE, *Lorna Doone,* ch. 57.

7
Contrary to male sentimentality and psychology, the confrontation of a hostile crowd, to a woman, is like a tonic.
WILLIAM BOLITHO, *Twelve Against the Gods.*

8
If a woman looks at her watch, it is a sure sign that someone is in the way.
SHELLAND BRADLEY, *An American Girl in India.*

9
Women are not a hobby—they're a calamity.
ALEXANDER BRAILOWSKY, *Interview* in Minneapolis, 1931.

10
Brigands demand your money or your life; women require both.
SAMUEL BUTLER.

11
Two are better than one, but the man who said that did not know my sisters.
SAMUEL BUTLER.

12
There is a tide in the affairs of women
Which, taken at the flood, leads—God knows where.
LORD BYRON, *Don Juan.*

13
No lady is ever a gentleman.
JAMES BRANCH CABELL, *Something About Eve.*

14
All women are natural born espionage agents.
EDDIE CANTOR, *The Way I See It.*

15
I often wish I had been dumped on the world with a plain face and a flat chest, but the sort of woman who, even if you see her eating fried fish with her fingers at a street stall, you'd know was a lady.
WYMOND CAREY, *Love the Judge.*

16
Bill Feather quotes this despairing paragraph from the writings of the French artist, Jean Gabriel Domergue: The world belongs to women. When a man is born people ask how his mother is. When he gets married people exclaim, "Isn't the bride sweet!" When he is dead, people ask, "How much did he leave her?"
BENNETT CERF, *The Laugh's on Me.*

17
Between a woman's Yes and No
There is not room for a pin to go.
(Entre el Si y el No de la mujer,
No me atreveria yo a'poner una punta de alfiler.)
MIGUEL DE CERVANTES, *Don Quixote.*

18
A woman is like your shadow—follow her, she flies; fly from her, she follows.
NICHOLAS CHAMFORT.

19
The sagacity of women, like the sagacity of saints, or that of donkeys, is something outside all questions of ordinary cleverness and ambition.
G. K. CHESTERTON, *A Handful of Authors.*

20
Twenty million young women rose to their feet with the cry *We will not be dictated to,* and promptly became stenographers.
G. K. CHESTERTON, quoted by HESKETH PEARSON, *Lives of the Wits.*

21
The same, I trust, as it has been since the days of Adam and Eve.
SIR WINSTON CHURCHILL, *Reply,* to an American feminist who asked about the role of women in the future.

22
There are three classes into which all elderly women that I ever knew were to be divided: first, that dear old soul; second, that old woman; third, that old witch.
SAMUEL TAYLOR COLERIDGE, *Table-Talk.*

23
You are a woman, you must never speak

what you think; your words must contradict your thoughts but your actions may contradict your words.
> WILLIAM CONGREVE, *Love for Love.* Act ii, sc. 11.

1
A lady is one who never shows her underwear unintentionally.
> LILLIAN DAY, *Kiss and Tell.*

2
Were there no women, men might live like gods.
> THOMAS DEKKER, *The Honest Whore.* Act iii, sc. 1.

3
Women never use their intelligence—except when they need to prop up their intuition.
> JACQUES DEVAL, *News summaries,* May 10, 1954.

4
Tongue; well that a wery good thing when it ain't a woman's.
> CHARLES DICKENS, *Pickwick Papers,* ch. 19.

5
In company with several other old ladies of both sexes.
> CHARLES DICKENS, *Little Dorrit.* Pt. i, ch. 17.

6
The average man is more interested in a woman who is interested in him than he is in a woman—any woman—with beautiful legs.
> MARLENE DIETRICH, *News summaries,* Dec. 13, 1954.

7
Women are most fascinating between the age of 35 and 40 after they have won a few races and know how to pace themselves. Since few women ever pass 40, maximum fascination can continue indefinitely.
> CHRISTIAN DIOR. (*Collier's,* June 10, 1955.)

8
Women are like hens; you never lay, but you cackle an hour after, to discover your nest . . .
> JOHN DRYDEN, *Marriage à la Mode.* Act iii, sc. 2.

9
Women are never stronger than when they arm themselves with their weaknesses.
> MADAME DU DEFFAND, *Letter,* to Voltaire.

10
She was tight as the paper on the wall.
> MIGNON EBERHART, *Escape the Night.*

11
When lovely woman stoops to folly and
Paces about her room again, alone,
She smoothes her hair with automatic hand,

And puts a record on the gramophone.
> T. S. ELIOT, *The Waste Land: The Fire Sermon.*

12
A woman should be good for everything at home, but abroad good for nothing.
> EURIPIDES, *Meleager,* frag. 525.

13
Women are like pictures, of no value in the hands of a fool, till he hears men of sense bid high for the purchase.
> GEORGE FARQUHAR, *The Beaux' Stratagem.* Act 2.

14
And as in the Dark all Cats are grey, the Pleasure of Corporal Enjoyment with an old Woman is at least equal and frequently superior; every Knack being by Practice capable of improvement.
> BENJAMIN FRANKLIN, *Letter* to an unidentified young friend, June 25, 1745. Franklin's fifth stated reason for preferring older women to young ones.

15
Discreet women have neither eyes nor ears.
(La femme de bien n'a ni yeux no oreilles.)
> OLD FRENCH PROVERB.

16
A woman, a dog, and a walnut tree,
The more you beat 'em the better they be.
> THOMAS FULLER, *Gnomologia,* No. 6404.

17
Women and music should never be dated.
> OLIVER GOLDSMITH, *She Stoops to Conquer.*

18
No lady begins now to put on jewels till she's past forty.
> OLIVER GOLDSMITH, *She Stoops to Conquer.*

19
What female heart can gold despise?
What cat's averse to fish?
> THOMAS GRAY, *Ode on the Death of a Favourite Cat.*

20
Women forgive injuries, but never forget slights.
> T. C. HALIBURTON (SAM SLICK), *The Old Judge,* ch. 15.

21
Directly domineering ceases in the man, snubbing begins in the woman.
> THOMAS HARDY, *A Pair of Blue Eyes,* ch. 27.

22
If men knew how women pass the time when they are alone, they'd never marry.
> O. HENRY, *Memoirs of a Yellow Dog.*

23
Women may be whole oceans deeper than we

are, but they are also a whole paradise better. She may have got us out of Eden, but as a compensation she makes the earth very pleasant.

JOHN OLIVER HOBBES, *Ambassador*, Act 3.

1
A woman never forgets her sex. She would rather talk with a man than an angel any day.

OLIVER WENDELL HOLMES. (*Wit and Wisdom of Oliver Wendell Holmes*, ed. by LESTER E. DENONN.)

2
'Tis a powerful sex; they were too strong for the first, the strongest and wisest man that was; they must needs be strong, when one hair of a woman can draw more than a hundred pair of oxen.

JAMES HOWELL, *Familiar Letters*, bk. 2.

3
Women are just like elephants to me; I like to look at them, but I wouldn't want one.

FRANK MCKINNEY (KIN) HUBBARD.

4
After all, a woman is a good deal like th' automobile—it hain't th' upholsterin' that counts.

FRANK MCKINNEY (KIN) HUBBARD, *Abe Martin's Primer*.

5
When a woman says somethin' wouldn' surprise her much she means it would please her.

FRANK MCKINNEY (KIN) HUBBARD, *Abe Martin's Primer*.

6
When a woman says "they say" she means herself.

FRANK MCKINNEY (KIN) HUBBARD, *Abe Martin's Primer*.

7
Women's intuition is the result of millions of years of not thinking.

RUPERT HUGHES.

8
When a woman writes her confession she is never further from the truth.

JAMES G. HUNEKER, *Pathos of Distance*, p. 58.

9
"Sayin' nothin'," says the goldsmith, "is a woman's rarest skill."
"Birds should sing," remarked the Doctor, "but a woman should be still."

WALLACE IRWIN, *The Chamber of Tranquillity*.

10
I want to make a policy statement. I am unabashedly in favor of women.

LYNDON B. JOHNSON, *Comment*, Mar. 4, 1964, upon announcing the appointment

of several women to high governmental posts.

11
A woman's preaching is like a dog's walking on his hind legs. It is not done well; but you are surprised to find it done at all.

SAMUEL JOHNSON, BOSWELL's *Life*, July 31, 1763.

12
I am very fond of the company of ladies. I like their beauty, I like their delicacy, I like their vivacity, and I like their silence.

SAMUEL JOHNSON, SEWARD's *Johnsoniana*, 617.

13
Nature has given women so much power that the law has very wisely given them little.

SAMUEL JOHNSON, *Letters*. Vol. i, p. 104.

14
If I had no duties and no reference to futurity, I would spend my life in driving briskly in a post-chaise with a pretty woman, but she should be one that could understand me, and would add something to the conversation.

SAMUEL JOHNSON, BOSWELL's *Life*, Sept. 19, 1777.

15
He knew women, as his brother Addison said, from the best homes and houses.

ALVA JOHNSTON, *Legend of a Sport; The New Yorker* (1942). Reference to Wilson Mizner.

16
It's a very venerable and useful superstition that one woman is perfectly safe if another woman is pretending to look after her.

HENRY ARTHUR JONES, *The Triumph of the Philistines*, Act 1.

17
One woman reads another's character without the tedious trouble of deciphering.

BEN JONSON, *New Inn*. Act iv, sc. 4.

18
When danger comes in an honorable way, a woman's heart grows chill with fear; but if she is doing a bold bad thing her courage never fails.

JUVENAL, *Satires*. Sat. vi, l. 94.

19
Although all womankind be nought, yet two good days hath she:
Her marriage day, and day of death, when all she leaves to thee.

TIMOTHY KENDALL, *Flower of Epigrams*, 143.

20
The outstanding talent of woman . . . the one which altogether differentiates her from all other living organisms . . . is her un-

believable ability to completely renew the structure of her whole conceptual apparatus, if the emotional stimulus happens to be sufficiently strong.

ALEXANDER KING, *Rich Man, Poor Man, Freud and Fruit*, ch. 1.

1

A fool there was and he made his prayer
(Even as you and I!)
To a rag and a bone and a hank of hair
(We called her the woman who did not care)
But the fool he called her his lady fair—
(Even as you and I!)

RUDYARD KIPLING, *The Vampire*, st. 1.

2

A woman's guess is much more accurate than a man's certainty.

RUDYARD KIPLING, *Plain Tales from the Hills*.

3

All a man could say of any woman was, what next?

EDWIN LANHAM, *Speak Not Evil*.

4

Talk to me tenderly, tell me lies;
I am a woman and time flies.

VIVIAN YEISER LARAMORE, *Talk To Me Tenderly*.

5

If a woman hasn't got a tiny streak of a harlot in her, she's a dry stick as a rule.

D. H. LAWRENCE, *Pornography and Obscenity*.

6

The woman was not taken
From Adam's head we know,
To show she must not rule him—
'Tis evidently so.
The woman she was taken
From under Adam's arm,
So she must be protected
From injuries and harm.

ABRAHAM LINCOLN, *Song*, written on the occasion of a friend's wedding.

7

Our ideal of womanhood in this present industrial society is that a woman should achieve the highest feminine attraction at the lowest cost to men.

LIN YUTANG, *With Love and Irony*.

8

How like an angel speaks the tongue of woman,
When pleading in another's cause her own!

HENRY WADSWORTH LONGFELLOW, *The Spanish Student*. Act iii, sc. 5.

9

To say why gals act so or so,
Or don't, 'ould be persumin';
Mebby to mean *yes* an' say *no*
Comes nateral to women.

JAMES RUSSELL LOWELL, *The Courtin'*.

10

. . . A lady is nothing very specific. One man's lady is another man's woman; sometimes, one man's lady is another man's wife. Definitions overlap, but they almost never coincide.

RUSSELL LYNES, *Look*, July 22, 1958.

11

A woman is no more mysterious than a race horse.

J. P. McEVOY, *Charlie Would Have Loved This*.

12

How it rejoices a middle-aged woman when her husband criticizes a pretty girl.

MIGNON McLAUGHLIN, *The Saturday Review*.

13

Men will make all sorts of allowances for a pretty woman, and women for an unmarried man.

MIGNON McLAUGHLIN, *The Neurotic's Notebook*.

14

Cleverness in a woman suggests somebody wide awake, and the quality is superfluous, save when a woman has been denied good looks.

S. MACNAUGHTON, *The Expensive Miss Du Cane*.

15

"The inconstancy of woman"—this is the most convenient phrase ever invented by man, for it condones in advance all his meditated indiscretions.

DON MARQUIS, *New York Herald*.

16

The Queen of Sheba never told what she thought of King Solomon's proverbs warning young men against women.

DON MARQUIS, *New York Herald*.

17

A woman will always sacrifice herself if you give her the opportunity. It is her favorite form of self-indulgence.

W. SOMERSET MAUGHAM, *The Circle*.

18

There must be some women who are not liars.

W. SOMERSET MAUGHAM, at 86. (*Time*, Oct. 17, 1960.)

19

He who teaches women letters feeds more poison to a frightful asp.

MENANDER, *Fragments*, No. 702.

20

I expect that woman will be the last thing civilized by man.

GEORGE MEREDITH, *The Ordeal of Richard Feverel*.

1
When a woman professes to know a good deal of men, you can be sure that all she knows is bad. Knowledge of man is with most women equivalent to a knowledge of one bad man.
FRANKFORT MOORE, *The Marriage Lease.*

2
What do you mean by a woman's better nature? I did not know that a woman had more than one nature, and that is . . . nature.
FRANKFORT MOORE, *The Marriage Lease.*

3
My only books were woman's looks,
And folly's all they've taught me.
THOMAS MOORE, *The Time I've Lost in Wooing.*

4
Woman was God's second mistake.
FRIEDRICH WILHELM NIETZSCHE, *The Antichrist:* aphorism, 48.

5
Where there is neither love nor hate in the game woman's play is mediocre.
FRIEDRICH WILHELM NIETZSCHE, *Beyond Good and Evil,* tr. by HELEN ZIMMERN.

6
In the background of all their personal vanity, women themselves have still their impersonal scorn—for "woman."
FRIEDRICH WILHELM NIETZSCHE, *Beyond Good and Evil,* tr. by HELEN ZIMMERN.

7
Mirages are like women—strictly unpredictable. They always look inviting, cool and attractive, but you can't pin one down.
HARRY OLIVER, *The Desert Rat Scrap Book.*

8
Whether they give or refuse, it delights women to have been asked. (Quae dant, quaeque negant, gaudent tamen esse rogatae.)
OVID, *Ars Amatoria.* Bk. i, l. 345.

9
Women often wish to give unwillingly what they really like to give. (Quod juvat, invitae saepe dedisse volunt.)
OVID, *Ars Amatoria.* Bk. i, l. 674.

10
Every woman is a source of annoyance, but she has two good seasons, the one in her bridal chamber and the other in her grave.
PALLADAS. (*Greek Anthology.* Bk. xi, epig. 381.)

11
Every woman is a potential Napoleon, with a possible empire in each successive man she meets.
G. SYDNEY PATERNOSTER, *The Folly of the Wise.*

12
Woman is as false as a feather in the wind.
F. M. PIAVE, *Libretto* for VERDI's *Rigoletto.*

13
Whoever it was who first called women the fair sex didn't know much about justice.
More Playboy's Party Jokes (1965).

14
A woman with a past attracts men who hope history will repeat itself.
More Playboy's Party Jokes (1965).

15
No woman ever hates a man for being in love with her, but many a woman hates a man for being a friend to her.
ALEXANDER POPE, *Thoughts on Various Subjects.*

16
A woman who meditates alone meditates evil. (Mulier cum sola cogitat, male cogitat.)
PUBLILIUS SYRUS, *Sententiae,* No. 369.

17
It takes a woman to tread on a man's corns while she is pretending to try to kiss his lips.
Reflections of a Bachelor.

18
It is better to be made a fool of by women than to be ignored by them.
Reflections of a Bachelor.

19
Women's rights begin where men's wrongs leave off.
Reflections of a Bachelor.

20
After men the animals that women take most interest in are boys.
Reflections of a Bachelor.

21
It is the feline strain of femininity which makes it claw what it loves and caress what it hates.
Reflections of a Bachelor.

22
As for the women, though we scorn and flout 'em,
We may live with, but cannot live without 'em.
FREDERICK REYNOLDS, *The Will,* Act 1.

23
I'm not a woman hater. Life is only long enough to allow even an energetic man to hate one woman—adequately.
FRANK RICHARDSON, *2835 Mayfair.*

24
For when a woman is left too much alone,
Sooner or later she begins to think;
And no man knows what then she may discover.
EDWIN ARLINGTON ROBINSON, *Tristram,* pt. 7.

1
The fact that women outlive men means, irrevocably, that the women—not necessarily the meek—are inheriting the earth.
> DONALD I. ROGERS, *Teach Your Wife to Be a Widow.*

2
As Abe Martin says, women is just like elephants: I like to look at 'em, but I'd sure hate to own one.
> WILL ROGERS, *Autobiography.*

3
Such, Polly, are your sex—part
  truth, part fiction;
Some thought, much whim,
  and all contradiction.
> RICHARD SAVAGE, *To a Young Lady.*

4
Friends' husbands always bore one: and friends' wives are—well—all women are cats.
> HUGH DE SELINCOURT, *A Boy's Marriage.*

5
She's beautiful and therefore
  to be woo'd:
She is a woman, therefore to
  be won.
> WILLIAM SHAKESPEARE, *Henry VI, Pt. I.* Act v, sc. 3.

6
Have you not heard it said full oft,
A woman's nay doth stand for naught?
> WILLIAM SHAKESPEARE, *The Passionate Pilgrim.*

7
Two women placed together makes cold weather.
> WILLIAM SHAKESPEARE, *Henry VIII.* Act i, sc. 4.

8
If her breath were as terrible as her terminations, there were no living near her; she would infect to the north star.
> WILLIAM SHAKESPEARE, *Much Ado About Nothing.* Act ii, sc. 1.

9
I thank God I am not a woman, to be touched with so many giddy offenses as he hath generally taxed their whole sex withal.
> WILLIAM SHAKESPEARE, *As You Like It.* Act iii, sc. 2.

10
You sometimes have to answer a woman according to her womanishness, just as you have to answer a fool according to his folly.
> BERNARD SHAW, *An Unsocial Socialist,* ch. 18.

11
Every woman who hasn't any money is a matrimonial adventurer.
> BERNARD SHAW, *Heartbreak House,* Act 2.

12
It is one of the mysterious ways of Allah to make women troublesome when he makes them beautiful.
> BERNARD SHAW, *The Adventures of the Black Girl in Her Search for God.*

13
. . . you are a lady; and wherever ladies are is hell.
> BERNARD SHAW, *Don Juan in Hell.*

14
I am glad that I am not a man, as I should be obliged to marry a woman.
> MADAME DE STAËL.

15
A wise woman never yields by appointment. It should always be an unforseen happiness.
> STENDHAL (HENRI BEYLE), *De l'Amour,* ch. 60.

16
Women and birds are able to see without turning their heads, and that is indeed a necessary provision, for they are both surrounded by enemies.
> JAMES STEPHENS, *The Demi-Gods,* ch. 2.

17
Women are wiser than men because they know less and understand more.
> JAMES STEPHENS, *The Crock of Gold,* ch. 2.

18
To say the truth, I never yet knew a tolerable woman to be fond of her own sex.
> JONATHAN SWIFT, *A Letter, to a Very Young Lady on Her Marriage.*

19
As divines say, that some people take more pains to be damned than it would cost them to be saved; so your sex employ more thought, memory and application to be fools than would serve to make them wise and useful.
> JONATHAN SWIFT, *A Letter, to a Very Young Lady on Her Marriage.*

20
It is said of the horses in the vision, that "their power was in their mouths and in their tails." What is said of horses in the vision, in reality may be said of women.
> JONATHAN SWIFT, *Thoughts on Various Subjects.*

21
Ladies, like soldiers, ought to keep their powder dry before going into action.
> HORACE SYNDHAM, *Reginald Auberon.*

22
There are some meannesses which are too mean even for man—woman, lovely woman alone, can venture to commit them.
> WILLIAM MAKEPEACE THACKERAY, *A Shabby Genteel Story,* ch. 3.

1
A woman without a laugh in her . . . is the greatest bore in existence.
WILLIAM MAKEPEACE THACKERAY, *Miscellanies*.

2
Woman is more impressionable than man. Therefore in the Golden Age they were better than men. Now they are worse.
LEO TOLSTOY, *Diary*.

3
Most women have small waists the world throughout,
But their desires are a thousand miles about.
CYRIL TOURNER, *The Revengers*, Act 5.

4
He is a fool who thinks by force or skill
To turn the current of a woman's will.
SAMUEL TURKE, *Adventures of Five Hours*.

5
Most women turn to salt . . . looking back.
UNKNOWN, *A Woman*.

6
Women are like Gods. They have a face for their worshippers, and one for their rivals.
UNKNOWN, *A Woman*.

7
For isn't it just those women who were not virtuous, who broke all laws, who were never faithful, who have lived in literature and made history?
UNKNOWN, *A Woman*.

8
Ashes to ashes,
Dust to dust,
If whiskey don't get you,
Women must.
UNKNOWN, from *The Book of Negro Humor* by LANGSTON HUGHES.

9
A woman should be seen at night, in the distance, or under an umbrella.
UNKNOWN, Japanese proverb, in *Oriental Humor*, ed. by R. H. BLYTH.

10
I'll sooner undertake to teach sincerity to a courtier, generosity to a usurer, honesty to a lawyer, than discretion to a woman I see has once set her heart upon playing the fool.
SIR JOHN VANBRUGH, *The Provoked Wife*, Act 2.

11
Let our weakness be what it will, mankind will still be weaker; and whilst there is a world, 'tis woman that will govern it.
SIR JOHN VANBRUGH, *The Provoked Wife*, Act 3.

12
Very learned women are to be found in the same manner as female warriors; but they are seldom or never inventors.
VOLTAIRE, *Dictionnaire Philosophique: Women*.

13
Whatever women do they must do twice as well as men to be thought half as good. Luckily, this is not difficult.
CHARLOTTE WHITTON, Mayor of Ottawa. Quoted in *Canada Month*, June, 1963.

14
Women never hit what they aim at: but if they just shut their eyes and shoot in the air they generally find themselves in the bull's eye.
KATE D. WIGGIN, *New Chronicles of Rebecca*.

15
Women represent the triumph of matter over mind, just as men represent the triumph of mind over morals.
OSCAR WILDE, *The Picture of Dorian Gray*, ch. 4.

16
I am on the side of the Trojans. They fought for a woman.
OSCAR WILDE, *The Picture of Dorian Gray*, ch. 17.

17
Womankind more joy discovers
Making fools than keeping lovers.
JOHN WILMOT, *A Dialogue*, l. 71.

18
Women are notoriously deficient in sporting blood.
P. G. WODEHOUSE, *The Brinkmanship of Galahad Threepwood*.

19
Ay, women are apt to tell before the intrigue, as men after it, and so show themselves the vainer sex.
WILLIAM WYCHERLEY, *The Country Wife*, Act 3.

20
Vain fops but court and dress, and keep a pother,
To pass for women's men with one another;
But he who aims by women to be prized,
First by the men, you see, must be despised.
WILLIAM WYCHERLEY, *The Country Wife*, Act 5: "A Dance of Cuckolds."

21
Only one thing I believe of a woman, and that is, that she will not come to life again after she is dead.
CURTIS YORKE, *The World and Delia*.

WORDS

See also Speech

22
People endowed with a gift of words out of proportion to their native intelligence, no

matter how much improved by training and learning—such people can become a public danger, socially, politically, and above all culturally.

BERNARD BERENSON, *Diaries* (1954).

1
Oaths are but words and words but wind.

SAMUEL BUTLER, *Hudibras*, pt. 2.

2
I wish he would explain his explanation.

LORD BYRON.

3
Words fascinate me. They always have. For me, browsing in a dictionary is like being turned loose in a bank.

EDDIE CANTOR, *The Way I See It.*

4
Alice had not the slightest idea what Latitude was, or Longitude either, but she thought they were nice grand words to say.

LEWIS CARROLL, *Alice's Adventures in Wonderland*, ch. 1.

5
Well, "slithy" means "lithe and slimy." . . . You see it's like a portmanteau—there are two meanings packed up into one word.

LEWIS CARROLL, *Through the Looking-Glass*, ch. 6. Hence "portmanteau word," word formed by combining the elements of two other words.

6
Weasel words are words that suck all the life out of the words next to them, just as a weasel sucks an egg and leaves the shell.

STEWART CHAPLIN, *Stained-Glass Political Platform.* See also THEODORE ROOSEVELT in this section.

7
Fair words butter no parsnips.

JOHN CLARKE, *Paraemiologia.*

8
He who wants to persuade should put his trust, not in the right argument, but in the right word. The power of sound has always been greater than the power of sense.

JOSEPH CONRAD, *A Personal Record.*

9
God is in heaven, and thou upon earth: therefore let thy words be few.

Ecclesiastes. III.

10
In two words: im-possible.

SAMUEL GOLDWYN, quoted by ALVA JOHNSON in *The Great Goldwyn.*

11
I had always assumed that cliché was a suburb of Paris, until I discovered it to be a street in Oxford.

PHILIP GUEDALLA, *Some Historians.*

12
Lexicographer: a writer of dictionaries, a harmless drudge.

SAMUEL JOHNSON, *Dictionary.*

13
I am not yet so lost in lexicography, as to forget that words are the daughters of earth, and that things are the sons of heaven.

SAMUEL JOHNSON, *Dictionary:* preface.

14
At the beginning there was the Word—at the end just the Cliché.

STANISLAW J. LEC, *Unkempt Thoughts*, tr. from the Polish by JACEK GALASKA.

15
Value your words. Each one may be the last.

STANISLAW J. LEC, *Unkempt Thoughts*, tr. from the Polish by JACEK GALASKA.

16
He can compress the most words into the smallest ideas of any man I ever met.

ABRAHAM LINCOLN, speaking of a fellow lawyer. (GROSS, *Lincoln's Own Stories*, p. 36.)

17
Similes are like songs in love:
They much describe; they nothing prove.

MATTHEW PRIOR, *Alma*, canto 3.

18
One of our defects as a nation is a tendency to use what have been called "weasel words." When a weasel sucks eggs the meat is sucked out of the egg. If you use a "weasel word" after another there is nothing left of the other.

THEODORE ROOSEVELT, *Speech*, 1916.

19
But, my lord, there is a Southern proverb—fine words butter no parsnips.

SIR WALTER SCOTT, *The Legend of Montrose*, ch. 3.

20
Syllables govern the world.

JOHN SELDEN, *Power.*

21
Thous art not so long by the head as honorificabilitudinitatibus.

WILLIAM SHAKESPEARE, *Love's Labour's Lost.* Act v, sc. 1.

22
Man does not live by words alone, despite the fact that sometimes he has to eat them.

ADLAI STEVENSON, *Speech*, Sept. 5, 1952.

23
Some of his words were not Sunday-school words. . . . Some of those old American words do have a kind of a bully swing to them.

MARK TWAIN, *A Tramp Abroad*, ch. 20.

1
Naturally, when baronets are threatening to pour vitriol down her neck, a refined and sensitive young girl cannot pick her words. This sort of thing must of necessity interfere with the selection of the *mot juste.*
P. G. WODEHOUSE.

WORK

See also Industry, Labor

2
My wife's idea of housecleaning is to sweep the room at a glance.
JOEY ADAMS, *Cindy and I,* ch. 1.

3
The shorter the hours, the larger the income. Don't get into the habit of putting in long hours or you may be set down into a permanent subordinate position.
GEORGE ADE, *Fables.*

4
We have it on good authority that it is lawful to pull an ass out of the pit on the Sabbath day. Well, there never was a bigger ass, nor a deeper pit.
HENRY WARD BEECHER, to his attorneys, who came to consult him one Sunday, during the Tilton-Beecher trial, in the fall of 1874. (*Dict. of American Biography.*)

5
Anyone can do any amount of work provided it isn't the work he is supposed to be doing at that moment.
ROBERT BENCHLEY, *Think.*

6
I do most of my work sitting down; that's where I shine.
ROBERT BENCHLEY.

7
Never work before breakfast; if you have to work before breakfast, get your breakfast first.
JOSH BILLINGS.

8
A wife is afraid of having her husband enjoy his work too much; she doesn't mind if he suffers at it—for her sake.
HAL BOYLE, *Column,* Associated Press, Oct. 21, 1964.

9
Many bring rakes but few shovels.
FRANK C. BROWN, *Collection of North Carolina Folklore.*

10
Of the professions it may be said that soldiers are becoming too popular, parsons too lazy, physicians too mercenary, and lawyers too powerful.
C. C. COLTON, *Lacon,* vol. 1.

11
It is better to wear out than to rust out.
RICHARD CUMBERLAND, Bishop of Peterborough. When a friend told him he would wear himself out by his incessant labors. (BOSWELL, *Tour to the Hebrides.*)

12
All work and no play makes Jack a dull boy,
All play and no work makes Jack a mere toy.
MARIA EDGEWORTH, *Harry and Lucy.*

13
It's better to be in love with your work than in love with your self.
B. C. FORBES, *Epigrams.*

14
The best grease is elbow-grease.
B. C. FORBES, *Epigrams.*

15
Work now, or wince later.
B. C. FORBES, *Epigrams.*

16
Sinecures are never long secure.
B. C. FORBES, *Epigrams.*

17
His sole concern with work was considering how he might best avoid it.
ANATOLE FRANCE, *Revolt of the Angels,* ch. 1.

18
Why work at Nothing, like the Wee Pig's Tail
That Wiggles all day long to no avail?
ARTHUR GUITERMAN, *A Poet's Proverbs: Old Irish Proverbs.*

19
Work is the greatest thing in the world, so we should always save some of it for tomorrow.
DON HEROLD.

20
Th' feller who quits work in th' evenin' like he wuz leavin' a penitentiary never reaches Easy Street.
FRANK MCKINNEY (KIN) HUBBARD, *Abe Martin's Primer.*

21
I like work; it fascinates me. I can sit and look at it for hours. I love to keep it by me: the idea of getting rid of it nearly breaks my heart.
JEROME K. JEROME, *Three Men in a Boat.*

22
It's all in the day's work, as the huntsman said when the lion ate him.
CHARLES KINGSLEY, *Westward Ho,* ch. 4.

23
And so we plough along, as the fly said to the ox.
HENRY WADSWORTH LONGFELLOW.

1
Isn't it nice that no one cares which twenty-three hours of the day I work?

> THURGOOD MARSHALL, during his years (1938–61) as special counsel for the National Association for the Advancement of Colored People. (SIDNEY E. ZION, *Thurgood Marshall Takes a New 'Tush-Tush' Job; The New York Times Magazine*, Aug. 22, 1965.)

2
I go on working for the same reason that a hen goes on laying eggs.

> H. L. MENCKEN, quoted by DURANT, *On the Meaning of Life*.

3
Work is the scythe of time.

> NAPOLEON BONAPARTE, on board H. M. S. Bellerophon, Aug., 1815.

4
The men who work hardest seem to do it by making other men do their work for them.

> *Reflections of a Bachelor*.

5
Set me anything to do as a task, and it is inconceivable the desire I have to do something else.

> BERNARD SHAW, quoted by GAMALIEL BRADFORD in *As God Made Them*.

6
Never buy anything with a handle on it. It means work.

> H. ALLEN SMITH, *H. Allen Smith's Almanac* (1965).

7
I think of a story my grandfather Stevenson, a devout Scotch-Presbyterian, told about the preacher who was driving along a back road in the South when he espied a parishioner wearily clearing up a poor, stony field. "That is a fine job you and the Lord have done, cleaning up that rocky field," he shouted. "Thank you, parson," the man replied. "But I wish you could have seen it when the Lord had it all to himself."

> ADLAI STEVENSON, *A. Powell Davies Memorial Lecture*, Jan. 18, 1959.

8
In the words of the young preacher, I'm working to beat hell.

> ADLAI STEVENSON, quoted in *Life*, July 23, 1965.

9
It is easier to admire hard work if you don't do it.

> UNKNOWN, *Meditations in Wall Street*.

10
Work is the curse of the drinking classes.

> OSCAR WILDE, quoted by HESKETH PEARSON in *Lives of the Wits*.

11
Boy to girl as they are about to wash dishes: "You wash, I'll drop."

> GEORGE WOLF, *Cartoon Caption, McCall's*.

WORLD

12
The world, which took but six days to make, is like to take six thousand to make out.

> SIR THOMAS BROWNE, *Christian Morals*.

13
The created world is but a parenthesis in eternity.

> SIR THOMAS BROWNE, *Christian Morals*.

14
I do not see any way of realizing our hopes about world organization in five or six days. Even the Almighty took seven.

> SIR WINSTON CHURCHILL, *Message* to President Roosevelt prior to Yalta Conference.

15
To me it seems as if when God conceived the world, that was Poetry; He formed it, and that was Sculpture; He colored it, and that was Painting; He peopled it with living beings, and that was the grand, divine, eternal Drama.

> CHARLOTTE CUSHMAN, quoted in STEBBINS, *Charlotte Cushman*.

16
He took the world for an enormous toy.

> EDUARDO DE FILIPPO, *Christmas with the Cupiellos*.

17
This is the way the world ends
Not with a bang but a whimper.

> T. S. ELIOT, *The Hollow Men*.

18
The world is a beautiful book, but of little use to him who cannot read it.

> CARLO GOLDONI, *Pamela*.

19
To understand the world, and to like it, are two things not easily to be reconciled.

> LORD HALIFAX, *Works*.

20
If the world were good for nothing else, it is a fine subject for speculation.

> WILLIAM HAZLITT, *Characteristics*, No. 302.

21
The world has narrowed to a neighborhood before it has broadened to brotherhood.

> LYNDON B. JOHNSON, *Response* to a toast proposed by Adlai E. Stevenson at a luncheon given by the latter in honor of Johnson and the leadership of the United Nations, New York City, Dec. 17, 1963. Johnson recalled at the time that he had first used substantially the

same words in an address at the high-school graduation of his daughter Lynda Bird.

1
The window to the world can be covered by a newspaper.
> STANISLAW J. LEC, *Unkempt Thoughts*, tr. from the Polish by JACEK GALASKA.

2
The world's as ugly, ay, as sin,—
And almost as delightful.
> F. LOCKER-LAMPSON, *The Jester's Plea*.

3
The world's a book writ by the *eternal art*
Of the great Maker; printed in man's heart;
'Tis falsely printed though divinely penned,
And all the errata will appear at the end.
> FRANCIS QUARLES, *Divine Fancies*.

4
. . . what the world calls originality is only an unaccustomed method of tickling it.
> BERNARD SHAW, *Three Plays for Puritans:* preface.

5
We are told that when Jehovah created the world he saw that it was good. What would he say now?
> BERNARD SHAW, *Maxims for Revolutionists*.

6
The world is so full of a number of things,
I'm sure we should all be as happy as kings.
> ROBERT LOUIS STEVENSON, *Couplet*.

7
Pray, Madam, who were the company? Why, there was all the world and his wife.
> JONATHAN SWIFT, *Polite Conversation*, Dial. 3.

8
'Tis a mad world, my masters.
> JOHN TAYLOR, *Western Voyage*.

9
Even if the world owes you a living, you have to be your own collector.
> UNKNOWN, quoted in *Chicago American Magazine*.

10
If this is the best of all possible worlds, what then are the others?
> VOLTAIRE, *Candide*, ch. 6.

11
The world is a comedy to those that think, a tragedy to those that feel.
> HORACE WALPOLE, *Letter* to Sir Horace Mann.

12
The world is full of care, and much like
> unto a bubble;
Women and care and care and women, and
> women and care and trouble.
> NATHANIEL WARD, *Epigram*.

WORRY

13
All the apostles of repose and the mental scientists tell the business slave not to worry, but an old trader's advice is to worry until you have had enough of it and then do something desperate.
> GEORGE ADE, *Fables*.

14
If the grass is greener in the other fellow's yard—let him worry about cutting it.
> FRED ALLEN, *Treadmill to Oblivion*.

15
Nobody should ever look anxious except those who have no anxiety.
> BENJAMIN DISRAELI.

16
As a cure for worrying, work is better than whiskey.
> THOMAS A. EDISON, *Interview*, on prohibition.

17
The reason worry kills more people than work is that more people worry than work.
> ROBERT FROST, *Vogue*, Mar. 15, 1963.

18
It's wonderful what a run ther is on worry when you consider that it never helped anything.
> FRANK MCKINNEY (KIN) HUBBARD, *Abe Martin's Primer*.

19
Worry, the interest paid by those who borrow trouble.
> GEORGE W. LYON. (*Judge*, Mar. 1, 1924, p. 6; *New York Times Book Review*, Oct. 23, 1932, p. 27.)

20
Common sense, in so far as it exists, is all for the bourgeoisie. Nonsense is the privilege of the aristocracy. The worries of the world are for the common people.
> GEORGE JEAN NATHAN, *Autobiography of an Attitude*.

21
Worry makes everybody thin except fat people who worry over their fatness.
> *Reflections of a Bachelor* (1903).

22
Let care kill a cat. We'll laugh and grow fat.
> UNKNOWN, *Shirburn Ballads*, 91 (1585). See also BEN JONSON in section headed "Sorrow."

23
Care to our coffin adds a nail, no doubt,
And every grin so merry draws one out.
> JOHN WOLCOT (PETER PINDAR), *Expostulary Odes*.

WRITING

See also Literature, Plagiarism, Poetry

1
Our Grub-street Biographers watch for the death of a great man, like so many undertakers, on purpose to make a penny of him.
> JOSEPH ADDISON, quoted in *Classic Quotations*, ed. by JAMES ELMES.

2
Drink deep, or cut out the Pierian spring altogether.
> GEORGE ADE, *Fables*.

3
I told Harold [Ross] that when I saw what you were writing I planned to insert my quill back into the fowl.
> FRED ALLEN, *Letter* to James Thurber. (*Fred Allen's Letters*, ed. by JOE MCCARTHY.)

4
With pen and pencil we're learning to say Nothing, more cleverly every day.
> WILLIAM ALLINGHAM, *Blackberries*.

5
The reason why so few good books are written is that so few people who can write know anything.
> WALTER BAGEHOT, *Literary Studies: Shakespeare*.

6
Art thou a pen, whose task shall be
  To drown in ink What writers think?
  Oh, wisely write, that pages white
Be not the worse for ink and thee!
> ETHEL LYNN BEERS, *The Gold Nugget*.

7
You know writing one's life has a sobering effect on one—you get it together and you think: "Well! look at the damn thing . . ."
> S. N. BEHRMAN, *Biography*.

8
First I tell them what I am going to tell them; then I tell them; and then I tell them what I've told them.
> HILAIRE BELLOC, quoted by HESKETH PEARSON, *Lives of the Wits*.

9
It took me fifteen years to discover I had no talent for writing, but I couldn't give it up because by that time I was too famous.
> ROBERT BENCHLEY.

10
Creative writing is or pretends to be a course in originality, although crabbed English teachers assert that creative writing is just a composition course in which the spelling is not corrected.
> MORRIS BISHOP, *The Perfect University; The Atlantic*, May, 1966.

11
There is probably no hell for authors in the next world—they suffer so much from critics and publishers in this.
> C. N. BOVEE, *Summaries of Thought: Authors*.

12
Being a writer in a library is rather like being a eunuch in a harem.
> JOHN BRAINE, quoted in *The New York Times*, Oct. 7, 1962.

13
They lard their lean books with the fat of others' works.
> ROBERT BURTON, *The Anatomy of Melancholy*.

14
The art of writing things that shall sound right and yet be wrong has made so many reputations and afforded comfort to such a large number of readers that I could not venture to neglect it.
> SAMUEL BUTLER, *Erewhon*.

15
That's not writing, that's typing.
> TRUMAN CAPOTE, quoted on work of Jack Kerouac.

16
A well-written life is almost as rare as a well-spent one.
> THOMAS CARLYLE, *Essays: State of German Literature*.

17
The composing room has an unlimited supply of periods available to terminate short, simple sentences.
> TURNER CATLEDGE, managing editor, *The New York Times. Memo* to his staff. (*Time*, Dec. 20, 1954.)

18
The pen is the tongue of the mind.
> MIGUEL DE CERVANTES, *Don Quixote*. Pt. ii, ch. 16.

19
It requires a great man to write so badly as that.
> G. K. CHESTERTON, *A Handful of Authors*. Comment on Dumas.

20
I couldn't write the things they publish now, with no beginning and no end, and a little incest in the middle.
> IRVIN S. COBB.

21
So that the jest is clearly to be seen,
Not in the words—but in the gap between:
Manner is all in all, whate'er is writ,
The substitute for genius, sense, and wit.
> WILLIAM COWPER, *Table Talk*.

22
He inquired of an old man whether it were sinful to write for money. And the old man

answered, "There be two kinds of writers, my son: to wit, those who write for money and get it, and those who write for money and don't get it."

T. W. H. CROSLAND, *Little Stories.*

1
Write disagreeably, if you like; as the man said of the rack, it will help me to pass an hour or two, at any rate.

MADAME DU DEFFAND, *Letters.*

2
Being an editor is a hard job, but a fascinating one. There's nothing so hard as minding your own business and an editor never has to do that.

FINLEY PETER DUNNE, *Mr. Dooley Remembers.*

3
Robert Benchley has a style that is weak and lies down frequently to rest.

MAX EASTMAN, *Enjoyment of Laughter.*

4
People do not deserve to have good writing, they are so pleased with bad.

RALPH WALDO EMERSON, *Journals.* Vol. vi, p. 132.

5
Good writing is a kind of skating which carries off the performer where he would not go.

RALPH WALDO EMERSON, *Journals.* Vol. vii, p. 334.

6
Mr. Faulkner, of course, is interested in making your mind, rather than your flesh, creep.

CLIFTON FADIMAN, *Review* in *The New Yorker*, Apr. 21, 1934.

7
Even those who call Mr. Faulkner our greatest literary sadist do not fully appreciate him, for it is not merely his characters who have to run the gauntlet but also his readers.

CLIFTON FADIMAN, *Review* in *The New Yorker*, Apr. 21, 1934.

8
To read some magazines makes one wonder what the editor has rejected.

Farmer's Almanac, 1966.

9
Who knows whether in retirement I shall be tempted to the last infirmity of mundane minds, which is to write a book.

GEOFFREY FISHER, Archbishop of Canterbury. Quoted in *Time*, May 12, 1961.

10
I never said anything good about an editor until he or she had published something of mine.

ROBERT FONTAINE, *That's a Good Question.*

11
"The Pen is mightier than the sword." Not unless you push it.

B. C. FORBES, *Epigrams.*

12
Sometimes it sounds like I walked out of the room and left the typewriter running.

GENE FOWLER, on his writing. (*Newsweek*, Nov. 1, 1954.)

13
At a literary party. Frogs and oxen. The frogs are the magazine and newspaper men, the agency men, the publishers, who rather pathetically try to equate knowing writers with actually creating something; the oxen are the writers, who are castrated by their own self-interest, their own vanities, their "shop." Both frogs and oxen are very well by themselves; but the syzygy is fatal. Their chatter deafens me and I feel like Alice at the tea-party. They are not even good "material."

JOHN FOWLES, *I Write Therefore I Am;* *Evergreen Review*, No. 33, Aug.–Sept., 1964.

14
The canny among the publishers know that an enormous popular appetite for the insulting of the famous must be gratified, and the modern biographer emerges from the editorial conference a sadist and a wiser man.

FLORENCE KIPPER FRANK, *Morrow's Almanac* (1929).

15
Unprovided with original learning, unformed in the habits of thinking, unskilled in the arts of composition, I resolved—to write a book.

EDWARD GIBBON.

16
Another damned, thick, square book! Always scribble, scribble! Eh! Mr. Gibbon?

WILLIAM HENRY, Duke of Gloucester. BEST'S *Literary Memorials.* (BOSWELL'S *Johnson*, vol. 2.)

17
No matter how much or how little, it is my contention people feel poets and novelists and scriptwriters are overpaid. On the other hand, baseball players, who ought to play for nothing, are a source of great concern.

HARRY GOLDEN, *Carl Sandburg.*

18
'Twas Arnold Bennett's habit to deplore
That younger writers did not publish more,
And yet it would be easier to assess
His own position had he written less.

KENSAL GREEN, *Premature Epitaphs.*

19
I don't want to be a doctor, and live by men's diseases; nor a minister to live by

their sins; nor a lawyer to live by their quarrels. So I don't see there's anything left for me but to be an author.

> NATHANIEL HAWTHORNE, *Remark* to his mother.

1
Bees are sometimes drowned (or suffocated) in the honey which they collect. So some writers are lost in their collected learning.

> NATHANIEL HAWTHORNE, *American Note-Books.*

2
No author is a man of genius to his publisher.

> HEINRICH HEINE, *Works.*

3
A serious writer is not to be confused with a solemn writer. A serious writer may be a hawk or a buzzard or even a popinjay, but a solemn writer is always a bloody owl.

> ERNEST HEMINGWAY, *Death in the Afternoon,* ch. 16.

4
Easy writing makes hard reading.

> ERNEST HEMINGWAY. (SAMUEL PUTNAM, *Paris Was Our Mistress.*) See also JOHNSON and SHERIDAN in this section.

5
I never saw an author in my life, saving perhaps one, that did not purr as audibly as a full-grown domestic cat on having his fur smoothed the right way by a skilful hand.

> OLIVER WENDELL HOLMES, *The Autocrat of the Breakfast-Table,* ch. 3.

6
Originality is undetected plagiarism.

> DEAN W. R. INGE.

7
The greatest part of a writer's time is spent in reading, in order to write: a man will turn over half a library to make one book.

> SAMUEL JOHNSON, BOSWELL'S *Life,* Apr. 6, 1775.

8
No man but a blockhead ever wrote except for money.

> SAMUEL JOHNSON, BOSWELL'S *Life,* 1776.

9
The worst thing you can do to an author is to be silent as to his works.

> SAMUEL JOHNSON, BOSWELL'S *Life.*

10
The promises of authors are like the vows of lovers.

> SAMUEL JOHNSON. *Boswell's Life.*

11
What is written without effort is in general read without pleasure.

> SAMUEL JOHNSON, *Miscellanies,* vol. 2.

12
He did not win his world public solely through mediocrity.

> ALVA JOHNSTON, *How to Become a Great Writer.* Reference to Edgar Rice Burroughs.

13
The incurable itch of writing possesses many. (Tenet insanabile multos scribendi cacoëthes.)

> JUVENAL, *Satires,* Sat. 7.

14
No man—especially a practicing writer—is perhaps ever entirely a hero to his ex-spouse.

> ALFRED KAZIN, *Contemporaries: Sinclair Lewis, Hail and Farewell.*

15
There are two literary maladies—writer's cramp and swelled head. The worst of writer's cramp is that it is never cured; the worst of swelled head is that it never kills.

> COULSON KERNAHAN, *Lecture,* Birmingham, England.

16
Brief history of a successful author: From ink-pots to flesh pots.

> RICHARD R. KIRK, from *Toaster's Handbook,* compiled by PEGGY EDMUND AND HAROLD WORKMAN WILLIAMS.

17
There is only one recipe for writing that I ever heard of: take a quart or more of life-blood, mix it with a bottle of ink and a teaspoonful of human tears, and ask God to forgive the blots.

> STEPHEN LEACOCK, *How to Write.* Credited to "a well-known novelist of today."

18
Today an editor is a man who has a keen sense of what the public wants to read and buys it from those who can write it. He has, as such, the same connection with literature that a hotel chef has with fish. But he is not a fisherman—unless, as is likely, "on the side."

> STEPHEN LEACOCK, *Charles Dickens.*

19
No fading beauty questioning the looking-glass suffers more keenly than the author drowsing toward old age.

> STEPHEN LEACOCK, *Charles Dickens.*

20
How pleasant to know Mr. Lear!
Who has written such volumes of stuff!
Some think him ill-tempered and queer,
But a few think him pleasant enough.

> EDWARD LEAR.

21
Authors in general are stark mad on the subject of their own works.

> ALAIN RENÉ LE SAGE, *Gil Blas.* Bk. vii, ch. 10.

1

I once said his prose is dipped in chicken fat.

OSCAR LEVANT, *Memoirs of an Amnesiac.* Reference to David Susskind.

2

This boy would rather write than eat. And if he keeps writing this junk he won't be eating at all.

JOE E. LEWIS, of Joey Adams. Quoted by JOEY ADAMS in *Cindy and I,* ch. 27.

3

When once the itch of literature comes over a man, nothing can cure it but the scratching of a pen.

SAMUEL LOVER, *Handy Andy,* ch. 36.

4

Though old the thought and oft exprest,

'Tis his at last who says it best.

JAMES RUSSELL LOWELL, *For an Autograph.*

5

His rhythms are erratic, his sense of character is nil, and he is as pretentious as a rich whore, as sentimental as a lollypop. Yet I think he has a large talent.

NORMAN MAILER, *Advertisements for Myself.* Comment on Jack Kerouac.

6

Salinger is everyone's favorite. I seem to be alone in finding him no more than the greatest mind ever to stay in prep school.

NORMAN MAILER, *Advertisements for Myself.* On J. D. Salinger.

7

Writing in America is largely a matter of plastering pink peppermint candy over the realities of life.

DON MARQUIS, *New York Sun.*

8

I decline to write about garters when I can write about souls.

BRUCE MARSHALL, *Father Malachy's Miracle.*

9

Arthur, they say, has wit; for what?

For writing? No, for writing not.

MARTIAL, *Epigrams.* From *Roman Culture,* ed. by GARRY WILLS.

10

Why don't I send my book to you

Although you often urge me to?

The reason's good, for if I did

You'd send me yours—which God forbid!

MARTIAL, *Epigrams.* From *Roman Culture,* ed. by GARRY WILLS.

11

The impulse to create beauty is rather rare in literary men. . . . Far ahead of it comes the yearning to make money. And after the yearning to make money comes the yearning to make a noise.

H. L. MENCKEN, *Prejudices,* ser. 5.

12

But I became a writer all the same, and shall remain one until the end of the chapter, just as a cow goes on giving milk all her life, even though what appears to be her self-interest urges her to give gin.

H. L. MENCKEN, quoted in DURANT, *On the Meaning of Life.*

13

A person who publishes a book willfully appears before the populace with his pants down . . .

EDNA ST. VINCENT MILLAY, from *Letters of Edna St. Vincent Millay* (1952).

14

The p'int of good writing is knowing when to stop.

L. M. MONTGOMERY, *Anne's House of Dreams.*

15

To write upon *all* is an author's sole chance

For attaining, at last, the least knowledge of *any.*

THOMAS MOORE, *Literary Advertisement.*

16

Though an angel should write, still 'tis *devils* must print.

THOMAS MOORE, *The Fudge Family in England,* letter 3.

17

There is no such thing as a dirty theme. There are only dirty writers.

GEORGE JEAN NATHAN, *Testament of a Critic.*

18

As artists they're rot, but as providers they're oil wells—they gush.

DOROTHY PARKER, on lady novelists. Quoted in *The Years with Ross* by JAMES THURBER.

19

In these days the greater part of whitewashing is done with ink.

GEORGE D. PRENTICE.

20

Many a writer seems to think he is never profound except when he can't understand his own meaning.

GEORGE D. PRENTICE.

21

A pin has as much head as some authors and a good deal more point.

GEORGE D. PRENTICE.

22

Let him be kept from paper, pen, and ink;

So he may cease to write, and learn to think.

MATTHEW PRIOR, *To a Person Who Wrote Ill.*

23

God have mercy on the sinner

Who must write with no dinner,

No gravy and no grub,

No pewter and no pub,
No belly and no bowels,
Only consonants and vowels.
> JOHN CROWE RANSOM, *Survey of Literature.*

1
Make 'em laugh; make 'em cry; make 'em wait.
> CHARLES READE, *Recipe for a Successful Novel.*

2
An original writer is not one who imitates nobody but one whom nobody can imitate.
> FRANÇOIS RENÉ (VICOMTE DE CHATEAUBRIAND). Quoted in WALTER SCOTT'S *Personality Parade* in *Parade* magazine, June 25, 1967.

3
There ain't nothing that breaks up homes, country, and nations like somebody publishing their memoirs.
> WILL ROGERS, *Autobiography.*

4
In a style, to be sure, of remarkable fullness,
Which nobody reads on account of its dullness.
> JOHN GODFREY SAXE, *Pyramus and Thisbe.*

5
. . . you must not suppose, because I am a man of letters, that I never tried to earn an honest living.
> BERNARD SHAW, *The Irrational Knot:* preface.

6
. . . I have not wasted my life trifling with literary fools in taverns as Johnson did when he should have been shaking England with the thunder of his spirit.
> BERNARD SHAW, *Parents and Children.*

7
. . . the money is a lifebelt thrown to a swimmer who has already reached the shore in safety.
> BERNARD SHAW, referring to the Nobel prize. Quoted by HESKETH PEARSON in *Lives of the Wits.*

8
An author of any sort must keep in training like an athlete. How else could he wrestle with God as Jacob did with the angel?
> BERNARD SHAW, to George Sylvester Viereck in an interview.

9
In England everything is twenty years out of date before it gets printed.
> BERNARD SHAW, *Dramatic Opinions.*

10
You write with ease to show your breeding,
But easy writing's vile hard reading.
> RICHARD BRINSLEY SHERIDAN, *Clio's Protest.*

11
A best-seller is the gilded tomb of a mediocre talent.
> LOGAN PEARSALL SMITH, *All Trivia.*

12
What I like in a good author is not what he says, but what he whispers.
> LOGAN PEARSALL SMITH, *All Trivia.*

13
As a general rule, run your pen through every other word you have written; you have no idea what vigour it will give your style.
> SYDNEY SMITH, from *Bon-Mots of Sydney Smith,* ed. by JERROLD.

14
It is the nobility of their style which will make our writers of 1840 unreadable forty years from now.
> STENDHAL (HENRI BEYLE), *Manuscript note* (1840).

15
Salinger, the Greta Garbo of American letters . . .
> HARVEY SWADOS, *A Radical's America.*

16
I am now trying an experiment very frequent among modern authors, which is to write upon nothing; when the subject is utterly exhausted, to let the pen still move on: by some called the ghost of wit, delighting to walk after the death of its body.
> JONATHAN SWIFT, *A Tale of a Tub.*

17
Pens are most dangerous tools, more sharp by odds
Than swords, and cut more keen than whips or rods.
> JOHN TAYLOR, *News from Hell, Hull and Halifax.*

18
With sixty staring me in the face, I have developed inflammation of the sentence structure and a definite hardening of the paragraphs.
> JAMES THURBER, quoted in *New York Post,* June 30, 1955.

19
Persons attempting to find a motive in this narrative will be prosecuted; persons attempting to find a moral in it will be banished; persons attempting to find a plot in it will be shot.
> MARK TWAIN, *The Adventures of Huckleberry Finn.*

1
I am sometimes charmed by the minor talent of J. D. Salinger, but when he puts on his Great Author suit I think one should point out that it doesn't fit.
> GORE VIDAL, *The Reporter,* Dec. 10, 1959.

2
Writing to me is not an exercise in addressing readers, it is more as though I were talking to myself while shaving.
> E. B. WHITE, quoted by CLIFTON FADIMAN in *Enter, Conversing.*

3
The good ended happily, the bad unhappily. That is what fiction means.
> OSCAR WILDE, *The Importance of Being Earnest.* Act 2.

4
The fact of a man being a poisoner is nothing against his prose.
> OSCAR WILDE, *Pen, Pencil and Poison.*
> The reference is to THOMAS GRIFFITHS WAINEWRIGHT.

5
His style is chaos, illumined by flashes of lightning. As a writer, he has mastered everything except language.
> OSCAR WILDE, *The Decay of Lying.* Referring to GEORGE MEREDITH.

6
The ancient historians gave us delightful fiction in the form of fact; the modern novelist presents us with dull facts under the guise of fiction.
> OSCAR WILDE, *The Decay of Lying.*

7
Trivial personalities decomposing in the eternity of print.
> VIRGINIA WOOLF, *The Common Reader.*

8
I found her in hospital typing away lugubriously. She had given her address as Bedpan Alley, and represented herself as writing her way out. There was a hospital bill to pay before she dared to get well . . .
> ALEXANDER WOOLLCOTT, *While Rome Burns.* Reference to DOROTHY PARKER.

9
Another writes because his father writ,
And proves himself a bastard by his wit.
> EDWARD YOUNG, *Epistles to Mr. Pope,* epis. 1.

WRONG

10
Fear not, then, thou child infirm;
There's no god dare wrong a worm.
> RALPH WALDO EMERSON, *Compensation.*

11
When Something's Wrong don't call it Right
For fear of seeming Impolite.
> ARTHUR GUITERMAN, *A Poet's Proverbs.*

12
Wrong no man and write no woman.
> ELBERT HUBBARD.

13
Can the cannibal speak in the name of those he ate?
> STANISLAW J. LEC, *Unkempt Thoughts,* tr. from the Polish by JACEK GALASKA.

14
The best book ever written by any man on the wrong side of a question of which the writer was profoundly ignorant.
> THOMAS BABINGTON MACAULAY, *Review* of Atterburg's *Defense of the Letters of Phalaris.*

15
The wrong way always seems the more reasonable.
> GEORGE MOORE, *The Bending of the Bough,* Act 4.

16
Napoleon: What shall we do with this officer, Giuseppe? Everything he says is wrong.
Giuseppe: Make him a general, excellency; and then everything he says will be right.
> BERNARD SHAW, *The Man of Destiny.*

17
The greatest right in the world is the right to be wrong.
> HARRY WEINBERGER, *The First Casualties in War; New York Evening Post,* Apr. 10, 1917.

Y

YAWN

18
Why doth one man's yawning make another yawn?
> ROBERT BURTON, *The Anatomy of Melancholy.*

19
A yawn is at least an honest opinion.
> *Farmer's Almanac,* 1966.

YEAR

20
One New Year is just about as happy as another.
> GEORGE ADE, *The Fable of Successful Tobias and Some of His Happy New-Years.*

21
The year expires placidly in Devonshire, like

a saintly clergyman unobtrusively breathing his last during an after-dinner nap.

MARGARET HALSEY, *With Malice Toward Some.*

1
Is that a birthday? 'Tis, alas! too clear;
'Tis but the funeral of the former year.

ALEXANDER POPE, *To Mrs. M.B. on Her Birthday.*

2
Years ago—years and years and donkey's ears, as the saying is.

E. M. WRIGHT, *Rustic Speech.*

YOUTH

See also Age

3
In case you're worried about what's going to become of the younger generation, it's going to grow up and start worrying about the younger generation.

ROGER ALLEN, *Grand Rapids Press.*

4
Sociologists agree that one of the worst things that can happen to an American child nowadays is youth.

RUSSELL BAKER, *"Observer" Column, The New York Times*, Feb. 27, 1966.

!5
Young fellows will be young fellows.

ISAAC BICKERSTAFFE, *Love in a Village.*

6
At 19, everything is possible and tomorrow looks friendly.

JIM BISHOP, *New York Journal-American*, May 9, 1961.

7
To youth I have but three words of counsel —work, work, work.

OTTO VON BISMARCK, from *Sayings of Bismarck.*

8
Young men are apt to think themselves wise enough, as drunken men are apt to think themselves sober enough.

LORD CHESTERFIELD, *Letters*, Jan. 15, 1753.

9
It is easy enough to praise men for the courage of their convictions. I wish I could teach the sad young of this mealy generation the courage of their confusions.

JOHN CIARDI, *Saturday Review*, June 2, 1962.

10
She still aims at youth, though she shot beyond it years ago.

CHARLES DICKENS.

11
Anybody that tries to do anything before he's an uncomfortable risk for the life insurance company is snubbed for youthful impertinence.

FINLEY PETER DUNNE, *Mr. Dooley Remembers.*

12
"And youth is cruel, and has no remorse
And smiles at situations which it cannot see."
I smile, of course,
And go on drinking tea.

T. S. ELIOT, *Portrait of a Lady.*

13
The teen-ager (Huck Finn remodeled by Charles Addams) has enormous energy, great ability to command publicity, and the Hitlerian capacity to dominate through incessant demands.

CLIFTON FADIMAN, *Enter, Conversing.*

14
To a boy of twenty-eight it would seem that anyone the other side of fifty should make out his will at once, and stay out of drafts.

GENE FOWLER, *Skyline.*

15
The young are always at pains to tell us they will never be surprised. They say they are hardened and skeptical but they forget that only the hardened and the skeptical are surprised.

HARRY GOLDEN, *Carl Sandburg.*

16
No young man believes he shall ever die.

WILLIAM HAZLITT, *The Feeling of Immortality in Youth.*

17
When you're young and strong, they can throw you down and the harder you hit the higher you bounce.

FREDERICK LAING, *The Giant's House.*

18
If youth only had a chance or old age any brains.

STEPHEN LEACOCK, *Charles Dickens.*

19
If youth be a defect, it is one that we outgrow only too soon.

JAMES RUSSELL LOWELL, *Address*, Cambridge, Mass., Nov. 8, 1886.

20
Youth is a malady of which one becomes cured a little every day.

BENITO MUSSOLINI, on his fiftieth birthday.

21
The atrocious crime of being a young man.

WILLIAM PITT, to Walpole.

22
Even the youngest of us may be wrong sometimes.

BERNARD SHAW, *Love Among the Artists.*

1
For God's sake give me the young man who has brains enough to make a fool of himself.
ROBERT LOUIS STEVENSON, *Crabbed Age.*

2
We are none of us infallible, not even the youngest.
WILLIAM HEPWORTH THOMPSON, quoted by JAMES STUART, *Reminiscences.*

3
The trouble with the lost generation is that it didn't get lost enough.
JAMES THURBER, *Credos and Curios.*

4
Consider well the proportions of things. It is better to be a young June-bug than an old bird of paradise.
MARK TWAIN, *Pudd'nhead Wilson's Calendar.*

5
Most parents think they know better than you do, and you can generally make more by humoring that superstition than you can by acting on your own better judgment.
MARK TWAIN, *Essays: Advice to Youth.*

6
Finally, the advertiser is responsible for the "teenager." That phenomenon never existed until the advertisers, aware of the growing affluence of the adolescent, invented him.
GORE VIDAL, *Rocking the Boat.*

7
The youth of America is their oldest tradition. It has been going on now for three hundred years.
OSCAR WILDE, *A Woman of No Importance,* Act 1.

8
Those whom the gods love grow young.
OSCAR WILDE, *Saturday Review,* Nov. 17, 1894.

9
Young scoundrels are more dangerous because they live longer.
YEVGENY YEVTUSHENKO, quoted in *The New York Times,* Nov. 8, 1966.

Z

ZEAL

See also Enthusiasm

10
Rash enthusiasm in good society
Were nothing but a moral inebrity.
LORD BYRON, *Don Juan.* Canto xiii, st. 35.

11
Passions are fashions.
CLIFTON FADIMAN, *The Selected Writings of Clifton Fadiman: Children's Reading* (1955).

12
Our Hero, whose homeopathic sagacity
With an ocean of zeal mixed his drop of capacity.
JAMES RUSSELL LOWELL, *A Fable for Critics.*

INDEX AND CONCORDANCE